ASCENT®

CENTER FOR TECHNICAL KNOWLEDGE

Autodesk® Vault 2027 for Inventor® and AutoCAD® Users

Learning Guide

Edition 1.0

ASCENT - Center for Technical Knowledge®
Autodesk® Vault 2027
for Inventor® and AutoCAD® Users
Edition 1.0

Prepared and produced by:

ASCENT Center for Technical Knowledge
11201 Dolfield Blvd, Suite 112
Owings Mills, MD 21117

866-527-2368
www.ASCENTed.com

ASCENT - Center for Technical Knowledge (a division of Rand Worldwide Inc.) is a leading developer of professional learning materials and knowledge products for engineering software applications. ASCENT specializes in designing targeted content that facilitates application-based learning with hands-on software experience. For over 25 years, ASCENT has helped users become more productive through tailored custom learning solutions.

We welcome any comments you may have regarding this guide, or any of our products. To contact us please email: feedback@ASCENTed.com.

AS-VLT2701-IAU1NU-SG // IS-VLT2701-IAU1NU-SG

Contents

Chapter 6: Working with Autodesk Inventor Files 6-1

Chapter 7: Working with AutoCAD Files 7-1

Chapter 9: File and Design Management 9-1

Preface

Autodesk® Vault 2027 for Inventor® and AutoCAD® Users introduces the Autodesk Vault 2027 software (Basic and Professional) to users. This learning content is intended for Autodesk CAD users who need to access their design files from the Autodesk Vault software. It provides an introduction to Vault and focuses specifically on features available to end-users for working with and managing Inventor and AutoCAD designs.

You can use the Autodesk Vault 2027 software and the desired Autodesk 2027 CAD software (such as Inventor or AutoCAD) to complete the practices in this learning content. Note that this content does not cover administrative functionality. Hands-on practices are included to reinforce how to manage the design workflow process using the Autodesk Vault software. Included with this learning content is a training vault that can be used alongside a production vault, to ensure that both vaults can be accessed from the Autodesk Vault software.

Topics Covered

- Introduction to Autodesk Vault features
- Using Autodesk Vault Client
- Working with non-CAD files
- Working with Inventor files
- Working with AutoCAD files
- Searching the Vault
- Data management and reusing design data
- Items and bill of materials management
- Change management
- Customizing the user interface

Prerequisites

- Access to the 2027.0 version of the software, to ensure compatibility with this learning content. Future software updates that are released by Autodesk may include changes that are not reflected in this content. The practices and files included are not compatible with prior versions of the software (e.g., 2026).
- Basic working knowledge of Autodesk CAD software such as Inventor and AutoCAD.

Using This Guide for Specific CAD Users

This guide covers Vault topics for two types of CAD users:

- Autodesk Inventor users
- AutoCAD users

While most of the chapters are common to both types of users, some chapters deal with topics that are relevant only to a specific user type. You can skip the chapter(s) irrelevant for your user type, if time or interest doesn't permit.

Note that the practice files for all chapters are included in the same dataset zip.

For your quick reference, a table listing the chapters applicable for each CAD user type has been provided below. Please refer to the appropriate column for a complete list of chapters for your user type.

For Autodesk Inventor Users	For AutoCAD Users
Chapter 1: Introduction to Autodesk Vault	Chapter 1: Introduction to Autodesk Vault
Chapter 2: Orientation to Autodesk Vault Client	Chapter 2: Orientation to Autodesk Vault Client
Chapter 3: Orientation to the Vault Add-in	Chapter 3: Orientation to the Vault Add-in
Chapter 4: Autodesk Inventor Vault Add-in Setup	**N/A**
Chapter 5: Working with Files	Chapter 5: Working with Files
Chapter 6: Working with Autodesk Inventor Files	**N/A**
N/A	Chapter 7: Working with AutoCAD Files
Chapter 8: Searching the Vault	Chapter 8: Searching the Vault
Chapter 9: File and Design Management	Chapter 9: File and Design Management
Chapter 10: Items and Bills of Materials Management	Chapter 10: Items and Bills of Materials Management
Chapter 11: Change Management	Chapter 11: Change Management
Chapter 12: Customizing the User Interface	Chapter 12: Customizing the User Interface
Chapter 13: Managing Prompts and Dialog Boxes	Chapter 13: Managing Prompts and Dialog Boxes

Note on Software Setup

This guide assumes a standard installation of the software using the default preferences.

Note on Learning Guide Content

ASCENT's learning guides are intended to teach the technical aspects of using the software and do not focus on professional design principles and standards. The practices aim to demonstrate the capabilities and flexibility of the software rather than following specific design codes or standards.

In This Guide

The following highlights the key features of this guide.

Feature	Description
Practice Files	The Practice Files page includes a link to the practice files and instructions on how to download and install them. The practice files are required to complete the practices in this guide.
Chapters	A chapter consists of the following: Learning Objectives, Instructional Content, Practices, Chapter Review Questions, and Command Summary. • **Learning Objectives** define the skills you can acquire by learning the content provided in the chapter. • **Instructional Content**, which begins right after Learning Objectives, refers to the descriptive and procedural information related to various topics. Each main topic introduces a product feature, discusses various aspects of that feature, and provides step-by-step procedures on how to use that feature. Where relevant, examples, figures, helpful hints, and notes are provided. • **Practice** for a topic follows the instructional content. Practices enable you to use the software to perform a hands-on review of a topic. It is required that you download the practice files (using the link found on the Practice Files page) prior to starting the first practice. • **Chapter Review Questions**, located close to the end of a chapter, enable you to test your knowledge of the key concepts discussed in the chapter. • **Command Summary** concludes a chapter. It contains a list of the software commands that are used throughout the chapter and provides information on where the command can be found in the software.

Errata Sheets

If there are any updates or corrections to this guide, they will be published in an errata sheet.

Access it here: ***https://resources.ascented.com/errata-sheets-autodesk***

or

visit **ASCENTed.com > RESOURCES > RESOURCE CENTER > Errata Sheets** and select **Autodesk** from the drop-down list.

Practice Files

To download the practice files for this guide, use the following steps:

1. Type the URL *exactly as shown below* into the address bar of your Internet browser to access the Course File Download page.

   Note: If you are using the ebook, you do not have to type the URL. Instead, you can access the page by clicking the URL below.

   https://www.ascented.com/getfile/id/rhizanthellaPF

2. On the Course File Download page, click the **DOWNLOAD NOW** button, as shown below, to download the .ZIP file that contains the practice files.

3. Once the download is complete, unzip the file and extract its contents.

   The recommended practice files folder location is:
   C:\Vault Data Management Practice Files

   Note: It is recommended that you do not change the location of the practice files folder. Doing so may cause errors when completing the practices.

Stay Informed!
To receive information about upcoming events, promotional offers, and complimentary webcasts, visit:
www.ASCENTed.com/updates

Installation and Setup

Software Installation

Install Autodesk Vault Professional Server and Autodesk Vault Professional Client on each computer. Vault Basic Server and Vault Basic Client can also be used; however, some functionality shown in the guide is specific to Vault Professional. If you are using AutoCAD and/or Autodesk Inventor in conjunction with Autodesk Vault, they must also be installed.

Download and Extract Practice Files

Follow the instructions in the ***Practice Files*** section to download and extract the contents of the Practices zip file into the correct folder location.

Database Setup

There are two methods of setting up the database. Please choose the method that works for your environment:

Method A: Attach the Database (works alongside other vaults and keeps current vault intact)

Method B: Restore the Database (overwrites current vault setup)

Note that Method B will overwrite the current datasets and file stores in your current Vault. Be sure to back up any necessary Vaults that might be required at a later time.

Method A: Attach the Database

1. From the practice files folder location (*C:\Vault Data Management Practice Files\Method A-Attachment),* move **Vault_Training.mdf** and **Vault_Training_log.ldf** to the *C:\Program Files\Microsoft SQL Server\MSSQL16.AUTODESKVAULT\MSSQL\DATA* folder.
2. From the Start menu, select **Autodesk>Autodesk Data Management>Autodesk Data Management Server Console 2027**.
3. Log in as **Administrator** without a password.
4. Select **Vaults**, as shown below:

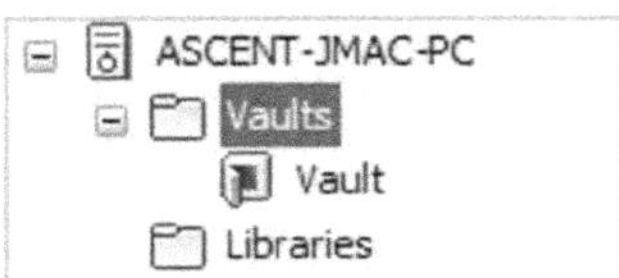

5. Select **Actions>Attach>***Advanced* tab to attach the Vault. Fill in the following details, as follows:
   - **Data File:** *C:\Program Files\Microsoft SQL Server\MSSQL16.AUTODESKVAULT\MSSQL\DATA\Vault_Training.mdf*
   - **Log File:** Filled in automatically
   - **File Store:** *C:\Vault Data Management Practice Files\Method A-Attachment [for Vault Professional or Vault Basic]\Vault_Training*
   - **Vault Name:** Filled in automatically
6. Click **OK**. The *Attach Progress* dialog box opens.
7. In the *Autodesk Data Management Server Console* dialog box, click **OK** when prompted that the vault was attached successfully.
8. Select the **Vault_Training** vault.
9. Select **Actions>Content Indexing Service**.
10. In the *Content Indexing Service* dialog box, select **Yes, enable the Content Indexing Service**.
11. Click **OK**.
12. Remain in the Autodesk Data Management Server Console to create users.

Set Up Users

1. If the Autodesk Data Management Server Console is not open, from the Start menu, select **Autodesk>Autodesk Data Management>Autodesk Data Management Server Console 2027** and log in as Administrator. No password is required. Select **Tools>Administration** and select the *Security* tab.
2. Click **Manage Access...**.
3. Ensure that the *Users* tab is active and select **New**.
4. Set the *Display Name* to **user1**.
5. Set the *First Name* to **user1**.
6. Click **Accounts...** and select the **Vault Account** option. Leave the password blank and click **OK**.
7. Click **Roles...** and select **Administrator**, **Document Editor (Level 2)**, **Change Order Editor (Level 2)**, **and Item Editor (Level 2)**. Click **OK**.

8. Click **Vaults...** and select **Vault_Training**. Click **OK**. The *New User Profile* dialog box should display as shown below.

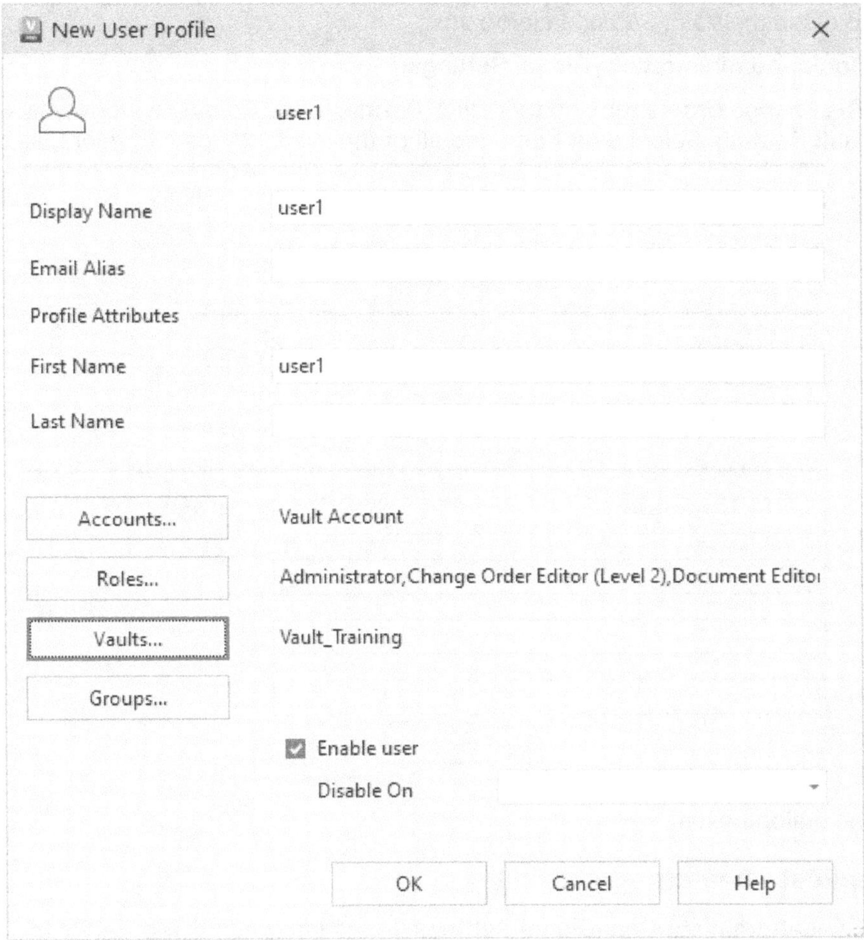

9. Click **OK**.
10. Create another user with a *Display Name* and *First Name* of **user2** using the same roles and vault as defined for user1.
11. Click **OK**. Close the dialog boxes.
12. Close the Autodesk Data Management Server Console.
13. Log in to the Autodesk Vault Client **Vault_Training** vault as **Administrator**, no password.
14. For Vault Revision Table, click **Tools>Administration>Vault Settings**. In the *Vault Settings* dialog box, select the *Behaviors* tab and click **Revision Table.**

15. In the *Revision Table Settings* dialog box, select the **Enable Revision Table Control** checkbox to enable the Vault Revision Table Functionality, and select **Yes** to load the suggested settings. Click **OK** to close the *Revision Table Settings* dialog box, then click **Close** to close the *Vault Settings* dialog box.
16. Select **Tools>Administration>Global Settings**.
17. Select the *Change Orders* tab and then click **Define**. In the *Routing* window, click **Edit** to edit the Default Routing. Select **user1** and add all of the available roles to **user1**, as shown below.

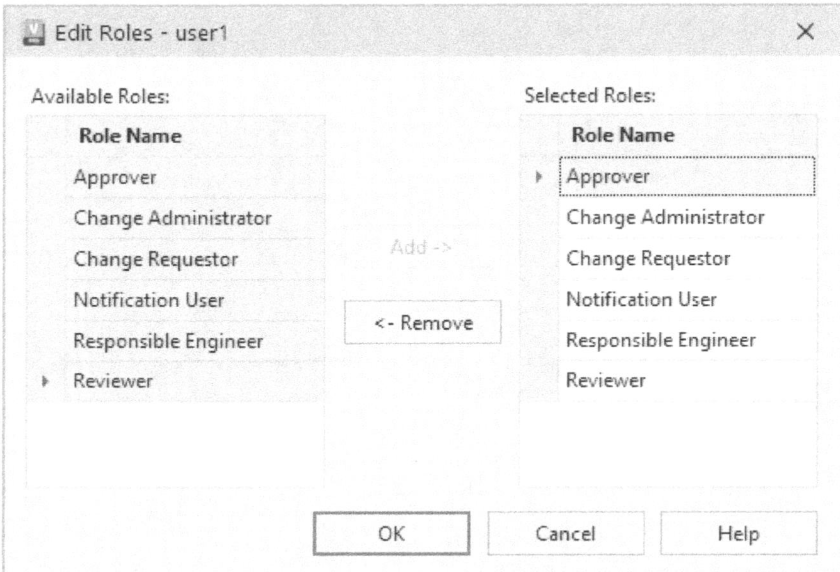

18. Close the dialog boxes.

Set Up Duplicate Search

1. Select **Tools>Administration>Global Settings**. In the *Integrations* tab, select the **Enable Job Server** option and click **Close**.
2. Select **Tools>Administration>Vault Settings**.

3. In the *Files* tab, click **Configure...** in the *Duplicate Search Settings* section, as shown below.

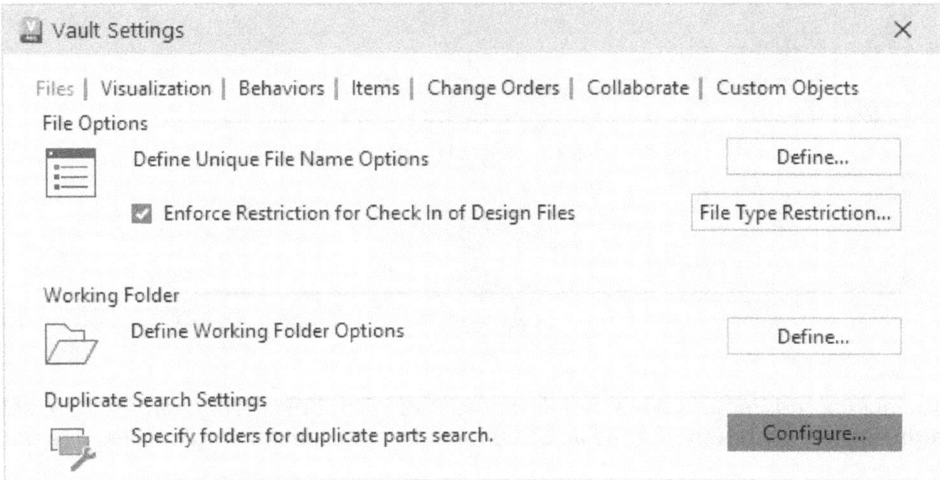

4. Ensure that the **Enable Duplicate Search** option is selected.
5. Click ➕ and select the **$** folder, then click **OK** to start indexing.
6. Close the *Vault Settings* dialog box.

Method B: Restore the Database

This method is intended for use in an instructor-led environment. If you plan to use the practice files and database on your own in a non-classroom environment, do not use a production vault server for the practices. It is recommended that you set up a separate vault server.

WARNING: ***The following procedure will overwrite the current datasets and file stores in your current Vault. Be sure to back up any necessary Vaults that might be required at a later time.***

1. Click **Start>All Programs>Autodesk>Autodesk Data Management>Autodesk Data Management Server Console 2027**.
2. In the *Log In* dialog box:
   - For *User Name*, enter **administrator**.
   - Leave *Password* blank.
   - Click **OK**.
   - The Autodesk Data Management Server Console displays.
3. Select **Tools>Backup and Restore**.
4. Select **Restore**, then click **Next**.

5. In the *Backup and Restore Wizard* dialog box, in *Select backup directory for restore:*, navigate to the location on your local C: drive where the files were extracted.

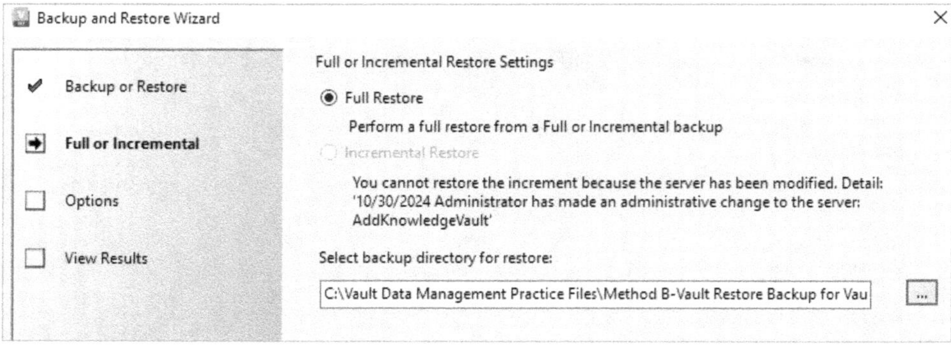

6. In the *Backup and Restore Wizard* dialog box, in the *Database data location* area, select **Default Restore Location**. In the *File Store location* area, select **Original Restore Location.**

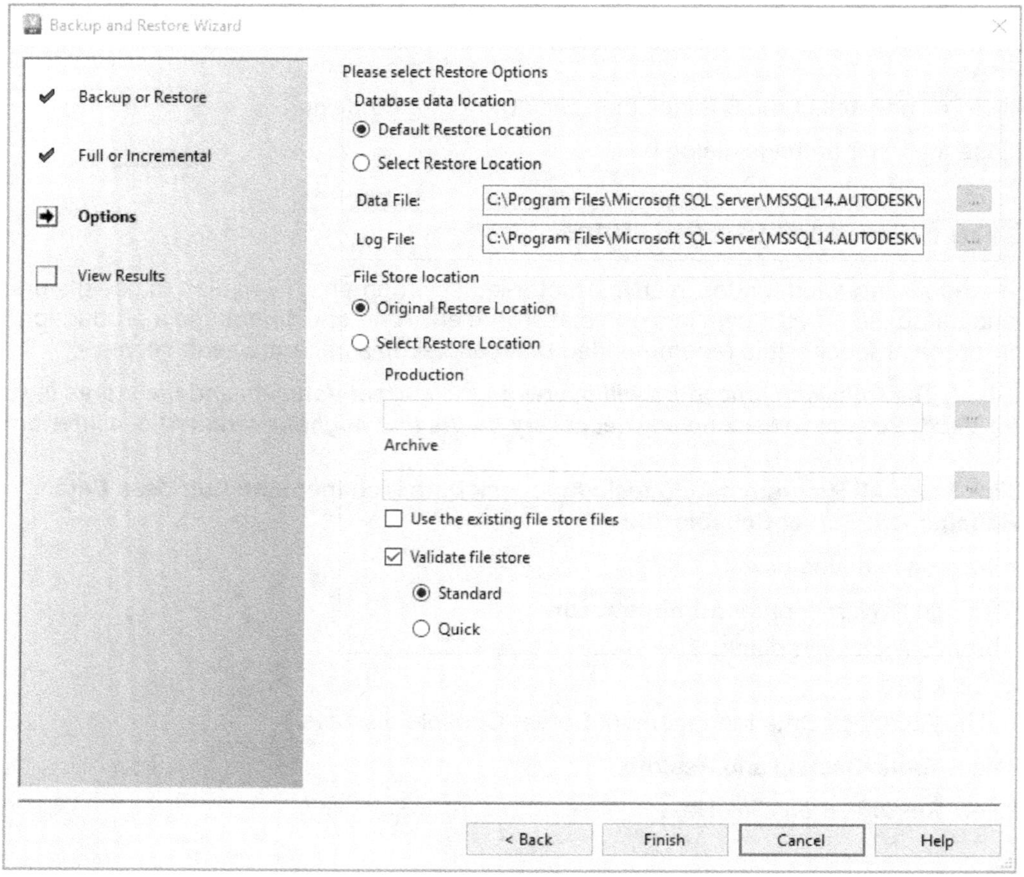

7. Click **Finish**.
8. In the prompt that displays, click **Yes** (as shown below) **only if you are sure that you want to delete the current datasets**.

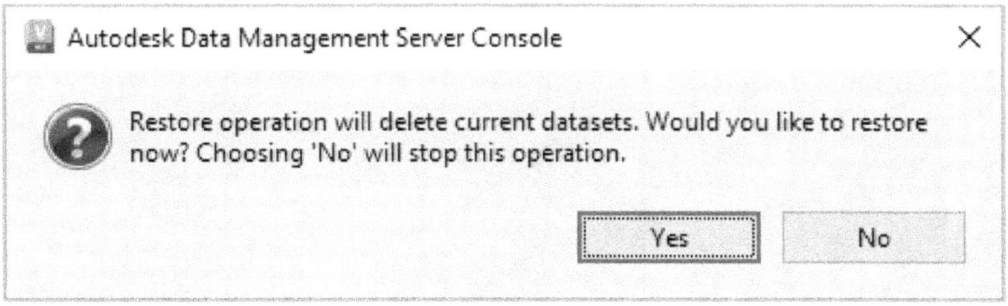

9. The *Restore Progress* dialog box displays the progress for restoring the database.
10. Click **Close** when complete.
11. In the *Autodesk Data Management Server Console* dialog box, click **File>Exit**.

Chapter 1

Introduction to Autodesk Vault

Autodesk® Vault is Product Data Management (PDM) software that enables you to secure, consolidate, and organize all product information for easy reference, sharing, and reuse. Autodesk Vault users can store and search both non-CAD data (such as Microsoft® Word and Microsoft® Excel® files) and CAD data (such as Autodesk® Inventor®, AutoCAD®, and DWF files).

Learning Objectives

- Describe the key features and benefits of the Autodesk Vault software.
- Differentiate between terms used in the Autodesk Vault software.
- Identify the ways that Autodesk Vault functions can be accessed.

1.1 Autodesk Vault Features

Autodesk Vault is Product Data Management (PDM) software that manages the life of a design from conception to retirement. The files associated with the design are tracked and managed. The software also manages who is permitted to work with files at specific times.

The Autodesk Vault software's capabilities include:

- Central repository for data.
- Security access control to data.
- Protection against accidentally overwriting design data.
- Object relationship management.
- Revision history tracking.
- Search and view tools to easily find and view design data.
- Management of CAD and non-CAD data.
- Direct CAD Integration with Autodesk CAD products: Autodesk Inventor, AutoCAD, AutoCAD Mechanical, Autodesk® Civil 3D®, and many more.
- Copy Design tool for copying an entire design, including all related files, and maintaining their relationships to each other in the new design.
- Change Management functionality.
- Items/Bill of Materials Management.

This guide covers the core functionality of the Autodesk Vault Basic and Professional software from a user's perspective.

1.2 Terms and Definitions

Before working with the software, it is recommended to become familiar with the fundamental terminology of the Autodesk Vault software. This section describes some of the commonly used Autodesk Vault terminology.

Object

Object is a generic term used to describe anything stored in the Autodesk Vault database, such as files and items.

File

File is the term used to describe files stored in the Autodesk Vault database. The vault can store any type of file, including Autodesk Inventor, Project files, AutoCAD, AutoCAD Mechanical, AutoCAD Electrical, Autodesk Revit, Autodesk Civil 3D, Microsoft Excel, Microsoft Word, etc.

By default, files stored in the Autodesk Vault database do not require unique filenames. To enforce unique file names, select **Tools>Administration>Vault Settings** and select **Define** in the *File Options* section. In the *File Name Options* dialog box, select **Enforce unique file name** (as shown in Figure 1–1) to ensure that the filenames are unique in the Autodesk Vault software. You can also allow duplicate file names for selected extensions or files in specified folders, if required.

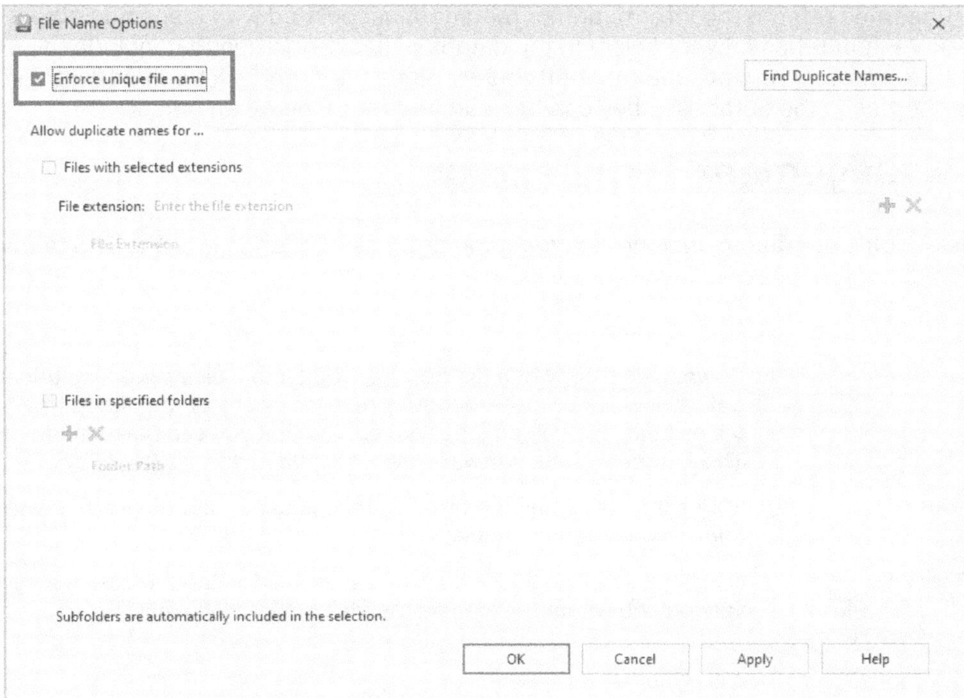

Figure 1–1

Best Practice: Using Unique Filenames

Enforcing unique filenames is a recommended best practice. If not previously enforced, you can search for duplicates by clicking Find Duplicates.

Item

An item is an object type that represents all information related to the end item part. It is a container for data that can include Autodesk Inventor files (and other associated reference files), ECOs (Change Order), and BOMs. Items refer to what a company manages, assembles, sells, and manufactures. An item is identified by its item number or part number. Not only can items represent parts and assemblies, they can also represent paint, lubricants, etc.

Change Order

A Change Order, also referred to as an ECO, is an object that describes why, how, and when changes are made to an Item and/or file. The result and purpose of a Change Order is to release these objects.

Properties/Metadata

Object properties refer to the information or metadata associated with a specific object in the Autodesk Vault database. Every object in the database has properties that include the object name, state, revision, version, and other attributes. Since the Autodesk Vault software stores these properties in the database, they can be searched for to locate an object.

File Management Terminology

Autodesk Vault's operations include recording the process of change in a file. The terminology related to these processes is described as follows:

Term	Description
Get	Downloads a copy of a file from the vault into a user's working folder. This option enables you to either get a read-only copy of the files, or mark the file as being worked on (checked out) so that you can make modifications. The Autodesk Vault software always contains the master copy of the file.
Check Out	Marks the file as being worked on (checked out) but does not download a copy to your working folder.
Undo Check Out	Checks the selected files back in, unmodified, without creating a new version and without uploading the files back to the vault.

Term	Description
Check In	Uploads a file from the user's working folder to the Autodesk Vault database. You are prompted to save a file before check in if you have not already done so.
Open	Opens the latest version of a file in the associated application. It downloads a copy of the file from the vault into a user's working folder.
Version	Defines the state of the file in the change process. It is an incremental numeric attribute that changes every time a file is changed and submitted (checked in) to the database.
Working Copy	A local copy of the file that has been downloaded from the vault and is located in a local directory or workspace on your machine. The downloading takes place during **Get** and **Open** operations.
File Status in Vault (Vault Status)	Defined by both the state of the file (checked in, checked out, etc.) and the state of the file in the vault compared to the local copy on the user's file system (newer, older, etc.).
Refresh	Updates the current state of the files in the vault.
Revision	Defines a collection of versions with a single character typically, such as A or B. A revision is created with the **Revise** command. Revisions can also be automatically generated through a Lifecycle State change.

Best Practice: Delete Working Copies

The vault contains all of the master files, which means you are working on a copy of the master file each time you check it out. When you check a file back into the Vault, it becomes the latest version of the master file. Consider your workspace or local working folders as a temporary location for your design files as they are being modified. A recommended best practice is to delete the working copies when you check them in.

Category

Categories are used to group objects and help to assign behaviors and rules to each group of objects. A category can automatically assign user-defined properties to objects in the Vault. Categories can also be used to automatically assign lifecycle definitions or revision values to files.

Lifecycle

Lifecycles are used to manage the stages of maturity of an object. Objects such as files, items and change orders move from state to state (e.g., **Work in Progress>For Review>Released,** etc.), as managed by the lifecycle definition. At each lifecycle state, an individual is responsible for performing some type of work. An example of a file or item lifecycle is shown in Figure 1–2. An example of a change order object or ECO lifecycle is shown in Figure 1–3.

File or Item Lifecycle Example

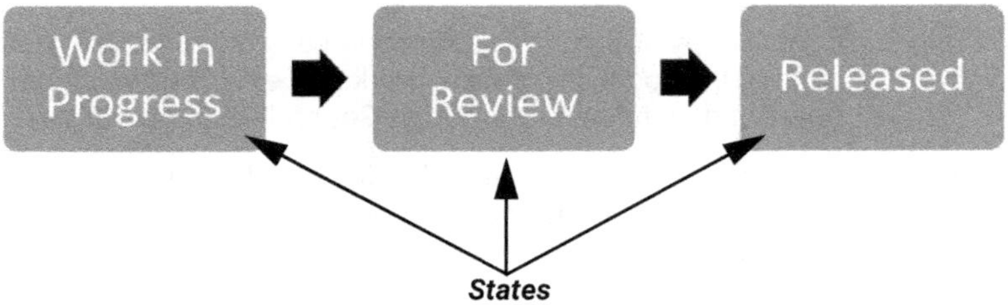

Figure 1–2

ECO (Change Order) Lifecycle Example

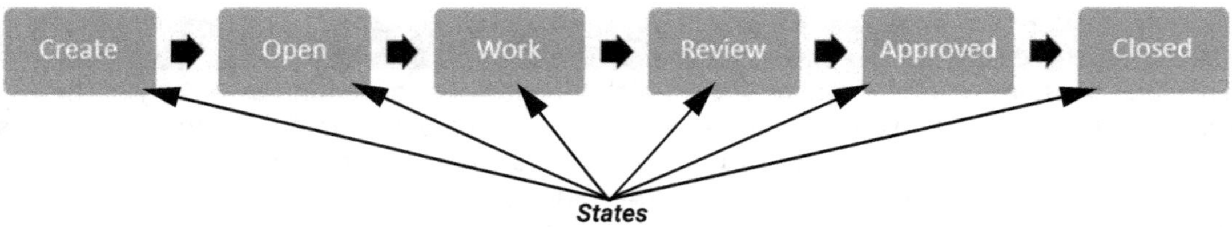

Figure 1–3

1.3 Accessing Autodesk Vault

There are two ways of accessing Autodesk Vault functions:

- Logging in to the Autodesk Vault Client.
- Logging in from the Autodesk CAD software or Microsoft Office product to use the Autodesk Vault Add-in.

Autodesk Vault Client

The Autodesk Vault Client (also referred to as Autodesk Vault Explorer), provides the user interface for accessing data in the vault. Tasks performed in the Autodesk Vault Client software include searching the vault, viewing file status and history, and checking files in and out.

The Autodesk Vault Client can be launched via the desktop icon or the Start menu. It can also be launched and accessed from the Autodesk CAD software or Microsoft application via the Add-In ribbon icon, as shown in Figure 1–4.

Figure 1–4

The Autodesk Vault Client software displays a complete view of the data in the vault, as shown in Figure 1–5.

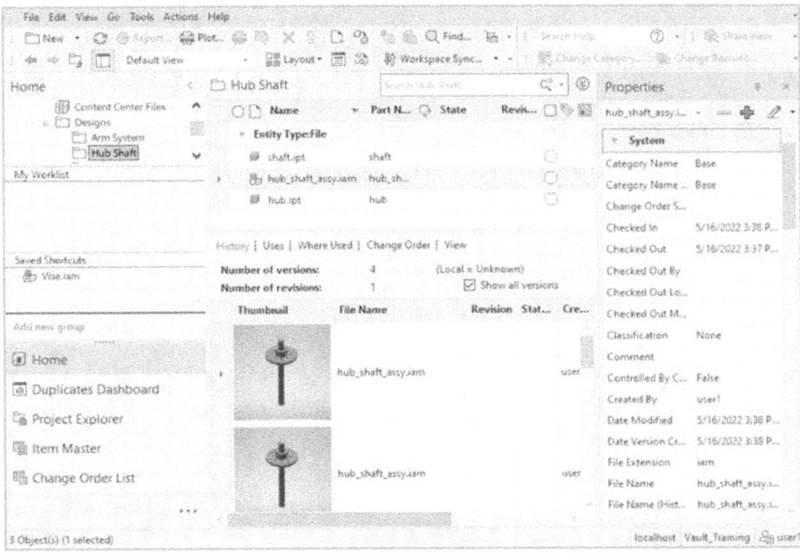

Figure 1–5

Autodesk Vault Add-in

Most Autodesk and Microsoft Office products have a direct integration with Autodesk Vault using the Autodesk Vault Add-in. This means that the products have a Vault menu or tab in its interface, providing quick access to the Autodesk Vault options. File operations, such as Check In and Check Out, can be performed from within the Autodesk CAD or Microsoft Office interface to maintain file relationship integrity. The add-in is typically used more on a daily basis than the Vault Client since it allows users to perform most of their tasks. It is also used to Check In (upload) files to vault for the first time.

An example of the integration interface is shown in Figure 1–6.

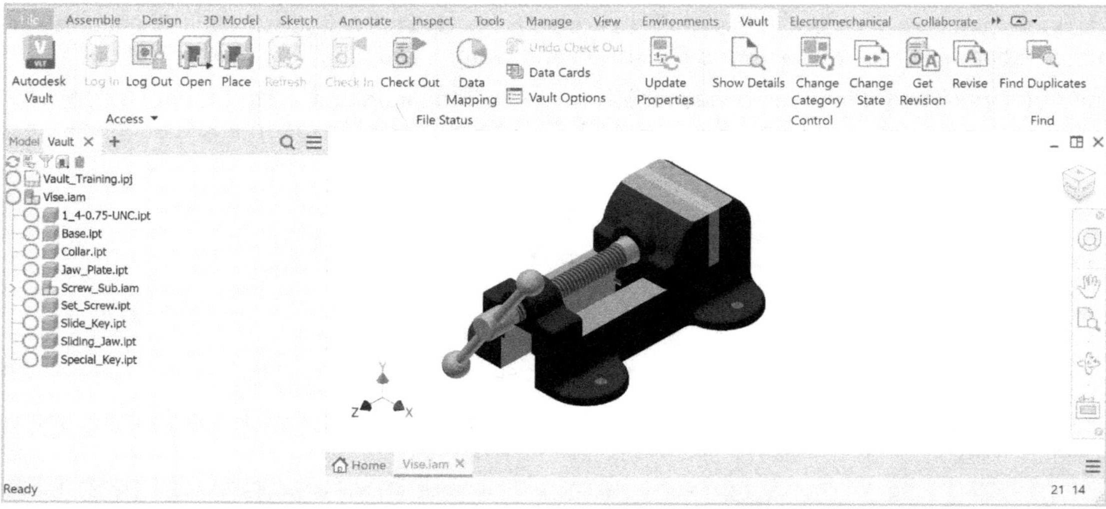

Figure 1–6

1.4 Accessing Help

To get information on how to use the Autodesk Vault software, you can use Help or the Autodesk Assistant that are available directly from the software interface.

Help

If you are connected to the Internet, you can access Online Help. To open the Help documentation:

- click (Help) in the top-right corner of the interface,
- select the **Help** menu > **Autodesk Vault Professional Help Topics**,
- or press <F1>.

You can then use the *Search* field in the browser to search for a topic or browse the available list of topics.

Autodesk Assistant in Vault

Autodesk Assistant is an AI-powered tool integrated into the software. It provides conversational support, self-service features, and personalized assistance within Autodesk Vault. You can ask questions in the chat box about workflows, commands, and features to receive context-specific answers, troubleshoot issues, and work more efficiently.

> **Note:** *To use the Autodesk Assistant in Vault, the user's profile must have the Autodesk ID authentication method enabled with their Autodesk ID email address. The user does not need to log into Vault using the Autodesk ID method but they must be signed into their Autodesk Account on the desktop.*

How To: Use Autodesk Assistant

1. In the Title Bar, click (Autodesk Assistant) to open the *Autodesk Assistant* panel shown in Figure 1–7.

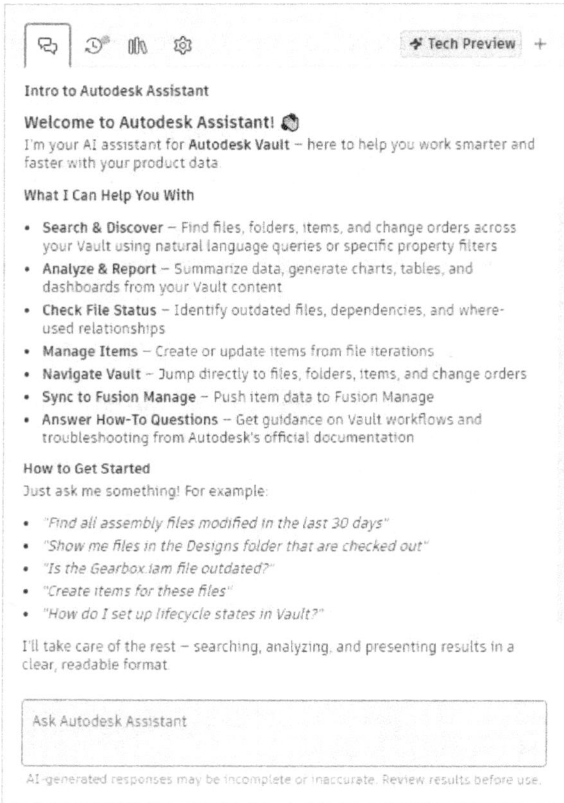

Figure 1–7

*Note: **Autodesk Assistant** was introduced in Autodesk Vault 2027, and its capabilities are expected to evolve in future releases. By default, **Tech Preview** mode is activated, but you can disable it by clicking Settings tab ( ) in the Autodesk Assistant panel and toggling off the option. Disabling **Tech Preview** mode does not disable all Autodesk Assistant features. Instead, it limits the Autodesk Assistant to offering guidance based only on existing Autodesk product documentation. With **Tech Preview** mode activated, the Autodesk Assistant can work with your Vault data to help you find files, update files, and sync data across systems.*

2. Enter your question in the chat box, as shown on the left in Figure 1–8. Autodesk Assistant responds with AI generated answers, as shown on the right in Figure 1–8.

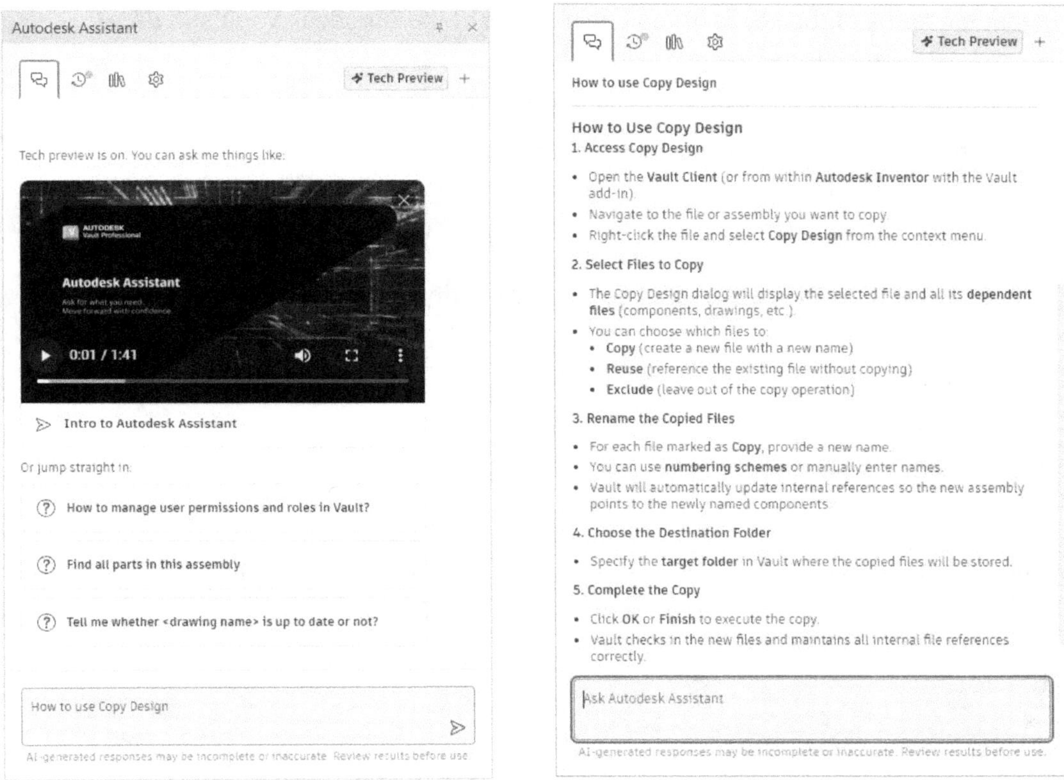

Figure 1–8

3. You can continue the conversation with Autodesk Assistant by entering additional prompts in the panel, or start a new chat by selecting + and **Got it**.

Note: Chat history is saved in the Chat History ( ) tab until you explicitly delete them. To delete a chat, hover over it in the list and click . The history also persists between Inventor sessions.

To use prompts more efficiently, consider the following:

- You can save existing prompts by hovering over them in the panel and clicking (Save prompt). All saved prompts are stored in the Prompt Library ( ) tab for reuse.
- You can copy an existing prompt from your conversation by hovering over it in the panel and clicking (Copy prompt).

Chapter Review Questions

1. What are some of the key features and benefits of the Autodesk Vault software?
   a. Central repository for data.
   b. Protection against accidentally overwriting design data.
   c. Search and display tools to easily find and view design data.
   d. All of the above.

2. What term is used to describe the stages of maturity of an object?
   a. Item
   b. Change Order
   c. Lifecycle
   d. Revision

3. The **Check Out** command downloads a copy of a file from the vault into a user's working folder.
   a. True
   b. False

4. Which of the following provides a complete view of all of the data files in the vault?
   a. Autodesk Vault Client (also known as Autodesk Vault Explorer)
   b. Autodesk Data Management Console
   c. Autodesk Inventor (or AutoCAD, Civil 3D, etc.)
   d. Vault Add-in

5. What term relates to the incremental numeric attribute that changes every time a file is changed, submitted, and checked in to the database?
   a. State
   b. Revision
   c. Version
   d. File Status

Chapter 2

Orientation to Autodesk Vault Client

Orientation to the Autodesk® Vault Client includes logging in to the software, setting up the vault folder structure, becoming familiar with the interface, and accessing data.

Learning Objectives

- Log in to the Autodesk Vault Client (Vault Explorer).
- Differentiate between the main areas of the Autodesk Vault interface.
- Describe the functions of each main area of the Autodesk Vault interface.
- Set the vault working folder.
- Set up the vault folder structure in the Autodesk Vault software.

2.1 Logging In to the Autodesk Vault Client

Use the following steps to log in to the Autodesk Vault Client software. Once logged in, you have access to the database, which includes the physical files and metadata.

How To: Log In to the Autodesk Vault Client

1. The Autodesk Vault Client can be started using one of the following methods:
   - Double-click on (Autodesk Vault Basic or Professional 2027) on the desktop.
   - Select **Autodesk Data Management>Autodesk Vault Basic or Professional 2027** from the **Start** menu.
   - Select **Autodesk Vault Basic or Professional 2027** in the desktop Apps list.
2. In the *Log In* dialog box, select a method from the *Authentication* drop-down list, as shown in Figure 2–1 (in this example, **Vault Account** is selected):
   - **Vault Account:** Enter a Vault account user name and password.

   Note: *If your current Vault account password does not meet the administrator's enforced password policy, you will be prompted to change it.*

   - **Windows Account:** Uses Windows Active Directory credentials, which are entered for you.
   - **Autodesk ID:** Uses Autodesk ID credentials.

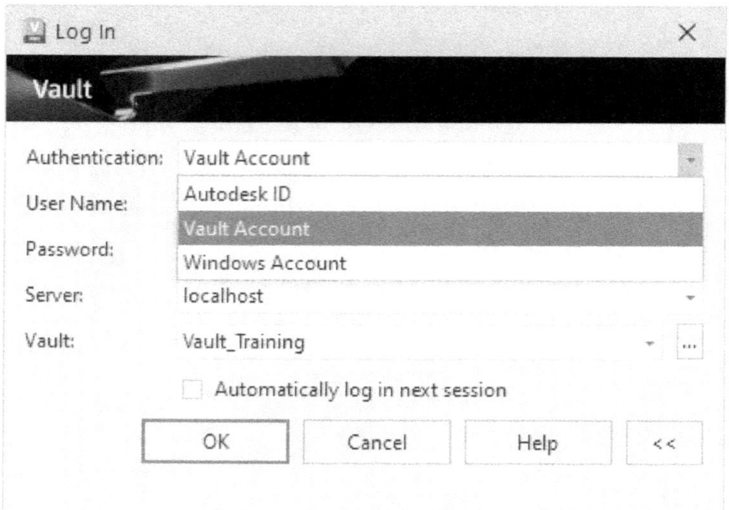

Figure 2–1

3. In the *Log In* dialog box, enter the *User Name* and *Password, as* shown in Figure 2–2.

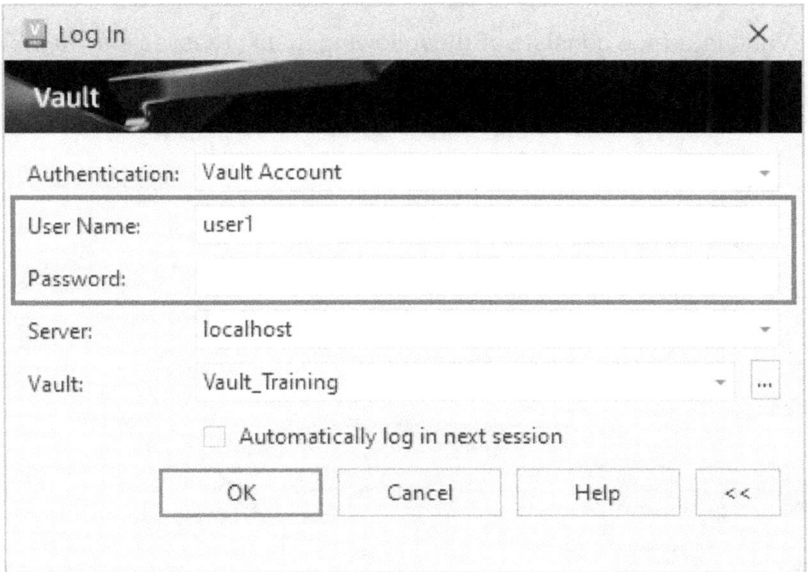

Figure 2–2

4. In the *Server* drop-down list, select the server, as required.

   Note: *The server and vault are set up and managed by the administrator; therefore, they will provide you with the Server: and Vault: selections.*

5. In the *Vault* drop-down list, select the vault, as required. You can also click ... (Browse) to display the list of active vaults.
6. Select **Automatically Log in next session**. In subsequent sessions, this enables you to be automatically logged into the vault as the previous specified user.
7. Click **OK**.

2.2 Autodesk Vault Interface Overview

The Autodesk Vault interface consists of the following main areas, as shown in Figure 2–3:

- Menu
- Toolbars
- Navigation pane
- Main table or pane
- Preview pane
- Properties grid

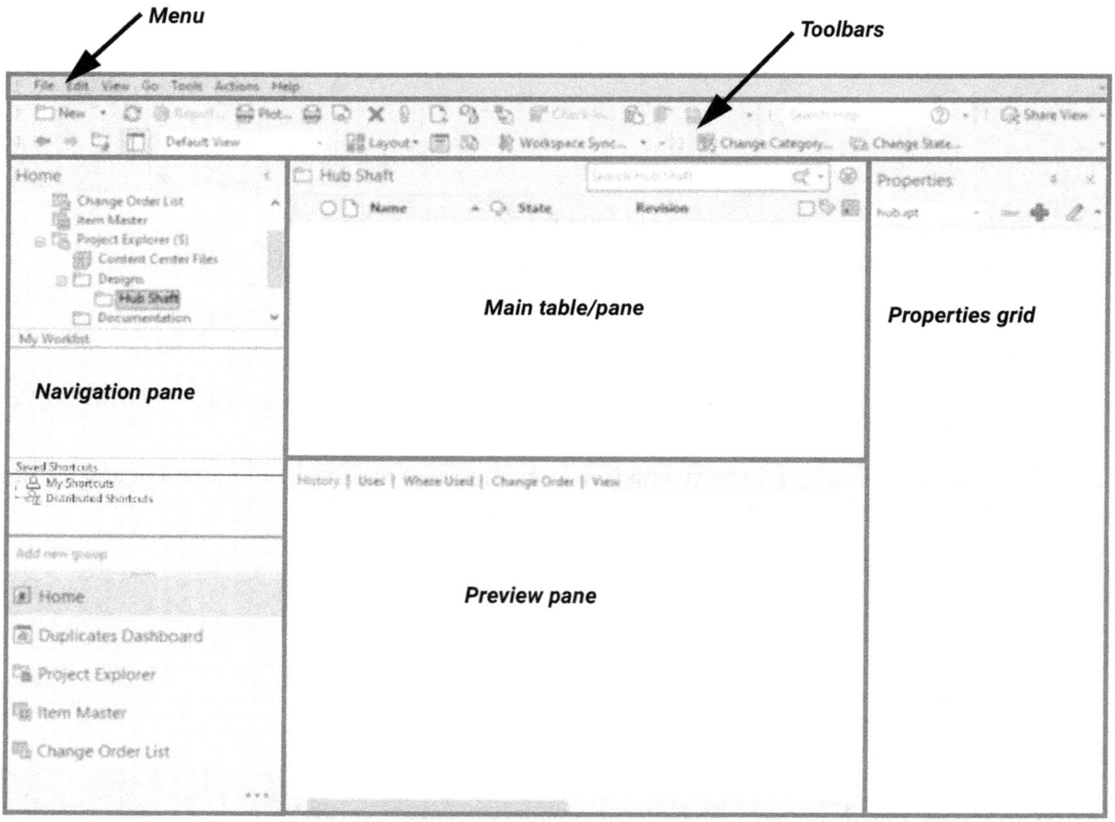

Figure 2–3

The Navigation pane shows the folder structure in a tree format, while the data displays in the Main and Preview panes in a column or grid format. An example is shown in Figure 2–4.

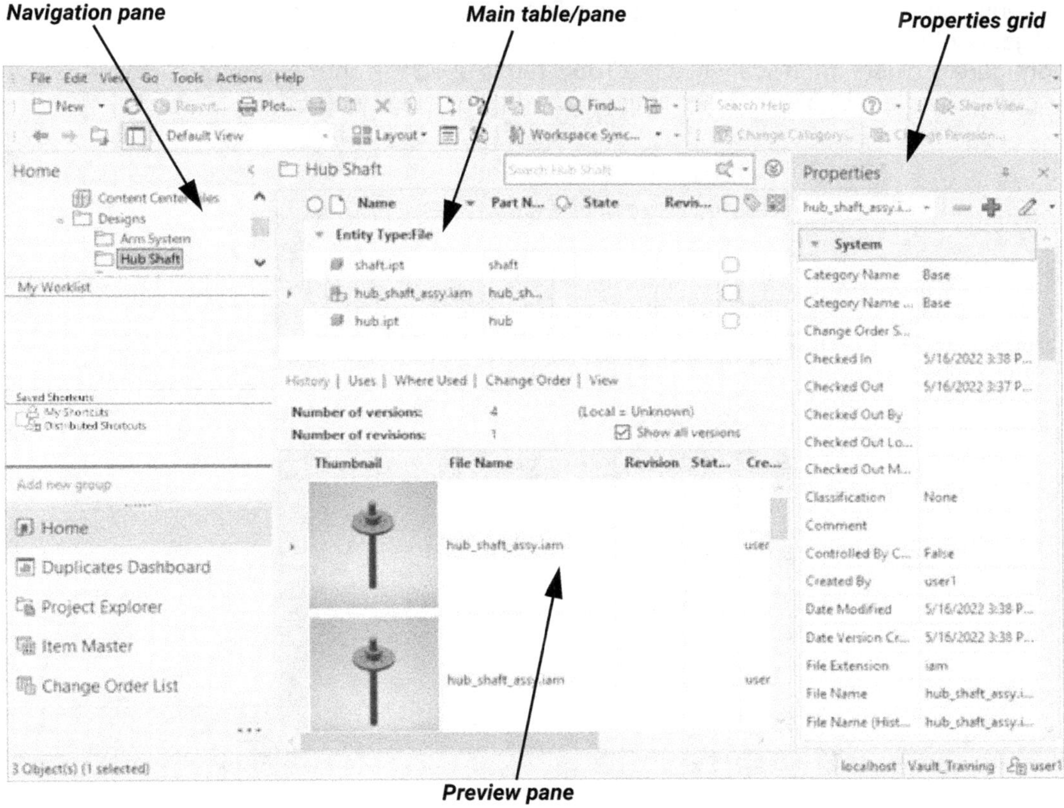

Figure 2–4

2.3 Menu

The menu consists of tabs, such as *File* and *Tools*, that provide access to operations and settings. For instance, the *File* tab is where you log in and out of the vault. The *View* tab is used to configure the user interface while the *Tools* tab is used to control settings. Click or hover your cursor over a tab to display its options, as shown in Figure 2–5.

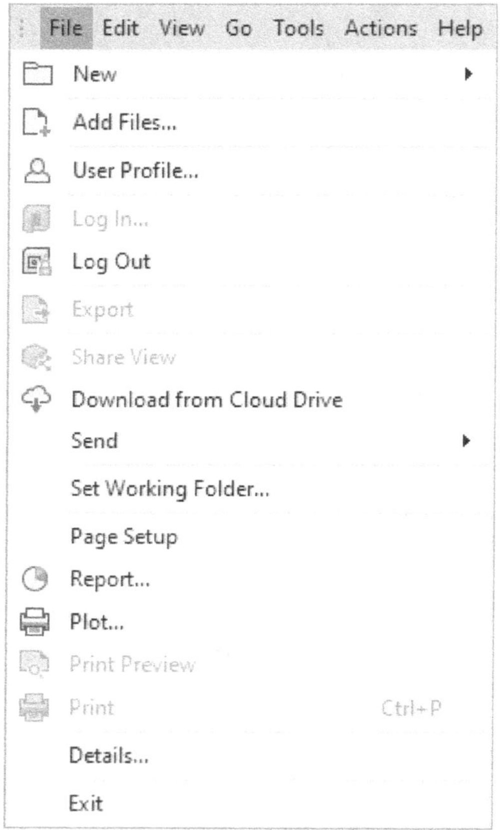

Figure 2–5

2.4 Toolbars

Autodesk Vault's standard and advanced toolbars, shown in Figure 2–6, provide fast access to many vault operations.

Figure 2–6

> **Note:** *The icons available depend on the files selected in the Main table.*

Standard Toolbar Icons

Icon	Name and Description
	**New Folder** or **New Library Folder:** Create a new folder or new library area.
	**Refresh:** Update the current state of the files in the vault.
	**Report:** Create report using selected template.
	**Plot:** Plot selected files.
	**Print Direct:** Print directly to the printer.
	**Print Preview:** Preview the output before it is printed.
	**Delete:** Delete the selected files.
	**Attachments:** Select a file and view its attachment or attach additional files, as required.
	**Add Files:** Add files to the vault.
	**Copy Design:** Copy an entire design, including all of the related files, parts, drawings, subassemblies, and attachments to a new design.
	**Copy Folder:** Copy an entire folder structure, including subfolders, folder permissions, and properties.

Icon	Name and Description
	**Check In:** Check in the selected files.
	**Get:** Download the selected files from the vault to the working folder and are read only by default.
	**Undo Check Out:** Undo the **Check Out** operation on selected files.
	**Find:** Search the vault by entering a specified text string.
	**Share View:** Upload to Autodesk Viewer and share views.
 	**Download from Cloud Drive:** Download the latest versions of the selected files from the Cloud Drive. **Upload to Cloud Drive:** Upload files to a selected Cloud Drive destination.

Advanced Toolbar Icons

Icon	Name and Description
	**Move Backward:** Moves you back to the previously selected folder in the Navigation pane.
	**Move Forward:** After moving backwards, click to return to the folder in which you started.
	**Up One Level:** Moves you back to the parent of the selected folder in the Navigation pane.
	**Preview Pane:** Toggles the Preview pane on and off.
	**Default View:** Controls whether the default view or a custom view is assigned to control the display of the Main table.
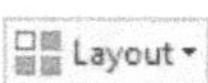	**Layout:** Controls the display of files in the Main table. Options include **Detail View**, **Small Icons**, or **Large Icons**.
	**Group By Box:** Groups column headings.
	**Auto Preview:** Displays comments for each file on a separate line below the file details.
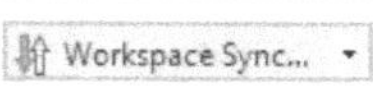	**Workspace Sync:** Synchronizes the contents of your local workspace with the contents of the corresponding Vault folders.

Icon	Name and Description
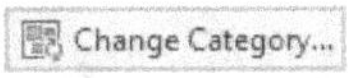	**Change Category:** Changes the category of the selected object.
	**Change State:** Changes the state of the selected object.
	**Change Revision:** Changes the revision of the selected object.

2.5 Navigation Pane

The Navigation pane, located on the left side of the interface, contains the *Home, Duplicates Dashboard, Project Explorer, Item Master,* and *Change Order List* tabs. The active tab is highlighted in gray in the lower half of the navigation window and the name displays at the top. When you select content within the tab, it is highlighted in blue and will display in the Main and Preview panes. The Duplicates Dashboard, Project Explorer, Item Master, and Change Order List data can be accessed by clicking on their respective links, or from the *Home* tab, as shown in Figure 2–7.

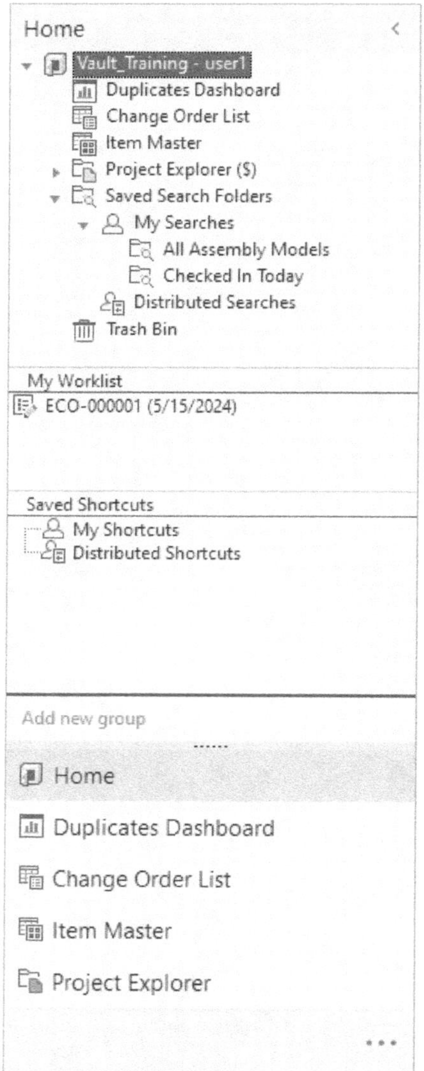

Figure 2–7

The Project Explorer displays the vault objects in a tree view, as shown in Figure 2–8.

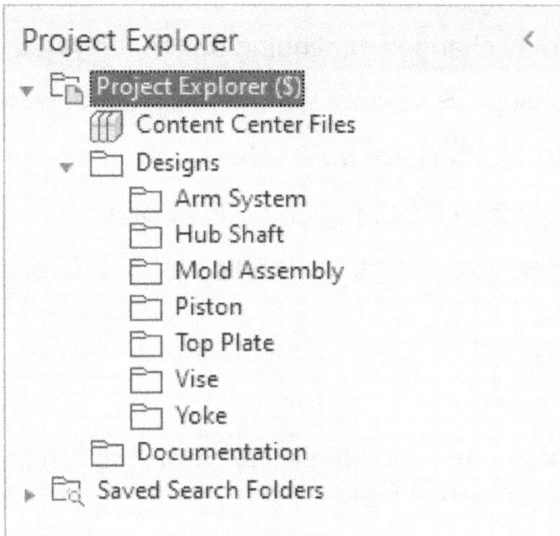

Figure 2–8

Folders with subfolders display (Expand) next to each folder name, which you can click to expand the branch. Expanded folders display (Collapse), which enables you to collapse the branch when clicked. Right-click on a folder to display the contextual options.

The Project Explorer also contains a folder called *Saved Search Folders*. You can use this to create saved searches for quick access.

> ***Note:*** *Saved Search Folders is also available on the Home, Change Order List, and Item Master tabs.*

2.6 Main Table

The Main table or pane display changes depending on the tab you are using:

- The *Project Explorer* tab displays objects that reside in the selected vault folder.
- The *Item Master* tab displays the Item Master list.
- The *Change Order List* tab displays the Change Order objects.
- The *Duplicates Dashboard* tab displays the Duplicate Parts Overview and Indexed Data Overview.

Project Explorer

When using the Project Explorer, the vault folder name displays in the Main table title bar. The Main table displaying files is shown in Figure 2–9.

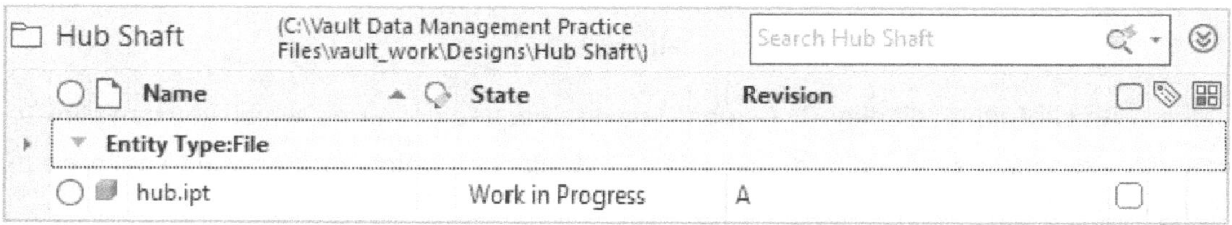

Figure 2–9

The default columns that display include: *Vault Status*, *Entity Icon*, *Name*, *State*, *Revision*, *Category Glyph*, *Property Compliance*, and *Linked to Item*.

By default, vault automatically generates .DWF files that are attached to all CAD files. These files are highly compressed versions of a CAD file that are used for visualization, such as preview thumbnails. The .DWF files are hidden by default. To display the .DWF file, select **Tools>Options...** and then select **Show hidden files** in the *Options* dialog box.

You can customize the columns in the Main table to show, remove, reorder, and sort additional file properties as required by right-clicking on a column header and using the **Customize View...>Fields...** option.

> **Note:** *It is a best practice to keep the DWF files hidden. If they display during checkout, they are also checked out.*

Item Master

If the *Item Master* tab is selected, the Main table displays the items in the table. The default columns that display include: *Vault Status, Number, Revision, State, Title (Item, CO), File Link State, Category Glyph, Property Compliance,* and *Controlled by Change Order,* as shown in Figure 2–10.

Figure 2–10

Change Order List

If the *Change Order List* tab is selected, the main table displays the Change Order objects in the table. The default columns that display include: *Vault Status, Number of File Attachments, Number, State, Title (Item, CO),* and *Due Date*, as shown in Figure 2–11.

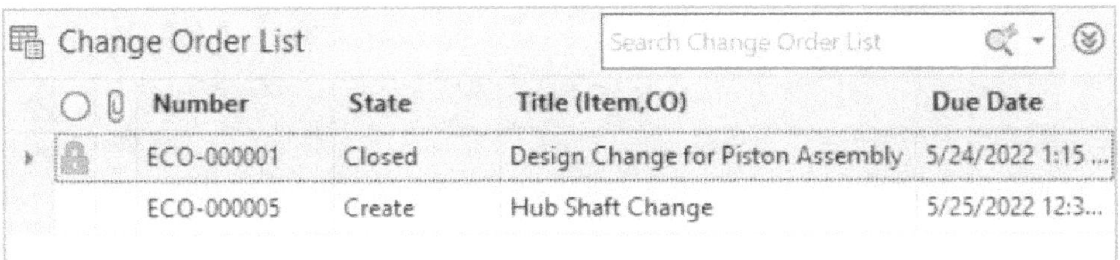

Figure 2–11

Duplicates Dashboard

If the *Duplicates Dashboard* tab is selected, the main table displays the Duplicate Parts Overview and Indexed Data Overview, as shown in Figure 2–12.

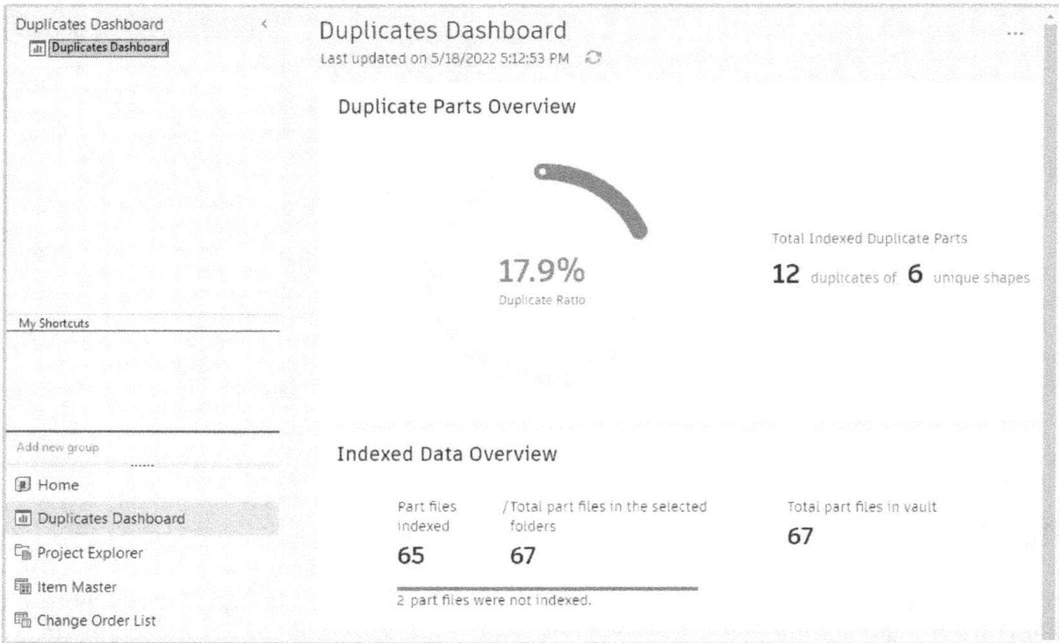

Figure 2–12

2.7 Preview Pane

The Preview pane is one of the main areas in the Autodesk Vault interface. When a file is selected, the Preview pane displays information, which is categorized into tabs. These tabs are different for the Project Explorer, Item Master, and Change Order List.

Project Explorer

When a file is selected in the Project Explorer, the tabs displayed in the Preview pane are *History*, *Uses*, *Where Used*, *Change Order*, and *View*.

History Tab

The *History* tab displays versions of the file that has been selected in the Main table. File properties display for each version. The default properties displayed include the *Thumbnail*, *File Name*, *Version*, *Created By* (which user checked in the file), *Checked In* (date of the version), and *Comment*, as shown in Figure 2–13.

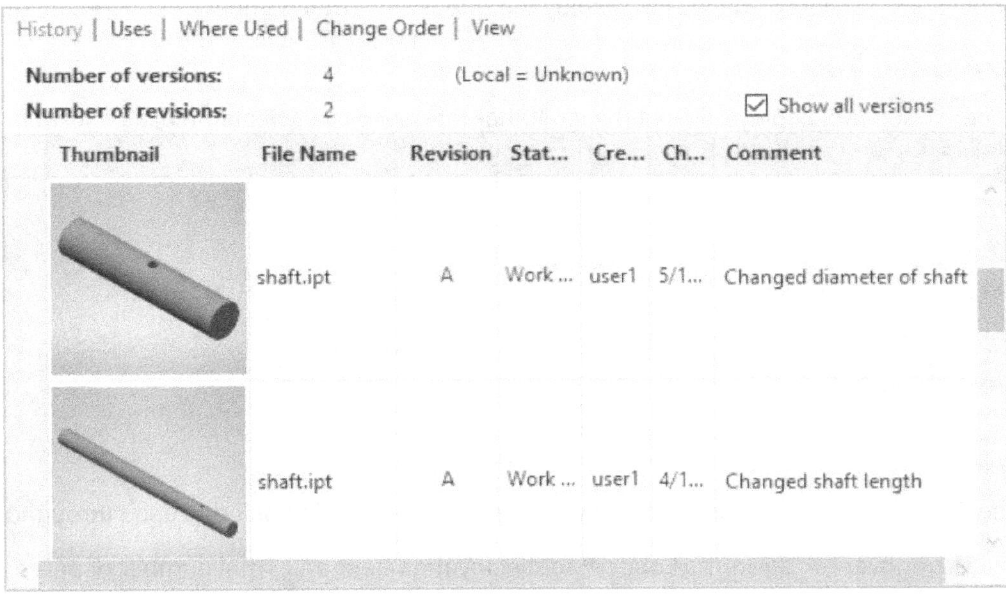

Figure 2–13

You can customize the columns to show, remove, reorder, and sort additional file properties as required by right-clicking on a column header and using the **Customize View...>Fields...** option.

Uses Tab

The *Uses* tab lists all of the files used in the selected file as shown in Figure 2–14.

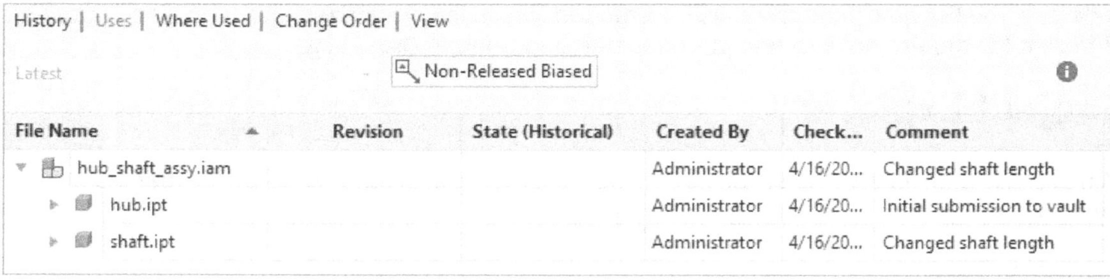

Figure 2–14

The *Revision* drop-down list enables you to see files that were used throughout the history of the selected file.

Hover over (Children Loaded) to display the Direct and Total number of children loaded.

Where Used Tab

The *Where Used* tab displays files in the vault that reference the selected file, as shown in Figure 2–15.

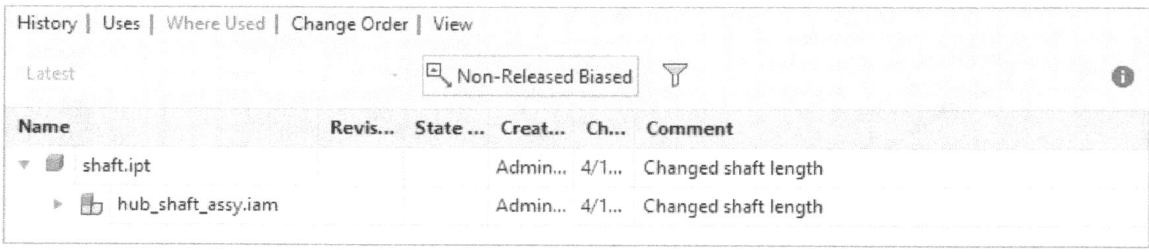

Figure 2–15

Use the *Revision* drop-down list to display where the selected file has been used throughout its history. Hover over (Parents Loaded) to display the Direct and Total number of parents loaded.

Change Order

The *Change Order* tab displays the change order associated with the file selected, if any exists, as shown in Figure 2–16.

Figure 2–16

Double-click on the change order item to open the change order dialog box.

View Tab

The *View* tab displays a carousel view of the selected file, as shown in Figure 2–17. The carousel view enables you to view thumbnails of the selected file and cycle through previous versions or revisions of the file. The file version or revision displays at the top of each thumbnail, and the last check in date displays at the bottom.

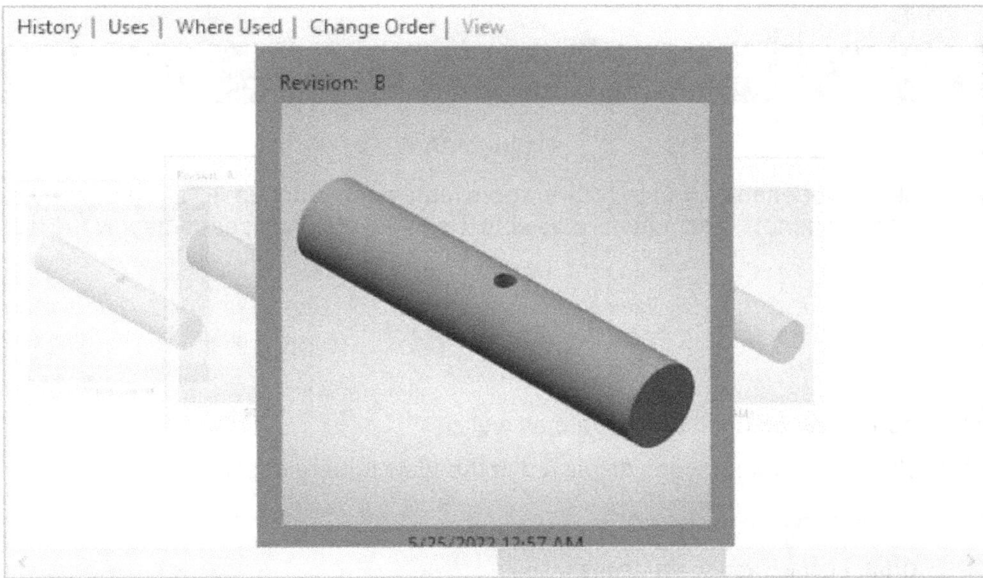

Figure 2–17

As previously mentioned, for CAD files (such as parts, assemblies, and Autodesk Inventor drawings), Autodesk Vault attaches a visualization file to the selected file. When the thumbnail is selected, the associated visualization file is loaded using the Autodesk Viewer (.IPT, .IAM, or .IDW) or a document previewer (.DOC, .XLS, .PPT, .XPS, .CSV, or .ZIP). When you select a previous version or release of a file, a warning displays. An example message is shown in Figure 2–18.

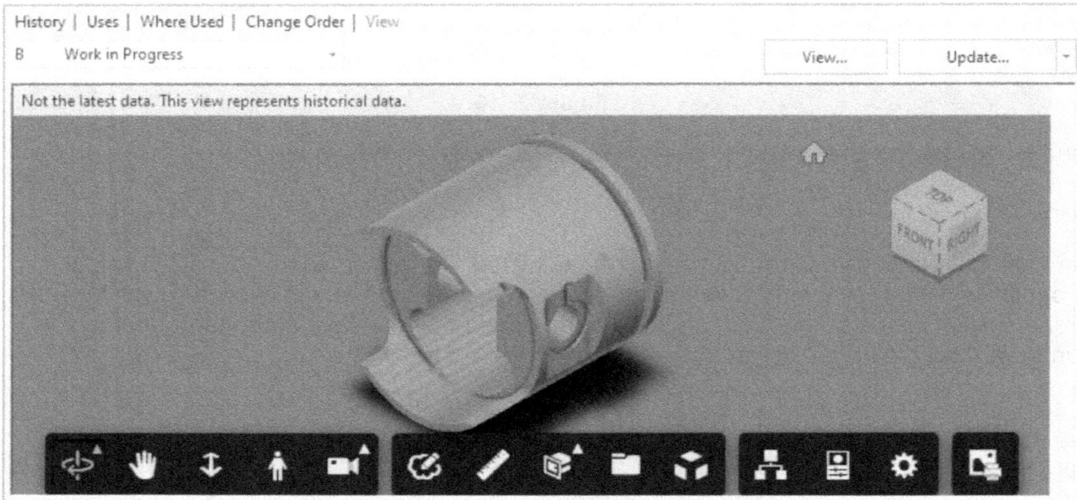

Figure 2–18

The Autodesk Viewer enables you to rotate, zoom, pan, print, mark up 2D and 3D objects, save and print image snapshots, and measure objects. Use the version slider to display the history of the file.

> ***Note:*** *You can select the Autodesk Viewer or Autodesk Design Review (ADR) under the Vault Options (Tools>Options) to view previews of files. By default, Autodesk Viewer is set to view the files.*

A wheeled mouse can be used to navigate as well.

The Autodesk Viewer toolbar icons displayed in the *View* tab are described below:

Icon	Name and Description
	**Orbit:** Enables you to rotate the object.
	**Pan:** Enables you to move the object.
	**Zoom:** Enables you to zoom in or out of the model.

<table>
<tr><th>Icon</th><th>Name and Description</th></tr>
<tr><td></td><td>First Person: Enables you to explore the object from a first person perspective.</td></tr>
<tr><td></td><td>Camera Interactions: Enables you to fit the object into the view window, to roll the object, and to set the focal length.</td></tr>
<tr><td></td><td>Markup: Enables you to create annotations for the object. These annotations, also known as markups, can be viewed, filtered, renamed, and deleted through the Markup Browsing Panel.
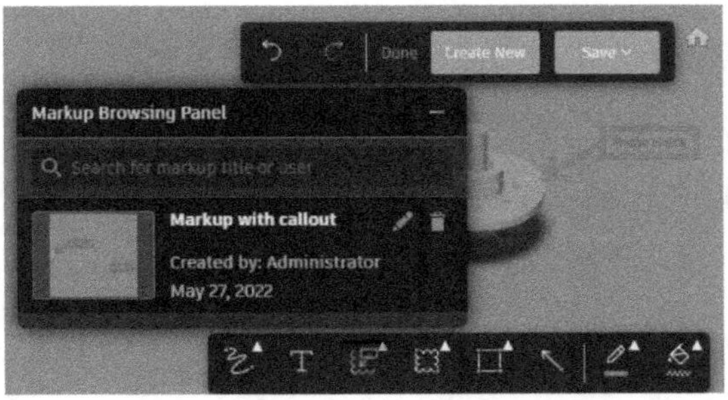

You can also save the markup as a screenshot image to your local machine or save it to the Vault as data. When saved to the Vault, the markup can be viewed again in the Markup Browsing Panel.
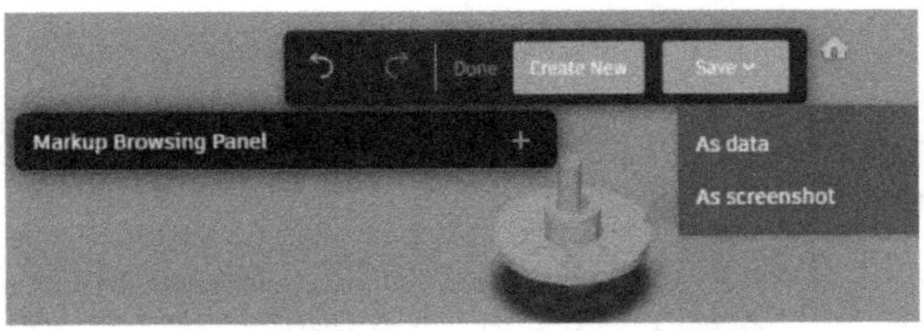
</td></tr>
<tr><td></td><td>Measure: Enables you to measure the distance between two points or an angle between three points.</td></tr>
<tr><td></td><td>Section Analysis: Enables you to cut through a design along an axis with a plane, or through a selected box.</td></tr>
<tr><td></td><td>Document Browser: Enables you to display model information.</td></tr>
<tr><td></td><td>Explode Model: Enables you to separate a model's geometry to view individual parts of the design.</td></tr>
<tr><td></td><td>Model Browser: Enables you to navigate the model's geometry and control the display of parts of a model.</td></tr>
</table>

Icon	Name and Description
	**Properties:** Enables you to display a design's properties such as part numbers, types of material, and mechanical properties.
	**Settings:** Enables you to configure settings such as reducing image quality to improve performance, changing the background color, and changing how navigational elements (such as zoom) interact with the design.
	**Print Snapshot:** Enables you to print what is rendered in the *View* tab.

Non-DWF documents can also be previewed, including the following file formats:

- Microsoft® Office Word (.DOC, .DOCX, .DOT, .DOTX, and .RTF)
- Microsoft® Office Excel® (.XLS, .XLSB, .XLSX, and .XLTX)
- Microsoft® Office PowerPoint® (.POT, .POTX, .PPS, .PPSX, .PPT, and .PPTX)
- Microsoft® Outlook® Email previewer (*.msg)
- PDF preview handler (.PDF)
- XPS viewer (.XPS)
- Comma separated values (.CSV)
- Compressed files (.ZIP)

To control which application will be used as the default viewer for the various file formats, select **Tools>Options** and click **Document Previewers...**.

For files that cannot be viewed with the DWF Viewer or a document viewer, right-click on the file and select **Open**, select **File>Open**, or click **Open...** in the Preview pane to launch the associated application and display the file.

Item Master

For Item Master, the tabs are *General*, *History*, *Bill of Materials*, *Where Used, Change Order*, and *View*.

Additional details will be covered in ***10.1 Items and Bills of Materials*** in ***Chapter 10 Items and Bill of Materials Management***.

Change Order List

For Change Order List, the tabs are *General*, *Records*, *Comments*, *Files*, *Routing*, and *Status*.

Additional details will be covered in ***Chapter 11 Change Management***.

2.8 Properties Grid

You can display properties in the Properties Grid, as shown in Figure 2–19.

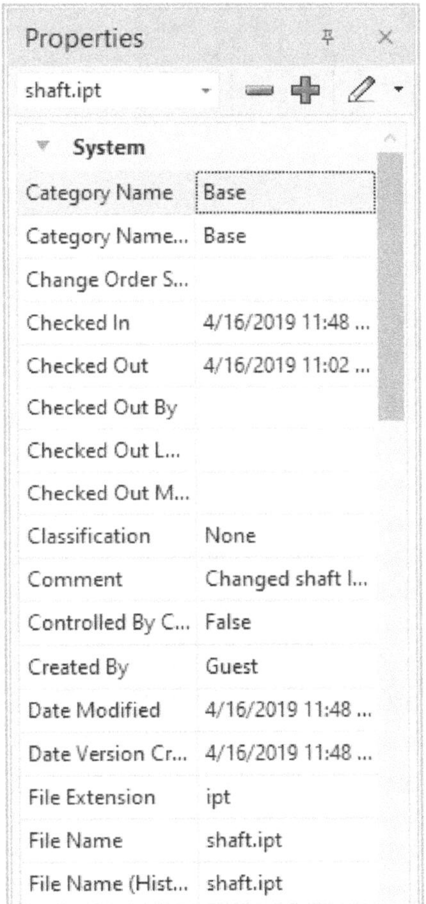

Figure 2–19

To manage file properties, select **Tools>Administration>Vault Settings**, and then in the *Behaviors* tab, click **Properties...** in the *Properties* area. The *Property Definitions* dialog box opens, as shown in Figure 2–20.

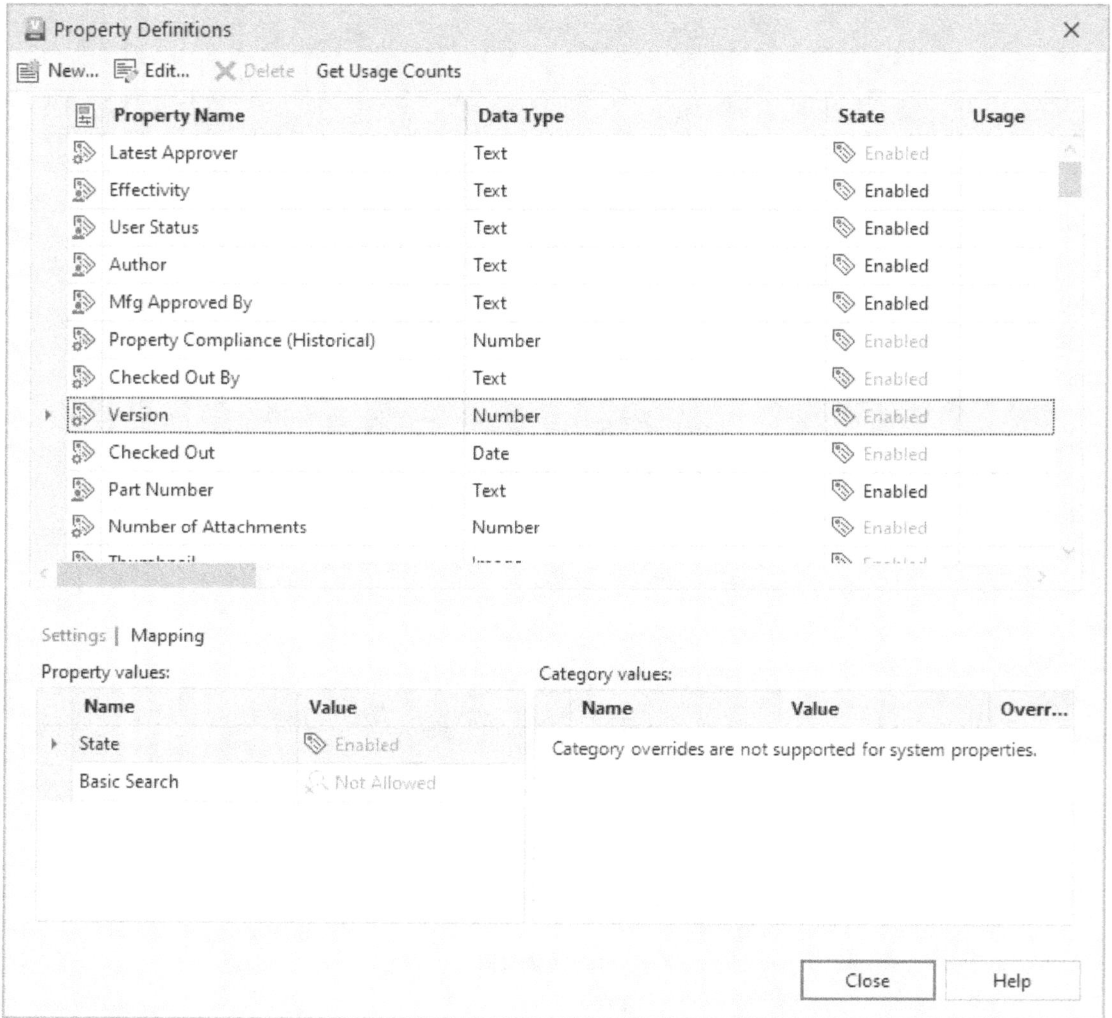

Figure 2–20

2.9 Folder Structure

Folder structure refers to where the files are located and accessed. It is very important to understand folder structure, because this is the area you interface with the most when working with vault, and it is what establishes the relationship between the file location in the vault relative to the local copy location. Each company determines what their folder structure standard will be based on their needs and processes.

After logging in to the Autodesk Vault Client for the first time, you should familiarize yourself with the vault folder structure in the Navigation pane and associated local folders.

Vault Folders

The Root in the Autodesk Vault Client (also known as the Project Explorer Root) is the top-level directory and is defined as $. Typically, a *Designs* folder or project folders are created below the Root to hold all of your designs. Library folders contain read-only library parts and require their own folder structure, separate from the *Designs* folder structure. They must also be located directly below the Root.

Working Folder

The working folder is the location on the client machine in which the user will work on the vault files. When design files from vault are copied (downloaded) to the client machine, the vault folders and files are placed in the working folder. The working folder is a direct duplicate of the folder and file hierarchy that is established in vault.

This is also the location that you will place new design folders and files before you upload them to vault. New folders and files need to be created in the proper structure within the working folder.

The working folder is set for the Root of the vault, not for each folder. This is because the folder structure used in the vault is automatically replicated below the working folder on the client machine when using the **Get** command. When the Autodesk Vault Client software is installed, a working folder is defined by default so that you can begin working with a vault. The default working folder is *My Documents>Vault*.

A new working folder can be defined if a consistent working folder for all users has not been enforced by the system administrator. If the administrator has enforced a consistent working folder, a warning message opens indicating that the working folder cannot be changed if you try to set a new one.

An example of the Vault Project Explorer and the working folder structure duplication is shown in Figure 2–21.

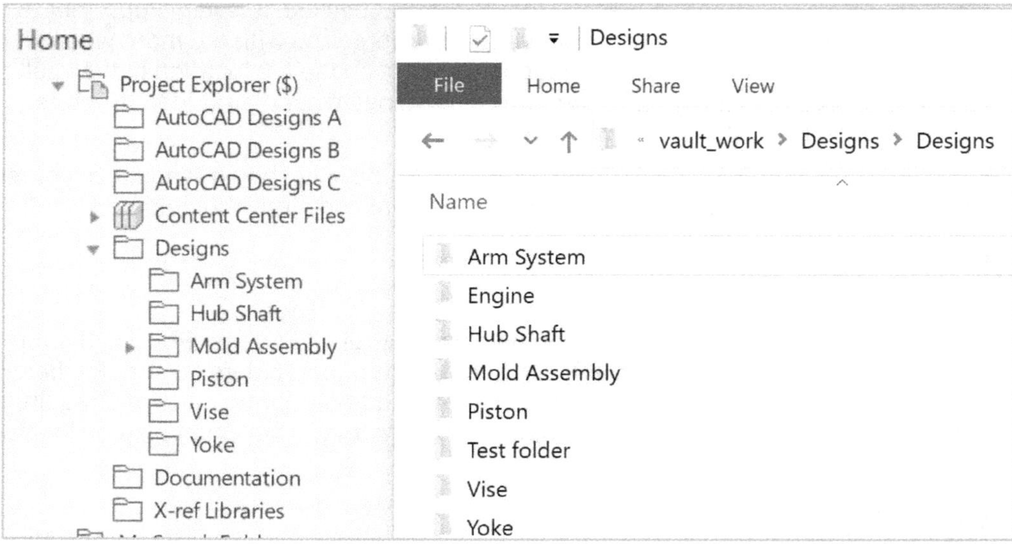

Figure 2–21

By default, the working folder path is not displayed in the Vault Client title bar. To display the path, select **Tools** (in **Menu**)>**Options** and select the **Show working folder location** option.

Best Practice: Store Files Temporarily in Working Folder

As a recommended best practice, the working folder should be considered a temporary folder in which to store files until they are checked back into the vault. Once checked back into the vault, the files should be deleted.

How To: Set Up the Vault Folder Structure

The folder structure is typically enforced by the system administrator or a third-party that implements your vault. Follow these directions only if you do not have an administrator.

1. To set the working folder, select the root folder of the vault in the Vault Client, then select **File** (in **Menu**)>**Set Working Folder...**, as shown in Figure 2–22.

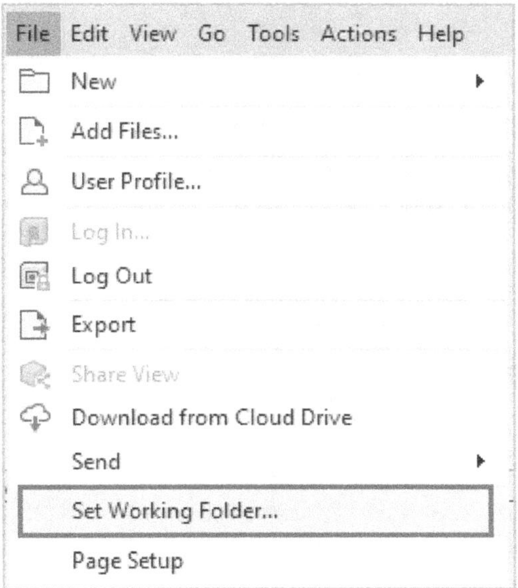

Figure 2–22

Note: *A working folder is set up for each user, machine, and vault.*

2. Browse to the folder on your machine that is at the top-level directory of all of your design folders. Click **OK** when the design folder is selected. If the folder does not exist, you can create one by clicking **Make New Folder**.
3. Create the top-level design folder if it has not already been created. Select the Project Explorer Root, right-click on it, and select **New Folder**, as shown in Figure 2–23.

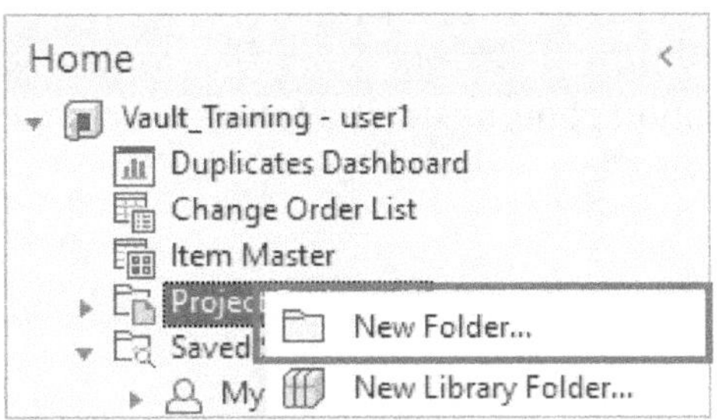

Figure 2–23

You can create as many subfolders for each design as required. If a folder hierarchy exists on the local machine, the folder hierarchy in the vault should match. However, if vault folders do not have a match on the local machine, the folder structure on the local machine is replicated to match the vault folder structure, as required, when using the **Get** command.

Similarly, if the *Designs* local folder structure contains additional subfolders in preparation for adding designs to the vault, these subfolders are automatically created (as required) in the vault as files are added. When you have created the required folders, you might need to make corrections or modifications to the folder structure, such as renaming or deleting folders.

- To rename a folder, right-click on it and select **Rename**.
- To delete a folder, right-click on it and select **Delete**.

4. Create the top-level library folder if it has not already been created. Select the Vault Explorer Root, right-click, and select **New Library Folder**, as shown in Figure 2–24.

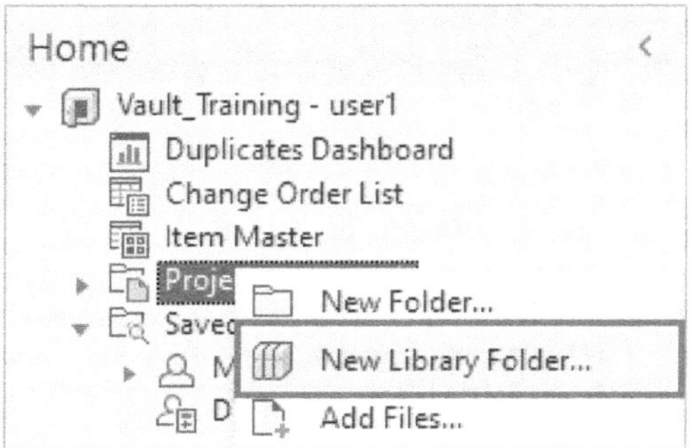

Figure 2–24

Copy Folder

To assist in maintaining proper folder structure and streamline the setup of a new project, you can use the **Copy Folder** command in the Vault Client to start with a known folder structure. This feature can copy a folder's original structure, including subfolders, folder permissions, and properties.

How To: Copy Folder

1. In the Vault Client Navigation pane, select the folder to be copied.

2. Right-click and select **Copy Folder...**, as shown in Figure 2–25.

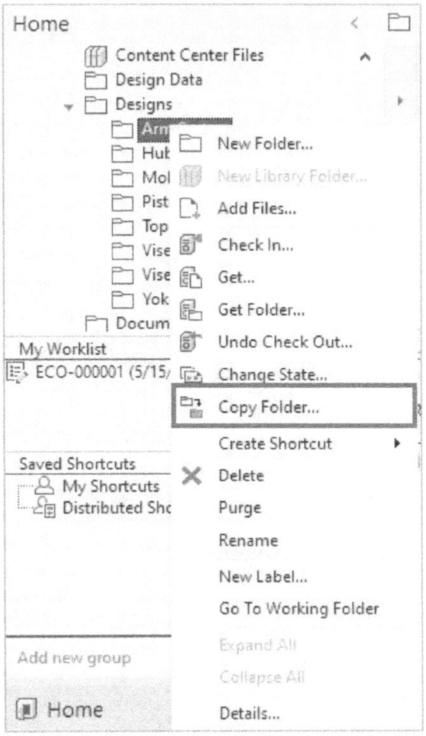

Figure 2–25

3. In the *Copy Folder* dialog box, define the new folder name, as shown in Figure 2–26.

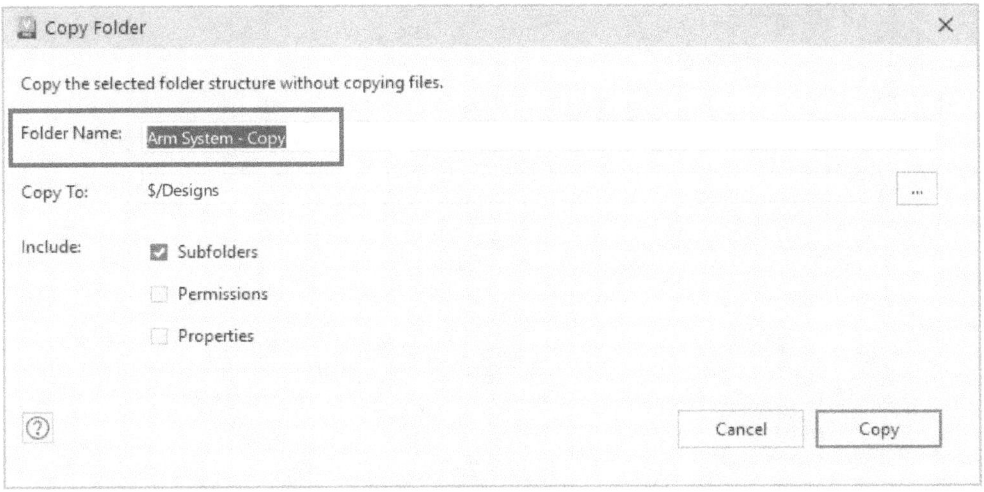

Figure 2–26

4. If desired, redefine the folder location by clicking on the icon adjacent to *Copy To:* (shown in Figure 2–27) and select the new folder location, as shown in Figure 2–28.

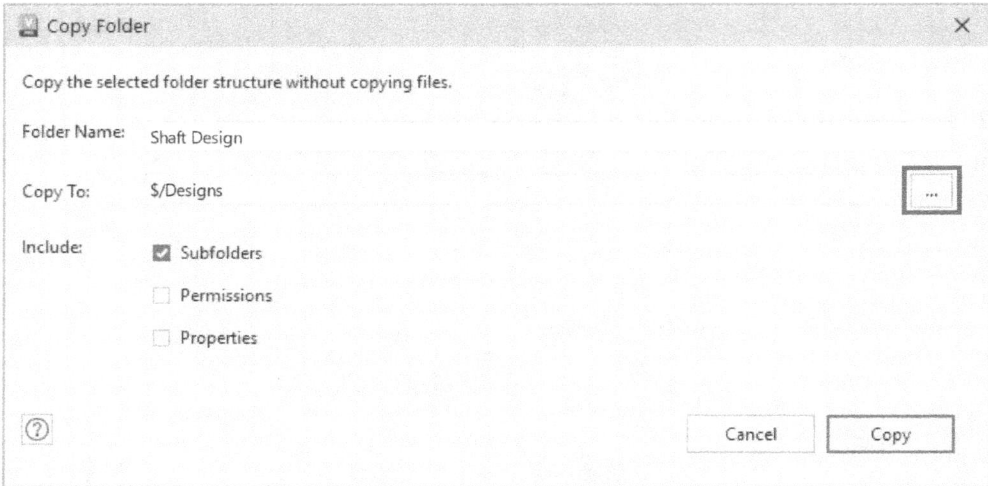

Figure 2–27

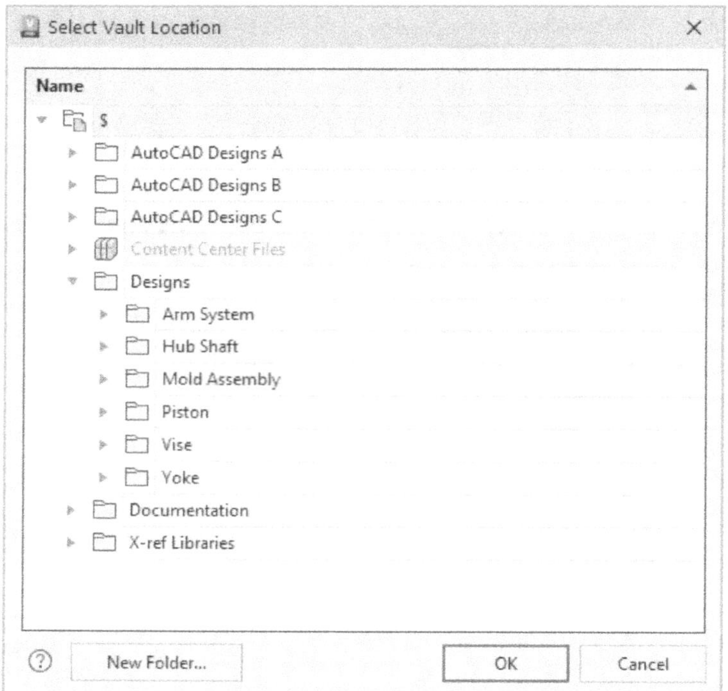

Figure 2–28

5. Define what information will be included by checking the boxes, shown in Figure 2–29, then click **Copy**.

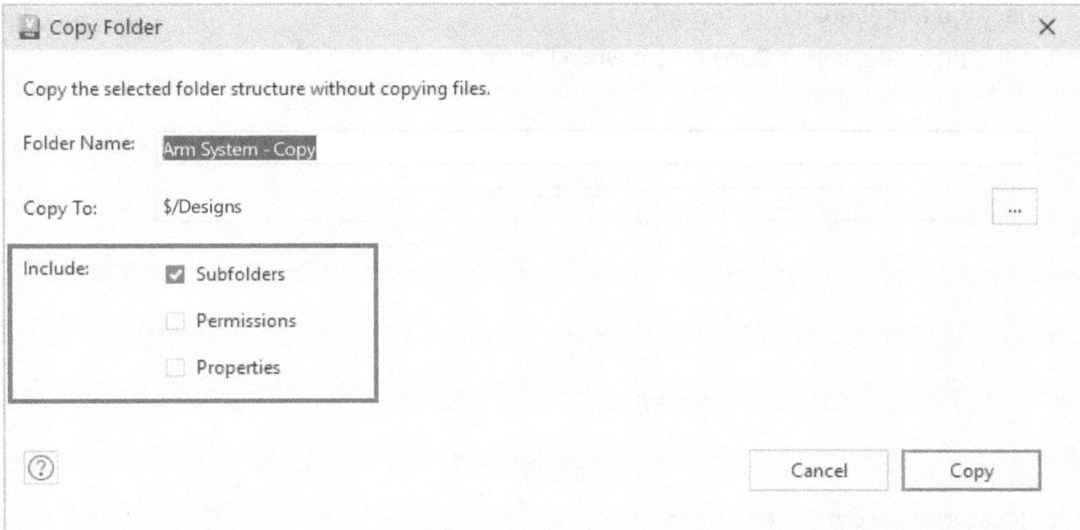

Figure 2–29

6. In the lower left corner of the *Copy Folder* dialog box, a message will display stating that the copy operation is completed. Click **Done**.

Links

Links can be created anywhere in the Project Explorer and point to a target object (such as a file, folder, item, or change order). The target object resides in one location only. Organizing objects and links in a project folder can facilitate management and reporting. Commands such as **Check Out** and **Check In** can be performed using a link and are executed on the target object. Note that the **Delete** and **Move** commands only affect the link and not the target object.

How To: Create a Link

1. Select the target object for the link.
2. In the Edit menu, select **Copy** as shown in Figure 2–30.

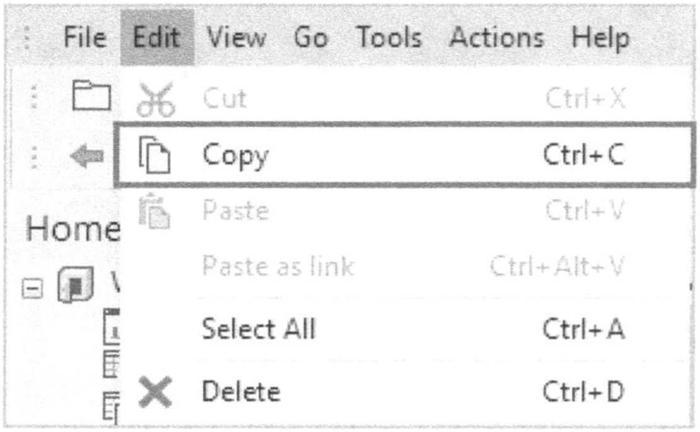

Figure 2–30

3. Select the link's destination folder.
4. In the Edit menu, select **Paste as link** as shown in Figure 2–31.

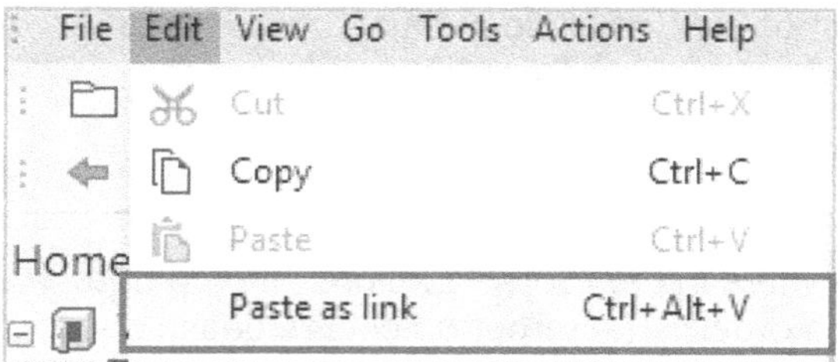

Figure 2–31

5. The link is created in that folder with an arrow included in the entity icon as shown in Figure 2–32.

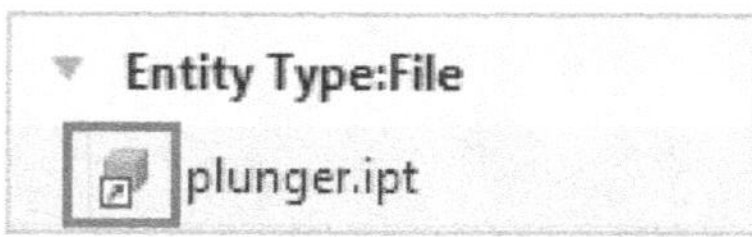

Figure 2–32

Practice 2a
Orientation to Autodesk Vault Client

Practice Objectives

- Log in to the Autodesk Vault software and set a working folder.
- Compare the working folder structure to the vault folder structure.
- View and analyze vaulted files.

In this practice, you will log in to Autodesk Vault Client and become familiar with the user interface. You will also set a working folder and compare the folder structure on the local machine to the vault folder structure.

Task 1: Log in to the Autodesk Vault Client software.

1. Log in to the Autodesk Vault Client software using one of the following methods:
   - Double-click on (Autodesk Vault 2027) on the desktop.
   - Select **Autodesk Data Management>Autodesk Vault Professional 2027** from the **Start** menu.
   - Select **Autodesk Vault Professional 2027** in the desktop Apps list.
2. The *Log In* dialog box opens as shown in Figure 2–33. In the *User Name field,* type **user1**.

   Verify that *Vault* is set to **Vault_Training** (click (Browse) to select it, as required). Leave the *Password* field blank.

   Note: *Refer to the Practice Files section of this guide to set up the Vault, if not already completed.*

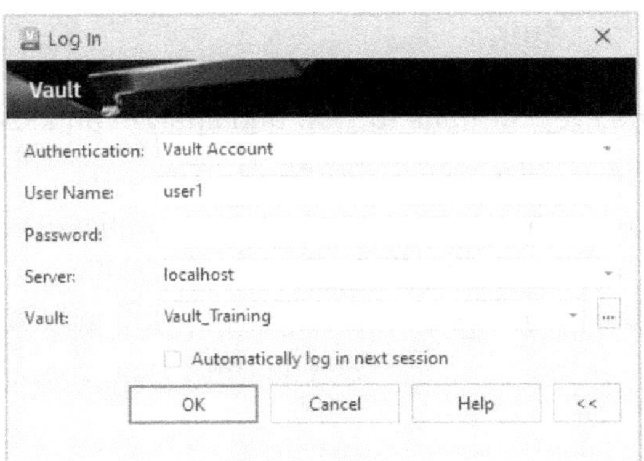

Figure 2–33

3. Select **Automatically log in next session** to automatically logged into the vault in subsequent sessions.

   Note: *Selecting this option saves login time.*

4. Click **OK**.

Task 2: Set a new working folder.

In this task, you will set a new working folder. The vault database has been created with the *AutoCAD Designs A*, *Content Center Files*, *Designs*, and *Documentation* folders in the Project Explorer ($) root.

1. Select **Project Explorer ($)** and select **File>Set Working Folder...**.
2. In the *Set Working Folder For '$' To:* dialog box, select **C:\Vault Data Management Practice Files\vault_work** and click **Select Folder**.
3. The working folder path can be displayed in the Main table's title bar. To display the path, if not already displayed, select **Tools>Options** and select **Show working folder location**. Click **OK**. Verify that the path is set to *...\vault_work*.

Task 3: Compare folder structures.

In this task, you will compare the folder structure in the working folder (*...\vault_work*) to the Vault folder structure.

1. To view the working folder, select **Actions>Go To Working Folder**. A File Explorer window opens displaying the working folder contents. Note that there is no *Hub Shaft* subfolder under the *Designs* folder in the local working folder structure.
2. In the Autodesk Vault software, expand **Project Explorer ($)>Designs**. Note that the subfolders in vault are different. Only the *Hub Shaft* folder exists in the vault.
3. Close File Explorer.

Task 4: View files in the vault.

In this task, you will use the Preview pane to view and analyze an assembly design.

1. In the *Designs>Hub Shaft* folder, select **hub_shaft_assy.iam**.
2. In the Preview pane, select the *View* tab to view the carousel of versions for this assembly. Select **Version 2** to view the visualization file of this version.
3. Use the ViewCube or the icons in the viewer to manipulate and analyze the assembly.
4. Use the Autodesk Viewer toolbar icons such as **Orbit**, **Pan**, **Zoom**, and **Measure** to explore the model's geometry.

5. Select the *History* tab and select the **Show all versions** checkbox to view the history of the assembly versions. Notice in the *Thumbnail* column that the shaft length is shorter in Version 1. The *Comment* column for Version 2 states that the shaft length was changed, as shown in Figure 2–34.

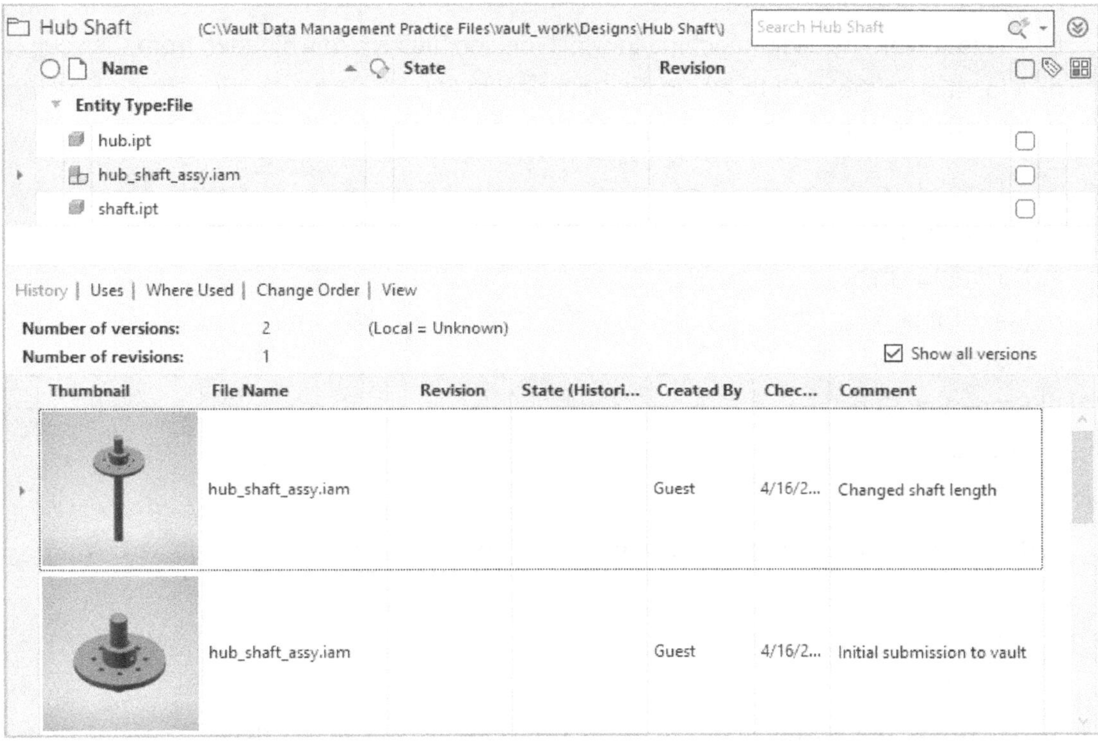

Figure 2–34

6. Select the *Uses* and *Where Used* tabs to display any children and whether any parents are associated with the selected file.

End of practice

Chapter Review Questions

1. What is a working folder?
   a. Central repository for data.
   b. A location on the client machine to which design files are downloaded from the vault.
   c. A location in the vault that contains your design files.
   d. All of the above.

2. What are the main areas of the Autodesk Vault interface? (Select all that apply.)
   a. Navigation pane
   b. Main Table
   c. Preview pane
   d. Properties Grid
   e. Toolbars

3. In the Preview pane, the *Where Used* tab lists all of the files used in the selected file.
   a. True
   b. False

4. In the Preview pane, what does the *Uses* tab display when a file is selected from the Project Explorer?
   a. The files that use the selected file.
   b. The files used in the selected file.
   c. The files that reference the selected file.
   d. Only files that are available to use in the selected file.

5. In the Preview pane, the latest version of the selected file displays in the *View* tab by default.
   a. True
   b. False

6. Which file format is used for the *View* tab to display an image of an Autodesk Inventor file?

a. DWF

b. PRT

c. DWG

d. PDF

Command Summary

Button	Command	Location
	Add Files	• **Standard toolbar**
	Attachments	• **Standard toolbar**
	Auto Preview	• **Advanced toolbar**
Check In...	**Check In**	• **Standard toolbar**
	Copy Design	• **Standard toolbar**
	Delete	• **Standard toolbar**
	Expand the query builder	• **Main Table pane**
Find...	**Find**	• **Standard toolbar**
	Get	• **Standard toolbar**
	Group By Box	• **Advanced toolbar**
Layout	**Layout**	• **Advanced toolbar**
	Move Backward	• **Advanced toolbar**
	Move Forward	• **Advanced toolbar**
New	**New Folder or New Library Folder**	• **Standard toolbar**
	Preview pane	• **Advanced toolbar**
	Print Direct	• **Standard toolbar**
	Print Preview	• **Standard toolbar**
	Refresh	• **Standard toolbar**

Button	Command	Location
	**Undo Check Out**	• **Standard toolbar**
	**Up One Level**	• **Advanced toolbar**

Chapter 3

Orientation to the Vault Add-in

Orientation to the Vault Add-in takes you through the process of logging in to a vault from the Autodesk® Vault Add-in and introduces you to the Vault Add-in interface.

Learning Objectives

- Log in to a vault from the Autodesk Vault Add-in.
- Identify areas of the Autodesk Vault Add-in interface.
- Describe the functions of each area of the Autodesk Vault Add-in.

3.1 Log In to a Vault from the Vault Add-in

The Vault Add-in consists of a *Vault* or *Autodesk Vault* tab, and sometimes an additional auxiliary tool, such as the Inventor Vault Browser. Most of the *Vault* tab content is grayed out until you are logged in. You can log in to the Autodesk Vault software from the Add-in *Vault* tab.

How To: Log In to a Vault from the Vault Add-in

1. Launch the desired software, and click on the *Vault* (or *Autodesk Vault*) tab.
   - For AutoCAD, the *Vault* tab is only accessible once you have a template or file open.
2. In the *Vault* tab>*Access* panel, click **Log In** as shown in Figure 3–1.

Figure 3–1

3. In the *Log In* dialog box, select a method from the *Authentication* drop-down list, as shown in Figure 3–2 (in this example, **Vault Account** is selected):
   - **Vault Account:** Enter a Vault account user name and password.
   - **Windows Account:** Uses Windows Active Directory credentials, which are entered for you.
   - **Autodesk ID:** Uses Autodesk ID credentials.

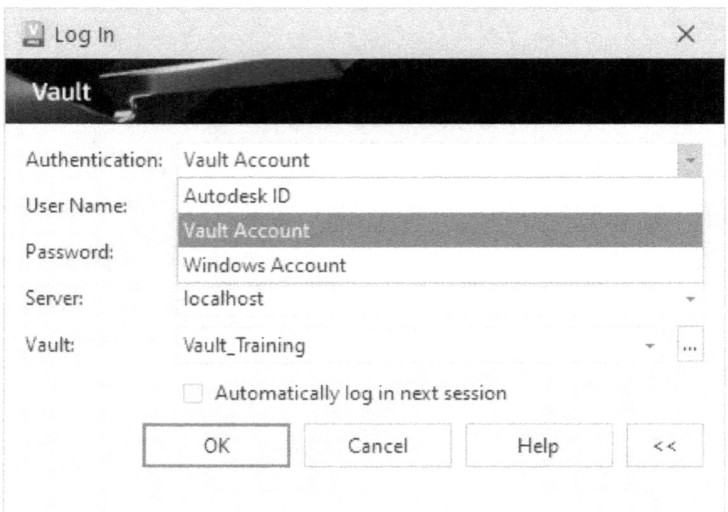

Figure 3–2

4. Enter the *User Name* and *Password* as shown in Figure 3–3.

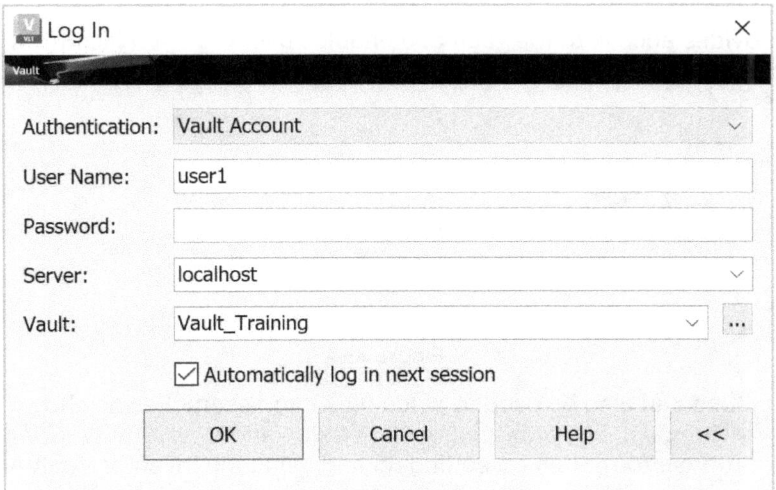

Figure 3–3

5. Click **OK**.

*Note: After you have logged in for the first time, the server and vault names are stored so that the same information displays each time you log in to the vault. Select **Automatically log in next session** to log in automatically and bypass the Log In window.*

3.2 Vault Tab

The *Vault* tab provides access to the vault and enables users to open files from Vault, perform file status functions such as Check In a file to Vault, and access advanced tools. An example is shown in Figure 3–4.

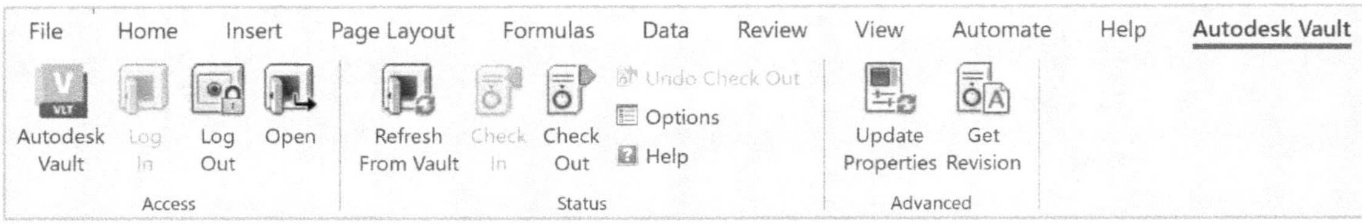

Figure 3–4

In Inventor, the ribbon can also be used to place files into assemblies as shown in Figure 3–5. Refer to ***Chapter 4 Autodesk Inventor Vault Add-in Setup*** and ***Chapter 6 Working with Autodesk Inventor Files*** for more information on setting up and using the Inventor Vault Add-In.

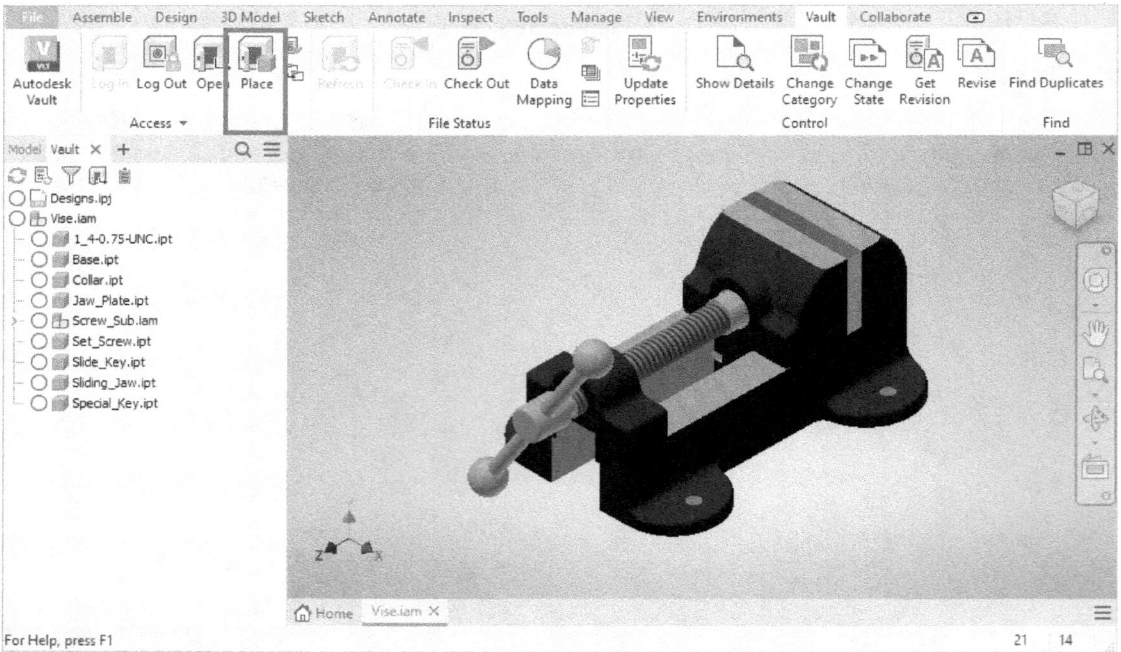

Figure 3–5

In AutoCAD, the ribbon can also be used to attach files from the Vault as shown in Figure 3–6. Refer to ***Chapter 7 Working with AutoCAD Files*** for more information on using the AutoCAD Vault Add-In.

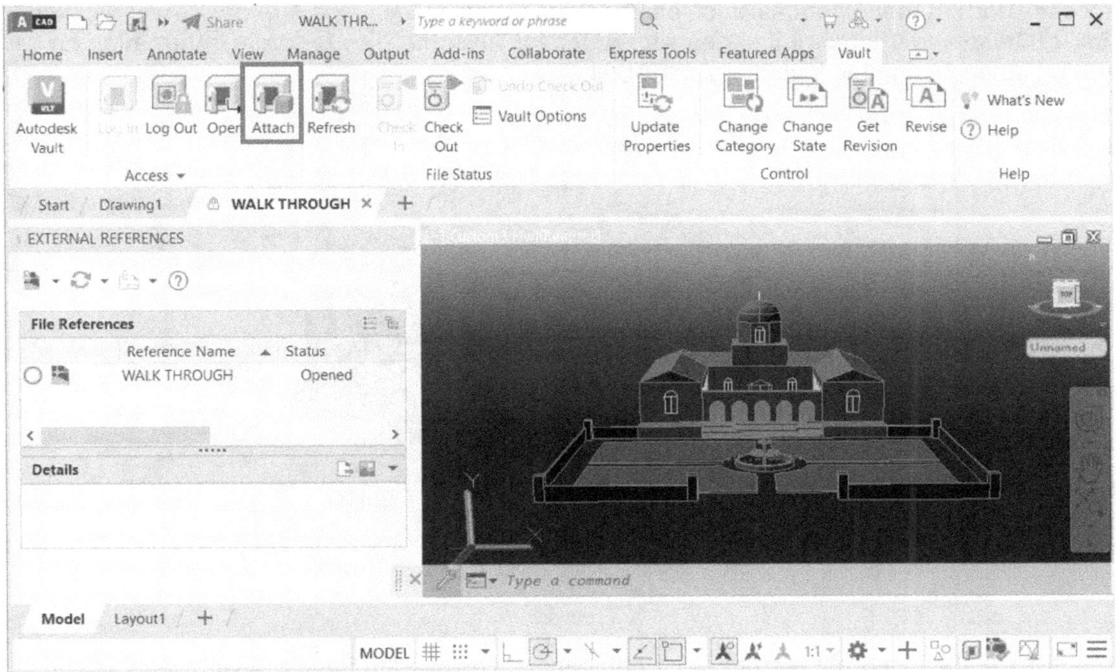

Figure 3–6

3.3 Vault Auxiliary Add-in

In Inventor, the Vault Browser (shown in Figure 3–7) can be used to view the file status and access shortcut menu options, such as Check In. Refer to ***Chapter 4 Autodesk Inventor Vault Add-in Setup*** and ***Chapter 6 Working with Autodesk Inventor Files*** for more information on setting up and using the Inventor Vault Add-In.

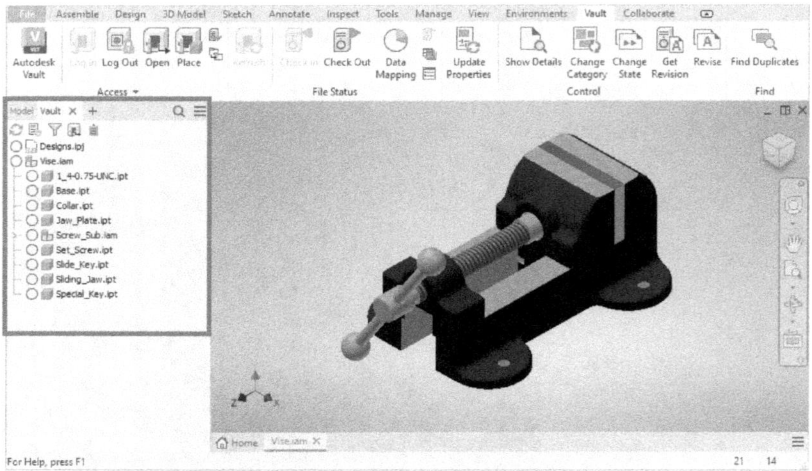

Figure 3–7

In AutoCAD, the External References palette can also be used to interface with vault as shown Figure 3–8. Refer to ***Chapter 7 Working with AutoCAD Files*** for more information on using the AutoCAD Vault Add-In.

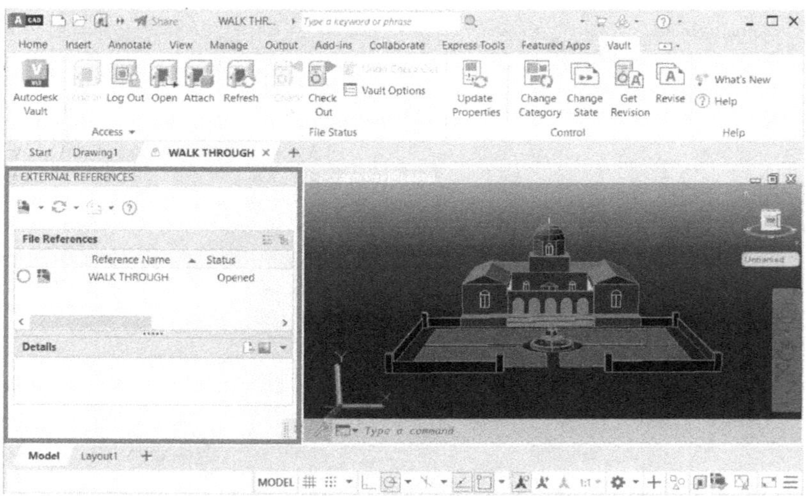

Figure 3–8

Practice 3a
Orientation to the AutoCAD Add-in Interface

Practice Objectives

- Log in to the Autodesk Vault software from within AutoCAD.
- Open a drawing and display the External References palette.

In this practice, you are oriented to the Vault AutoCAD Add-in interface. You first launch AutoCAD and log in to the vault. Then you activate and set up the External References palette.

Task 1: Launch AutoCAD and log in to the vault.

1. Launch the AutoCAD software. Create a new drawing and select a template so that the *Vault* tab becomes active.
2. In the *Vault* tab>*Access* panel, click **Log In**.
3. Type **user1** as the user name. Do not enter a password, as shown in Figure 3–9.

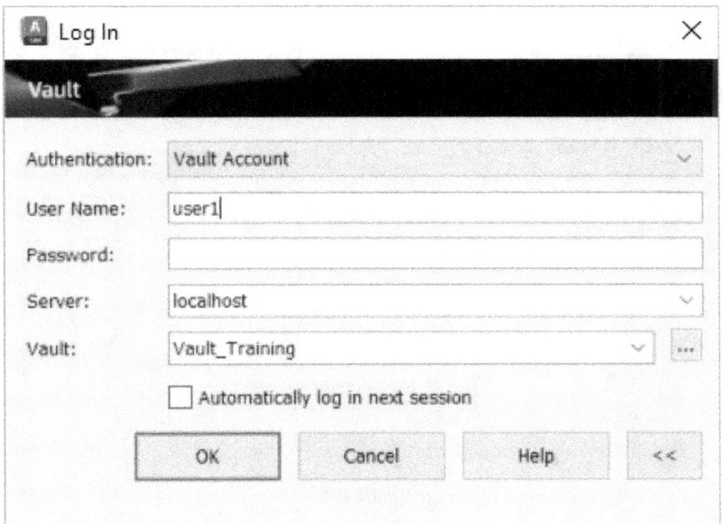

Figure 3–9

4. Click **OK**.

Task 2: Open an AutoCAD drawing.

In this task, even though you are now logged in to the vault, you open an AutoCAD drawing from your local folders using the **Open** command.

1. Select **Open** from the Application Menu or from the Quick Access Toolbar.
2. Select **TANK.dwg** from the ...*\vault_work\AutoCAD Designs B* directory, as shown in Figure 3–10.

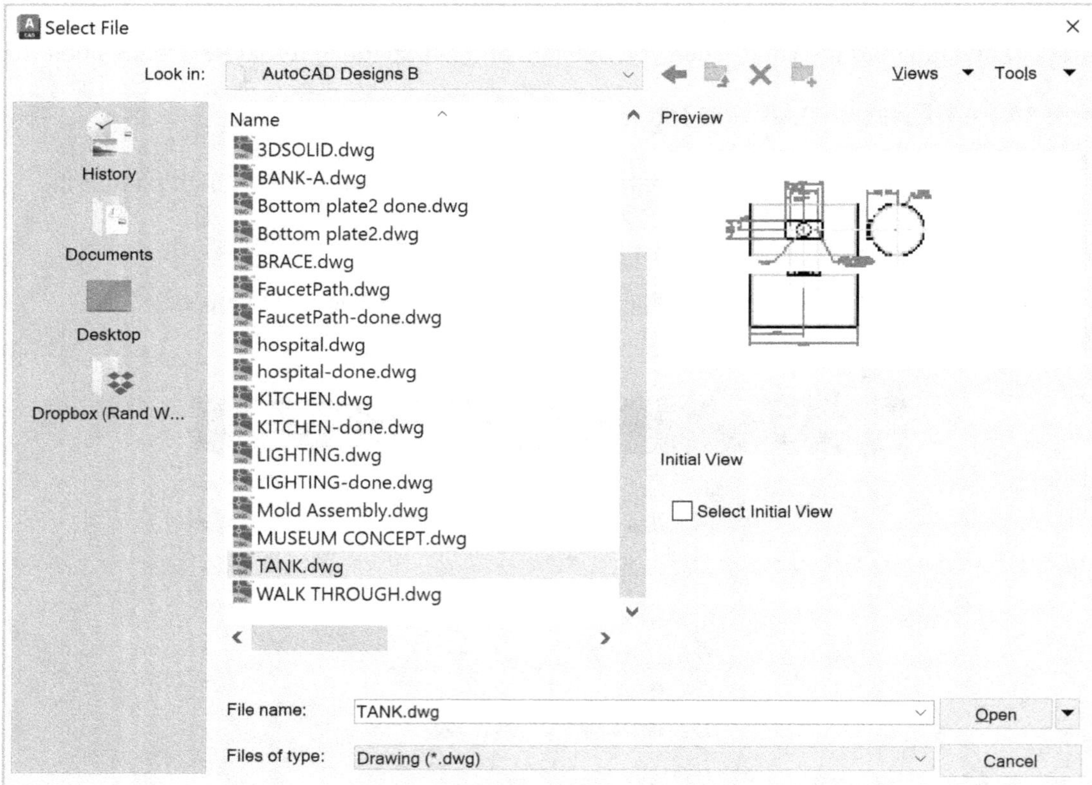

Figure 3–10

3. Select **Open** to display the drawing in the AutoCAD software.

Task 3: Display the External References palette.

In this task, you display the External References palette (also known as the Xref Manager), which is used for vault activities in addition to its standard Xref capabilities. For ease of use, you dock the External References palette and set it to auto-hide.

1. Open the External References palette by clicking (External References Palette) in the *View* tab>*Palettes* panel, as shown in Figure 3–11.

Figure 3–11

2. Right-click on the *EXTERNAL REFERENCES* vertical column and ensure that **Allow Docking**, **Anchor Left**, and **Auto-hide** are selected, as shown in Figure 3–12.

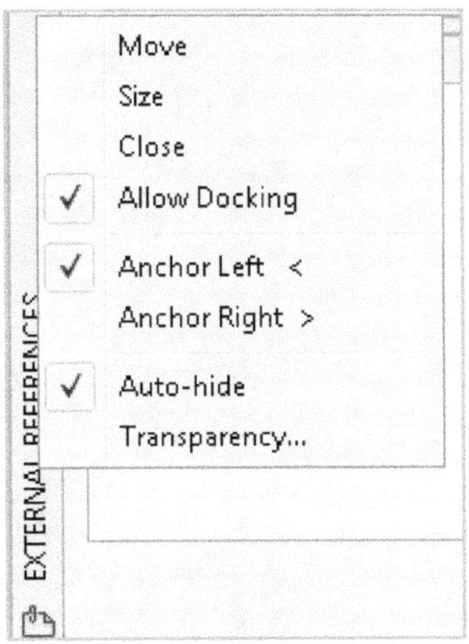

Figure 3–12

3. Close the file and exit AutoCAD.

End of practice

Chapter Review Questions

1. All of the *Vault* (or *Autodesk Vault*) tab commands are accessible when there is no file open.
    a. True
    b. False

2. In Inventor, what can the *Vault* tab also be used for?
    a. Opening files from the working folder
    b. Accessing the Main Table
    c. Placing files into assemblies
    d. Accessing the Item Master

3. Non-CAD files have an auxiliary Add-in, such as the Vault Browser.
    a. True
    b. False

Chapter 4

Autodesk Inventor Vault Add-in Setup

The Autodesk Vault Add-in is an integration software that provides direct access to the Autodesk® Vault software from other apps, such as Autodesk Inventor. This add-in enables you to perform many of the tasks available in the Autodesk Vault software. Inventor requires setup of the Add-in before it can be utilized, which includes creating a vault project and mapping folders.

Learning Objectives

- Configure the integration between Autodesk Inventor and Autodesk Vault by creating a vault master project file and mapping your local folder structure to the vault.
- Log in to the Autodesk Vault software from the Autodesk Inventor software.

4.1 Autodesk Vault Projects

When working with the Autodesk Inventor software, projects are used for organizing and accessing all files that are associated with a particular design job. When you are using Inventor with the Autodesk Vault software, the project must be an Autodesk Vault project rather than an Autodesk Inventor project. The key difference between an Autodesk Inventor project file and an Autodesk Vault project file is that workgroup search paths are not permitted in the Autodesk Vault project files. You must consolidate all of the project folders under the single workspace search path for the project.

One method of integrating an Autodesk Vault project into your Autodesk Inventor environment is to use the single project or *vault master project* method. This uses one project file for the entire vault instead of setting up separate project files for each project/design. With the single project method, you create a folder for each design with all designs referencing one master project file. Recommended by Autodesk, the single project method is the simplest and most robust way of setting up your Autodesk Inventor Vault integration.

The vault master project file can be located under the Project Explorer Root ($) or in a subfolder under Project Explorer Root ($). When you want to work with the vault, use this vault project file.

How To: Create a Vault Master Project File

1. In the Autodesk Inventor software, select **File>Manage>Projects**. The Project Editor opens as shown in Figure 4–1.

   Note: *You can also click* ***Projects...*** *from the Open dialog box to display the Project Editor or use the icon in the Quick Access Toolbar.*

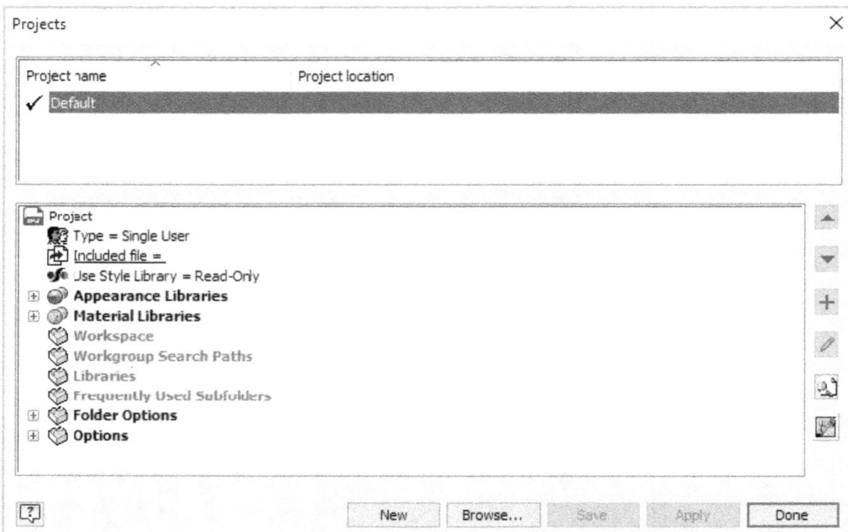

Figure 4–1

2. Click **New** to create a project file.
3. Select **New Vault Project** and click **Next**.
4. Enter the Project Name and specify the location of the project file, as shown in Figure 4–2.

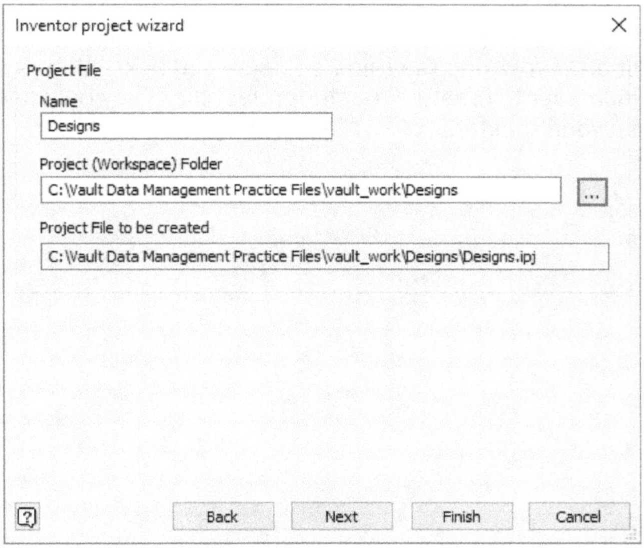

Figure 4–2

5. Click **Next** and click **Finish**.
6. Expand Folder Options, right-click on the *Content Center Files* folder, and select **Edit**, as shown in Figure 4–3. Enter the new Content Center Files directory path.

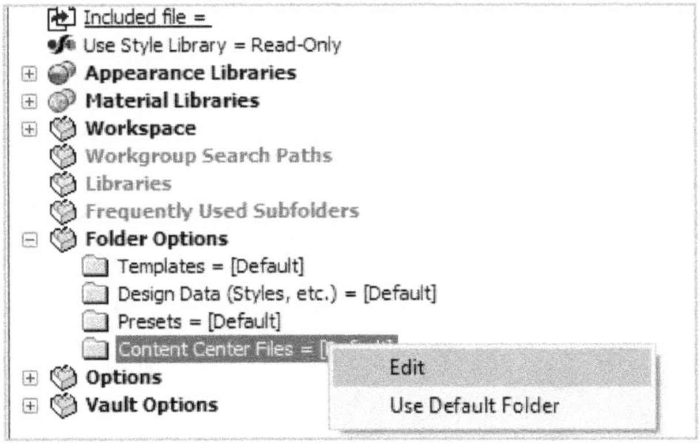

Figure 4–3

Note: *Content Center Files are stored in a user's C: drive by default. Step 6 is used to redirect the Content Center Files to a location in the Vault folder structure that all users can access.*

7. Specify any other settings, such as locations for the styles library, templates, etc.
8. Click **Save** to save the changes to the project file.
9. In the Project Editor, double-click on the project name and then click **Done** to make the new project active.

The project file is created in the specified location, but is not added to the vault. You add the project file to the vault after you map the folders (discussed next). With a single project file, there is no need for each user to create a master project file. They only need to perform a **Get** operation on the single vault master project file and then activate it in the Autodesk Inventor software.

> ***Note:*** *A default project file can be set by your administrator, otherwise Autodesk Inventor's last vault controlled project file is used.*

4.2 Mapping Folders

When you add or access Autodesk Inventor files in the vault, the local folder paths displayed in the project file need to match the folders in the vault. The Autodesk Inventor software uses this information when storing the files. The information is then saved in the master project file. The Project Root mapping displays in the project file in the **Vault Options>Virtual Folder** branch of the Project Editor, as shown in Figure 4–4.

Figure 4–4

How To: Map the Local Folder Structure to the Vault

1. In the Autodesk Inventor software, in the *Vault* tab, expand the *Access* panel and click (Map Folders) as shown in Figure 4–5.

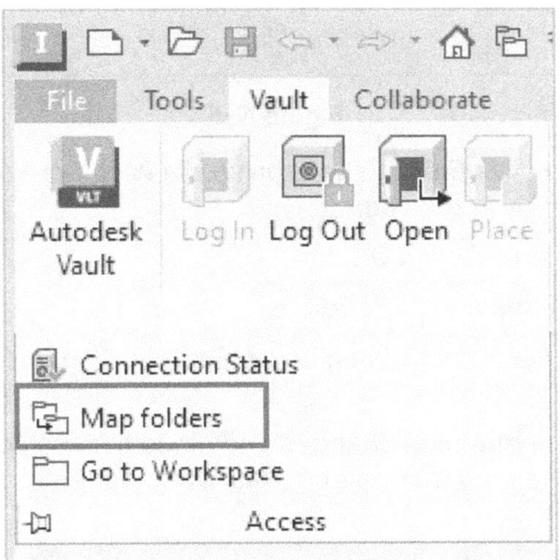

Figure 4–5

2. The *Project Folder Mapping* dialog box opens, as shown in Figure 4–6.

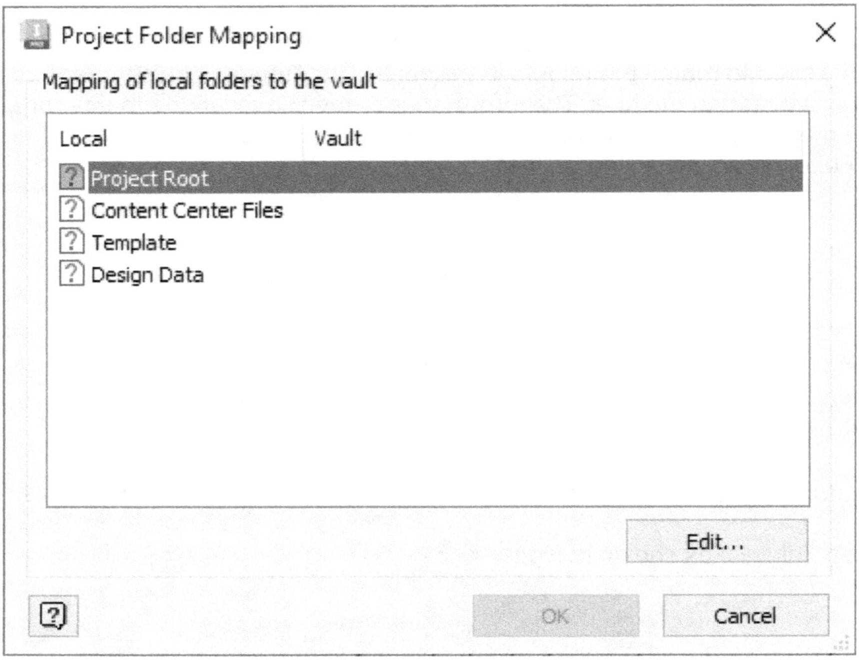

Figure 4–6

3. Select **Project Root** and click **Edit...**. The *Browse the vault For Folder* dialog box opens, listing the folders currently in the vault.
4. Select the *Designs* folder and click **OK**.
5. Select **Content Center Files** and click **Edit...**.
6. In the *Browse the vault For Folder* dialog box, select the *Content Center Files* folder and click **OK**.
7. Click **OK** to complete the mapping changes and close the *Project Folder Mapping* dialog box. The vault folders are now mapped for your workspace.

4.3 Log In to Vault from Autodesk Inventor

When you have set up the master project file and mapped your folder paths, you can log in to the Autodesk Vault software from the Autodesk Inventor interface.

How To: Launch Autodesk Inventor and Log In to the Vault

1. Launch the Autodesk Inventor software.
2. Select **File>Manage>Projects**.
3. In the *Projects* dialog box, double-click on an Autodesk Vault Project to activate it and click **Done**, as shown in Figure 4–7. You have to create an Autodesk Vault Project if one does not exist.

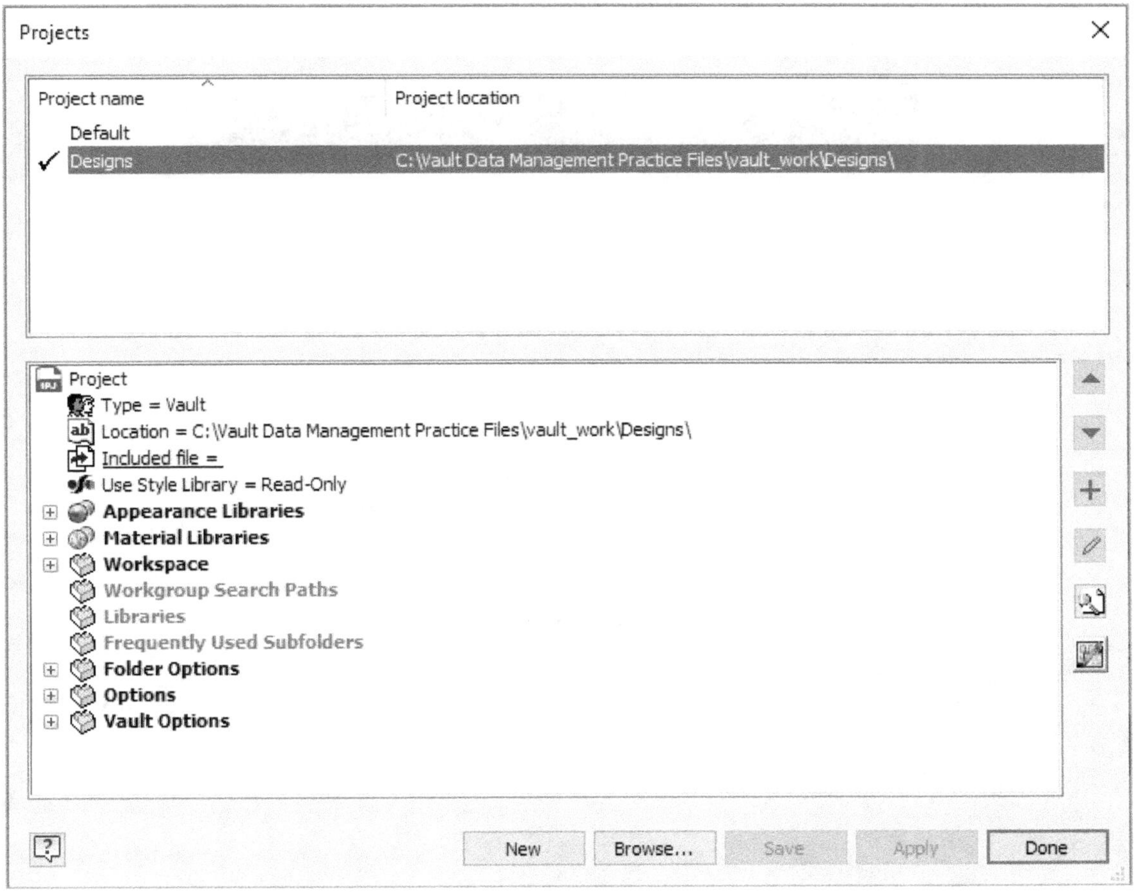

Figure 4–7

4. In the *Vault* tab>*Access* panel, click  (Log In) as shown in Figure 4–8.

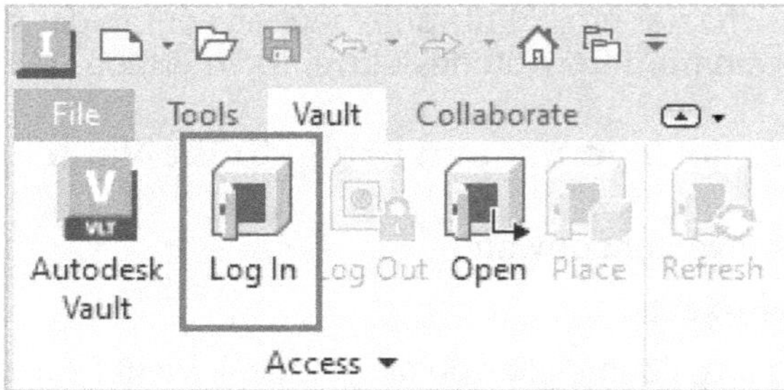

Figure 4–8

5. Enter your user name and password as shown in Figure 4–9.

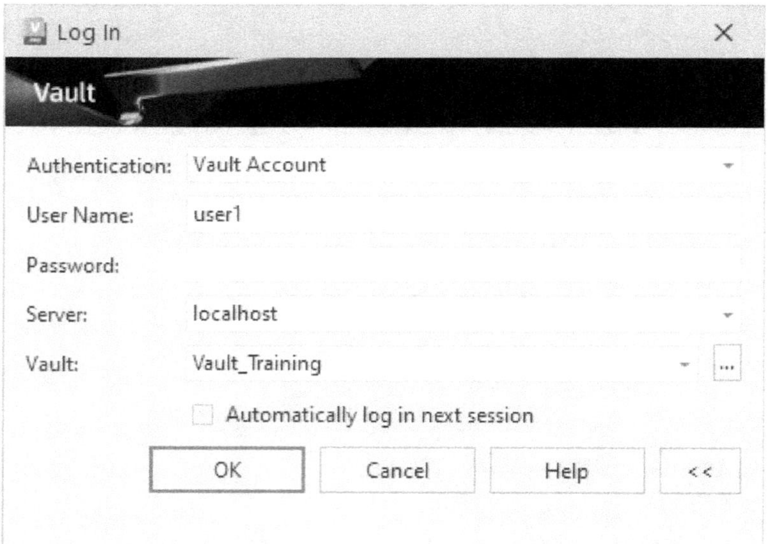

Figure 4–9

Note: *After you have logged in for the first time, the server and vault names are stored so that the same information displays each time you log in to the vault. Select* ***Automatically log in next session*** *to log in automatically and bypass the Log In window.*

6. Click **OK**.

Practice 4a
Create a Vault Project and Map Folders

Practice Objective

- Create a vault project and map folders.

In this practice, you will set up a vault master project for the database and map the local folders (i.e., the active project's workspace) to the vault folders. This enables Autodesk Inventor files to be added to the vault and accessed from it.

Task 1: Create a vault project.

In this task, you will create a vault master project file to use for all vault designs.

1. Launch the Autodesk Inventor software.
2. Select **File>Manage>Projects**.
3. Click **New** to create a new project file.
4. Select **New Vault Project** and click **Next**.
5. For *Name*, type **Designs**. Set the *Project (Workspace) Folder* to ***C:\Vault Data Management Practice Files\vault_work\Designs***, as shown in Figure 4–10.

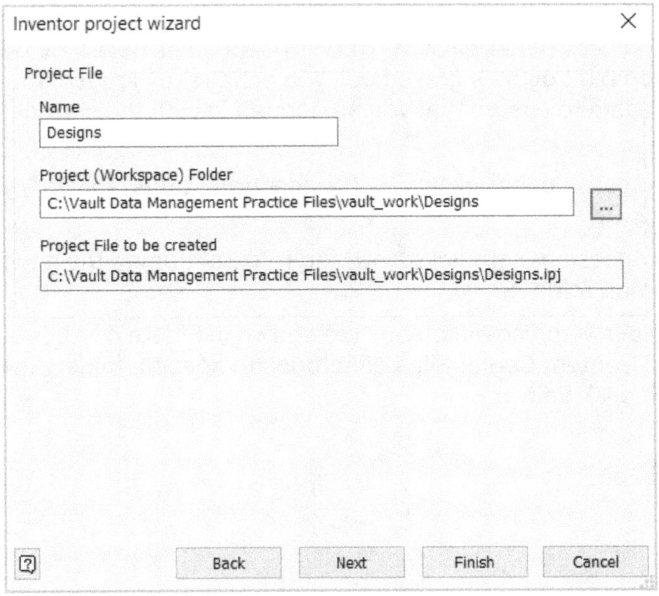

Figure 4–10

6. Click **Finish**.

7. In the *Projects* dialog box, double-click on the Designs project name to make the new project active, if a check mark is not already displayed next to the new project name indicating that it is the active project.
8. In the *Project Details* area, expand Folder Options. Right-click on Content Center Files and select **Edit**. Browse to the directory path shown in Figure 4–11. Click **OK** and press <Enter>.

   Note: *If the Content Center Files folder is missing, create the folder.*

Figure 4–11

9. Click **Save** to save the changes.
10. Click **Done** to complete the creation of the master vault project that can be used for all vault designs.

Task 2: Map folders.

In this task, you will map the local folders (i.e., the active project's workspace) to the vault folders so that Autodesk Inventor files can be added to and accessed from the vault. This operation only needs to be performed once.

1. In the *Vault* tab>*Access* panel, click (Log In). Log in as **user1**, no password, to the *Vault_Training* vault. If **Log In** is grayed out, you are already logged into the vault. Log out and log back in again to ensure that you are logged in with the correct User Name and Vault.
2. In the *Vault* tab>*Access* panel, click (Connection Status) to verify your login and vault information. Click **OK**.
3. In the *Vault* tab>*Access* panel, click (Map folders) to map the newly created master vault project to vault folders.
4. In the *Project Folder Mapping* dialog box (as shown in Figure 4–12), you will map the Project Root and Content Center Files directories to specific folders in the vault. Select **Project Root** and click **Edit...**.

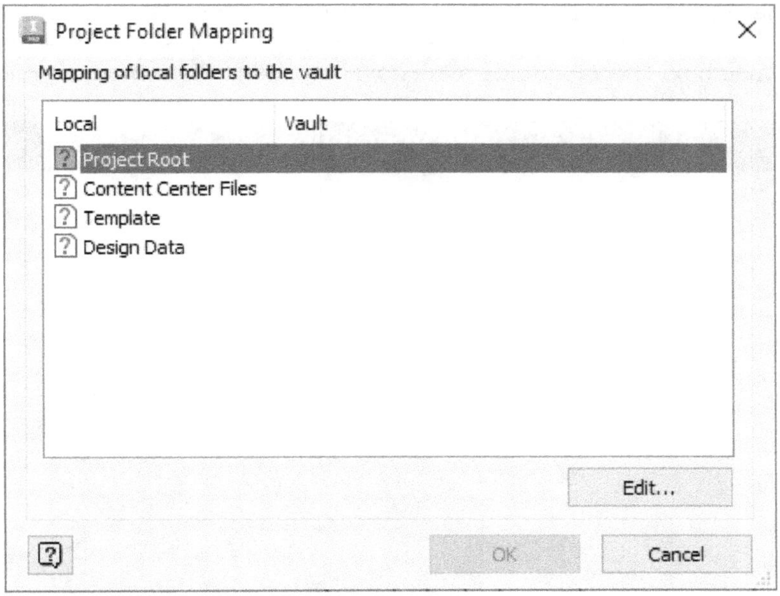

Figure 4–12

5. The *Browse the vault For Folder* dialog box opens listing the folders that are currently in the vault.
6. Select the *Designs* subfolder and click **OK**.
7. In the *Project Folder Mapping* dialog box, select **Content Center Files** and click **Edit...**.
8. Select the *Content Center Files* subfolder and click **OK**. The *Project Folder Mapping* dialog box updates as shown in Figure 4–13.

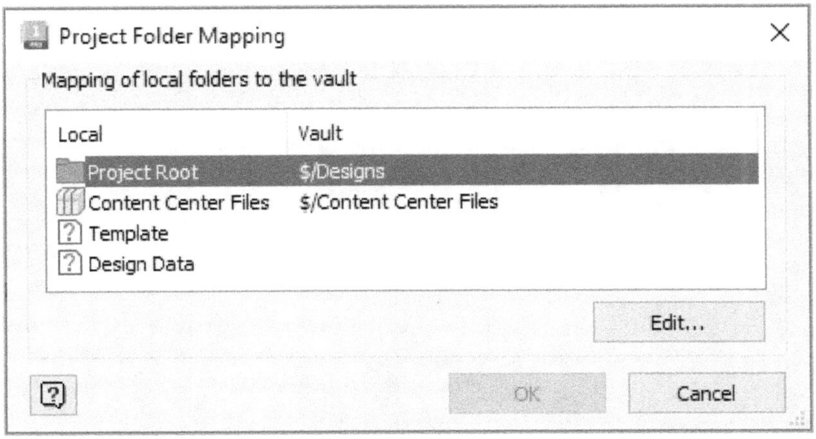

Figure 4–13

9. Map **Template** and **Design Data** to *$/Template* and *$/Design Data*, respectively, by creating these vault folders. Click **OK** to complete the mapping changes and close the *Project Folder Mapping* dialog box. The vault folders are now mapped for your master project workspace.

End of practice

Chapter Review Questions

1. When you are using Inventor with the Autodesk Vault software, the project must be an Autodesk Vault project rather than an Autodesk Inventor project.
    a. True
    b. False

2. What is true of the single vault project method? (Select all that apply.)
    a. All projects or designs reference the one master project file.
    b. Not recommended by Autodesk.
    c. The simplest and most robust way of setting up your Autodesk Inventor Vault integration.
    d. All of the above.

3. In the Autodesk Inventor software, which operation enables you to associate the local folder structure to the corresponding folder structure in the vault so that Autodesk Inventor files can be added and/or accessed?
    a. Place from Vault
    b. Check In Project
    c. Open from Vault
    d. Map Folders

Command Summary

Button	Command	Location
	**Log In**	• **Autodesk Inventor Ribbon:** *Vault* tab>*Access* panel
	**Map Folders**	• **Autodesk Inventor Ribbon:** *Vault* tab>*Access* panel
	**Projects**	• **Autodesk Inventor Ribbon:** *Get Started* tab>*Launch* panel

Chapter 5

Working with Files

The Autodesk® Vault Client and Vault Add-in are used to control the presence and status of the files in vault. They are used to add files from your local workspace (working folder), or get (download) and modify files from vault. Vault records the process of change in any file when you use the Autodesk Vault Client and Vault Add-in.

Learning Objectives

- Add (upload) files to the Vault for the first time.
- **Get** (download) files from the Vault.
- Open (download) files from the Vault.
- Modify vault files using **Check Out** and **Check In**.
- Undo a **Check Out** operation using **Undo Check Out**.
- Differentiate between the file status (vault status) icons.
- Retrieve a previous version of a file.
- Change the categories of files.
- Change the lifecycle states and create new revisions of files.

5.1 Add Files to the Vault

You can add any file format to a vault (database). Once a file is transferred to the vault, the file in the vault becomes the master or vaulted file. Make sure the file, or files, are in the proper folder structure before adding it to the vault.

> ***Note:*** *Your user role must be defined as Editor or Administrator to add files to the vault.*

Non-CAD files can be added using the Vault Client or a non-CAD application's Add-in, while CAD files can only be added using **Check In** with the Add-in.

How To: Add a Non-CAD File to the Vault Using Vault Client

1. Ensure the file is in the proper folder structure in your local workspace.
2. In the Vault Client Navigation pane, select Project Explorer.
3. Select the folder in which you want the file to be stored.
4. Right-click and select **Add Files...**.

   Note: *You can also drag and drop files from File Explorer to the Autodesk Vault software to add non-CAD files to the vault.*

5. In the *Add Files* dialog box, navigate to the file location and select the file. Click **Open**.
6. If desired, select **Keep files checked out** to keep the file writable so you can continue editing the file.
7. Select **Delete working copies** to delete the file from your computer. This is a recommended best practice if you have finished modifying the file and have not selected **Keep files checked out**. When you need to modify it again or to view the file, you can retrieve it from the vault to ensure you are working with the latest.
8. In the *Enter comments to include...* area, type a description of the file, such as **Initial submission to vault**. It is best practice to provide a comment for file version tracking.
9. Click **OK** to add the file to the vault.

How To: Add a CAD File to the Vault

1. Ensure the file is in the proper folder structure in your local workspace.
2. Open the file in the appropriate CAD software (Inventor or AutoCAD, as required).

   Note: *You cannot use the drag-and-drop method to add CAD files to the vault.*

3. Use the Add-in for the CAD software you opened and check in the file. For instructions, refer to ***Chapter 6 Working with Autodesk Inventor Files*** for Inventor and ***Chapter 7 Working with AutoCAD Files*** for AutoCAD.
4. Once added to the vault, the file displays in the Vault Client. The *Vault Status* column indicates that the file is available for check out. If the local copy was deleted, the column indicates that you do not have a local copy. Refer to ***5.8 File Status*** for more information on File Status icons.

5.2 Get Vault Files

Once files are in a vault, they can be downloaded from the server to your local device for viewing or modification purposes.There are several methods to download files from a vault. Getting a file typically means that you are downloading a read-only copy to your local workspace (working folder) for viewing purposes.

The method used depends on the purpose for the download. If you want to just view the file, the action you take to download the file will be different than if you intend to modify the file. In this chapter, the topics of Getting, Opening, Modifying, Checking Out, and Checking In files are discussed.

Get is only available in Vault Client and downloads a read-only copy of a file or files. When using the **Get** command, you also have the choice to check out specific versions or revisions of files for editing.

How To: Get Files from Vault

1. In the Vault Client, select the file(s) in the Navigation pane or Main pane, right-click, and select **Get...**. The *Get* dialog box opens as shown in Figure 5–1.

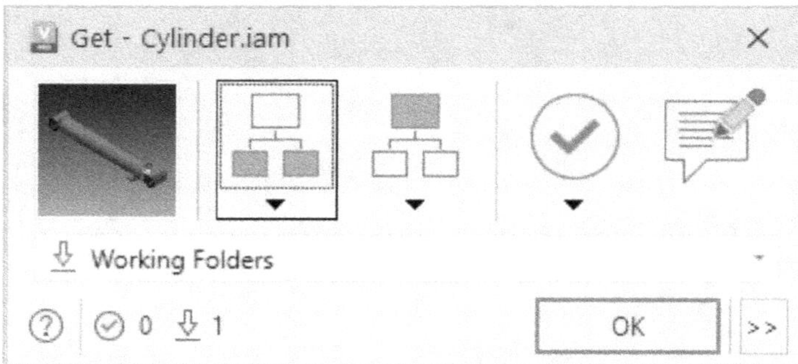

Figure 5–1

2. Click >> (Expand to show details), if desired, to view what files are being downloaded. The expanded view of the *Get* dialog box displays, as shown in Figure 5–2.

   Note: *By default, the Get dialog box is collapsed. If you want the dialog box to stay expanded every time you open it, click (Select the pin to lock the detail view).*

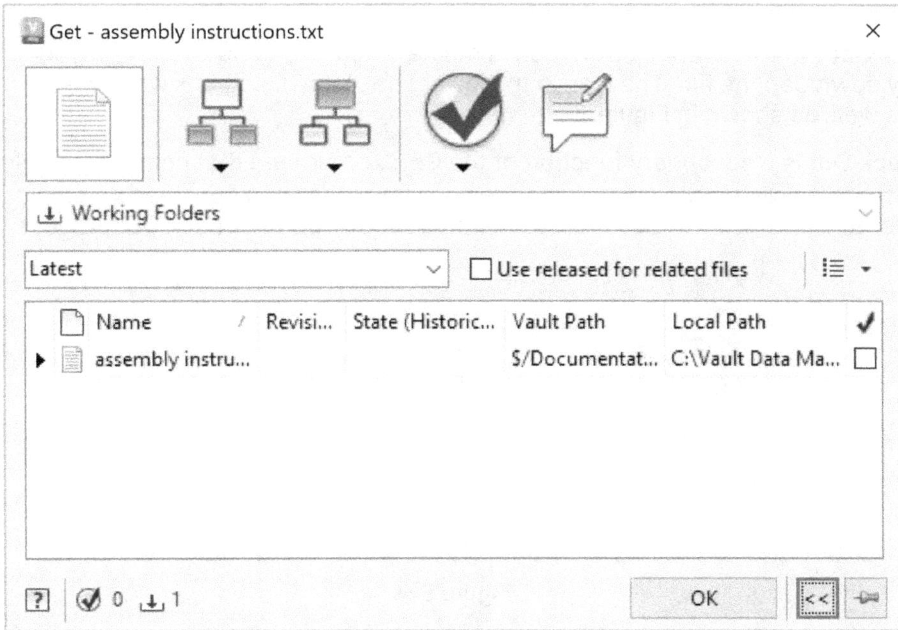

Figure 5–2

3. If required, determine what associated files also get downloaded by clicking on the **Include Children** and **Include Parents** to make the proper selections, as shown in Figure 5–3.
   - This is particularly important when working with Inventor files as this controls whether you download a single part/assembly file, or all files associated with an assembly.
   - The icon will turn blue if it is activated.
   - Expand **Include Children** and **Include Parents** using the down arrow to further define what child or parent is included.
   - The file count being downloaded displays at the bottom of the dialog box, as shown in Figure 5–3.

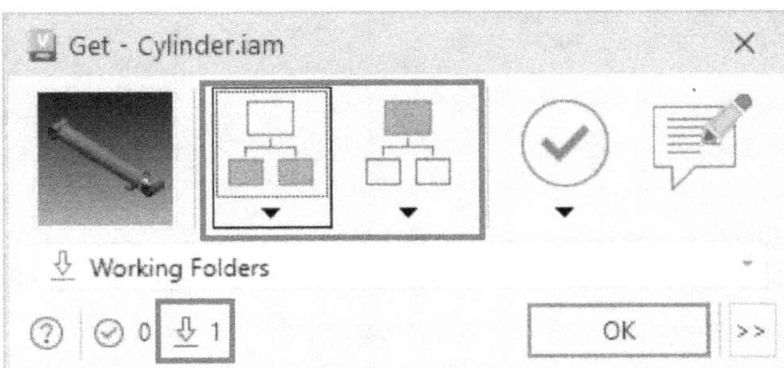

Figure 5–3

4. Ensure that the  (Check Out) icon is not selected (it should be grey), if your intention is to only download the file. The icon in the lower left of the dialog box will have a 0 (zero) next to it as well, as shown in Figure 5–4.
   - **Check Out** is a secondary function of the **Get...** command that changes the file from read-only to read/write so that changes can be made for a specified version or revision. Refer to ***5.4 Check Out Files*** for further instructions on the Check Out process.

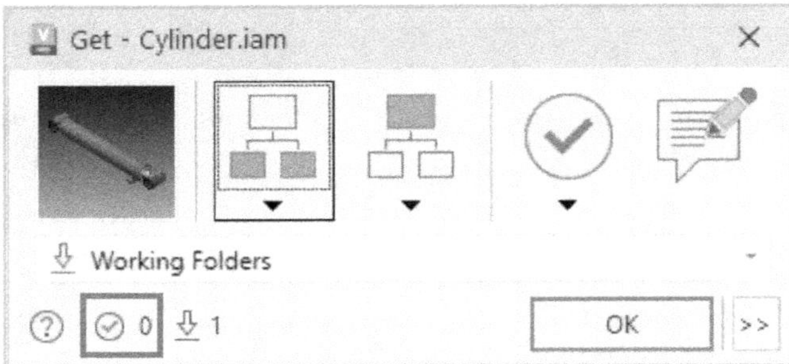

Figure 5–4

5. By default, the latest version of the file is downloaded. To change the revision selection, click the (Expand to show details) icon in the lower right corner of the *Get* dialog box. Then expand and make a selection as shown in Figure 5–5.

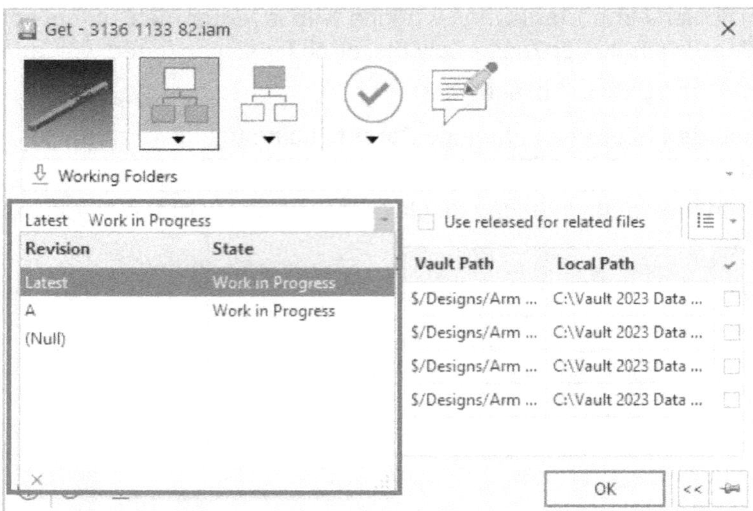

Figure 5–5

6. Click **OK**. The file is now downloaded to your local working folder.

7. To open the file, do one of the following:
    - In the Vault Client, right-click on the file and select **Go to Working Folder**. This will open File Explorer in the appropriate location.
    - In File Explorer, navigate to the appropriate working folder. Double-click on the file to launch and open the file in the appropriate software.
    - In the appropriate software, such as AutoCAD, open the file as you normally would using the Open option (not the Open from Vault option via the Add-in).

5.3 Open Vault Files

Opening a file gets (downloads) the file and opens it in the proper software. You can open a file from the vault using the CAD Add-In (preferred method) or from the Vault Client. Use whichever application you are in at the time you want to open a file.

> **Note:** *You can only open one file at a time when opening from the Vault Client.*

Open a Vault File Using the Add-in

When you have launched the Autodesk CAD or Microsoft software, you can open a file from vault.

- If you click (Open) in the Quick Access Toolbar in CAD or **File>Open**, rather than (Open) in the *Vault* tab>*Access* panel, you are opening a file from the local workspace, not from vault. The workspace is a local folder that is mapped to the corresponding folder in the vault. The workspace can be a single folder, or can include a hierarchy of subfolders to help organize the design.
- The recommended best practice is to use (Open) in the *Vault* tab>*Access* panel to open the file from the vault instead of from the local working folder. This ensures that you are always working with the latest version of the project.

> **Note:** *If you click (Open) without logging in, you are prompted to login.*

- (Open) in the *Vault* tab>*Access* panel in the integrated user interface is available after you log in to the vault, as shown in Figure 5–6.

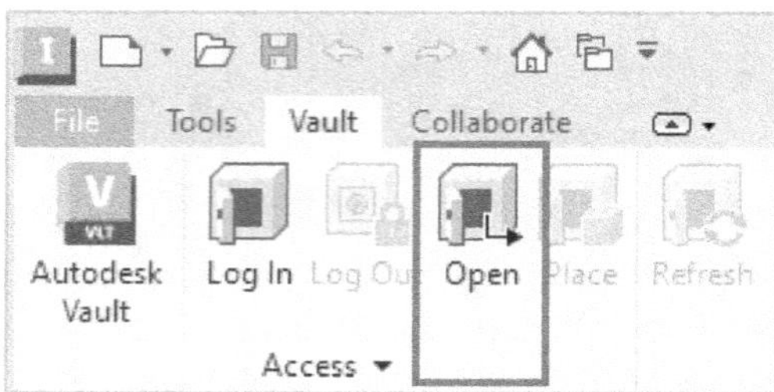

Figure 5–6

How To: Open a File from the Vault Using Add-In

1. In the desired software, in the *Vault* tab>*Access* panel, click (Open). The *Select File From Vault* dialog box opens, as shown in Figure 5–7 (CAD) and Figure 5–8 (Microsoft Office).

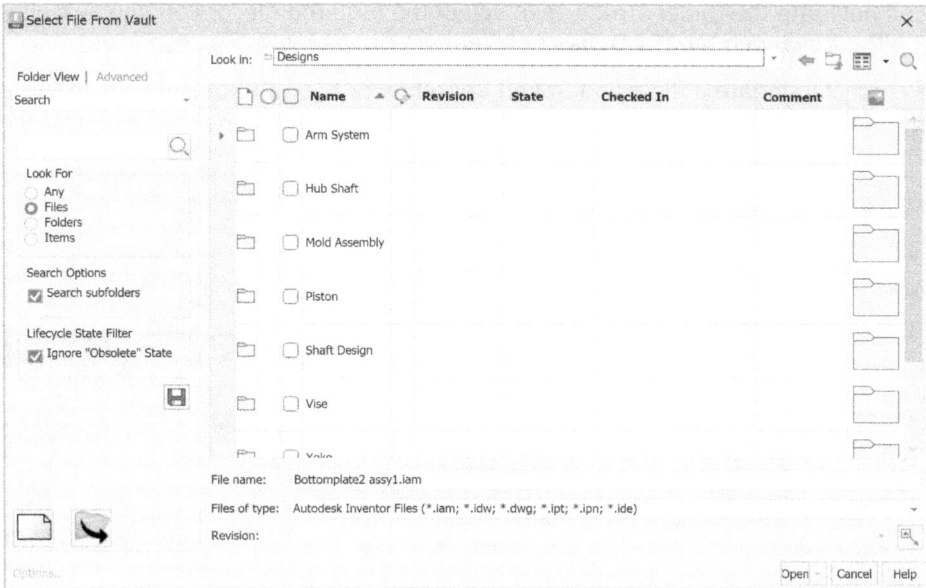

Figure 5–7

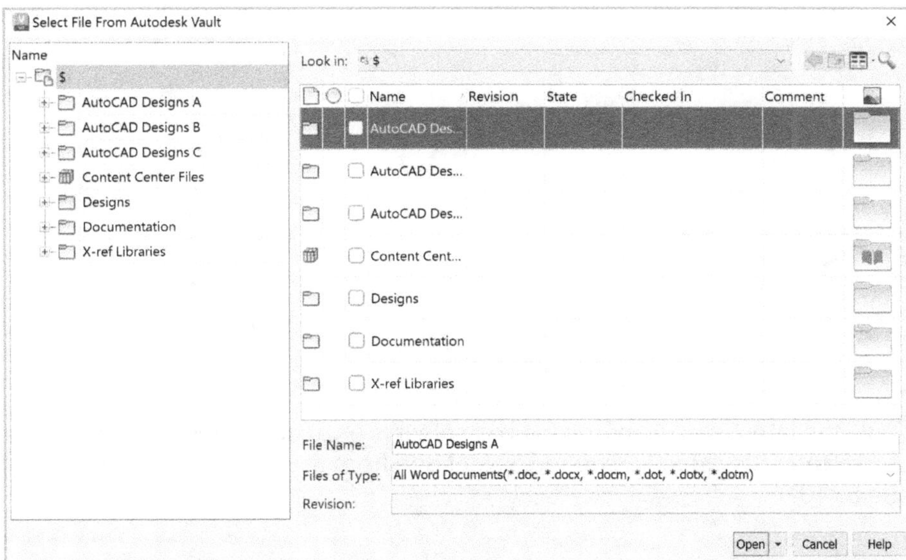

Figure 5–8

Note: *You can use [search icon] to access the Find dialog box. Once the search is executed, you can use [save icon] to save your search for reuse purposes.*

2. You can navigate the folder structure to select the required file, or you can search using the field on the *Advanced* tab (CAD files only) shown on the left in Figure 5–9.
   - You can also locate a file using **Saved Searches** or **Saved Shortcuts**, as shown on the right in Figure 5–9.

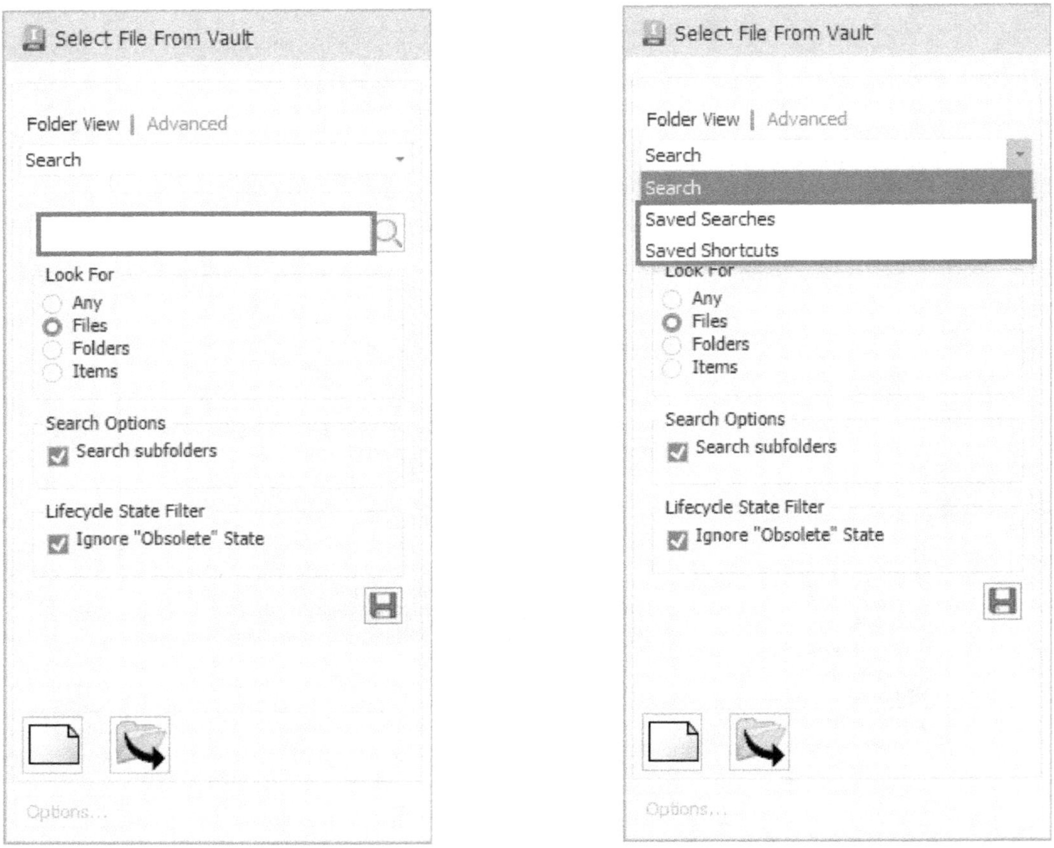

Figure 5–9

3. By default, the latest version of the file you select is used and **Latest** displays in the *Revision* field. If a different revision is required, select one from the *Revision* drop-down list, as show in Figure 5–10.

Figure 5–10

4. Select **Open** to retrieve the file from the vault.
5. A dialog box displays prompting you to check out the file:
    - Select **No** to open the file in read-only mode.
    - Select **Yes** to check out and open the file to modify it.

Open a File from the Vault Client

How To: Open a File from the Vault Client

1. In the Vault Client, select the file, right-click, and select **Open**.
    - If the file is present in your local workspace before you click **Open**, the software application will immediately launch and the files will open. Depending on the file type, other prompts may display before the file opens.
2. The *Open File* dialog box displays prompting you to check out the file:
    - Select **No** to open the file in read-only mode.
    - Select **Yes** to check out and open the file to modify it.

5.4 Check Out Files

A file is checked out from the vault so that only one user can perform changes to the file. While the file is checked out, other users cannot modify the checked out files while they are in your control. They can only retrieve a read-only copy of the files until you perform a check in. Checking out temporarily increments the version of the file in the vault (e.g., a file at Version 1 becomes Version 2 on check out). After the changes to the file have been completed, you can check the file back into the vault server, where it remains at the incremented version (e.g., Version 2) and is available again for other users to check out and modify.

Figure 5–11 shows a file that is crossed out, indicating that the file is checked out to another user, and a file that you currently have checked out as indicated by the checkmark and **bold blue** lettering. In both those cases, you have downloaded the copy locally as indicated by the circle.

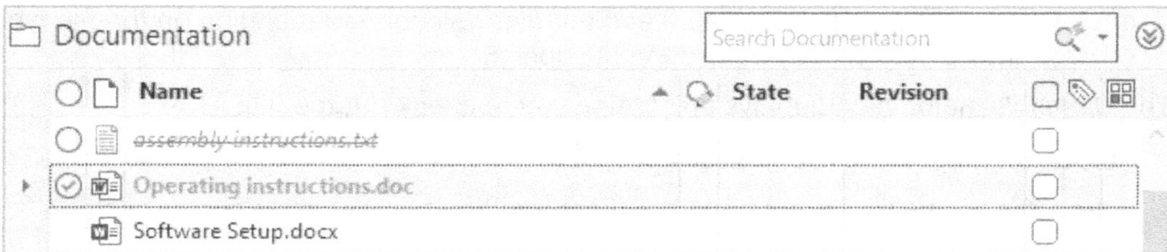

Figure 5–11

You can check out files via the Vault Add-in or the Vault Client.

Check Out Using Open in the Vault Add-in

You can use (Open) in the *Vault* tab>*Access* panel of the CAD or non-CAD application Add-in ribbon to check out the latest version file from the vault. This is the preferred option and is used when you need to download the file, open it, and check it out. You can also right-click on a file in the Inventor Vault Browser or AutoCAD Xref palette and select **Check Out**.

How To: Check Out Using Open in the Add-in *Vault* tab

1. In the *Vault* tab>*Access* panel in the ribbon, click (Open).

2. In the *Select File From Vault* dialog box, expand *Open* and select one of the check out options: **Open (Check Out)** or **Open (Check Out All)**, as shown in Figure 5–12.

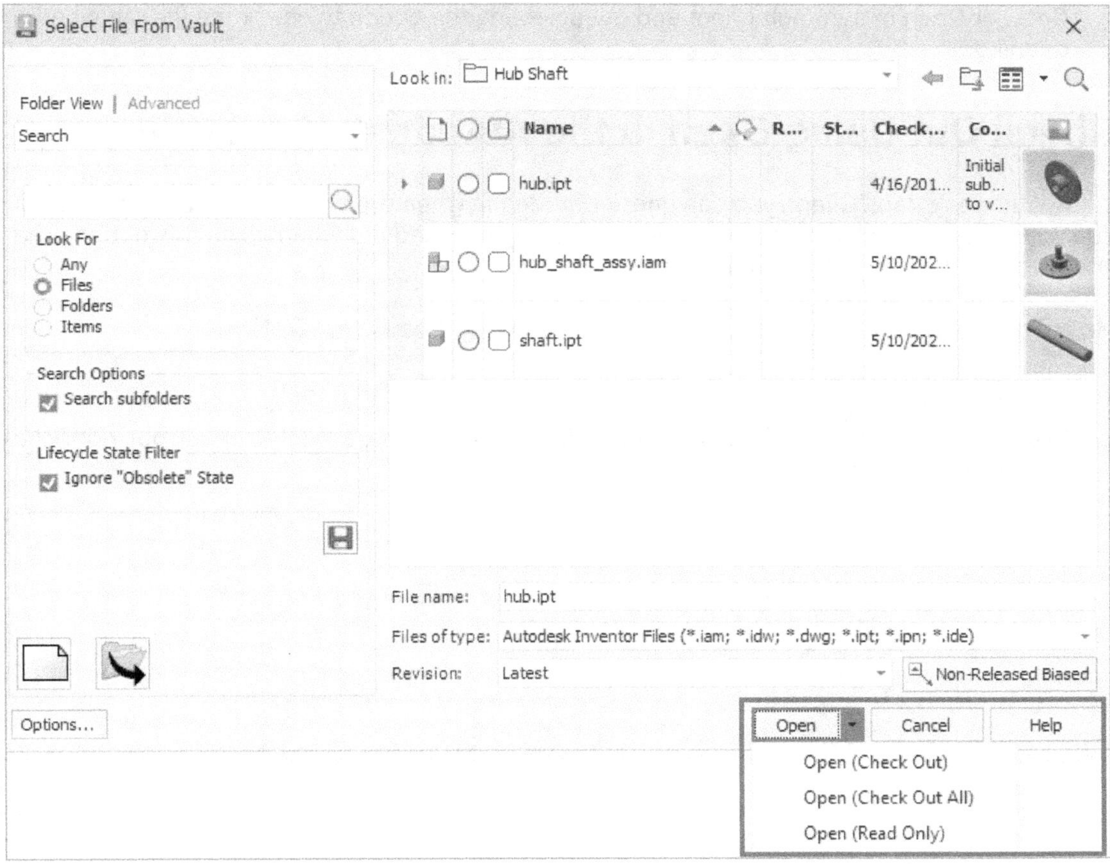

Figure 5–12

If you don't expand for options and just click **Open** when retrieving a file and the file is available for check out, a warning box opens prompting you to check the file out, as shown in Figure 5–13.

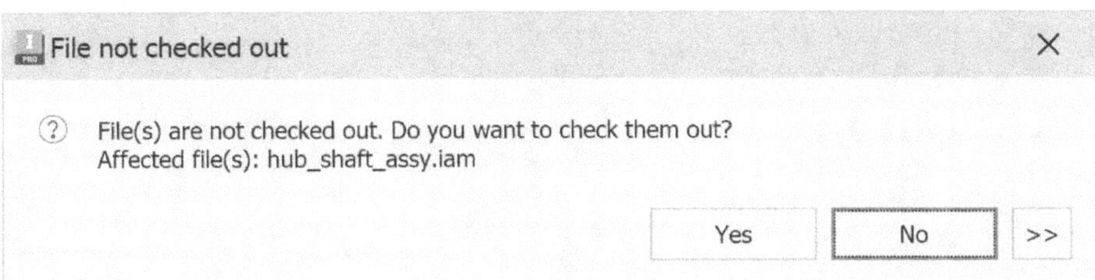

Figure 5–13

3. If you do not select **Yes** to check out the file, you can do so at a later time by selecting (Check Out) in the *Vault* tab>*Status* panel of the ribbon. This option is used after using **Get...** or **Open** in the Vault Client and not selecting the option to check the file out when opening.

Check Out Using Open in the Autodesk Vault Client

In the Autodesk Vault Client, you can check out the file when prompted, using the **Open** option. You cannot specify which version of the file is being checked out when using this option. The latest version is automatically checked out.

How To: Check Out an Autodesk CAD File Using the Open Option

1. Locate the file or search for the required files using the search tools.
2. In the Main table or search results area, select the file that you want to check out, right-click, and select **Open**, as shown in Figure 5–14.

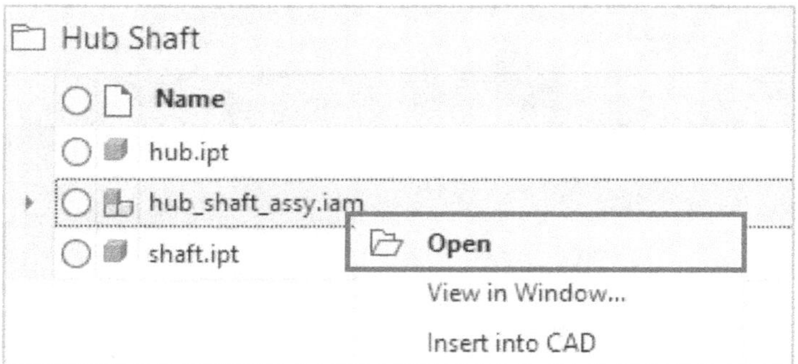

Figure 5–14

3. In the *Open File* dialog box, select **Yes** to open and check out the file, or **No** to open without checking out the file, as shown in Figure 5–15.

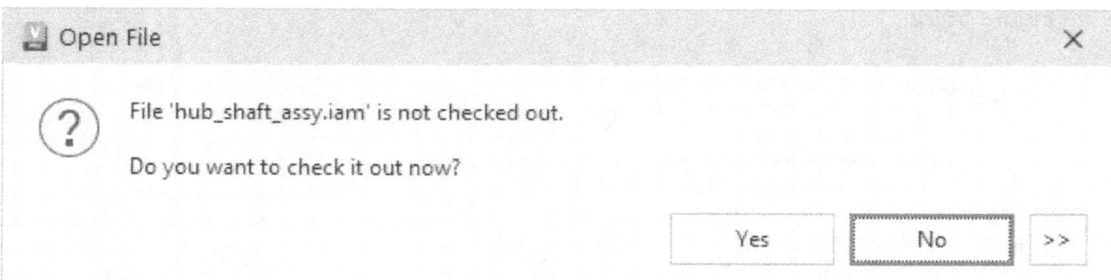

Figure 5–15

Get and Check Out a File in the Vault Client

The **Get** function was discussed earlier, however this section includes additional instructions required for checking out files. You can select more than one file to Get and Check Out.

How To: Check Out Files Using Get in the Vault Client

1. In the Vault Client, select the file(s) in the Navigation pane or Main pane, right-click, and select **Get...**. The *Get* dialog box opens as shown in Figure 5–16.

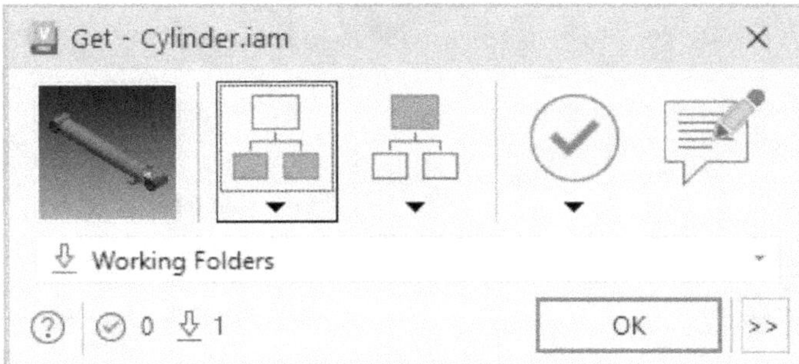

Figure 5–16

Note: *If you right-click on a file then select* ***Check Out****, the latest version of the file is immediately checked out. Note that this option is not usually used as it does not download the file. However, it is useful to prevent the latest version of the file from being modified by another user.*

2. Click (Expand to show details), if desired, to view what files are being downloaded. The expanded view of the *Get* dialog box displays, as shown in Figure 5–17.

   Note: *By default, the Get dialog box is collapsed. If you want the dialog box to stay expanded every time you open it, click*  *(Select the pin to lock the detail view).*

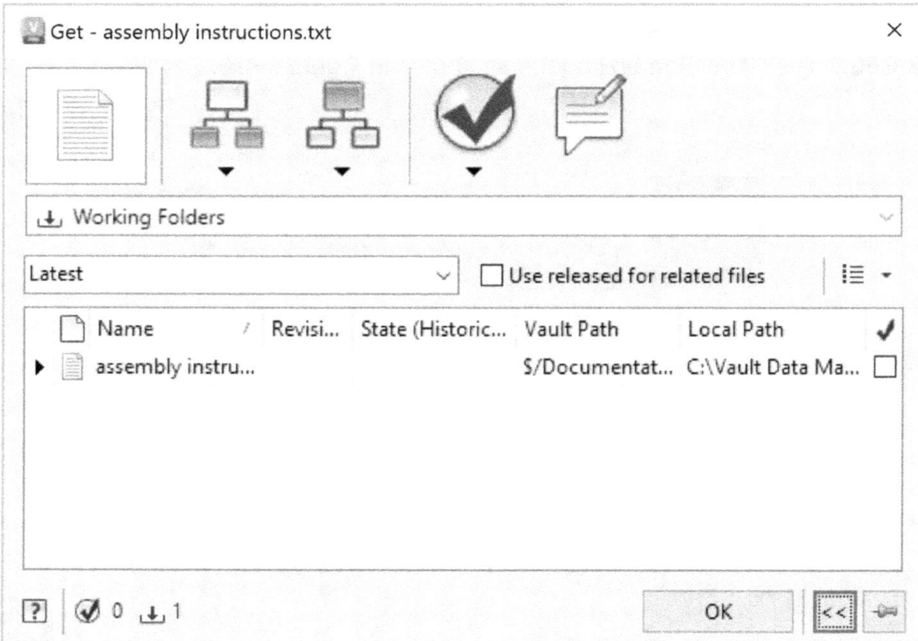

Figure 5–17

3. If required, determine what associated files also get downloaded by clicking on the **Include Children** and **Include Parents** to make the proper selections, as shown in Figure 5–18.

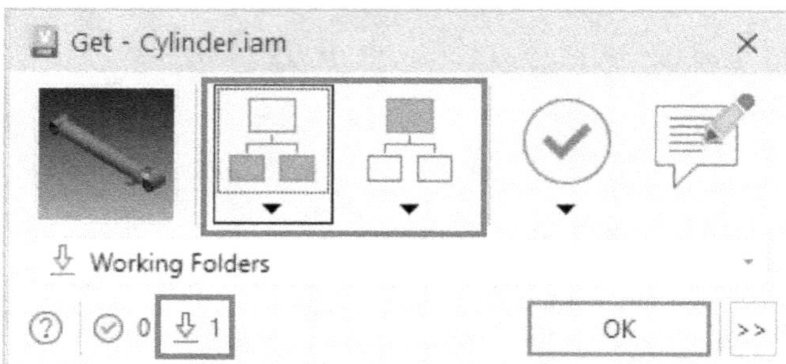

Figure 5–18

- This is particularly important when working with Inventor files as this controls whether you download a single part/assembly file, or all files associated with an assembly.
- The icon will turn blue if it is activated.
- Expand **Include Children** (as shown on the left in Figure 5–19) and **Include Parents** (as shown on the right) using the down arrow to further define what child or parent is included.

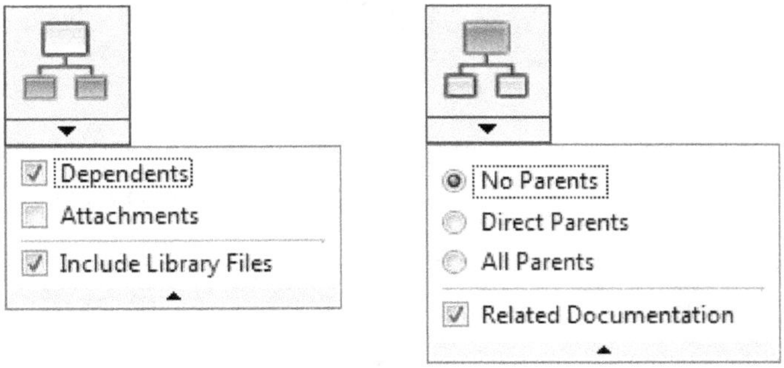

Figure 5–19

- The file count being downloaded displays at the bottom of the dialog box, as shown previously in Figure 5–18.

Note: *By default, the* **Get** *command downloads a read-only version of the file to the working folder without checking it out.*

4. If you want to check out the file(s), click the checkbox in the *Check Out* column, as shown in Figure 5–20. You can also click  (Check Out Files) to automatically add the checkmark.

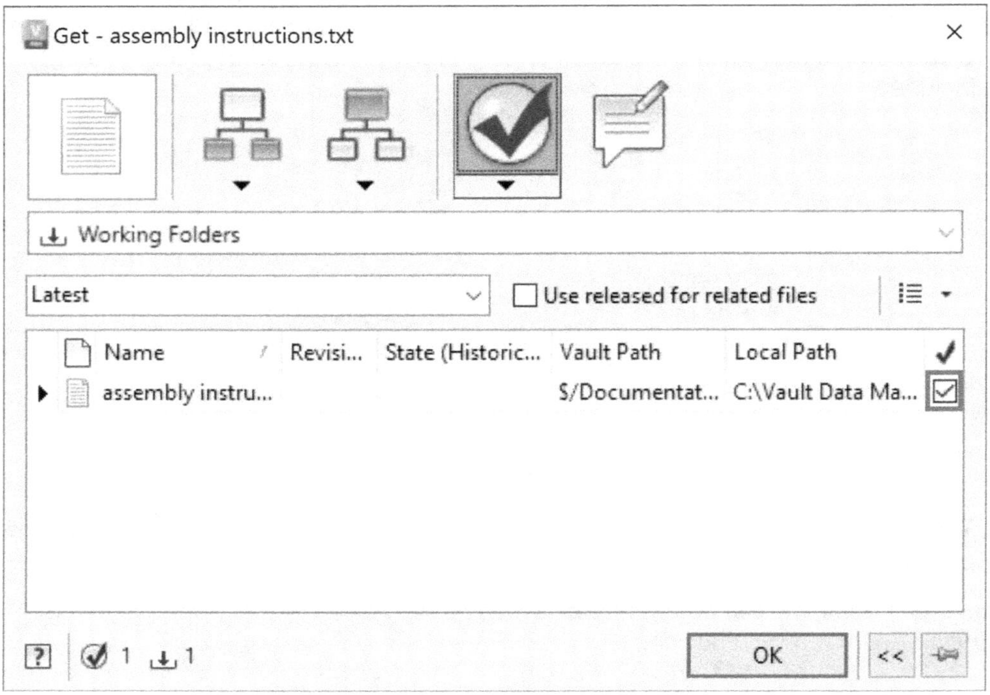

Figure 5–20

- If the file you selected has dependents (children) and you chose for them to participate in the download, you can define here if they are also going to be checked out by expanding the check out box and selecting **All Files**, as shown in Figure 5–21.

Figure 5–21

5. By default, the latest version of the file is downloaded and checked out. To change the revision selection, click the (Expand to show details) icon in the lower right corner of the *Get* dialog box, then expand and make a selection as shown in Figure 5–22.

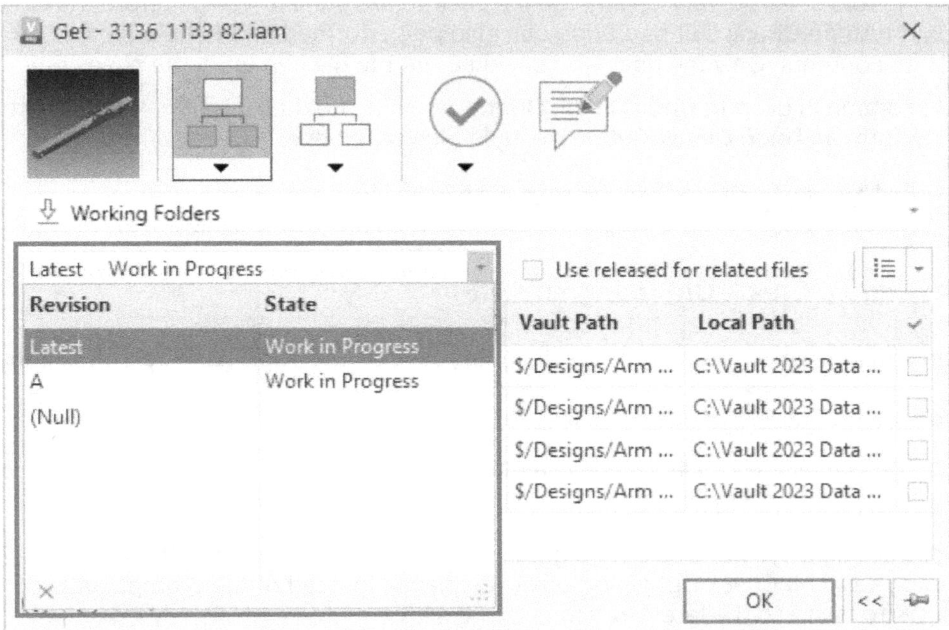

Figure 5–22

6. Click **OK**. The file is now downloaded to your local working folder.
7. To open the file, do one of the following:
   - In the Vault Client, right-click on the file and select **Go to Working Folder**. This will open File Explorer in the appropriate location.
   - In File Explorer, navigate to the appropriate working folder. Double-click on the file to launch and open the file in the appropriate software.
   - In the appropriate software, such as AutoCAD, open the file as you normally would using the Open option (not the Open from Vault option via the Add-in).

5.5 Undo Check Out

If you have checked out a file but do not need to make changes to it, you can perform an **Undo Check Out** operation. This cancels the change operation to the selected file in the vault and your working folder, effectively setting the file back to the state it was in before the check out operation. An **Undo Check Out** operation can also be performed on multiple files, or on a folder and all of its contents. Only the user who checked out the file can undo the check out.

The Add-in option is used to **Undo Check Out** for one file at a time. Use the Vault Client if you want to perform an **Undo Check Out** on multiple files or folders.

Undo a Check Out Using an Add-in

How To: Undo a Check Out Using an Add-in

1. In the software application, with the file open, click on the *Vault* tab>*File Status* panel in the ribbon, then click (Undo Check Out).

   Note: *You can also right-click in the Inventor Vault Browser or in the AutoCAD Xref palette and select* ***Undo Check Out****.*

2. If a prompt displays (as shown in Figure 5–23), click **Yes** to revert to the latest version. For Inventor, an *Undo Check Out* dialog box is displayed instead of the prompt, and you can click **OK** to revert to the latest version.

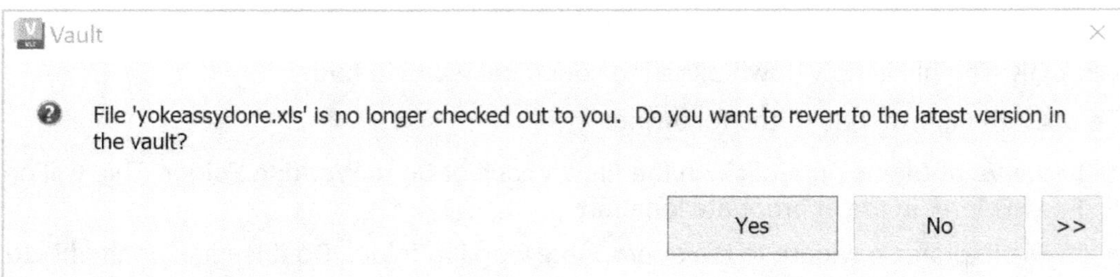

Figure 5–23

3. The check out is canceled and the file is reverted back to a checked-in state with no change to the version number.

Undo a Check Out Using the Vault Client

How To: Undo Check Out Using the Vault Client

1. Locate the files or search for the required files using the available search tools.
2. Select the files in the Main table or search results list, right-click, and select **Undo Check Out**. The *Undo Check Out* dialog box opens as shown in Figure 5–24.

   Note: *Multiple objects can be selected using <Ctrl>.*

   - You can also select **Actions>Undo Check Out** or click (Undo Check Out) in the Standard toolbar.

   Note: *To perform an **Undo Check Out** operation on an entire folder, select the folder, right-click, and select **Undo Check Out**.*

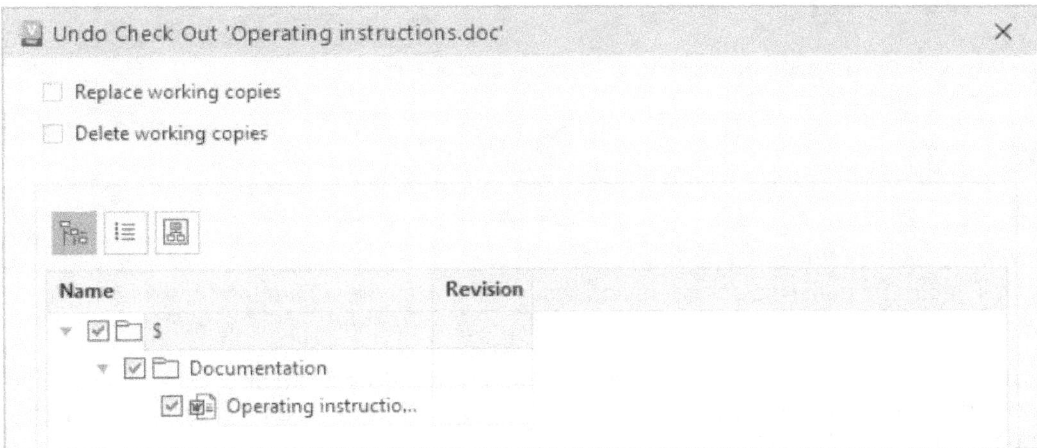

Figure 5–24

3. Select **Replace working copies** if you want the file in your working folder to return to the state it was in before you checked it out.
4. Select **Delete working copies** if you want the file in your working folder to be removed. This is a recommended best practice to ensure that you are always working with the latest version of the file.
5. Click (Settings) to control the inclusion settings of the children, parents, and related documentation of the selected files. The children are included by default.
6. Click **OK** to complete the operation.

5.6 Modify Vault Files

To modify files, the files must be downloaded from the Vault to the user's working folder, using **Get** or **Open**, along with the **Check Out** option to allow for changes to be made. Once the files are modified, they must be checked in to the vault to overwrite the master files with the updated files.

The vault enables multiple users to access the same design project and work on different parts of the design.

For example, user1 can be working on file A of a design and user2 on file B of the same design. They can both retrieve a read-only copy of the referenced file, such as an assembly, to their working folders and only check out the necessary file for modification.

If you try to modify a file that has not yet been checked out, a message box opens prompting you to do so, as shown in Figure 5–25.

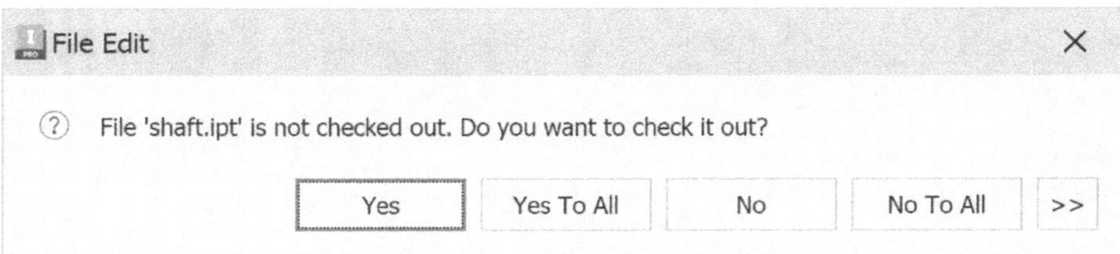

Figure 5–25

> ***Note:*** *To change the settings for the* ***File Edit*** *prompt, in the Vault Add-in ribbon, Vault tab>File Status panel, select* ***Vault Options*** *(in CAD Add-in), or* ***Options*** *(in non-CAD Add-in), click* ***Prompts...*** *and change the response or frequency for* ***File Edit****.*

After modifications are performed, a file must be saved before a **Check In** operation can be performed. By default, if you try to close a checked out file without checking it in, the system prompts you to save the file and check it in.

5.7 Check In Files

Check In can be used for two reasons: to add (upload) a CAD file to vault for the first time or to override the master copy that resides in Vault when a file is modified. After modifications are made to the file in the local working folder and it is saved, the file must be checked back into the vault so that other users can access the file containing the latest changes.

The Add-in is used to **Check In** files for the first time. It is also used to check in files that have been downloaded to your local device, checked out, and modified.

The Vault Client **Check In** options allow for you to check in files that are checked out for modification. You can check in multiple files across multiple projects using the Vault Client.

Check In Using the Add-In

These instructions define the general process for checking in files using the Add-in. To learn how to bulk load CAD files, refer to ***Chapter 6 Working with Autodesk Inventor Files*** for Inventor and ***Chapter 7 Working with AutoCAD Files*** for AutoCAD.

How To: Check In a File Using the Add-In

1. In the *Vault* tab>*Access* panel, select (Check In). The *Check In* dialog box opens as shown in Figure 5–26.

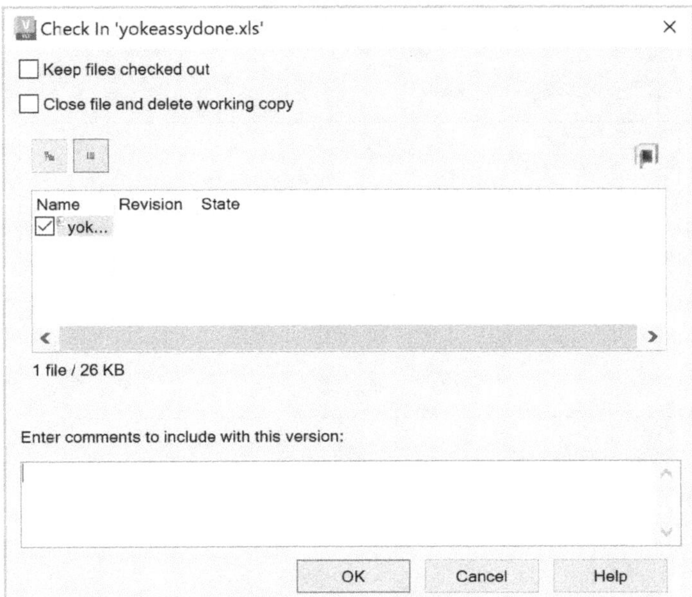

Figure 5–26

Note: *You can also right-click in the Inventor Vault Browser or in the AutoCAD Xref palette and select* ***Check In****. You must save your changes before checking files into the vault.*

2. Select **Keep files checked out** if you want to check the files back out immediately after checking them in.
3. Select **Close file and delete working copy** to close the file and to remove the local copy after the file is checked into the vault.
4. In the *Enter comments to include with this version:* area, enter any notes regarding this version.

   Note: *Best Practice is to always submit a comment such as "Initial Upload", or notes on modifications made, for communication and tracking purposes.*

5. Click **OK** to complete the operation.

Check In Using the Vault Client

How To: Check In a File Using the Vault Client

1. Locate the files or search for the required files using the search tools.
2. In the Main table or search results list, select the files to check in, right-click, and select **Check In**. The *Check In* dialog box opens, as shown in Figure 5–27.

   Note: *Multiple objects can be selected using <Ctrl>.*

   - You can also select **Actions>Check In** or click (Check In) in the Standard toolbar.

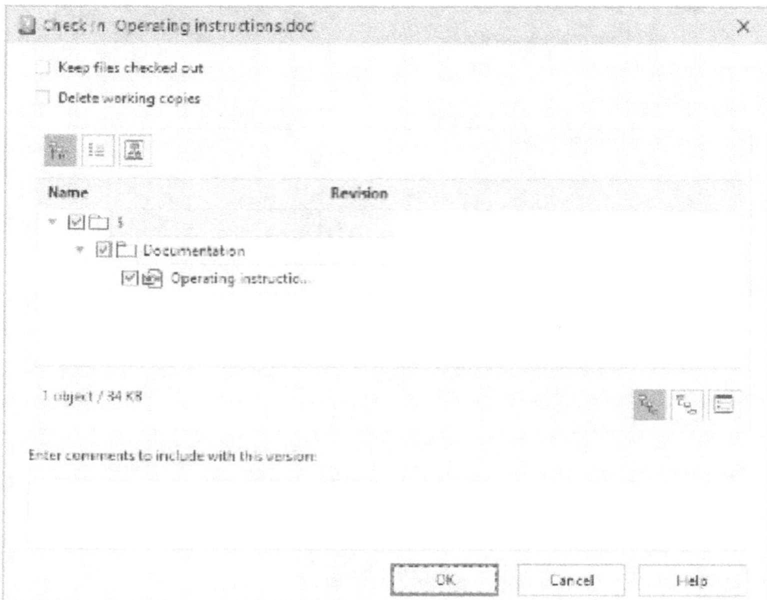

Figure 5–27

3. Select **Keep files checked out** if you want to check the files back out immediately after checking them in.
4. Select **Delete working copies** to remove the local copy after the file is checked into the vault.
5. Click (Settings) to control the inclusion settings of the children, parents, and related documentation of the selected files. By default, the children are included.
6. In the *Enter comments to include...* area, enter any notes regarding this version.
7. Click **OK** to complete the operation.

5.8 File Status

The status of a file in the vault, shown with vault status icons, status fonts, and modifiers, displays in the Autodesk Vault Client and in the CAD Add-in.

Vault Basic Status Icons

If you are using the Vault Basic software, the vault status icons are shown in the table below.

Icon	Description	Required Action
No icon	Indicates that the file is in the vault in a checked in state and that you do not have a local copy.	The file is available to be checked out, or a local copy can be retrieved using the **Get** command.
(empty)	The file is in the vault in a checked in state and the read-only version you are working on is the same as the one in the vault (also known as *Latest Version* or *leading version of the leading revision* of the file).	The read-only file is available to be checked out.
(green)	The file is in the vault in a checked in state, but the version you are working on is newer than the latest version in the vault.	Typically means that your local file was changed without checking it out.
(red)	The file is in the vault in a checked in state but the local copy is out of date.	Get the latest version from the vault
	The file is checked out to you but you do not have a local copy. May have been checked out to a location other than your working folder.	Get the latest version from the vault.
	The file is checked out to you and the version you are working on is the same as the one in the vault (also known as *Latest Version*).	Use **Check In** to check the file back into the vault or select **Undo Check Out** to cancel any changes.
(green)	The file is checked out to you but the version you are working on is newer than the latest version in the vault.	Typically means you made changes to the file since it was checked out but have not yet checked it back in.
	The file is checked out to you and the local copy is older than the latest version in the vault.	You can check it in to promote it to the latest.
	The file is checked out by another user and you do not have a local copy.	You can get/download the latest version.

Icon	Description	Required Action
	The file is checked out by another user and your local copy is the same as the vault.	The other user can check in their changes.
	The file is checked out by another user and the local copy is newer than the latest version in vault.	The other user can check in their changes before you make your changes.
	The file is checked out by another user and the local copy is older than the latest version in vault.	You can get/download the latest version.
	The file is not in the vault.	Use **Check In** to add the file to the vault.

Vault Professional Status Icons

- **Black/Normal font:** The file is not checked out.
- **Blue/Bold:** The file is checked out to you. An asterisk will display at the end of the file name if the file has been modified but not been saved.
- **Gray/Italic/Strikethrough:** The file is checked out to another user.
- **Vault Status Modifier (+):** The file's edits have been saved locally.

Vault Status Icons

Icon	Description	Required Action
No icon	Indicates that the file is in the vault in a checked in state and that you do not have a local copy.	The file is available to be checked out, or a local copy can be retrieved using the **Get** command.
(empty)	The file is in the vault in a checked in state and the read-only version you are working on is the same as the one in the vault (also known as *Latest Version* or *leading version of the leading revision* of the file).	The read-only file is available to be checked out.
(green)	The file is in the vault in a checked in state, but the version you are working on is newer than the latest version in the vault.	Typically means that your local file was changed without checking it out.

Icon	Description	Required Action
	The file is checked out to you and the version you are working on is the same as the one in the vault (also known as *Latest Version*).	Use **Check In** to check the file back into the vault or select **Undo Check Out** to cancel any changes.
	The local copy is a historical revision of the leading revision in the vault.	
(green)	The file is checked out to you but the version you are working on is newer than the latest version in the vault.	Typically means you made changes to the file since it was checked out but have not yet checked it back in.
	The file is not in the vault.	Use **Check In** to add the file to the vault.
	The local copy does not match the latest version in the vault.	Use the **Refresh from Vault** command to obtain the latest version of the file.
	The file is locked and the local copy is up-to-date.	
	The file is locked and the local copy is not up-to-date.	
	There has been an unexpected revision with the file, or the status could not be determined.	Review the tooltip for the action required.

5.9 Get Previous Versions

To retrieve older versions of files from Vault, you must be in the Vault Client and use the **Get** command. It cannot be done directly in the Autodesk Inventor software.

How To: Revert to a Previous Version

1. Select the file, right-click on it, and then select **Check Out**.
2. Select the *History* tab.
3. Select **Show all versions**.
4. Select the version of the file that you would like to download.
5. Right-click on the file and click **Get**, as shown in Figure 5–28.

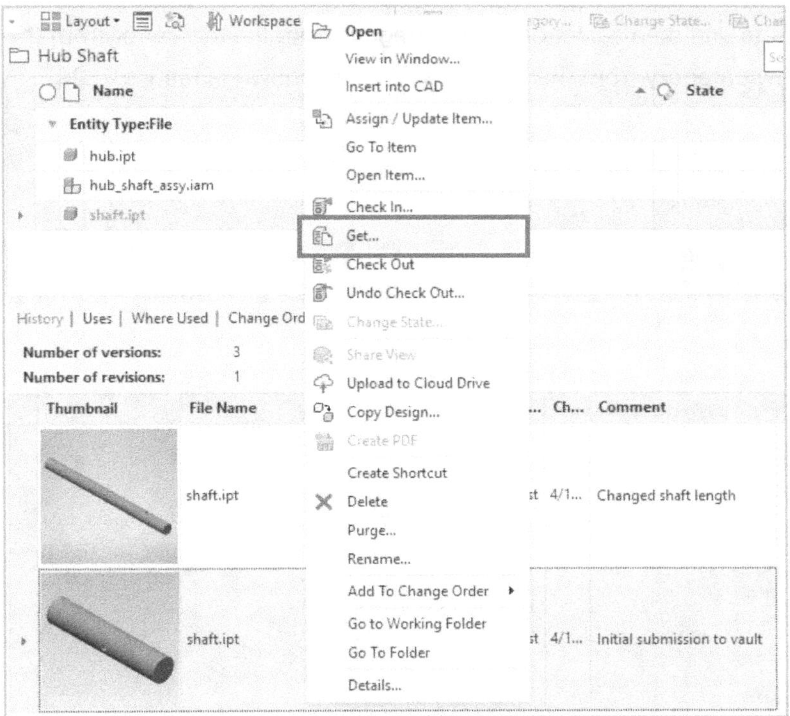

Figure 5–28

6. The previous version of the file is shown in the dialog box. Click **OK** to download to the working folder.
7. Click **Yes** when prompted to overwrite the working folder file with the file from the vault.
8. Now you can open the file from the working folder in the CAD or non-CAD application and make any changes. Once it is checked back in to the vault, it will be the latest version.

5.10 Categories

Categories enable you to group objects and assign a defined set of behaviors and rules to objects. For example, a category can automatically assign user-defined properties to objects in the Vault, automatically assign lifecycle definitions, or automatically set revision values to files.

Categories can be assigned to CAD or non-CAD files in the Add-in (not available for non-CAD applications) or in the Vault Client. Using the Vault Client is the most efficient method as it allows you to change the category on a group of files. The file(s) must be checked in to assign categories.

Change a Category in the Vault Client

How To: Change a Category in the Vault Client

1. Select objects and then select **Change Category** from the toolbar or from the **Actions** menu.
2. Select a new category from the drop-down list, as shown in Figure 5–29.

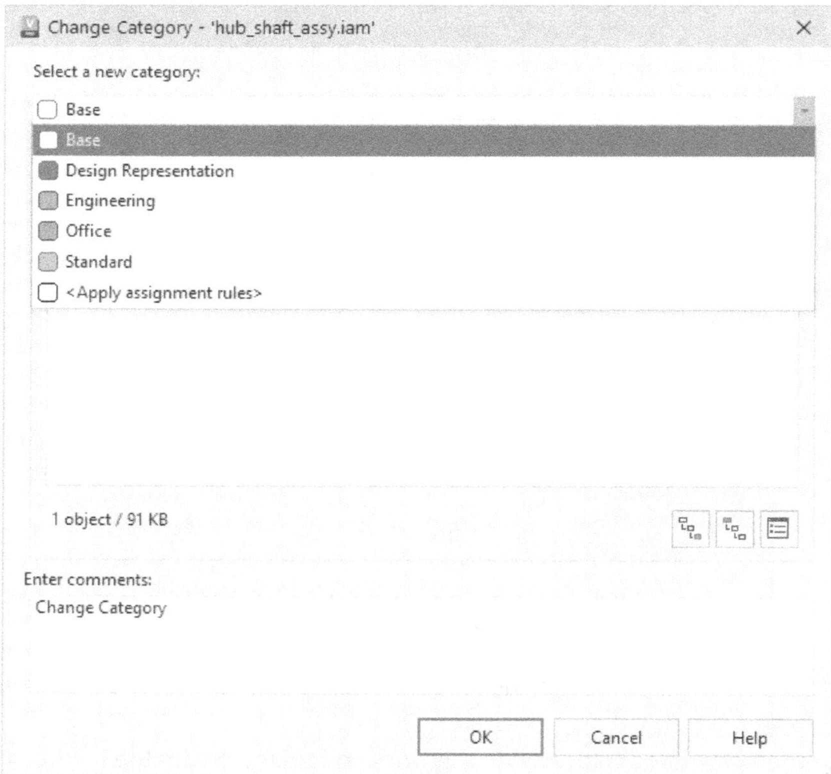

Figure 5–29

3. Click **OK**.

4. The category column of the Preview pane displays the assigned category, the *Revision* changes to **A**, and the *State* becomes **Work in Progress**, as shown in Figure 5–30.

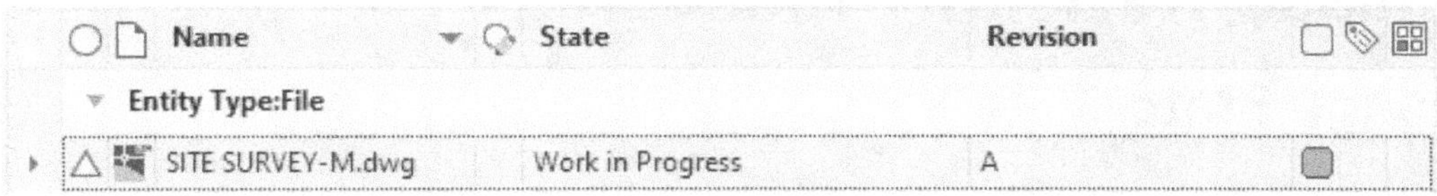

Figure 5–30

Change a Category in the Add-In

How To: Change a Category in the Add-In

1. With a file open and checked in, click on the  (Change Category) icon in the *Vault* tab>*Control* panel.
2. Select a new category from the list and add a comment, if desired, as shown in Figure 5–31.

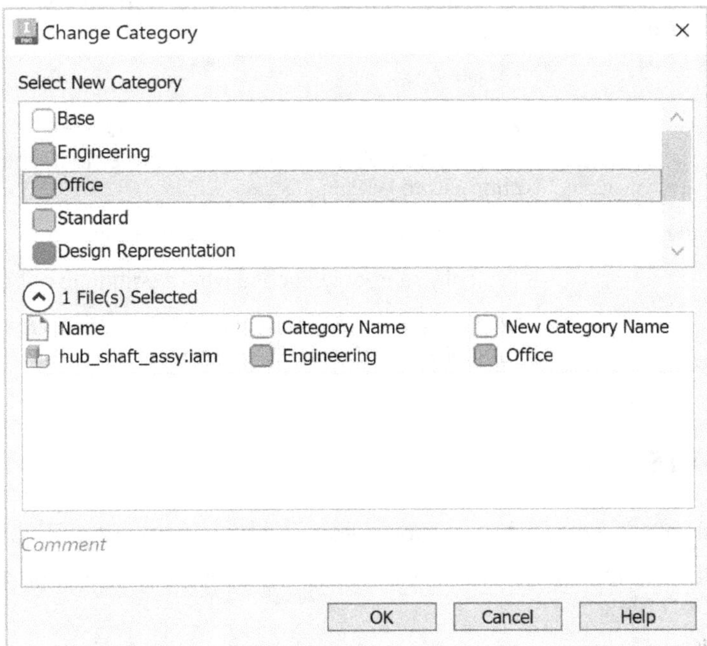

Figure 5–31

Note: *Categories can also be assigned by right-clicking on a file in the Inventor Vault Browser or in the AutoCAD External References palette.*

3. Click **OK**.

5.11 Changing Lifecycle States and Next Release/Revision Procedures

Change State

The **Change State** command enables you to change the lifecycle state of a selected object.

How To: Change State

1. Select the objects from the main pane.
2. Click **Change State**, or right-click and select **Change State**.
3. Select a lifecycle definition, if required, and then select the lifecycle state from the drop-down list.
4. Click **Settings** for children and parent options, if required.
5. Type a comment or select from a list of predefined comments.
6. Click **OK**.

The following is a list of predefined Lifecycle States for the Flexible Release Process that is associated with the Engineering Category:

Lifecycle State	Description
Work In Progress	Also known as WIP, this state typically involves the editing of the files. By default, the Revision will increment when the state is changed to WIP.
For Review/In Review	In general, no editing is permitted at this state.
Released	Typically read-only access where editing is not permitted.
Obsolete	Designs are no longer active and therefore access is restricted. Typically, no edits can be made.

Change Revision/Revise

The **Change Revision** and **Revise** commands create a new revision of a file or item.

The **Revise** command is found in Autodesk Inventor or AutoCAD in the *Vault* tab. It is not available for non-CAD files.

The **Change Revision** command is found in Autodesk Vault in the **Actions** menu or toolbar.

When you need to make changes to a file or item that has already been released into production, you must first create a new revision. This protects the integrity of the existing released version, and creates a new version on which to make the changes. When a file is revised, its revision is incremented following a predefined sequence, and the version number is reset to 1.

How To: Create a New Revision in Autodesk Inventor or AutoCAD

1. In Autodesk Inventor or AutoCAD, open the file you want to revise.
2. In the *Vault* tab, click **Revise**, as shown in Figure 5–32.

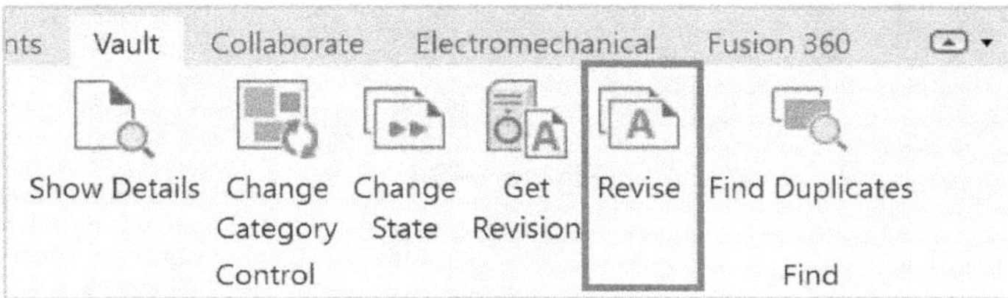

Figure 5–32

3. Select one of the format options shown in Figure 5–33.

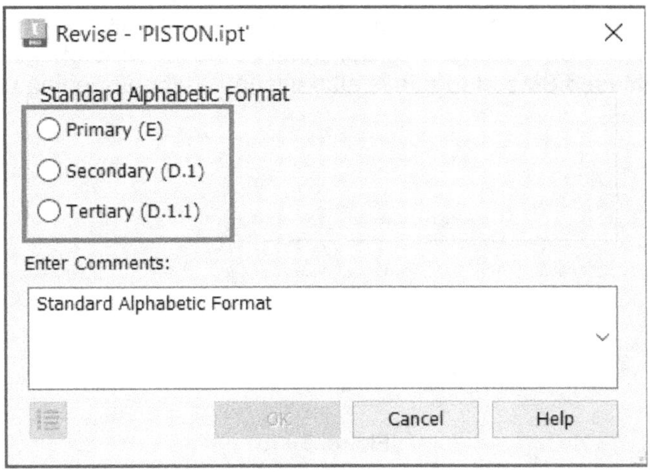

Figure 5–33

4. Click **OK**.

How To: Create a New Revision in Autodesk Vault Client

1. In Autodesk Vault Client, select a file and then in the toolbar, select **Change Revision**.
2. In the *Select next revision* drop-down list, select **Primary**, **Secondary**, or **Tertiary**, as shown in Figure 5–34.

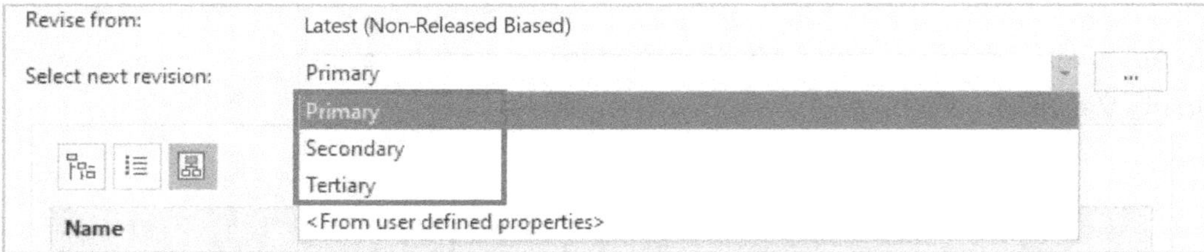

Figure 5–34

3. Click **OK**.

Released Biased

Released Biased is an option that determines if released objects should take priority over unreleased objects. This option can be toggled on and off. An example of a **Non-Released Biased** configuration is shown in Figure 5–35, and a **Released Biased** example is shown in Figure 5–36. The **Released Biased** toggle is also available when opening or placing/attaching files.

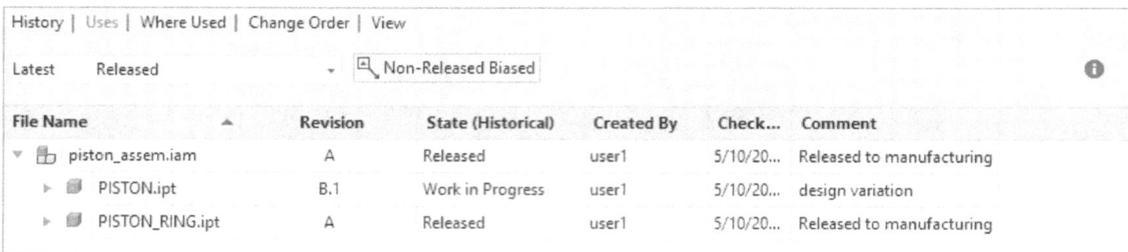

Figure 5–35

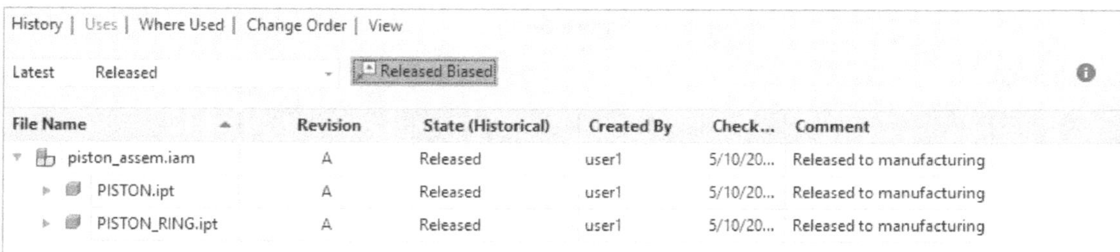

Figure 5–36

5.12 Get Revision

You can retrieve a specific revision of a file, if and when required. Get Revision is only available in the Add-in for CAD files.

How To: Get a Specific Revision

1. In the desired application, such as Autodesk Inventor software, select **Get Revision** on the *Vault* tab, as shown in Figure 5–37.

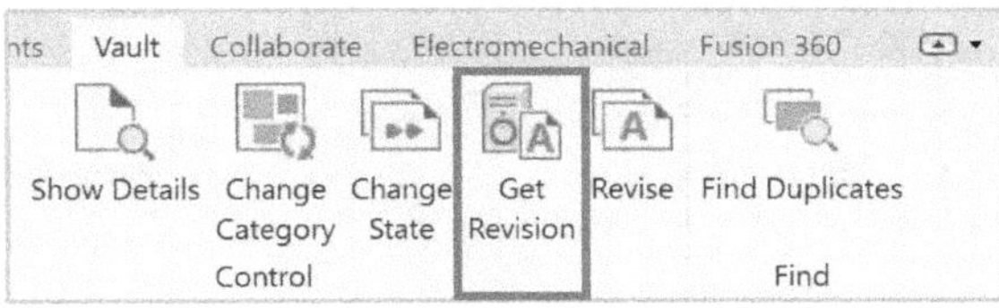

Figure 5–37

2. Select a revision from the *Select Revision:* drop-down list, as shown in Figure 5–38. The dialog box might look different depending on the application.

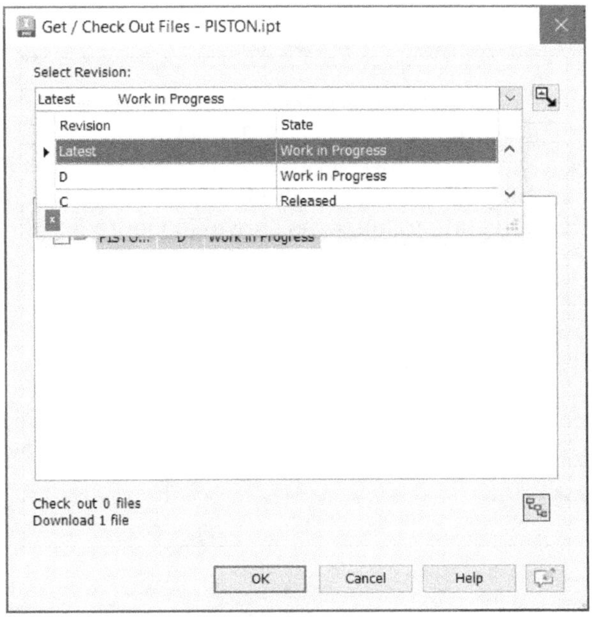

Figure 5–38

> ***Note:*** *The Revision drop-down list is also available when opening or placing Autodesk Inventor files or attaching AutoCAD files in the vault.*

3. Click **OK**.

Roll Back Lifecycle State Change

Another method to revert to a previous revision is to undo the revision change using the **Roll Back Lifecycle State Change** command.

How To: Roll Back a File's Lifecycle State

1. Select a file in the main table and select **Actions>Roll Back Lifecycle State Change...**, as shown in Figure 5–39.

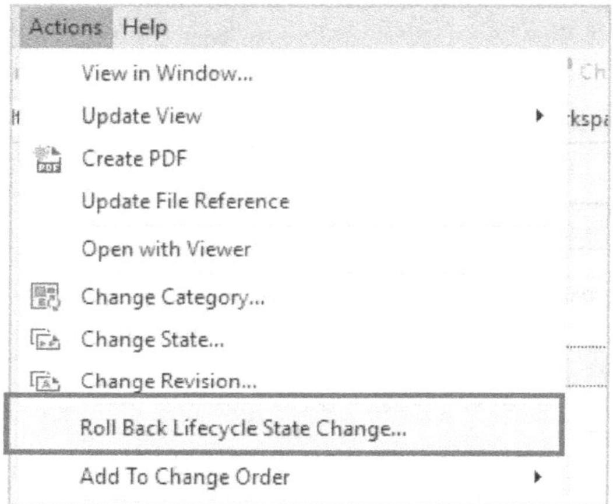

Figure 5–39

2. A window opens describing to which state the file will be rolled back. Click **Yes** to continue and complete the lifecycle state rollback, as shown in Figure 5–40.

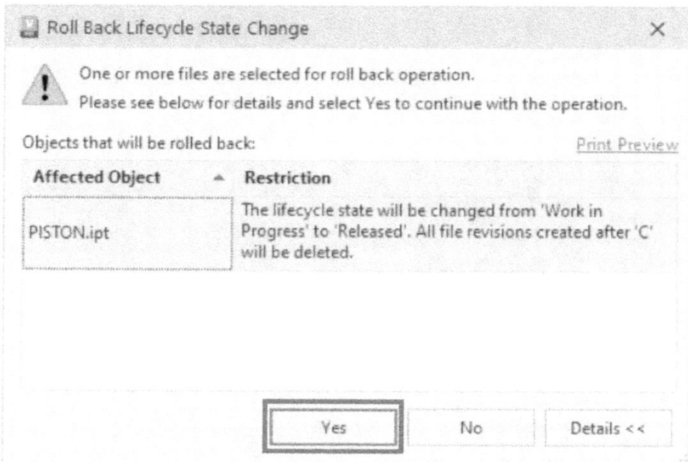

Figure 5–40

Practice 5a
Add Non-CAD Files to the Vault

Practice Objectives

- Add a non-CAD file to the vault using the **Add Files** command and the drag-and-drop method.
- View a non-CAD file in the vault.

In this practice, you will add non-CAD files to the vault using multiple methods, and then you will view them in the Preview pane of the Vault client.

Task 1: Add non-CAD files to the vault using Add Files.

In this task, you will add a PDF file to the vault using the **Add Files** command.

1. In the Navigation pane, select the *$\Documentation* folder, right-click, and select **Add Files**.
2. In the *C:\Vault Data Management Practice Files\vault_work\Documentation* folder, select the document **Using Autodesk Vault with Single Inventor Project.pdf**, and click **Open**.

3. In the *Add Files...* dialog box, select **Delete working copies**. In the *Enter comments to include...* area, enter **Initial submission** as shown in Figure 5–41.

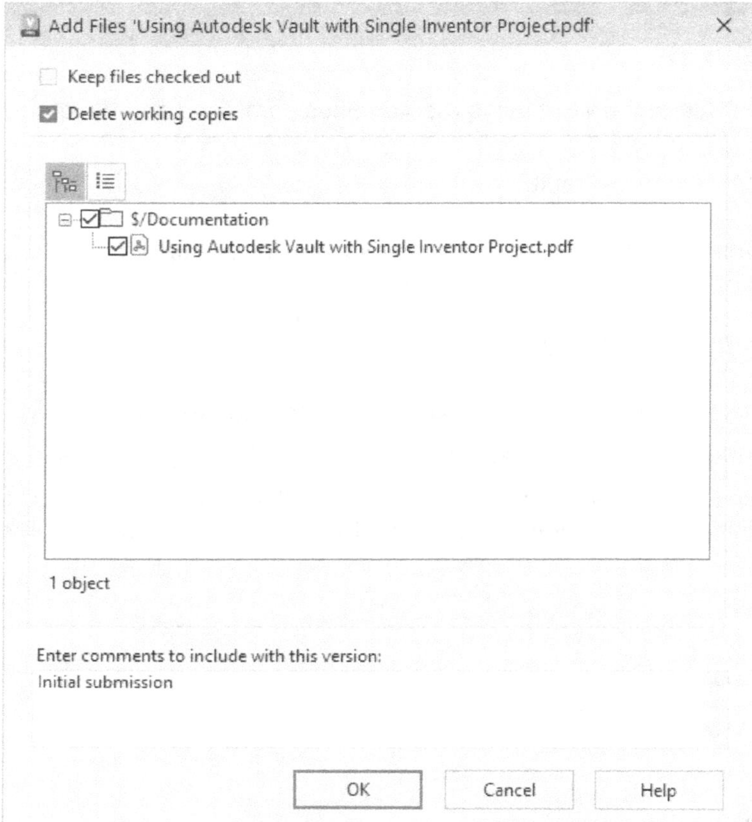

Figure 5–41

4. Click **OK**.

Task 2: Add non-CAD files to the vault using drag and drop.

In this task, you will add a Word file to the vault using drag and drop.

1. In the Navigation pane, select the *$\Documentation* folder to view its current files.
2. In a File Explorer window, navigate to the *C:\Vault Data Management Practice Files\vault_work\Documentation* folder.
3. Drag **Software Setup.docx** and drop it into the vault *Documentation* folder.
4. In the *Add Files...* dialog box, select **Delete working copies**. In the *Enter comments to include...* area, enter **Initial submission** as shown in Figure 5–42.

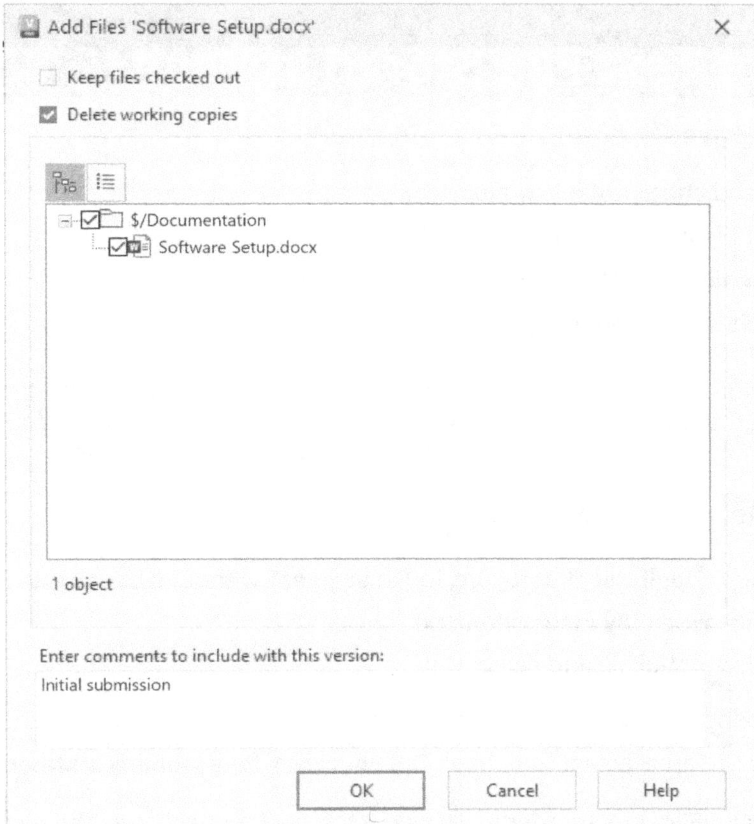

Figure 5–42

5. Click **OK**.

Task 3: View the non-CAD files in the vault.

In this task, you will view the non-CAD files in the vault.

1. In the Main table, select the document **Using Autodesk Vault with Single Inventor Project.pdf**.
2. Select the *View* tab to display the thumbnail of Version 1. Click the thumbnail to display the PDF in the Preview pane.
3. Select the *History* tab to view the comment in the *Comment* column.
4. In the Main table, select **Software Setup.docx**. Click the thumbnail in the *View* tab to display the document in the Preview pane.

End of practice

Practice 5b
Modify a Text File Stored in Vault

Practice Objectives

- Locate, get, and check out a text file.
- Modify a text file and check it back into the vault.
- Check out the file as another user.
- View the Vault Status and display the file's Version History.

In this practice, you will make modifications to an assembly instructions file. You will locate the file, check it out, make modifications, and then check it back into the vault. You will then check out the file as another user and as the original user, display the file's history.

Task 1: Locate, get, and check out a text file.

1. In the Autodesk Vault Client software, log in as **user1** without a password.
2. Locate the file **assembly instructions.txt**.
3. Select the file, right-click, and select **Get**.
4. In the *Get* dialog box, click >> (Expand to show details) and note that it is set to **Latest**.
5. In the *Check Out* area, select the Check Out checkbox for **assembly instructions.txt**, or click (Check Out Files) to automatically select the file for check out. The dialog box updates showing that one file will be checked out and one file will be downloaded, as shown in Figure 5–43.

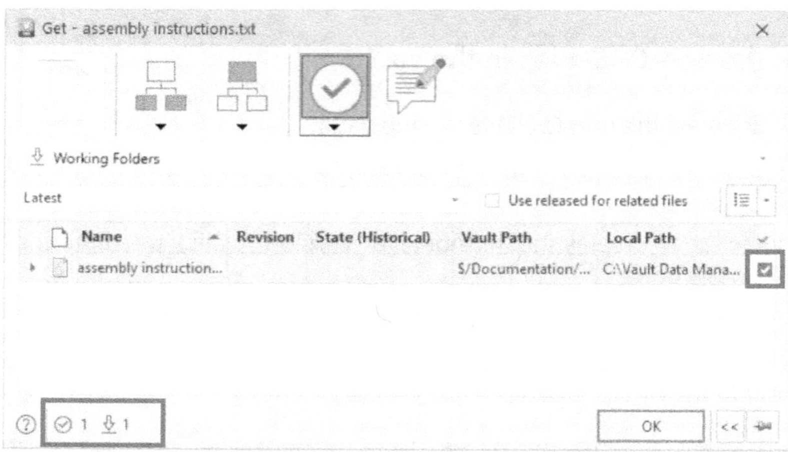

Figure 5–43

6. Click (Comments). In the text field, type **Changes required** as shown in Figure 5–44. Adding comments is optional.

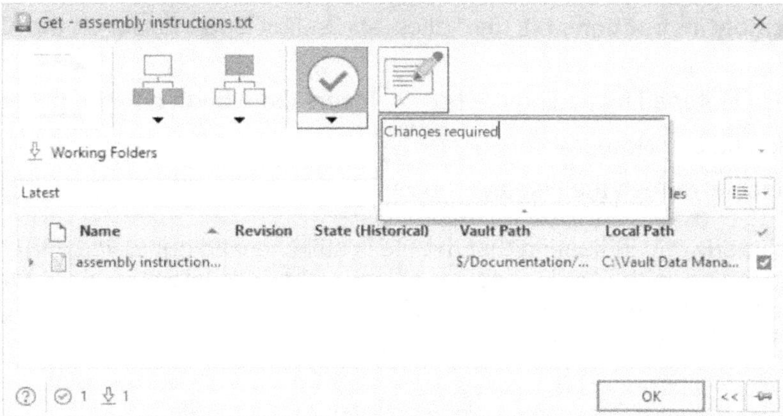

Figure 5–44

7. Click **OK**.

8. The Main table updates. Note that the vault status icon has updated to display and that the filename has a blue bold font. The file is checked out to you and the version you are working on is the same as the one in the vault (also known as the *Latest Version* or *leading version* of the leading revision of the file).The comments entered are also shown in the *History* tab of the Preview pane, as shown in Figure 5–45.

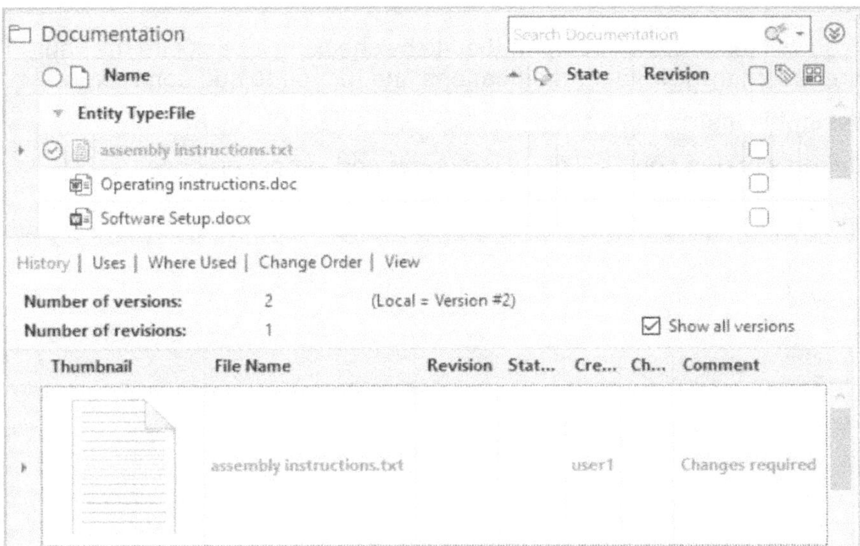

Figure 5–45

Task 2: Open the text file and edit it.

In this task, you will open the text file in Notepad for modification.

1. Select **assembly instructions.txt**, right-click, and select **Open** to launch the Notepad application.
2. Edit the file in Notepad by adding the text: **4. Insert the 4 bolts into the holes.**
3. Save the file and exit Notepad.
4. In the Main table, refresh the display. The vault status icon updates to display a green circle with a checkmark, indicating that the file is still checked out to you and that the version you are working on, in the working folder, is newer than the latest version in the vault. There is also a plus sign (+) in the *Vault Status Modifier* column, indicating the file's edits have been saved locally, as shown in Figure 5–46.

Figure 5–46

Task 3: Check in the document.

In this task, you will release ownership of the file by checking it back into the vault. This is done to enable other users to view your modifications and for you to add comments.

1. Select **assembly instructions.txt**, right-click, and select **Check In**.
2. Select **Delete working copies**. This is a recommended best practice.

3. In the *Enter comments to include...* area, type **Added step 4.** as shown in Figure 5–47. Click **OK**.

Figure 5–47

Task 4: Check out the document as another user.

A co-worker now needs to add to the instructions.

1. Log out of the Autodesk Vault software by selecting **File>Log Out**.
2. Log back in as **user2** without a password.
3. Locate the **assembly instructions.txt** file, right-click and select **Get**.
4. Click (Check Out Files) to select the file for check out.
5. For the comment, type **Further modifications required** and click **OK** to perform the check out.
6. Log out of the Autodesk Vault software.

Task 5: View vault status and display version history.

In this task, you will log back in as **user1** and view the vault status and version history of the assembly instructions file.

1. Log in to the Autodesk Vault software as **user1**.
2. Locate the **assembly instructions.txt** file. Note that the file is crossed out, indicating that the file is checked out by someone else, as shown in Figure 5–48.

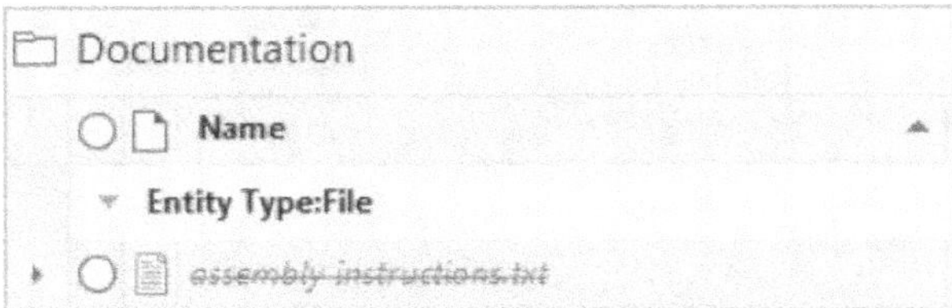

Figure 5–48

3. Select the file, right-click, and click **Get**. Click (Expand to show details). Note that the **Check Out** option is not available in the *Get* dialog box because the file is checked out by **user2**, as shown in Figure 5–49.

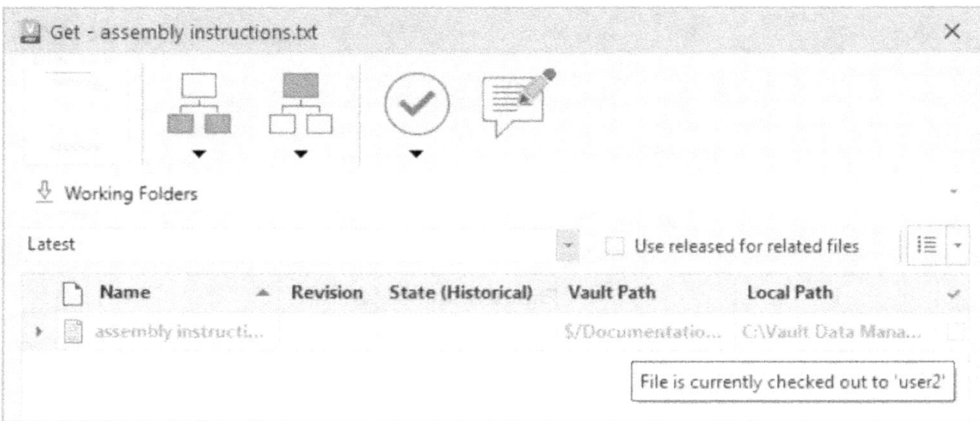

Figure 5–49

4. Close the *Get* dialog box.

5. In the Preview pane, select the *History* tab to view the version history, as shown in Figure 5–50. Select **Show all versions** to show the version history.

Figure 5–50

End of practice

Chapter Review Questions

1. A file, regardless of it being a CAD or non-CAD file, needs to be checked out to modify it.
   a. True
   b. False

2. If a file is checked out to a user, another user cannot check it out at the same time to make modifications.
   a. True
   b. False

3. What file operation cancels the change operation, setting a file back to the state it was in before a check out operation?
   a. Check In
   b. Open
   c. Undo Check Out
   d. Get

4. The **Check Out** command downloads and checks out a selected file(s).
   a. True
   b. False

5. What file operation can change a file to be in a released state?
   a. Change Category
   b. Change State
   c. Check Out
   d. Check In

Command Summary

Button	Command	Location
	**Check In**	• **Inventor Ribbon:** *Vault* tab>*File Status* panel • Shortcut menu in the Vault Browser
	**Get**	• **Menu:** Actions>Get • **Shortcut:** (*right-click on selected file*) • **Standard Toolbar**
	**Check Out**	• **Menu:** Actions>Check Out • **Shortcut:** (*right-click on selected file*)
	**Undo Check Out**	• **Inventor Ribbon:** *Vault* tab>*File Status* panel • Shortcut menu in the Vault Browser
	**Change Category**	• **Menu:** Actions>Change Category • **Advanced Toolbar**

Chapter 6

Working with Autodesk Inventor Files

The Vault Add-in for Inventor provides direct access to Vault within the Autodesk Inventor interface and is used to manage your Inventor files and maintain parent/child relationships between Inventor files. The Add-in's *Vault* tab and Vault Browser are used to work with Inventor files.

Learning Objectives

- Add (upload) Inventor files to the Vault for the first time.
- Use the *Vault* tab to open and place Inventor files from Vault.
- Use the Vault Browser to perform Vault file operations.
- Retrieve a previous version of an Inventor file.
- Modify, release, and revise an Inventor design.
- Accelerate design documentation.
- Use the **Find Duplicates** command in Autodesk Inventor to search for duplicate parts.

6.1 Add Inventor Files to Vault

The **Check In** and **Check In Project** operations are used if you are adding files to the vault for the first time. The separate **Autoloader** utility can also be used. Autodesk .DWF files are automatically created and attached for files that have changed or for files that do not already have .DWF files published.

A CAD file becomes the master when it is added or checked into the vault. Use the **Get Revision** operation to update the local working folder with the latest version (leading version of the leading revision) of the selected files. Use **Check Out** when you want to modify the files. These operations copy the requested files to your local working folder again and ensure that you are working with the latest versions.

Best Practice: Temporarily Store Files in the Local Working Folder

As a recommended best practice, the working folder should be considered a temporary folder in which to store files until they are checked back into the vault. Once checked back into the vault, the temporary files should be deleted.

Check In

The **Check In** operation adds files to the vault folders specified during the **Map Folders** operation in the Autodesk Inventor software. These mapped folders are stored in the project file and become the default file storage locations each time you add files. If the files are already in the vault, a Warning box opens.

How To: Check In Files to the Vault for the First Time

1. Ensure the files are located in the proper folder structure.
2. After logging into the vault in the Autodesk Inventor software, select the *Vault* tab.
3. Select the file, right-click, and select **Check In**. The *Check In* dialog box displays all of the files that are going to be added to the vault and their folder structure.

   Note: *The vault creates any folders required to support the structure displayed in the dialog box.*

4. Select **Keep files checked out** to check the files into the vault and then check them out again so that you can keep working with them.
5. Select **Close files and delete working copies** to close the files after they have been checked in and delete them from the local working folder.
6. Click **Settings** to set the .DWF attachment settings. The **Create visualization attachment** option is selected by default. The **Apply to all files** option is disabled because all of the parts and assemblies are added by default.

7. In the *Enter comments to include...* area, enter comments as required.
8. Click **OK**.

Check In Project (Bulk Load)

The **Check In Project** operation bulk loads design projects into the vault in one operation, while maintaining file relationships. This operation locates all of the files related to the project using the defined search paths. The files added include the presentations (.IPN), parts (.IPT), assemblies, (.IAM) and drawings (.IDW or .DWG) that are associated with the project. The operation does not add files that are already in the vault.

To add Autodesk Inventor project files to the vault, they must be Vault projects and the project folders must be mapped to vault folders.

- The *OldVersions* folder and its contents, lock files (.LCK), and other project files in the active project, are not added.

How To: Bulk Load Multiple Designs

1. In the Inventor Application Menu, expand **Vault Server** and select **Check In Project**. A scan is performed on the project files to find files that are not currently in the vault. Files not found in the vault are listed in the *Check In Project* dialog box.
2. In the *Enter comments to include...* area, enter comments as required.
3. Click **OK** to add all of the files to the vault. If you need to remove the files from the local directories after they have been loaded into the vault, you must remove them manually.

Autoloader

Autodesk Autoloader for Vault is a utility that is provided with the Autodesk Vault installation kit. It includes tools to assist with gathering, analyzing, and loading Autodesk Inventor designs into the vault. This utility is used outside the Autodesk Inventor software. During the analysis or scanning phase, you are informed of any issues (such as missing references and duplicate files) so they can be addressed before the files are loaded into the vault. The Autodesk Autoloader for Vault is recommended when bulk loading large Autodesk Inventor projects. It can also upload legacy projects. This utility can be accessed via the Windows Start menu>Autodesk Data Management folder.

Add Library Files

Library files can also be added to the vault using the **Check In** and **Check In Project** operations. Library files can be added if the library path in the project file is mapped to a vault folder. Library files are the only files located outside the workspace that are added to the vault using the **Check In Project** option.

6.2 Inventor Add-in Vault Browser

The Vault Browser enables you to view the status of Autodesk Inventor files in the vault and perform other operations, such as Check In and Check Out. In the Autodesk Inventor software Model browser, select the *Vault* tab in the Browser panel bar, as shown in Figure 6–1.

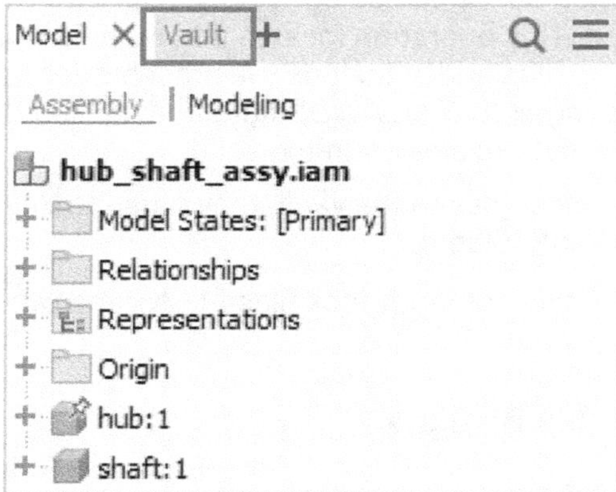

Figure 6–1

The Vault Browser opens as shown in Figure 6–2. The Vault Browser toolbar with icons is shown and each component listed in the browser displays a Vault status icon and the filename by default.

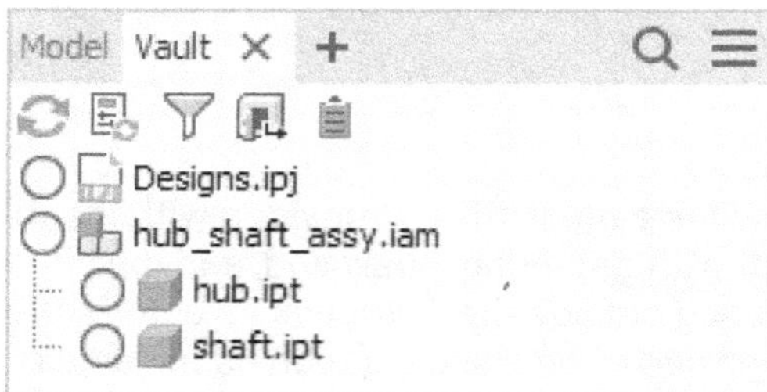

Figure 6–2

Note: *If the Vault tab is not available, click*  *(Show tabs) on the Model browser panel bar and select* ***Vault****.*

Vault Browser Toolbar Icons

The icons located at the top of the Vault Browser provide access to useful tools, such as refreshing a file status. Below is a description of each icon and their usage. The Vault Browser can be left docked next to the Inventor Model browser so that the two browsers can be viewed simultaneously or undocked to float separately.

Icon	Name and Description
	**Refresh Vault status:** Refreshes the file's status to reflect the current state of the files in the vault.
	**Update Properties:** Updates the properties for the active file and all of its children.
	**Filter:** Options to filter the Vault Browser display. Options are shown below.

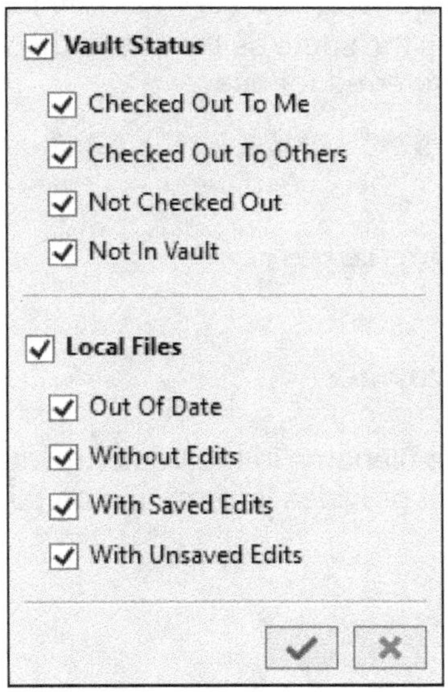

Icon	Name and Description
	**Logged in as:** Displays current log in information and launches the Autodesk Vault software.
	**Choose Properties:** Enables you to specify which Vault Properties display in the Vault Browser after the filename.

Vault Status Icons

Vault Status Icons communicate if you are logged into the vault and the relationship of the local files relative to the vault files. Using these icons is vital to ensure that there are no mistakes made during file operations.

- An exclamation mark in a yellow triangle ( ) indicates that you are not logged into the vault in the Autodesk Inventor software.
- A white circle with a plus sign ( ) indicates that the files are not in the vault.
- If a filename displays in **blue bold font**, the file is checked out to you. An asterisk beside the filename means that you have changes in memory that have not been saved, and it requires a save before it can be added to the vault.
- A white circle containing a checkmark ( ) or nothing ( ) indicates that the version of file you are working with is the same as the one in the vault. This is also known as the *Latest Version* and is typically preferred for use.

  Note: *When multiple users are working on the same design, use the* ***Refresh*** *toolbar icon to see the current status of the loaded files.*

Using the Vault Browser

How To: Use the Vault Browser

1. Hover the cursor over the filename in the Vault Browser to display the vault status tooltip, as shown in Figure 6–3. It provides information on the action that needs to be performed on the file.

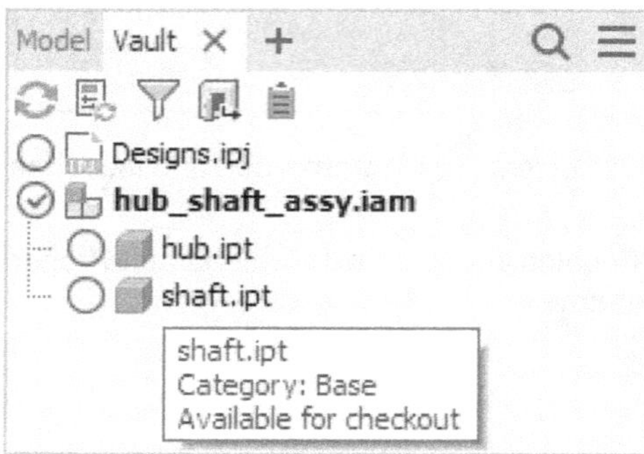

Figure 6–3

2. Select a file and right-click to display the shortcut menu. The options available depend on the file format and how the file was opened. For example, if you checked out the file when opening it, the **Check In** option is available but not the **Check Out one**. If you opened the file as **Read Only**, **Check Out** is available.
3. The Vault Browser operation options are described as follows:

Option	Description
Open	Opens the selected file in a new Inventor window.
Refresh File	Downloads a copy of a file's latest checked in version to your local working folder.
Get Revision	Copies a file's selected revision from the vault to the local working folder, enabling it to be modified
Check In	Copies a file from the local working folder to the vault.
Check Out	Copies a file from the vault to the local working folder, enabling it to be modified.
Undo Check Out	Checks the selected files back in, unmodified.
Revert to Latest	Reverts to the latest revision of the file.
Change Category	Changes the category of the selected file.
Change State	Changes the state of the selected file.
Revise	Creates a new revision of the selected file.
Data Cards	Toggles the Data Cards display on and off.
Show Details	Opens the *Show Details* dockable panel displaying historical data for the file, including revision and state information, thumbnail image, and checked-in date. You can also see which other files use the selected file. If applicable, you can also view the file's change order details and bill of materials.
Expand All Children	Expands the Vault Browser tree to display the assemblies children (available for assemblies).
Collapse All Children	Collapses the Vault Browser tree to display only the assembly (available for assemblies).
Find in Window	Highlights the selected component in the Autodesk Inventor window.
Go to Vault Folder	Opens a new Vault Client session showing the version and revision of the selected component inside its vault folder.

How To: Search in the Vault Browser

1. To search the contents of the Vault Browser, select the search icon in the browser, as shown in Figure 6–4.

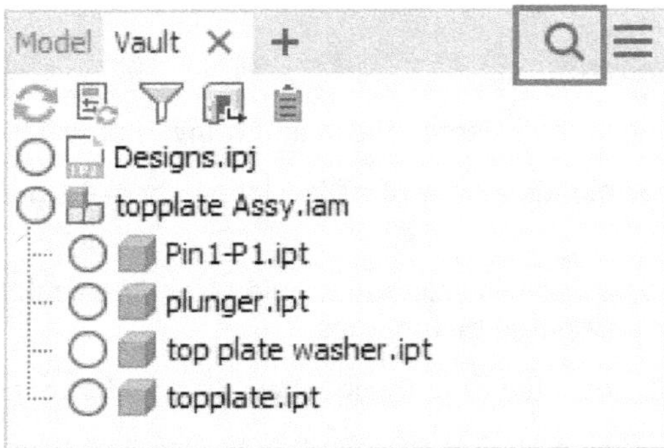

Figure 6–4

Note: *If Vault properties were added using the Choose Properties dialog box, you can search the value of those properties.*

2. Enter a keyword in the *Type Keyword* field, as shown in Figure 6–5.

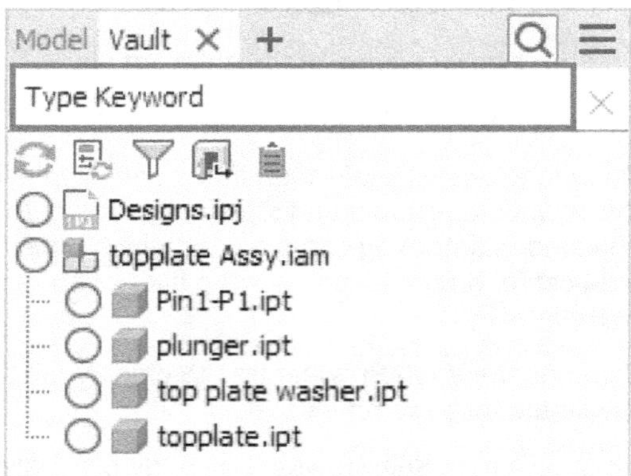

Figure 6–5

Note: *Multiple keywords can be entered, separated by a space.*

3. The results of the keyword search display as shown in Figure 6–6.

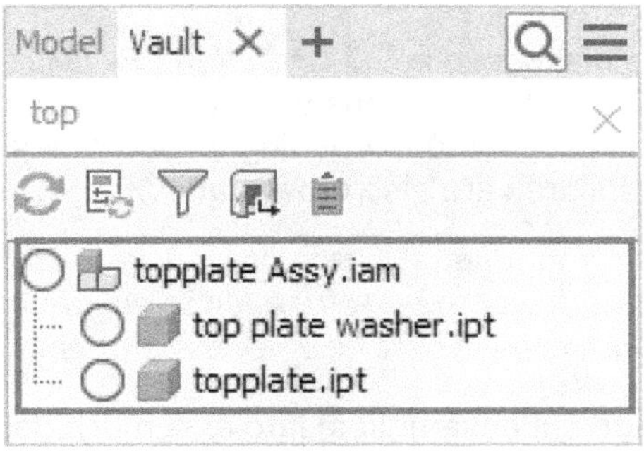

Figure 6–6

Note: *Both expanded and collapsed file nodes will be searched.*

6.3 Open and Place Vault Files in Inventor

Opening files via the Add-in is discussed in ***5.3 Open Vault Files*** in ***Chapter 5 Working with Files***. This is a review with the addition of the options that can be used to load Inventor files, such as loading Express. Something else specific to opening Inventor files from Vault is that when an assembly file is opened, the children are also downloaded.

> ***Note:*** *You can open files from the Vault Client, but it is best practice and highly recommended to use the Add-in or the* ***Get*** *function to ensure that the latest version is downloaded. You have more control over how the file is opened when you use the Add-in.*

Placing components (parts and subassemblies) into assembly files is another function specific to Inventor. Information is provided in this chapter on how to place files into assemblies from Vault using the Add-in.

Open a Vault File from the Add-in

When you have launched the Autodesk Inventor software and selected the active project file, you can open an Autodesk Inventor file. If you click (Open) in the Quick Access Toolbar, rather than (Open) in the *Vault* tab>*Access* panel, you are prompted to select a file from the local workspace.

The workspace is a local folder that is mapped to the corresponding folder in the vault. The workspace can be a single folder, or can include a hierarchy of subfolders to help organize the design. The recommended best practice is to use (Open) in the *Vault* tab>*Access* panel to open the file from the vault instead of from the local working folder. This ensures that you are always working with the latest version of the project.

(Open) in the *Vault* tab>*Access* panel in the integrated user interface (as shown in Figure 6–7) is available after you log in to the vault.

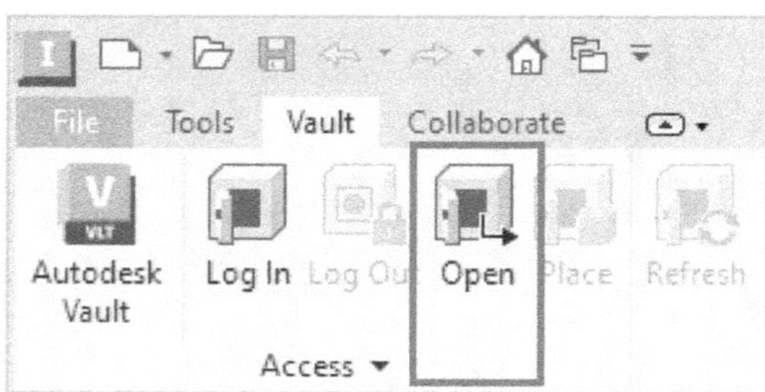

Figure 6–7

> ***Note:*** *If you click (Open) without logging in, you are prompted to login.*

How To: Open a Vault File from Add-in

1. In the Autodesk Inventor software, in the *Vault* tab>*Access* panel, click (Open). The *Select File From Vault* dialog box opens, as shown in Figure 6–8.

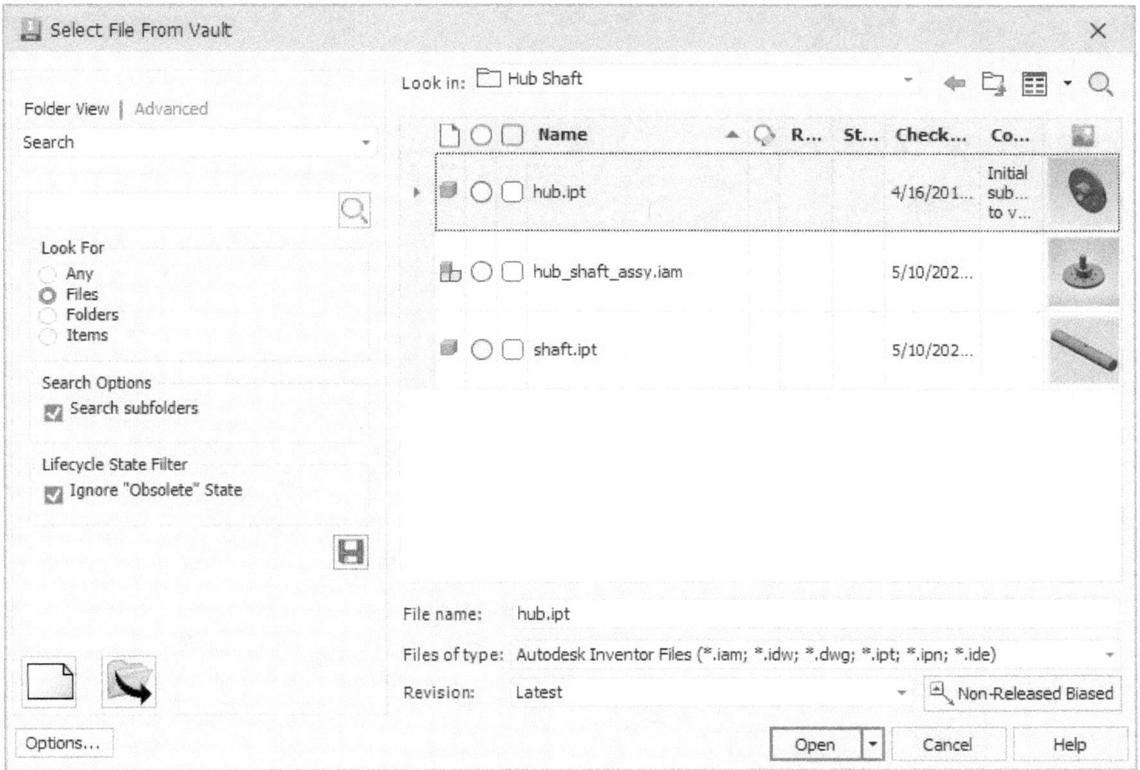

Figure 6–8

Note: *You can use to access the Find dialog box.*

2. You can navigate the folder structure to select the required file, or you can search using the field shown in Figure 6–9.

Figure 6–9

Note: *Once you execute a search, you can use*  *to save that search to **My Searches** for reuse purposes.*

3. You can also locate a file using **Saved Searches** or **Saved Shortcuts,** as shown in Figure 6–10.

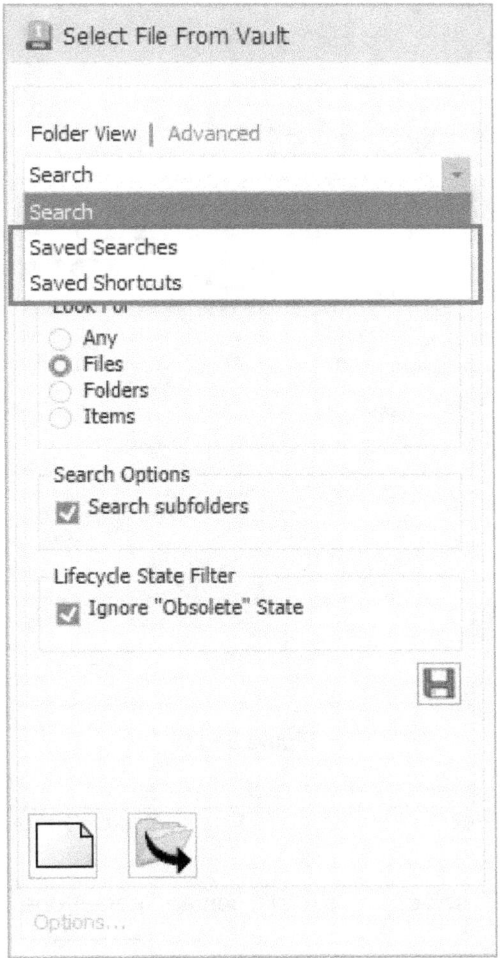

Figure 6–10

4. To open files in Express mode, select **Options** to open the *File Open Options* dialog box and select **Express**, as shown in Figure 6–11.

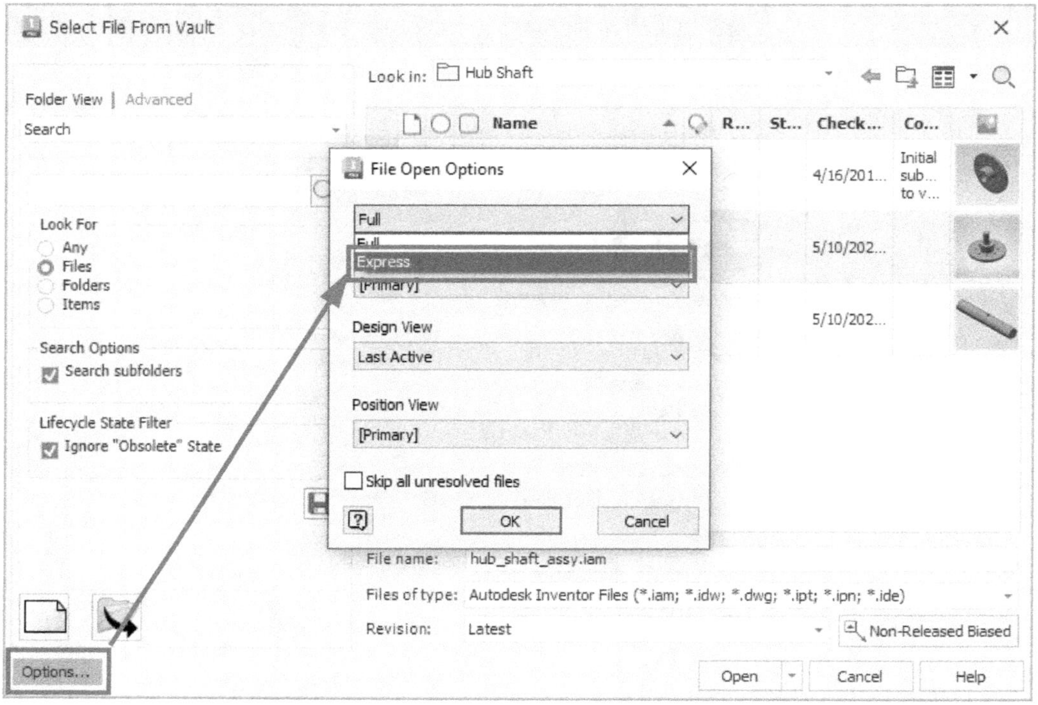

Figure 6–11

***Note: Full** loads all component data and makes all commands available. **Express** is 3-5x faster when opening large assemblies, but some commands are not available.*

5. Once the file is selected, select ▾ next to **Open** and select one of the open methods, as shown in Figure 6–12.

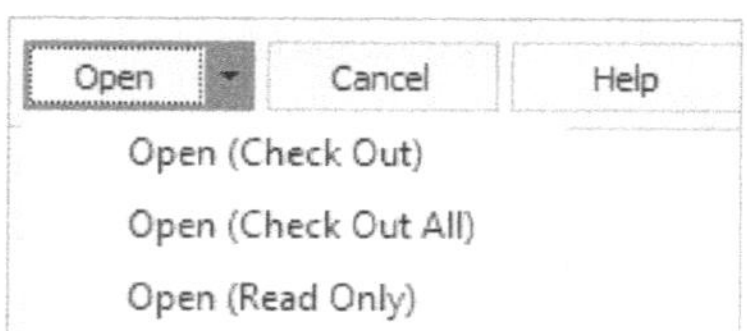

Figure 6–12

- **Open (Check Out):** Check out and open the file.
- **Open (Check Out All):** Check out and open the selected file and all of its children.
- **Open (Read Only):** Open the file without checking it out.

6. If you do not select one of the methods shown in Figure 6–12, you can click **Open** to retrieve the file from the vault into the Autodesk Inventor software. You are prompted to check out the file. Click **No** to open the file as read-only or click **Yes** and then **OK** to check the file out of the vault.

Place Files into Assemblies from Vault

To add a component from the vault to an Autodesk Inventor assembly, click  (Place) in the *Vault* tab>*Access* panel. The *Select File From Vault* dialog box opens.

The options in this dialog box are similar to the ones displayed when **Open From Vault** is selected, with the addition of the iMate functionality when placing components, as shown in Figure 6–13.

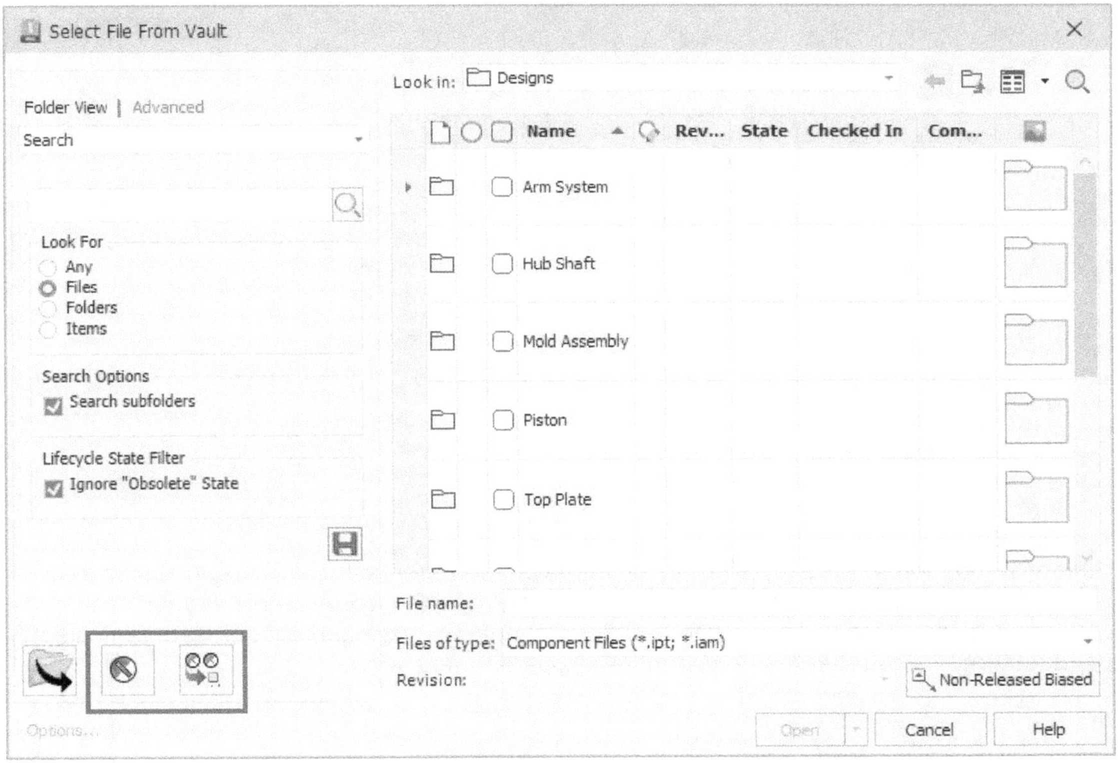

Figure 6–13

Opening and Placing Model States from Vault

Model states in Autodesk Inventor offer capabilities similar to those found in iParts/ iAssemblies; however, all configurations are stored in a single file instead of in multiple files. When opening or placing files with model states from Vault, select **Options...** then select the *Model State* and *View* options, as shown in Figure 6–14.

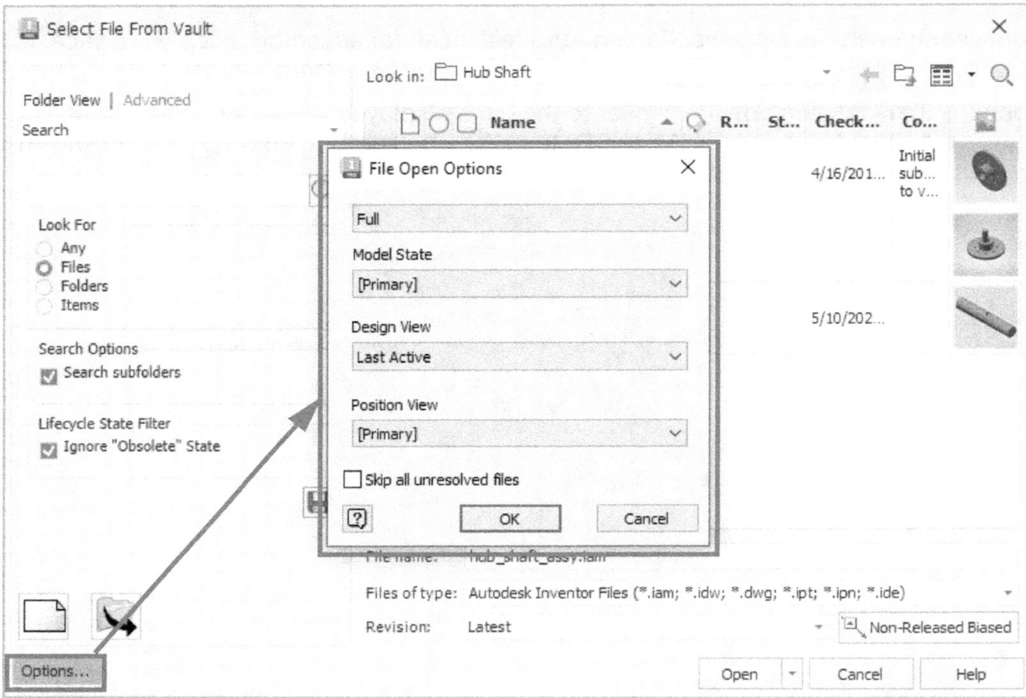

Figure 6–14

Additional functionality is available if using items in Vault Professional. You can assign items to model states to view each model state's individual iProperties, for example. If your Vault implementation does not include items, an Inventor file that contains model states will display the master model's properties (e.g., iProperties, parameters, etc.).

Insert into CAD

To place a component from the vault into an Autodesk Inventor design directly from the Autodesk Vault Client, use the **Insert into CAD** command. This command downloads the file from the vault and places it into the active Inventor session.

How To: Use the Insert into CAD Command

1. In the Autodesk Vault Client, select the file to place in the Autodesk Inventor design, right-click, and select **Insert into CAD**, as shown in Figure 6–15.

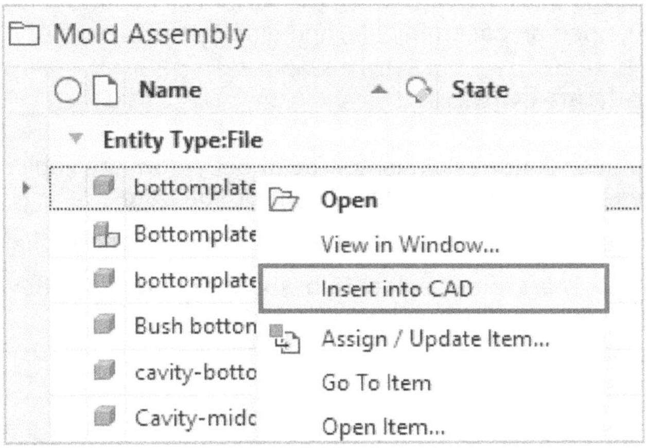

Figure 6–15

2. Finish placing the file into the design.

Practice 6a
Use Open from Vault and the Vault Browser

Practice Objectives

- Open a file from the vault from in the Autodesk Inventor software.
- Use the Vault Browser to check in a project file to the vault.
- Display the history of a design file in Vault Browser.

In this practice, you will log in to the vault from the Autodesk Inventor software, check in a project file to the vault, open an assembly file, and display the history of the assembly's design.

Task 1: Open a file from the vault.

In this task, you will open an Autodesk Inventor file directly from the vault using the **Open** option in the *Vault* tab>*Access* panel in the Autodesk Inventor software.

1. In the Autodesk Inventor software, in the *Vault* tab>*Access* panel, click (Open).
2. In the $\Designs\Hub Shaft* folder, select **hub_shaft_assy.iam** as shown in Figure 6–16.

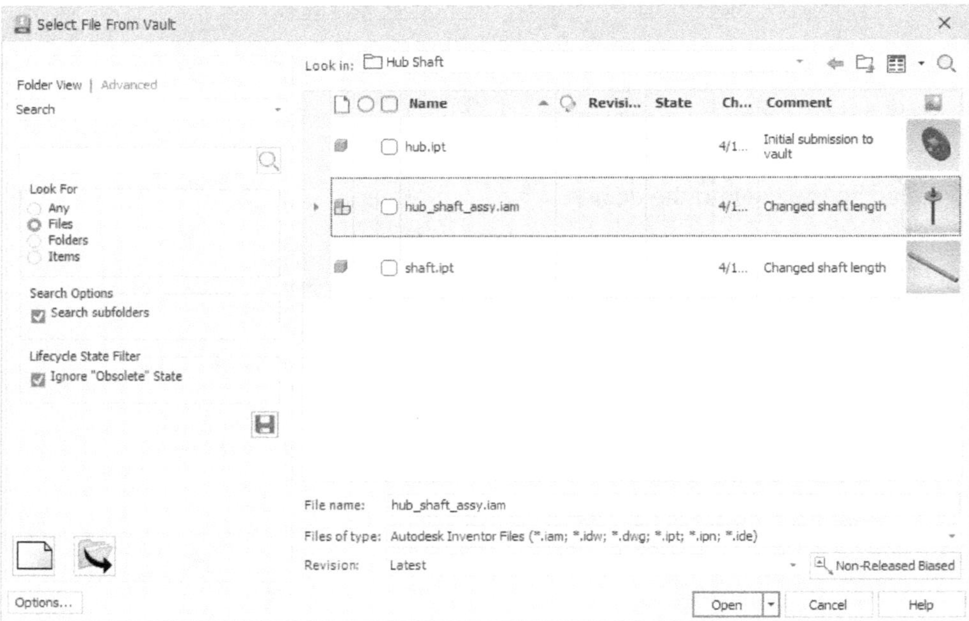

Figure 6–16

3. Click **Open**.
4. Click **No** if prompted to check out the assembly. A read-only copy of the file opens.

Task 2: Use the Vault Browser.

In this task, you will use the Vault Browser to view the vault status of the listed Autodesk Inventor files.

1. In the Browser panel, select **Vault,** as shown in Figure 6–17, to open the Vault Browser.

   ***Note:** If the Vault tab does not display, click + and select **Vault**.*

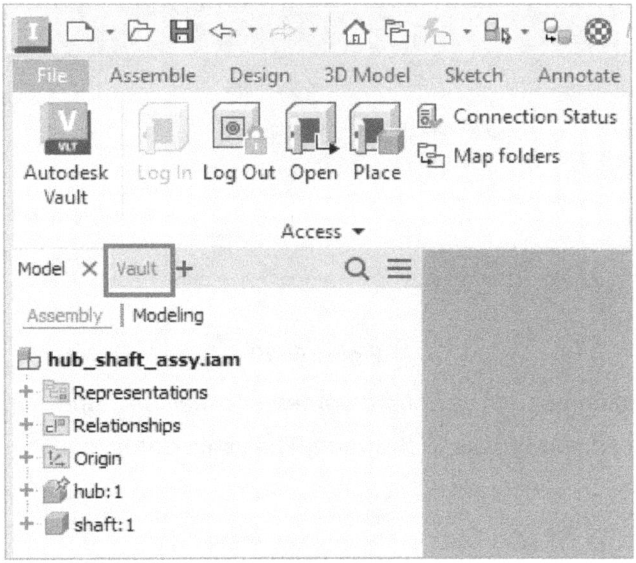

Figure 6–17

2. A circle with a plus sign ( ) displays next to the **Designs.ipj** project file, as shown in Figure 6–18. Move the cursor over the project file to display the tooltip indicating that it is not in the vault. All of the other files display a plain white circle, indicating that the version of the file copied to the working folder that you are working on is the same as the one in the vault, also known as the *Latest Version*.

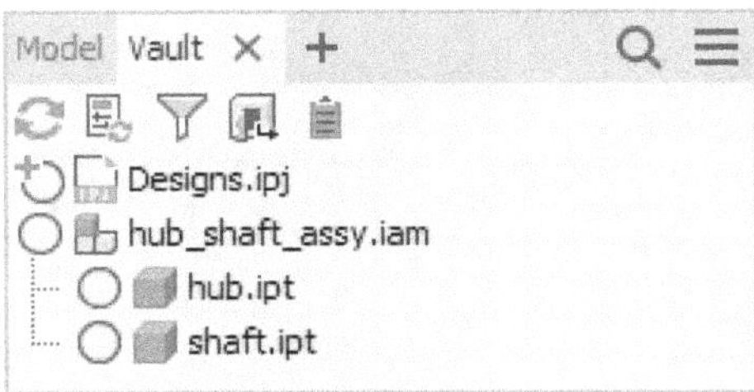

Figure 6–18

Task 3: Check in a project file to the vault.

In this task, you will add the project file to the vault as required, which will change the vault status icon.

1. In the Vault Browser, select **Designs.ipj**, right-click, and select **Check In**, as shown in Figure 6–19.

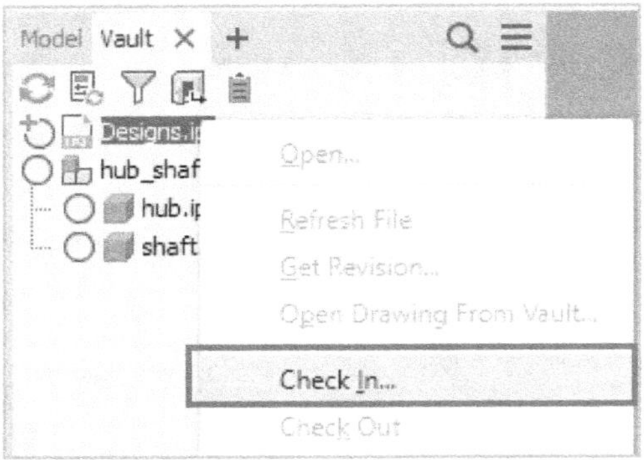

Figure 6–19

2. In the *Check In* dialog box, in the *Enter comments to include...* area, type **Initial submission**.
3. Click **OK** to finish adding the file to the vault. The vault status icon is now the same as that of the other files.

Task 4: Show details of the file.

In this task, you will show the details of the file, similar to how you would view the file's details within the Preview pane in Autodesk Vault Client.

1. In the Vault Browser, select **hub_shaft_assy.iam**, right-click, and select **Show Details....** You can also click **Show Details** in the *Vault* tab>*Control* panel. The *Show Details* dockable panel displays, as shown in Figure 6–20.

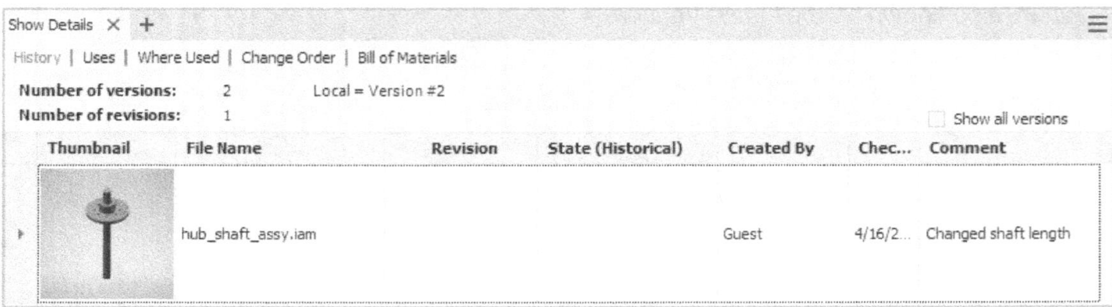

Figure 6–20

Task 5: Display the history of the file.

In this task, you will view the history of the Autodesk Inventor design in the *Show Details* dockable panel.

1. In the *Show Details* panel, in the *History* tab, select the **Show all versions** checkbox, if not already selected. The two versions currently in the vault are displayed, as shown in Figure 6–21.

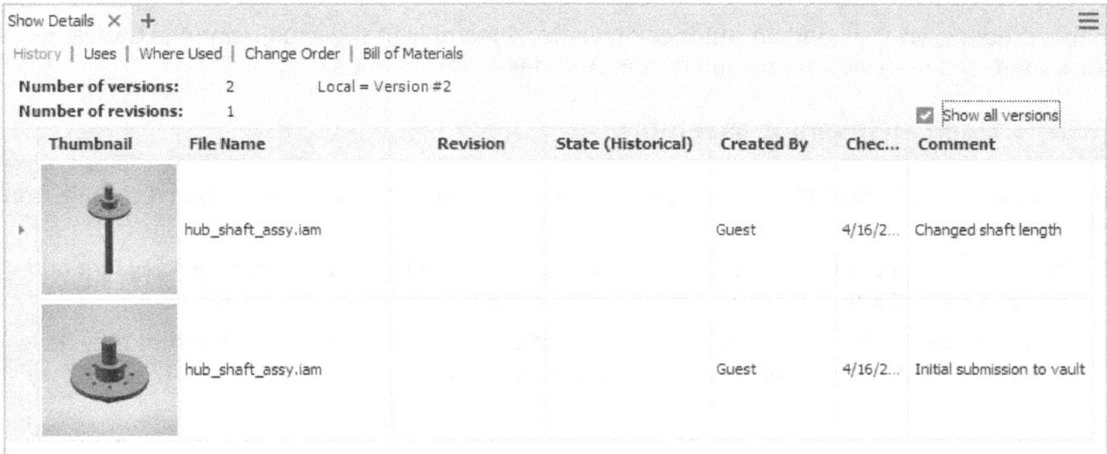

Figure 6–21

2. Close the *Show Details* panel.
3. Close **hub_shaft_assy.iam**.

End of practice

Practice 6b
Add an Inventor Design to the Vault

Practice Objectives

- Use the **Check In** command to add an Autodesk Inventor design to the vault.
- Verify the added files in the Autodesk Vault software.

In this practice, you will add an Autodesk Inventor assembly to the vault using the **Check In** command, and then view its design files in Autodesk Vault client.

Task 1: Open an Inventor assembly.

In this task, you will retrieve an Autodesk Inventor assembly, that is not already in the vault, from a local directory.

1. In Inventor, select **File>Open>Open**. In the *Top Plate* folder, select **topplate Assy.iam** and open the assembly in the Autodesk Inventor software.
2. Open the Vault Browser. The files display circles with plus signs indicating that they have not been added to the vault, as shown in Figure 6–22.

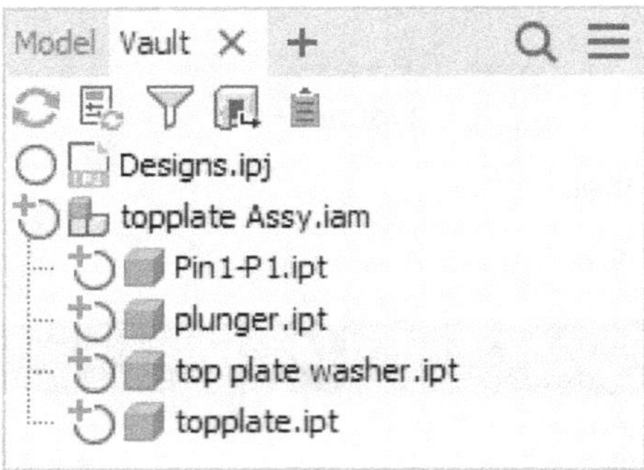

Figure 6–22

Task 2: Check in the assembly using the Vault browser.

In this task, you will add the Autodesk Inventor assembly to the vault using the Vault Browser.

1. In the Vault Browser, select **topplate Assy.iam**, right-click, and select **Check In**.
2. The *Check In* dialog box opens displaying all of the files to be added to the vault, including the folder structure that will be created, as shown in Figure 6–23. Ensure that the **Keep files checked out** option is not selected.

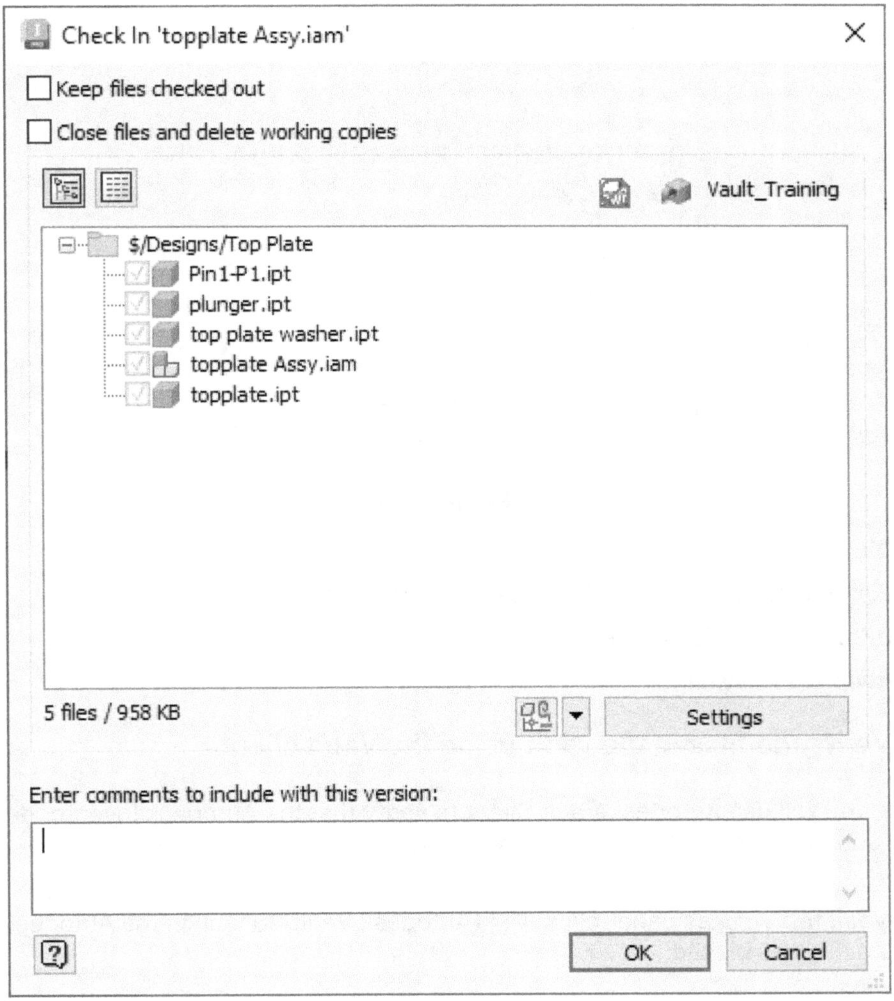

Figure 6–23

3. Note at the top of the dialog box. It indicates that the **Create visualization attachment** option is disabled. Click **Settings**. Select **Create during check-in** and **Apply to all files**, as shown in Figure 6–24.

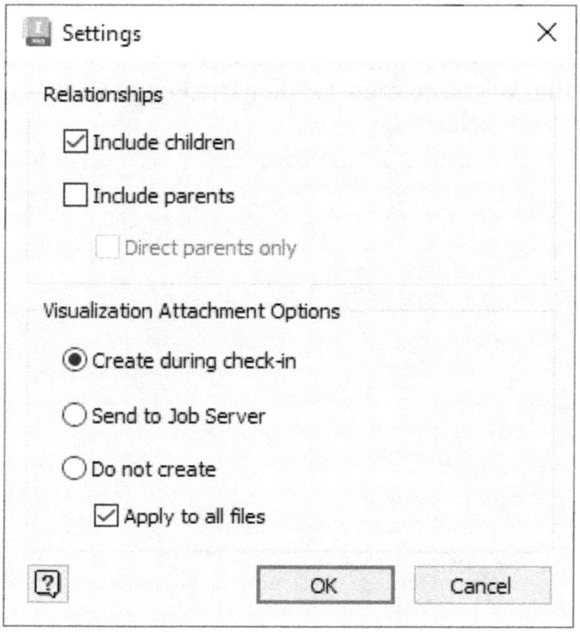

Figure 6–24

4. Click **OK**.
5. In the *Enter comments to include...* area, type **Initial Submission**.
6. Click **OK** to add the files to the vault.
7. Close **topplate Assy.iam**.

Task 3: Verify the files in the vault using the Vault client.

In this task, you will use Autodesk Vault Client to verify that the Autodesk Inventor design files have been added to the vault and that the relationships have been maintained.

1. In the *Vault* tab>*Access* panel, click (Autodesk Vault) to launch the Autodesk Vault software if it was closed.
2. Click (Refresh) to update the vault display.
3. In the Navigation pane, expand the $*Designs* folder structure and select the *Top Plate* folder to view the files that have just been added to the vault, as shown in Figure 6–25. The *Top Plate* folder was automatically created when the design files were added.

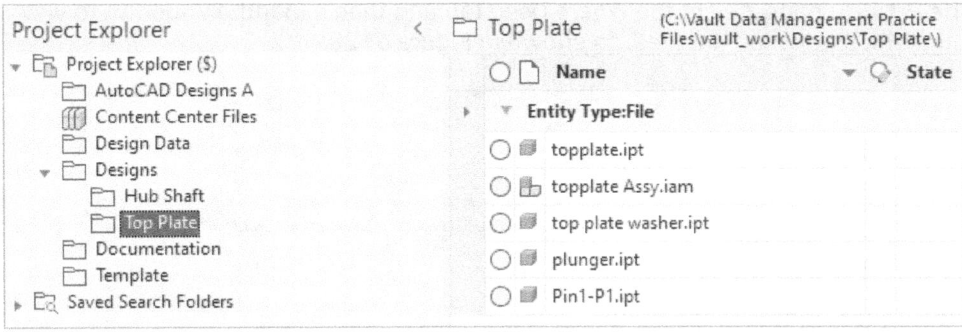

Figure 6–25

4. Select **plunger.ipt** in the Main table.
5. In the Preview pane, select the *History* tab. The file displays Version 1 because it was just added by **user1**, as shown in Figure 6–26. All of the other files that were checked in as part of the **topplate Assy.iam** file are also version 1.

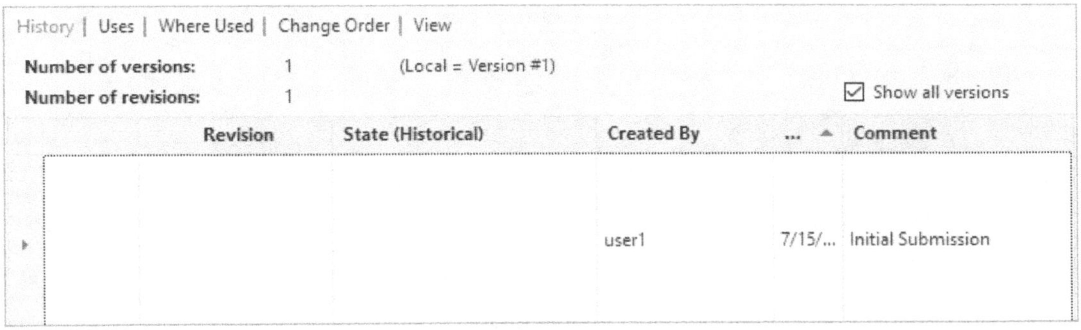

Figure 6–26

6. Select the *View* tab and select the **Version 1** thumbnail, as shown in Figure 6–27. The model displays because the .DWF was created when the files were added to the vault.

Figure 6–27

7. In the Preview pane, select the *Where Used* tab and then expand **plunger.ipt** to view the relationships between the files, as shown in Figure 6–28.

Figure 6–28

8. In the Main table, select **topplate Assy.iam** and select the *Uses* tab to view the files used by the assembly, as shown in Figure 6–29.

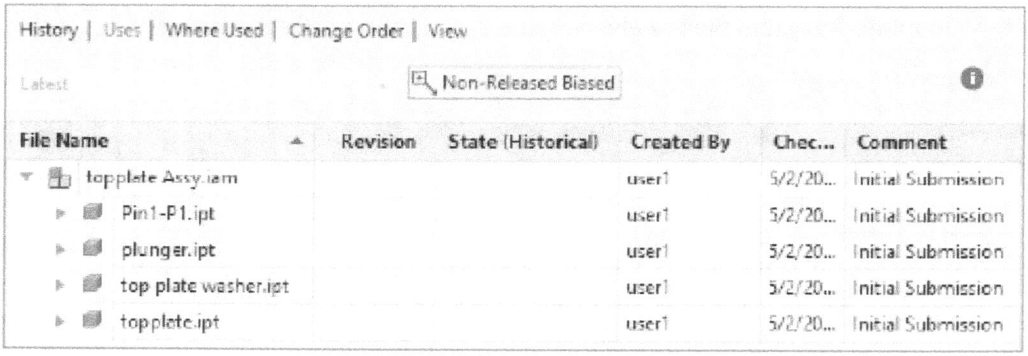

Figure 6–29

End of practice

Practice 6c
Bulk Load Inventor Files into the Vault

Practice Objective

- Use the **Check In Project** command to bulk load multiple design projects into the vault.

In this practice, you will use the **Check In Project** operation to bulk load multiple design projects into the vault. You will then verify the results of the bulk loading and change the category on some of the design files.

Task 1: View design files in the working folder and add them to the vault.

In this task, you will open the working folder to view the design files and then use the **Check In Project** operation to add them to the vault.

1. In the Autodesk Inventor software, in the *Vault* tab, expand the *Access* panel, and click (Go to Workspace). A File Explorer window opens displaying the workspace folder structure.
2. Compare this folder structure to the *Designs* folder structure in the Autodesk Vault software. The designs: *Arm System*, *Mold Assembly*, *Piston*, *Vise*, and *Yoke* have not been added to the vault.
3. In the Autodesk Inventor software, select **File>Vault Server**, and then hover the cursor over at the bottom of the menu to scroll down. Click (Check In Project) to bulk load these designs into the vault. All of the files in the selected folder are bulk loaded.
4. In the *Check In Project* dialog box, in the *Enter comments to include...* area, type **Initial Submission** and click **OK**.
5. Close the Autodesk Inventor software.

Task 2: Verify the bulk load results in the Autodesk Vault client.

In this task, you will verify that the new Autodesk Inventor designs have been added to the vault successfully using the **Check In Project** operation.

1. In the Autodesk Vault software, click (Refresh) and expand the $\Designs folder to verify that the bulk upload process has added the new design folders and all of their design files as shown in Figure 6–30.

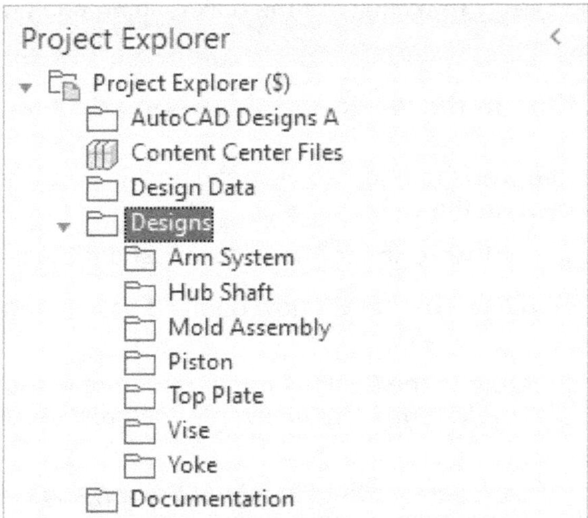

Figure 6–30

Task 3: Remove the files from the local working folder.

Now that the files have been loaded into the vault, you will remove all of the *Design* folders (including their contents) from the local working folder, with the exception of the **Designs.ipj** project file. This is a recommended best practice to ensure that you are always using the latest version of the files from the vault.

1. In the Vault, select the ...*Designs* folder, right-click and select **Go To Working Folder**. Delete the folders and their contents from File Explorer, keeping only **Designs.ipj**.
2. Close File Explorer.

Task 4: Change the category of the Vise files to Engineering.

In this task, you will change the category to Engineering for the Vise design files.

1. In the Autodesk Vault software, in the ...*\Designs\Vise* folder, use <Ctrl>+<A> to select all of the files, then click **Change Category** on the toolbar.
2. Select **Engineering** from the *Select a new category* drop-down list, as shown in Figure 6–31.

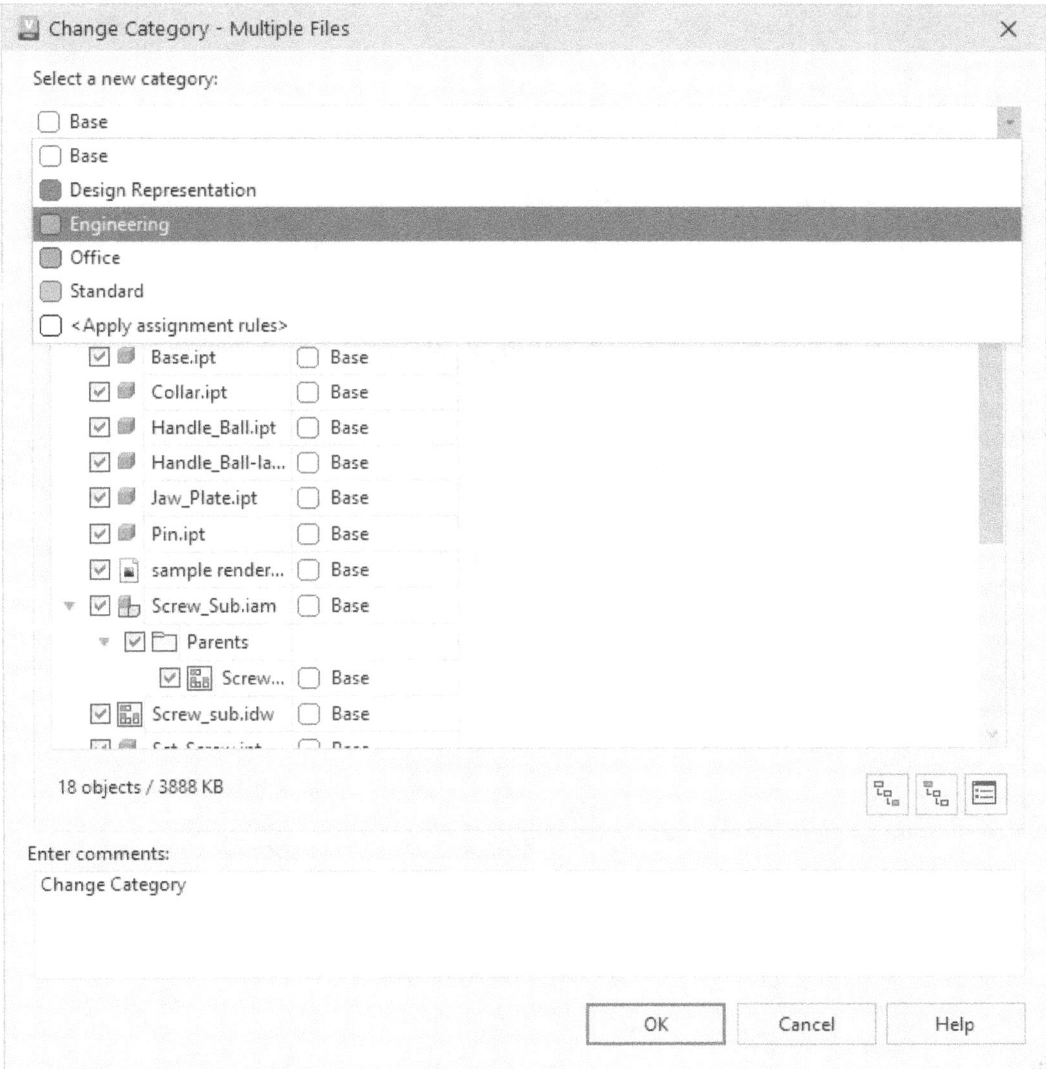

Figure 6–31

3. Click **OK**.

4. Note that the files in the *Vise* folder are now updated with the blue **Engineering** category and display **Revision A**, as shown in Figure 6–32.

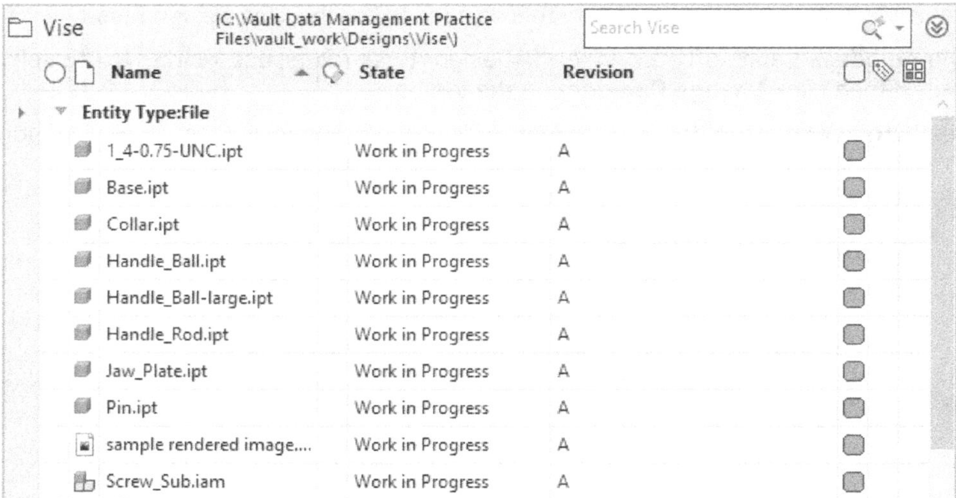

Figure 6–32

Note: *If the files have a lock symbol, select **Tools>Administration>Vault Settings**. In the Behaviors tab, select **Lifecycles** and **Flexible Release Process**, then select **Edit** and add user1 to the Security tab with **Allow** permissions, as shown in Figure 6–33. Click **OK**, then close the Lifecycle Definitions and Vault Settings dialog boxes.*

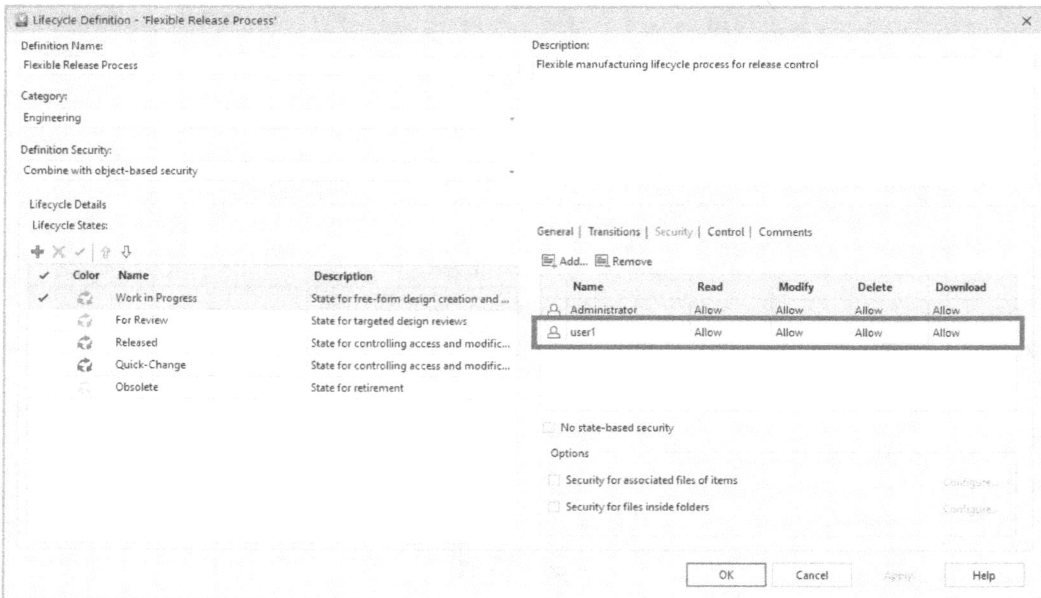

Figure 6–33

Task 5: Change the category of the Piston design files to Engineering.

In this task, you will perform the same Change Category operation, this time on the Piston design files.

1. In the Autodesk Vault software, in the ...*\Designs\Piston* folder, use <Ctrl>+<A> to select all of the files, then click **Change Category** on the toolbar.
2. Select the **Engineering** category for all of the Piston design files.
3. Click **OK**.

End of practice

6.4 Modifying an Inventor Design

The vault enables multiple users to access the same design project and work on different parts of the design.

For example, **user1** can be working on part A of an assembly and user2 on part B of the same assembly. They can both retrieve a read-only copy of the assembly to their working folders and only check out the part for modification.

This section discusses how to make modifications to an Inventor design that is in a Work In Progress (WIP) lifecycle state and not released. See ***6.5 Releasing an Inventor Design*** and ***6.6 Revise a Released Inventor Design*** to learn how to release an Inventor design and make changes to a released Inventor design.

How To: Modify an Inventor Design

1. In Inventor, open the file(s) you want to modify using (Open from Vault) on the *Vault* tab>*Access* panel in the ribbon. Expand *Open* and select **Open (Check Out)**, which checks out just the assembly file, or **Open (Check Out All)** to check out all children.
   - If you are modifying an assembly, only check out the part files that will be modified. You must check out the assembly drawing file, if one exists, and open it for it to receive the updates.
   - If you are modifying a part file, you must check out the part drawing file, if one exists, and open it for it to receive the updates.
   - If your local working folder contains the latest version because you performed a **Get**, or Open and then saved the file and didn't check it back into Vault, use the standard open procedure, such as Open in the Quick Access Toolbar, and navigate to your local working folder to open the file.
   - If you try to modify a file that has not yet been checked out, a message box opens prompting you to do so, as shown in Figure 6–34.

   Note: *To change the settings for the* ***File Edit*** *prompt, in the Vault tab>File Status panel, select* ***Vault Options****, click* ***Prompts...*** *and change the response or frequency for* ***File Edit****.*

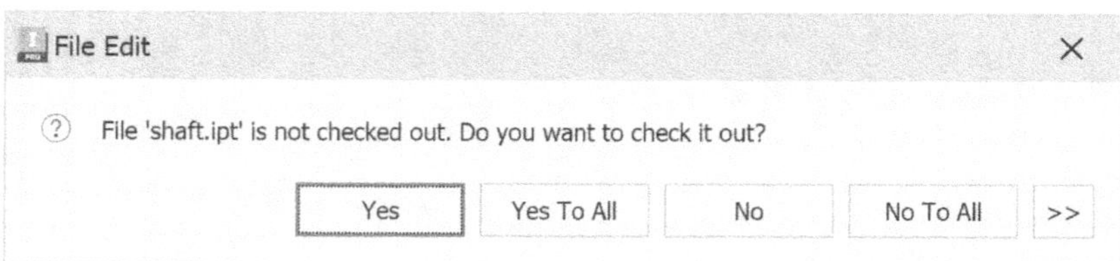

Figure 6–34

2. Once you confirm the check out, the *Check Out* dialog box displays, as shown in Figure 6–35. Uncheck any file(s) that you do not want checked out.

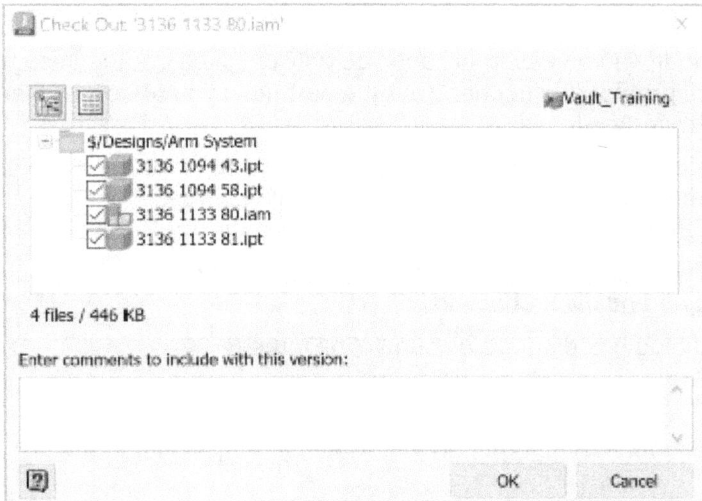

Figure 6–35

- You might get a prompt indicating the properties are out of date (as shown in Figure 6–36). Click **Yes** or **Yes To All** to update the properties when checking out the files. Any time properties are updated, the software recognizes it as an update and wants to keep the files up to date.

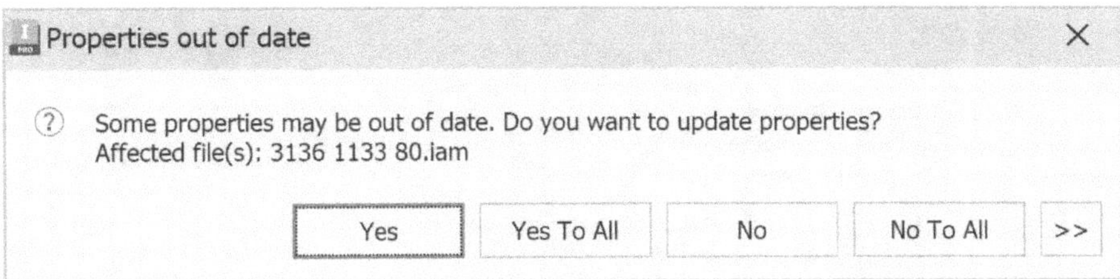

Figure 6–36

3. Use the Vault Browser, shown in Figure 6–37, to review the file status before you perform modifications. If a file status is not proper, right-click on it in the Vault Browser, and select **Refresh File**.

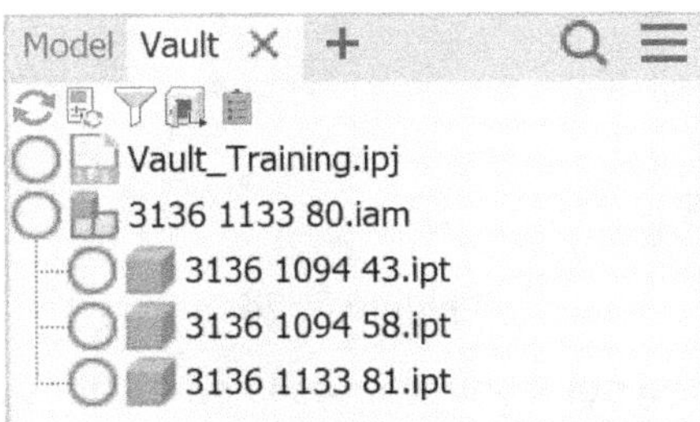

Figure 6–37

4. Once the file(s) are checked out, make modifications as you normally would.
   - If you are modifying an assembly and you only checked out the assembly file, the software will prompt you to check out the part file if you try to make any changes to it, including iProperty edits.
5. After modifications are performed, a file must be saved in Autodesk Inventor before a **Check In** operation can be performed. By default, if you try to close a checked out Autodesk Inventor file without checking it in, the system prompts you to save the file and check it in.
6. Check In the file(s) using the *Vault* tab>*Access* panel>**Check In**, or right-click on the file(s) in the Vault Browser and click **Check In**.
7. The *Check In* dialog box displays as shown in Figure 6–38.

   Note: *For manual check in operations, you can scan and then include or exclude local documentation related to the 3D model by toggling between*  *(Related files are included for the check-in operation) and*  *(Related files are excluded for the check-in operation).*

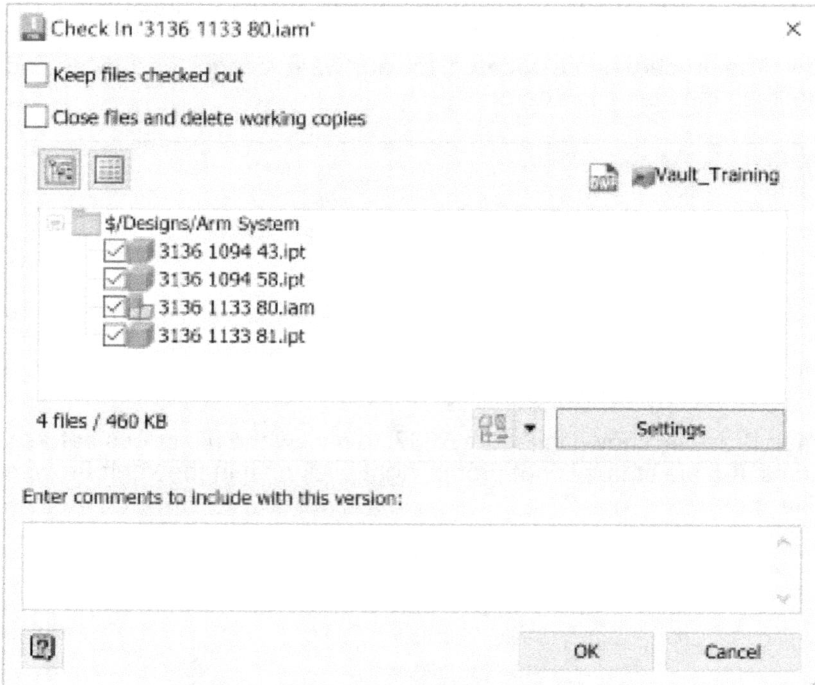

Figure 6–38

- Select **Keep files checked out** if you want to keep the files checked out for further modifications.

- Select **Close files and delete working copies** to remove the local copy after the file is checked into the vault. This is a recommended best practice. If required, close the file in the Autodesk Inventor software.
- Click **Settings** to control the inclusion settings of the children, parents, and related documentation of the selected files. By default, the children are included, as shown in Figure 6–39.

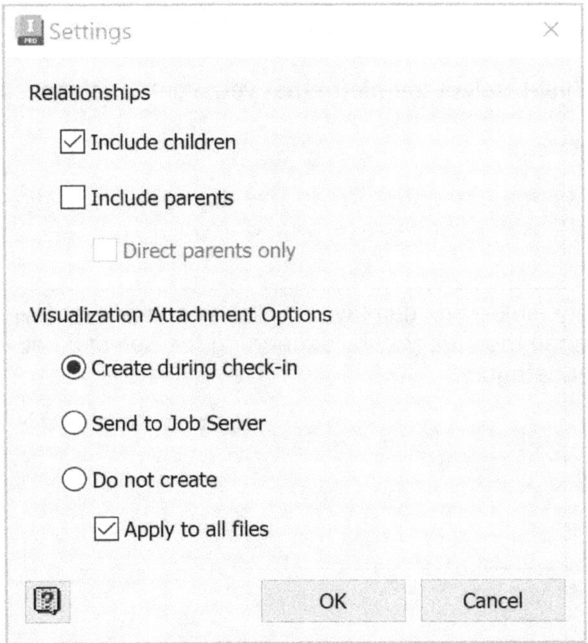

Figure 6–39

- In the *Enter comments to include...* area, enter any notes regarding this version.

8. Click **OK** to complete the operation.
9. Close Inventor.

6.5 Releasing an Inventor Design

Once the Inventor design is complete, it needs to be released in the Vault. Prepping files for release includes assigning Categories and managing Lifecycle states. See ***5.10 Categories*** and ***5.11 Changing Lifecycle States and Next Release/Revision Procedures*** in ***Chapter 5 Working with Files*** for more details.

How To: Release an Inventor Design Using Change State

1. In Autodesk Vault Client, select the file(s) that you want to release. In the toolbar, select (Change Category...).

   Note: *You can also assign Categories in the Inventor software in the Vault tab>Control panel or the Vault Browser>right-click>Change Category. This only changes the category for the file that is open.*

2. The *Change Category* dialog box displays. You can change the view using the icons shown in Figure 6–40. Change the category by expanding the *Select a new category:* area and selecting the proper category.

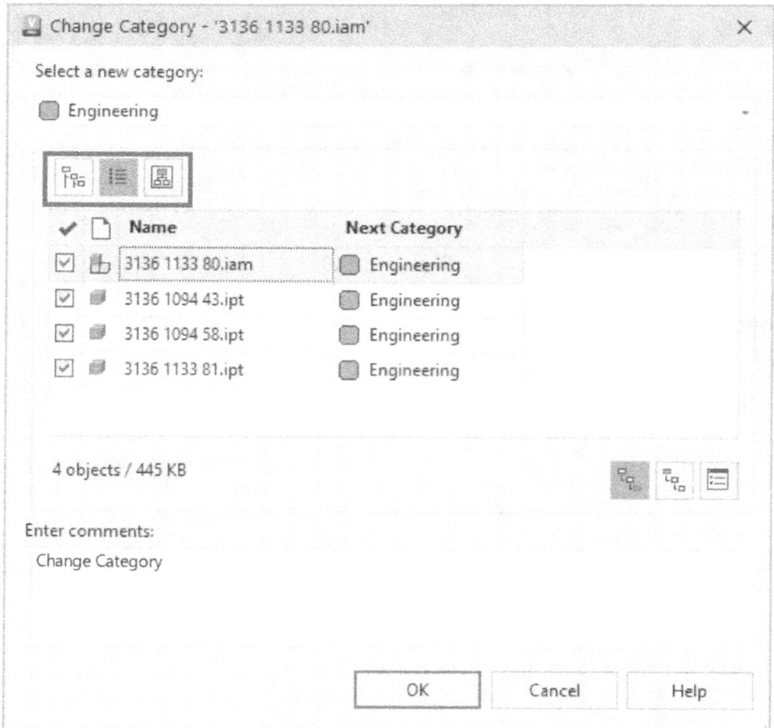

Figure 6–40

- Select (Include Dependents) to include the children of assembly files.
- Select (Include Parents) to include the parents of part files or subassemblies.
- Click (Settings) to control the inclusion settings of the children, parents, and related documentation of the selected files. By default, the children the related documentation is included, as shown in Figure 6–41.

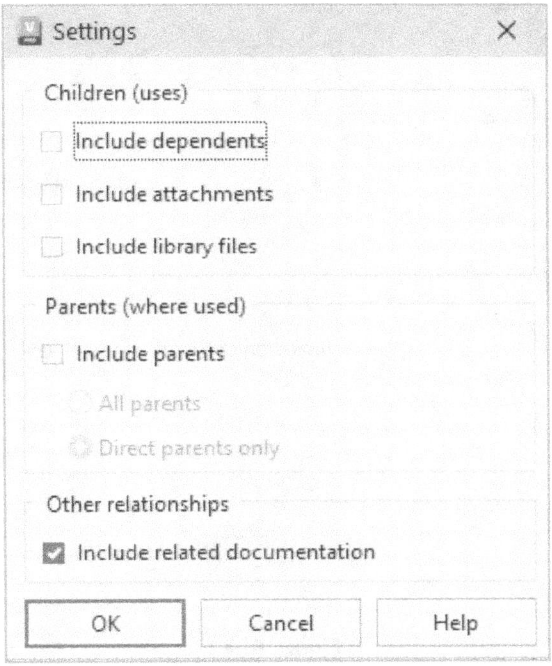

Figure 6–41

- In the *Enter comments to include...* area, "Change Category" is auto filled.

3. Click **OK** to complete the operation.
4. Select all of the files again and in the toolbar, select (Change State...).

5. The *Change State* dialog box displays. You can change the view using the View icons shown in Figure 6–42.

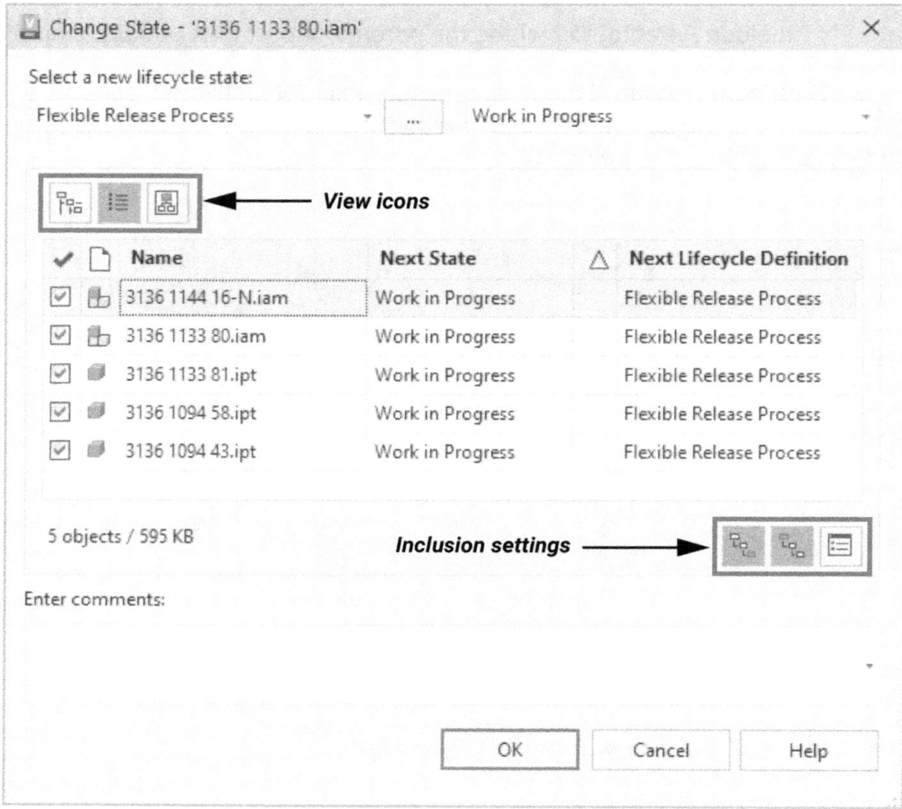

Figure 6–42

6. You can configure the inclusion options using the three inclusion settings shown in Figure 6–42.

- Select (Include Dependents) to include the children of assembly files.
- Select (Include Parents) to include the parents of part files or subassemblies.
- Click (Settings) to control the inclusion settings of the children, parents, and related documentation of the selected files. By default, the related documentation is included as shown in Figure 6–43.

Figure 6–43

7. Expand the *Work in Progress* area and click ***Released***, as shown in Figure 6–44.

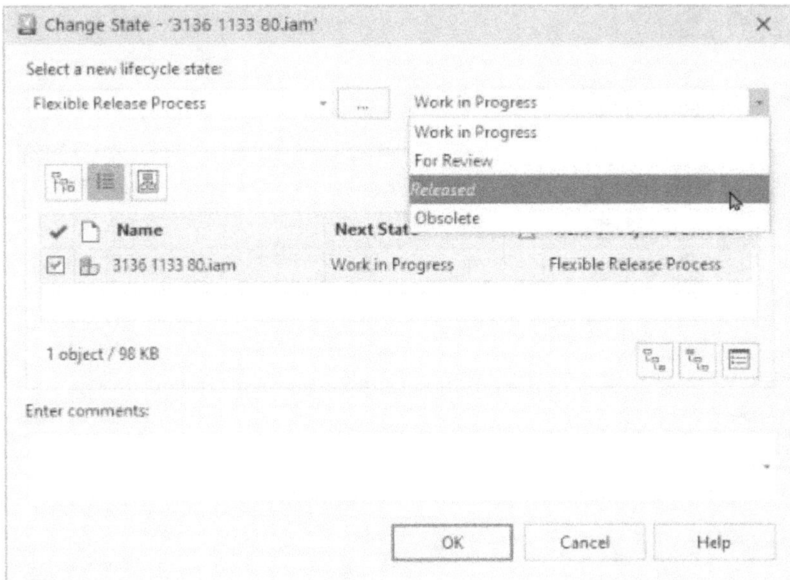

Figure 6–44

- In the *Enter comments to include...* area, "Released to manufacturing" is auto filled.

8. Click **OK** to complete the operation.

6.6 Revise a Released Inventor Design

Once the Inventor design is released and it needs to be modified, the lifecycle state has to be changed before the files can be checked out and edited.

How To: Revise a Released Inventor Design Using Change State

1. In Autodesk Vault Client, select the file(s) that you want to edit. In the toolbar, select  (Change State...).

   Note: *You can also change the state of a file in Inventor via Vault tab>Control panel or by right-clicking on the file in the Vault Browser and selecting* ***Change State****.*

2. The *Change State* dialog box displays. You can change the view using the icons shown in Figure 6–45.

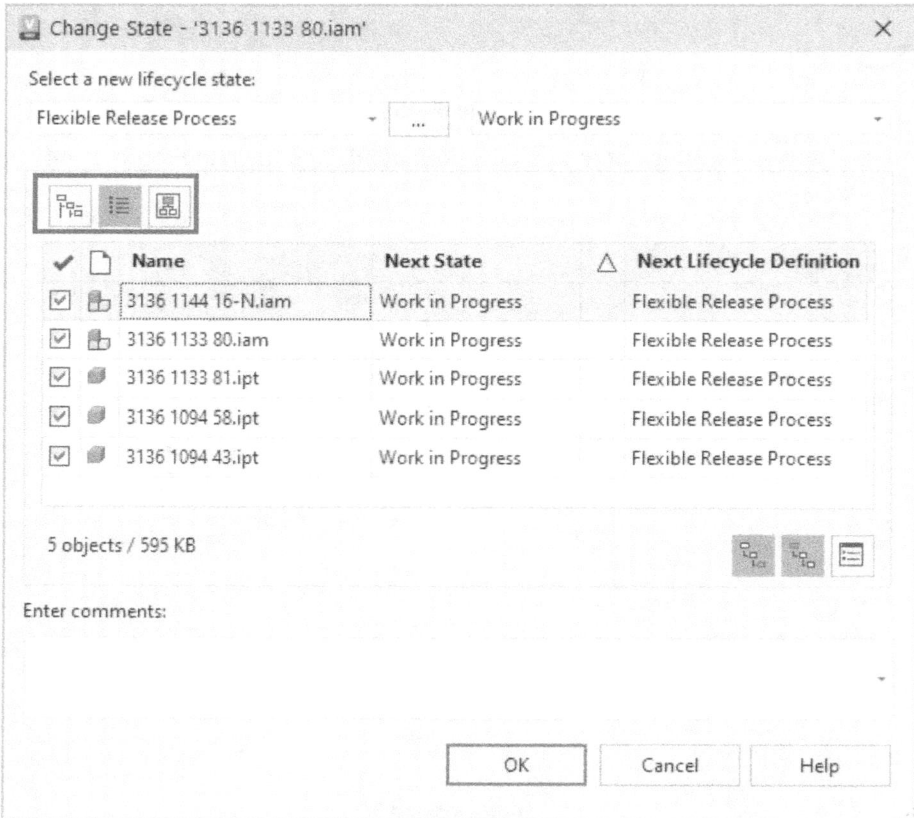

Figure 6–45

- Select (Include Dependents) to include the children of assembly files.
- Select (Include Parents) to include the parents of part files or subassemblies.
- Click (Settings) to control the inclusion settings of the children, parents, and related documentation of the selected files. By default, the children the related documentation is included, as shown in Figure 6–46.

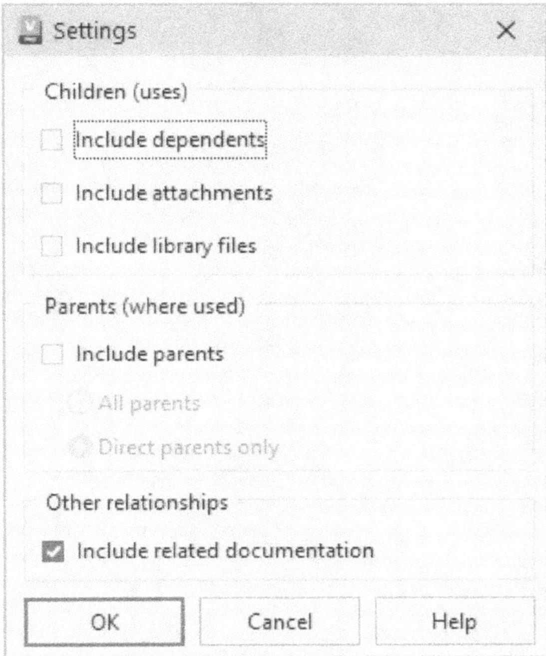

Figure 6–46

3. Expand the *Released* drop-down list and select **Work in Progress**, as shown in Figure 6–47.

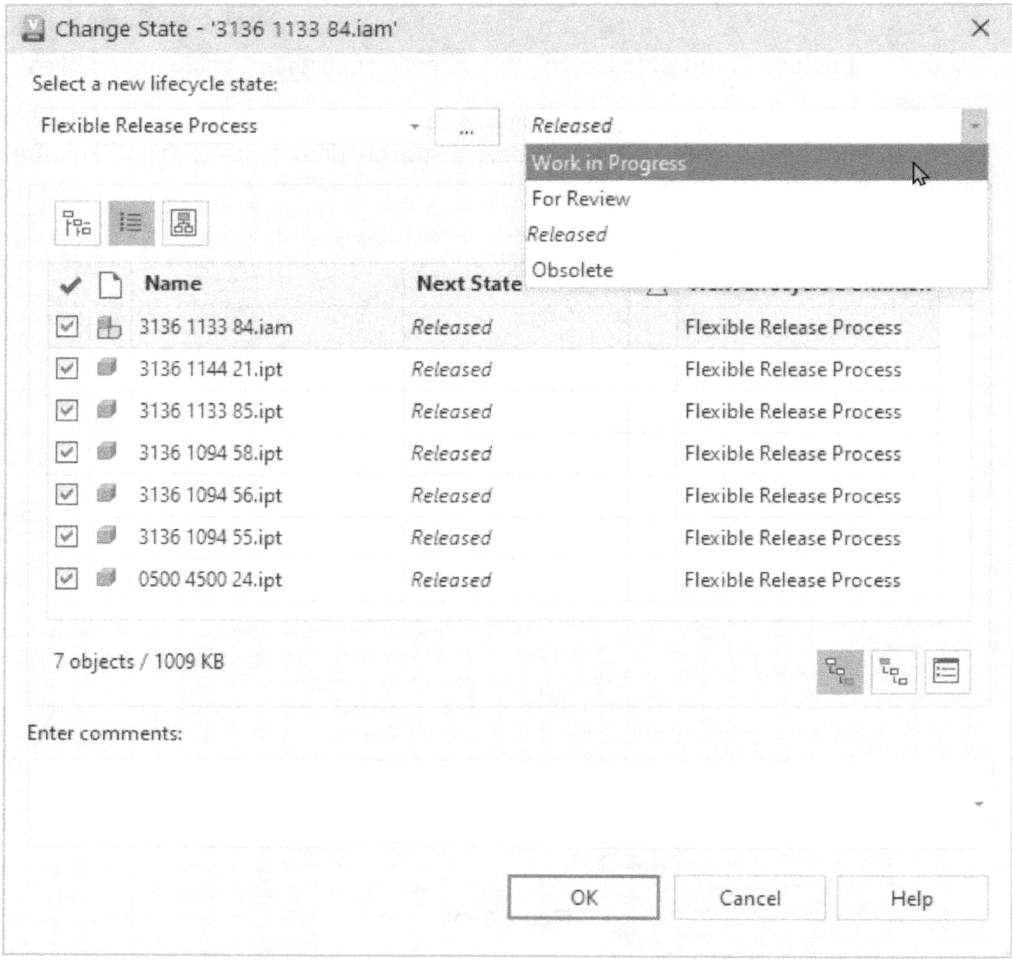

Figure 6–47

- In the *Enter comments to include...* area, "Available for editing" is auto filled.

4. Click **OK** to complete the operation.
5. Check out the files, make the modifications, check the files in and then change the state to ***Released***.

6.7 Vault Revision Tables

The Vault Revision Table feature enables you to automatically update a drawing's revision table with Vault data when its properties are synchronized through the Job Server. You can also synchronize the properties manually.

How To: Add a Vault Revision Table to a Drawing

1. In the *Annotate* tab, click **Vault Revision**, as shown in Figure 6–48.

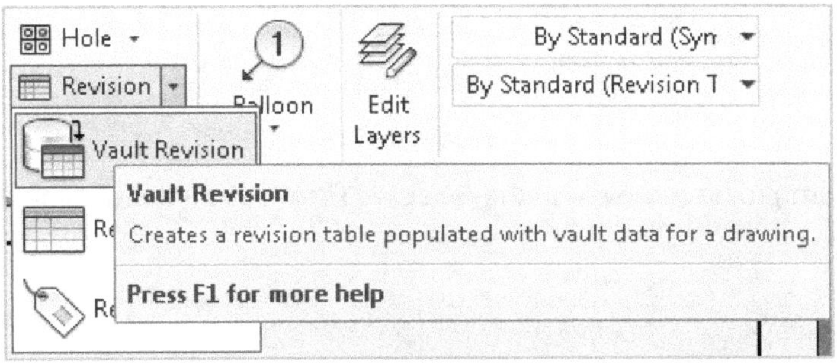

Figure 6–48

2. Insert the table in the drawing, as shown in Figure 6–49.

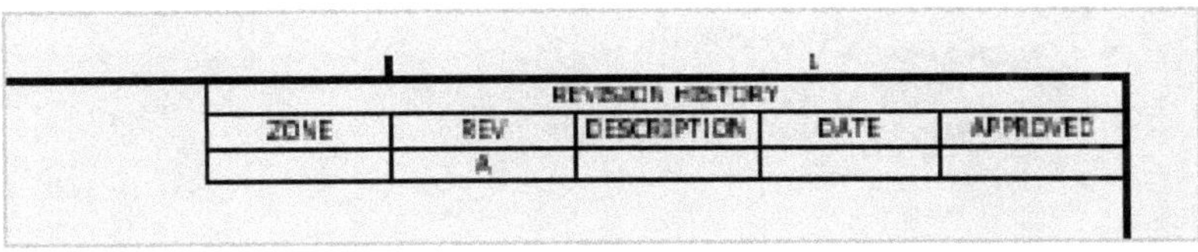

Figure 6–49

3. To edit the table, right-click on the revision table and select **Edit**, as shown in Figure 6–50.

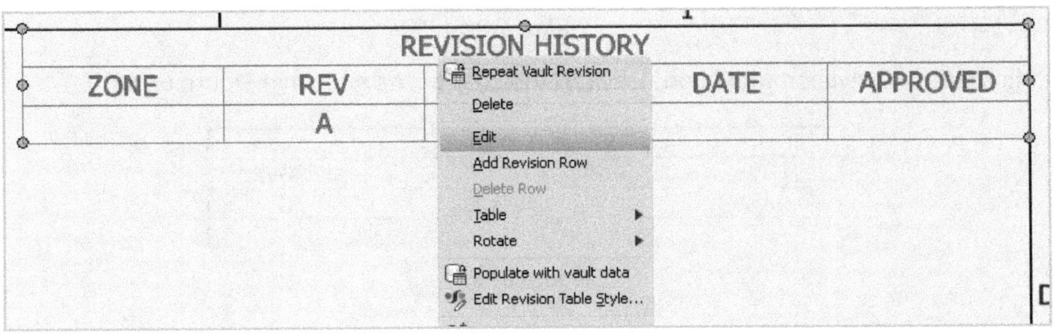

Figure 6–50

4. To remove a column, right-click on a column header and click **Column Chooser...**, as shown in Figure 6–51.

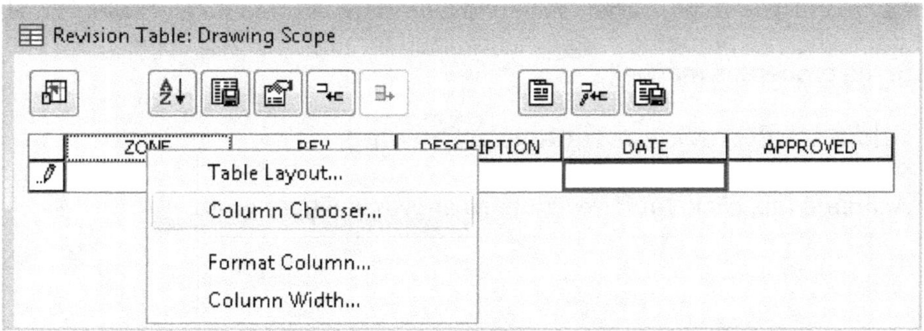

Figure 6–51

5. Select the column to be removed in the *Selected Properties* list and click **Remove**, as shown in Figure 6–52.

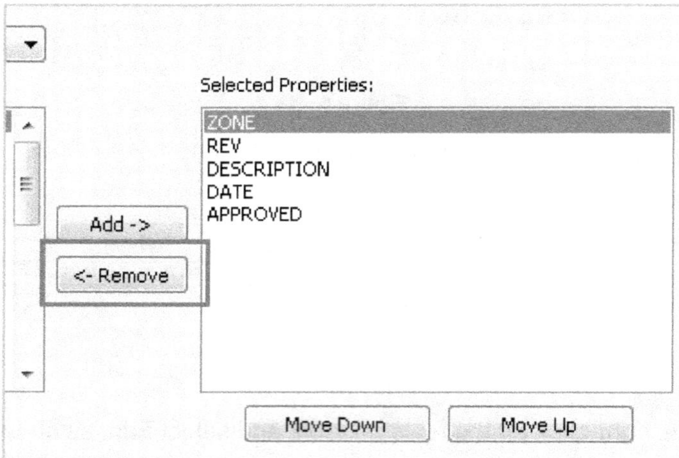

Figure 6–52

6. Click **OK**. The revision table updates with the change, as shown in Figure 6–53.

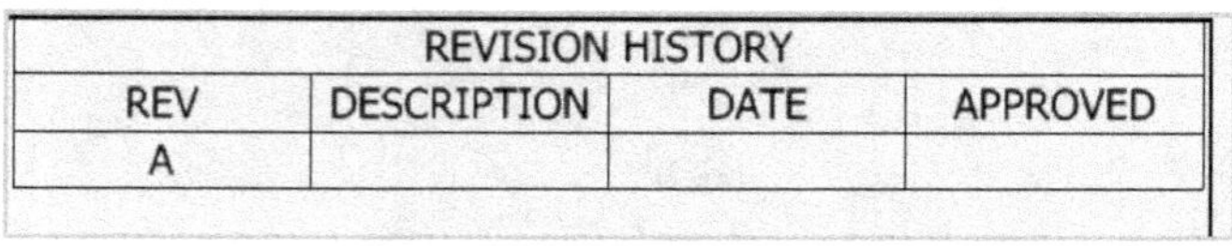

Figure 6–53

Update Properties

The Update Properties feature is integrated with the vault revision table, ensuring that revision block data is synchronized with vault release information. You can manually update the properties if mapped properties are edited in several ways, as shown in Figure 6–54 by using **Update Properties** in the Vault Browser or *Vault* tab, or by right-clicking on the Vault Revision table and selecting **Populate with vault data**.

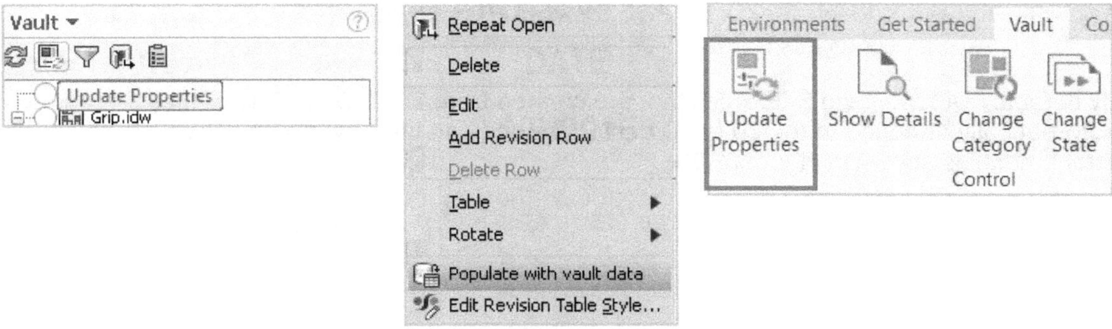

Figure 6–54

6.8 Accelerate Design Documentation

You can automatically publish your Autodesk 2D CAD files as PDF or DXF files and 3D CAD files as DXF or STEP files during design release or at any other lifecycle state. You can also manually create a PDF or DXF of a 2D CAD file using the **Create PDF or Create DXF** command. To manually created DXF or STEP files of 3D CAD files, use the **Create DXF** or **Create STEP** command

> ***Note:*** *To be able to use the **Create PDF, Create DXF**, or **Create STEP** commands, you must have the required access privileges set by your administrator.*

By default, PDF, DXF, and STEP files that are created from 2D CAD or 3D CAD files are automatically attached to the 2D or 3D design file and can be viewed in the *Uses* tab as an attachment, as shown in Figure 6–55.

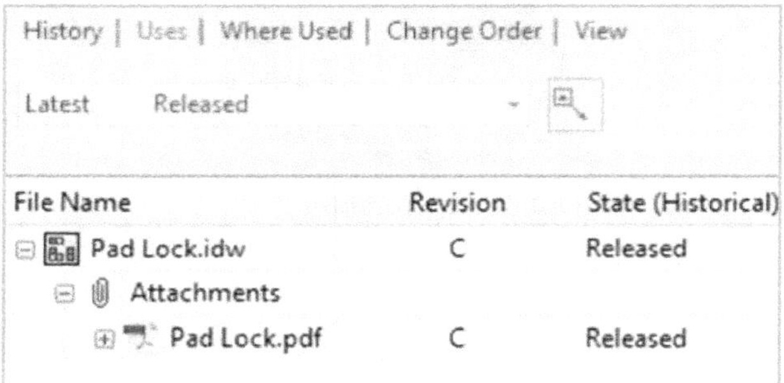

Figure 6–55

How To: Create a PDF, DXF, or STEP Manually Using the Create PDF, Create DXF, or Create STEP Command

1. Select the file in the Main table, then select **Actions>Create** and select the desired option, or right-click>**Create** and select the desired option.

   Note: *By default, automatically generated PDF, DXF, and STEP files are hidden. Select **Tools>Options** to display hidden files.*

2. The PDF, DXF, or STEP is created.

   The location of the file depends on the setting for the Publish Location set by the administrator. The three options are:

   - **Save in Vault (local copies will not be created)**: Select to save your published file in Vault.
   - **Save on a local drive in one folder:** Select to store all published files in a single folder on the local computer.
   - **Save on local drive using the Vault folder structure:** Select to store local copies of the files in a folder structure that duplicates the structure used in Vault Client.

6.9 Find Duplicates and the Duplicates Dashboard

The **Find Duplicates** command and associated Duplicate Search functionality is available in the Autodesk Professional software and can be used in Autodesk Inventor to search for duplicate parts in specified folders of the Vault database. Duplicate Search is based on geometric properties of the Inventor part files. A part file is considered a duplicate if the solid bodies in the Autodesk Inventor part files have exactly the same geometry. The part file can contain multiple solid bodies.

> ***Note:*** *An Administrator is required to enable the Duplicate Search functionality and select folders containing parts to index.*

How To: Find Duplicate Parts

1. In Inventor, open an assembly.
2. In the *Vault* tab>*Find* panel, click (Find Duplicates). Alternatively, in the Vault Browser, you can select **Find Duplicates** from the right-click menu.

   > ***Note:*** *You also have options to check Content Center and released parts during the search by selecting the* ***Check Content Center parts*** *and the* ***Check released parts in the selected assembly*** *checkboxes.*

3. In the *Input Geometry* section, select a component (part, assembly, sub-assembly) for duplicate search, as shown in Figure 6–56.

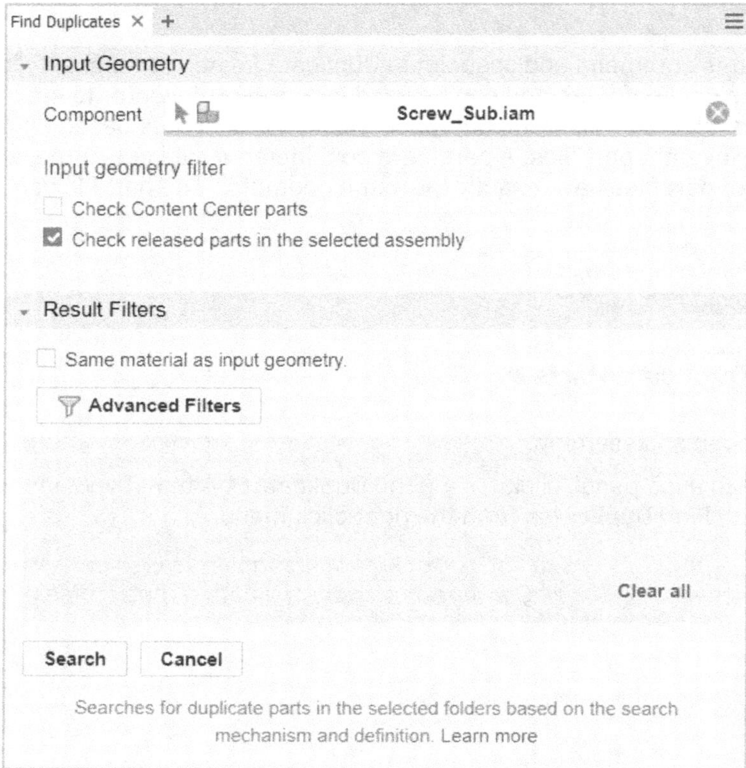

Figure 6–56

Note: *If desired, select the* ***Same material as input geometry*** *checkbox.*

4. In the *Results Filters* section, if specifying filters on the search results, click **Advanced Filters**. You can specify filters before or after the search for duplicates.
5. Click **Search**.
6. Duplicates of the parts files within the assembly are displayed. Click a group to view details, as shown in Figure 6–57.

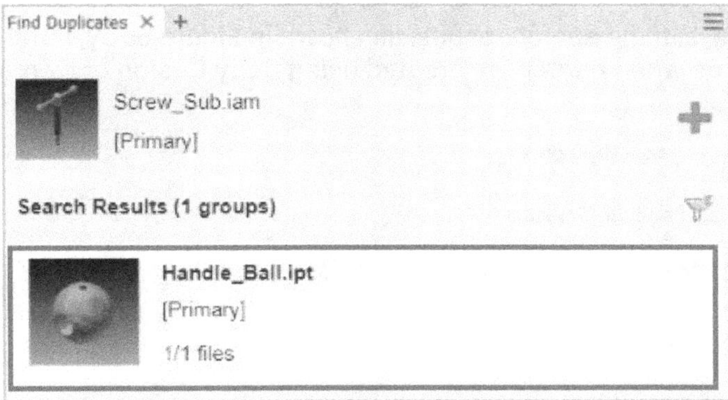

Figure 6–57

7. The duplicate part files from Vault are displayed. Click 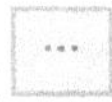 to view the actions that can be performed, as shown in Figure 6–58. Options to go to the Vault folder, open, replace, place, and show details are available for each duplicate file.

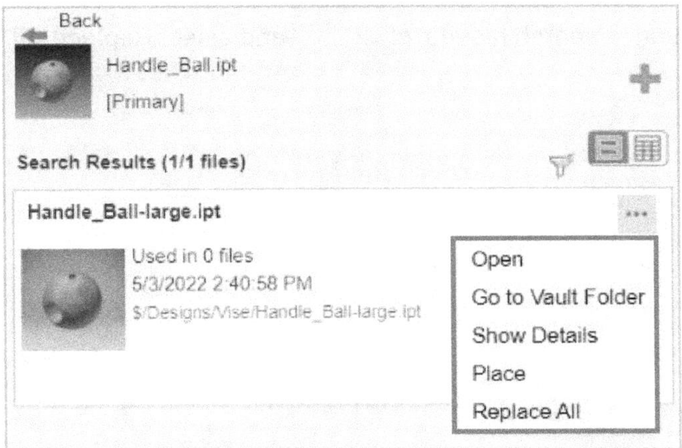

Figure 6–58

The table below details the actions that can be performed.

Action	Description
Open	Opens the selected part in Autodesk Inventor.
Go to Vault	Opens the selected part in Autodesk Vault Client.
Show Details	Displays details about the part such as its number of versions and where it is used.
Place	Places the selected part into the active assembly.
Replace All	Replaces all instances of the part in the assembly.

Note that displays in the search results, as shown in Figure 6–59, if the parts share the same source, such as when parts were created using **Copy Design** or by manually copying.

Figure 6–59

How To: Replace Duplicate Parts

1. In the Find Duplicates search results, click and select **Replace All**, as shown in Figure 6–60.

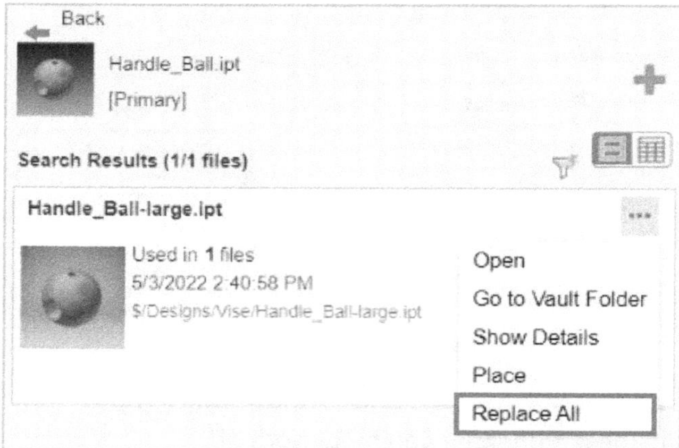

Figure 6–60

2. Click **Yes** to check out, if not already checked out. The replacement is performed, as shown in Figure 6–61.

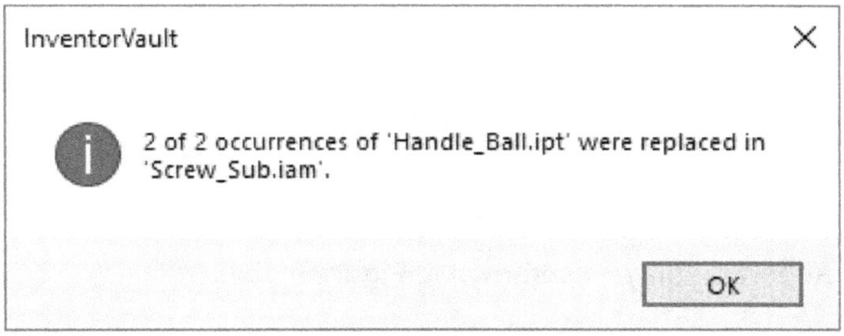

Figure 6–61

3. Click **OK**.

How To: View Duplicates Report

1. In the Navigation pane of the Vault Client, click **Duplicates Dashboard**. The *Duplicates Dashboard* displays as shown in Figure 6–62.

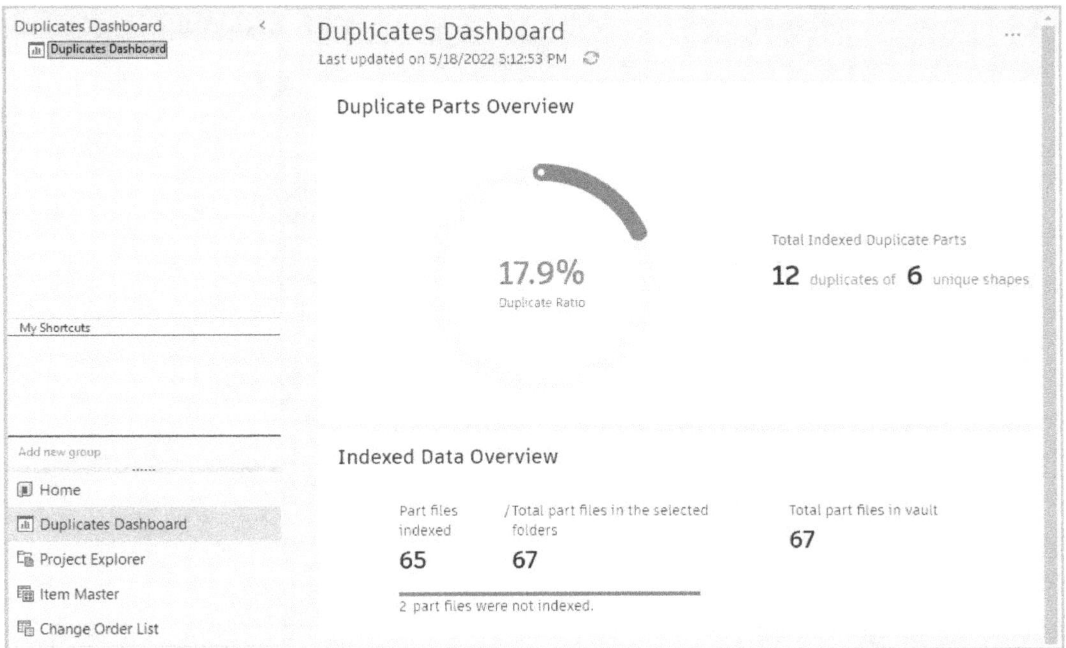

Figure 6–62

2. In the top right corner of the *Duplicates Dashboard*, click ··· and select **View Duplicates Report**, as shown in Figure 6–63.

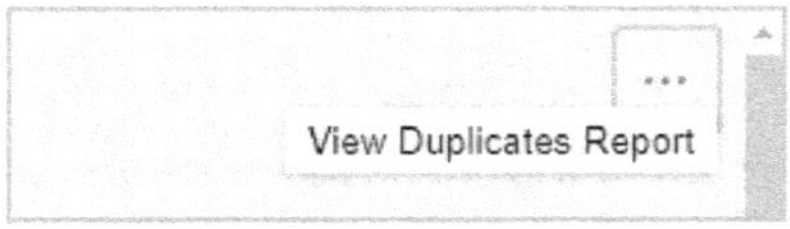

Figure 6–63

3. The *Duplicates Report* displays, as shown in Figure 6–64.

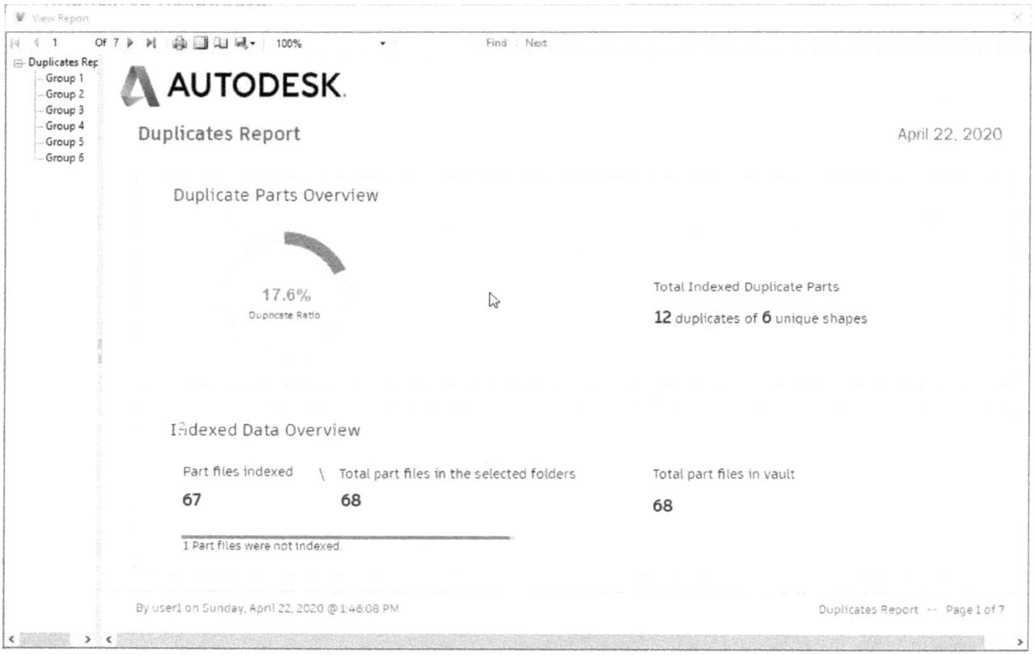

Figure 6–64

4. Use the page controls to view the details of each Duplicate group, or click a Group name to view that group's details, as shown in Figure 6–65.

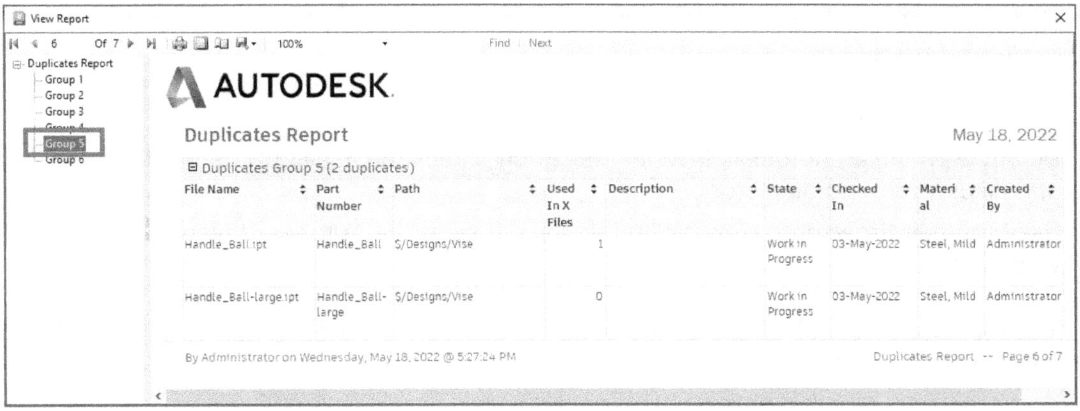

Figure 6–65

5. Select  (Export) and select **Excel**, **PDF**, or **Word** to export the report to an Excel, PDF, or Word file, respectively.

Practice 6d
Modify an Autodesk Inventor Design

Practice Objectives

- Locate and check out an Autodesk Inventor assembly.
- Modify a part in an Autodesk Inventor assembly, check the assembly back into the vault and display the version history.
- Use the Vault Browser to view vault status and display the Autodesk Inventor design's version history.

In this practice, you will check out an Autodesk Inventor assembly, make changes, and then check it back into the vault.

Task 1: Set the Inventor project file within the Autodesk Vault client.

In this task, you will set the Inventor project file in Autodesk Vault before checking out an assembly located in Autodesk Vault.

1. In the Autodesk Vault software, select the *$\Designs* folder. Select **Designs.ipj**, right-click, and select **Set Inventor Project File**.

Task 2: Open an assembly from the vault.

In this task, you will open and check out an assembly from the Autodesk Vault software using the **Open** option.

1. In the Autodesk Vault software, select the *$\Designs\Mold Assembly* folder. Select **Final Mold Assy.iam**, right-click, and select **Open** to launch the Autodesk Inventor software. Click **Yes** to check out the assembly. The Autodesk Inventor software is launched (if this is not already done) and the assembly is opened.
2. Log into Vault as **user1**.

Task 3: Modify a part in the assembly.

In this task, you will make a modification to the height of the Grip Handle part. Since only the assembly was originally checked out, you will be prompted to check out the Grip Handle part when making the modification.

1. In the Model Browser, right-click on **Grip handle:1** and select **Edit**.
2. Select **Extrusion1**, right-click, and select **Show Dimensions**.
3. Modify the height of the Grip Handle from *1.5 inches* to **6 inches**.
4. In the Warning box, click **Yes** to check out **Grip handle.ipt**.

5. Update the model in the Autodesk Inventor software and return to the assembly. The assembly updates as shown in Figure 6–66.

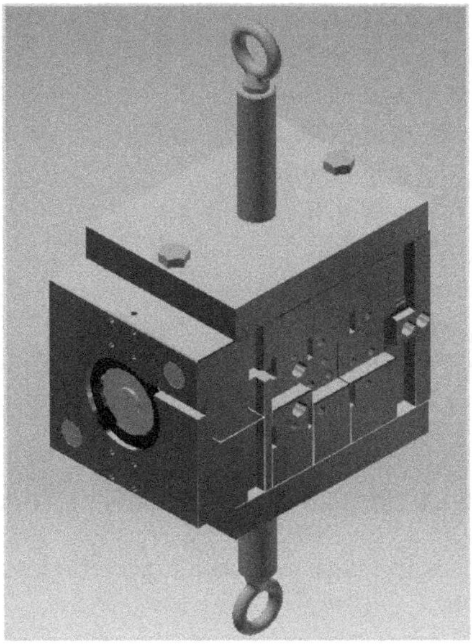

Figure 6–66

Task 4: View the status icons in the Vault browser.

In this task, you will view the Vault browser to see how it changes after the part has been modified.

1. Open the Vault browser to display the files, as shown in Figure 6–67. The Grip Handle part file name displays in bold (as does **Final Mold Assy.iam**) with an asterisk, indicating that it has been changed and requires a save.

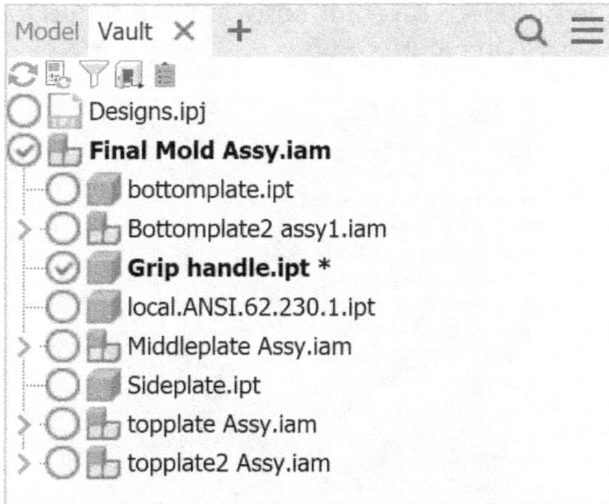

Figure 6–67

In the Vault Browser, the vault status icon for the checked out files is a circle with a checkmark ( ). It indicates that you are working on the latest version of the files and that they are checked out to you.

2. In the Quick Access Toolbar, select (Save).
3. Click **OK** to save **Final Mold Assy.iam** and **Grip handle.ipt**. The vault status icon for the saved assembly and saved Grip handle part turns green, as shown in Figure 6–68. This indicates that the file you are working on has been modified and therefore is newer than the one in the vault.

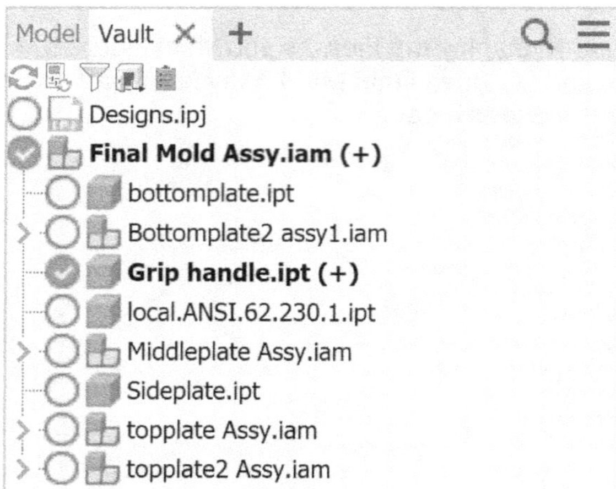

Figure 6–68

Task 5: Check in the modified files.

In this task, you will check the modified files in to the vault to make them accessible to other users.

1. In the Vault Browser, right-click on **Final Mold Assy.iam** and select **Check In**.
2. Note that the modified part is also shown along with the assembly in the *Check In* dialog box. In the *Enter comments to include...* area, type **Modified the grip handle**, as shown in Figure 6–69.

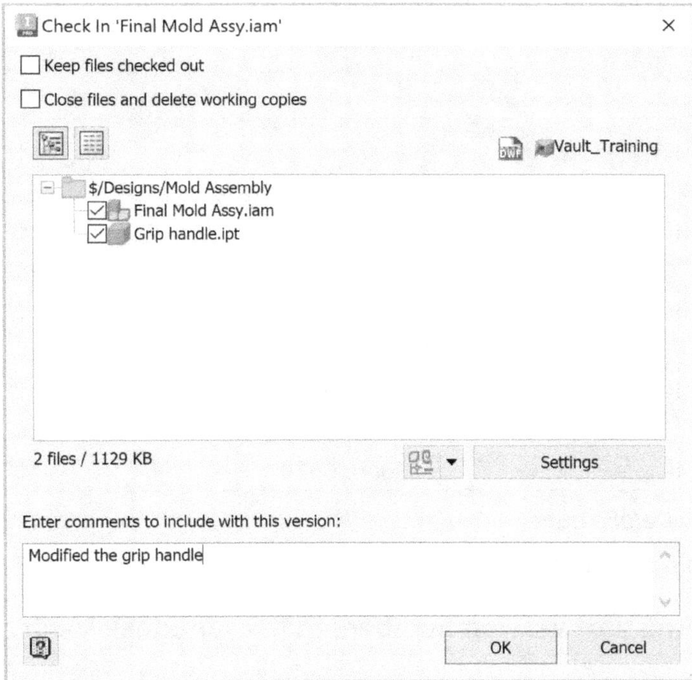

Figure 6–69

3. Click **Settings** to view whether or not children and parents are included when checking in and if .DWF attachments are to be created. Ensure **Include children**, **Create during check-in**, and **Apply to all files** are selected. Click **OK**.
4. In the *Check In* dialog box, click **OK** to complete the check in.
5. Close **Final Mold Assy.iam**.

Task 6: Display the assembly design history.

In this task, you will open **Final Mold Assy.iam** again (this time using **Open** (from Vault) in Inventor) and view its design history.

1. In the Autodesk Inventor software, in the *Vault* tab>*Access* panel, click (Open).
2. In the *$\Designs\Mold Assembly* folder, double-click on **Final Mold Assy.iam** to open the assembly as read-only (default).
3. In the Warning box, click **No** to not checking out the assembly.
4. Open the Vault browser.
5. Right-click on **Final Mold Assy.iam** and select **Show Details...**. The Details window opens, displaying the history with images of **Final Mold Assy.iam**. Select **Show all versions**.

   Note the Grip Handle change, as shown in Figure 6–70.

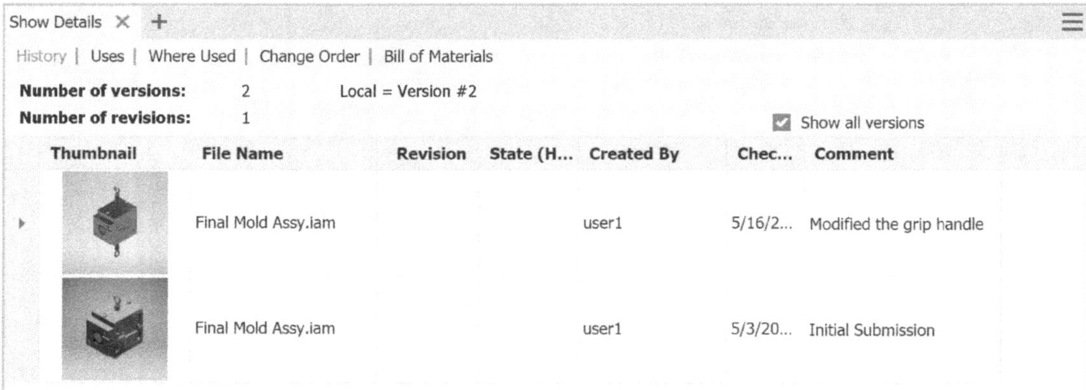

Figure 6–70

6. Close the *Show Details* panel.
7. Close **Final Mold Assy.iam**.

Task 7: Display the part version numbers in the Autodesk Vault client.

In this task, you will view the part version numbers in the Vault client that are associated with **Final Mold Assy.iam**.

1. In the Autodesk Vault software, click (Refresh). Only **Final Mold Assy.iam** and **Grip handle.ipt** have two versions. All other parts in the design remain at one version. The status icon also indicates that all of the files are checked in.

End of practice

Practice 6e
Get a Previous Version of an Inventor Part

Practice Objectives

- Use the **Get** command to download a previous version of an Autodesk Inventor part file to your working folder.
- Make changes to the part, save it, check it back in to the vault and view its version history.
- Modify the dialog box default for checking in files.

In this practice, you will use **Get** to roll back an Inventor part file to a previous version, because changes in the latest version are no longer required. You will make changes to the previous version part to create a new latest version. You will also change the dialog default used for checking in files.

Task 1: Get (download) a previous version of a file.

In this task, you will use the **Get** command to download a previous version of the shaft part to your local working folder.

1. In the Autodesk Vault software, in the Navigation pane, select the *$\Designs\Hub Shaft* folder to display its design files.
2. In the Main table, right-click on **shaft.ipt** and select **Check Out**.
3. In the Preview pane for **shaft.ipt**, select the *History* tab. Select **Show all versions**, if required. You need to go back to the original version, Version 1, with the original, shorter shaft length.

4. Select **Version 1**, and then right-click on **shaft.ipt** and select **Get**, as shown in Figure 6–71. Note that the image shows the shorter length of the shaft.

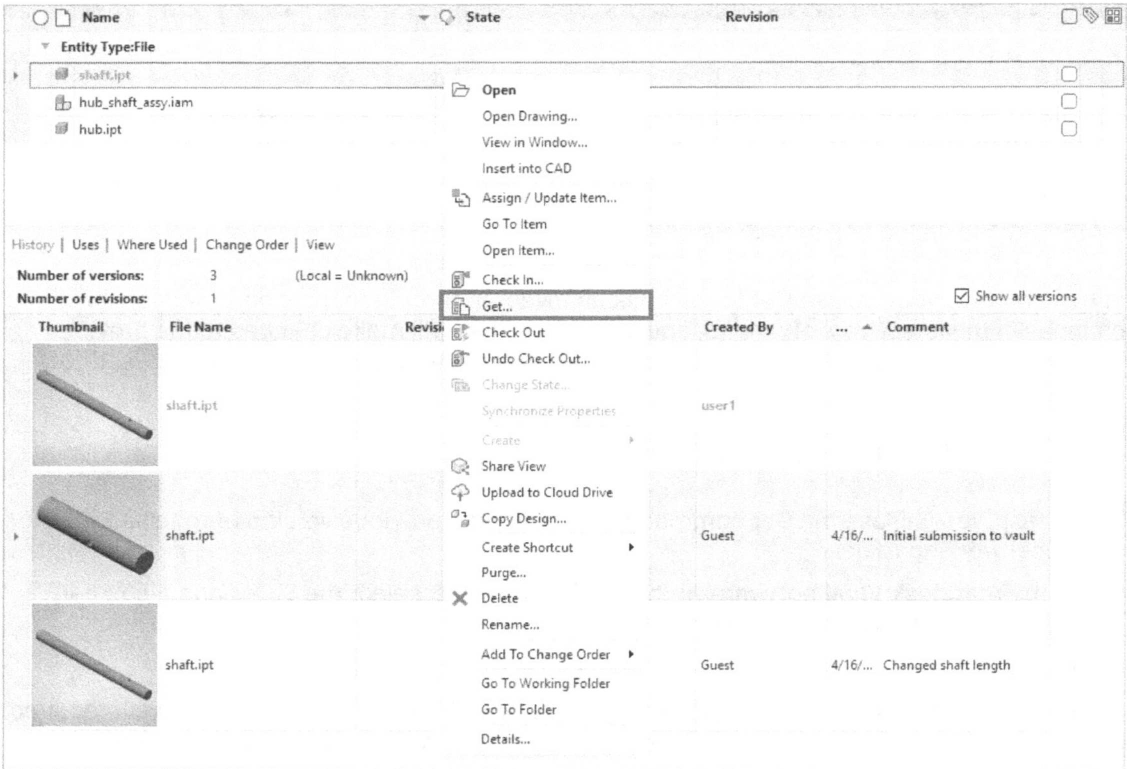

Figure 6–71

5. Click **OK** to download the file to the working folder.
6. If prompted, select **Yes** to overwrite the file in the working folder with the file from the vault.

The Vault status icon updates to show (as shown in Figure 6–72) with the tooltip showing incorrect version, which is the desired effect in this case. In other words, the local copy does not match the latest version in the vault.

Figure 6–72

7. Now you can open the file from the working folder in Autodesk Inventor and make any changes, as shown in the next tasks. Once it is checked back in to the vault, it will be the latest version.

Task 2: Open the downloaded previous version in Autodesk Inventor.

In this task, you will open Version 1 of the Shaft part into the Autodesk Inventor software from the local working folder.

1. In the Autodesk Inventor software, click **File>** (Open). You are not selecting **Open** in the *Vault* tab because you need to retrieve the local copy of the file.
2. In the *Hub Shaft* folder, select **shaft.ipt** and open it. This is the version with the shorter shaft.

Task 3: Make changes and save the modified part.

In this task, you will make modifications to make that version the latest.

1. Open the Vault browser. In the Autodesk Inventor software, the vault status icon also shows the red arrows , indicating the version you are working with is older than the latest version in the vault.
2. Open the Model browser, right-click **Extrusion1**, and select **Show Dimensions**. Modify the diameter from 30 to **25 mm**.
3. Open the Vault browser. **shaft.ipt** displays in bold font with an asterisk, indicating that a save is required. as shown in Figure 6–73.

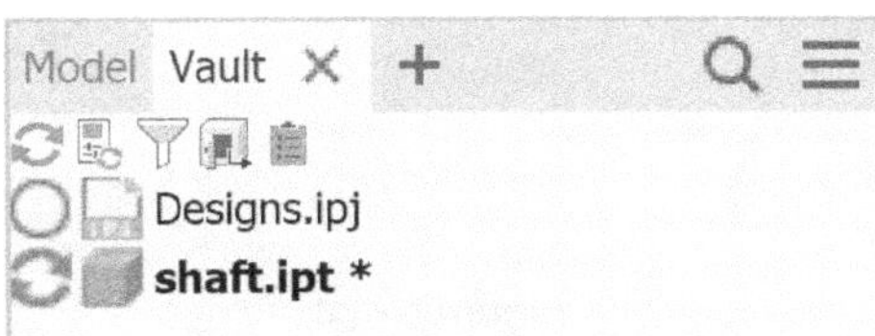

Figure 6–73

4. In the Quick Access Toolbar, click (Save).
5. If the *Data Format Has Changed* dialog box opens, click **OK**. The Data Format has changes if Version 1 was created in a previous Autodesk Inventor version and you are now saving it in the latest Autodesk Inventor version. The vault status icon changes to green, indicating that a check in is required.

Task 4: Check in the modified part to make it the latest version.

In this task, you will check in the modified part.

1. In the Vault browser, select **shaft.ipt**, right-click, and select **Check In**.
2. In the *Check In* dialog box, in the *Enter comments to include...* area, type **Changed diameter of shaft**. Clear the **Close files and delete working copies** option, if required.
3. Click **OK**. The file was not closed because **Close files and delete working copies** was not selected when checking in. The vault status icons indicate that you are now working on the latest version.
4. Select **shaft.ipt,** right-click on it, and select **Show Details....** Select **Show all versions**. The latest version is displayed with a shorter shaft and changed diameter, as shown in Figure 6–74.

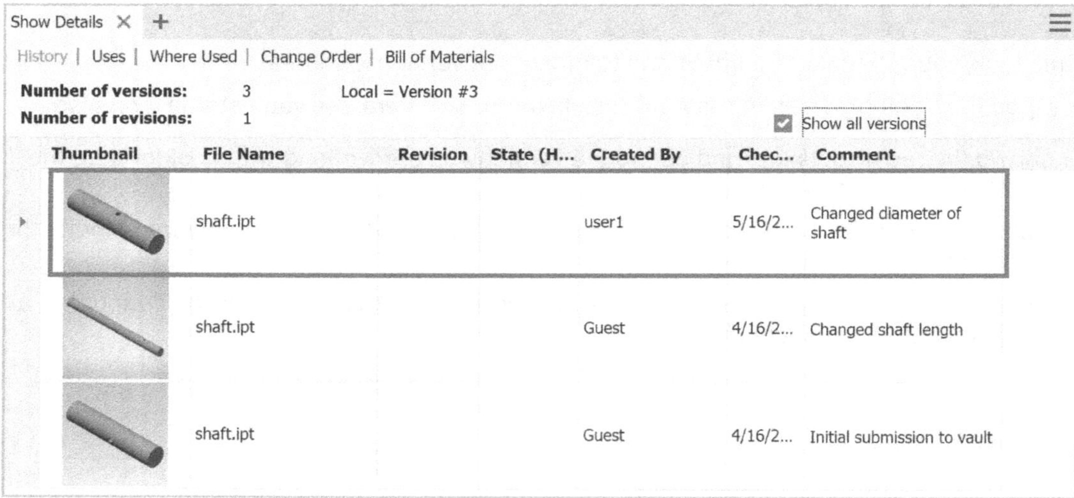

Figure 6–74

5. Close the *Show Details* panel.
6. Close **shaft.ipt**.

Task 5: Modify the dialog box default for checking in.

In this task, you will modify the default settings when checking in an Autodesk Inventor file so that working copies are deleted by default.

1. In the *Vault* tab>*File Status* panel, click (Vault Options).
2. Select **Check In dialog** and click **Settings** next to **Check in dialog**.
3. Select **Delete working copy** and click **OK** to set that option as the new default.
4. In the *Options* dialog box, click **OK**.

Task 6: Open, check out, and check in an assembly file to see changes.

In this task, you will see the effect of setting the **Delete working copy** option as the default when checking in an Autodesk Inventor file.

1. In Inventor, click **Open Vault** on the *Home* page or from the *Vault* tab>*Access* panel.
2. In the *Select File From Vault* dialog box, select the $\Designs\Hub Shaft folder, then select **hub_shaft_assy.iam**, right-click, and select **Open**. Check out and open the assembly in the Autodesk Inventor software.
3. Log in to Autodesk Vault, if required. **Check In** the assembly file.
4. Click **Yes**, as shown in Figure 6–75 to accept that the files will be deleted.

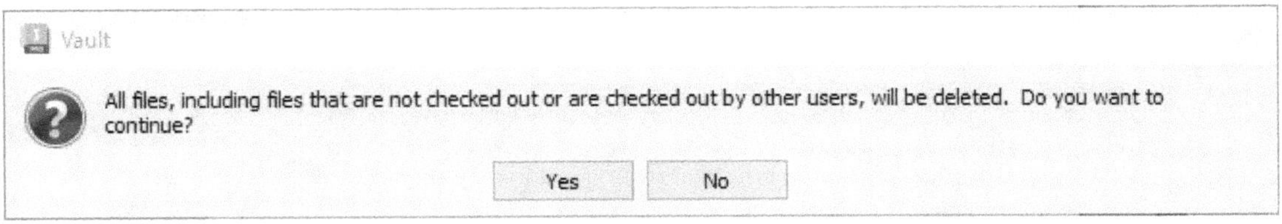

Figure 6–75

5. In the *Vault* tab, expand the *Access* panel, and click (Go to Workspace). Browse to the *$\Designs\Hub Shaft* folder to see that the files have now been deleted.
6. Close the Workspace File Explorer window.

End of practice

Practice 6f
Revise an Inventor Design

Practice Objectives

- Change the lifecycle state and revisions of files using **Change State**.
- Change the revision of a file using **Change Revision**.

In this practice, you will revise design files using the **Change State** and **Change Revision** commands.

Task 1: Release a design using Change State.

1. In the Autodesk Vault software, navigate to the *$\Designs\Piston* folder. Note that all files are at *Revision* **A** and that the *States* are all **Work in Progress**.
2. Select **piston_assem.iam**, right-click on it, and then select **Change State**.
3. Click **Include Dependents,** then select **Released** from the drop-down list. The comments automatically display *Released to manufacturing*, as shown in Figure 6–76.

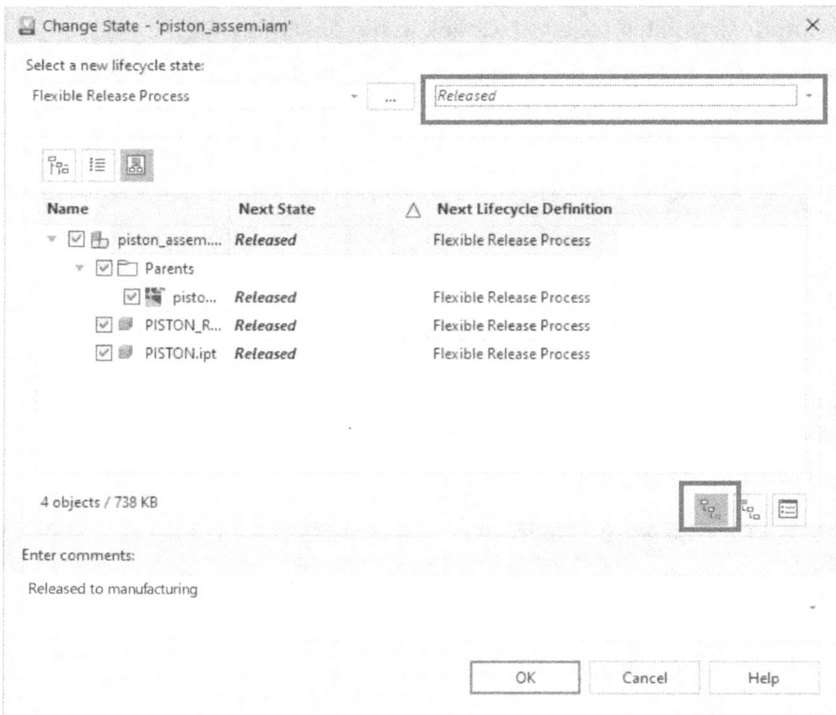

Figure 6–76

4. Click **OK**. The results display as shown in Figure 6–77. Note that all of the design files are still at *Revision* **A**, and that *State* is now set to **Released** with the files locked.

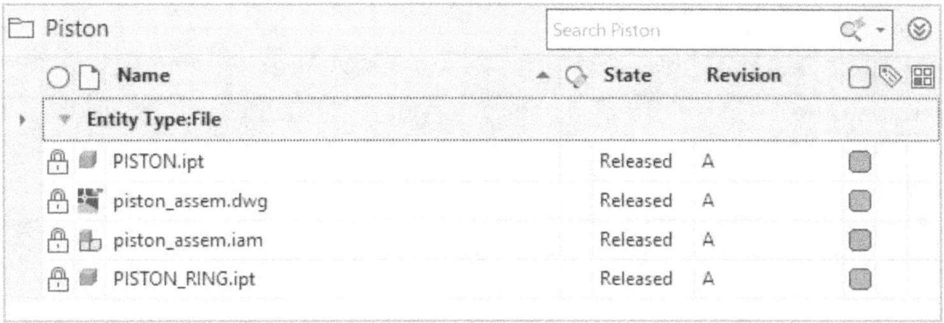

Figure 6–77

Task 2: Create a new revision using Change State.

1. In Autodesk Vault, select **PISTON.ipt**, right-click on it, and select **Change State**.
2. Select **Work In Progress**, as shown in Figure 6–78.

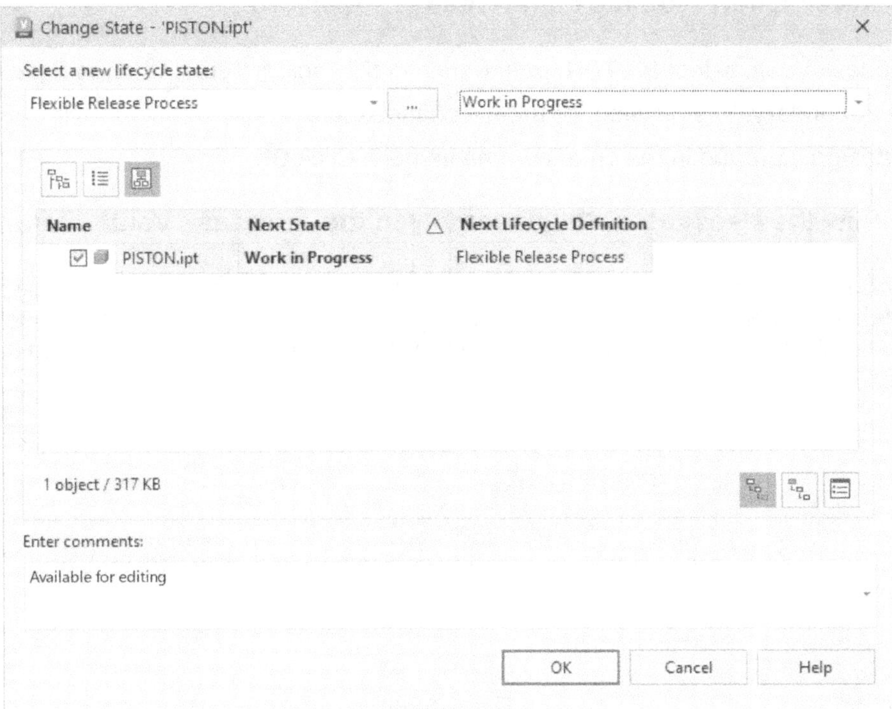

Figure 6–78

3. Click **OK**. The *Revision* changes to **B** and it becomes available for modification, as shown Figure 6–79.

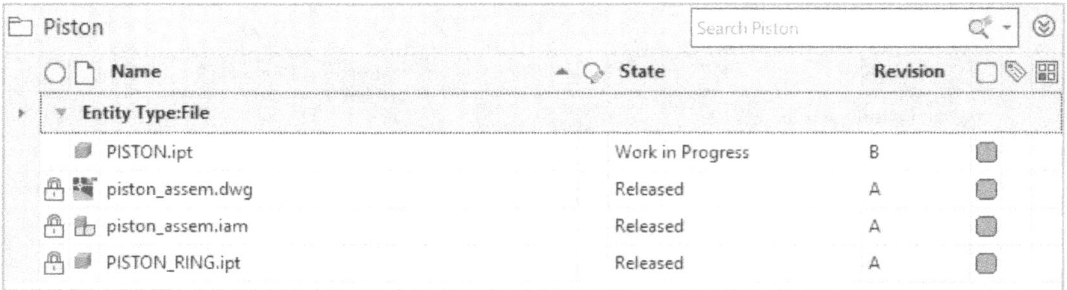

Figure 6–79

4. Open **PISTON.ipt** in Autodesk Inventor and click **Yes** to check out the file. Typically you would now make a design change and check in the file again. In the Vault browser, right-click on **PISTON.ipt** and select **Check In**, then click **OK**.
5. View the results in Autodesk Vault. Refresh the display. Note that the file is still at *Revision* **B**.

Task 3: Create a new revision using Change Revision.

1. In Autodesk Vault, select **PISTON.ipt** and then in the toolbar select **Change Revision**.
2. Select **Secondary**. The revision for the file changes to **B.1**.
3. Enter **design variation** in the *Enter comments* field. Click **OK**.

Task 4: View the Uses tab of the assembly in the Autodesk Vault client.

1. In Autodesk Vault, select **piston_assem.iam** and select the *Uses* tab. The display shows the **Non-Released Biased** configuration. Expand **piston_assem.iam**. The Piston assembly shows the Work In Progress B.1 version of the **PISTON.ipt** as a child, as shown in Figure 6–80.

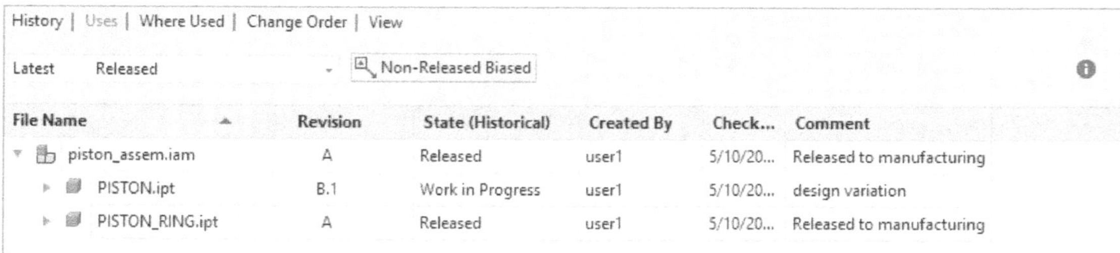

Figure 6–80

2. Select **Non-Released Biased** in the *Uses* tab to change it to **Released Biased**. Review the results. Note that when you use the **Released Biased** option, the Piston Assembly displays the released **A** *Revision* of the **PISTON** as a child, as shown in Figure 6–81.

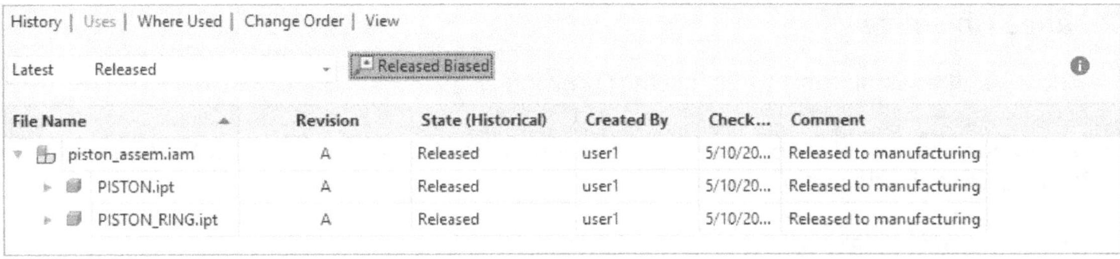

Figure 6–81

3. Change the *State* of **PISTON** to **Released** and note the change in the *Uses* tab for Piston Assembly when set to **Released Biased**, as shown in Figure 6–82.

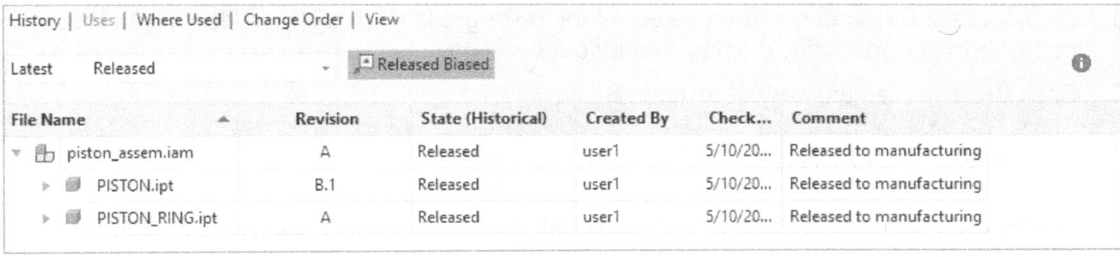

Figure 6–82

4. In the Main table, select **PISTON.ipt** and then select **Actions>Roll Back Lifecycle State Change** twice to change the state from **B.1** to **B**, then to **A**.

End of practice

Practice 6g
Create a Vault Revision Table

Practice Objective

- Add a Vault revision table to an Inventor drawing.

In this practice, you will first create a new revision of a design and then you will add a Vault revision table to the design's drawing.

Task 1: Create a new revision of a design.

1. In Vault Client, navigate to the *$\Designs\Piston* folder. Note that all files are at revision **A** and that the states are all **Released**.
2. Select **piston_assem.iam**, right-click, and select **Change State**.
3. Click **Include Dependents**, then select **Work in Progress** from the drop-down list. The comments automatically display *Available for editing*.
4. Click **OK**. The files are now at revision **B**.

Task 2: Add a Vault revision table to the drawing.

1. In Inventor, open and check out **piston_assem.dwg** from the vault's *Piston* folder.
2. In the *Annotate* tab, click **Vault Revision**, as shown in Figure 6–83.

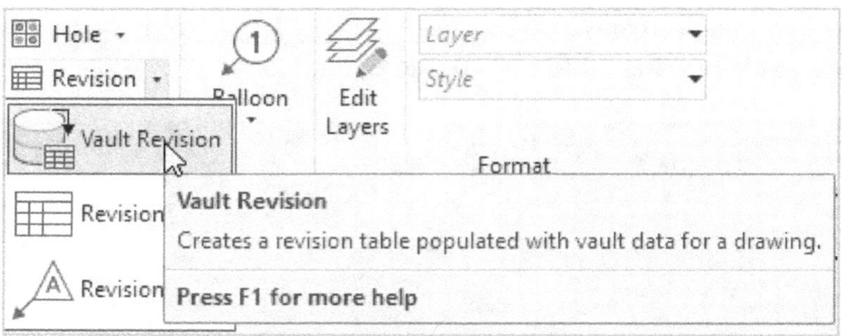

Figure 6–83

3. Insert the table in the top right corner of the drawing.
4. Right-click on the revision table and select **Edit**. Remove the *Zone* column.
5. Save the drawing and check it into the vault.
6. Now you can use the **Change State** command to release the files and then change state to *Work in Progress* again. Open the drawing in Inventor and view the Vault Revision Table.

7. Click **Update Properties** in the Vault Browser, then click **OK** to manually update the table to view all the revisions and release dates. Alternatively, the Vault administrator can set the environment to update the properties automatically when revisions are made to files in the Vault.
8. Close the drawing.

End of practice

Chapter Review Questions

1. In Figure 6–84, the highlighted Open icon retrieves files from the local workspace and not from the vault.

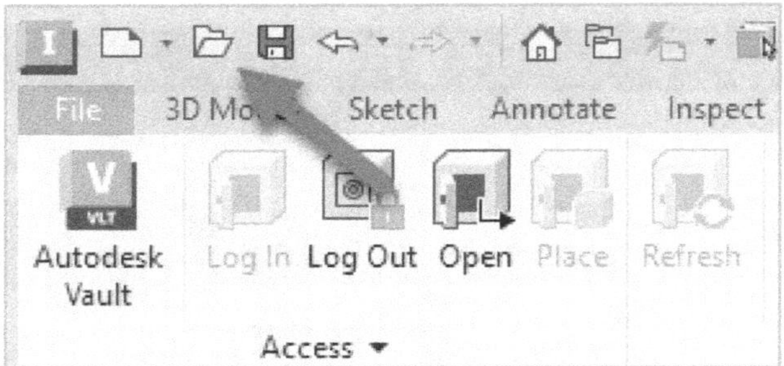

Figure 6–84

   a. True

   b. False

2. You can use the **Open (Read Only)** option in the *Open* drop-down list if you only want to view an Autodesk Inventor file and not make changes.

   a. True

   b. False

3. In the Vault Browser, what could the reason be when a filename displays with a white circle and a plus sign?

   a. The files are not yet in the vault.

   b. You are not working on the Latest Version.

   c. The file is not available for Check Out.

   d. All of the above.

4. How can Autodesk Inventor files be added to the vault for the first time to ensure all file relationships stay intact? (Select all that apply.)
    a. In the Autodesk Inventor software, use the Check In command.
    b. In the Autodesk Vault Client software, use the Check In command.
    c. In the Autodesk Inventor software, use the Check In Project command.
    d. Use the Autodesk Autoloader utility.

5. An Inventor file needs to be checked out to modify it.
    a. True
    b. False

6. What are the steps for reverting to a previous version of a part file?
    a. Use Check Out, and then open the file from the working folder.
    b. Check Out the file. In the file's History tab, ensure that the Show all versions option is selected, and then select the required version. Right-click, select Get, and then click OK to download.
    c. Use Get, select the previous version from the list, then use the Open from Vault command to open the previous version from the vault database.
    d. Use Get, select the previous version from the list, then open the file from the working folder.
    e. Use Get, select the latest version from the list, then open the file from the working folder.

7. In Figure 6–85, what does the highlighted button indicate?

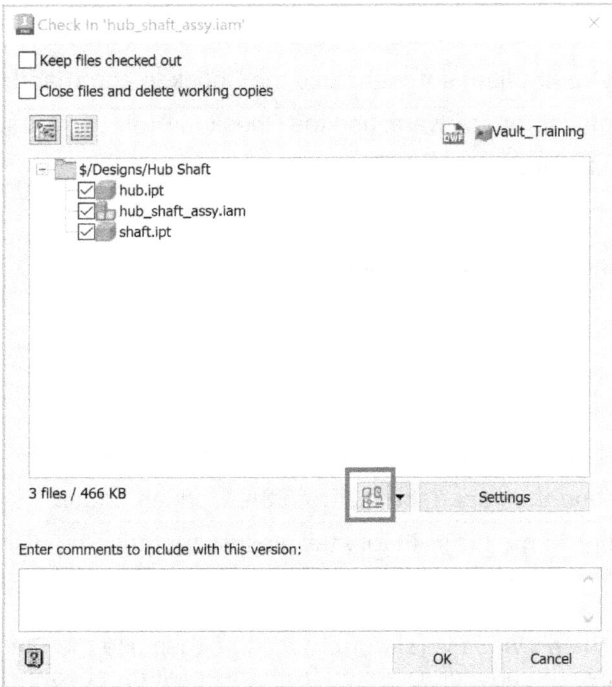

Figure 6–85

a. Related files are included for the check-in operation.
b. Related files are excluded for the check-in operation.

8. By default, .DWF files are automatically created and attached to the files on check in.
   a. True
   b. False

9. What does the red arrows () vault status icon indicate?
   a. The file is locked and the local copy is up-to-date
   b. The local copy is a historical revision of the leading revision in the vault.
   c. The file is not in the vault. Use Check In to add the file to the vault.
   d. The local copy does not match the latest version in the vault.

Command Summary

Button	Command	Location
	**Open**	• **Autodesk Inventor Quick Access Toolbar**
	**Open**	• **Autodesk Inventor Ribbon:** *Vault* tab>*Access* panel
	**Options**	• **Autodesk Inventor Ribbon:** *Vault* tab>*File Status* panel
	**Place**	• **Autodesk Inventor Ribbon:** *Vault* tab>*Access* panel
	**Check In**	• **Inventor Ribbon:** *Vault* tab>*File Status* panel • Shortcut menu in the Vault Browser
	**Get**	• **Menu:** Actions>Get • **Shortcut:** (*right-click on selected file*) • **Standard Toolbar**
	**Check Out**	• **Menu:** Actions>Check Out • **Shortcut:** (*right-click on selected file*)
	**Refresh File**	• **Inventor Ribbon:** *Vault* tab>*File Status* panel • Shortcut menu in the Vault Browser
	**Undo Check Out**	• **Inventor Ribbon:** *Vault* tab>*File Status* panel • Shortcut menu in the Vault Browser
	**Change Category**	• **Menu:** Actions>Change Category • **Advanced Toolbar**
	**Change State**	• **Menu:** Actions>Change State • **Shortcut:** (*right-click on selected file*) • **Advanced Toolbar**
	**Change Revision**	• **Menu:** Actions>Change Revision • **Advanced Toolbar**

Chapter

7

Working with AutoCAD Files

The Vault Add-in for AutoCAD provides direct access to Vault within the AutoCAD interface and is used to manage your AutoCAD designs. You will learn how to work with AutoCAD files using the *Vault* tab and the *EXTERNAL REFERENCES* (Xref) palette.

Learning Objectives

- Add (upload) files to the Vault for the first time.
- Use the *Vault* tab to Open AutoCAD files from Vault.
- Use the *EXTERNAL REFERENCES* palette to perform Vault file operations.
- Retrieve a previous version of an AutoCAD file.
- Modify, release, and revise an AutoCAD design.
- Accelerate design documentation.

7.1 Add AutoCAD Files to Vault

Since the Autodesk Vault software does not track and maintain relationships between AutoCAD files, it is recommended that you use the Vault Add-in for AutoCAD to add AutoCAD files to the Vault (i.e., use the *EXTERNAL REFERENCES* palette or the *Vault* tab options instead of the Autodesk Vault Client).

The **Check In** and **Check In Folder** operations can be used to add your files to the vault for the first time. Autodesk .DWF files are created and attached automatically for files that have changed or for files that do not already have .DWF files published. Vault hides the published .DWF files from the Main table.

Only one file can be checked in at a time unless it is a host file that references other files. When a host file is added to the vault, all dependent files are added automatically, retaining the saved paths to all the files it references.

A CAD file becomes the master when it is added or checked into the vault. Use the **Get Revision** operation to update the local working folder with the latest version (leading version of the leading revision) of the selected files. Use **Check Out** when you want to modify the files. These operations copy the requested files to your local working folder again and ensure that you are working with the latest versions.

Best Practice: Temporarily Store Files in the Local Working Folder

As a recommended best practice, the working folder should be considered a temporary folder in which to store files until they are checked back into the vault. Once checked back into the vault, the temporary files should be deleted.

Check In

How To: Check In Files to the Vault

1. Log in to the Vault and open an AutoCAD drawing from a local folder.

   Note: *Only DWG and image files can be checked into the vault in AutoCAD. To check other file types into the vault, use the Autodesk Vault Client interface.*

2. Use one of the following methods to access the **Check In** command:
   - Select **Check In** in the *Vault* tab>*Access* panel.
   - In the *EXTERNAL REFERENCES* palette, select the file, right-click, and select **Check In**.

3. The *Select Vault Location* dialog box opens, as shown in Figure 7–1.

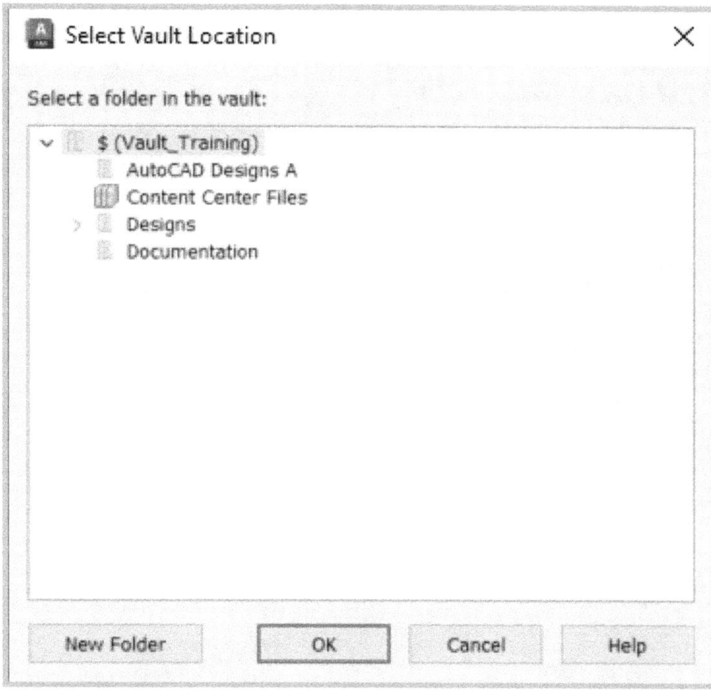

Figure 7–1

4. Select the Vault Location by selecting the existing vault folder. You can also select **New Folder** to create a new vault folder.
5. Select **OK** in the *Select Vault Location* dialog box.
6. If you have not saved the files, you will be prompted to do so. Select **Yes** to save.

7. The *Check In* dialog box opens, as shown in Figure 7–2.

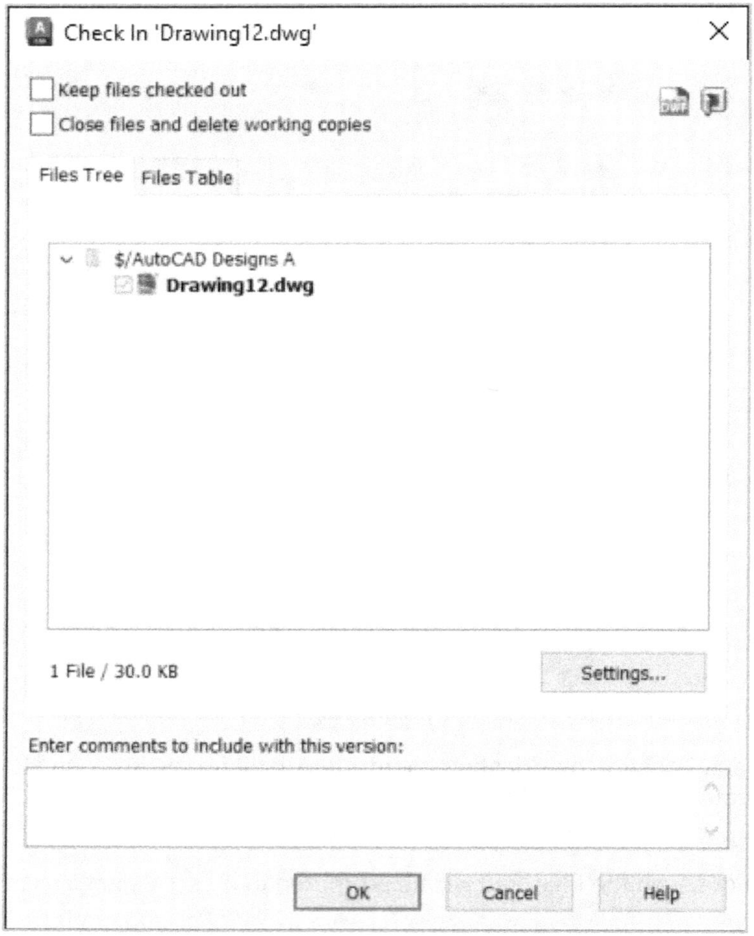

Figure 7–2

Note: *The vault creates any folders required to support the structure displayed in the dialog box.*

8. Select **Keep files checked out** to check the files into the vault and then check them out again so that you can keep working with them.
9. Select **Close files and delete working copies** to close the files after they have been checked in and delete them from the local working folder.

10. Click **Settings** to set the .DWF attachment settings. To create the visualization files, select either the **Create during check-in** option or the **Send to Job Server** option. The **Apply to all files** option can also be selected with preferences regarding Model Tab and Layout Tabs, as shown in Figure 7–3.

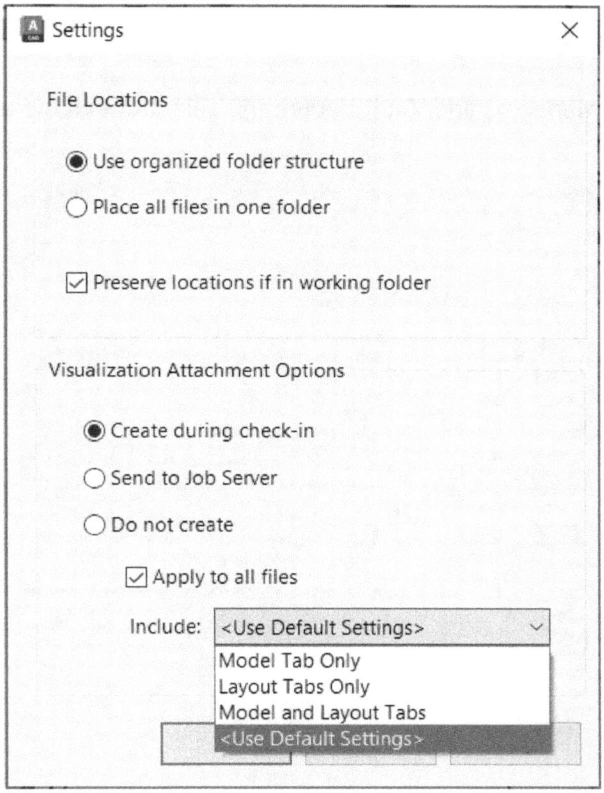

Figure 7–3

11. Click **OK**.
12. In the *Enter comments to include...* area, enter comments as required.
13. Click **OK**.

Check In Folder

The **Check In Folder** operation enables you to add an entire folder and its recursive contents to the vault in a single operation.

How To: Check In a Folder of Files

1. In the Application Menu, expand **Vault Server** and select **Check In Folder**, as shown in Figure 7–4.

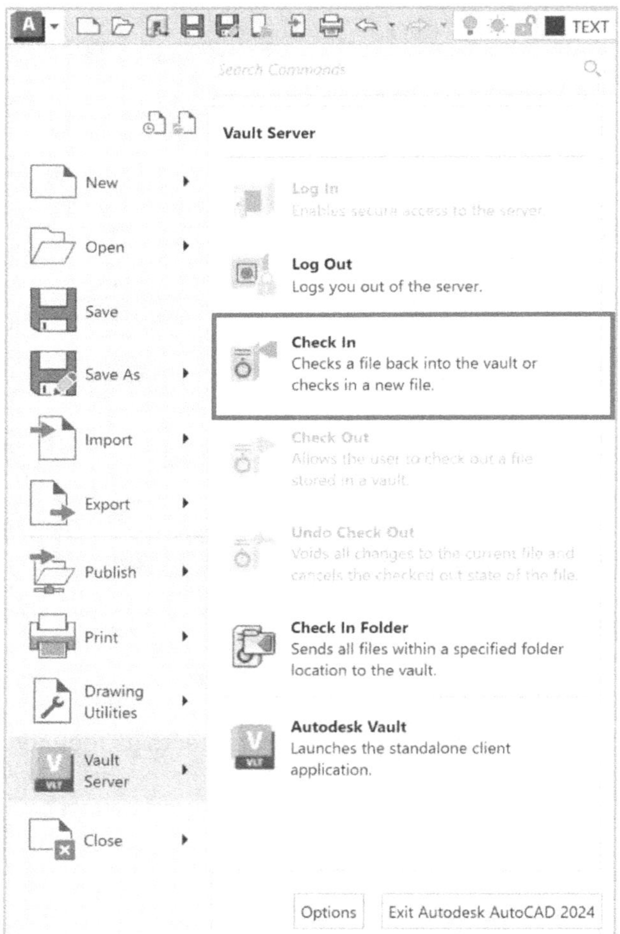

Figure 7–4

2. In the *Check In Folder* dialog box, select the folder to check in and the target vault location, if required, as shown in Figure 7–5.

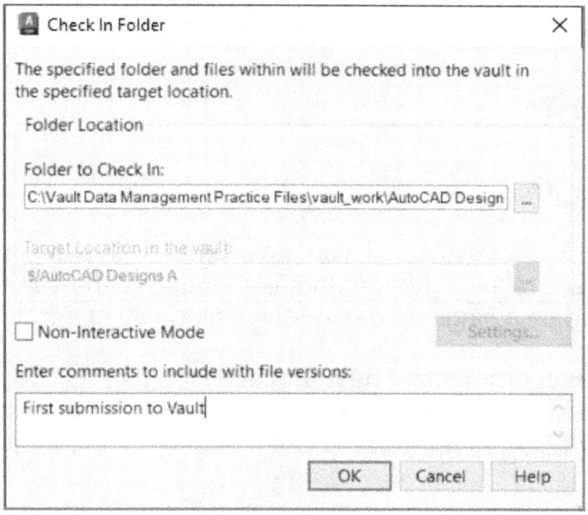

Figure 7–5

3. In the *Enter comments to include...* area, enter comments as required.
4. Click **OK**.
5. A *Check In Details* dialog box will open showing the results of the check in, as shown in Figure 7–6.

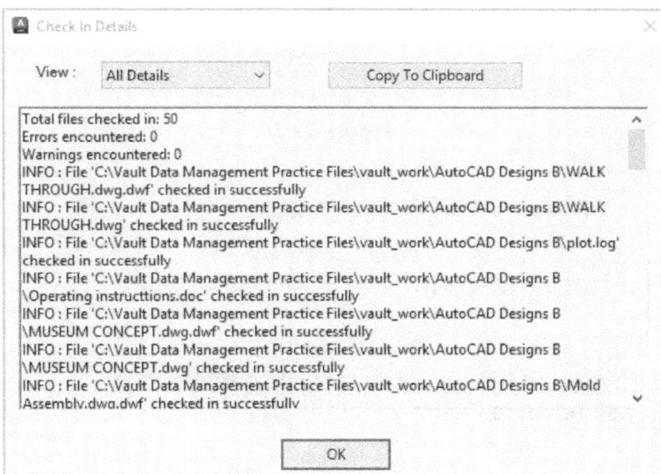

Figure 7–6

6. Click **OK**.

Add Library Files

Library files can also be added to the vault using the **Check In** and **Check In Folder** operations.

7.2 Open and Attach Vault Files in AutoCAD

Open from Vault

In the AutoCAD software, if you click (Open) in the Quick Access Toolbar rather than (Open) in the *Vault* tab>*Access* panel, you are prompted to select a file from the local workspace. The workspace is a local folder that is mapped to the corresponding folder in the vault. The workspace can be a single folder, or can include an hierarchy of subfolders to help organize the design. The recommended best practice is to use (Open) in the *Vault* tab>*Access* panel to open the file from the vault instead of from the local working folder. This ensures that you are always working with the latest version of the project.

(Open) in the *Vault* tab>*Access* panel in the integrated user interface is available after you log in to the vault, as shown in Figure 7–7.

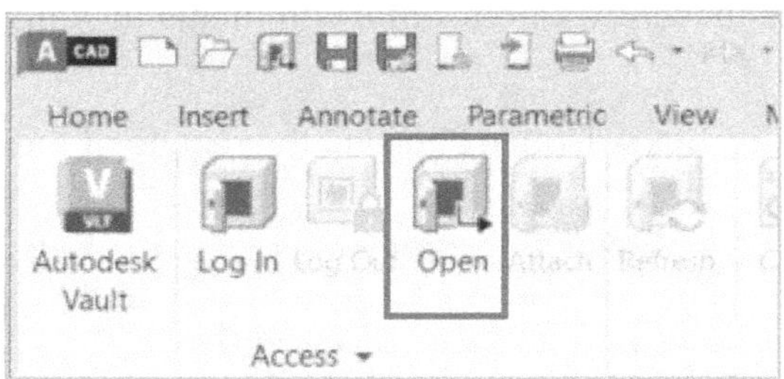

Figure 7–7

> ***Note:*** *If you click (Open) without logging in, you are prompted to log in.*

How To: Open a File from the Vault

1. In the AutoCAD software, in the *Vault* tab>*Access* panel, click (Open). The *Select File* dialog box opens, as shown in Figure 7–8.

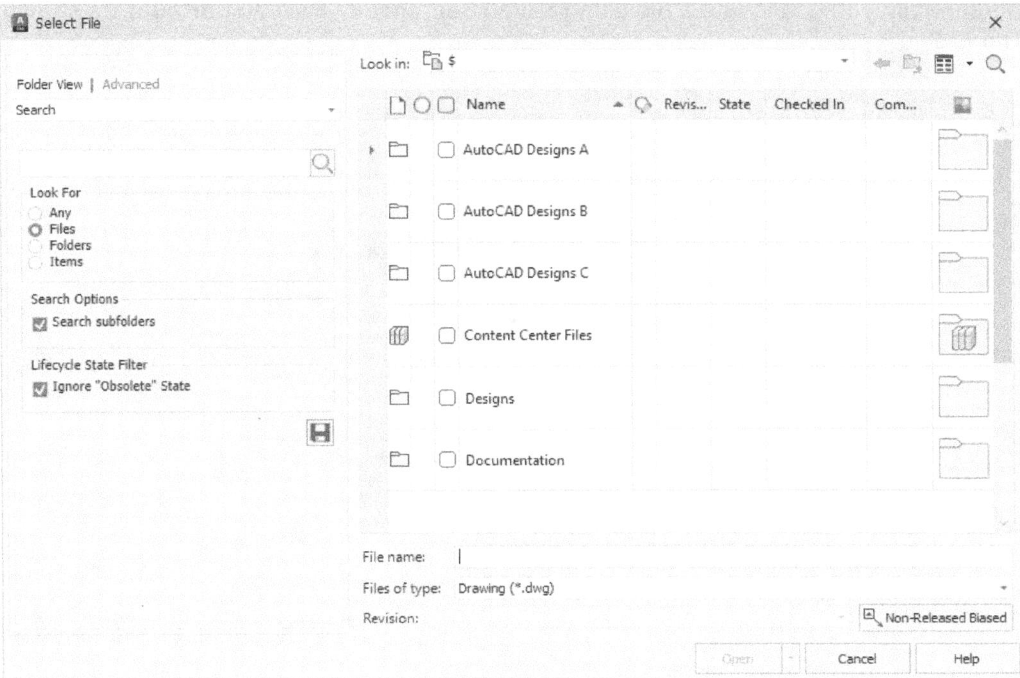

Figure 7–8

2. You can navigate the folder structure to select the required file, or you can search using the field shown in Figure 7–9.

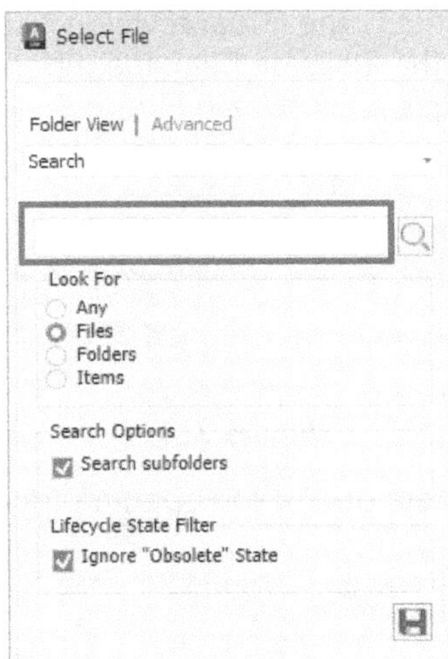

Figure 7–9

Note: *In the Select File dialog box, you can also use*  *(Advanced Search) to access the Find dialog box.*

3. Additionally, you can locate a file using **Saved Searches** or **Saved Shortcuts**, as shown in Figure 7–10.

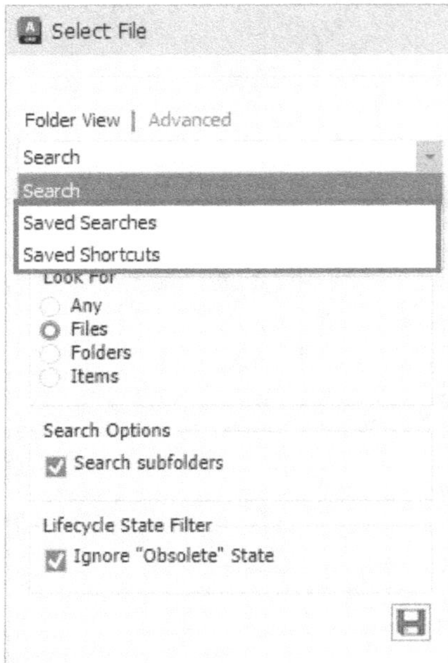

Figure 7–10

Note: *You can use [save icon] to save your search, once executed, to **Saved Searches** for reuse purposes.*

4. When you click on a file to select it, the latest revision of that file in the vault is selected by default and **Latest** displays in the *Revision* field. If a different revision is required, select one from the *Revision* drop-down list, as shown in Figure 7–11.

Figure 7–11

5. Select [drop-down icon] next to **Open** and select one of the open methods, as shown in Figure 7–12.

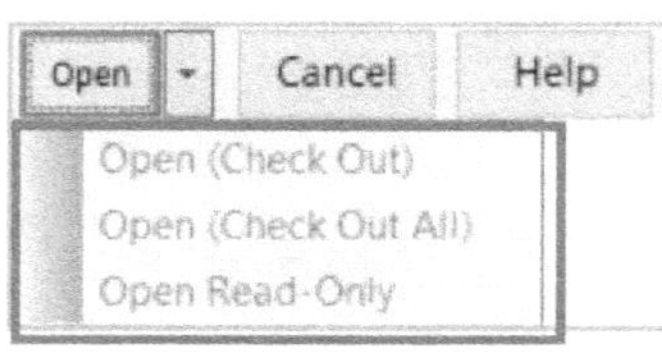

Figure 7–12

- **Open (Check Out):** Check out and open the file.
- **Open (Check Out All):** Check out and open the selected file and all of its children.
- **Open (Read Only):** Open the file without checking it out.

6. If you do not select one of the open methods, you can click **Open** to retrieve the file from the vault into the AutoCAD software. You are prompted to check out the file.
7. Click **No** to open the file as read-only or click **Yes** and then **OK** to check the file out of the vault.

Attach from Vault

To add an image or drawing from the vault to an AutoCAD drawing, click (Attach) in the *Vault* tab>*Access* panel. The *Select File* dialog box opens.

The options in this dialog box are the same as the ones displayed when **Open From Vault** is selected, as shown in Figure 7–13.

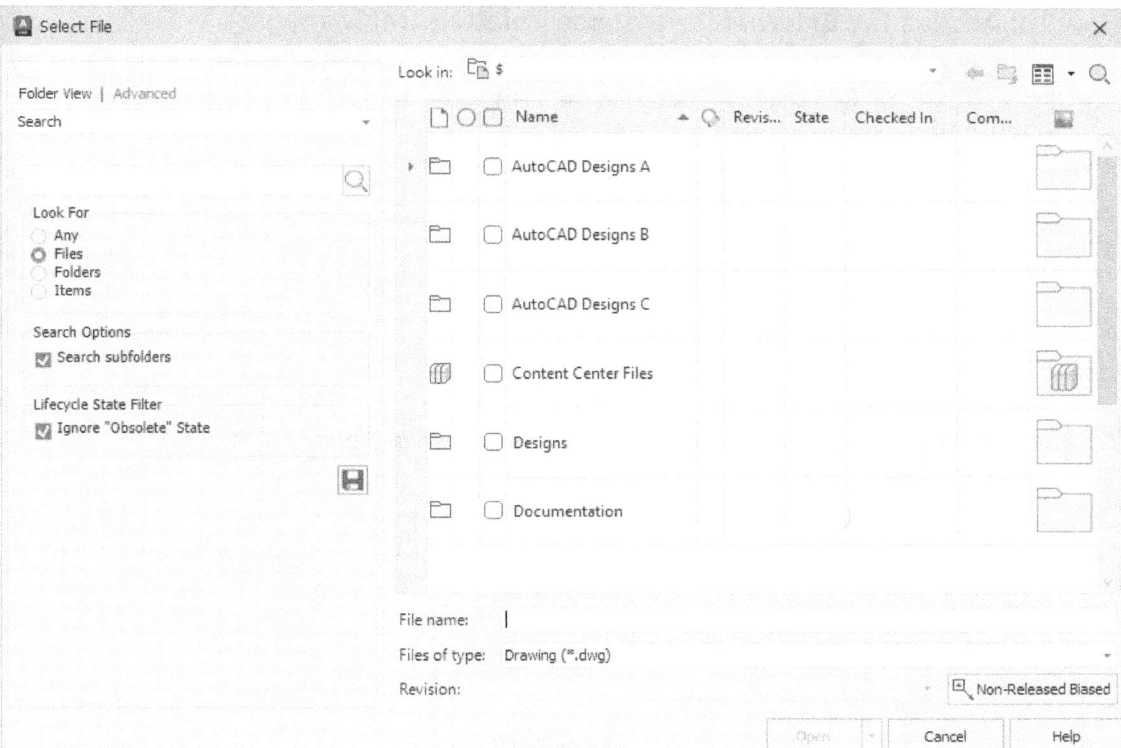

Figure 7–13

7.3 AutoCAD Add-In External References (Xref) Palette

The AutoCAD Vault Add-in adds vaulting functionality to the *EXTERNAL REFERENCES* palette (also known as the Xref Manager). In addition to performing standard Xref operations such as managing relationships between a host file and its Xrefs, the *EXTERNAL REFERENCES* palette enables you to perform all vaulting tasks when logged into the vault, including viewing the status of AutoCAD files within the vault.

When AutoCAD Vault is installed, the *EXTERNAL REFERENCES* palette becomes a dockable Enhanced Standard Window (ESW) that supports both drawing Xrefs and image files in the same window.

Accessing the Xref Manager

How To: Access the External References Palette (Xref Manager)

1. Click (External References Palette) in the *View* tab>*Palettes* panel, as shown in Figure 7–14.

Figure 7–14

2. The *EXTERNAL REFERENCES* palette displays as shown in Figure 7–15.

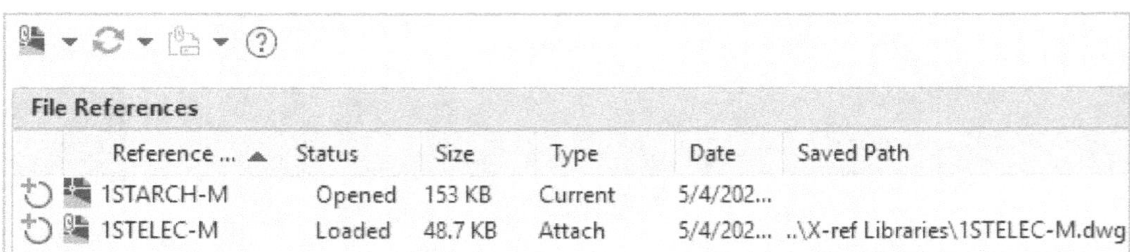

Figure 7–15

3. Once it displays, you can choose to dock the palette to the left- or right-hand side of the window and set to auto-hide for ease of use. To do this, right-click on the EXTERNAL REFERENCES vertical column and select **Allow Docking**, **Anchor Left** (or **Anchor Right**) and **Auto-hide**, as shown in Figure 7–16.

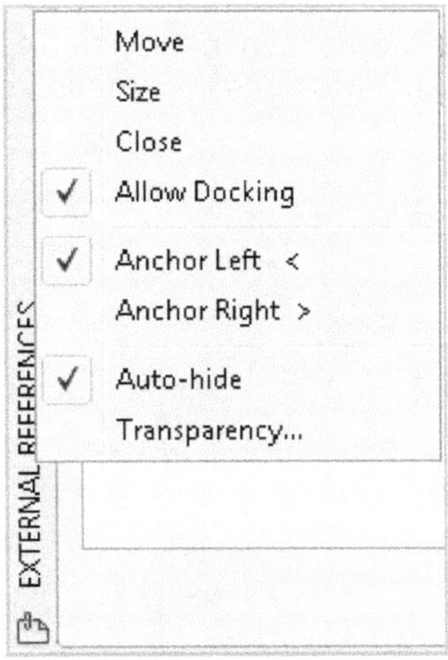

Figure 7–16

Note: *If the column containing the vault status icon is hidden, stretch the right-hand side of the column until the icon displays.*

In the *EXTERNAL REFERENCES* palette, to the left-hand side of each reference name, is the standard AutoCAD document icon. If you are logged into the vault, another column appears on the left-hand side of the AutoCAD document icon, displaying the vault status icon. The vault status icons are as follows:

- A white circle with a plus sign indicates that the files are not yet in the vault.
- A plain white circle or a white circle with a checkmark indicates that the version of file you are working with is in sync with the Latest Version that is in the vault.

Viewing the File Status Using Xref Manager

How To: View the Vault Status in the External References Palette

1. Hover the cursor over the vault status icon in the palette to view the vault status tool tip, as shown in Figure 7–17. This tooltip provides information on the action to be performed on the file.

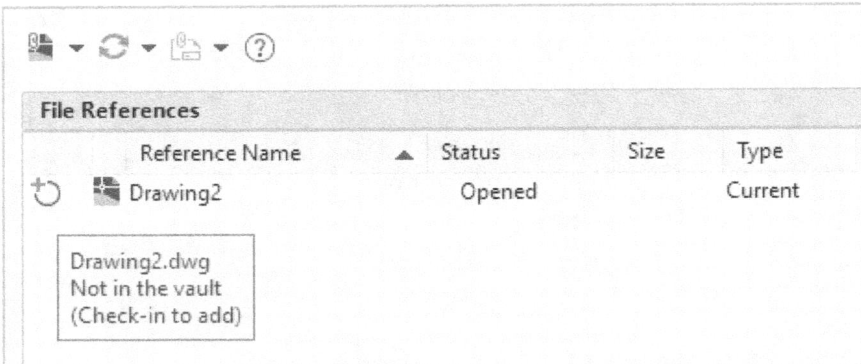

Figure 7–17

2. Select a file and right-click to see the commands. The commands available depend on how the file was opened and if it is an Xref or a host file. For example, if you checked out the file when opening it, **Check In** is available but not **Check Out**.

Xref Operations

The list of Xref operations available for the host and Xref files in the *EXTERNAL REFERENCES* palette is described in the following table.

Option	File Type	Description
Open	Xref only	Opens the selected Xref to view it.
Attach	Xref only	Attaches another instance of the Xref to the drawing.
Unload	Xref only	Unloads the selected Xrefs. The reference can be loaded at a later time.
Reload	Host and Xref	Opens a copy of a file's latest checked in version to your computer and loads it into memory. **Note:** When you currently have a file checked out to you and it is newer than the one in the vault, the reload command reloads from the working folder, and not from the vault.
Detach	Xref only	Detaches one or more Xrefs from your drawing, erasing all instances of a specified Xref.
Bind	Xref only	Converts a selected Xref into a block, making it part of your drawing permanently.
Check In	Host and Xref	Uploads a file from the working folder to the vault.
Check Out	Host and Xref	Copies a file from the vault to the client working folder to perform a change operation.
Undo Check Out	Host and Xref	Checks the selected file(s) back in, unmodified.

Vault Status Icons

- A white circle with a plus sign ( ) indicates that the files are not in the vault.
- If a filename displays in **bold font**, it means that the file is checked out to you. An asterisk beside the filename indicates that you have changes in memory that have not been saved, and it requires a save before it can be added to the vault.
- A white circle containing a checkmark ( ) or nothing ( ) indicates that the version of file you are working with is the same as the one in the vault. This is also known as the *Latest Version* and is typically preferred for use.

Practice 7a
Check In an AutoCAD Drawing

Practice Objectives

- Log in to the Autodesk Vault software from within AutoCAD.
- Open a drawing and display the *EXTERNAL REFERENCES* palette.
- Check in a drawing to the vault from the *EXTERNAL REFERENCES* palette.
- Use the *EXTERNAL REFERENCES* palette to view vault status.

In this practice, you are oriented to the Vault AutoCAD Add-in interface. You first launch AutoCAD and log in to the vault. Using the *EXTERNAL REFERENCES* palette with its vault capabilities you view the vault status of an AutoCAD drawing file and check it in to the vault.

Task 1: Launch AutoCAD and log in to the vault.

1. Launch the AutoCAD software. Create a new drawing and select a template so that the *Vault* tab becomes active.
2. In the *Vault* tab>*Access* panel, click **Log In**.
3. Type **user1** as the user name. Do not enter a password, as shown in Figure 7–18.

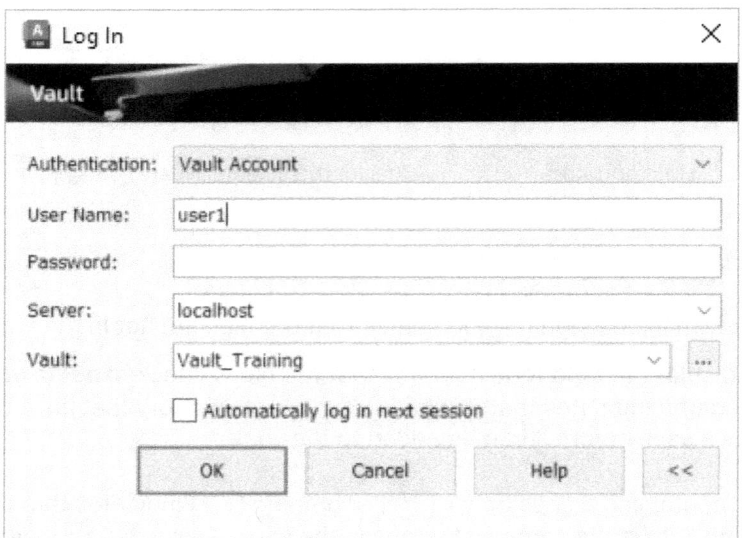

Figure 7–18

4. Click **OK**.

Task 2: Open an AutoCAD drawing.

In this task, even though you are now logged in to the vault, you open an AutoCAD drawing from your local folders using the Open command.

1. Select **Open** from the Application Menu.
2. Select **TANK.dwg** from the ...*\vault_work\AutoCAD Designs B* directory, as shown in Figure 7–19.

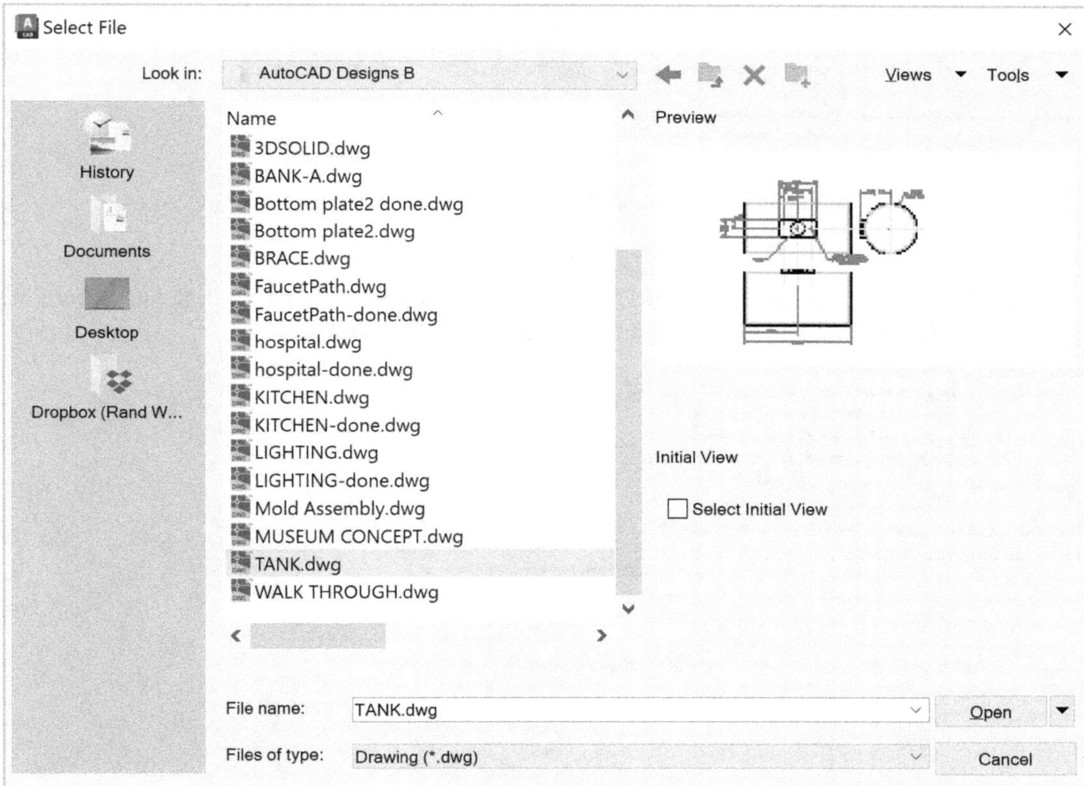

Figure 7–19

3. Select **Open** to display the drawing in the AutoCAD software.

Task 3: Display the External References palette.

In this task, you display the *EXTERNAL REFERENCES* palette (also known as the Xref Manager), which is used for vault activities in addition to its standard Xref capabilities. For ease of use, you dock the *EXTERNAL REFERENCES* palette and set it to auto-hide.

1. Open the *EXTERNAL REFERENCES* palette by clicking (External References Palette) in the *View* tab>*Palettes* pane, as shown in Figure 7–20.

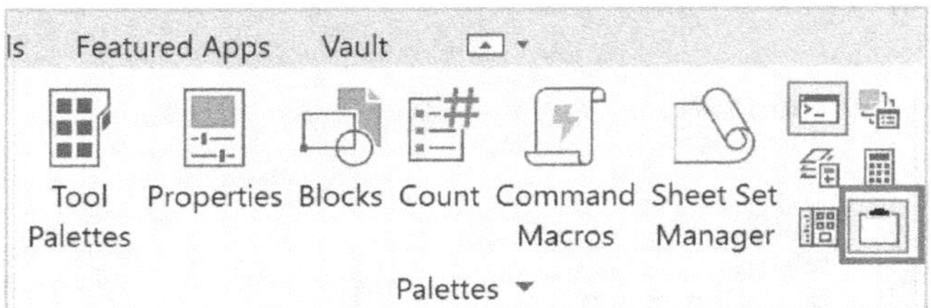

Figure 7–20

2. Right-click on the *EXTERNAL REFERENCES* vertical column and ensure that **Allow Docking**, **Anchor Left**, and **Auto-hide** are selected, as shown in Figure 7–21.

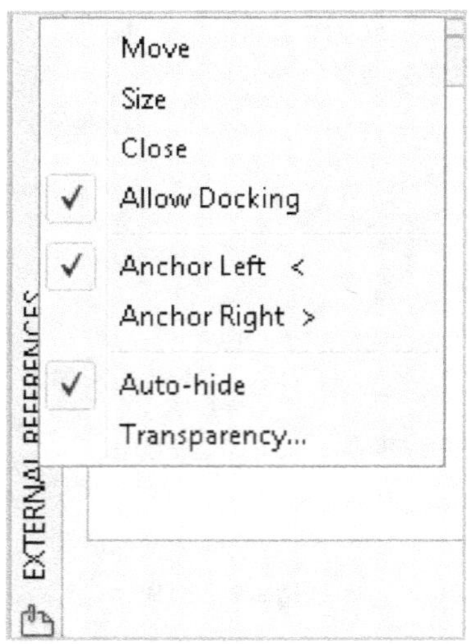

Figure 7–21

Task 4: View the vault status using the External References palette.

In this task, you become familiar with using the *EXTERNAL REFERENCES* palette to view the vault status of AutoCAD files.

1. In the *EXTERNAL REFERENCES* palette (Xref Manager), there is a white circle with a plus sign () next to the reference name, as shown in Figure 7–22.

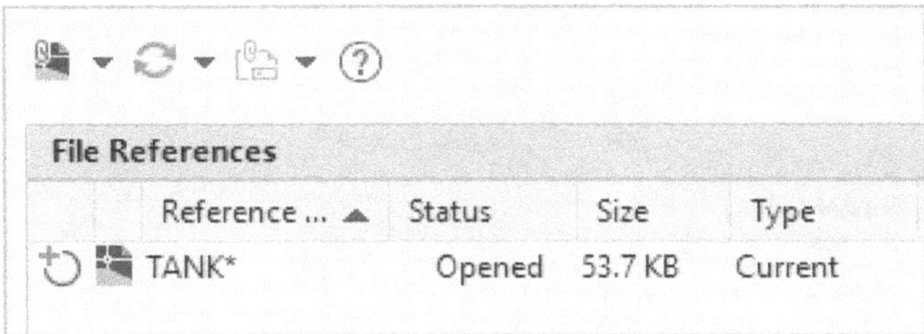

Figure 7–22

2. Move your cursor over the circle with the plus sign icon to see a tooltip indicating that the file is not in the vault and a recommendation to use **Check In**.

Task 5: Check in the drawing from the External References palette.

1. Select **TANK** in the *EXTERNAL REFERENCES* palette, right-click, and click **Check In** in the pop-up menu, as shown in Figure 7–23.

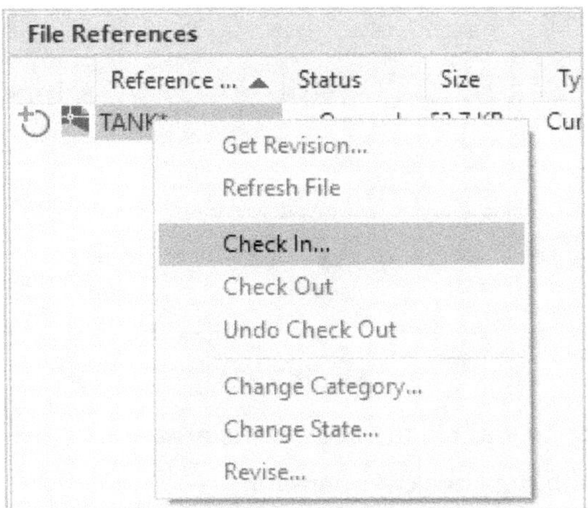

Figure 7–23

2. Click **Yes** to save the file, if prompted.

3. The file was opened from the working folder structure, therefore in the *Check In* dialog box, *$/AutoCAD Designs B* is automatically selected as the vault folder location, as shown in Figure 7–24.

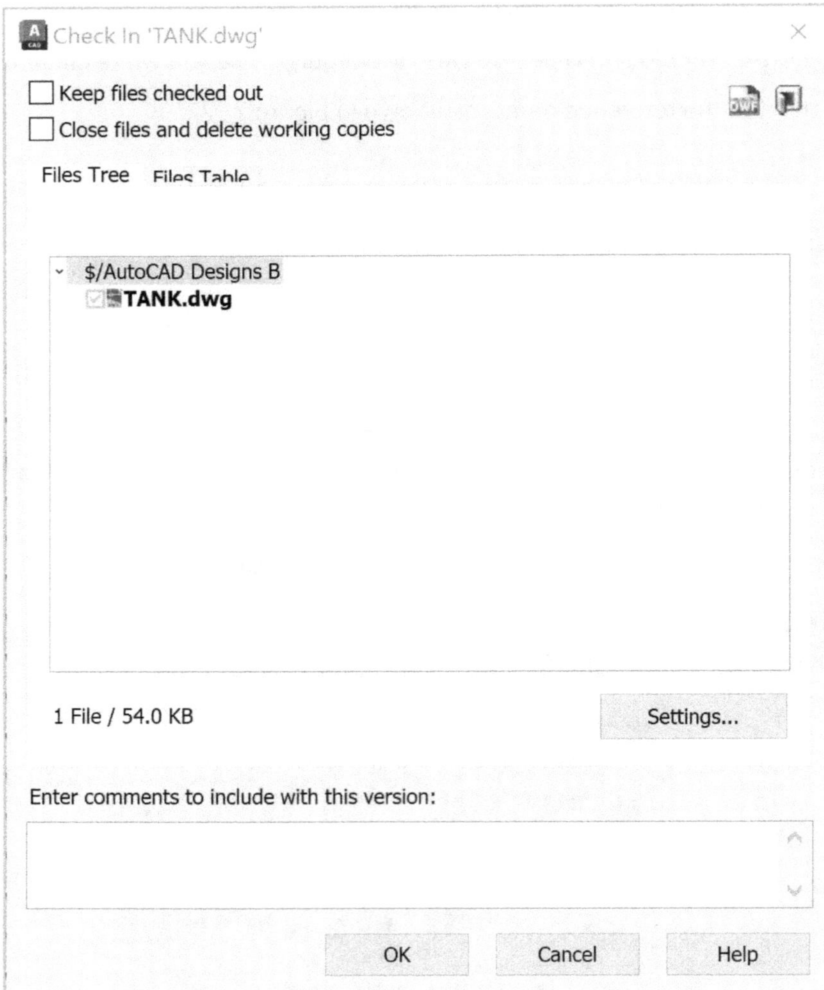

Figure 7–24

4. Type **Initial submission to vault** in the comments area.
5. Click **OK** to proceed with the check in operation.

Task 6: View the vault status in the External References palette after check in.

1. In the *EXTERNAL REFERENCES* palette, the vault status icon has changed to just a white circle, indicating that the file is now in the vault and that you are working with the latest version, as shown in Figure 7–25.

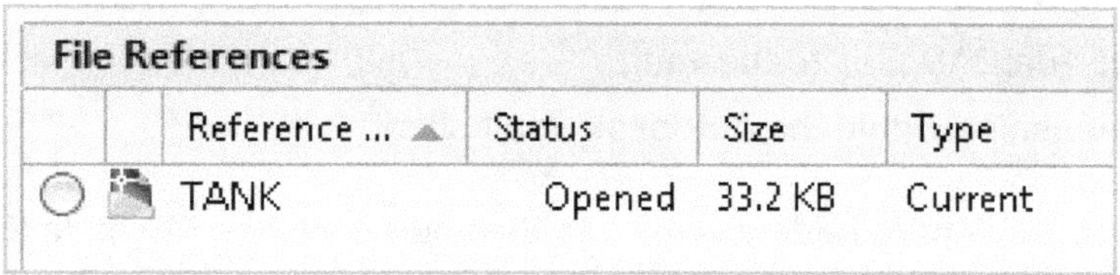

Figure 7–25

2. Close the drawing.

End of practice

Practice 7b
Add a Folder of Files to the Vault

Practice Objectives

- Open a drawing with an Xref and open the *EXTERNAL REFERENCES* palette.
- Add folders of AutoCAD files to the vault.
- View file relationships within the Autodesk Vault client.

In this practice, you add entire folders of files to the vault using the **Check In Folder** command. Some of these files are host files with Xrefs that also need to be added and their relationships maintained.

Task 1: Open a drawing with an Xref and display the External References palette.

In this task, you open a drawing containing an Xref and display the *EXTERNAL REFERENCES* palette to show the Xref information and its vault status.

1. Open **1STARCH-M.dwg** from *...vault_work\AutoCAD Designs B*, as shown in Figure 7–26.

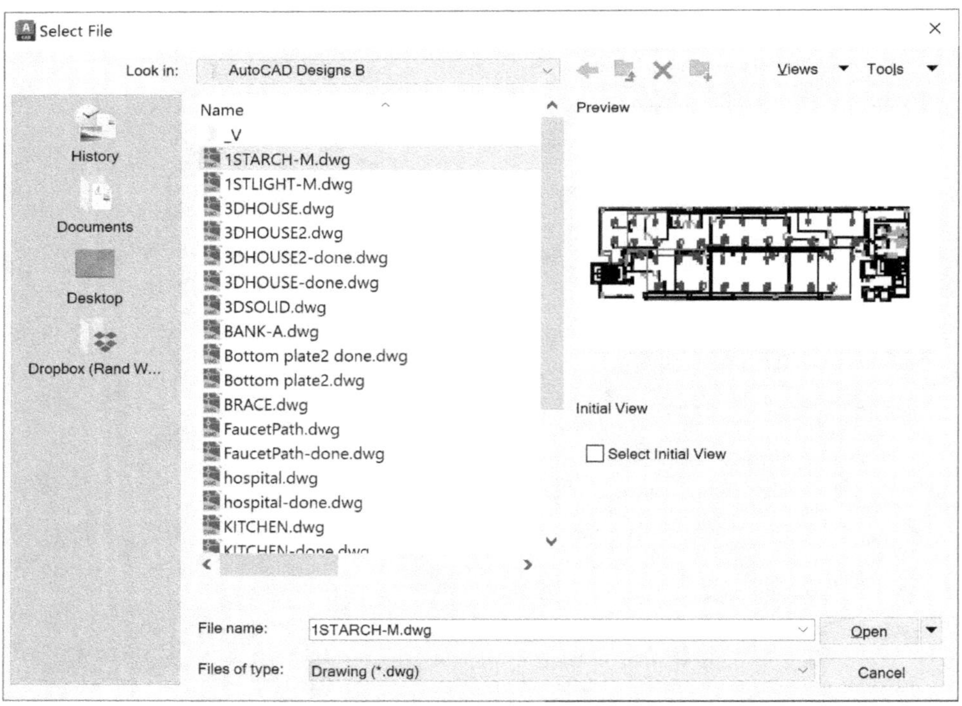

Figure 7–26

2. Select **Open** to display the drawing in AutoCAD.

3. Open the *EXTERNAL REFERENCES* palette. The white circles with plus signs beside the reference names indicate that they are not in the vault, as shown in Figure 7–27.

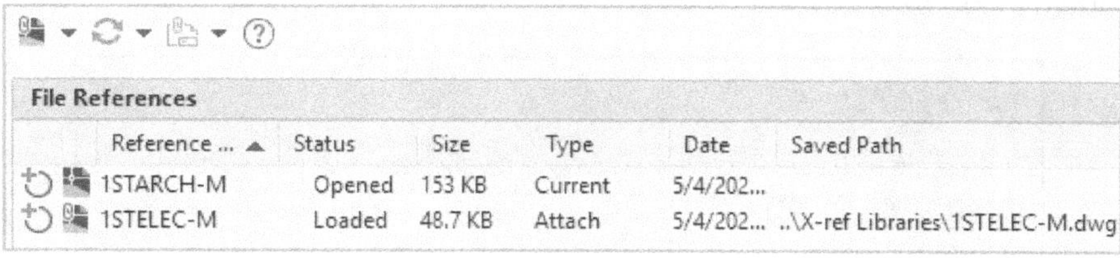

Figure 7–27

- **1STELEC-M** is an Xref, as indicated by the *Type* column displaying **Attach** and the *Status* column displaying **Loaded**. The Xref resides in the folder ...*vault_work\X-ref Libraries*, which can be seen in the saved path location for **1STELEC-M**.

Task 2: Check in the first folder of AutoCAD files into the vault.

In this task, you check into the vault the entire folder of AutoCAD files where **1STARCH-M.dwg** resides.

1. Select **Vault Server>Check In Folder** from the Application Menu, as shown in Figure 7–28.

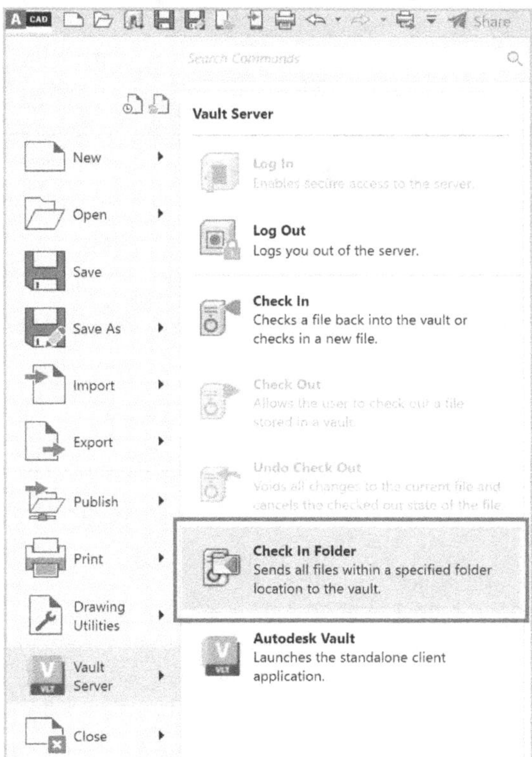

Figure 7–28

2. Select *...\vault_work\AutoCAD Designs B* as the folder to check in and type **First submission to Vault** in the comments area. The target vault location is specified as *$/AutoCAD Designs B*, as shown in Figure 7–29.

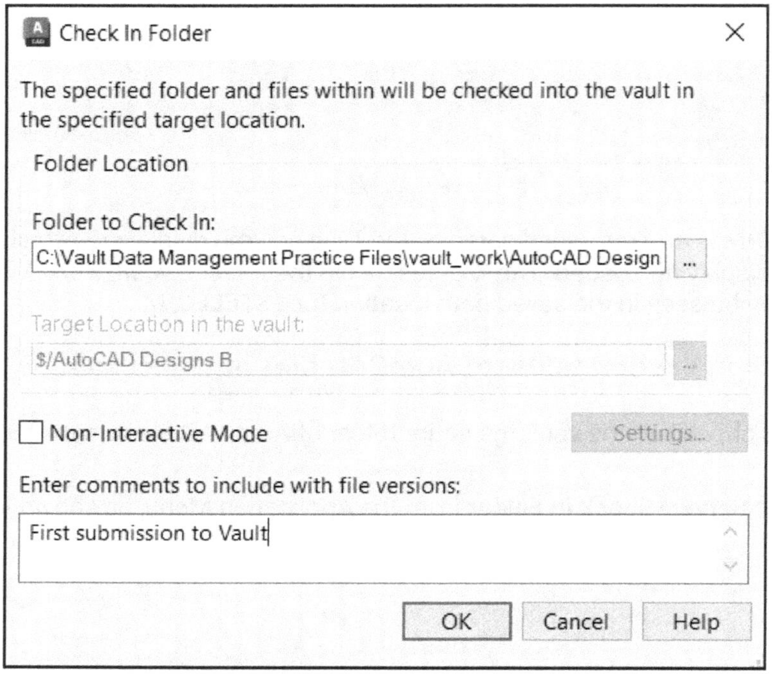

Figure 7–29

3. Select **OK**.

4. The *Check in Folder* dialog box appears showing all files to be added to the vault, including the folder structure that is created, as shown in Figure 7–30. The **1STELEC-M.dwg** is shown under the *X-ref Libraries* folder.

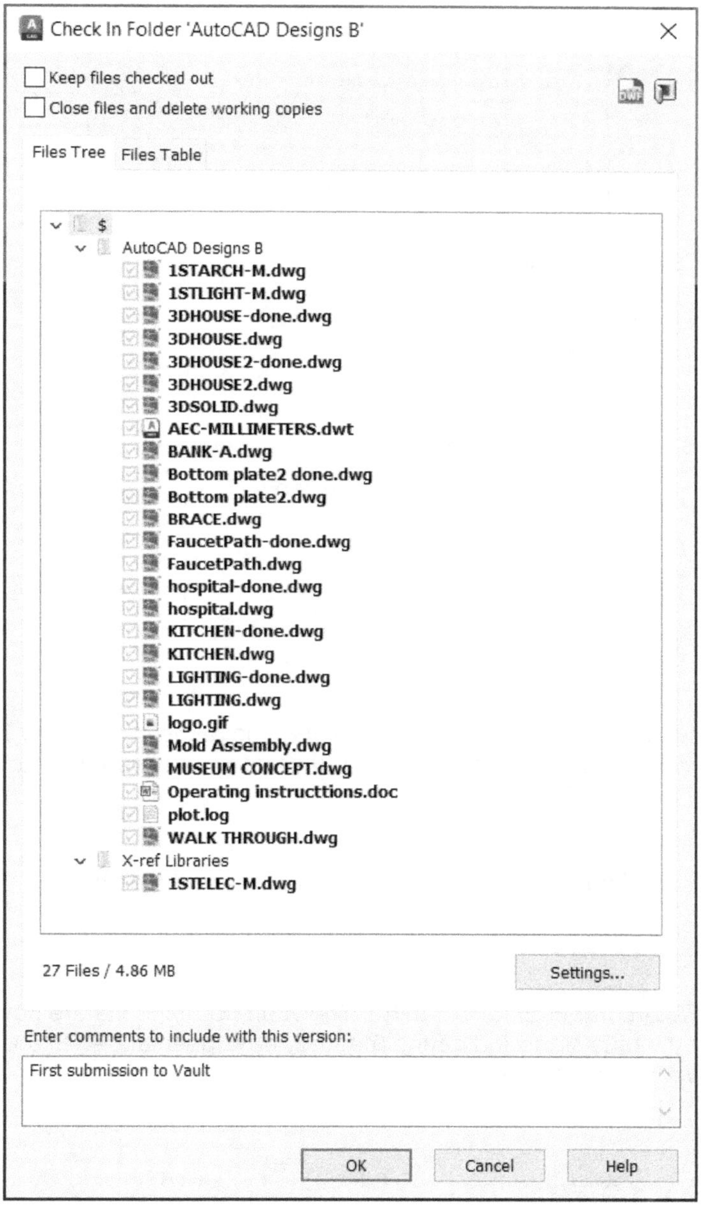

Figure 7–30

5. Select **Settings**. Select the options as shown in Figure 7–31.

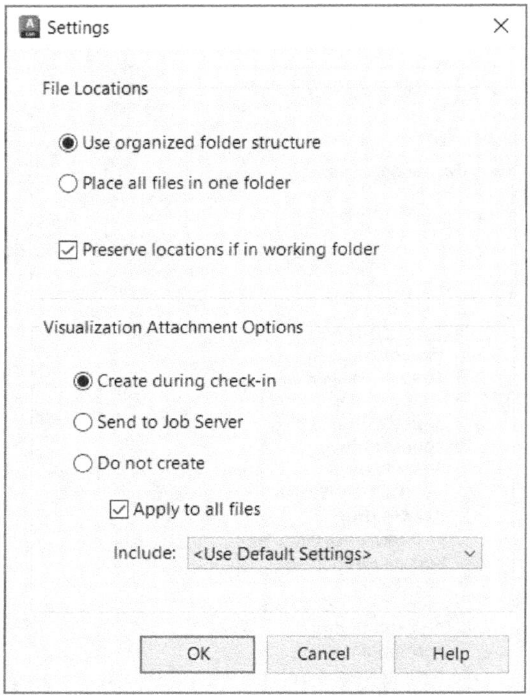

Figure 7–31

6. Select **OK** in the *Settings* dialog box. You can also move the cursor over the icon in the *Check In Folder* dialog box to see that the DWF Create visualization attachment option is toggled On.
7. Select **OK** to check the files in to the vault.
8. Select **OK** after confirming results in the *Check In Details* dialog box.

Task 3: View vault status of the drawing and Xref.

1. Open the *EXTERNAL REFERENCES* palette. The vault status icons are now displaying white circles without the plus signs, indicating that they have been added to the vault, and that the copy you are working on is the latest version, as shown in Figure 7–32.

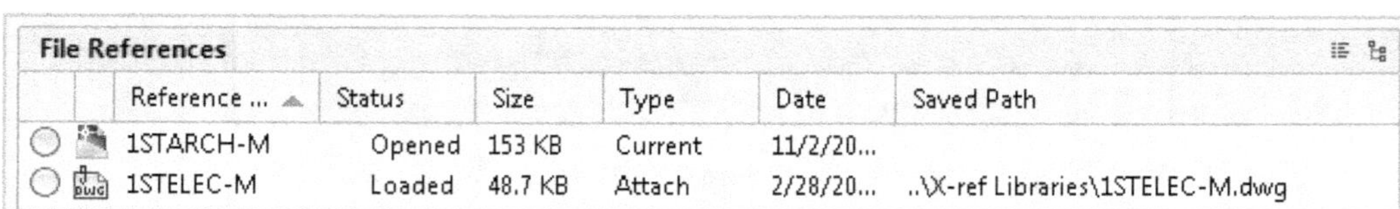

Figure 7–32

Task 4: Open a drawing from a second folder.

1. Open **Site Survey-done.dwg** from ...*\vault_work\AutoCAD Designs C*.
2. Display the *EXTERNAL REFERENCES* palette as shown in Figure 7–33.

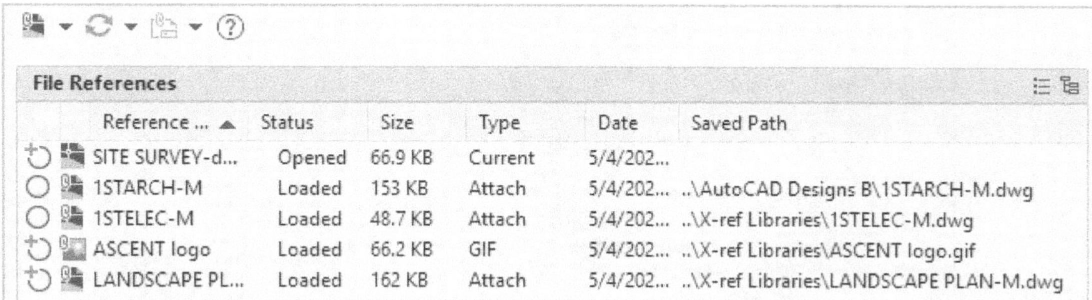

Figure 7–33

3. The **Site Survey-done.dwg** references the **1STELEC-M Xref** and the **1STARCH-M.dwg,** which are indicated as already being added to the vault.

Task 5: Check in the second folder of AutoCAD files into the vault.

In this task, you check in another folder of AutoCAD files into the vault.

1. Select **Vault Server>Check In Folder** from the Application Menu.
2. Select ...*\vault_work\AutoCAD Designs C* as the folder to check in and type **First submission to Vault** in the *comments* area. The vault target location is automatically selected as *$/AutoCAD Designs C*.
3. Select **OK**.

4. The *Check in Folder* dialog box appears showing all files to be added to the vault, including the folder structure that is used and/or created, as shown in Figure 7–34.

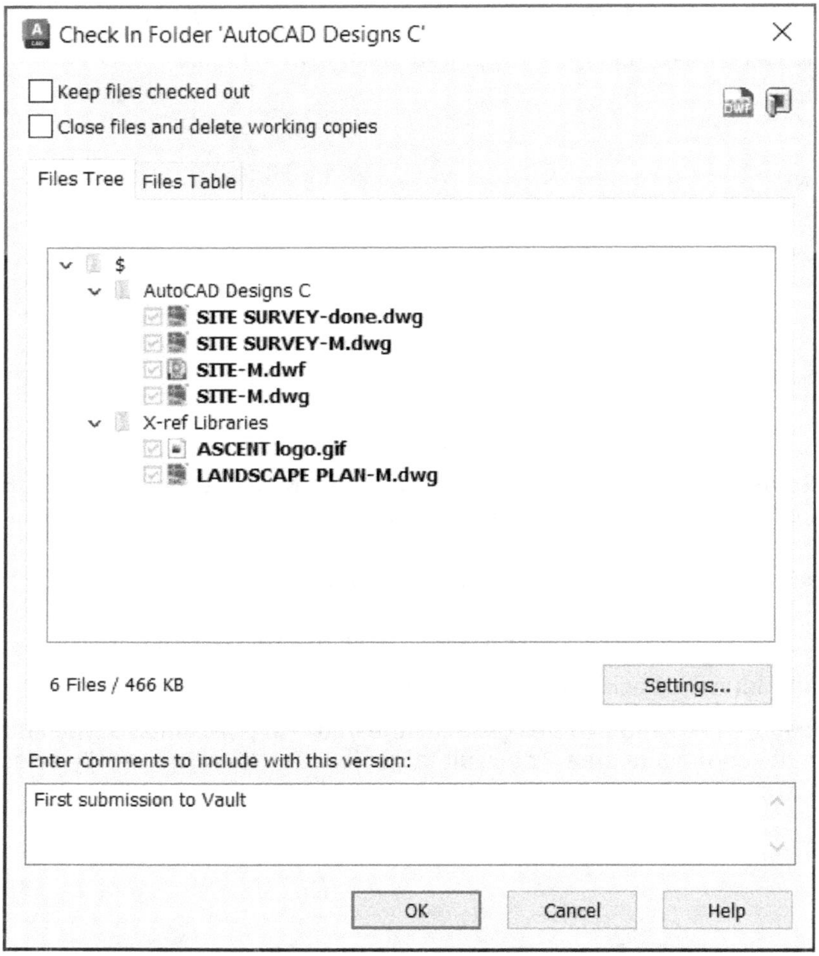

Figure 7–34

5. Select **OK** to add the files to the vault.
6. Select **OK** after confirming the results in the *Check In Details* dialog box.
7. Close the two drawings.

Task 6: Verify files in the vault using the Autodesk Vault client.

In this task, you verify that the files in the folder have been added to the vault and the relationships have been maintained.

1. If Autodesk Vault was closed, launch it again by clicking Autodesk Vault in the *Vault* tab> *Access* panel, as shown in Figure 7–35.

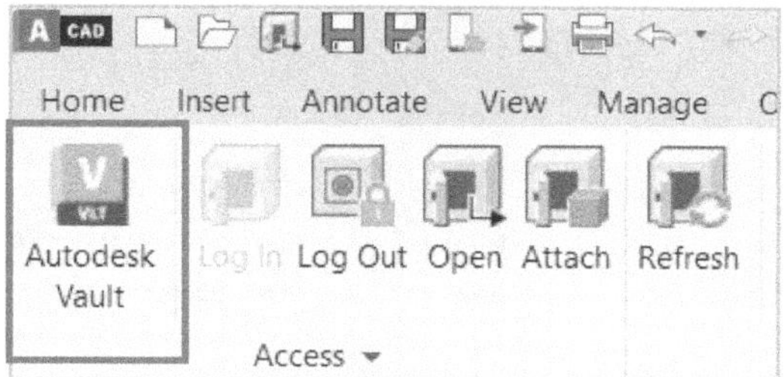

Figure 7–35

2. Log in as **user1** with no password.
3. Select  (Refresh) to update the vault folders.
4. In the Navigation pane, the *AutoCAD Designs B*, *AutoCAD Designs C*, and *X-ref Libraries* folders were created under *$* during the **Check In Folder** operations.
5. Select *$/AutoCAD Designs B*.
6. Select the *History* tab for several of the files to see that they are all Version 1 since they were all just added to the Vault for the first time.
7. Select **1STARCH-M.dwg**. Select the *View* tab in the Preview pane. Select the Version 1 thumbnail. The drawing is displayed, as shown in Figure 7–36, because a .DWF was created during the process of adding the files.

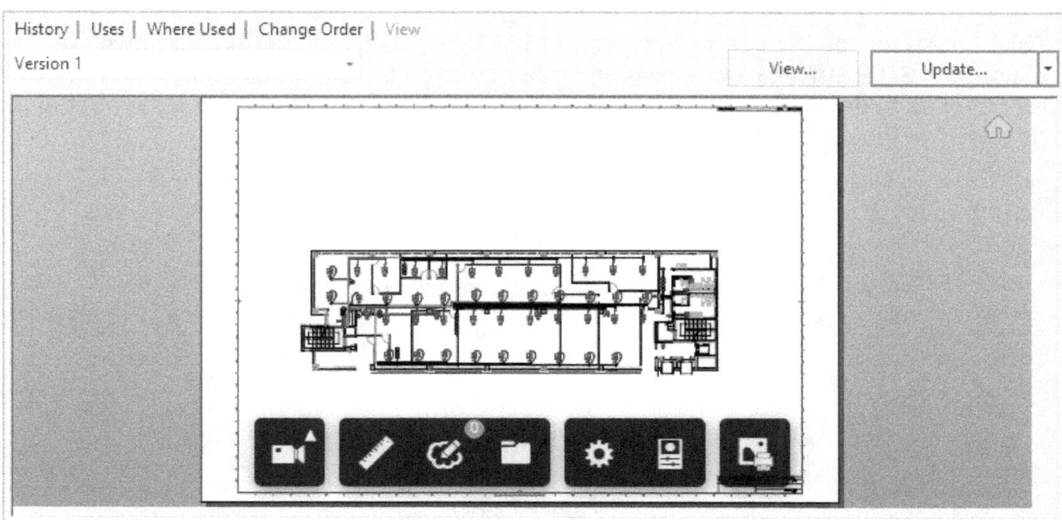

Figure 7–36

8. Select the *Where Used* tab in the Preview pane. Relationships have been maintained between the files, as shown in Figure 7–37.

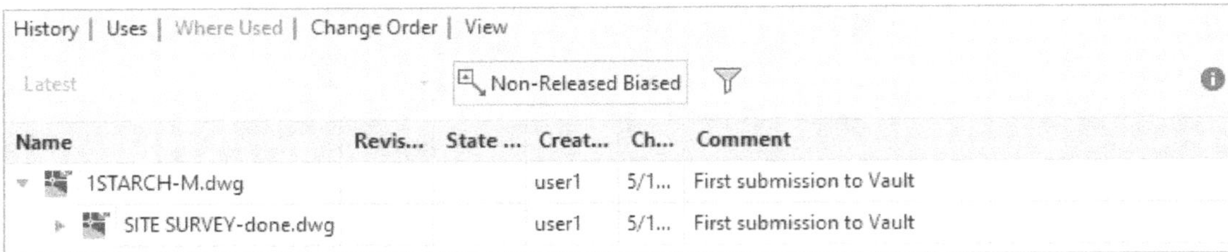

Figure 7–37

9. Select the *Uses* tab in the Preview pane. **1STELEC-M.dwg** is a child of **1STARCH-M.dwg** and their relationship was maintained upon check in, as shown in Figure 7–38.

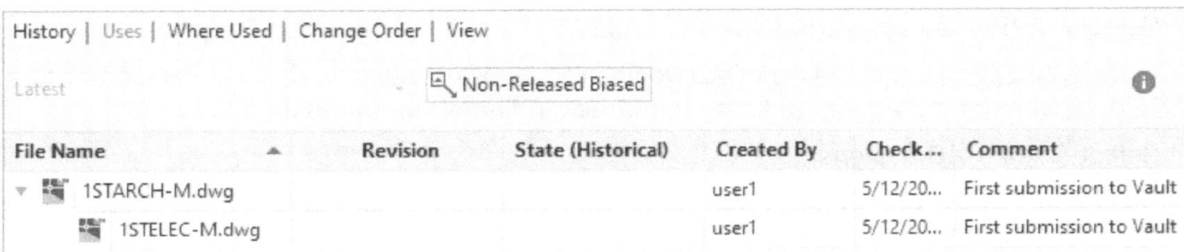

Figure 7–38

10. Select *$/AutoCAD Designs C* in the Navigation pane and select **SITE SURVEY-done.dwg** in the Main Table.

11. Select the *Uses* tab in the Preview pane. **1STARCH-M.dwg** and **1STELEC.M.dwg** are children of **SITE SURVEY-done.dwg** and other children are being referenced from the *$/X-ref Libraries* folder with their relationships intact after the two **Check In Folder** operations, as shown in Figure 7–39.

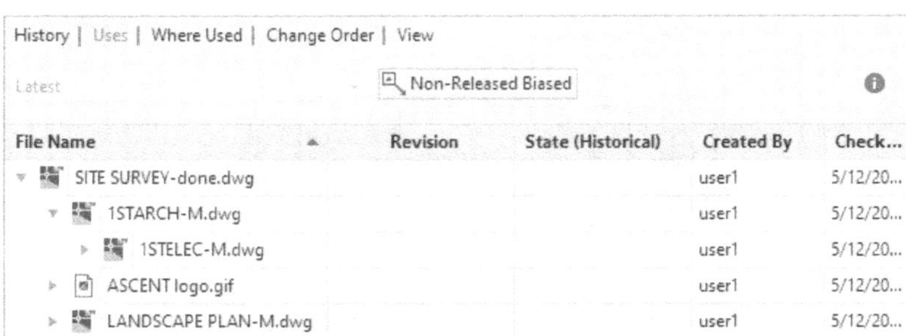

Figure 7–39

End of practice

Practice 7c
Use Open from Vault and Attach from Vault

Practice Objectives

- Use **Open from Vault** to open an AutoCAD drawing from the vault.
- Use **Attach from Vault** to attach a reference file from the vault to an AutoCAD drawing.

In this practice, you use **Open from Vault** to open an AutoCAD design from the vault. You will then use **Attach from Vault** to attach an Xref from the vault to an AutoCAD drawing.

Task 1: Open an AutoCAD drawing from the vault.

In this task, you open **Mold Assembly.dwg** using the **Open from Vault** command.

1. In AutoCAD, open any template.
2. From the *Vault* tab>*Access* panel, click  (Open from Vault). It opens directly into the vault folder structure.
3. Browse to the *$/AutoCAD Designs B* vault folder and then select the **Mold Assembly.dwg**, as shown in Figure 7–40.

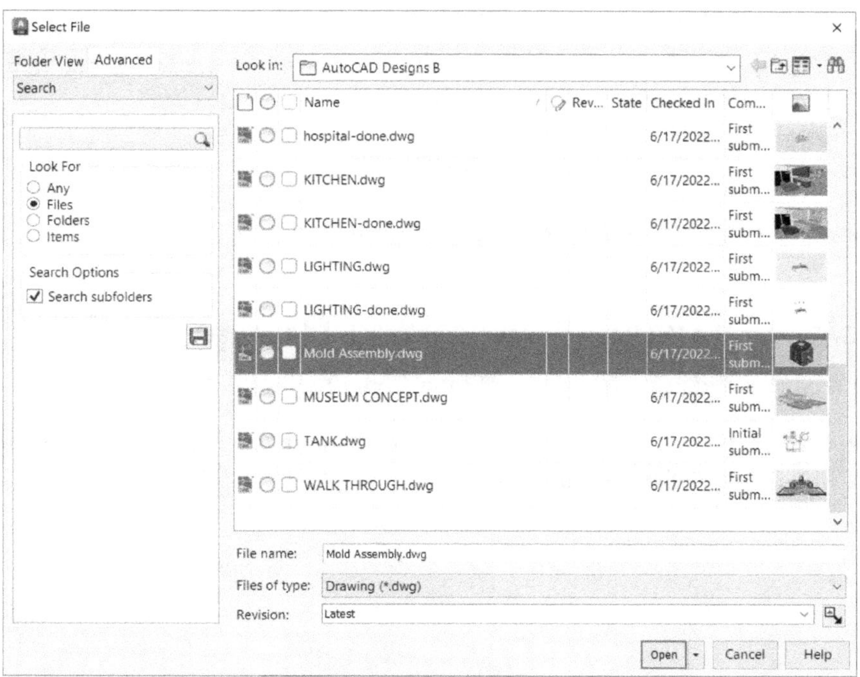

Figure 7–40

4. Select **Open**.
5. A warning message appears indicating that the file has not been checked out and prompts whether you want to check it out now, as shown in Figure 7–41.

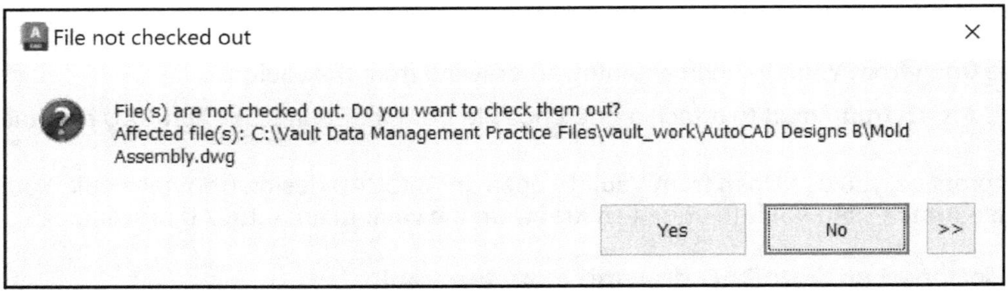

Figure 7–41

6. Select **Yes** to check out the drawing.
7. Open the *EXTERNAL REFERENCES* palette. The vault status icon displays a white circle with a check mark indicating that the file is checked out to you and is the latest version, as shown in Figure 7–42.

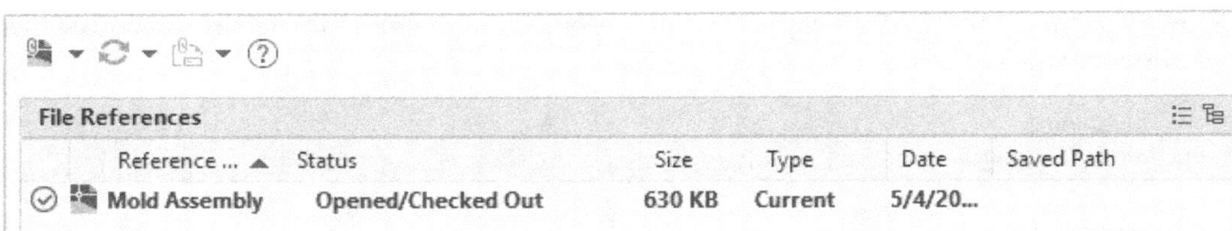

Figure 7–42

Task 2: Attach an external reference from the vault to a drawing.

1. In AutoCAD, from the *Vault* tab>*Access* panel, click (Attach from Vault).

   Note: *You can also access* ***Attach from Vault*** *from the EXTERNAL REFERENCES palette.*

2. In the *Select File* dialog box, select Files of type to **All image files** then browse to *$/X-ref Libraries* and select **ASCENT logo.gif**, as shown in Figure 7–43.

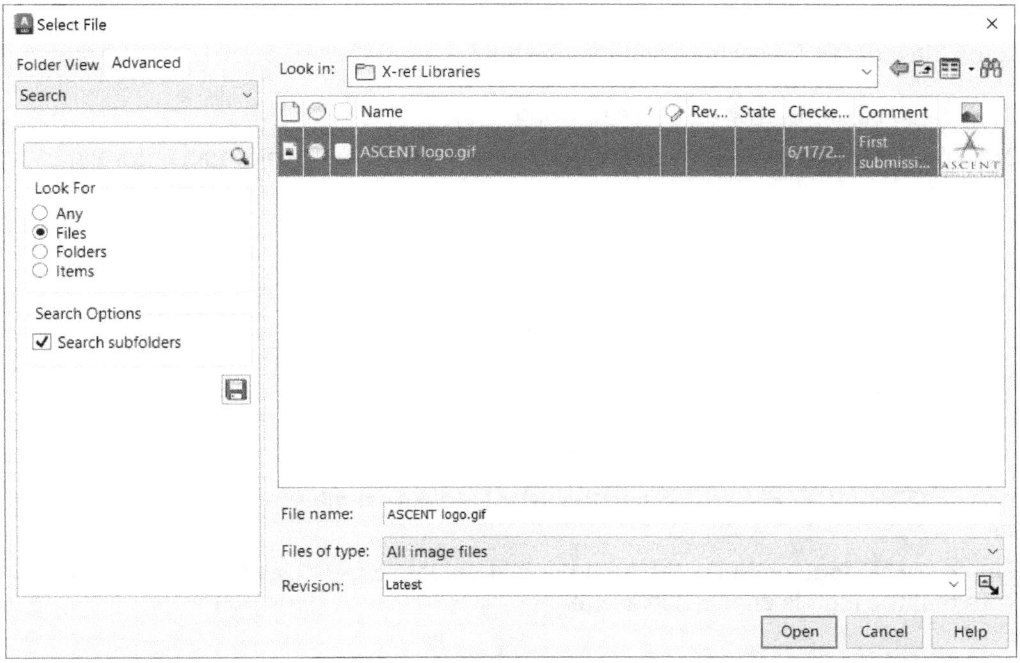

Figure 7–43

3. Select **Open** and **Yes** to check out.
4. To place the Xref, select the **Specify on-screen** option in the *Attach Image* dialog box as shown in Figure 7–44.

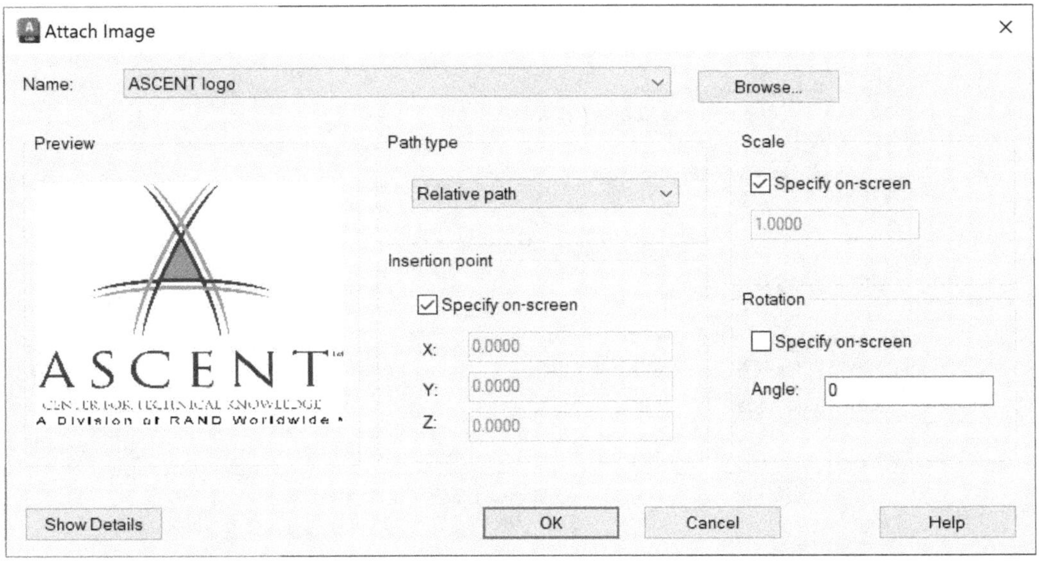

Figure 7–44

5. Click **OK**.
6. Place the logo Xref anywhere on the assembly.
7. Click to save the change to the drawing.
8. Open the *EXTERNAL REFERENCES* palette. The vault status displays as shown in Figure 7–45.

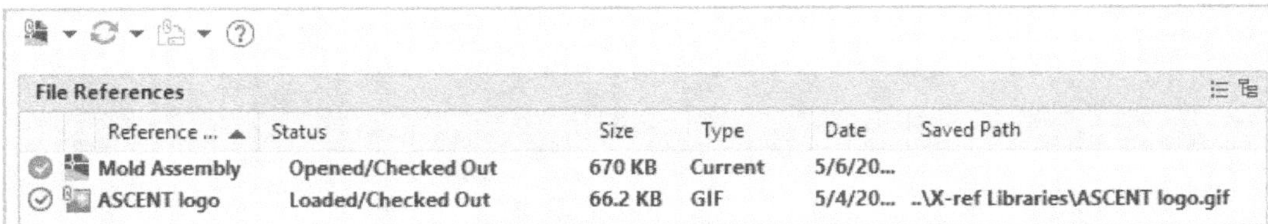

Figure 7–45

9. In the *EXTERNAL REFERENCES* palette, select **Mold Assembly**, right-click, and click **Check In**.
10. Type **ASCENT logo added** in the comments area and click **OK**, as shown in Figure 7–46. Note that the logo is checked in as well.

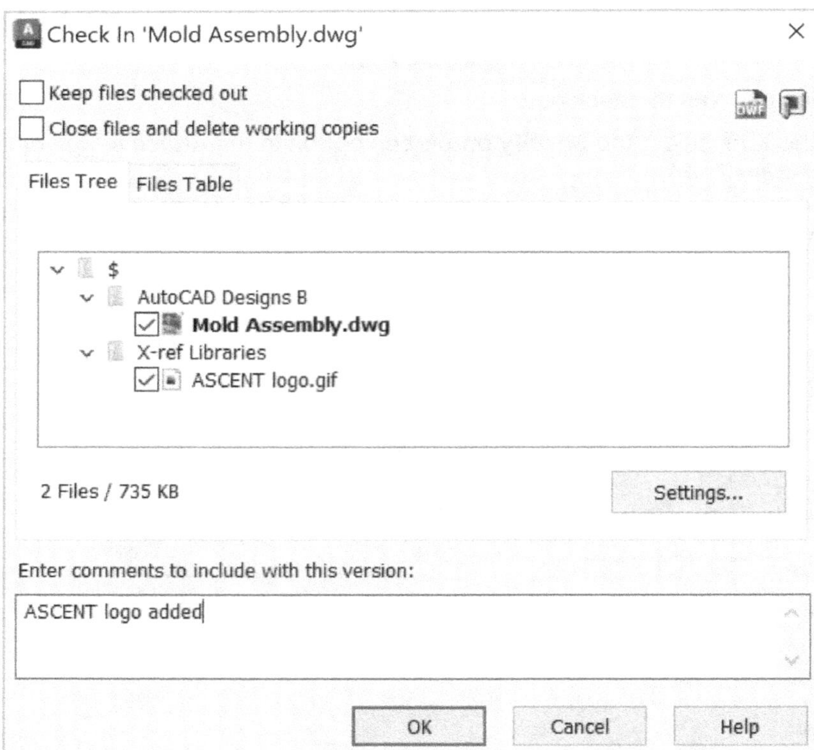

Figure 7–46

11. Click **Yes** to save and continue.
12. Close **Mold Assembly**.
13. In Autodesk Vault, select **Mold Assembly.dwg** from the *$/AutoCAD Designs B* vault folder.
14. In the *View* tab, select a thumbnail, then display both **Version 1** and **Version 2** of the design using the *Version* drop-down list, as shown in Figure 7–47.

Figure 7–47

Note: *Selecting a version to view may cause the Autodesk Vault application to crash. This is a known issue and as of the release of this guide, the issue has not been resolved. For more details, refer to this link - https://www.autodesk.com/support/technical/article/caas/sfdcarticles/sfdcarticles/Vault-Professional-2027-Client-crashes-silently-after-Windows-Lock-Unlock-or-Click-in-client-session-after-View.html*

15. Notice that the logo displays in **Version 2**.

End of practice

7.4 Modifying an AutoCAD Design

The vault enables multiple users to access the same design project and work on different parts of the design.

For example, **user1** can be working on Xref A of a drawing and user2 on Xref B, which is used in the same drawing. They can both retrieve a read-only copy of the host drawing to their working folders and only check out the Xref for modification. If you try to check out a file that has already been checked out to someone else, you will see that Check Out is grayed out and cannot be selected.

This section discusses how to make modifications to an AutoCAD design that is in a Work In Progress (WIP) lifecycle state and not released. See ***7.5 Releasing an AutoCAD Design*** and ***7.6 Revise a Released AutoCAD Design*** to learn how to release an AutoCAD design and make changes to a released AutoCAD design.

How To: Modify an AutoCAD Design

1. In AutoCAD, open the file(s) you want to modify using (Open from Vault) in the *Vault* tab>*Access* panel in the ribbon. Expand **Open** and select **Open (Check Out)**, which checks out just the assembly file, or **Open (Check Out All)** to check out all children.
    - If your local working folder contains the latest version because you performed a **Get** or **Open**, and then saved the file and didn't check it back into Vault, use the standard open procedure, such as Open in the Quick Access Toolbar, and navigate to your local working folder to open the file.
    - If you try to modify a file that has not yet been checked out, a message box opens prompting you to do so, as shown in Figure 7–48.

    Note: *To change the settings for the* ***File Edit*** *prompt, in the Vault tab>File Status panel, select* ***Vault Options****, click* ***Prompts...*** *and change the response or frequency for* ***File Edit****.*

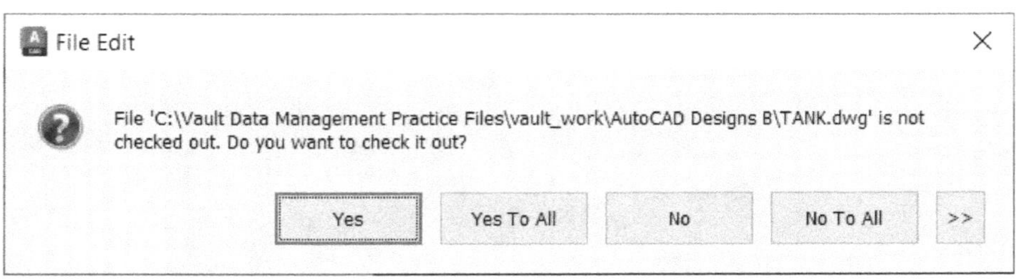

Figure 7–48

2. Once you click Open, the file is open and checked out.

- You might get a prompt indicating the properties are out of date (as shown in Figure 7–49), click **Yes** to update the properties when checking out the files. Anytime properties are updated, the software recognizes it as an update and wants to keep the files up-to-date.

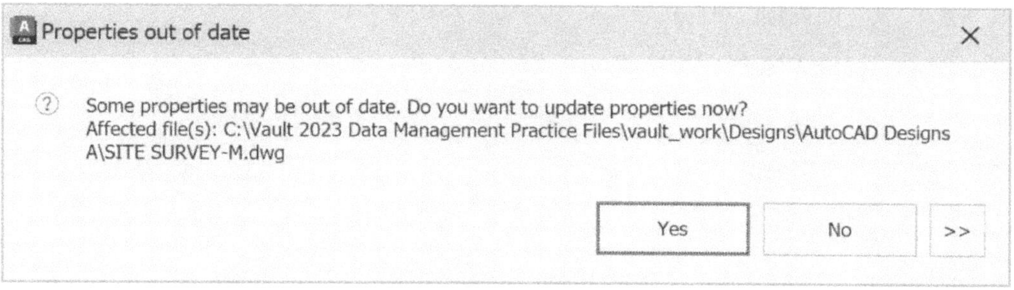

Figure 7–49

3. Use the *EXTERNAL REFERENCES* palette, shown in Figure 7–50, to review the file status before you perform modifications. If a file status is not proper, right-click on it and select **Refresh File**.

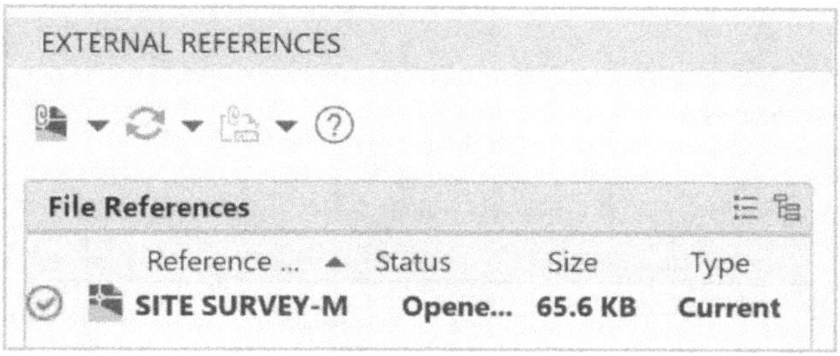

Figure 7–50

4. Once the file(s) are checked out, make modifications as you normally would.
5. After modifications are performed, a file must be saved in AutoCAD before a **Check In** operation can be performed. By default, if you try to close a checked out AutoCAD file without checking it in, the system prompts you to save the file and check it in.
6. Check In the file(s) using the *Vault* tab>*Access* panel>**Check In**, or right-click on the file(s) in the *EXTERNAL REFERENCES* palette and click **Check In**.

7. The *Check In* dialog box displays, as shown in Figure 7–51.

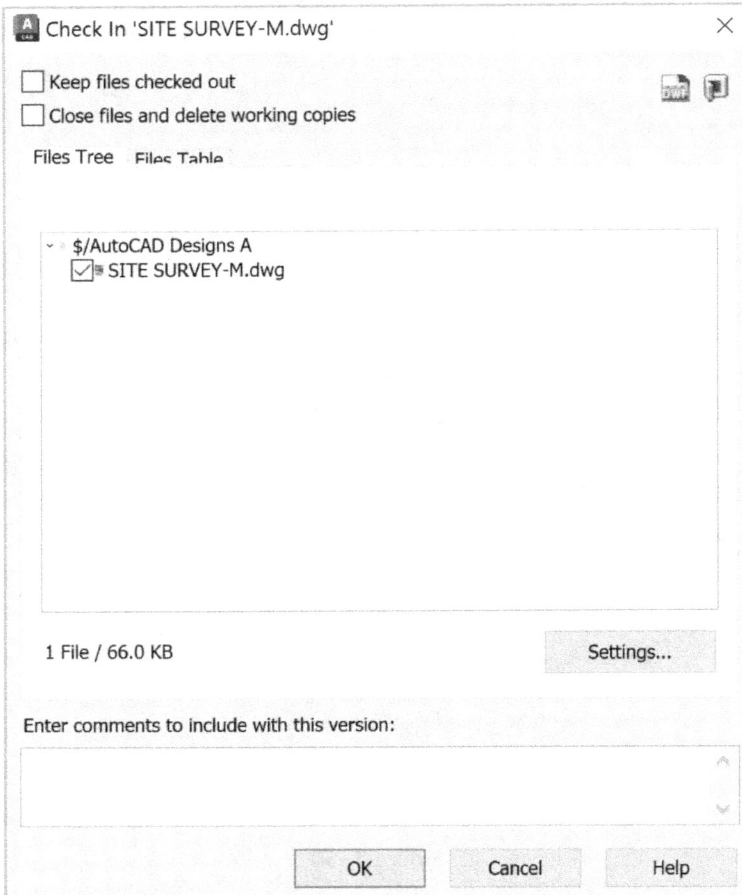

Figure 7–51

- Select **Keep files checked out** if you want to keep the files checked out for further modifications.
- Select **Close files and delete working copies** to remove the local copy after the file is checked into the vault. This is a recommended best practice. If required, close the file in the AutoCAD software.

- Click **Settings** to control the visualization attachment options, as shown in Figure 7–52.

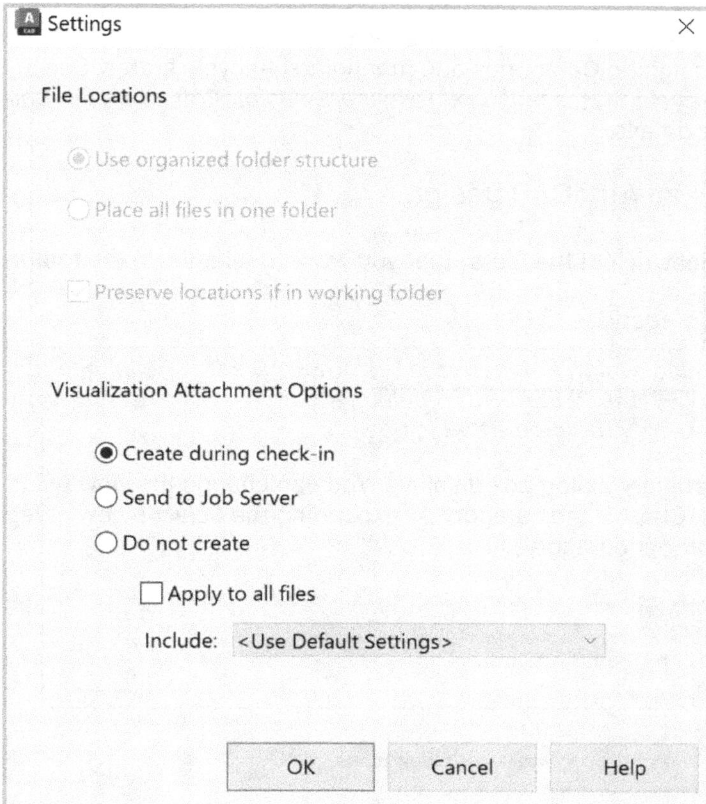

Figure 7–52

- In the *Enter comments to include...* area, enter any notes regarding this version.

8. Click **OK** to complete the operation.

7.5 Releasing an AutoCAD Design

Once the AutoCAD design is complete, it needs to be released in the Vault. Prepping files for release includes assigning Categories and managing Lifecycle states. See ***5.10 Categories*** and ***5.11 Changing Lifecycle States and Next Release/Revision Procedures*** in ***Chapter 5 Working with Files*** for more details.

How To: Release an AutoCAD Design

1. In the Vault Client, select the file(s) that you want to release. In the toolbar, select  (Change Category...).

   Note: *You can also assign Categories in the AutoCAD software in the Vault tab>Control panel or the EXTERNAL REFERENCES palette>right-click>Change Category. This only changes the category for the file that is open.*

2. The *Change Category* dialog box displays. You can change the view using the icons shown in Figure 7–53. Change the category by expanding the *Select a new category:* area and selecting the proper category.

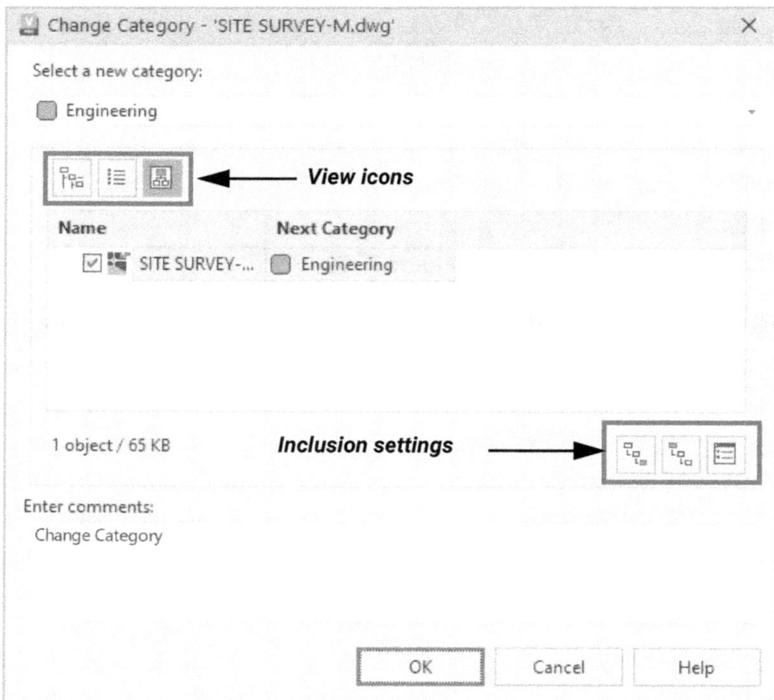

Figure 7–53

3. You can configure the inclusion options using the three inclusion settings shown previously in Figure 7–53.

   - Select (Include Dependents) to include the children of assembly files.
   - Select (Include Parents) to include the parents of part files or subassemblies.
   - Click (Settings) to control the inclusion settings of the children, parents, and related documentation of the selected files. By default, the related documentation is included, as shown in Figure 7–54.

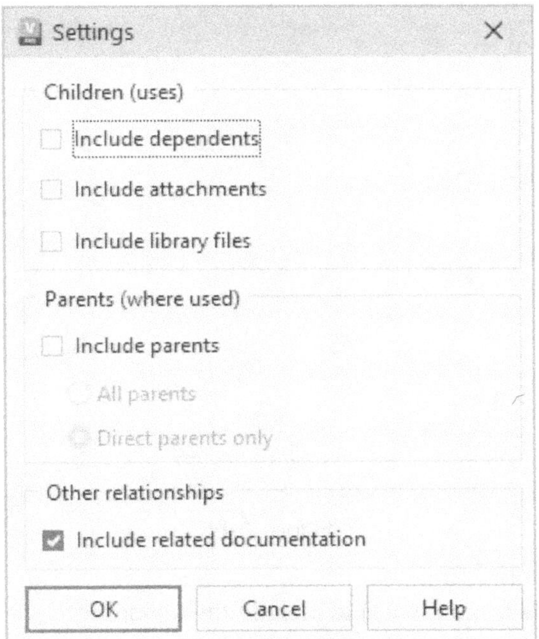

Figure 7–54

   - In the *Enter comments to include...* area, "Change Category" is auto filled.

4. Click **OK** to complete the operation.
5. Select all of the files again and in the toolbar, select (Change State...).

6. The *Change State* dialog box displays. You can change the view using the icons shown in Figure 7–55.

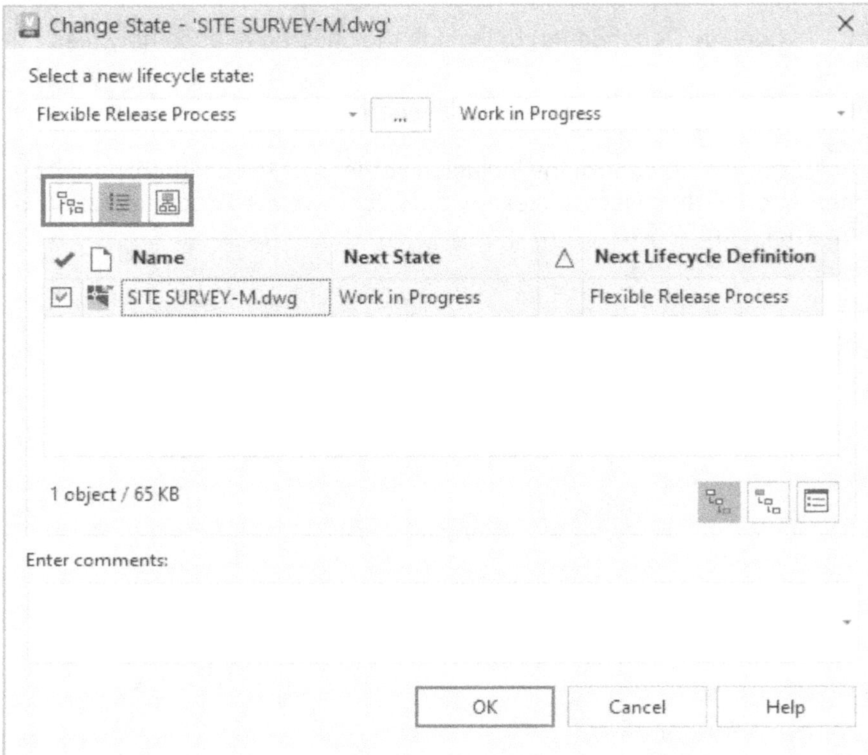

Figure 7–55

- Select (Include Dependents) to include the children.
- Select (Include Parents) to include the parents.
- Click (Settings) to control the inclusion settings of the children, parents, and related documentation of the selected files. By default, the children the related documentation is included, as shown in Figure 7–56.

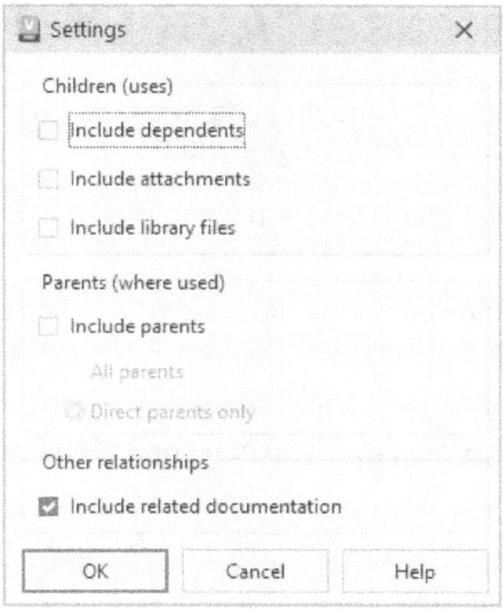

Figure 7–56

7. Expand the *Work in Progress* drop-down list and click ***Released***, as shown in Figure 7–57.

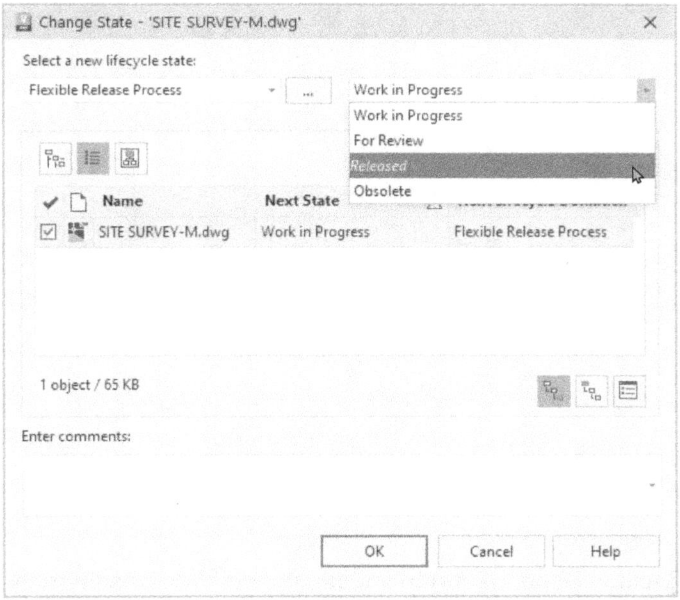

Figure 7–57

- In the *Enter comments to include...* area, "Released to manufacturing" is auto filled.

8. Click **OK** to complete the operation.

- Once the files are released, they will have to be revised if changes are required.

7.6 Revise a Released AutoCAD Design

Once the AutoCAD design is released and it needs to be modified, the lifecycle state has to be changed before the files can be checked out and edited.

1. In the Vault Client, select the file(s) that you want to edit. In the toolbar, select (Change State...).

   Note: *You can also change the state of a file in AutoCAD via Vault tab>Control panel or by right-clicking on the file in the EXTERNAL REFERENCES palette and selecting **Change State**.*

2. The *Change State* dialog box displays. You can change the view using the icons shown in Figure 7–58.

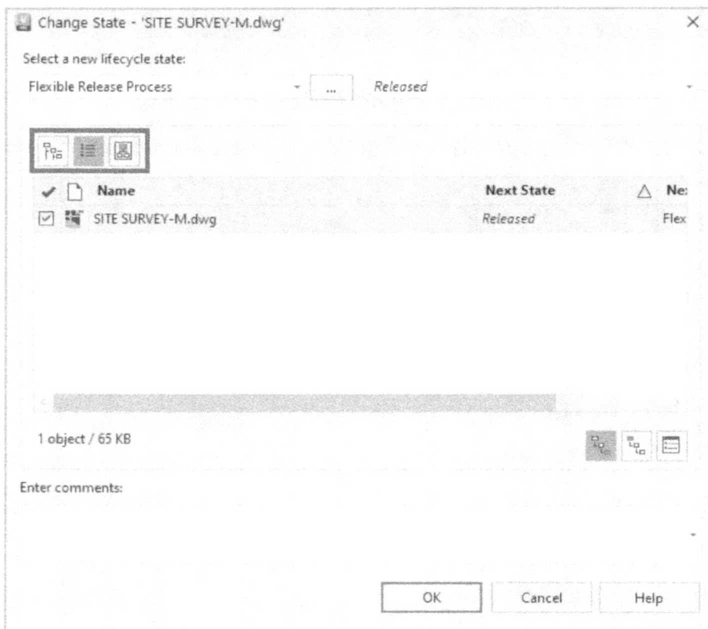

Figure 7–58

- Select (Include Dependents) to include the children of assembly files.
- Select (Include Parents) to include the parents of part files or subassemblies.
- Click (Settings) to control the inclusion settings of the children, parents, and related documentation of the selected files. By default, the children the related documentation is included, as shown in Figure 7–59.

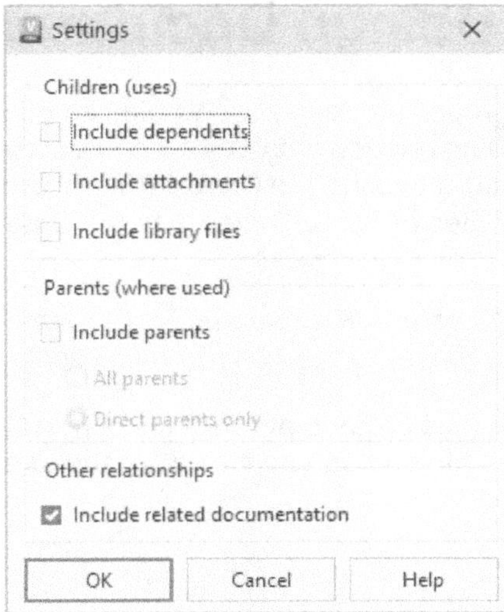

Figure 7–59

3. Expand the *Released* drop-down list and click **Work in Progress**, as shown in Figure 7–60.

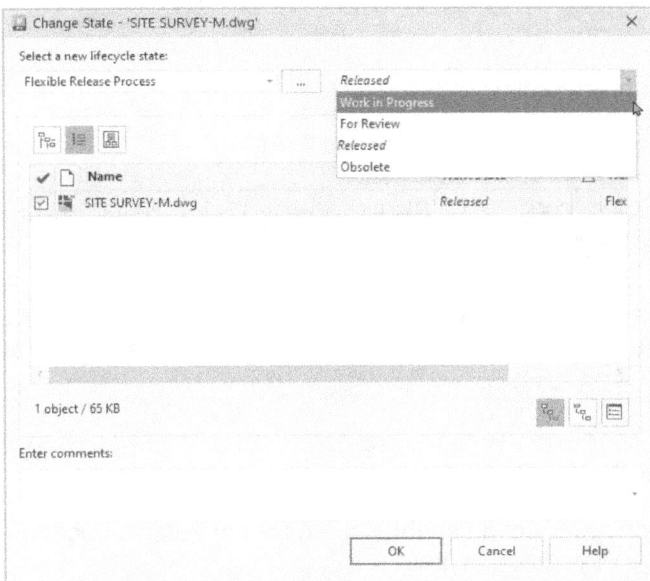

Figure 7–60

- In the *Enter comments to include...* area, "Available for editing" is auto filled.

4. Click **OK** to complete the operation.

Check out the files, make the modifications, check the files in and then change the state to ***Released***.

7.7 Accelerate Design Documentation

You can automatically publish your Autodesk 2D CAD files as PDF or DXF files and 3D CAD files as DXF or STEP files during design release or at any other lifecycle state. You can also manually create a PDF or DXF of a 2D CAD file using the **Create PDF or Create DXF** command. To manually created DXF or STEP files of 3D CAD files, use the **Create DXF** or **Create STEP** command.

> ***Note:*** *To be able to use the **Create PDF**, **Create DXF**, or **Create STEP** commands, you must have the required access privileges set by your administrator.*

By default, PDF, DXF, and STEP files created automatically from 2D CAD or 3D CAD files are attached to the 2D or 3D design file and can be viewed in the *Uses* tab as an attachment, as shown in Figure 7–61.

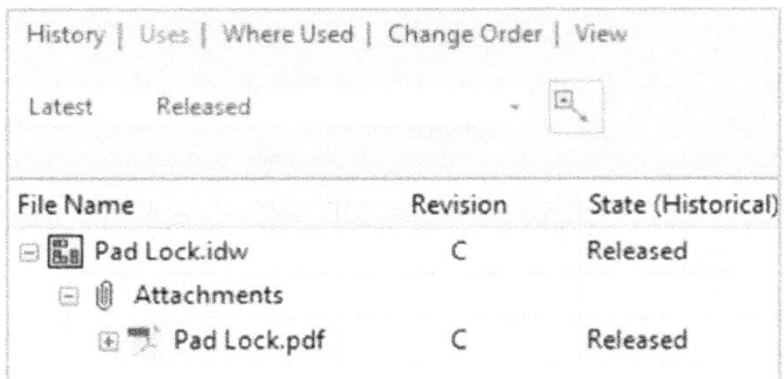

Figure 7–61

How To: Create a PDF, DXF, or STEP Manually Using the Create PDF, Create DXF, or Create STEP Command

1. In Autodesk Vault Client, select the file in the Main table, then select **Actions>Create** and select the desired option or right-click>**Create** and select the **desired option**.
2. The PDF, DXF, or STEP is created.

   > ***Note:*** *By default, automatically generated PDF, DXF, and STEP files are hidden. Select **Tools>Options** to display hidden files.*

   The location of the file depends on the setting for the Publish Location set by the administrator. The three options are:

   - **Save in Vault (local copies will not be created)**: Select to save your published file in Vault.
   - **Save on a local drive in one folder:** Select to store all published files in a single folder on the local computer.
   - **Save on local drive using the Vault folder structure:** Select to store local copies of the files in a folder structure that duplicates the structure used in Vault Client.

Practice 7d
Modify an AutoCAD Design

Practice Objectives

- Locate and check out an AutoCAD drawing.
- Modify an AutoCAD drawing and check it back into the vault.
- Use the **Undo Check Out** command to undo the changes made while the drawing was checked out.

In this practice, you check out an AutoCAD drawing, make changes, and then check it back into the vault. You then make some additional changes and use the **Undo Check Out** command to undo your changes.

Task 1: Open a drawing from the vault.

1. In AutoCAD, click (Open from the vault) in the *Vault* tab>*Access* panel.
2. Browse to the *$/AutoCAD Designs B* vault folder and select **WALK THROUGH.dwg**. Select **Open**.
3. Select **Yes** to check out the drawing and select **Yes** to update the properties.

Task 2: Modify the drawing, save, and check in.

In this task, you make a change to the drawing by removing the fountain. You then save the changes and check back in the drawing.

1. In AutoCAD, select the fountain, and press <Delete> to erase it, as shown in Figure 7–62.

Figure 7–62

2. Save the changes.

3. Open the *EXTERNAL REFERENCES* palette to view the vault status icon of a green circle with a checkmark. This indicates that the file saved to the disk is more recent than the one in the vault and is checked out to you, as shown in Figure 7–63.

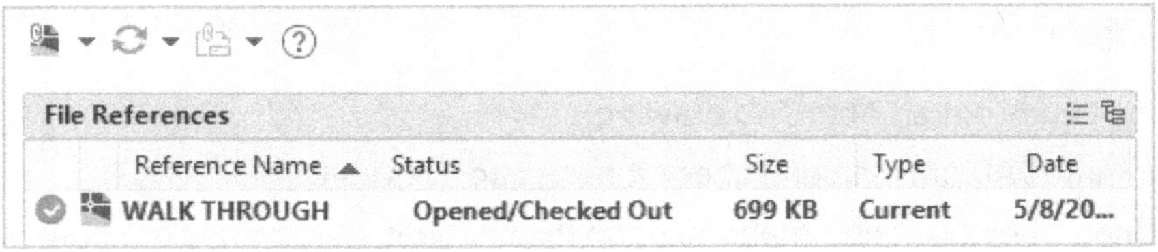

Figure 7–63

4. Hover the cursor over the Vault Status icon to view the tooltip.
5. In the *EXTERNAL REFERENCES* palette, select **WALK THROUGH**, right-click, and select **Check In**.
6. Type **Removed fountain** in the *Check In* dialog box comments area, as shown in Figure 7–64.

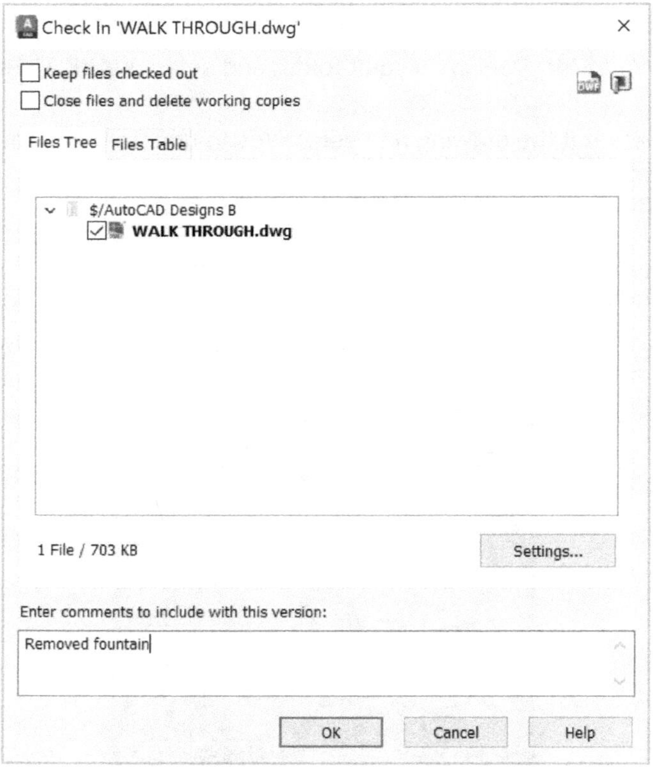

Figure 7–64

7. Click **OK**. The drawing remains on screen but is not checked out.

Task 3: Use Undo Check Out to undo your changes.

In this task, you remove the stairs of the drawing and then decide to replace the drawing with the latest version in the vault by selecting **Undo Check Out** in the *EXTERNAL REFERENCES* palette.

1. In the *EXTERNAL REFERENCES* palette, select **WALK THROUGH**, right-click, and click **Check Out**.
2. Remove the stairs in the drawing by selecting the stairs and pressing <Delete>.
3. You now decide you want to return to the version with the stairs. In the *EXTERNAL REFERENCES* palette, select **WALK THROUGH**, right-click, and click **Undo Check Out**.
4. Select **Yes** to confirm that you want to replace the drawing with the latest version in the vault. Notice that the stairs are now back in the drawing.
5. Close **WALK THROUGH.dwg**.

Task 4: View the version history in the Autodesk Vault client.

In this task, you view the version history in Autodesk Vault.

1. In AutoCAD, click (Autodesk Vault) in the *Vault* tab>*Access* panel.
2. In Autodesk Vault, click (Refresh).
3. Locate **WALK THROUGH.dwg**.

4. View the two versions in the *History* tab and note the comments, as shown in Figure 7–65.

Figure 7–65

End of practice

Practice 7e
Roll Back an AutoCAD Design

Practice Objective

- Use the **Get** command to retrieve a previous version of an AutoCAD design.

In this practice, you view the version history of a drawing in the vault. You then use the **Get** command to roll back the drawing to a previous version, since the changes in the latest version are no longer desired.

Task 1: View the version history of a drawing in the Autodesk Vault client.

1. In Autodesk Vault, log in as **user1**. Locate **Office.dwg** and view its version history in the *View* tab.
2. Compare the two versions of the drawing. The elevation view was removed in Version 2.

Task 2: Get the previous version of the drawing.

In this task, you use the **Get** command to retrieve Version 1 of Office.dwg with the elevation view added.

1. In Autodesk Vault, locate and select **Office.dwg**, right-click, and then click **Check Out**.

2. In the *History* tab, select version 1 of **Office.dwg** with the elevation view, right-click, and select **Get**, as shown in Figure 7–66.

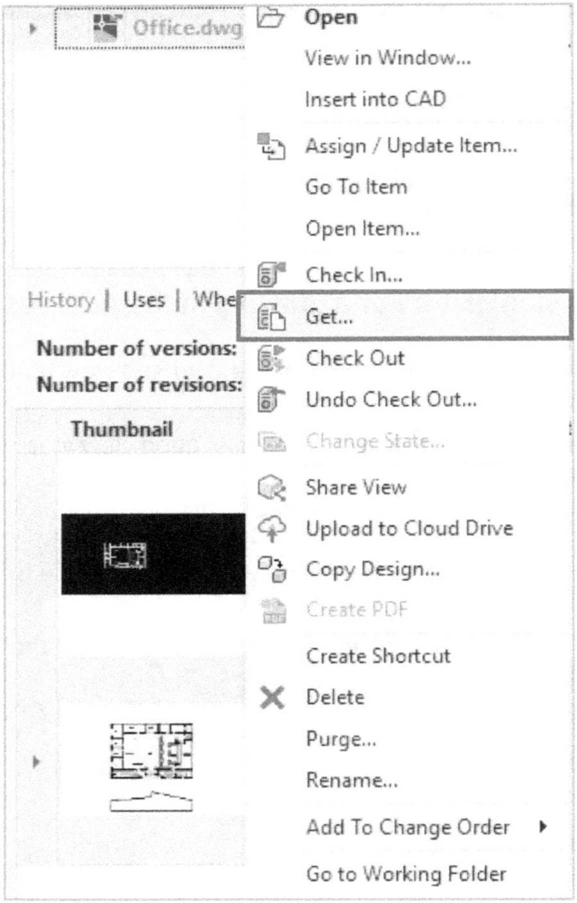

Figure 7–66

3. Click >> to expand the details of the *Get* dialog box.

4. Notice that it shows version 1 with the elevation view, as shown in Figure 7–67.

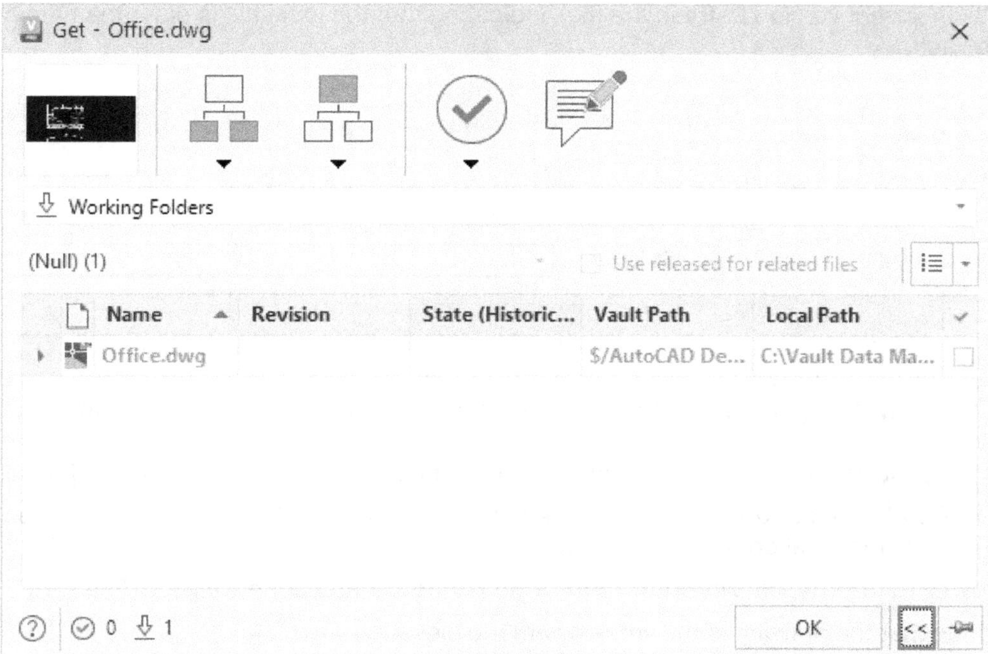

Figure 7–67

5. Click **OK** to copy the Version 1 file to your local working folder.
6. If prompted, click **Yes** to overwrite the file with data from the vault, as shown in Figure 7–68.

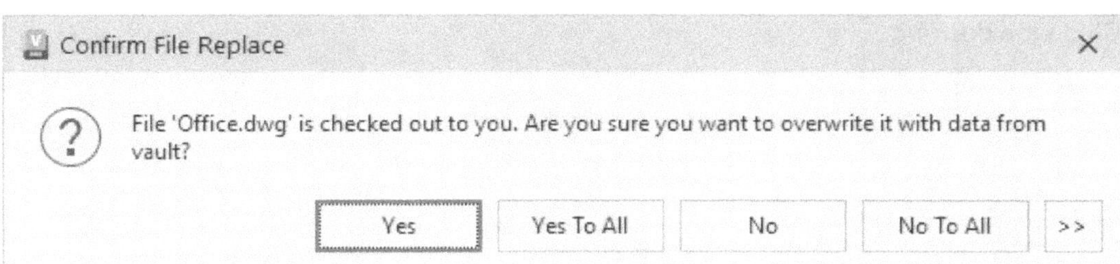

Figure 7–68

7. Notice that, as expected and as shown in Figure 7–69, the vault status icon changes to (Incorrect version Refresh the file), indicating that the local file is older than the one in the vault.

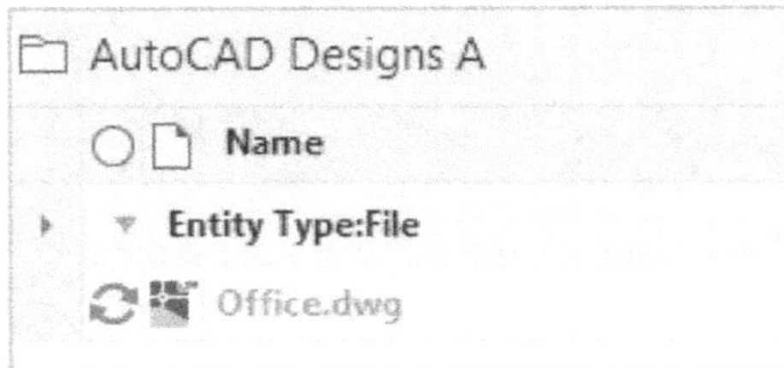

Figure 7–69

Task 3: Open the previous version in AutoCAD and perform a check in.

In this task, you open version 1 of **Office.dwg** into AutoCAD from the local working folder.

1. In AutoCAD, click **Open**. You are not selecting **Open from Vault**, because this time you want to retrieve the local copy of the drawing.
2. Browse to the ...*\vault_work\AutoCAD Designs A* folder and double-click **Office.dwg**.
3. Notice that the drawing is the version with the elevation view.
4. Open the *EXTERNAL REFERENCES* palette. The vault icon has changed there as well to (Incorrect version Refresh the file) indicating that it is older than the latest version in the vault.
5. Save the drawing and perform a Check In. Type **Rolled back to design with elevation** in the comments area, then click **OK**.
6. Close the drawing.

Task 4: View the drawing history in the Autodesk Vault client.

1. In Autodesk Vault, click the **Refresh** icon and view the version history of **Office.dwg** specifically to ensure that the latest version has the elevation view, as shown in Figure 7–70.

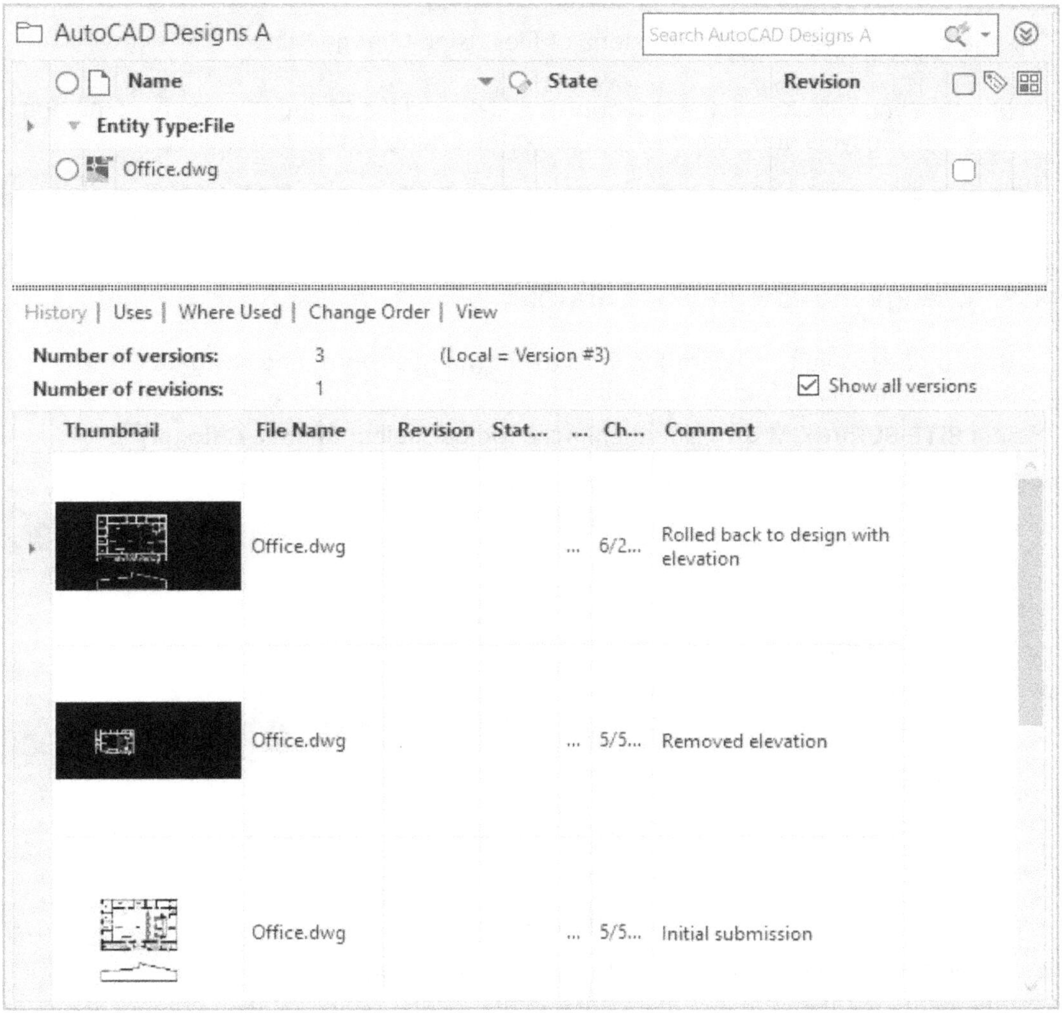

Figure 7–70

In summary, you retrieved an earlier version of the drawing, and then checked in the drawing, making it the latest version. This procedure is also known as the Leap Frog Approach.

End of practice

Practice 7f
Release an AutoCAD Design

Practice Objectives

- Change the category of a file using **Change Category**.
- Change the lifecycle state and revisions of files using **Change State**.

In this practice, you will change the category of a file using the **Change Category** command and then change its lifecycle state and revision using the **Change State** command.

> ***Note:*** *Typically, your files will already be assigned to a category and therefore, all that would be needed is to use the* ***Change State*** *command to release a file or set of files.*

Task 1: Change the category of a drawing.

1. In the Autodesk Vault software, log in as **user1** (no password) and navigate to the *$\AutoCAD Designs C* folder. Notice that the files have no State or Revision listed.
2. Select **SITE SURVEY-M.dwg**, and then in the toolbar, select **Change Category**.
3. Select **Engineering**, as shown in Figure 7–71.

Figure 7–71

4. Click **OK**. The *State* now displays as **Work In Progress** with a *Revision* of **A**.

Task 2: Release a drawing using Change State.

1. Select **SITE SURVEY-M.dwg**, right-click, and select **Change State**.
2. Select **Released** from the drop-down list. The comments automatically display *Released to manufacturing*, as shown in Figure 7–72.

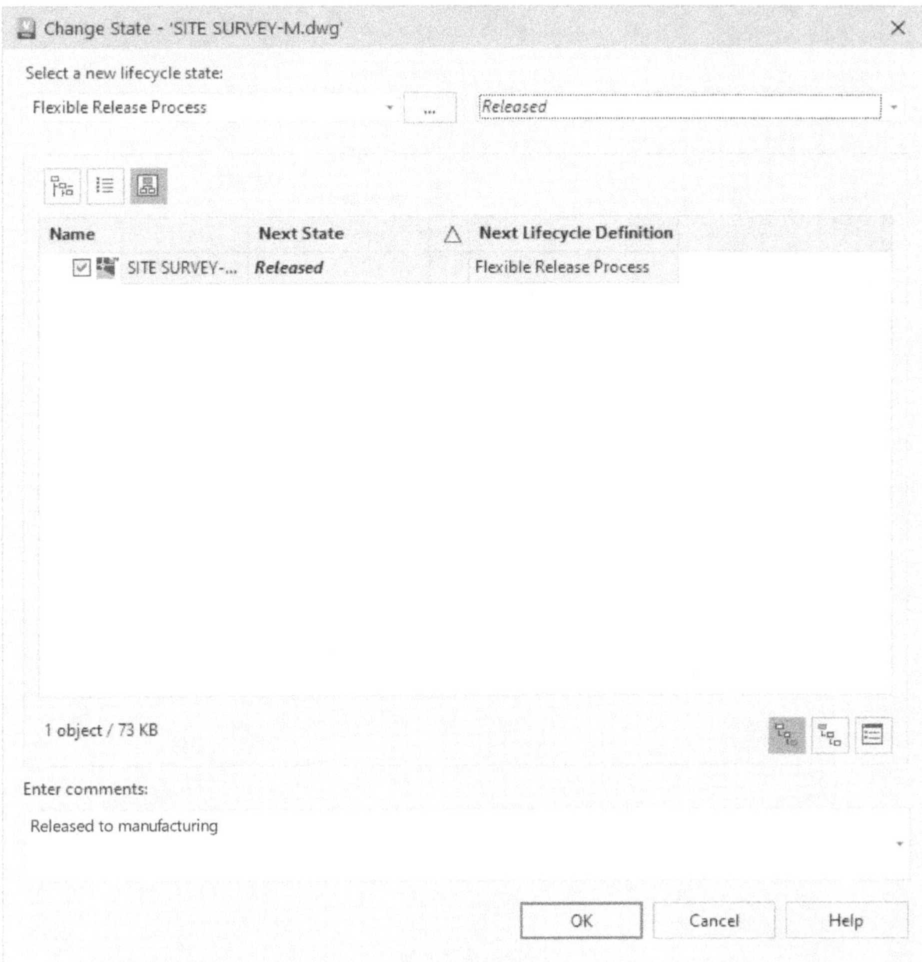

Figure 7–72

3. Click **OK**. The result displays as shown in Figure 7–73. Note that the file is still at *Revision* **A**, and the *State* is now set to **Released**.

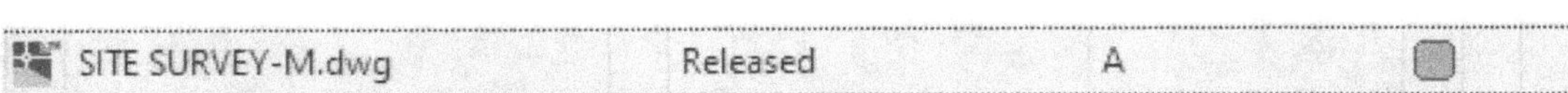

Figure 7–73

Task 3: Create a new revision of a drawing using Change State.

1. In Autodesk Vault, select **SITE SURVEY-M.dwg**, right-click, and select **Change State**.
2. Select **Work In Progress**, as shown in Figure 7–74.

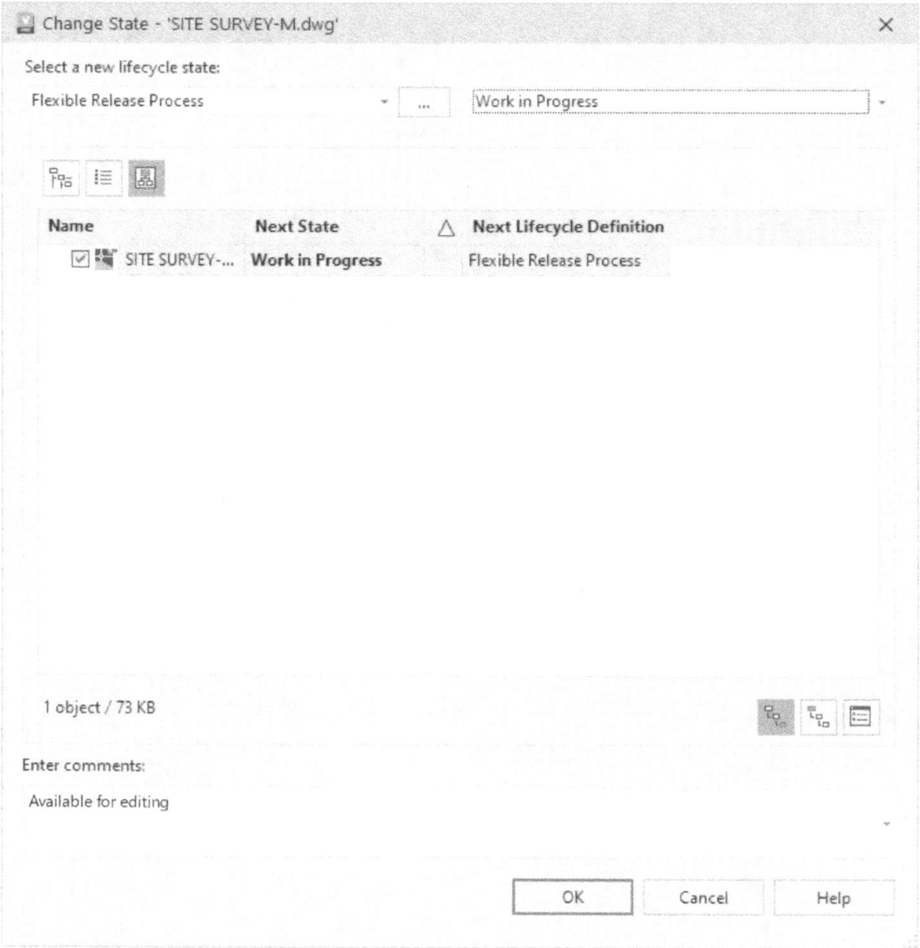

Figure 7–74

3. Click **OK**. The *Revision* changes to **B**.
4. Typically, you would now open the file in AutoCAD, check it out, make a design change and then check in the file.

End of practice

Chapter Review Questions

1. When you use **Open** from the *Vault* tab in AutoCAD, what are the three options to open your file that are located in the *Open* drop-down list? (Select all that apply.)
    a. Open (Check Out All)
    b. Open Read-Only
    c. Open (Check Out)
    d. Open (Check In)

2. The Xref Manager is another name for the *EXTERNAL REFERENCES* palette.
    a. True
    b. False

3. In the *EXTERNAL REFERENCES* palette, what does it mean when a file name appears with a white circle and plus sign beside it?
    a. The files are not yet in the vault.
    b. You are not working on the Latest Version.
    c. The file is not available for Check Out.
    d. All of the above.

4. What does the vault status icon look like when the version you are making changes to is the same as the one in the vault? (Select all that apply.)
    a. Question mark
    b. White circle with plus sign
    c. White circle with checkmark
    d. White circle

5. The **Check In Folder** command can be used to load your legacy data into the vault.
    a. True
    b. False

6. What does the red arrows ( ) vault status icon indicate?
    a. The file is locked and the local copy is up to date.
    b. The local copy is a historical revision of the leading revision in the vault.
    c. The file is not in the vault. Use Check In to add the file to the vault.
    d. The local copy does not match the latest version in the vault.

Command Summary

Button	Command	Location
	**Check In**	• **AutoCAD Ribbon:** *Vault* tab>*File Status* panel • Shortcut menu in the Vault Browser
	**Get**	• **Menu:** Actions>Get • **Shortcut:** (*right-click on selected file*) • **Standard Toolbar**
	**Check Out**	• **Menu:** Actions>Check Out • **Shortcut:** (*right-click on selected file*)
	**Undo Check Out**	• **AutoCAD Ribbon:** *Vault* tab>*File Status* panel • Shortcut menu in the Vault Browser
	**Change Category**	• **Menu:** Actions>Change Category • **Toolbar** (Behaviors)
	**Change State**	• **Menu:** Actions>Change State • **Toolbar** (Behaviors) • **Shortcut:** (*right-click on selected file*)

Chapter 8

Searching the Vault

Autodesk® Vault provides a variety of search methods and tools to locate files in the database. You can use a basic text string search or an advanced search on one or more file properties. Vaults can also be configured by the administrator to perform a full content search of known file formats. Specialized searches enable you to easily locate specific objects in a large database.

Learning Objectives

- Search for files in the Autodesk Vault software using the search methods of browsing folders, Quick Search, Basic Find, and Advanced Find.
- Differentiate between search methods.
- Create a saved search, edit a saved search, and run a saved search.
- Manage saved searches using **Rename**, **Copy**, and **Delete** operations.
- Create a search report.

8.1 Overview of Search Methods

Locating a file quickly and easily becomes important when design projects and databases contain a large number of files. Since Vault stores file properties and indexes them in the database, they can quickly be queried to locate a particular file.

Four main search operations enable you to locate files in the database: **Browse Folders**, **Quick Search**, **Basic Find**, and **Advanced Find.**

Use this table to compare search methods and decide which method best suits your needs.

Search Tool	Description
Browse Folders	Enables you to navigate the folder structure in the Navigation pane to find and view design folders and files. Click (Expand) to expand the folder structure and (Collapse) to collapse it (similar to File Explorer). 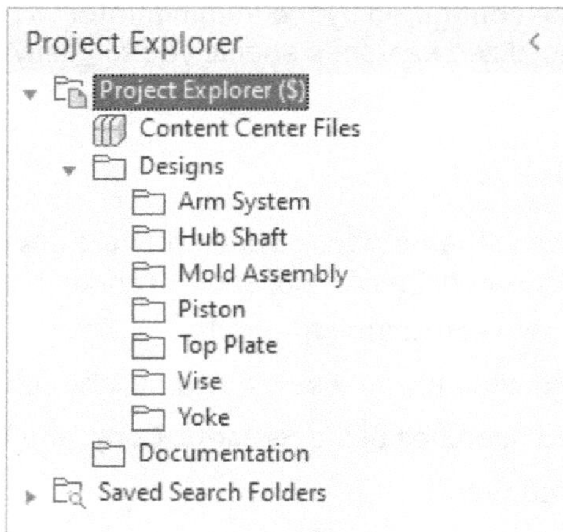
Quick Search	The Quick Search is located in the Main table title bar. Quick Search enables you to search on all of the file properties in the folders based on a specified text string.  You can also click (Expand the query builder) to set specific property search criteria and (Show search options menu) to access additional search options.

Search Tool	Description
Basic Find	The Basic Find is located in the *Find* dialog box and enables you to search by entering a specified text string. The search locates any file or object in the vault that contains the search string in any of the file properties. 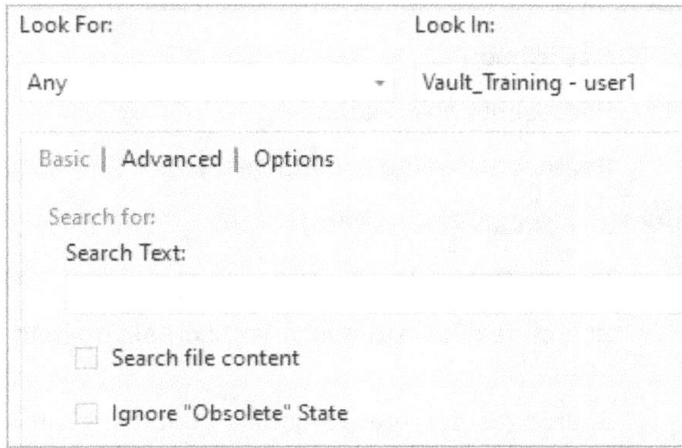
Advanced Find	The Advanced Find is located in the *Find* dialog box and enables you to create advanced searches by specifying file property criteria. The search locates the files and objects that match that criteria. 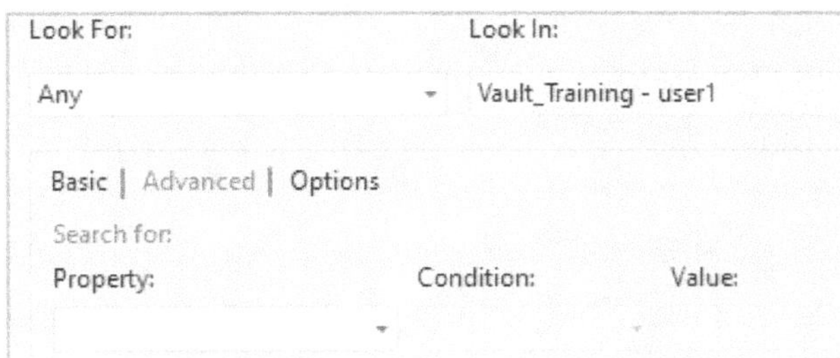

Searches defined using Quick Search or the *Find* dialog box (**Basic** or **Advanced**) can be saved to be used again. For quick access, any saved search can be added to *My Search Folders* in the Navigation pane.

You can also select the saved search for Inventor and AutoCAD from the corresponding dialog boxes shown below:

- *Open From Vault* and *Place From Vault* dialog boxes in the Autodesk Inventor software
- *Select File* dialog box in the AutoCAD software

Wildcard and Boolean Operators

You can use wildcards and boolean operators when specifying search criteria. Leading wildcards are supported.

Wildcard Operators	
Wildcard	**Description**
*	Represents any characters
?	Represents a single character
Boolean Operators (case insensitive)	
Operator	**Description**
and	Search results return anything containing both words. Searches for x AND y in any order.
or	Search results return anything containing either word. Searches for x OR y.
not	The search results exclude anything containing the specified word.
" "	The search results return everything containing the exact phrase in the quotes.

8.2 Browsing Folder Structure

In the Autodesk Vault software, you can browse the created folder structure to search for files. This is useful when you know the folder or design name and want to view its associated files.

To browse, click (Expand) to display the expanded folder structure. When the design folder is found and selected, its associated files display in the Main pane on the right side. An example of a selected design file is shown in Figure 8–1.

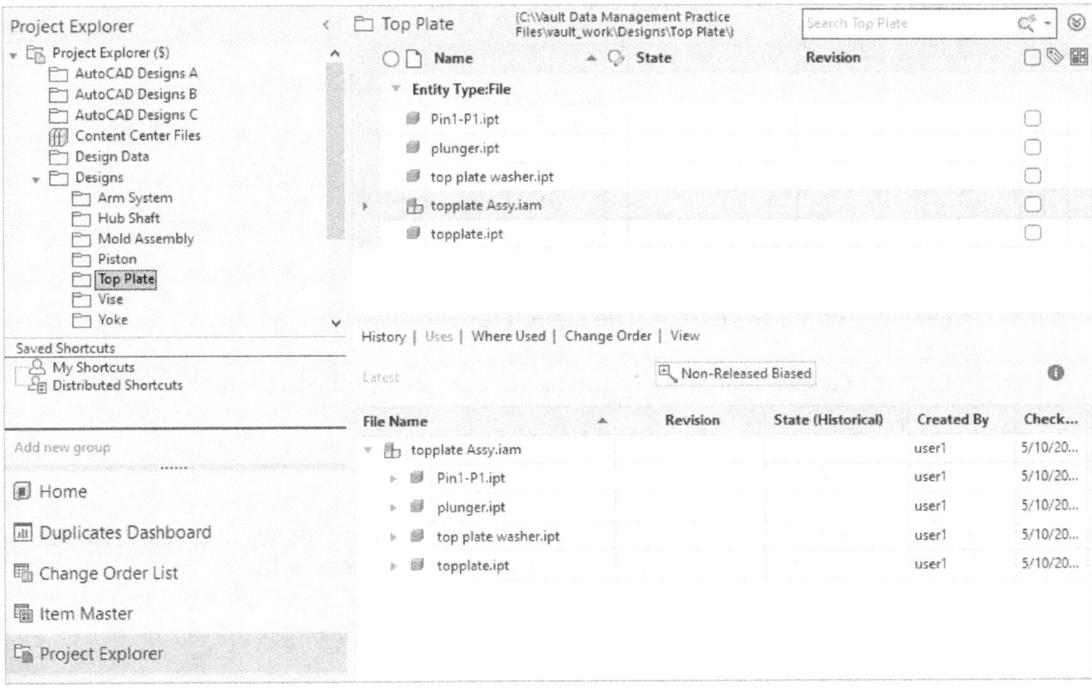

Figure 8–1

8.3 Quick Search

The **Quick Search** performs a search on all of the file properties in the folders based on the specified text string. **Quick Search** is located in the Main table's title bar, as shown in Figure 8–2.

Figure 8–2

How To: Perform a Quick Search

1. In the *Search* field, enter a text string.
2. Click (Search) or press <Enter>. The search results display.
3. Click (Clear or cancel search) to return to the contents of the main table.

Recent Searches

To access a list of recent searches, click (Show search options menu) and select **Recent Searches**. Select a recent search (as shown in Figure 8–3) to execute the search.

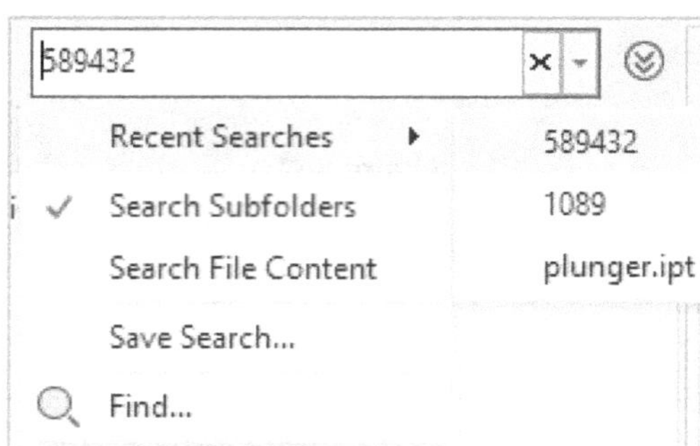

Figure 8–3

Query Builder

To specify additional criteria for your search, click (Expand the query builder) in the title bar to expand the Query Builder, as shown in Figure 8–4.

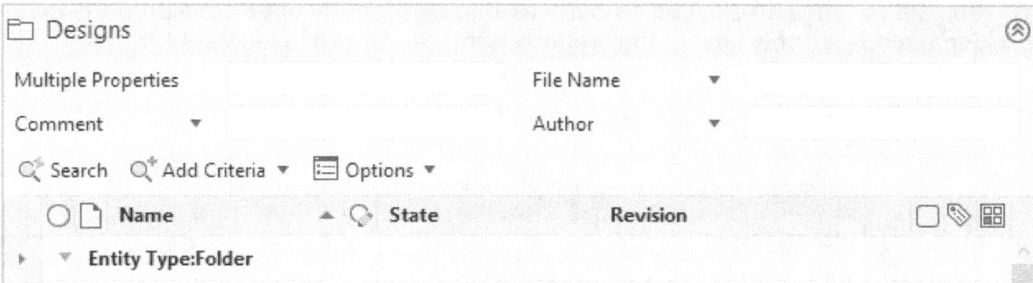

Figure 8–4

How To: Add Search Criteria Using the Query Builder

1. Click  to expand the Query Builder.
2. In the *Multiple Properties* field, enter the value that you want to search for in the properties.
3. If required, enter values in the *File Name*, *Comment,* and *Author* fields.
4. To add a search for a specific property, click **Add Criteria** and select the property.

   Note: *The Query Builder properties selected are kept from session to session.*

   - For example, the **Part Number** property is selected as shown in Figure 8–5, and added as a property to search as shown in Figure 8–6.

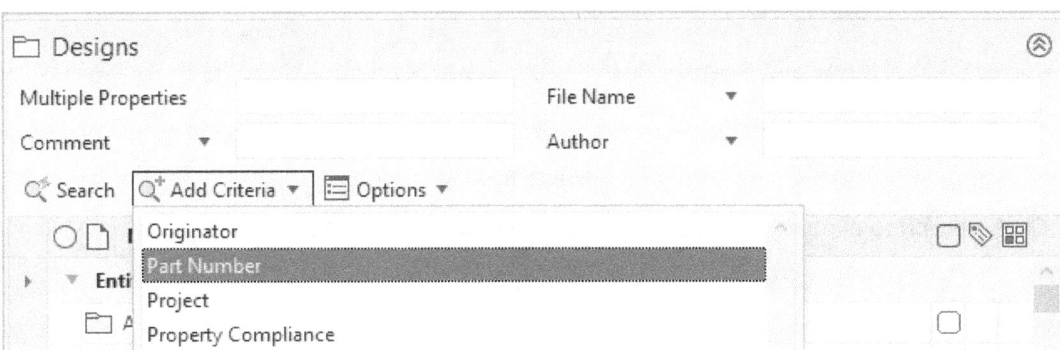

Figure 8–5

Figure 8–6

5. You can also change an existing property to another property or delete a property by clicking the down arrow next to the property name, as shown in Figure 8–7.

Figure 8–7

6. Click **Search** to execute the search and display the search results.

8.4 Basic Find

The **Basic Find** performs a search on all file properties in the folders based on the specified text string. You can access the **Basic Find** functionality in the *Basic* tab in the *Find* dialog box, as shown in Figure 8–8. Click **Find...** in the Standard toolbar to open the *Find* dialog box. You can also open the *Find* dialog box by selecting **Tools>Find** or pressing <Ctrl>+<F>.

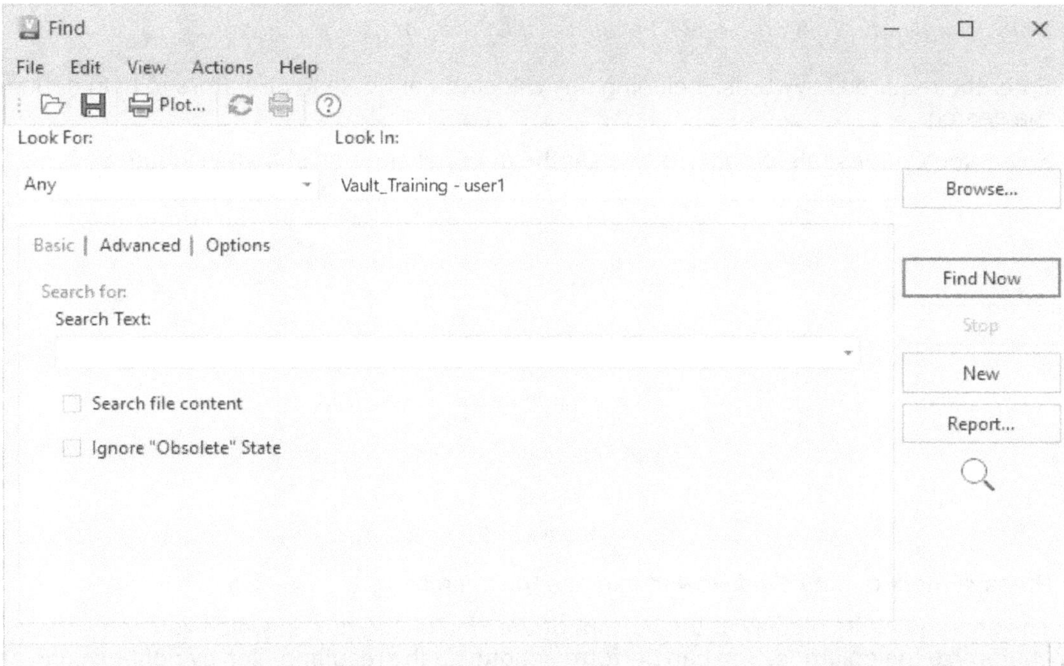

Figure 8–8

Specify which folders to search by clicking **Browse...** next to *Look In*. Select **Search file content** to search the contents of files.

The Content Indexing Service must be enabled in the Autodesk Vault Manager to perform a full content search.

> ***Note:*** *Content Indexing Service can be enabled in the Autodesk Data Management Server (ADMS) console by the administrator.*

How To: Perform a Basic Find

1. In the *Find* dialog box, select the *Basic* tab.
2. For *Look In*, browse to the vault folder that you want to search. By default, the entire vault is searched. To refine the search, click **Browse...** and select the folders to be searched. To search the contents of the files, select **Search file content**.

   Note: *The Search Text drop-down list stores the 10 most recent searches.*

3. Enter the required keywords, including any wildcards or boolean operators to help define the search.
4. Select the *Options* tab to confirm or clear the optional settings shown in Figure 8–9.

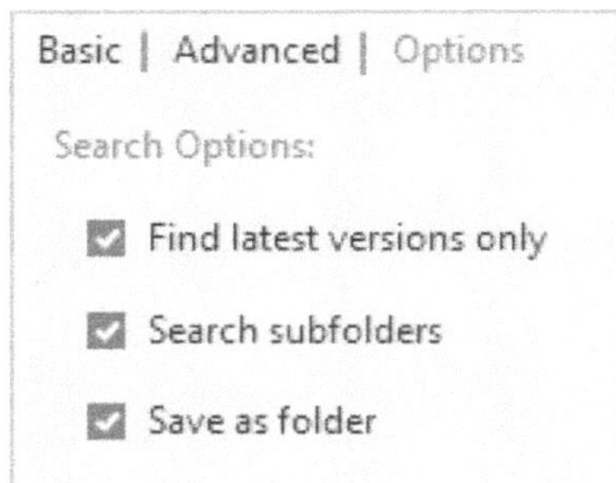

Figure 8–9

5. Press <Enter> or click **Find Now** to execute the search.
6. The search results display at the bottom of the *Find* dialog box, in which you can sort or customize the columns. You can perform actions on the resulting files by right-clicking and selecting an option.

   Note: *You can also expand* ***Actions*** *and select an option to modify the files.*

7. Click **New** if you want to define a new search.

8.5 Advanced Find

An **Advanced Find** provides greater flexibility over the search criteria. In the *Advanced* tab in the *Find* dialog box, you can define more in-depth search criteria using *Property*, *Condition*, and *Value*, as shown in Figure 8–10.

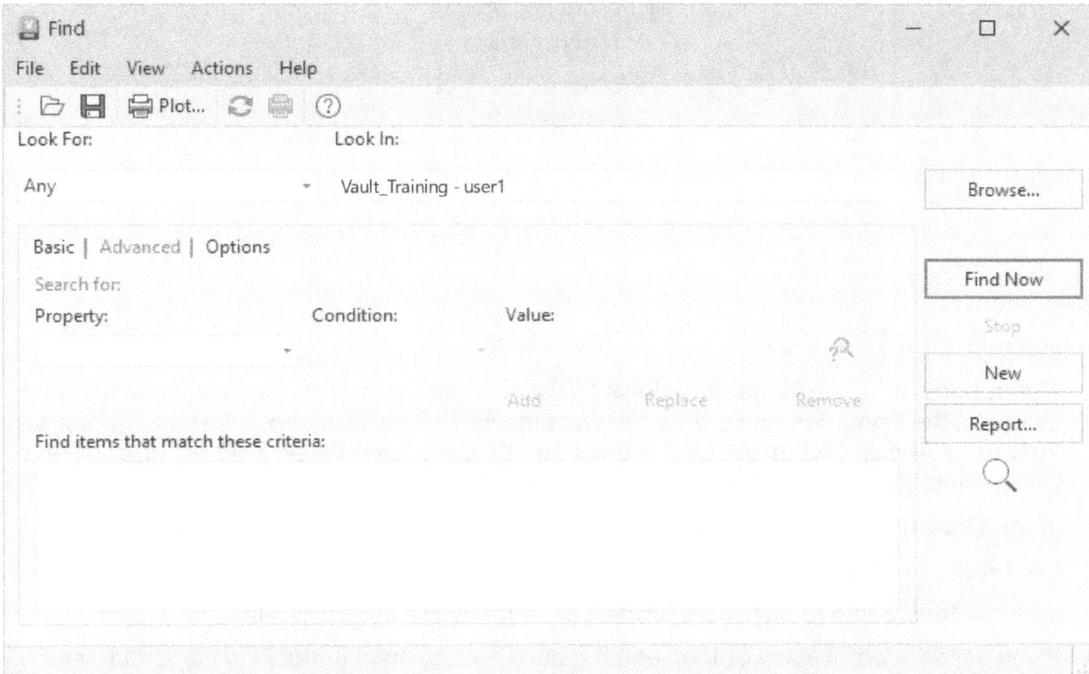

Figure 8–10

How To: Perform an Advanced Find

1. In the *Find* dialog box, select the *Advanced* tab.
2. For *Look In*, browse to the vault folder that you want to search. By default, the entire vault is searched. Click **Browse...** to refine the search by selecting specific folders.
3. Expand the *Property:* drop-down list and select an option.

   Note: *Custom properties are also available for searching.*

4. Expand the *Condition:* drop-down list and select an option. The conditions for a text field are shown in Figure 8–11.

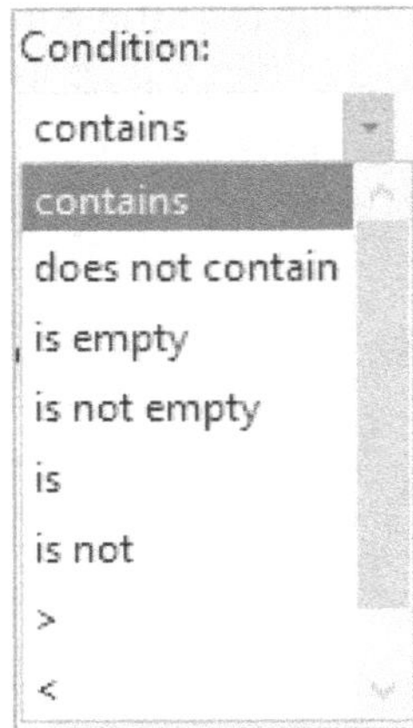

Figure 8–11

5. The options available in the drop-down list depend on the type of Property selected. For example, the Conditions for a date field include: **is**, **before**, **after**, **on or before**, **on or after**, **Yesterday**, **Today**, **Tomorrow**, **Last # Days**, **Next # Days**, **Last Week**, **This Week**, and **Next Week**, while those for a numeric field include **is**, **<=**, **<**, **>=**, **>**, **is not**, etc.
6. In the *Value* field, enter the value for the condition.
7. Click **Add** to add the properties to the list of criteria.
8. Repeat Steps 3 to 6 to add more properties to refine the search results.
9. If you need to remove any of the search criteria, select them in the *Find items that match these criteria* field and click **Remove**.
10. Select the *Options* tab to confirm or clear the optional settings shown in Figure 8–12.

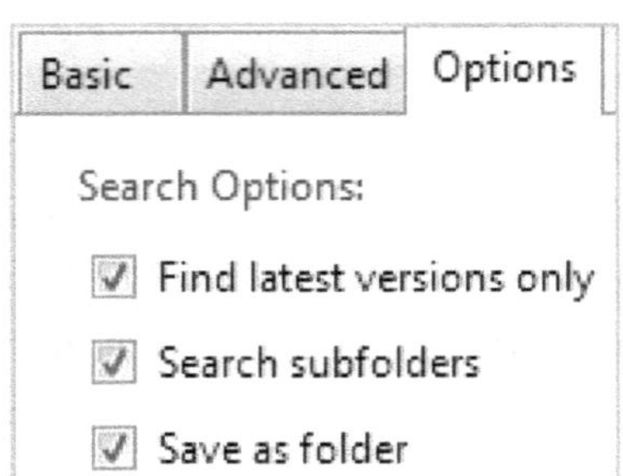

Figure 8–12

11. When the search criteria and settings have been defined, click **Find Now** to execute the search.
12. The search results display at the bottom of the dialog box.You can sort or customize the columns, and perform actions on the files by right-clicking and selecting an option.

    Note: *You can also expand* ***Actions*** *and select an option to modify the files.*

13. Click **New** to define a new search.

8.6 Saving Searches

Once you have defined a search, you can save the search criteria so that you can perform the same search again. In addition to defining and saving searches, the *Find* dialog box enables you to open and manage saved searches.

How To: Save a Search for Reuse

1. In the *Find* dialog box, select **File>Save Search** when your search results display.

   Note: *You can also click*  *(Save Current Search) in the Find toolbar.*

2. For *Search Name*, type a name for the saved search in the *Save Search* dialog box, as shown in Figure 8–13.

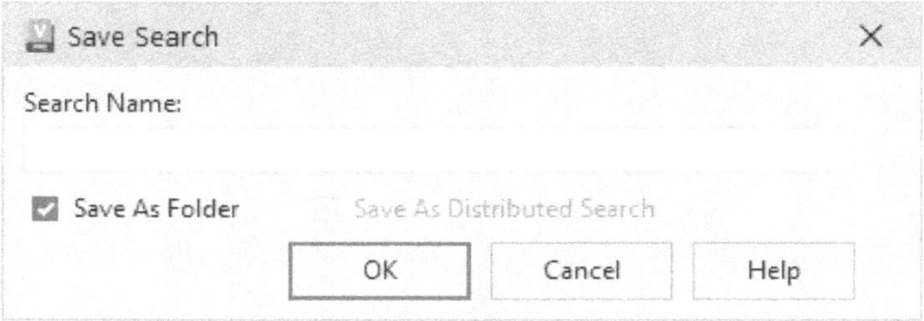

Figure 8–13

   Note: *If you are an administrator, you can select* ***Save As Distributed Search*** *to save the search as a distributed search to be used by the users.*

3. By default, the **Save As Folder** option is selected. It saves the search as a folder in the *Saved Search Folders* area so that it can be quickly accessed later.
4. Click **OK** to finish saving the search.

Save a Quick Search

To save a Quick Search, click ▾ (Show search options menu) and select **Save Search** as shown in Figure 8–14.

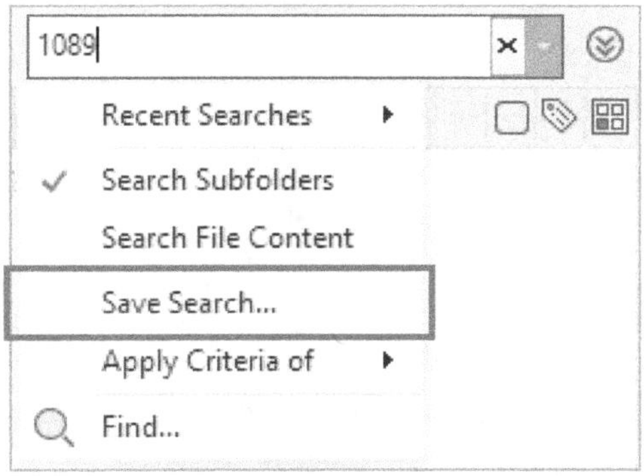

Figure 8–14

Save a Query Builder Search

To save a search from Query Builder, click **Options** and select **Save Search**, as shown in Figure 8–15.

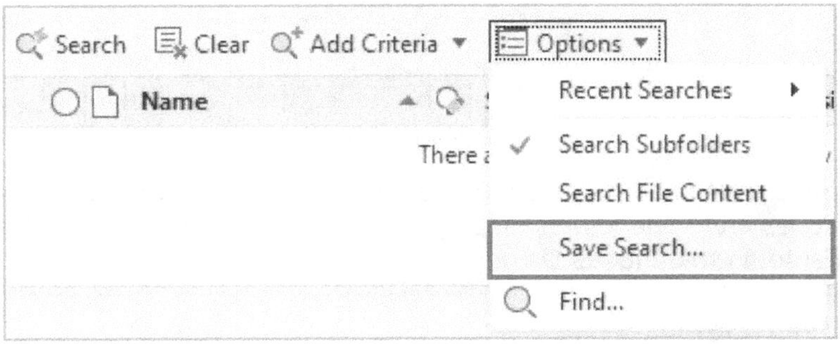

Figure 8–15

Saved Search Folders

Searches saved with the **Save As Folder** option selected display in the *Saved Search Folders> My Searches* area in the Navigation pane in the Autodesk Vault software, as shown in Figure 8–16.

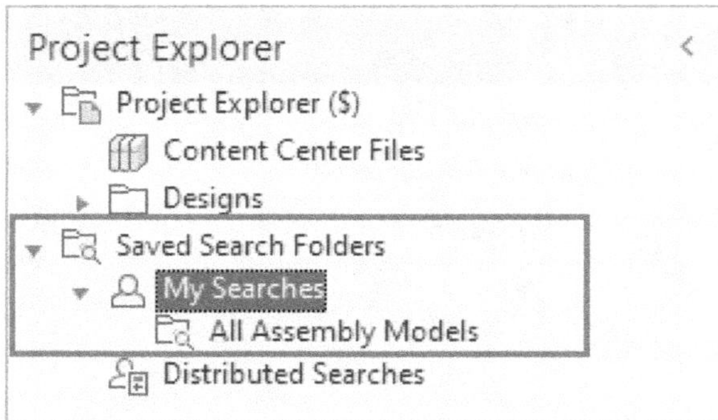

Figure 8–16

If an administrator saves a search using **Save As Distributed Search** then the search would show under the *Distributed Searches* folder, as shown in Figure 8–17.

Figure 8–17

To display and run a saved search, select the required search folder name in the *Saved Search Folders>My Searches* area. The results display in the Main table. A **Find** can also be performed on a search folder to narrow the results.

Run a Saved Search

You can use the *Open Saved Search* dialog box to run searches that were not saved in the *Saved Search Folders>My Searches* area. In the *Find* dialog box, select **File>Open Search...** and then select a saved search in the *Open Saved Search* dialog box, as shown in Figure 8–18.

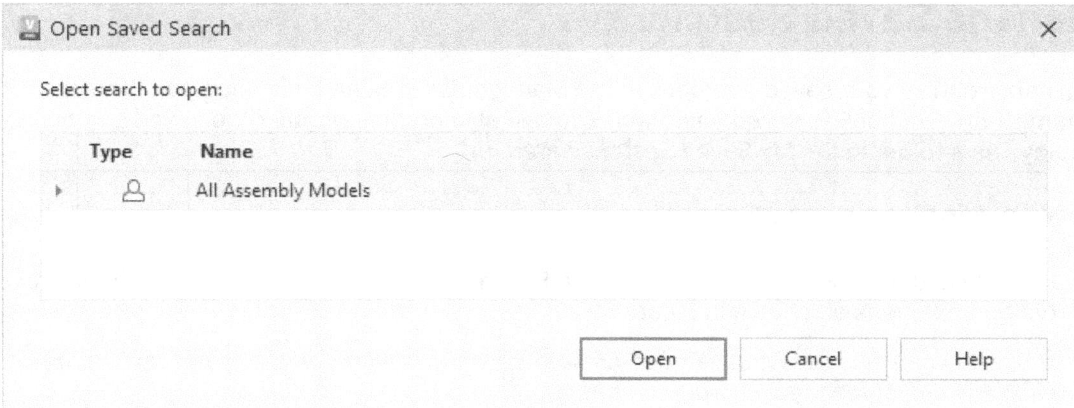

Figure 8–18

How To: Run a Saved Search

1. In the *Find* dialog box, select **File>Open Search...**.

   Note: *You can also click (Open Search) in the Find dialog box toolbar.*

2. In the *Open Saved Search* dialog box, select the saved search from the list.
3. Click **Open** to execute the search. The search results display in the *Find* dialog box. The dialog box switches to the tab in which the save was created: *Basic* or *Advanced*.

   Note: *You can also select a saved search to run from the Quick Search by clicking (Show search options menu)>**Apply Criteria of**, as shown in Figure 8–19.*

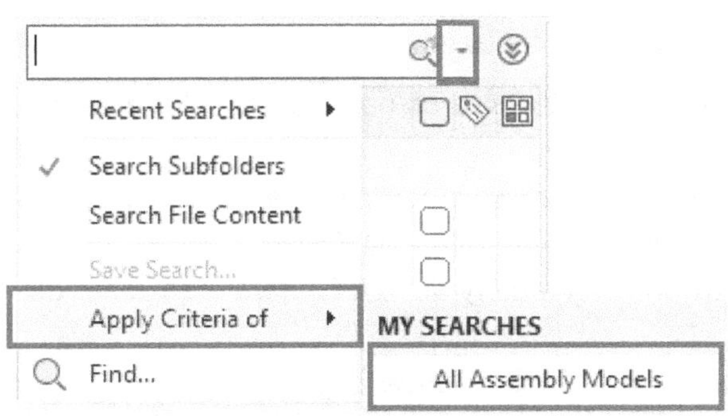

Figure 8–19

Manage Saved Searches

You can organize your saved searches in the *Manage Saved Searches* dialog box. You can rename, copy, and delete saved searches. You can also control whether the saved search displays as a folder in the *My Saved Searches* area.

How To: Modify a Saved Search

1. In the *Find* dialog box, select **File>Manage Saved Searches...**. The *Manage Saved Searches* dialog box opens as shown in Figure 8–20.

   Note: *You can also select* ***Saved Search Folders*** *in the Navigation pane, and then right-click and select* ***Manage Saved Searches...****.*

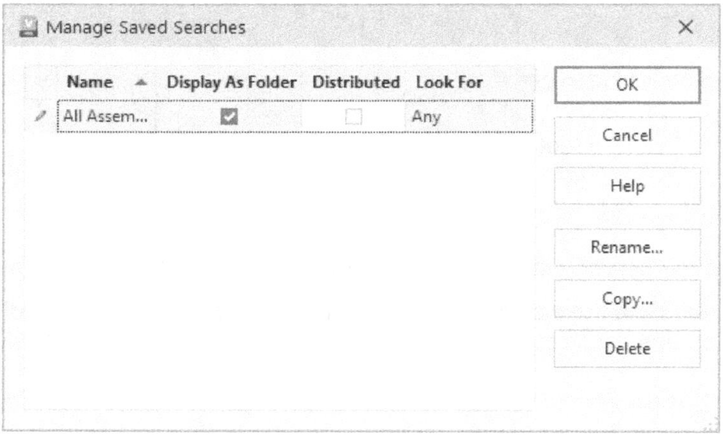

Figure 8–20

2. Perform the following tasks as required:
   - To rename a search, select the search name and click **Rename...**. Enter the new name and click **OK**.
   - To copy a search, select the search name in the *Manage Saved Searches* dialog box and click **Copy...**. Enter the new name and click **OK**.
   - To remove the search from the *My Search Folders* area, clear the **Display As Folder** option.
   - For administrators, select the **Distributed** option to save the search on the server to be deployed on the Vault Client of all users.

   Note: *If a search is saved as a search folder, you can also rename the search in the Search Folder list in the Navigation pane by right-clicking and selecting* ***Rename****.*

3. Click **OK** to save the changes and close the *Manage Saved Searches* dialog box.

Edit Search

You can edit the saved search criteria in the *Find* dialog box or *My Search Folders* area.

How To: Edit a Saved Search from the Find Dialog Box

1. In the *Find* dialog box, select **File>Open Search...**.
2. In the *Open Saved Search* dialog box, select the saved search from the list.
3. Click **Open** and make your changes.
4. Click (Save Current Search) to save the search with your changes.

How To: Edit a Saved Search from *My Search Folders* Area

1. In the *Saved Search Folders>My Searches* area, right-click on your saved search and select **Open Saved Search**, as shown in Figure 8–21.

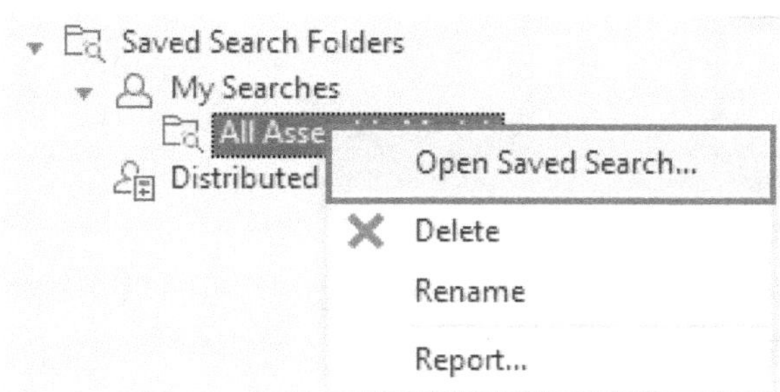

Figure 8–21

2. The *Find* dialog box opens with the saved search selected.
3. Make the required changes and click (Save Current Search) to save the search with the changes.

Deleting a Saved Search

If a search is saved as a search folder, you can delete the search from the *Saved Search Folders>My Searches* area in the Navigation pane or in the *Manage Saved Searches* dialog box. You are prompted to confirm the deletion of the selected saved search.

How To: Delete a Saved Search

1. In the *Find* dialog box, select **File>Manage Saved Searches**.

   Note: *In the My Search Folders area, right-click and select* ***Delete****.*

2. In the *Manage Saved Searches* dialog box, select the search that you want to delete.
3. Click **Delete**.
4. In the Warning box, click **Yes** to confirm the deletion.
5. In the *Manage Saved Searches* dialog box, click **OK** to save the changes and close the dialog box.

8.7 Reports

There are a number of default report templates available in the Autodesk Vault software. You can use these templates to create Reports. The following lists a few ways to access the Report functionality.

- In the *Find* dialog box, when Search Results display, click **Report**, as shown in Figure 8–22.

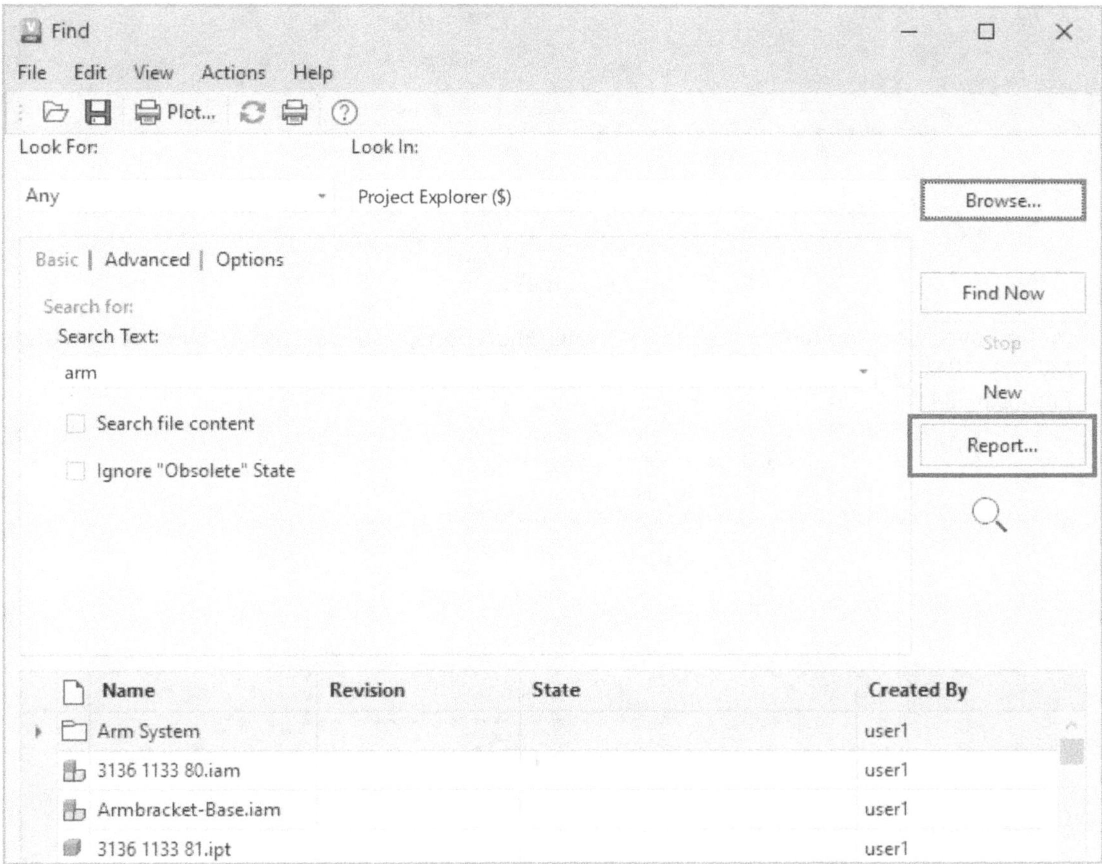

Figure 8–22

- With a folder selected in the Navigation pane, click **Report** on the toolbar, as shown in Figure 8–23. You can also use this button if the folder is selected in the Main table.

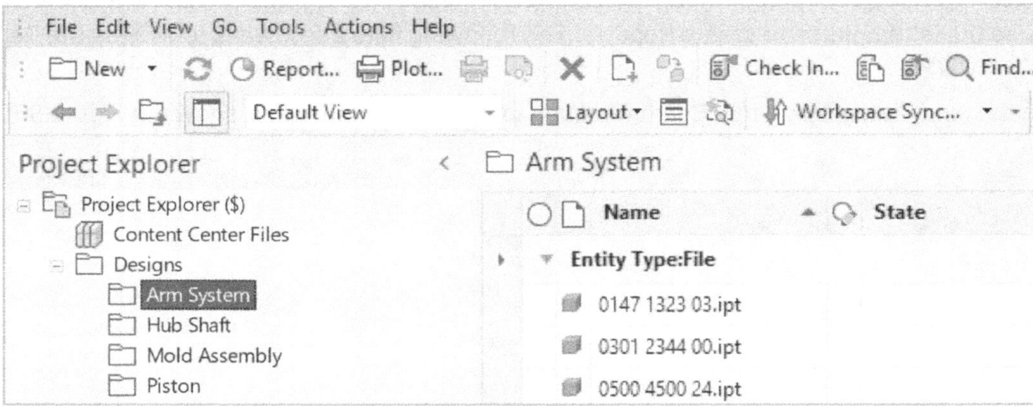

Figure 8–23

- In the *Saved Search Folders* area of the Navigation pane, right-click on a saved search under *My Searches* (or *Distributed Searches* for administrators) and select **Report**, as shown in Figure 8–24.

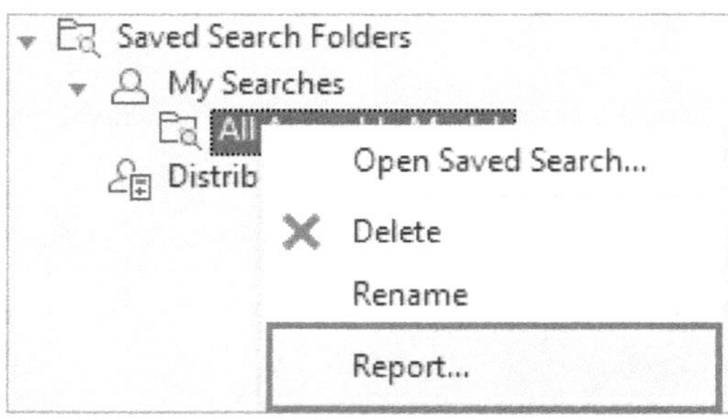

Figure 8–24

Practice 8a
Search

Practice Objective

- Search using a **Basic Find, Quick Search, and Advanced Find** operation.

In this practice, you will run a variety of searches, including Quick Search, Basic Find, and Advanced Find, to locate files in the database. Each search will produce a view of the database that contains the files that meet the search criteria. You will also use different methods of verifying the search results.

Task 1: Search using Quick Search.

In this task, you will search for the keyword **arm*** using the Quick Search.

1. Select the *Designs* folder in the Navigation pane, then in the *Search* field in the Main pane, type **arm*** as shown in Figure 8–25.

Figure 8–25

2. Click (Search) or press <Enter>. The search results display.

Task 2: Search using the Basic Find tab.

In this task, you will use the *Basic Find* tab to locate all files in the $\Designs folder that contain the word *arm* in their file properties, using the same search criteria as the previous task.

1. In the Autodesk Vault software, click **Find** to open the *Find* dialog box.
2. Select the *Basic* tab.
3. In the *Search Text* field, type **arm*** as shown in Figure 8–26.

Figure 8–26

4. Click **Find Now**. The search results display the same files that were found in the previous task, some of which are shown in Figure 8–27. Some of the files display the word *arm* in their filenames. However, some do not, such as **3136 1149 25.iam**.

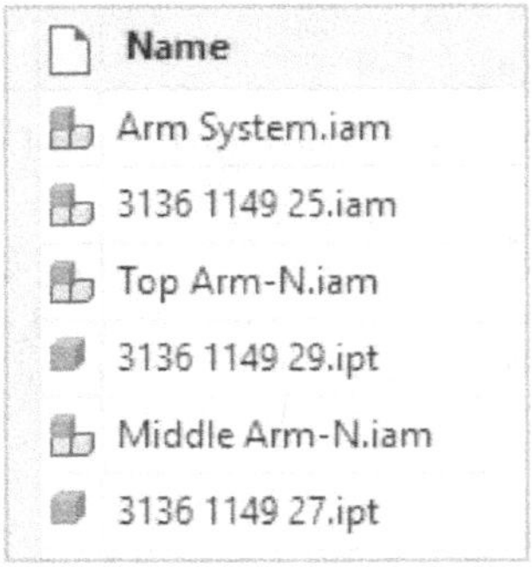

Figure 8–27

5. To determine which file property in **3136 1149 25.iam** contains the word *arm*, select the file, right-click, and select **Go to Folder**.
6. In the *Properties* grid, scroll down to the *User Defined* properties and note that the *Description* is **Armbracket**, as shown in Figure 8–28. This verifies that the word **arm** was found in the *Description* file property.

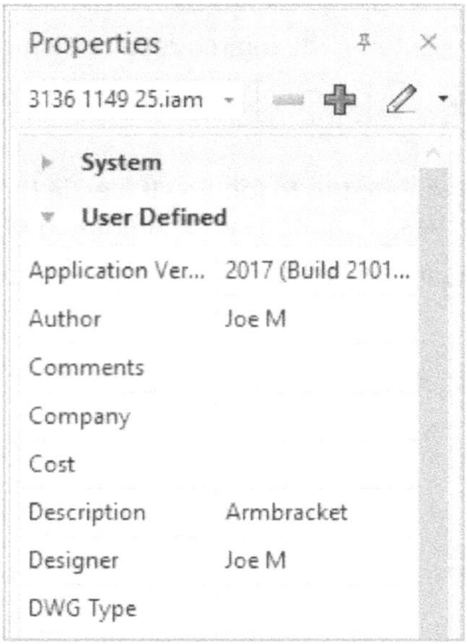

Figure 8–28

7. Close the *Find* dialog box.

Task 3: Search using the Advanced tab.

In this task, you will find all of the files in the vault in which the file property called *Designer* has the value of **Administrator**. You will first run a **Basic Find** with the keyword **Administrator** to display its results. You will then run the search again using the **Advanced Find** search and compare the results to identify the benefits of using each method.

1. Click **Find**. In the *Find* dialog box, in the *Basic* tab, in the *Search Text* field, type **Administrator**.
2. Click **Find Now** or press <Enter> to execute the search.
3. The search results include all of the files that have been created by the Administrator user and any files that contain the string *Administrator* as a property. Since you only want to display files in which the Designer file property is *Administrator*, you need to use the **Advanced Find**.
4. Select the *Advanced* tab.
5. Set the following:
    - *Property*: **Designer**
    - *Condition*: **is**
    - *Value*: **Administrator**
6. Click **Add** to add the criteria. The search criteria is displayed as shown in Figure 8–29.

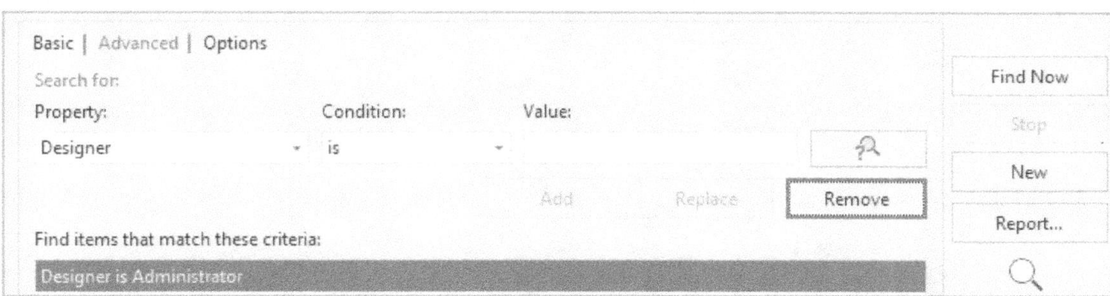

Figure 8–29

7. Click **Find Now** to execute the search. The search results list only displays **yoke.ipt** this time.
8. To verify the results, select **yoke.ipt**, right-click, and select **Go to Folder.**

9. In the Properties grid, scroll down and note that the *Designer* user-defined property contains the text: **Administrator**, as shown in Figure 8–30.

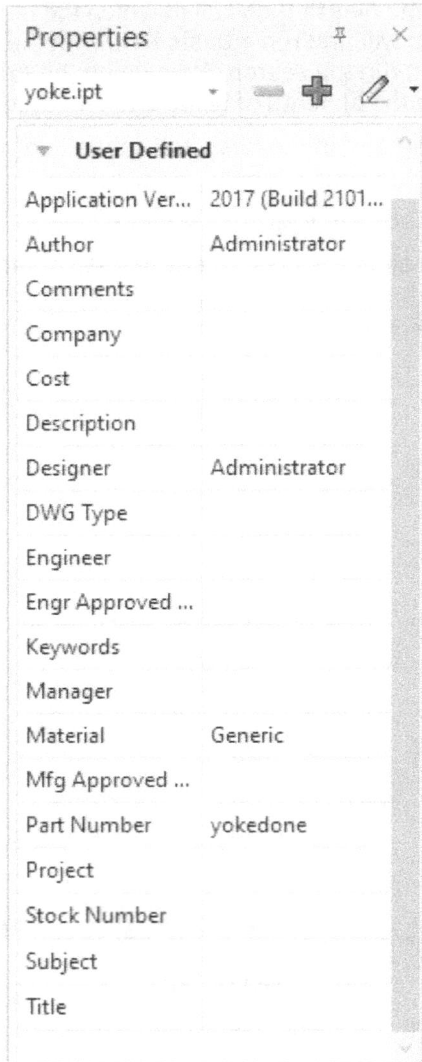

Figure 8–30

10. Leave the *Find* dialog box open.

Task 4: Perform another Advanced Find.

In this task, you will find all assemblies that use a specific library part. You are provided with a portion of the description for the library part *hex bolt*. However, you do not know the filename.

1. In the *Find* dialog box, click **New** to start a new search.
2. Set the *Property* to **Description**, set the *Condition* to **contains**, and set the *Value* to **hex bolt**.
3. Click **Add** to add the criteria.
4. Click **Find Now** to execute the search. The search results display one result: **local.ANSI.62.230.1.ipt**.
5. Select the library part in the results list, right-click, and select **Go To Folder**. Autodesk Vault displays the vault folder in which the library part is located (*Mold Assembly* folder).
6. Close the *Find* dialog box.
7. Select **local.ANSI.62.230.1.ipt**. In the Preview pane, select the *Where Used* tab. Expand the part and note that the part is used in **Final Mold Assy.iam**, as shown in Figure 8–31.

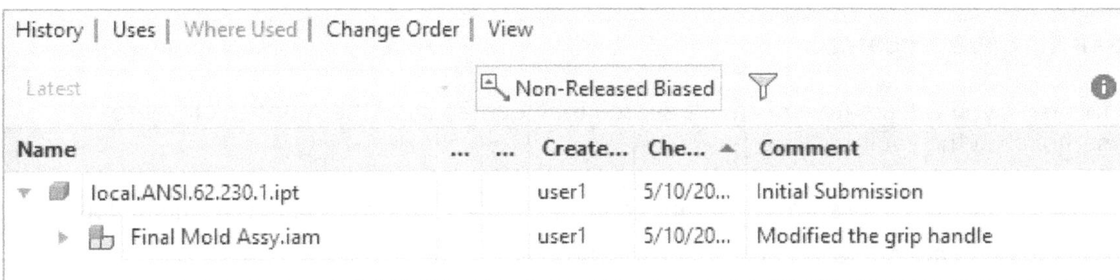

Figure 8–31

End of practice

Practice 8b
Saved Searches

Practice Objectives

- Save a search.
- Run a saved search.
- Run a search report.
- Modify a saved search.
- Delete a saved search.
- Save a search to *Saved Search Folders*.

In this practice, you will create several saved searches so that you can run them later for quick access to files that meet the search criteria. You will also modify a saved search, save a search in *Saved Search Folders*, and delete a saved search.

Task 1: Save a search.

In this task, you will create and save a search that locates all of the Autodesk Inventor assemblies in the vault.

1. Click Find... in the standard toolbar and select the *Advanced* tab in the *Find* dialog box.
2. In the *Search for* area, add the following criteria:
   - In the *Property:* drop-down list, select **File Extension**.
   - In the *Condition:* drop-down list, select **contains**.
   - In the *Value:* field, type **.iam**.
3. Click **Add** to add the criteria.
4. Click **Find Now** to run the search.
5. In the *Find* dialog box, select **File>Save Search**.
6. For the *Search Name*, type **All Assemblies**.
7. Clear the **Save As Folder** option and click **OK**. Your search is saved in the following location:
   - *C:\Users\[Username]\AppData\Roaming\Autodesk\ VaultCommon\Servers\ Services_Security_*\localhost\Vaults\[Vault_name]\Searches*
8. Click **New** to clear the search and its results.

Task 2: Run a saved search.

In this task, you will run the **All Assemblies** saved search.

1. In the *Find* dialog box, select **File>Open Search...**.
2. Select **All Assemblies** and click **Open** to run the search.

Task 3: Run a search report.

In this task, you will run a search report using the search results from the **All Assemblies** saved search.

1. In the *Find* dialog box, click **Report**, as shown in Figure 8–32.

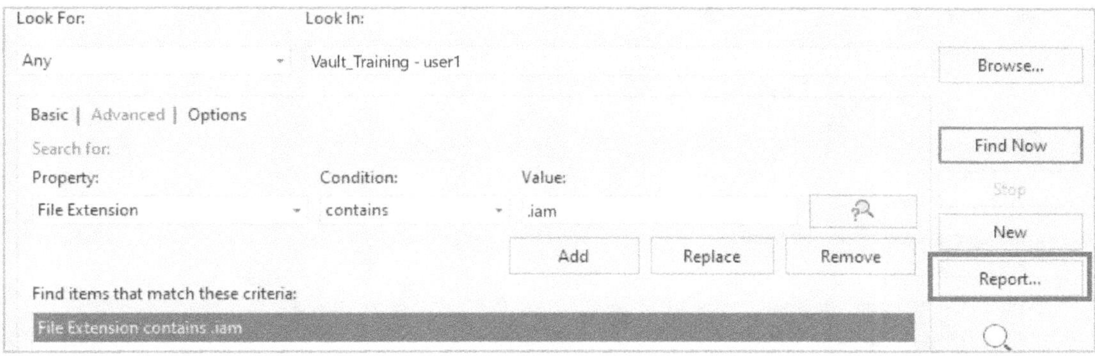

Figure 8–32

2. Select ... in the *Select Report Template* dialog box (as shown in Figure 8–33) and select **File Detail.rdlc** (as shown in Figure 8–34).

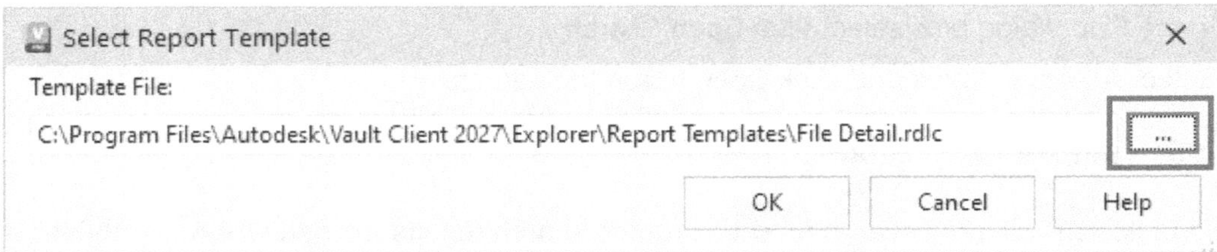

Figure 8–33

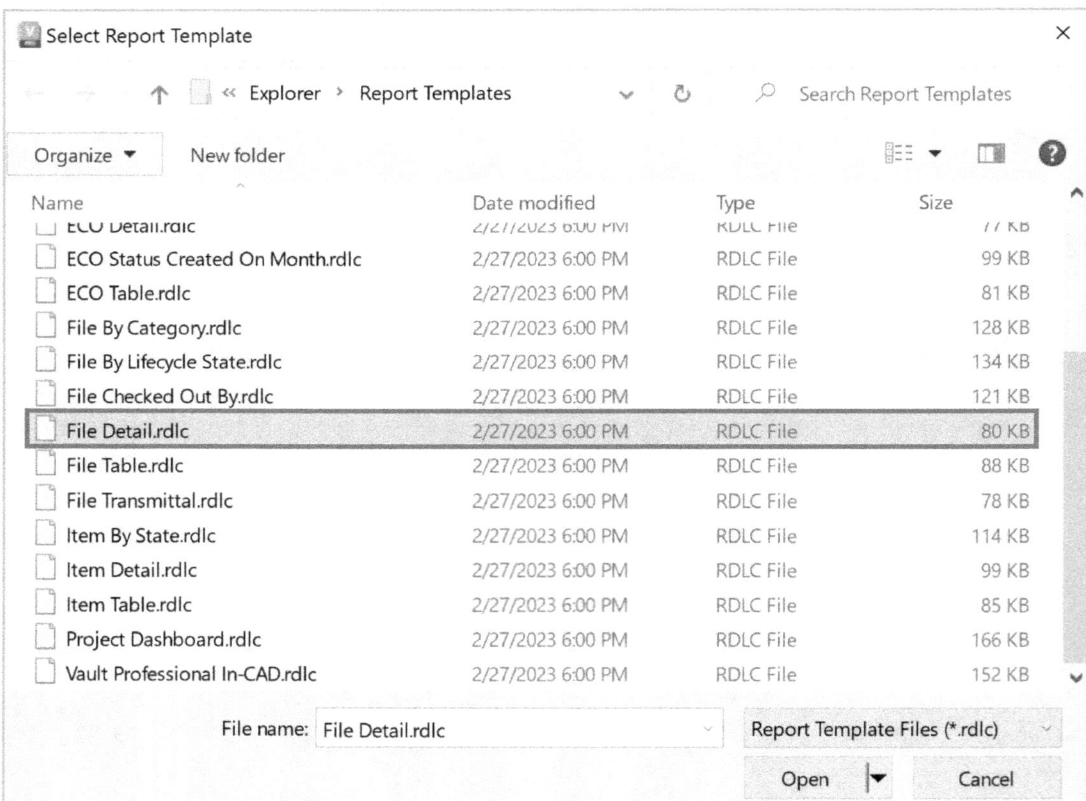

Figure 8–34

3. Click **OK**. The report will display as shown in Figure 8–35.

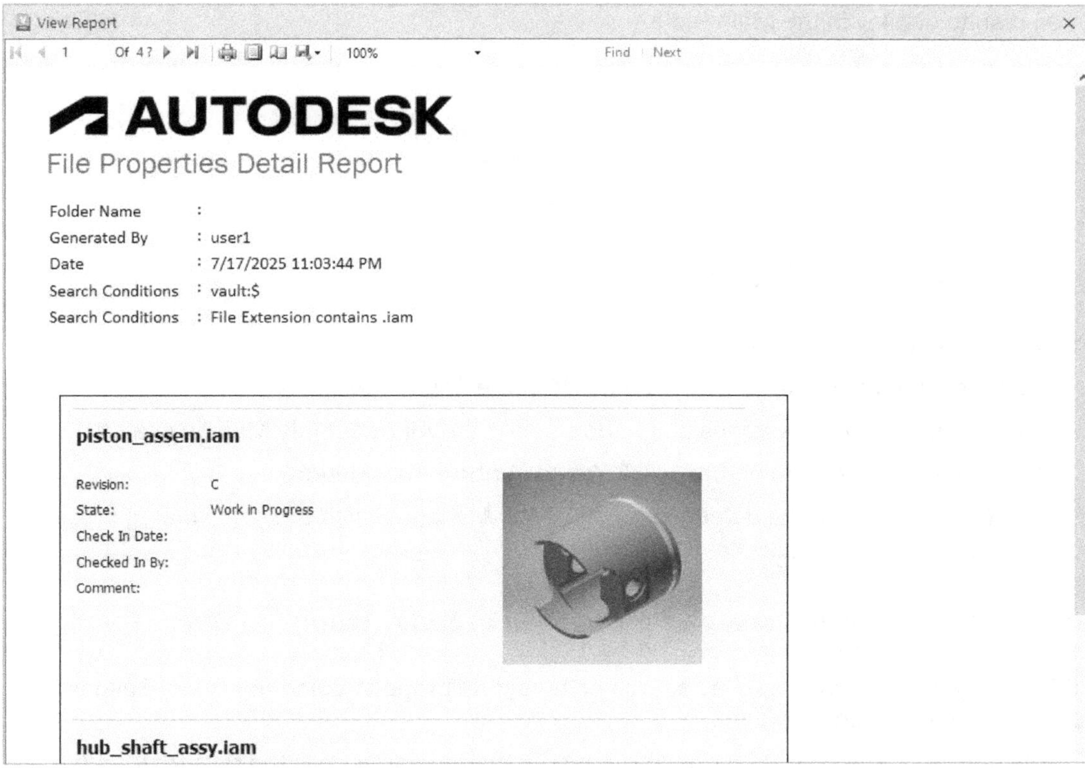

Figure 8–35

4. Close the report.

Task 4: Modify a saved search.

In this task, you will modify the **All Assemblies** saved search to display as a search folder and rename it **All Assembly Models**.

1. In the *Find* dialog box, select **File>Manage Saved Searches**.
2. In the *Manage Saved Searches* dialog box, select the **All Assemblies** search and click **Rename....**
3. For the *Search Name*, type **All Assembly Models** as the new name and click **OK**.
4. In the *Manage Saved Searches* dialog box, select **Display As Folder**.
5. Click **OK** to save the changes. Close the *Find* dialog box.

6. The *All Assembly Models* search folder displays in the Navigation pane, in the *Saved Search Folders* area under *My Searches*, as shown in Figure 8–36. Select ***All Assembly Models*** and all results display in the Main table.

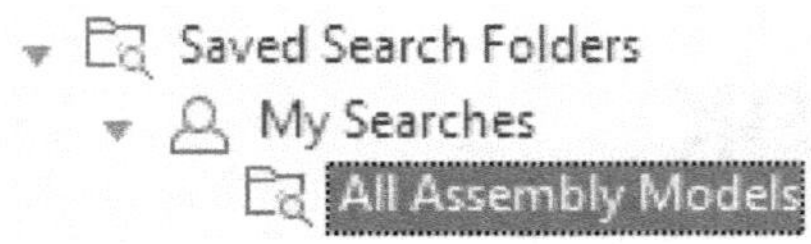

Figure 8–36

Task 5: Delete a saved search.

In this task, you will delete a saved search.

1. Open the *Find* dialog box and select **File>Manage Saved Searches**.
2. In the *Manage Saved Searches* dialog box, select the **All Assembly Models** search.
3. Click **Delete**. In the Warning box, click **Yes** to confirm the deletion.
4. Click **OK** to complete the deletion and close the *Manage Saved Searches* dialog box.
5. Close the *Find* dialog box.

Task 6: Create a saved search for Checked In Today using the Query Builder.

In this task, you will create a saved search using a date property using the Query Builder, and then save it to *My Search Folders*.

1. Select **Project Explorer ($)** in the Navigation pane to search from the root folder. Click  (Expand the query builder) next to the Quick Search.
2. The Query Builder displays as shown in Figure 8–37.

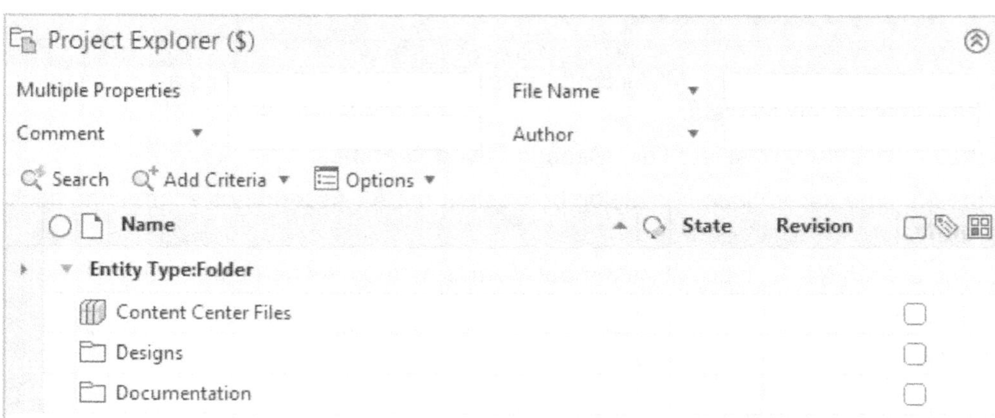

Figure 8–37

3. Click **Add Criteria** and select **Checked In**, as shown in Figure 8–38.

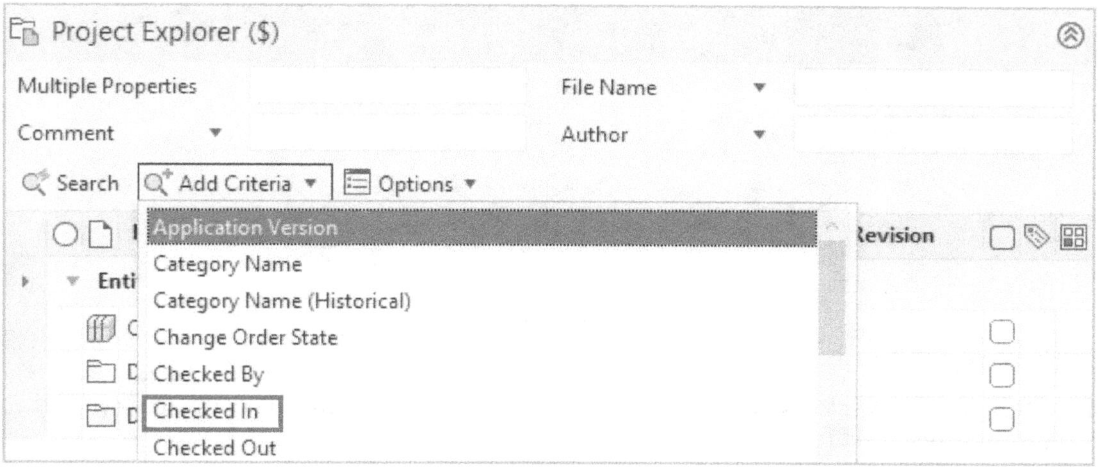

Figure 8–38

4. Expand the *Checked In* drop-down list as shown in Figure 8–39.

Figure 8–39

5. Select today's date from the calendar and click **Search**. The search results display.
6. Click **Options** and select **Save Search**, as shown in Figure 8–40.

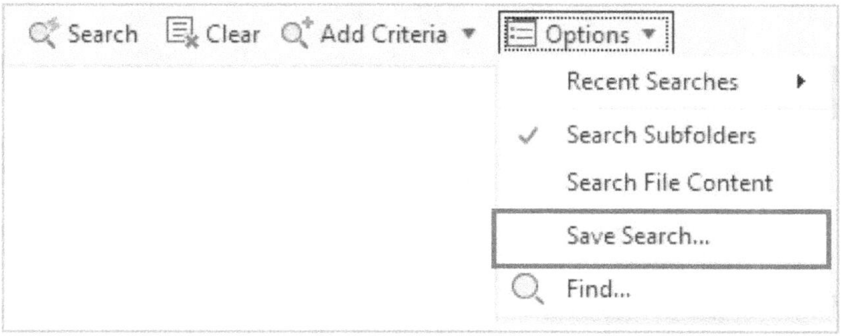

Figure 8–40

7. For the *Search Name*, enter **Checked In Today**.

8. Ensure that the **Save As Folder** option is selected, as shown in Figure 8–41.

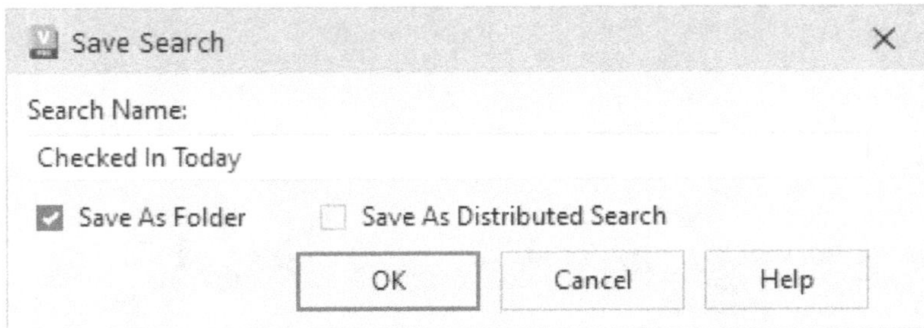

Figure 8–41

9. Click **OK**.
10. In *Saved Search Folders>My Searches*, select the **Checked In Today** search to view the results in the Main table.

Task 7: Edit the Checked In Today saved search.

1. Under *Saved Search Folders>My Searches*, right-click **Checked In Today** and select **Open Saved Search...**, as shown in Figure 8–42.

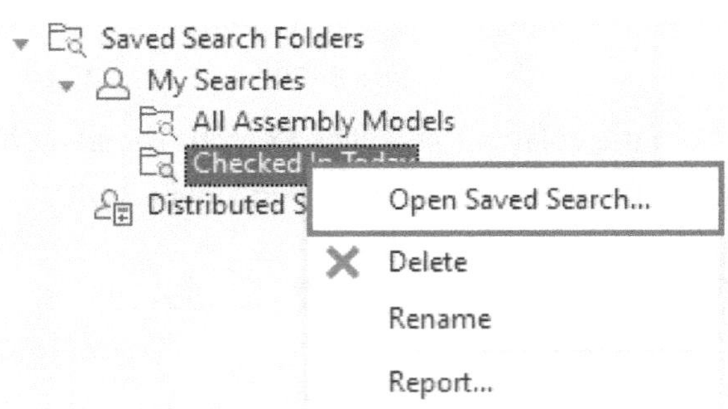

Figure 8–42

2. Highlight the criteria then change the Condition to **Today** and click **Replace**, as shown in Figure 8–43.

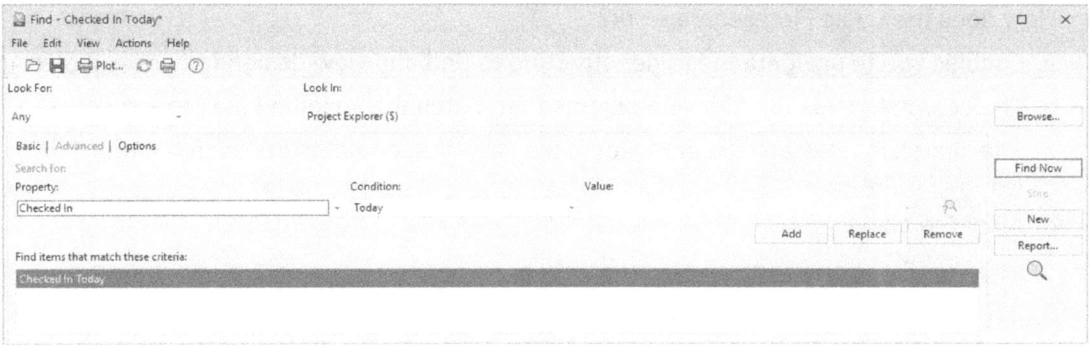

Figure 8–43

3. Click (Save) to save the changes. Now the saved search can be used on any day to view what files have been checked in on that day.

End of practice

Chapter Review Questions

1. How does the Basic Find search work?
   a. Enables you to navigate the folder structure to find and view design folders and files.
   b. The search locates the files and objects that match the specified file property criteria.
   c. The search locates any file or object in the vault that contains the search string in any of the file properties.
   d. All of the above.

2. What is not a valid search operator for a Basic or Advanced Find?
   a. *
   b. ?
   c. &
   d. NOT

3. What does the Advanced Find enable you to specify to refine your search? (Select all that apply.)
   a. Property Condition (e.g., is, <, >, etc.).
   b. Property Name
   c. Property Value
   d. Location in vault

4. Where can saved searches be executed? (Select all that apply.)
   a. In the Actions menu.
   b. *My Searches* in the Navigation pane.
   c. *My Shortcuts* in the Navigation pane.
   d. In the *Find* dialog box, select **File>Open Search**.

5. Custom properties can be selected as search criteria.
   a. True
   b. False

Command Summary

Button	Command	Location
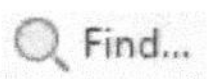	**Find**	• **Standard toolbar**
	**Open Search**	• **Find dialog box:** Toolbar
	**Save Current Search**	• **Find dialog box:** Toolbar

Chapter 9

File and Design Management

One of the Autodesk® Vault software's key features is its ability to consolidate and manage all product information for easy reference, sharing, and reuse. Tools for managing files in the vault include editing object properties and the **Copy Design** tool, which copies an entire design, including all related files, while maintaining their relationships to each other in the new design file.

Learning Objectives

- Use the **Move**, **Delete**, and **Attachments** operations to move, delete, and attach files to other files in the vault.
- Use the **Edit Properties** operation to edit object properties.
- Create a label to capture a project milestone.
- Use the **Rename** operation to rename files and update all related files that reference the renamed files.
- Use the **Replace** operation to replace files with new files and update the parent references.
- Use the **Pack and Go** command to copy all referenced files to a single location outside the Autodesk Inventor software.
- Use **Workspace Sync** to clean up files in your project workspace.
- Use the **Copy Design** operation to create a new design.

9.1 Managing Data in the Vault

Autodesk Vault's data management functionality includes the ability to move, delete, rename, and attach files to other files in the vault.

Required for Autodesk Inventor Files

To ensure file resolution when performing data management operations, the project specified in Autodesk Inventor's Project Settings is used. An administrator can set up an Autodesk Inventor project file to be used for all of the clients. If you are not an administrator, you can specify the Autodesk Inventor project file in the Autodesk Vault software by selecting **Tools>Options** or by right-clicking on the project file and selecting **Set Inventor Project File,** as shown in Figure 9–1.

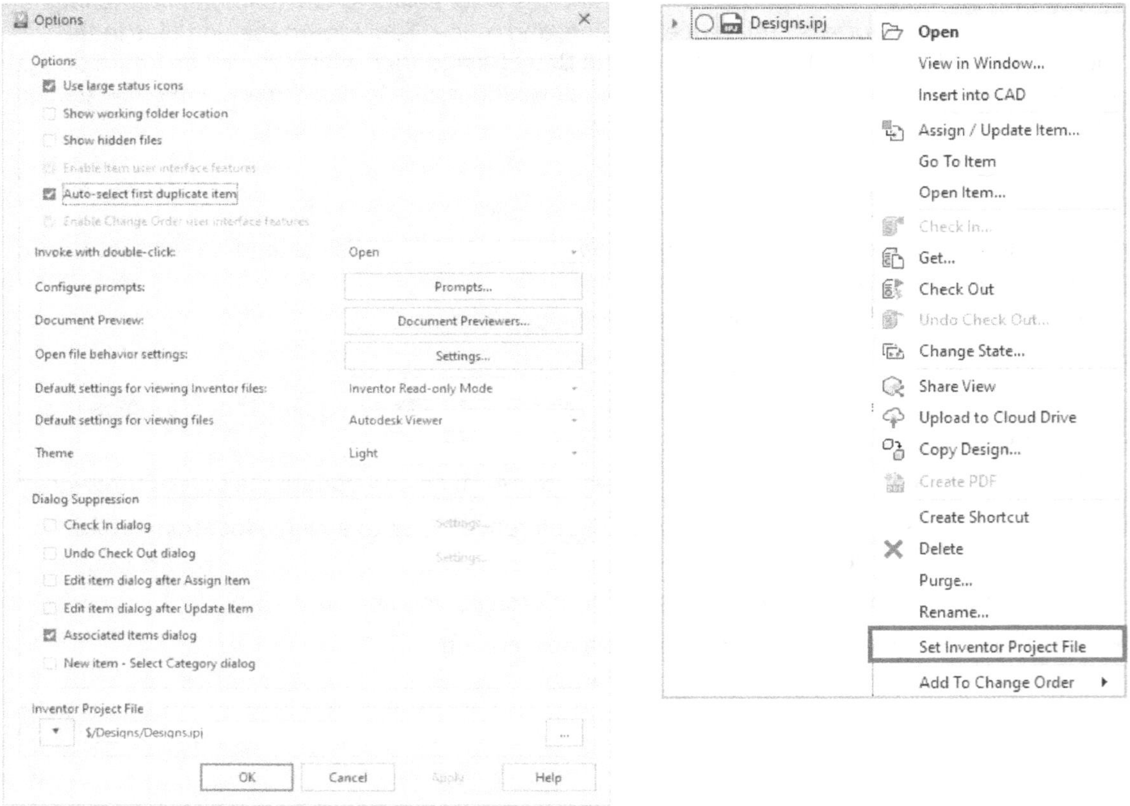

Figure 9–1

Moving Files

To move files from one folder to another, select the files in the Main table, hold the right mouse button, and drag them into the target folder. When you release the right mouse button after dragging, select **Move** as shown in Figure 9–2.

> ***Note:*** *You can also move a file by dragging and dropping it into its new folder using the left mouse button.*

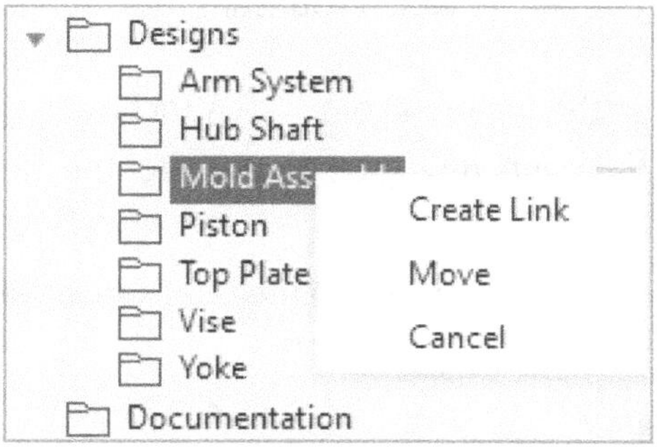

Figure 9–2

The file remains the same in the new location and is still referenced by its children and parents.

Deleting Files

To delete vault files, select them in the Main table, right-click, and select **Delete**. You are prompted to confirm the action. The **Delete** operation deletes all versions of the selected files.

You can also delete files by clicking  (Delete) in the Main toolbar.

When using the **Delete** operation:

- Parents need to be deleted before children.
- A file must be in a **Checked In** state.
- If a file label exists, it needs to be deleted before the file is deleted.

Attaching Files to Other Files

Files can be attached to other files in the vault, which creates a link between the files so that they act as a unit when being checked out and checked in. For example, you might want to attach a Microsoft Word document containing operating instructions to a design file.

How To: Attach a File to Another File

1. In the Main table, select the files to which you want to attach a file and select **Actions>Attachments...** in the file menu or (Attachments) in the standard toolbar.
2. Click **Attach...** in the *Attachments* dialog box and select the file(s) to attach.
3. Click **OK**.

Attachments display with a paper clip symbol, in the *Uses* tab, as shown for **yoke.ipt** in Figure 9–3.

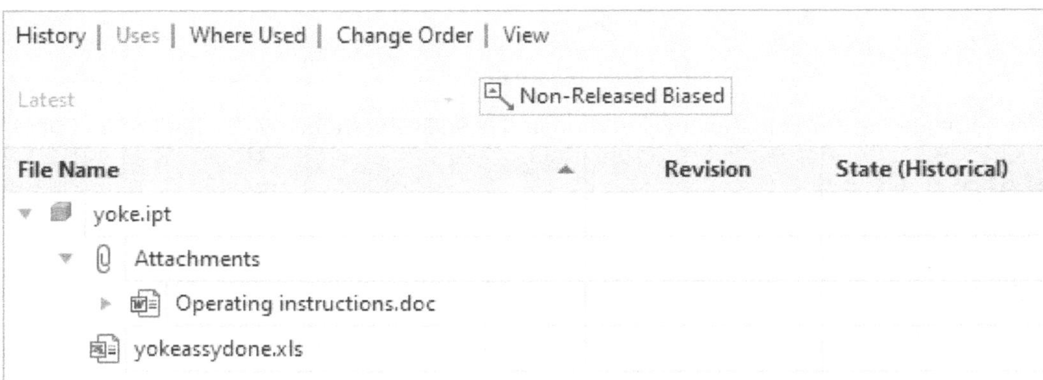

Figure 9–3

How To: Remove Attachments from a File

1. In the Main table, select the file from which you want to remove an attachment and select **Actions>Attachments** in the file menu or (Attachment) in the main toolbar.
2. Select the attachment filename and click **Detach**.
3. Click **OK**.

9.2 Properties

Editing Properties

The Autodesk Vault software includes both System-Defined Properties and User-Defined Properties (UDPs). The **Edit Properties** command in the Autodesk Vault software enables you to edit User-Defined Properties of selected objects, such as files, items, and change orders.

> ***Note:*** *Your user role must be defined as Editor or Administrator to edit file properties. Items can only be edited by an Item Editor Level 1, Item Editor Level 2, or an Administrator.*
>
> *You can also select multiple object types for editing.*

How To: Edit File Properties

1. In the Autodesk Vault software main table view, with the objects selected, select **Edit>Edit Properties**. Alternatively, with the objects selected, in the Properties grid, click (Edit Properties), as shown in Figure 9–4.

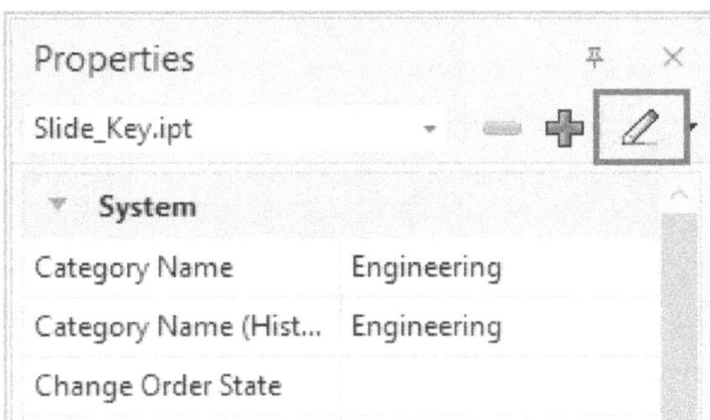

Figure 9–4

2. The *Property Edit* dialog box opens displaying the objects to edit. You can add additional objects or remove any objects using **Add** and **Remove**, respectively. By default, the properties of **Name**, **Author**, and **Description** display.
   - Properties that display with a gray background are read-only.
   - Properties that display with a white background can be edited. Double-click the property and type a new value.
3. Click (Select Properties) to add more properties.
4. In the *Customize Fields* dialog box, in the *Select available fields from*: drop-down list, select one of the following options to determine the type of properties to be displayed: **All fields**, **Change Orders**, **Files**, **Folders**, **Items**, or **Frequently-used fields**.

5. In the *Available fields* area, select a property (or properties).
6. Click **Add** to add the property to the *Show these fields in this order:* area.
7. In the *Show these fields in this order:* area, use **Move Up** or **Move Down** to organize the properties.
8. In the *Show these fields in this order:* area, use **Remove** to remove a property from the list.
9. Click **OK**.
10. Edit the properties by double-clicking on a cell and changing its value. You can also right-click on a cell to access the **Copy**, **Paste**, **Select All**, **Capitalize**, **Find**, and **Replace** options, as shown in Figure 9–5.

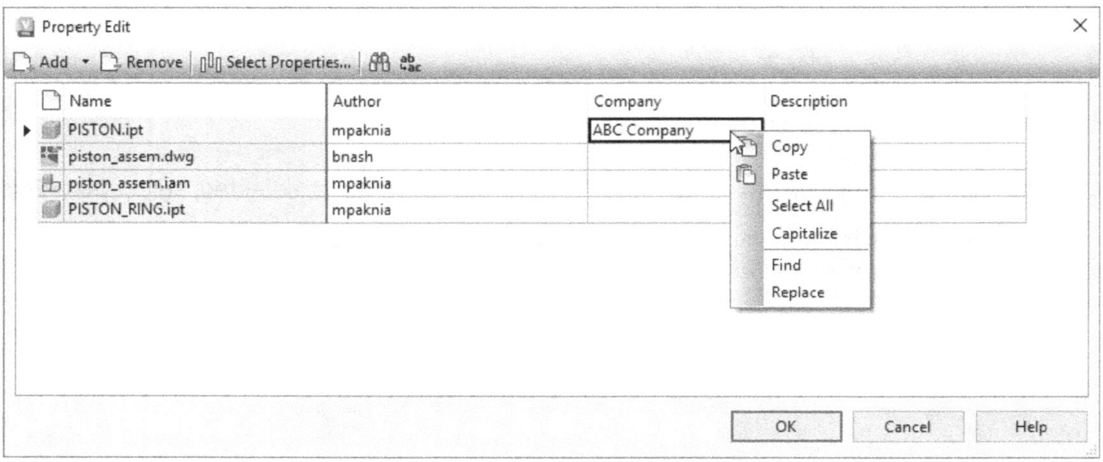

Figure 9–5

Note: *The new value for a file property must be the appropriate data type or it displays as incorrect.*

11. Drag the small black square at the bottom right corner of the selected cell to fill the other cells with the same value.
12. Click **OK**.
13. The *Property Edit Results* dialog box opens displaying the updated properties as shown in Figure 9–6.

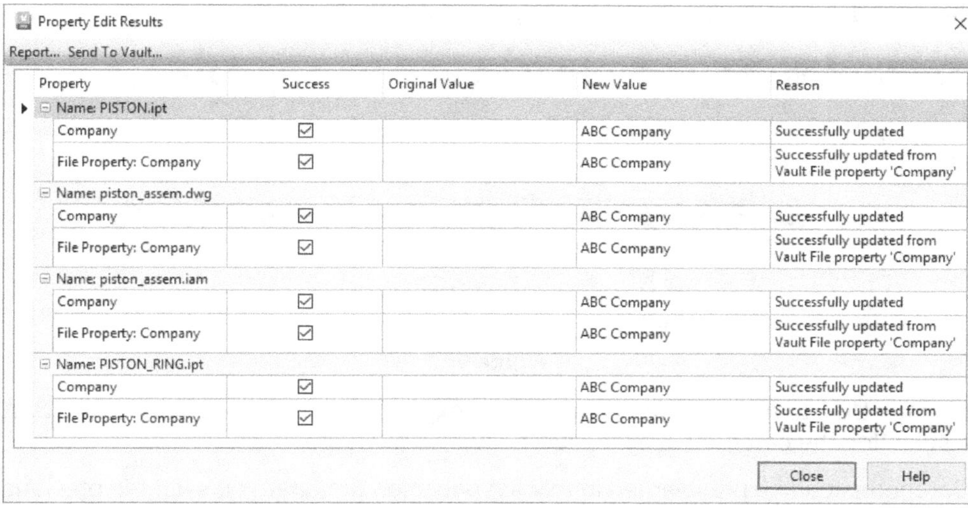

Figure 9–6

14. Select **Report** to print or export the results. The Preview window enables you to use the following options to modify, print, or export the report:
    - Add a header or footer, adjust the margins, and set the display to **Portrait** or **Landscape**.
    - Add a watermark or change the color of the background.
    - Export the report as a .PDF, .HTML, .MHT, .RTF, .XLS, .XLSX, .CSV, .TXT, or image file.
    - Send the report via email.
    - Customize how the report is going to print by selecting which items are going to print (header, footer, lines, etc.) and how the report is going to fit on the printed page.
15. In the *Property Edits Results* dialog box, select **Send To Vault** to save the report in the vault. In the *Save As* dialog box, select the vault in which to save the report, enter the report name, and click **Save**.
16. Click **Close**. The *Comment* field displays **Property Edit** to explain the version change for files with modified properties.

Creating UDPs

How To: Create a New User-Defined Property

1. Click **Tools (located in the Menu)>Administration>Vault Settings**.
2. Select the *Behaviors* tab and click **Properties...** in the *Properties* area.
3. In the *Property Definitions* dialog box, click **New**.
4. In the *New Property* dialog box, enter a name.

5. In the *Type* drop-down list, select the property type, as shown in Figure 9–7.

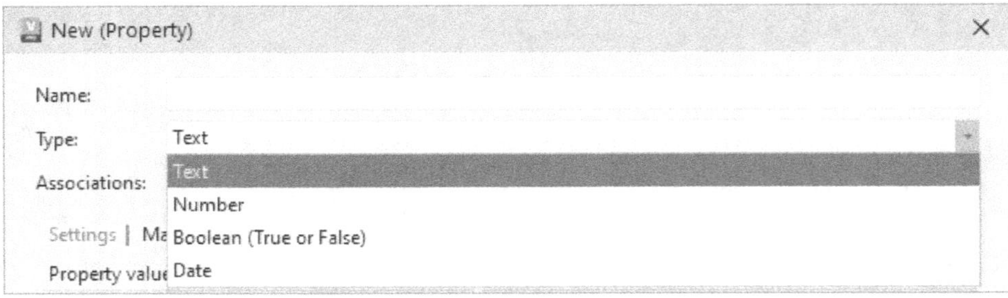

Figure 9–7

6. Assign the UDP to one or more categories by expanding the *Associations* drop-down list and selecting the category checkboxes, as shown in Figure 9–8.
   - Categories can be preselected in this list based on the filter you selected previously in the *Property Definitions* dialog box.
   - You can select or clear categories as required.

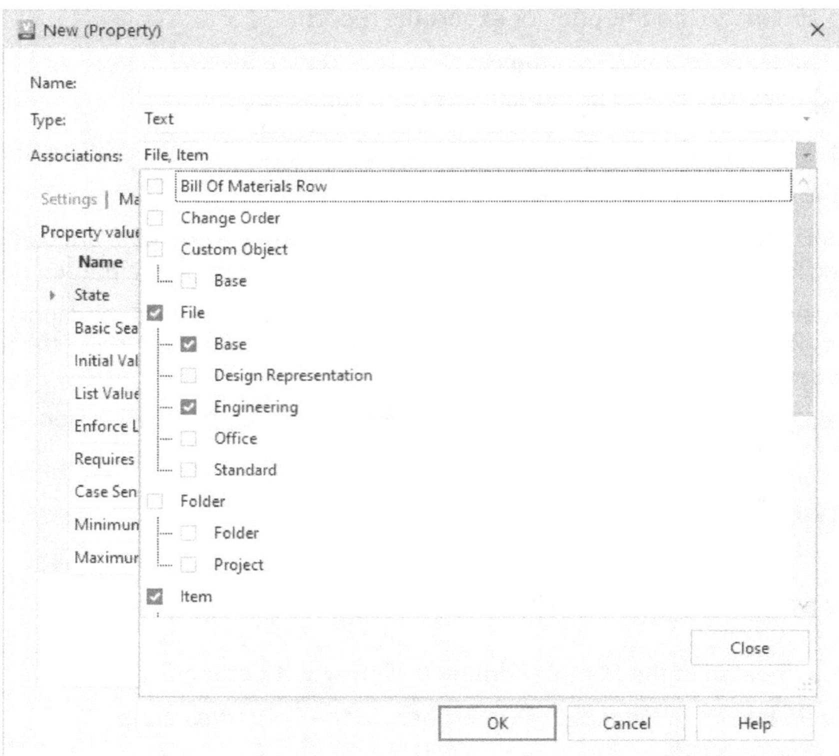

Figure 9–8

Add or Remove Properties

How To: Add or Remove Properties from Files or Items

1. Select the required objects and then select **Actions** (located in the Menu)**>Add or Remove Property**.
2. Locate the property and select **Add** or **Remove** from the *Action* drop-down list, as shown in Figure 9–9.

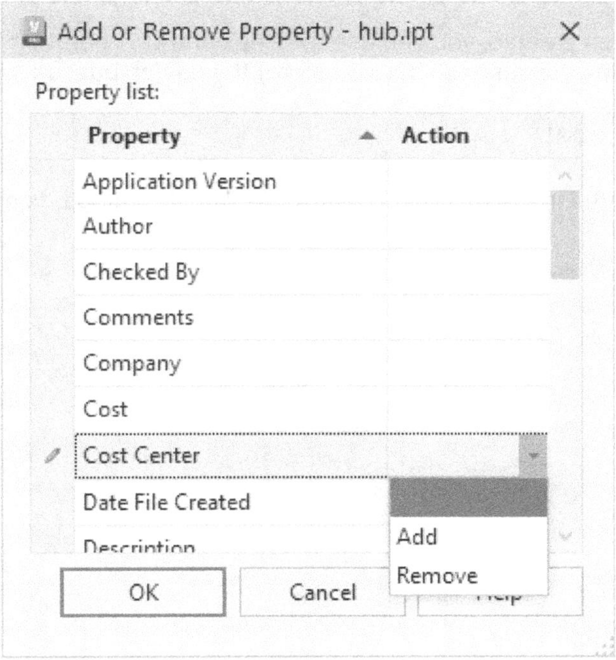

Figure 9–9

9.3 Labels

In the Autodesk Vault software, labels can be created to capture project milestones, such as customer proposals and design reviews. They act as snapshots of your data at a specific point in the design process. You can assign specific documents to these labels.

Labels can only be assigned to folders, not to files, items, etc. Labels do not include folder information, only the project files are labeled.

> ***Note:*** *All vault users can view labels; however, only user accounts assigned the role of Editor or Administrator can create and manage labels.*

Once the label has been created, you can use the **Pack and Go** operation to create a package based on that label. You can also roll back (restore) the design based on a label.

How To: Create a Label

1. Select **Tools** (located in the Menu)**>Labels...**. The *Labels* dialog box opens as shown in Figure 9–10.

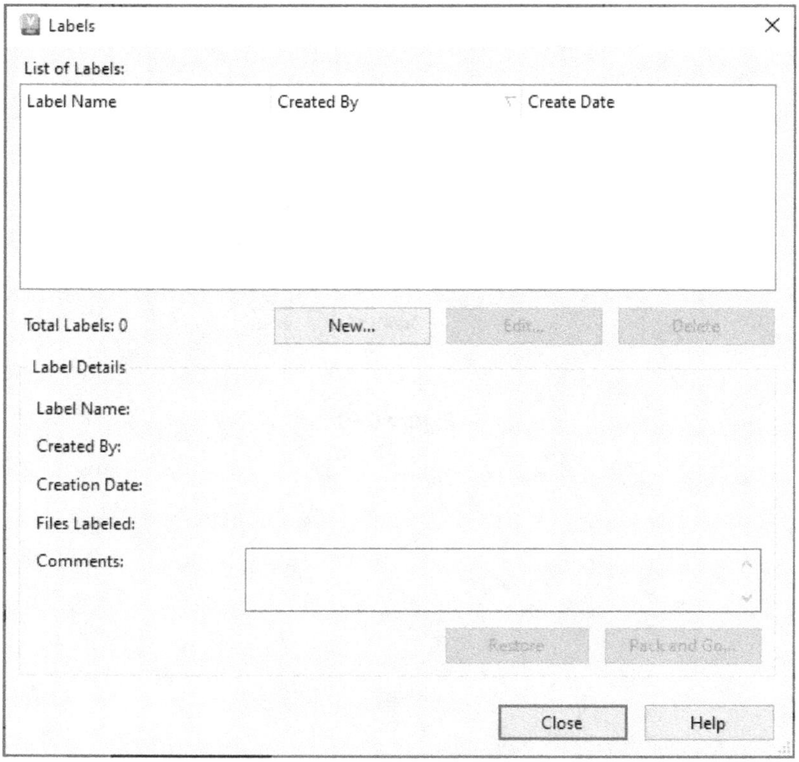

Figure 9–10

The *Labels* dialog box displays the list of labels that have already been defined and enables labels to be created, deleted, renamed, archived, and restored. It displays the *Created By* and *Create Date* information on a label, the number of files assigned to it, and any associated comments.

Note: *You can also create a new label by selecting a vault folder, right-clicking, and selecting* ***New Label...****.*

2. In the *Labels* dialog box, click **New...** to create a new label. The *New Label* dialog box opens as shown in Figure 9–11.

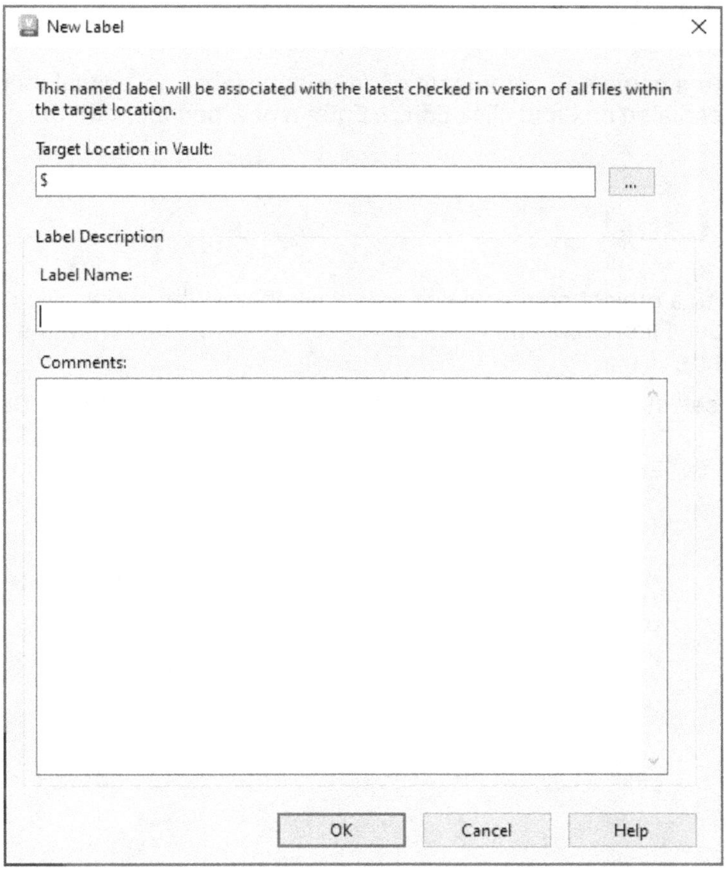

Figure 9–11

Note: *There is no limit to the number of labels that can be assigned to a project. Label names must be unique in the database and can contain any alpha-numeric text (excluding \ / : * ? " < > |).*

3. Select the target location for the label. The latest version of all of the files at that location is assigned that label. If child references exist outside the specified location, those files are also assigned that label.
4. Enter the name of the label that indicates the milestone. Since the folder information is not included, it is a good idea to include it in the name.
5. Enter comments that clearly summarize the content of the label.
6. Click **OK**.

Editing a Label

You can only edit the name and comments of an existing label. To edit a label, select one from the list in the *Label* dialog box and click **Edit...**. Enter a new name or edit the comments and click **OK**.

Deleting a Label

Assigning a label to a project creates a dependency between the project files and the corresponding label. Files associated with labels cannot be deleted from the vault unless the label is deleted first.

To delete a label, select a label from the list in the *Label* dialog box and click **Delete**. Click **Yes** to confirm deletion.

Extracting a Label

To extract a label, select a label from the list in the *Label* dialog box, then click **Pack and Go** to create a package of the label contents. Specify the Pack and Go details, as shown in Figure 9–12, including selecting which label to retrieve.

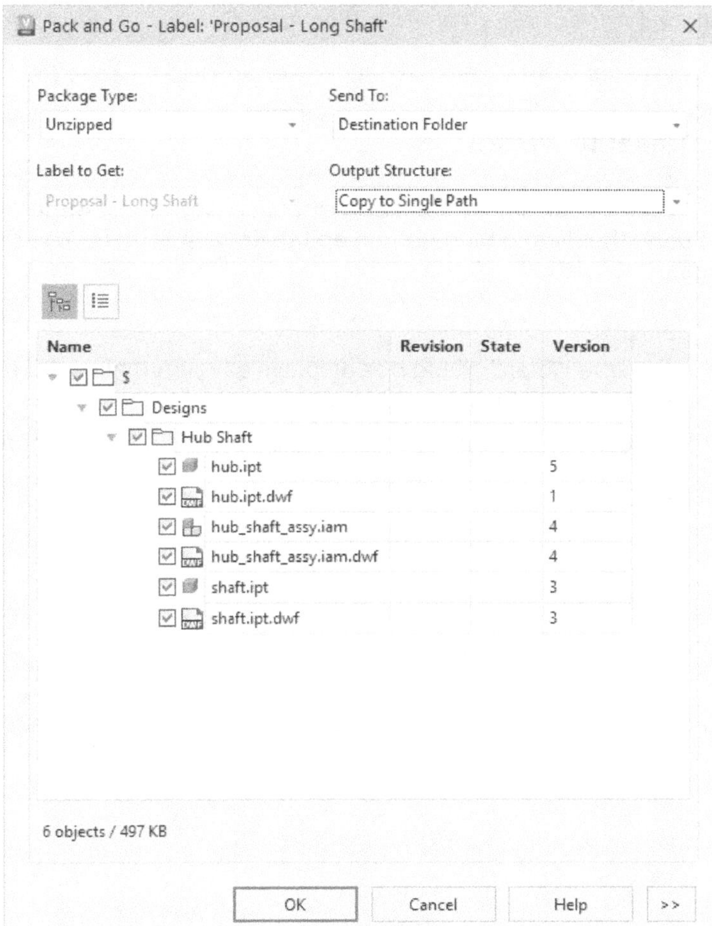

Figure 9–12

Restoring

When restoring a label, the version of the file(s) associated to the label becomes the current version.

To restore a label, select one from the list in the *Label* dialog box and click **Restore**. Click **Yes** to confirm the restore and creation of the new version.

9.4 Rename Wizard

The **Rename** operation in the Autodesk Vault software uses the Rename Wizard. In addition to renaming files, this operation updates all related files that reference the renamed files to ensure that all relationships remain intact. You must have permission to check out the files. Any file in the vault can be renamed using the Rename Wizard, except for .DWF files which are automatically published.

> ***Note:*** *Your user role must be defined as Editor or Administrator to use the Rename Wizard.*

How To: Use the Rename Wizard

1. In the Autodesk Vault Client, select the files, right-click, and select **Rename**. The Rename Wizard opens listing the files to be renamed and their vault folders. You can add or remove files in this page.

   Note: *You can also select a file and then select* ***Edit*** *(located in the Menu)>****Rename****.*

2. Click **Next>**. The *Rename Wizard* dialog box displays all related files and their vault locations that are affected by the name change.
3. Click **Next>**. Enter the new name for each file in the list, as shown in Figure 9–13.

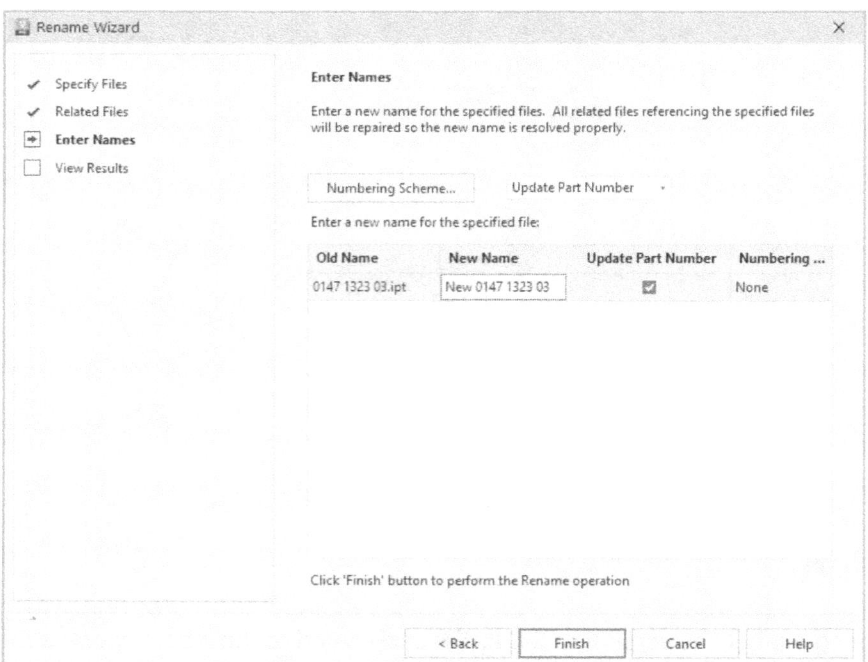

Figure 9–13

- You can click on **Numbering Scheme...** to edit or remove the prefix, add a suffix or choose to increment.

4. Select the checkbox in the *Update Part Number* column if you want to assign the new filename to the Part Number iProperty for Autodesk Inventor files.
5. Click **Finish**. The Rename Wizard performs the operation and displays the results.
6. Click **Save...** to export the results. Select the folder in which to save the report, enter the report name, and click **Save...**
7. Click **Send to Vault...** to save the report in the vault. Select the vault in which to save the report, enter the report name, and click **Save...**.
8. Click **Close**.

9.5 Replace Wizard

The *Replace Wizard* enables you to replace files with new files, which automatically updates the parent references. The file being replaced is not removed from the vault, versioned, or modified in anyway. Only the immediate parent files are changed to reference the new file. As a result, a new version of the parent file is created. Previous versions of the parent file will reference the old file, while new versions of the parent file will reference the new file.

How To: Use the Replace Wizard

> ***Note:*** *You must have permission to check out all related files before replacing files.*

1. In the Autodesk Vault Client, select the files, and select **Edit** (located in the Menu)>**Replace**. The *Replace Wizard* dialog box opens listing the files to be replaced and their vault folders. You can add or remove files from this page by clicking on the **Add Files...** button.
2. Click **Next>**.

> ***Note:*** *Replace can also be accomplished using the* ***Copy Design*** *option.*

3. On the *Related Files* page, all parent files display by default. To exclude a parent file from being updated with the new reference, clear the associated file checkbox.
4. Click **Next>**.

5. On the *Specify Replacement Files* page, shown in Figure 9–14, click ⋯ (Browse) to select a new file to replace the old file. Do this for each listed file.

   Note: *The status of the new file that replaces the old file does not matter.*

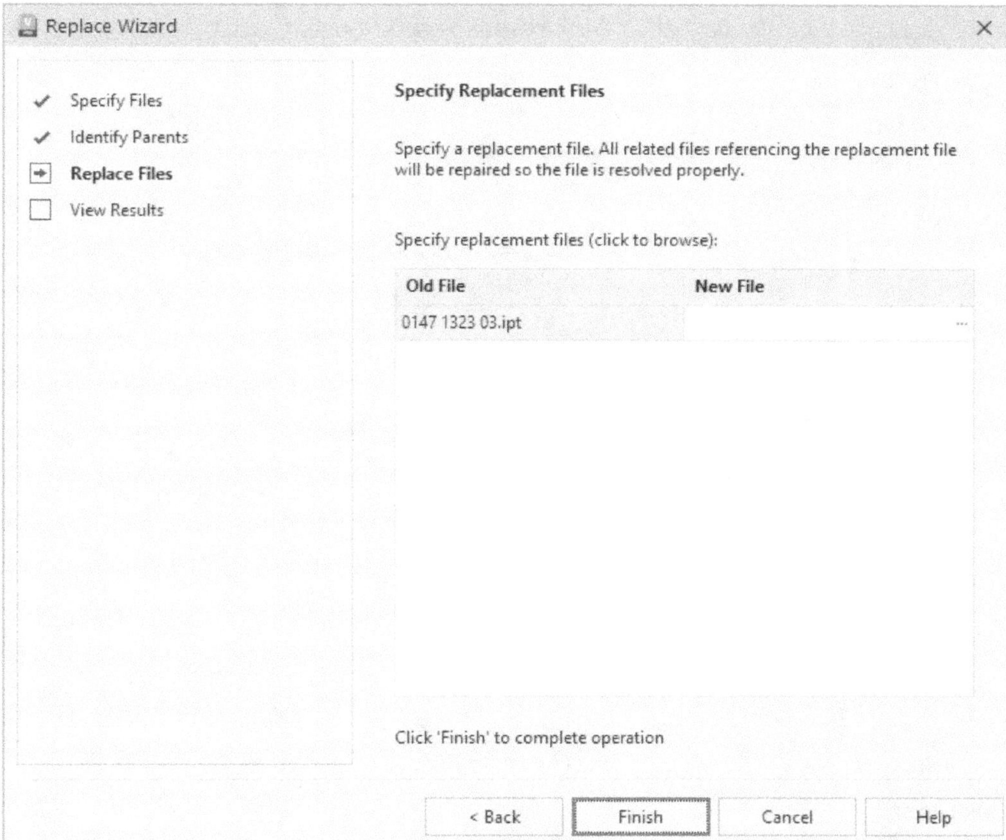

Figure 9–14

6. Click **Finish**. The *Replace Wizard* performs the operation and displays the results.
7. Click **Save...** to export the results to a text file.

8. Click **Send to Vault...** to save the report in the vault as shown in Figure 9–15. Select the vault in which to save the report, enter the report name, and click **Save...**.

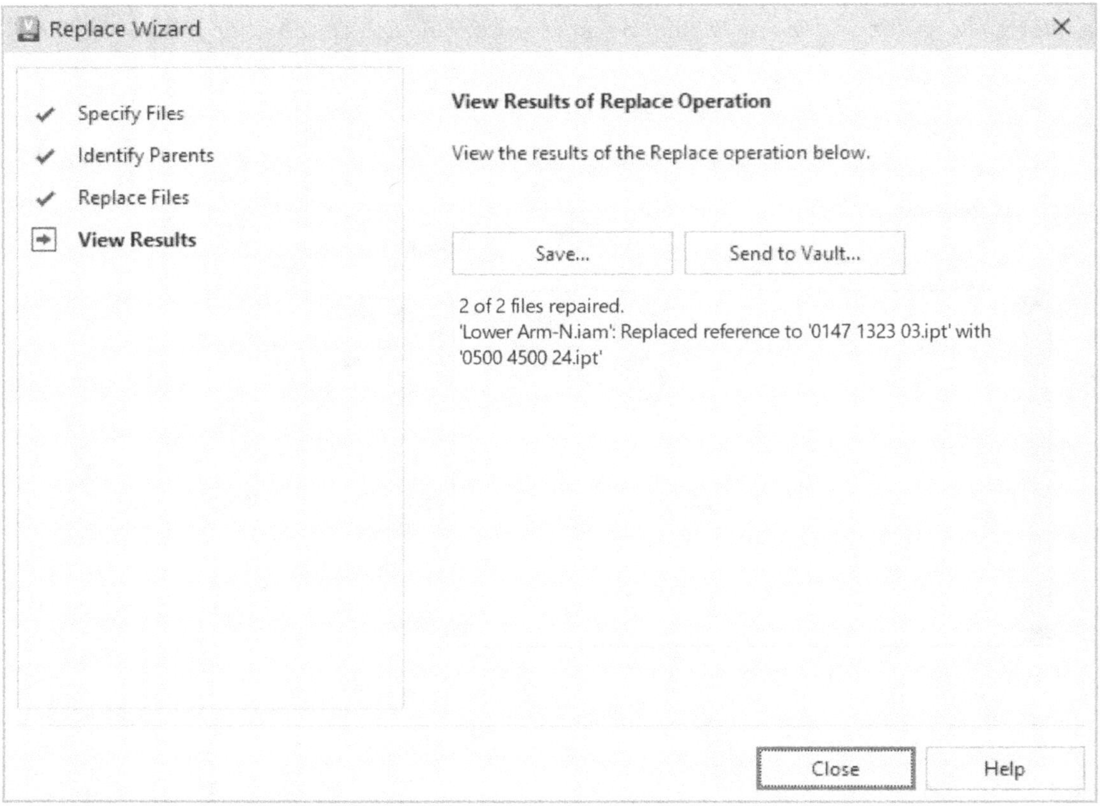

Figure 9–15

9. Click **Close**.

9.6 Pack and Go

The **Pack and Go** tool enables you to copy all of the referenced files to a single location outside of the CAD software, while also maintaining links to the referenced files. **Pack and Go** can be accessed from File Explorer or the Autodesk Vault software.

The **Pack and Go** tool is useful for archiving files, isolating a design for experimentation, and providing a complete project to a vendor who might not have access to the Autodesk Vault software. When using **Pack and Go**, you can specify the version of the files to retrieve, and whether you want to keep the folder hierarchy.

For Inventor, the **Pack and Go** tool can make it easier to add Autodesk Inventor projects that reside outside the vault. It creates a single-user project file that can then be converted into a vault project for use in the vault.

How To: Package a File and Its References in Autodesk Vault

1. In the Autodesk Vault Client, select the file that you want to package.
2. Select **File**(located in the Menu)**>Pack and Go...**. All of the files referenced by the selected file display as shown in Figure 9–16.

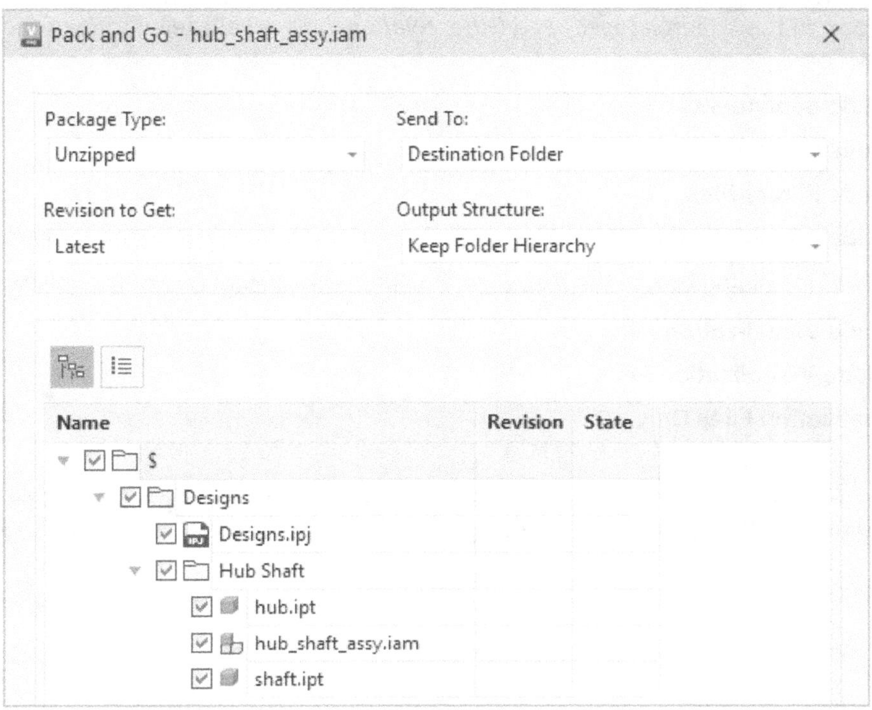

Figure 9–16

3. Set the *Package Type:* option to one of the following:
   - **Zip file (*.zip)**
   - **Unzipped**
   - **DWF Package**
   - **DWFx Package**
4. Set the *Send To:* option to one of the following:
   - **Destination Folder**
   - **Mail Recipient**
   - An installed Autodesk cloud drive (e.g., **Autodesk Drive** or **Fusion 360**)
5. Set the *Revision to Get*: option to the revision you want to package (**Latest**).
6. Set the *Output Structure:* option to one of the following:
   - **Copy to Single Path**
   - **Keep Folder Hierarchy**
7. Click (Settings) in the bottom right corner of the *Pack and Go* dialog box. In the *Settings* dialog box, in the *Children (uses)* and *Other relationships* areas, select one of the following options:
   - **Include dependents**
   - **Include attachments**
   - **Include library files**
   - **Include related documentation**
8. In the *Settings* dialog box, in the *Visualization Filter* area, select one of the following options:
   - **Include Visualization Files**
   - **Exclude Visualization Files**
   - **Visualization Files Only**
9. Click >> if you would like to append a transmittal report to the package. Select the **Append transmittal report to package** option and a template file, as shown in Figure 9–17.

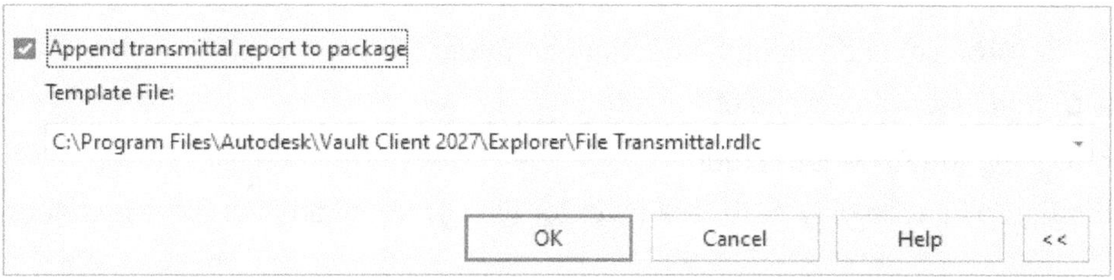

Figure 9–17

10. Click **OK**. If **Mail Recipient** was selected in the *Send To:* field, an email message opens. Depending on the Package Type selected, you are prompted for a folder or filename.

How To: Package a File and Its References in File Explorer

1. In File Explorer, right-click on the file you want to package and select **Pack and Go**. The *Pack and Go* dialog box opens. Click **More>>** to display the entire dialog box, as shown in Figure 9–18.

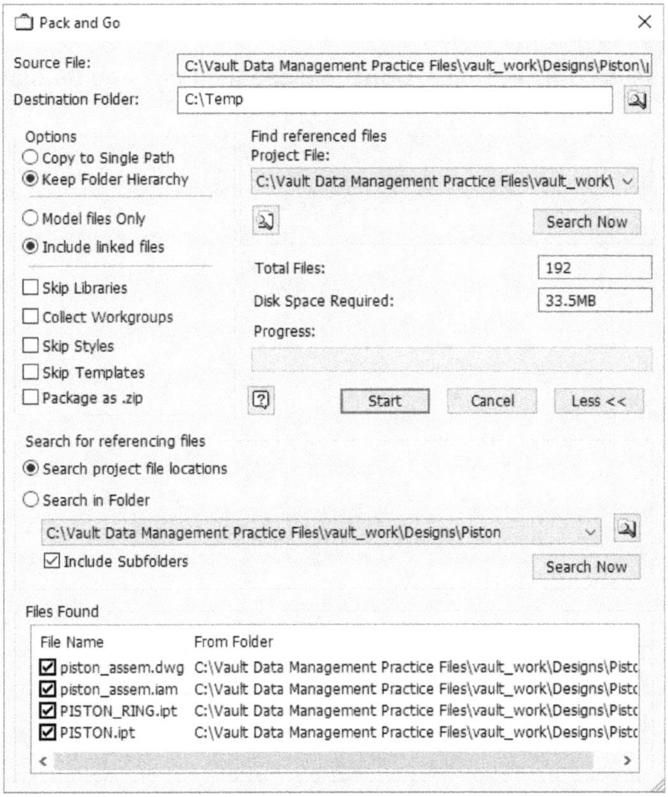

Figure 9–18

2. Click  (Browse) and select the destination folder.
3. In the *Options* area, select the options for:
    - Controlling the folder structure,
    - Whether to include only Autodesk Inventor files or all linked files (spreadsheets, etc.), and
    - Whether to skip libraries, templates, and styles or to collect workgroups.
4. In the *Find referenced files* area, set the *Project File* by selecting a project from the drop-down list, or by clicking  (Select project to use) and browsing to the project file.
5. In the *Find referenced files* area, click **Search Now**. The child files are listed in the *Files Found* area.
6. In the *Search for referencing files* area, click **Search Now**. Any files referencing the selected files are listed in the dialog box, which enables you to select which files to add to the list.

    Note: *Referenced files are typically drawing or presentation files.*

7. Click **Start** to begin copying the files.
8. When the process is complete, click **Done** to close the *Pack and Go* dialog box.

9.7 Synchronize Your Workspace

You can synchronize the contents of your local workspace with the corresponding Vault folders using the Vault Client. This operation either updates the files in either location, or removes files from the workspace.

You can click **Workspace Sync** to manually select the local files to synchronize and select the Settings for additional options. Alternatively, you can select **Quick Sync** from the drop-down list to synchronize immediately using the default settings.

How To: Synchronize Your Workspace

1. Select **Workspace Sync** from the toolbar, as shown in Figure 9–19.

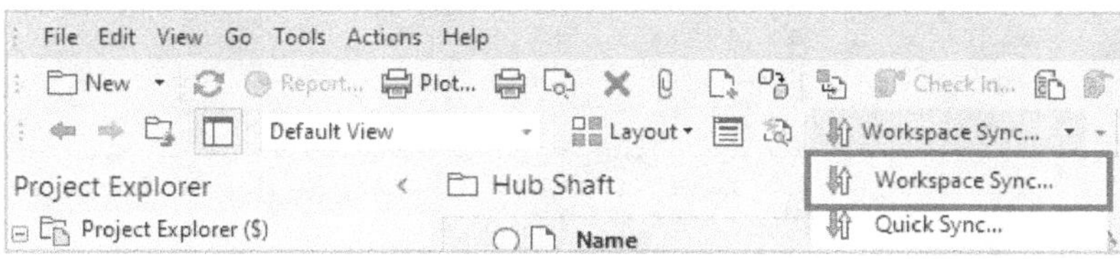

Figure 9–19

2. Select the check boxes for the files you would like to synchronize, as shown in Figure 9–20. Removed files are placed in the Windows Recycle Bin.

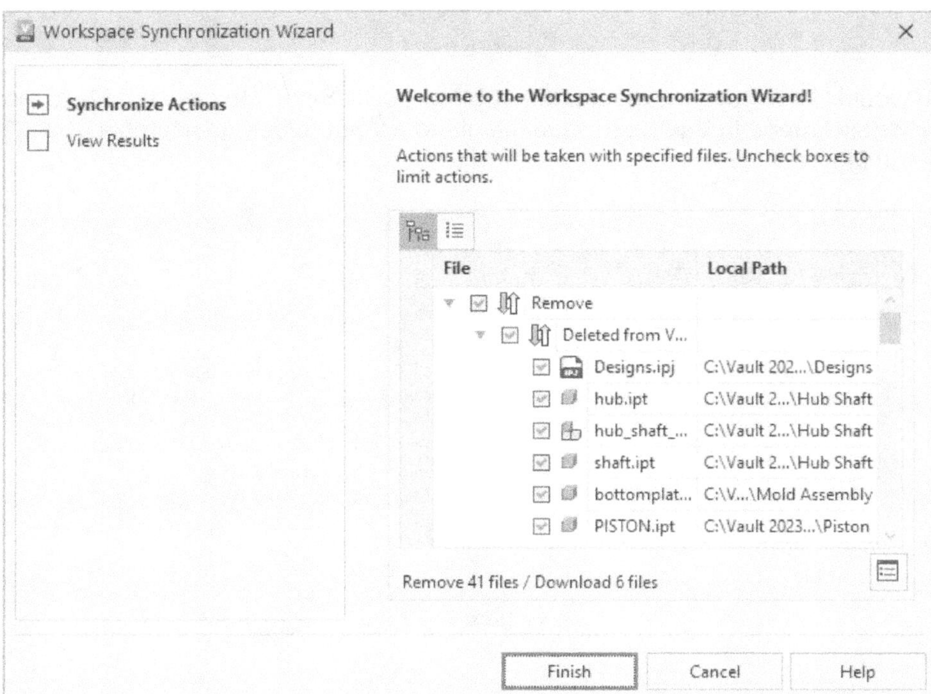

Figure 9–20

3. Select **Finish**. The results display as shown in Figure 9–21.

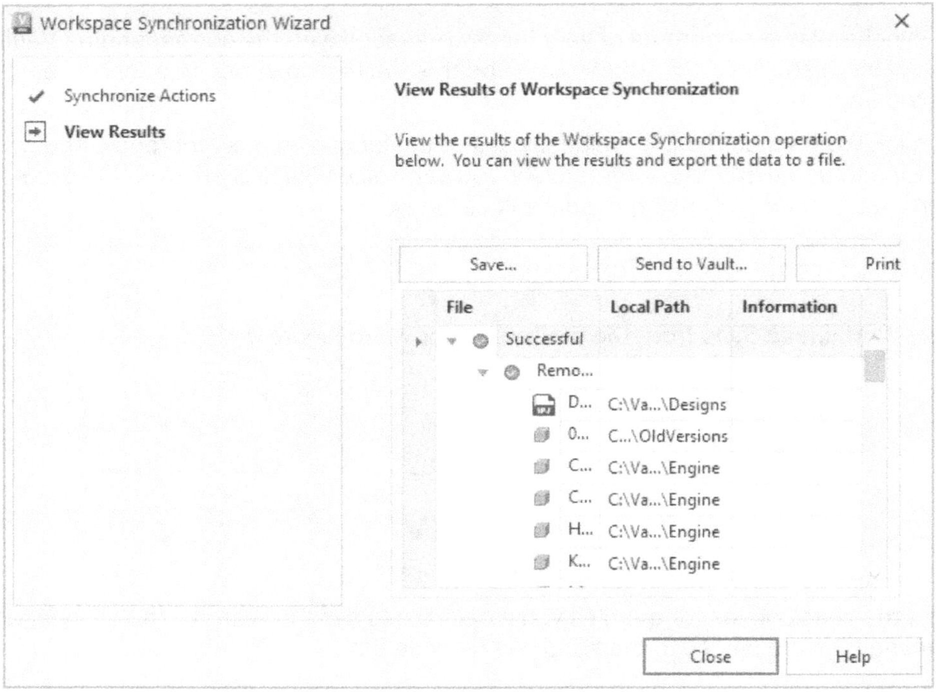

Figure 9–21

4. If you would like to save the results to a .CSV file, click **Save...** to save the file to a specified folder, or click **Send to Vault...** to save the file to a Vault folder. An example of a .CSV file is shown in Figure 9–22.

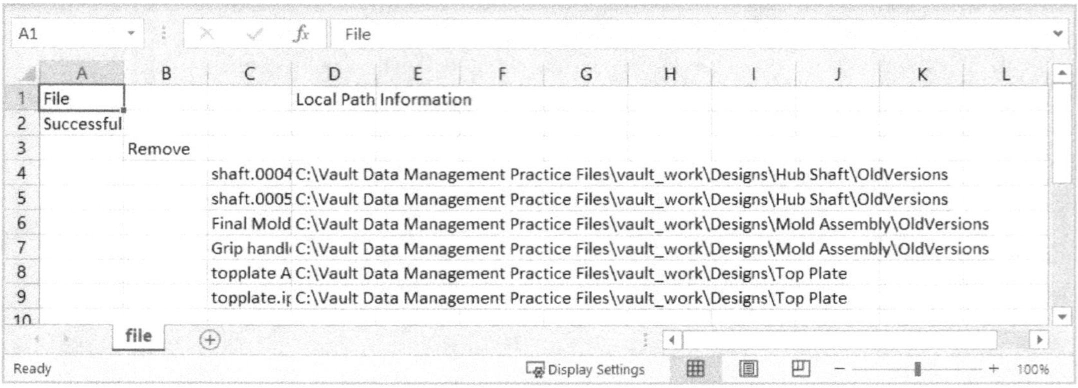

Figure 9–22

9.8 Copy Design

The **Copy Design** command enables you to copy an entire design (including all related files, parts, drawings, subassemblies, and attachments), and maintain their relationships to the new design. **Copy Design** commands can include copying, reusing, replacing, and excluding specified files from the existing design to create the new design.

Accessing Copy Design

Copy Design can be executed in Autodesk Vault using the **Edit** menu>Copy Design icon in the standard toolbar, or from the right-click menu. The Copy Design interface is launched in a modeless dialog, therefore, allowing you to perform work within Autodesk Vault while performing a Copy Design. Copy Design can also be executed as a standalone application from the Windows Start menu.

Copy Design Interface

There are three major sections of the *Copy Design* interface: the menu and toolbars, main view, and the Navigation panel, as shown in Figure 9–23.

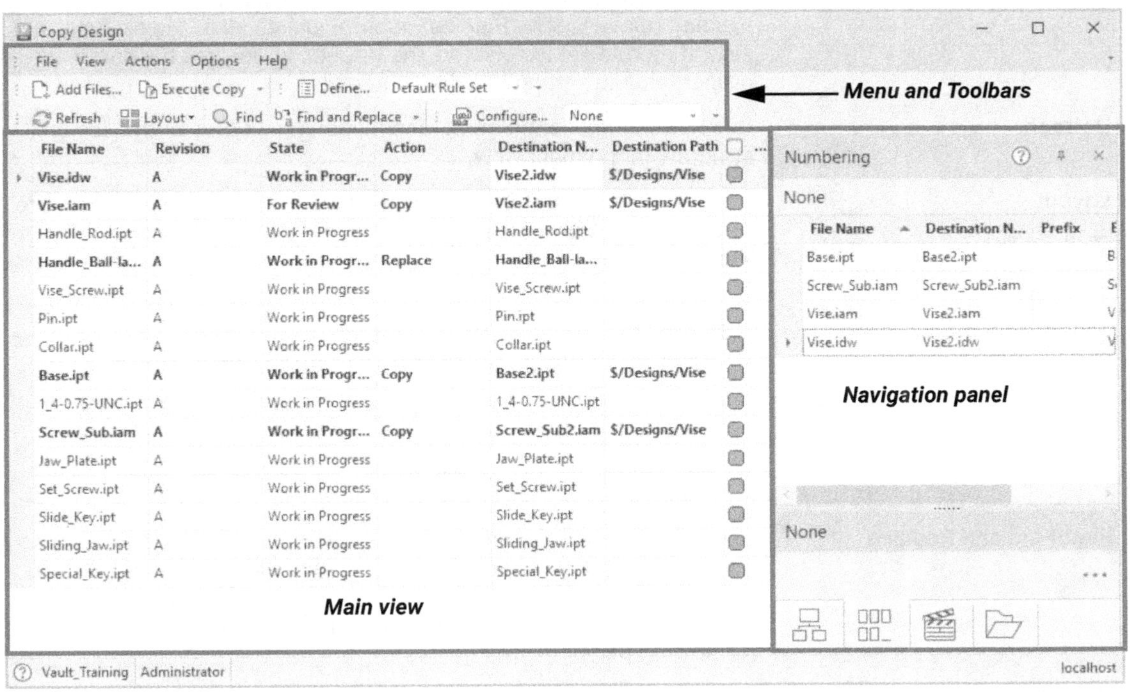

Figure 9–23

Menu and Toolbars

The menu includes the following menus: **File**, **View**, **Actions**, **Options**, and **Help**. Many of the commands found in these menus are also found in the toolbars and context (right-click) menus.

The toolbars can be used to add files to the main view, find and replace files, control copy settings or action rule sets, and create copies. The toolbar commands are described in the table below.

Command	Description
Log In/Log Out	If Copy Design is started from the Start menu, select **Log In**, to log into a vault to access designs for copying. Use **Log Out** to log out of a vault when you are finished or when you want to switch to a different vault.
Add Files	Add the files that you want to copy to the main view with **Add Files**.
Execute Copy	Once everything is configured, select **Execute Copy** to begin the copy operation.
Select Rule Set	A Rule set determines the file properties and settings for copied files when certain conditions are met. Users can select from a list of existing rule sets. The Rule Set sub-menu lists all of the existing rule sets. If no rule set is selected, the target file receives the same file properties and settings as the source file.
Refresh	Use Refresh to see the most recent changes to files or the design structure in the main view.
Layout	Use Layout to control the view of the files in the main view. There are three options: **Show Tree View**, **Show List View**, and **Show Folder View**. 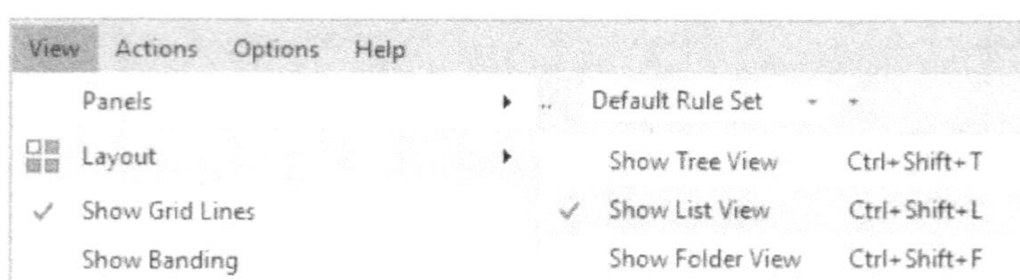
Find/Find and Replace	Use Find to search for words or characters; Use Find and Replace to search for words or characters and replace them with the ones you want (This is handy when you want to replace all instances of a word). You can perform the operation in the main window or the *Numbering* panel.
Configure	Enables you to configure the Numbering Scheme.

The Main View Grid

The main Copy Design view shows the name of the files available to copy, destination folder, the action that will be performed on the file, the revision and state of the file, and how many instances (Count) of the file occur in the current list.

Tip: By default, reference file names are set to the destination file name when an action is assigned. You can view the *Numbering* panel to identify files by their original name, or add *File Name (Historical)* to the main view. You can also manage copy actions and customize the view, including filtering columns, from the main view, as shown in Figure 9–24.

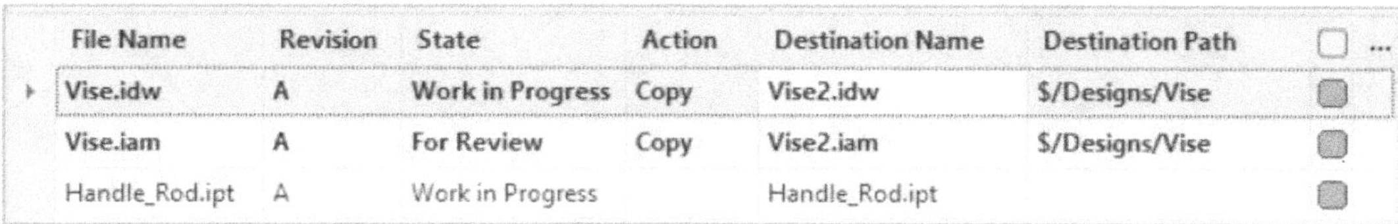

File Name	Revision	State	Action	Destination Name	Destination Path
Vise.idw	A	Work in Progress	Copy	Vise2.idw	$/Designs/Vise
Vise.iam	A	For Review	Copy	Vise2.iam	$/Designs/Vise
Handle_Rod.ipt	A	Work in Progress		Handle_Rod.ipt	

Figure 9–24

To change a copy action, select the file, right-click and select **Copy**, **Copy To...**, **Replace...**, **Exclude** or **Reuse**. **Copy To...** and **Replace...** prompt you to select the destination folder and replacement file, respectively.

The available file actions depend on the type of file selected. These are described as follows:

Action	Description
Copy	Generates a new file that is independent of the selected source file.
Copy To...	Enables you to change the destination folder of the selected file.
Reuse	Keeps the selected file in the new design while maintaining all links.
Exclude	Omits the selected file from the new design.
Replace...	Enables you to substitute the selected file with another one.

The Navigation Panel

There are four different navigation panels, each located on their own tab:

- Where Used
- Actions
- Numbering
- Folders

The *Actions* panel displays with its tab selected, as shown in Figure 9–25.

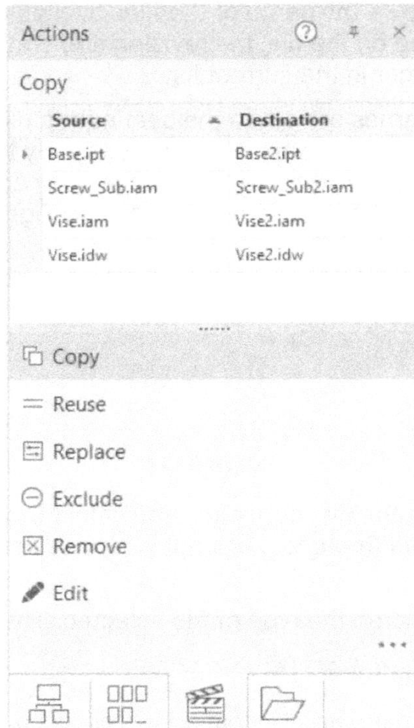

Figure 9–25

The options available in the four navigation panels are as follows:

Panel	Details
Where Used 	The *Where Used* panel lets users track the origin of the copy objects and their destination. Since you can replace existing files with uncommitted instances of files that are being copied, this means that the copied instance can have numerous destinations. Use the *Where Used* tab to ensure that the files are copied to the correct locations.
Actions 	The *Actions* panel enables you to review which operations are going to be performed on files in the main view. Once you have configured the files in the main view, you can use the *Actions* panel to filter the files based on their assigned operation. Assigned operations include copied, reused, replaced, excluded, or edited. Use the *Actions* panel to verify the copy design configuration in the main view and to make changes. Note that you can also set Action operations by dragging and dropping files from the main grid onto the required operation button in the *Actions* panel.

Panel	Details
Numbering 	The *Numbering* panel lists all of the files selected for copying. It also shows the original and new name for each selected file. The grid displays the renaming options based on available numbering schemes. In the *Numbering* panel grid, you can edit certain fields and individual numbering schemes.
Folders 	The *Folders* panel enables you to review the source and destination folders for the copy design operation. This helps you verify that the required files are selected and are being copied to the correct location. You can group selected files for operations based on the folder location. You can also drag and drop files between folders or from the main grid to perform a copy. You can also display the files in a Tree View or List View. There is **Find and Replace** functionality in the List View, in the shortcut menu, as shown below. 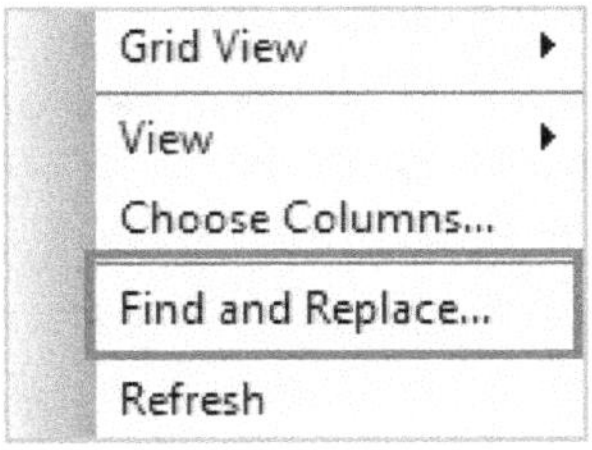

Performing a Copy Design (Vault Professional)

How To: Use Copy Design to Create a New Design Using Vault Professional

1. Select and right-click on a file from the main table and then select **Copy Design**.
2. If desired, select **Options** from the menu and select which of the following options do you want enabled:
   - **Automatically Copy Parents**
   - **Link Drawings and Model**
   - **Remove BOM Object**
   - **Select References**

   Notes: You can also access Action Rules and Numbering Schemes from this menu or from the toolbars.
3. If desired, select **Add Files** from the toolbar to select additional files that you want to copy and then click **Open**. The files are added to the main view of the *Copy Design* dialog box.

4. If desired, select **View** from the menu and select **Show Drawing View** to display the drawings that are participating in the copy design or **Show Children** to select **Attachments**, **Library Files**, or both in the Copy Design view.
5. If desired, turn on **Show Drawing View** in the View Menu to see the drawings participating in the Copy Design.
    - By default, associated drawings receive the same copy action as the associated file and is denoted by a value of **Auto** in the *Action* column. In Model View, documentation set to **Auto** takes the same name as the dependent file being replaced or copied. This can result in file name duplication. Select **View>Show Drawing View** to turn on the Drawing View to help resolve file naming conflicts.
    - When using Show Drawing View, view the files in Tree View by selecting **View>Layout>Show Tree View.**

    Note: *Click* ***Refresh*** *to display the latest version of the listed files.*
6. If you want to perform a different action other than copy, on a file, right-click on the file and select the action from the context menu.
7. In the toolbar, select the rule set from the drop-down list that you want to apply to the copy operation. The file properties and behavior settings determined by the rule set are applied to the destination files.

    Note: *To apply a numbering scheme, select a numbering scheme from the button list in the Numbering panel.*
8. To review the settings before executing the copy, display the **Actions**, **Folders**, **Numbering** and **Where Used** panels under **View>Panels**. View each panel and confirm all settings are correct.
9. Once everything is configured, select **Execute Copy** from the toolbar or from the **File** menu to start the copy operation.

All successful copy operations receive a green checkmark in the main view. If a copy operation failed, a red cross displays. To perform another copy operation, modify your settings and click **Execute Copy**.

Practice 9a
Data Management and Rename Wizard

Practice Objectives

- Use the Move operation to move a file from one folder to another folder.
- Attach one file to another file.
- Rename an assembly and a part.

In this practice, you will use Autodesk Vault's file management functionality to move and rename files. In addition, you will attach a file to another file to have them behave as one unit.

Task 1: Set the Autodesk Inventor project file (if not already set earlier).

1. In the Main table of the Autodesk Vault software, in the *$\Designs* folder, locate **Designs.ipj**.
2. Right-click **Designs.ipj** and select **Set Inventor Project File,** as shown in Figure 9–26.

   Note: *You can also set the Autodesk Inventor project file in Autodesk Vault by selecting **Tools>Options**.*

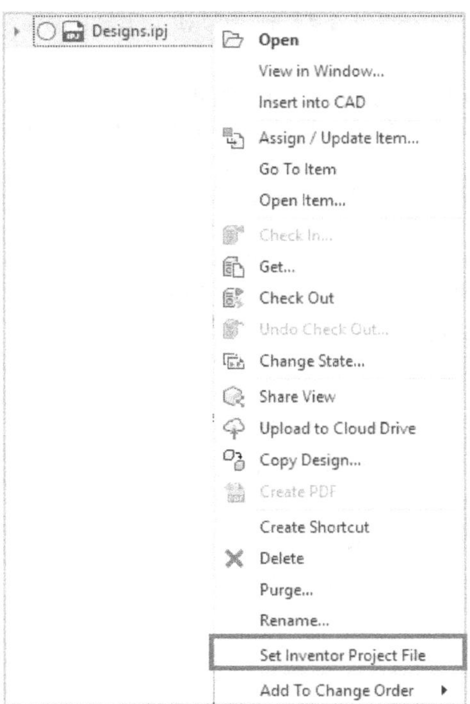

Figure 9–26

Task 2: Move a file from one folder to another folder.

1. Locate the file **3136 1094 44.ipt**.
2. In the Search Results, right-click on the file and select **Go To Folder**. It is located in the *$\Designs\Arm System* folder and is being used in three assemblies as shown in the *Where Used* tab of the Preview pane (**3136 1133 82.iam**, **Middle Arm-N.iam**, and **Arm System.iam**) as shown in Figure 9–27.

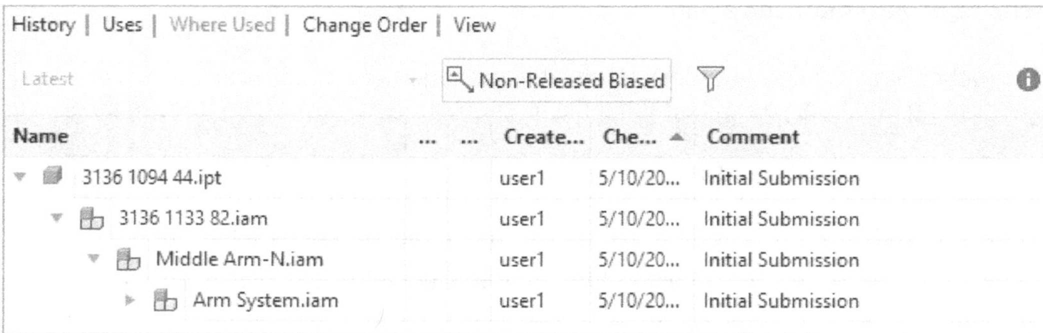

Figure 9–27

3. In the Main table, select **3136 1094 44.ipt** and drag it into the *$\Designs\Yoke* folder. Click **Yes** to confirm the move.
4. In the *$\Designs\Yoke* folder, select **3136 1094 44.ipt**. In the Preview pane, select the *Where Used* tab to see that it maintains the child relationships to the three assemblies.

Task 3: Attach one file to another file.

In this task, you will attach a Microsoft Word document to an Autodesk Inventor part file so that they behave as one unit when checking out and checking in.

1. Locate and select **yoke.ipt**.
2. Select **Actions>Attachments**.
3. In the *Attachments* dialog box, click **Attach...**.
4. In the *Select File to Attach* dialog box, in the *$>Documentation* folder, locate and select the file **Operating instructions.doc**. Click **Open**.
5. In the *Attachments* dialog box, click **OK**.

6. In the Preview pane, select the *Uses* tab. Note that the *Attachments* node contains an entry, as shown in Figure 9–28.

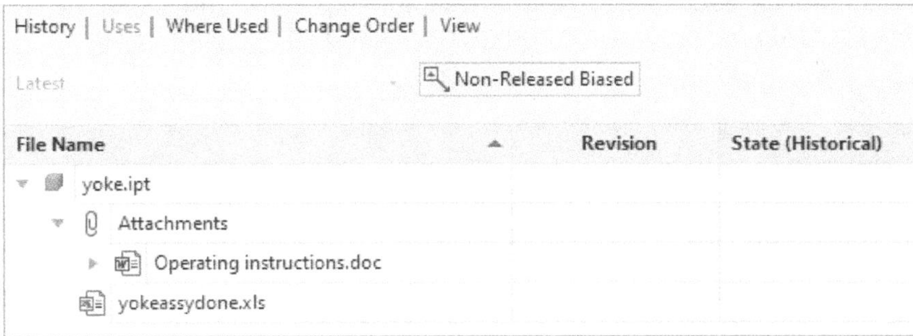

Figure 9–28

Task 4: Rename an assembly and a part.

In this task, you will use the *Rename Wizard* to rename **topplate Assy.iam** and **topplate.ipt**.

1. In Autodesk Vault, browse to the *$\Designs\Top Plate* folder.
2. Select the two files **topplate Assy.iam** and **topplate.ipt**, right-click, and select **Rename**. The *Rename Wizard* opens, as shown in Figure 9–29.

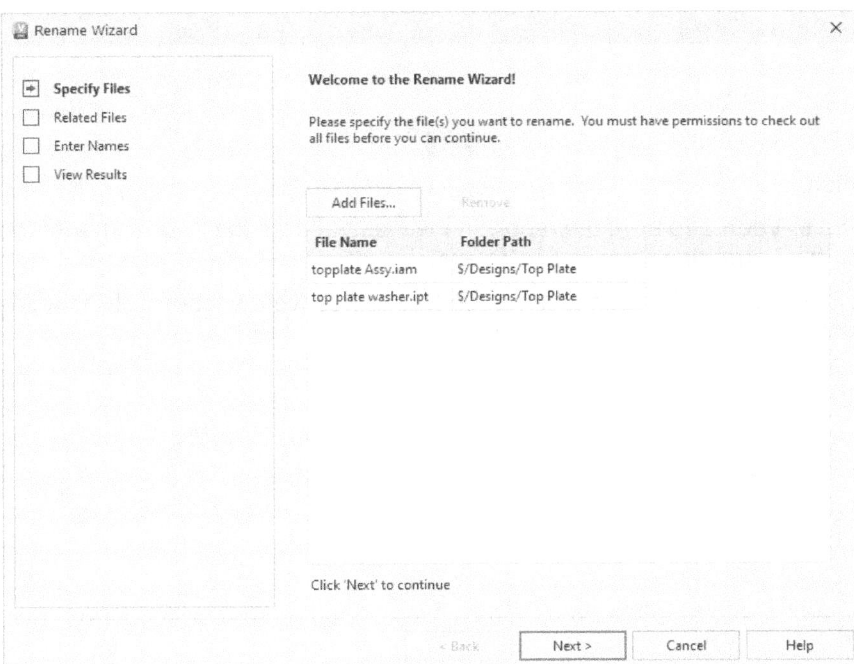

Figure 9–29

3. Click **Next>** to continue. There are no files affected by the rename so the *Related Files* page was automatically skipped.
4. Enter new names for each file, **Top Plate Assy** and **Top Plate**, and select the checkbox in the *Update Part Number* column for both parts, as shown in Figure 9–30.

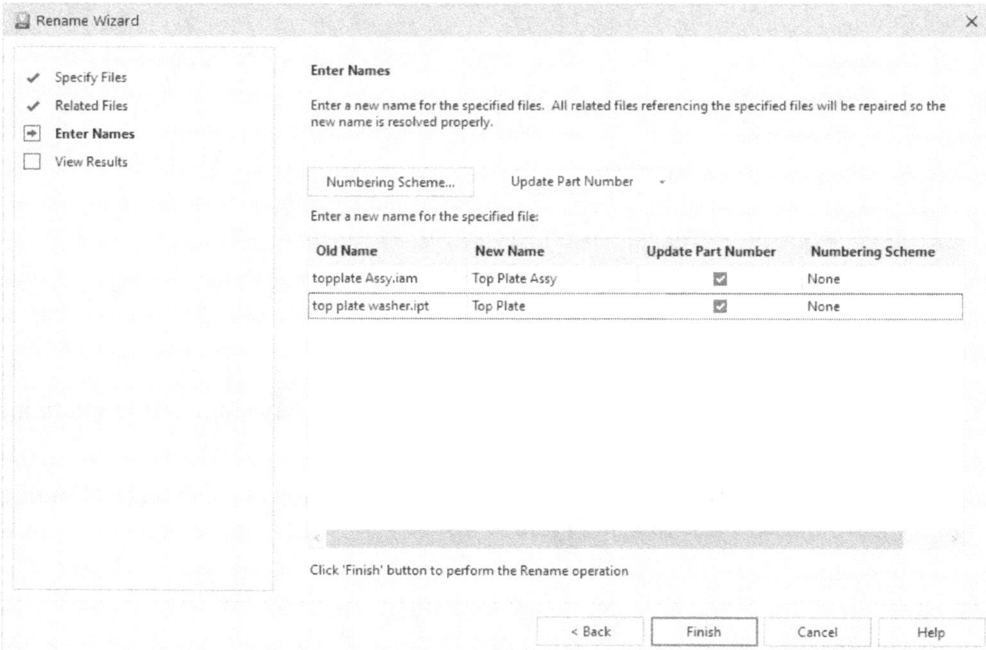

Figure 9–30

5. Click **Finish**.
6. Click **Send to Vault...** to save the report in the vault. Locate the ...*Documentation* folder and name the file **Renaming Report**. Click **Save**.
7. On the *View Results* page, confirm that both renames were successful, including the part number updates, as shown in Figure 9–31.

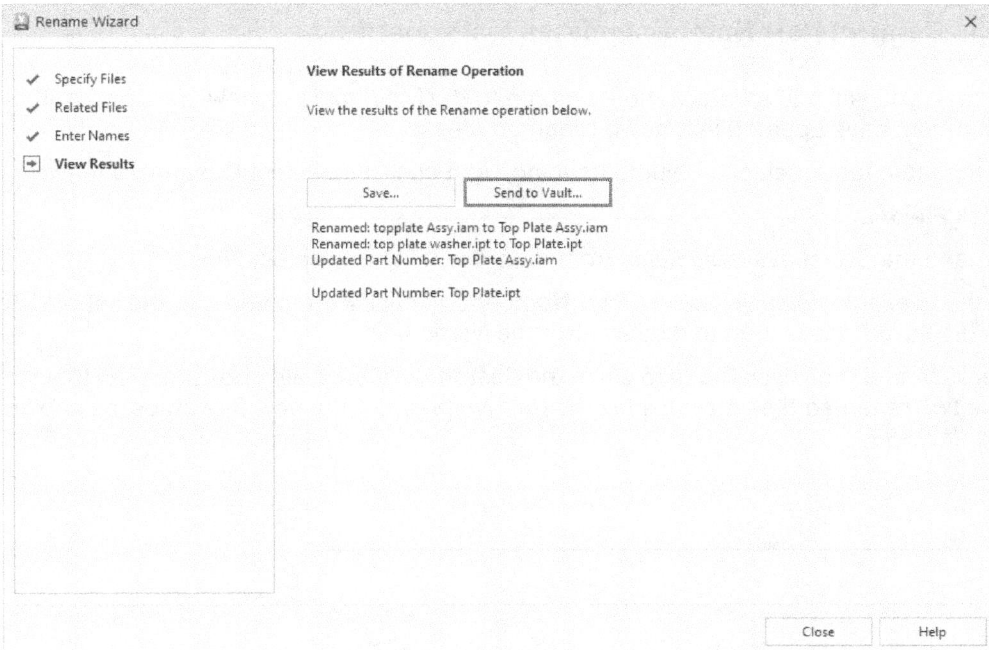

Figure 9–31

8. Click **Close**.
9. In the Main table, select **Top Plate Assy.iam**. In the Preview pane, select the *History* tab. The **Rename** operation has created Version 2 of the file and the comments have been filled in automatically, as shown in Figure 9–32.

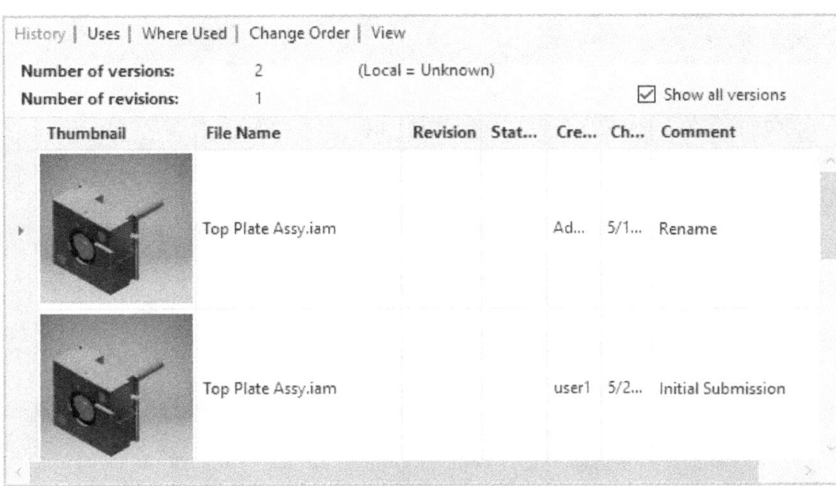

Figure 9–32

Task 5: Confirm Part Number updates in iProperties.

In this task, you will add a *Part Number* column to the Main table to view and confirm that the Part Numbers have updated in the two renamed files.

1. In the Main table, select a column heading, right-click, and select **Customize View**.
2. Click **Fields...**.
3. Expand the *Select available fields from* drop-down list and select **Files**.
4. In the *Available fields* list, select **Part Number** and click **Add** to add it to the list of fields to be displayed. Move it up to display after the *Name* field.
5. Click **OK** and then click **Close** to close the *Customize View* dialog box and view the changes. The two renamed files now display the *Part Numbers* of the new filenames, as shown in Figure 9–33.

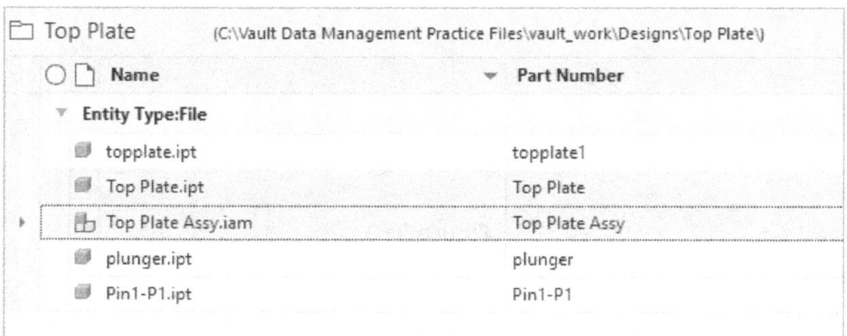

Figure 9–33

End of practice

Practice 9b
Edit File Properties and Create Labels

Practice Objectives

- Edit the file properties of an assembly.
- Create a label.

In this practice, you will edit file properties in the Autodesk Vault client interface and create a label to mark a design milestone for the hub shaft assembly.

Task 1: Edit the file properties of an assembly.

In this task, you will edit the file properties of an assembly and two of its parts. The file property that requires editing, **Company**, first needs to be displayed so that it can be edited.

1. In Autodesk Vault, navigate to the *$\Designs\Piston* folder. If the *State* of the files is not set to Work In Progress, use the **Change State** command to change all of the files in the folder to **Work In Progress**. Also, use **Undo Check Out** if the files are checked out.
2. Select all of the files in the *$\Designs\Piston* folder (**piston_assem.dwg, piston_assem.iam, piston.ipt**, and **piston_ring.ipt**) and, in the Properties grid, click (Edit Properties).
3. Click (Select Properties) to customize the list of file properties to edit.
4. Expand the *Select available fields from* drop-down list and select **Files**.
5. Select **Company** and click **Add** to add it to the list of file properties to edit.
6. Move **Company** so that it displays after **Author** in the list and click **OK**.
7. Double-click in the *Company* cell for the file in the first row. Enter **ABC Company** and press <Enter>. Drag the small black box in the bottom right corner of the cell to the bottom row to copy the value to the other *Company* cells.
8. Click **OK**.

9. The *Property Edit Results* window opens displaying the results with the new **Company** value, as shown in Figure 9–34.

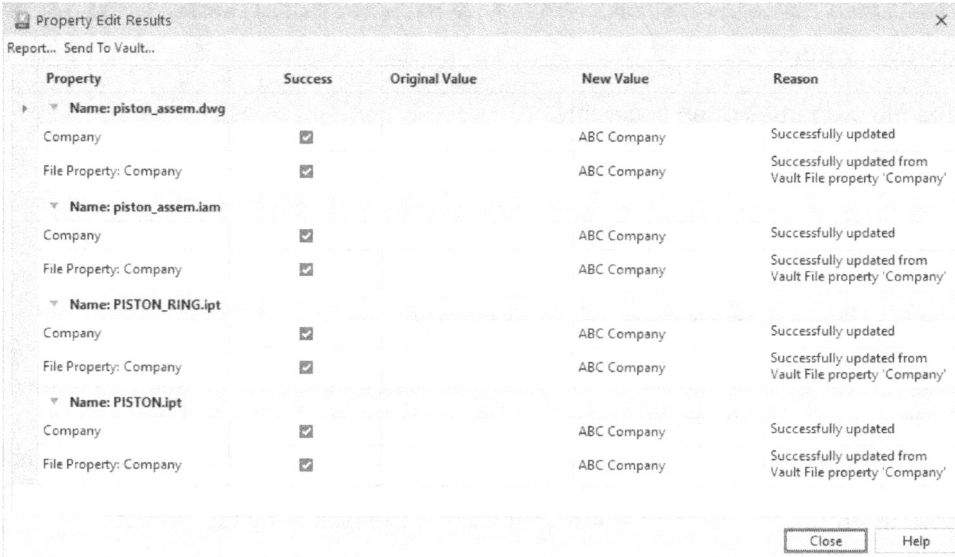

Figure 9–34

10. Select **Send To Vault** to save the report in the vault. Navigate to the *$\Documentation* folder and name the file **New Company Report**. Click **Save**.

11. Click **Close**.

Task 2: Verify the iProperties in Autodesk Inventor and then edit them.

In this task, you will open the file **piston_assem.iam** in the Autodesk Inventor software and verify the iProperty edit. You will then edit it again in the Autodesk Inventor software.

1. In the Autodesk Inventor software, in the *Vault* tab>*Access* panel, click  (Open).

2. In the *Search* field, enter **piston** and press <Enter>, as shown in Figure 9–35.

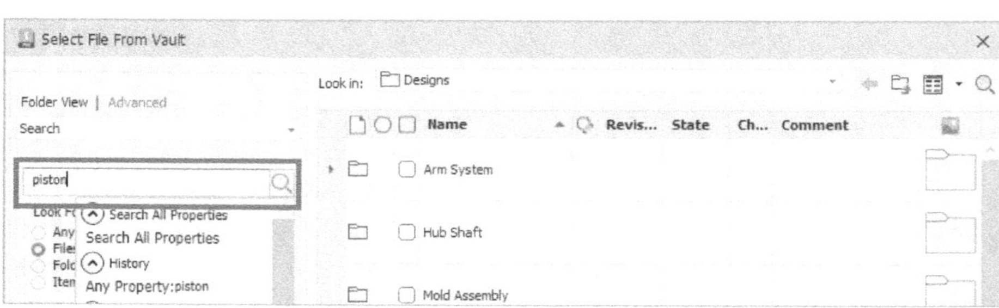

Figure 9–35

3. In the search results window, double-click on **piston_assem.iam**.
4. Click **Yes** to check out and modify the file.
5. In the *Check Out* dialog box, click **OK**.
6. In the Model Browser, select **piston_assem.iam**, right-click, and select **iProperties**. Select the *Summary* tab and verify that the *Company* is **ABC Company**.
7. Change the company name to **XYZ Company** and click **OK**.
8. Switch to the Vault Browser. The file displays in bold font with an asterisk, indicating that a save is required.
9. In the Quick Access Toolbar, click (Save) and click **OK**.
10. Select **piston_assem.iam**, right-click, select **Check In**, and click **OK**.

Task 3: Verify the iProperty change made in Autodesk Inventor.

In this task, you will confirm that the iProperty change made in the Autodesk Inventor software reflects correctly in the Autodesk Vault software.

1. In the Autodesk Vault software, click (Refresh) to update the Main table view in the *$\Designs\Piston* folder.
2. Select **piston_assem.iam**. In the Properties grid *User Defined* section, note that *Company* is now **XYZ Company**.

Task 4: Create a label.

In this task, you will create a label to mark a proposal milestone that displays the hub shaft design with a longer shaft.

1. Select **Tools>Labels**.
2. Click **New...** to create a new label.
3. The *New Label* dialog box opens. For the target location, click (Browse). Expand the *$\Designs* folder and select the *Hub Shaft* subfolder. Click **OK**.
4. For the label name, enter **Proposal - Long Shaft**.

5. In the *Comments* area, enter **The shaft was increased in length and proposed to ABC Company**, as shown in Figure 9–36.

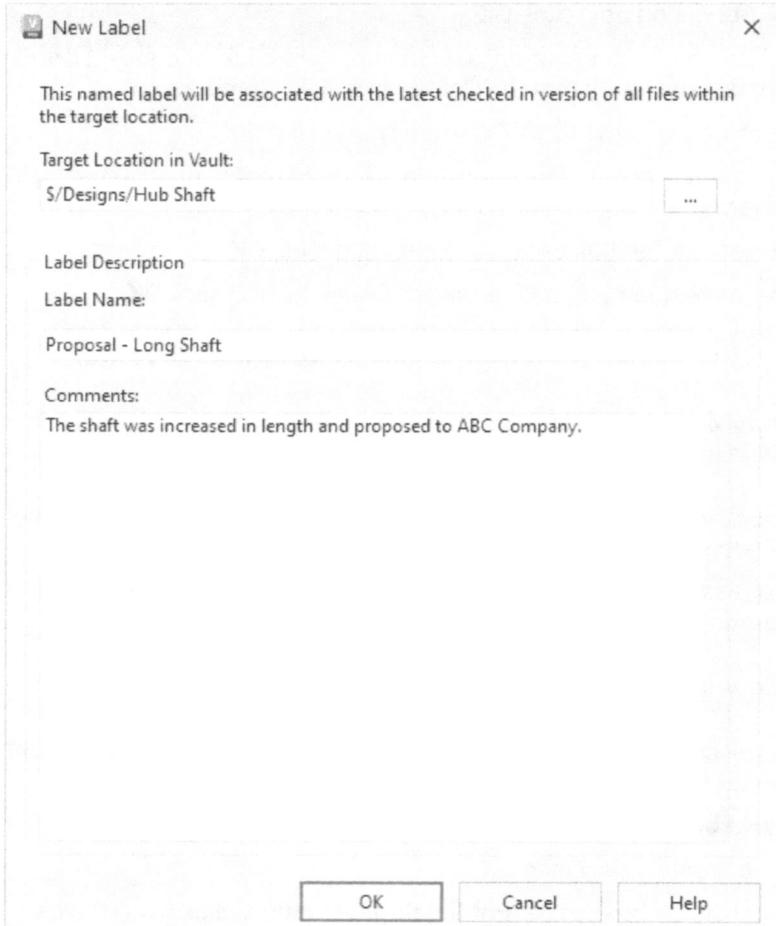

Figure 9–36

6. Click **OK**. In the *Labels* dialog box, the details of the new label display.
7. Click **Close** to close the *Labels* dialog box.

End of practice

Practice 9c
Copy Design

Practice Objective

- Create a new design using the Copy Design command.

In this practice, you will make a copy of **Vise.idw** using the **Copy Design** command. The files from Vise.idw will be set to be copied, replaced, or reused.

Task 1: Set up for the Copy Design command.

In this task, you start the **Copy Design** command and select the files you want to copy, reuse, and replace.

> ***Note:*** *If you need to remove all files from the dialog box, select the root node, right-click, and select* ***Clear Root Node****.*

1. Navigate to the *Vise* folder. In the Main table, right-click on **Vise.idw** and select **Copy Design**.
2. To display the files in a list, select **View>Layout>Show List View**.
3. Using <Ctrl>, select files **Vise.idw, Vise.iam, Base.ipt**, and **Screw_Sub.iam**, and then right-click and select **Copy**.
4. Select **Handle_Ball.ipt,** right-click and select **Replace.** Navigate to the *Vise* folder, select **Handle_Ball-large.ipt,** then click **Replace**. The *Copy Design* window displays as shown in Figure 9–37.

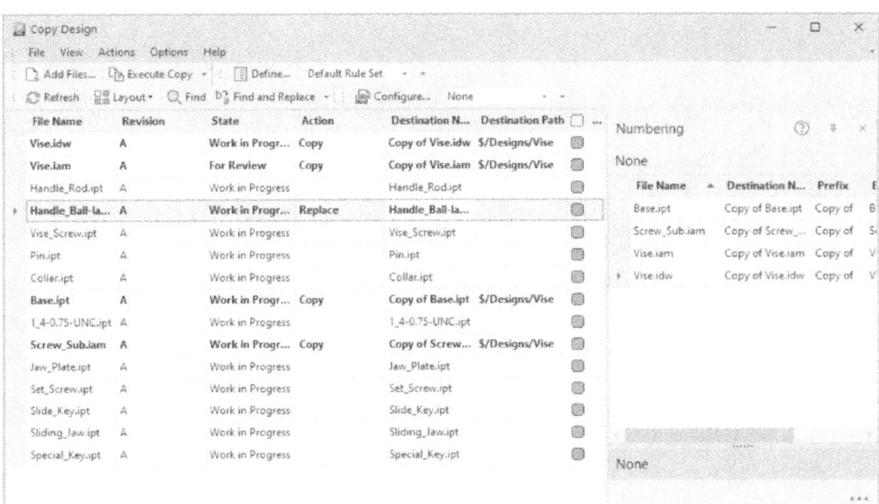

Figure 9–37

5. In the *Numbering* panel on the right, right-click in the white background and select **Set Values>Prefix**. Click **OK** to remove the values for *Prefix*. Set the value of the *Suffix* to **2**. Note that the *Destination Name* column updates as shown in Figure 9–38.

Numbering

None

File Name	Destination Name	Prefix	Base Name	Suffix
Base.ipt	Base2.ipt		Base	2
Screw_Sub.iam	Screw_Sub2.iam		Screw_Sub	2
Vise.iam	Vise2.iam		Vise	2
Vise.idw	Vise2.idw		Vise	2

Figure 9–38

Note: *If the Numbering panel is not displayed, select* ***View>Panels>Numbering****.*

6. Click in the *Destination Path* field for **Vise.idw**, and then click to create a new folder under *Designs* named **Vise2**. Change the *Destination Path* for the copied files to *Vise2*, as shown in Figure 9–39.

Destination Name	Destination Path
Vise2.idw	**$/Designs/Vise2**
Vise2.iam	**$/Designs/Vise2**
Handle_Rod.ipt	
Handle_Ball-large.ipt	
Vise_Screw.ipt	
Pin.ipt	
Collar.ipt	
Base2.ipt	**$/Designs/Vise2**
1_4-0.75-UNC.ipt	
Screw_Sub2.iam	**$/Designs/Vise2**
Jaw_Plate.ipt	
Set_Screw.ipt	
Slide_Key.ipt	
Sliding_Jaw.ipt	
Special_Key.ipt	

Figure 9–39

Task 2: Create a copy of the files and view the copied files.

In this task, you will create a copy of the selected files.

1. Click **Execute Copy** in the toolbar to start the copy operation. When successful, a green checkmark will display for the **Copy** and **Replace** actions, as shown in Figure 9–40.

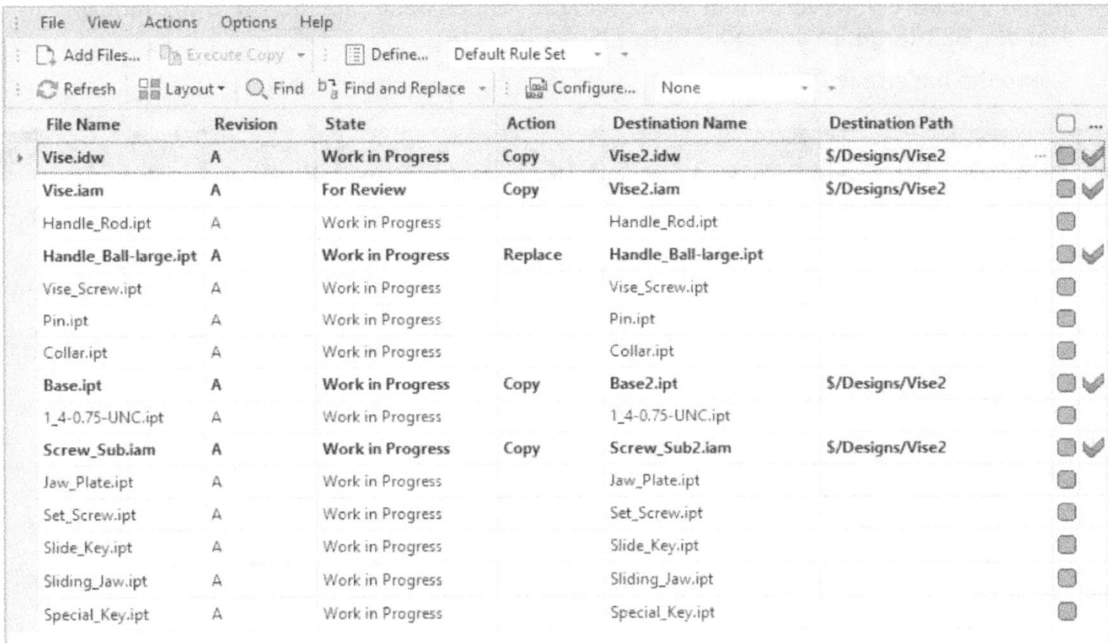

Figure 9–40

2. Close the *Copy Design* window. In Autodesk Vault Client, browse to the *Vise2* folder to view the copied files, as shown in Figure 9–41.

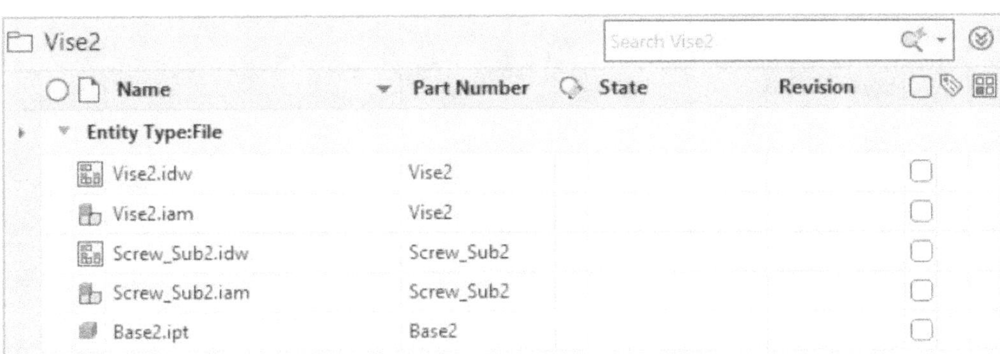

Figure 9–41

Task 3: Open the copied Vise2 assembly.

In this task, you will open the Vise2 assembly.

1. Select **Vise2.iam**, right-click, and select **Open** to open it in the Autodesk Inventor software. Click **No** to when prompted to check out the assembly.
2. In the Vault Browser, verify that **Vise2.iam** references **Base2.ipt**, **Screw_Sub2.iam**, and **Handle_Ball-large.ipt** are under **Screw_Sub2.iam**.
3. Close the assembly.

End of practice

Chapter Review Questions

1. When you move a file from one location to another, the file effectively remains the same in the new location and is still referenced by its children and parents.
   a. True
   b. False

2. What do you need to remember when using the **Delete** operation? (Select all that apply.)
   a. Parents need to be deleted before children.
   b. Children need to be deleted before parents.
   c. A file must be in a Checked In state.
   d. If a file label exists, it needs to be deleted before the file is deleted.

3. When a label has been created, which operation is used to create a package based on that label?
   a. Edit
   b. Copy Design
   c. Pack and Go
   d. Restore

4. When files are attached to other files in the vault, a link is created between the files so that they act as a single unit when they are checked out or checked in.
   a. True
   b. False

5. When using **Copy Design**, what operations can be performed on the files? (Select all that apply.)
   a. Copy
   b. Reuse
   c. Exclude
   d. Replace

Command Summary

Button	Command	Location
	**Select Properties**	• **Property Edit dialog box**

Chapter 10

Items and Bill of Materials Management

Items and bills of materials (BOMs) can be created in Autodesk Vault. You will learn how to view, modify, and compare BOMs and differentiate between methods of creating BOM detail reports.

Learning Objectives

- Use the New Item, Assign/Update Item, and drag-and-drop methods to create new items and bills of materials (BOMs).
- Use the *Bill of Materials* tab to view BOMs.
- Modify BOMs to add, remove, and reorder items.
- Use the **Compare** command to compare BOMs.
- Use the **Save BOM View** and **BOM Export** commands to export a BOM to a file.
- Use the **BOM Report** command to create BOM reports.

10.1 Items and Bills of Materials

Items can be created either from the Item Master or from Autodesk Inventor design files. The Item Master contains the list of all items in the Autodesk Vault. Items can be viewed from the Item Master, as shown in Figure 10–1.

Figure 10–1

When viewing an Item in the *Item* dialog box, the Bill of Materials (BOM) can be viewed on the *Bill of Materials* tab, as shown in Figure 10–2.

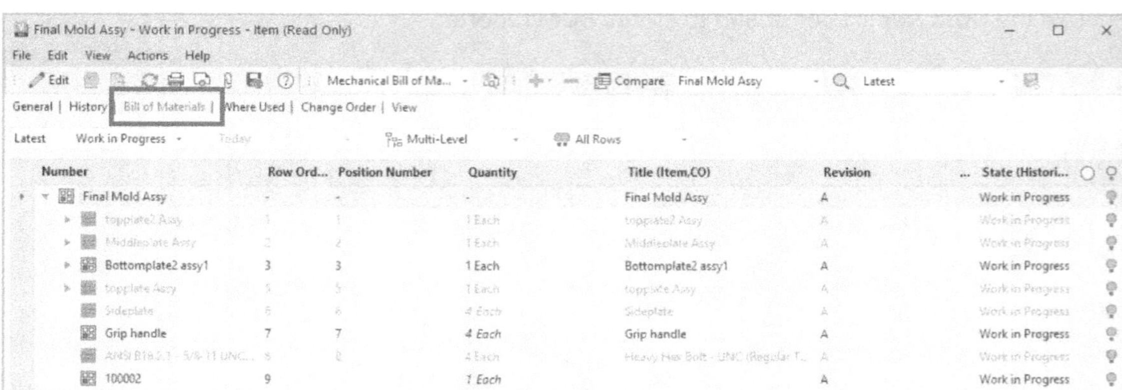

Figure 10–2

10.2 Creating Items and BOMs

Inventor design files stored in Autodesk Vault can be assigned to items in order to create a BOM. Alternatively, items can be created first in the Item Master and then associated with design files, also known as the "BOM first" workflow.

Assign Items

How To: Assign an Item to a File

1. In Project Explorer, select one or more files, right-click and select **Assign/Update Item**, (as shown in Figure 10–3), or click on the Assign/Update Item icon in the toolbar.

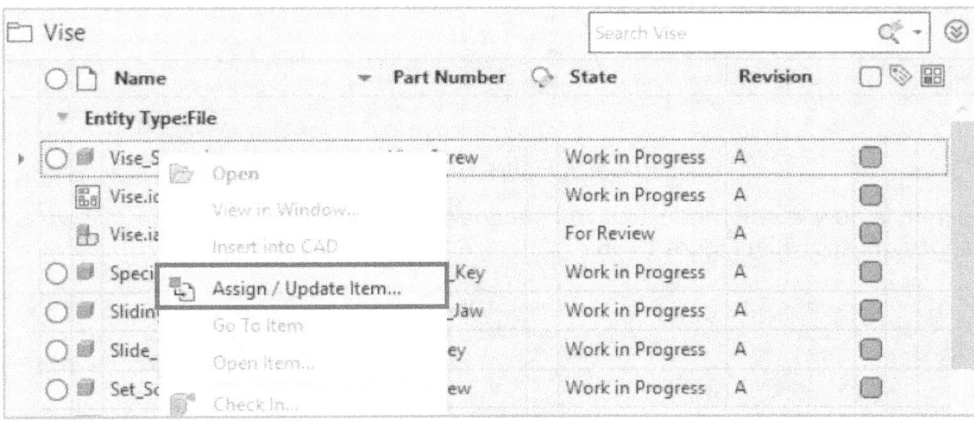

Figure 10–3

2. The items are created in the Item Master. Select *Item Master* to view the new items, as shown in Figure 10–4.

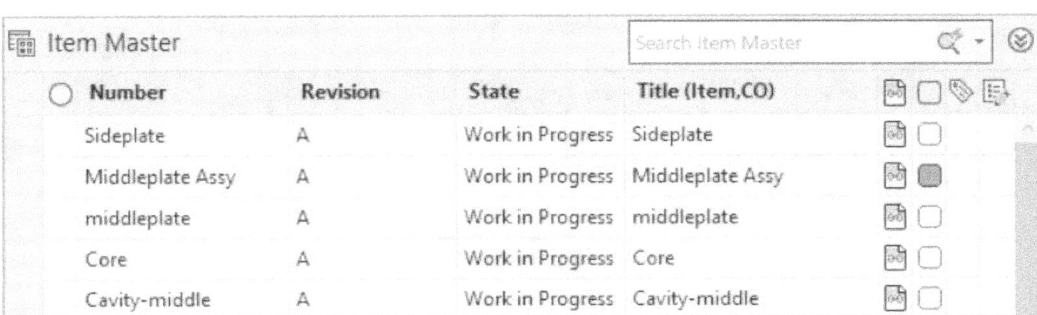

Figure 10–4

3. To edit the item, double-click on the item to open it in its own dialog box and then click **Edit**, as shown in Figure 10–5.

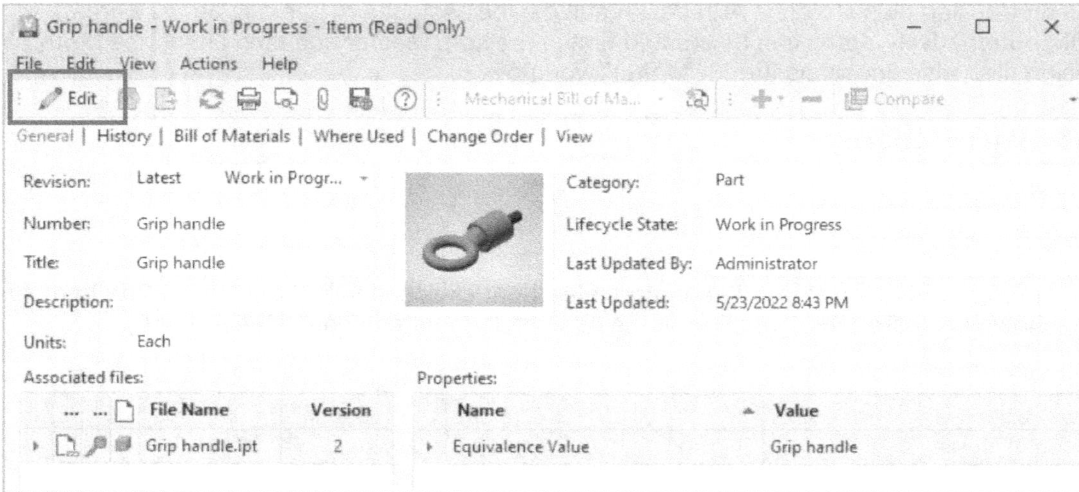

Figure 10–5

4. The item is now in edit mode, and you can make changes to it. Click **Save** to save any changes, as shown in Figure 10–6.

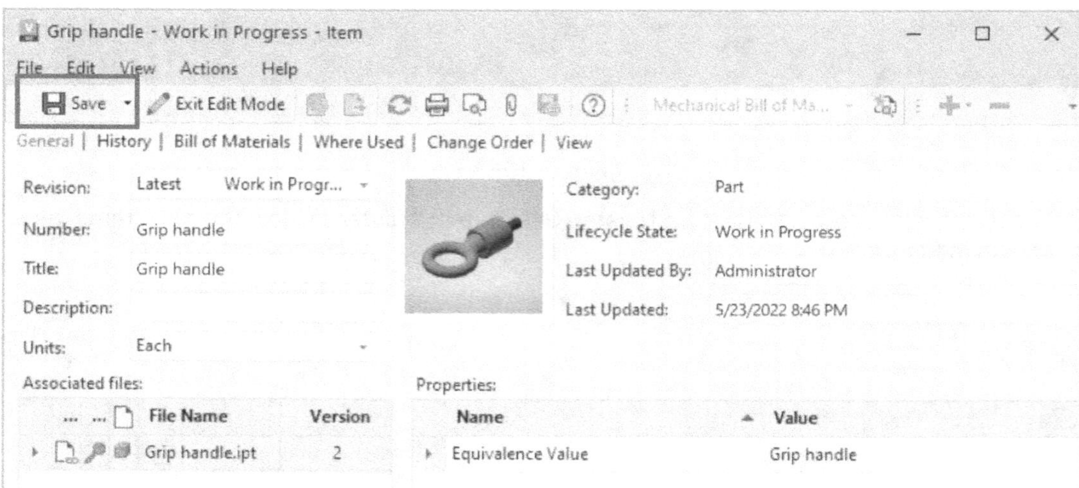

Figure 10–6

Create Items Using New Item

How To: Create Items Using the New Item Command

1. Click **Item Master.**
2. In the toolbar, click **New**, and then click **New Item,** as shown in Figure 10–7.

Figure 10–7

Note: *You can also create new items by dragging and dropping files onto the Item Master node in the browser.*

3. If applicable, select a category, as shown in Figure 10–8. Click **OK**.

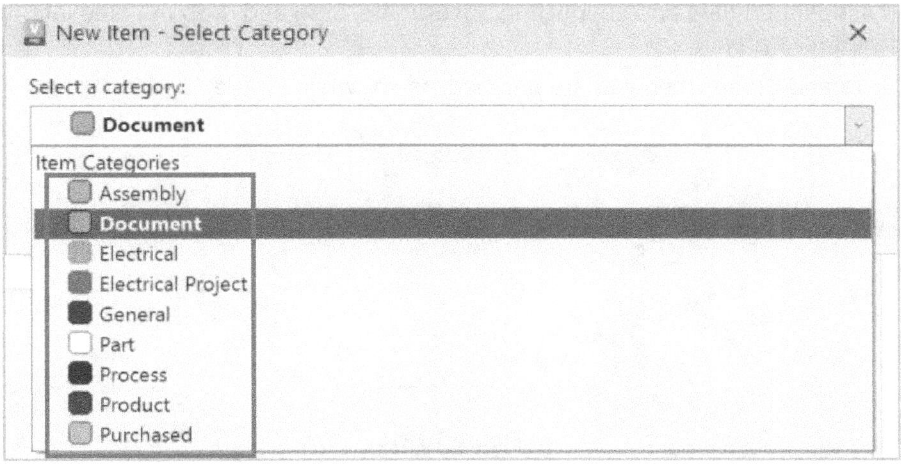

Figure 10–8

4. In the *Item* dialog box, in the *General* tab, enter the required values (e.g., Title, Description, Units, etc.), as shown in Figure 10–9.

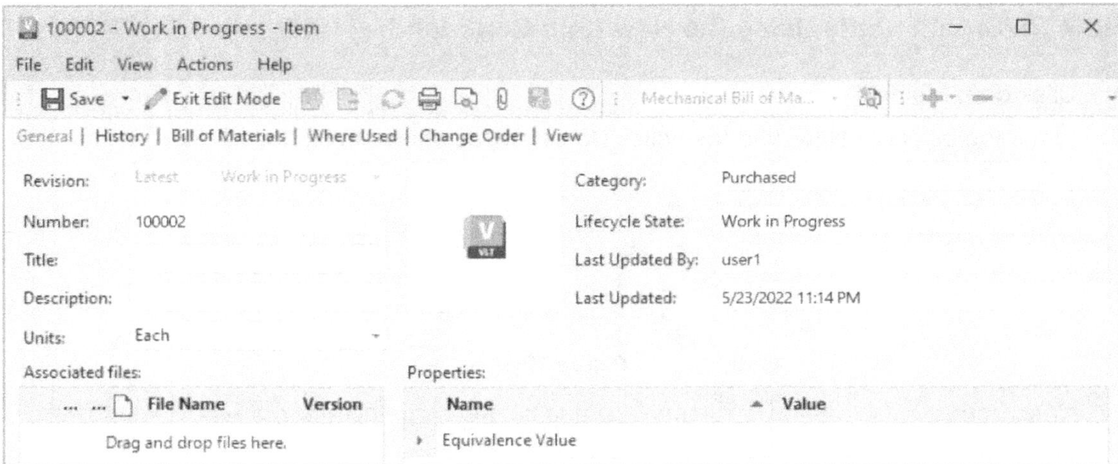

Figure 10–9

5. To add associated files and supporting documents, drag and drop the files into the *Associated files* area.
6. Click **Save and Close** when you are finished, as shown in Figure 10–10.

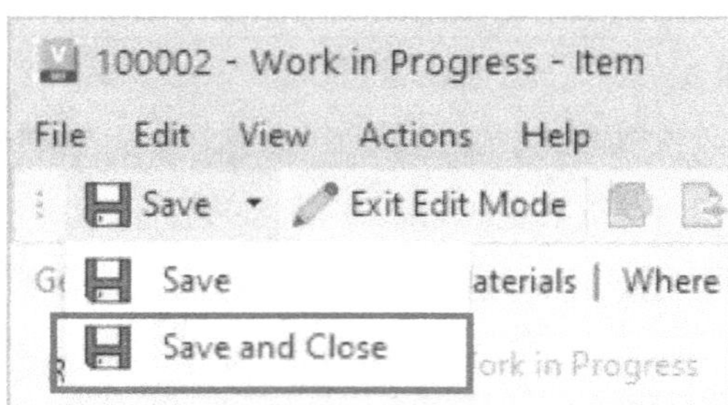

Figure 10–10

10.3 Working with BOMs

BOM management takes place in the *Bill of Materials* tab on the item record.

Viewing BOMs

You can view BOMs in Autodesk Vault's Main pane by double-clicking on an item, or through the Preview pane after selecting an item.

How To: View BOMs

1. Select the *Item Master* tab in the bottom half of the Navigation pane, then select the desired item.
2. In the Preview pane, select the *Bill of Materials* tab to view the BOM, or double-click to open the item in a new window, as shown in Figure 10–11.

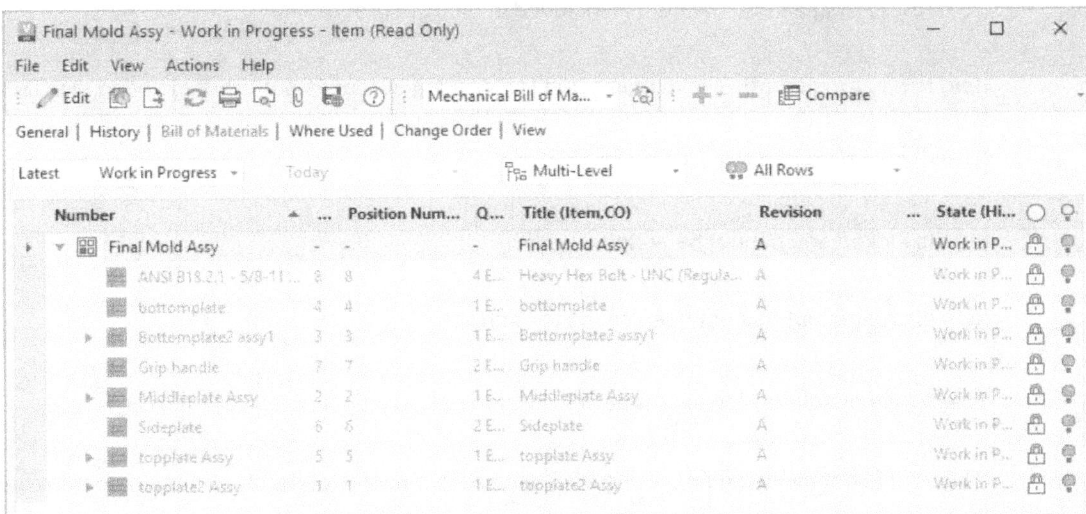

Figure 10–11

Note: *You can also show individual component instances' assigned properties. You first create new Bill of Materials Row properties that map to file properties with instance properties values. You then customize the view to add the column to display these values.*

BOM Status Icons

The BOM status icons can help you manage your BOM more effectively. These are described as follows:

Icon	Description
	Item exists in the vault.
	Item exists but the row is toggled off in the BOM.
	No item is assigned. The file is the child of a parent with an assigned item, however no item has been assigned to the child file.
	Item row consists of multiple rows that have been grouped together.
	Item row is toggled on. The item is included in all BOM processes.
	Item row is toggled off. The item is listed for tracking purposes but is not included in BOM processes.
	Item can be edited.
	Item is locked and cannot be edited.
	Item is created but has not been saved to vault yet.
	The item is obsolete. However, a newer revision may exist.
	The item is not available for editing because another user is currently editing the parent file.

Modifying BOMs

BOM modifications can include changing quantities, adding rows, deleting rows, toggling rows on or off, and reordering rows. In all cases, first click **Edit** to begin the modifications. Note that modifications can only be made when the BOM is set to a Multi-Level structure view.

How To: Change Quantity

1. Click in the *Quantity* field of an item and enter the new quantity, as shown in Figure 10–12.

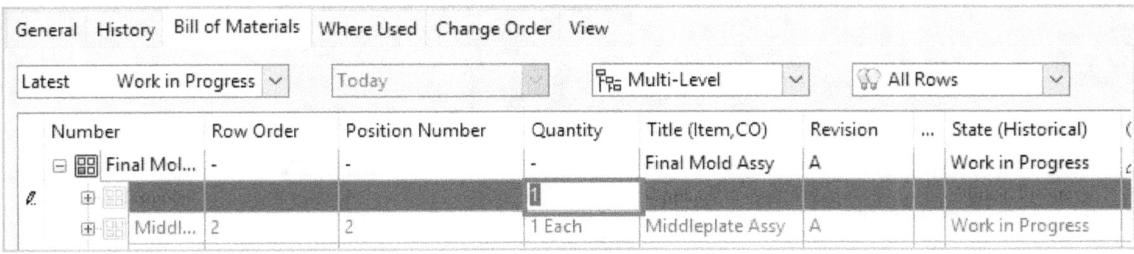

Figure 10–12

How To: Add Rows

1. Right-click on the top-level item and select **Add Row>From Existing Item** or **From New Item**, as shown in Figure 10–13.

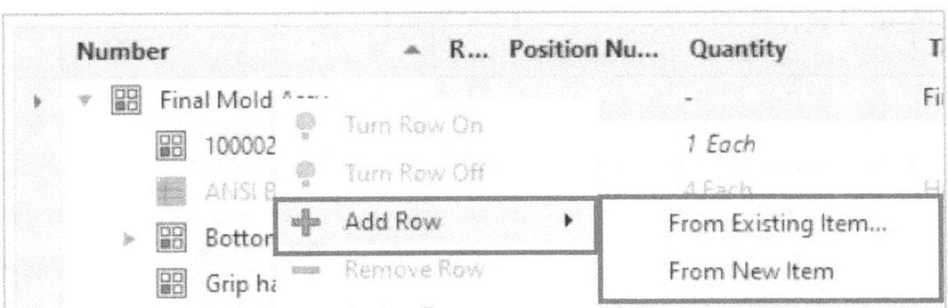

Figure 10–13

2. Follow the prompts to add a new or existing item.

How To: Delete Rows

1. Right-click on the top-level item and select **Remove Row**, as shown in Figure 10–14.

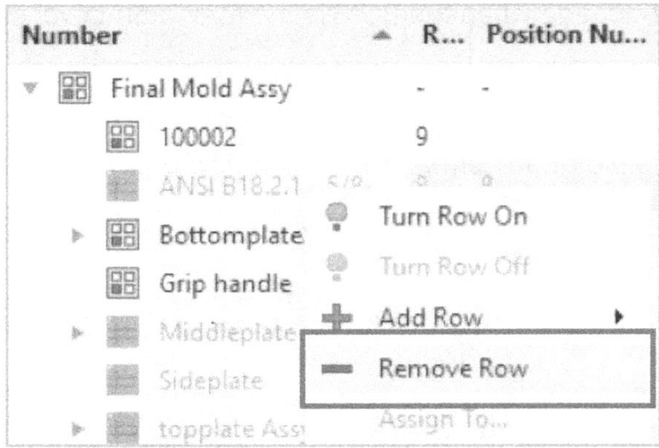

Figure 10–14

How To: Reorder Rows

1. To reorder rows, either:
    - Change the *Row Order* column values, or
    - Drag and drop the number to a different position in the same parent, as shown in Figure 10–15.

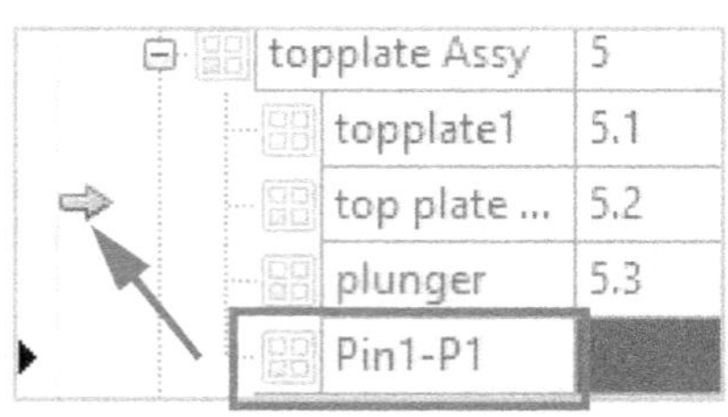

Figure 10–15

Note: *Select (Restore Saved Order) in the toolbar to revert back to the last saved order.*

How To: Toggle Rows On or Off

You can include items on the BOM but then hide them if you do not want them included in the BOM process.

1. In the *On/Off Row* column, click on a light bulb for an item to toggle it on or off, as shown in Figure 10–16.

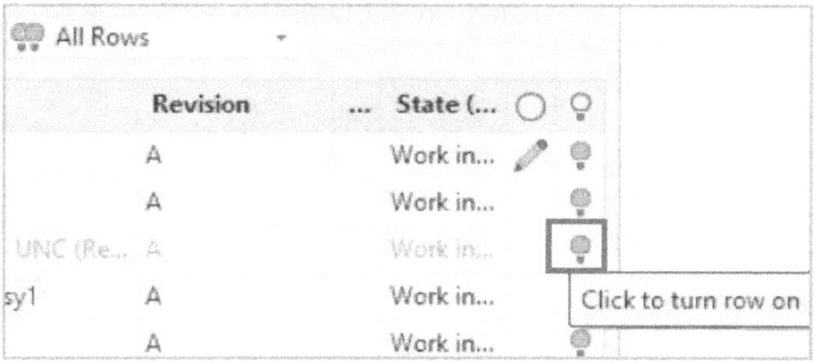

Figure 10–16

2. To control the display of on and off rows, select either **All Rows**, **On Rows Only** or **Off Rows Only** from the drop-down list, as shown in Figure 10–17.

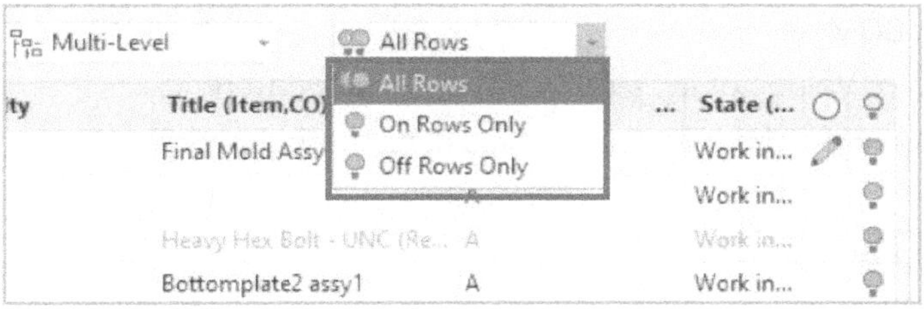

Figure 10–17

Comparing BOMs

How To: Compare BOMs

1. To compare the BOM of two different items, or a version of a BOM with the displayed revision, or different versions of the same item, select the items or values from the fields as shown in Figure 10–18.

Figure 10–18

2. Click **Compare**, as shown in Figure 10–19.

Figure 10–19

3. The differences between the two BOMs are highlighted in the current BOM view, as shown in Figure 10–20.

Number	Quantity	Title (Item,CO)	Revision	L...	State (Historical)
topplate2 Assy	1 Each	topplate2 Assy	B		Work in Progress
100002	1 Each		B		Work in Progress
Middleplate Assy	1 Each	Middleplate Assy	B		Work in Progress
Bottomplate2 assy1	1 Each	Bottomplate2 assy1	B		Work in Progress
topplate Assy	1 Each	topplate Assy	A		Work in Progress
Grip handle	4 Each	Grip handle	A		Work in Progress
Sideplate	4 Each	Sideplate	A		Work in Progress
ANSI B18.2.1 - 5/8-11 UNC - 2.5	4 Each	Heavy Hex Bolt - UNC (Regular...	A		Work in Progress

Figure 10–20

- **Blue font:** Either the row was added or toggle on in the displayed BOM, but not in the comparison BOM or the row has an item now but was a BOM component in the comparison BOM.
- **Blue Bold font:** Values of individual properties are different.
- **Red Strikethrough:** The row does not exist, or is toggled off in the displayed BOM.

Save the BOM View

How To: Save the BOM View

1. To save the view of the BOM, in the *Item* dialog box, in the *Bill of Materials* tab, select **File>Save BOM View**, as shown in Figure 10–21.

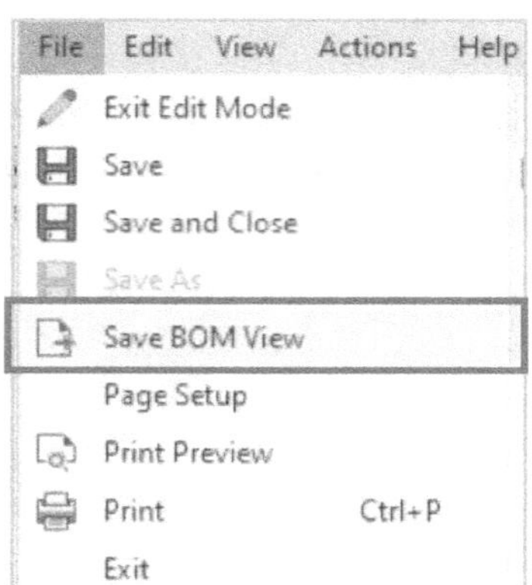

Figure 10–21

2. Select a destination and name for the Microsoft Excel file.

BOM Report

How To: Create a BOM Report

1. In the *Item* dialog box, select the *Bill of Materials* tab.
2. In the *BOM Structure* drop-down list, select **Multi-Level**, **First-Level,** or **Parts Only**, as shown in Figure 10–22.

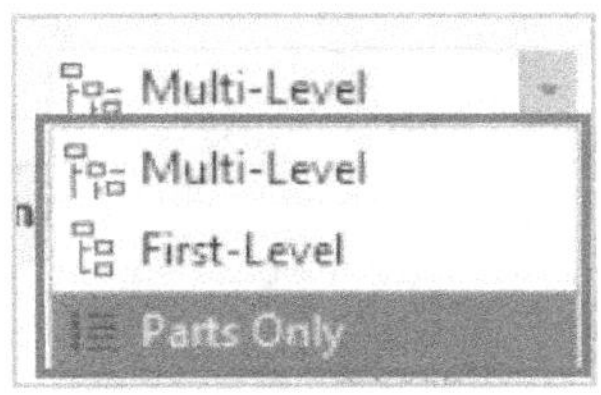

Figure 10–22

3. Right-click on any item in the list and select **BOM Report**, as shown in Figure 10–23.

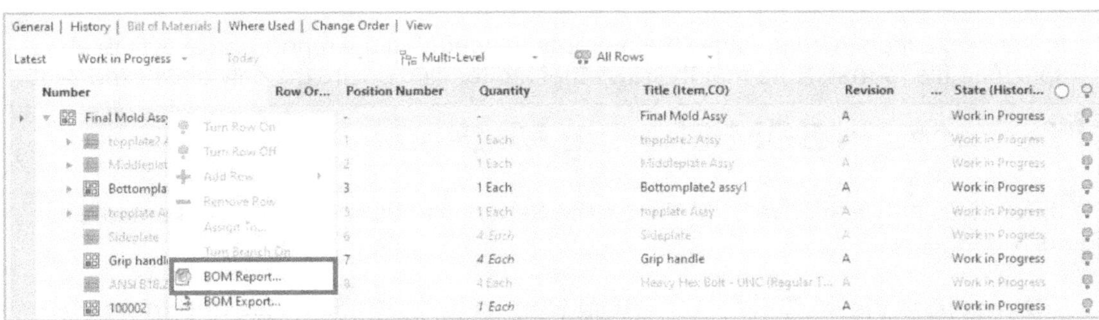

Figure 10–23

4. Select a BOM template that matches the selected structure (e.g., **BOM - First-Level.rdls, BOM - Multi-Level.rdlc**, or **BOM - Parts-Only.rdlc**).
5. Click **OK**. The report opens in a new window.

BOM Export

How To: Export a BOM

1. In the *Item* dialog box, select the *Bill of Materials* tab.

2. Right-click on any item in the list and select **BOM Export**, as shown in Figure 10–24.

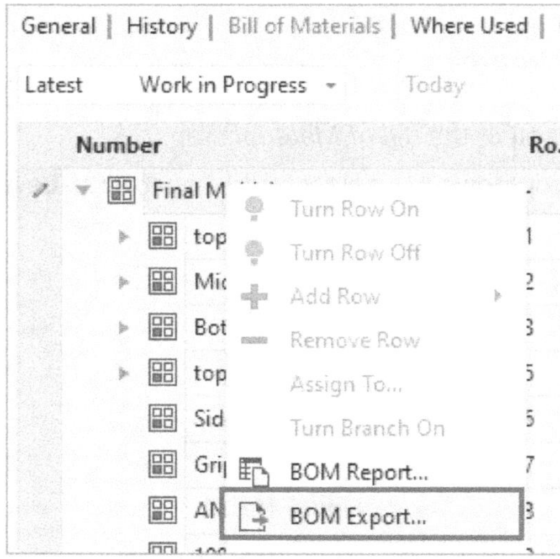

Figure 10–24

3. In the *Item Export Wizard*, follow the prompts to configure the report and export to a specified file format. Note that the rows that are toggled on are the only ones exported.

Differences in BOM Sharing Methods

The differences between **Save BOM View**, **BOM Report**, and **BOM Export** are summarized in Figure 10–25.

Save BOM View	BOM Report	BOM Export
• In the *Bill of Materials* tab, select **File>Save BOM View**. • Matches BOM View. • Excel/.CSV file formats. • Exports all rows.	• In the *Bill of Materials* tab, right-click top level, then select **BOM Report**. • Pre-defined report layout. • Exports all rows (T/F).	• In the *Bill of Materials* tab, right-click top level, then select **BOM Export**. • Select properties to show. • Multiple file formats. • Exports only "on" rows.
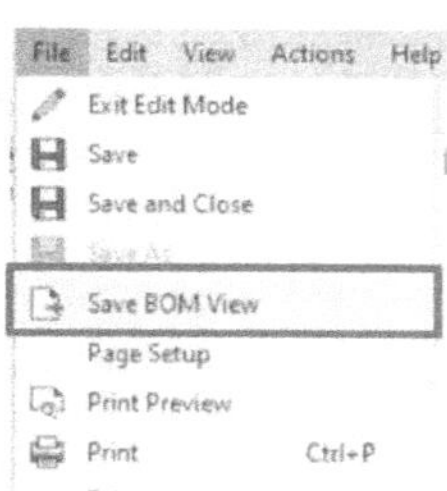	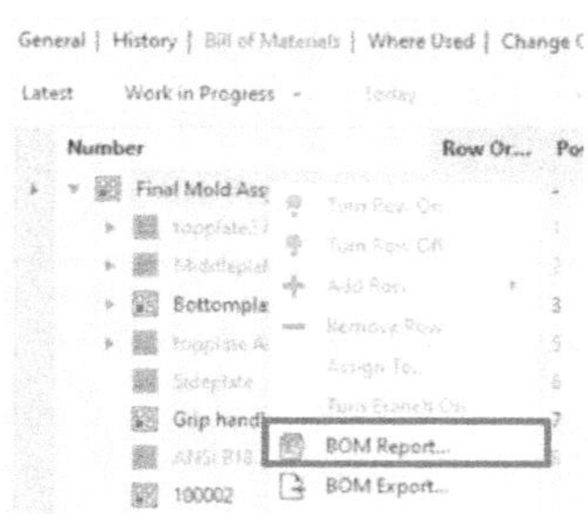	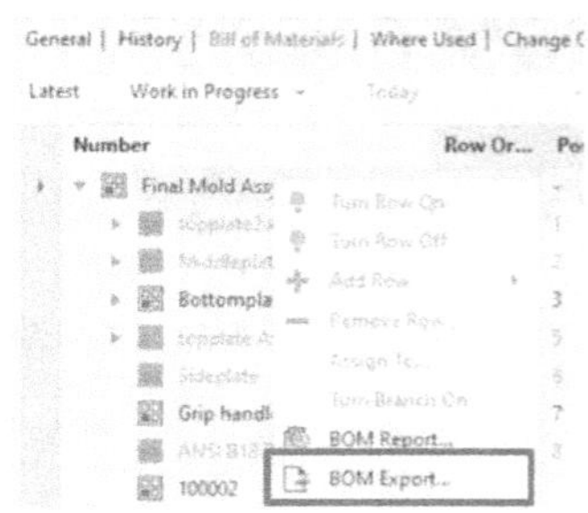

Figure 10–25

Practice 10a
Work with Items and BOMs

Practice Objectives

- Create an item using Assign/Update Item.
- Modify a bill of materials.
- Save a BOM view.
- Export a BOM.

In this practice, you will create items based on existing Autodesk Inventor files. You will then modify the BOM of the items created, save a BOM view, and export the BOM to an Excel file.

Task 1: Create items from design files using Assign/Update Item.

1. From the Main table of the Autodesk Vault Client software, open the *Mold Assembly* folder.
2. Use <Ctrl>+<A> to highlight all files in the folder, right-click and select **Assign/Update Item,** as shown in Figure 10–26.

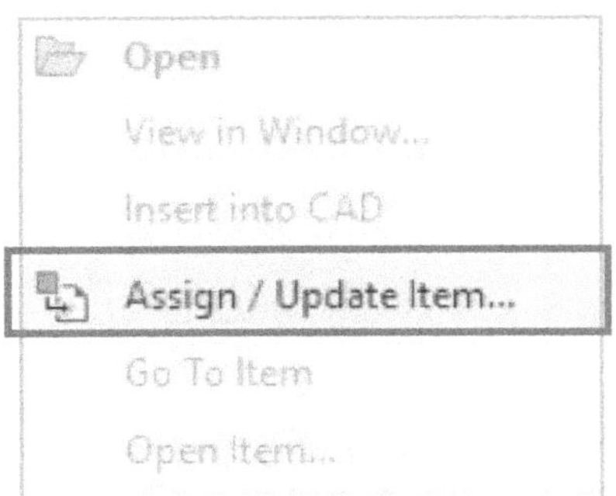

Figure 10–26

3. Click **Item Master** in the Navigation pane to view the created items.

***Note:** If the files have a lock symbol, select **Tools>Administration>Vault Settings**. In the Behaviors tab, select **Lifecycles** and **Item Release Process**, then select **Edit** and add user1 to the Security tab, as shown in Figure 10–27. Click **OK**, then close the Lifecycle Definitions and Vault Settings dialog boxes.*

Figure 10–27

Task 2: Modify the BOM by changing a quantity and removing an item.

1. Double-click on the item for **Final Mold Assy.iam** in the Item Master.
2. Select the *Bill of Materials* tab to view the BOM, as shown in Figure 10–28.

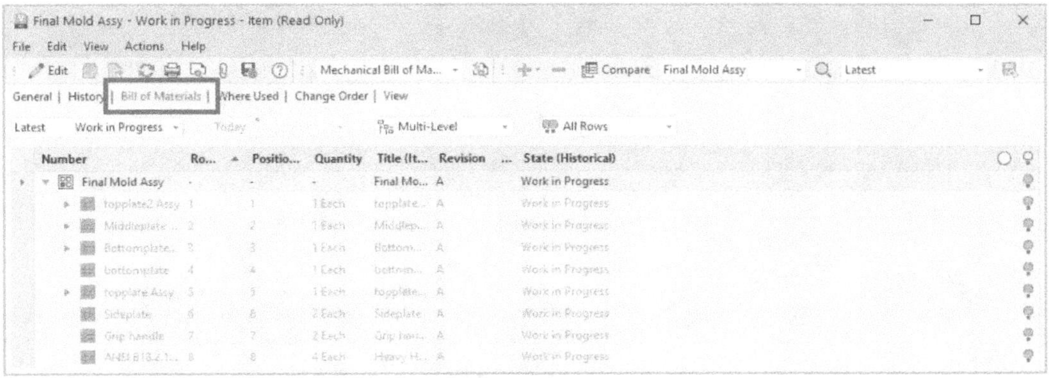

Figure 10–28

3. Click **Edit** in the top left corner.
4. Change the quantity for the **Sideplate** and **Grip handle** from **2** to **4**, as shown in Figure 10–29.

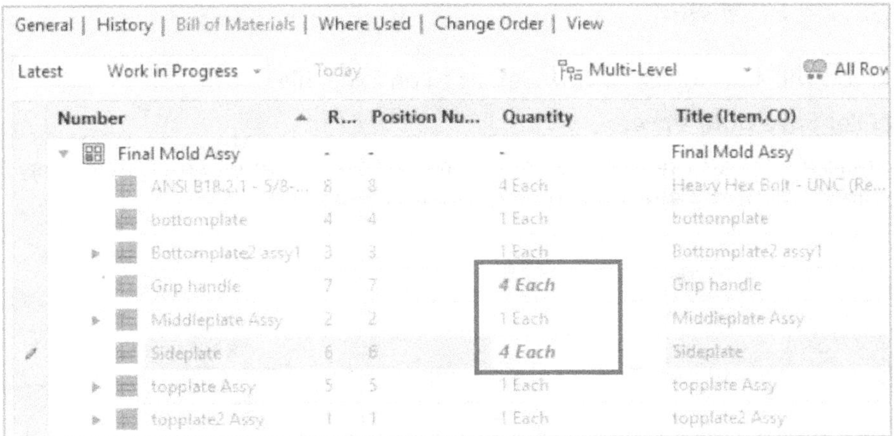

Figure 10–29

5. Right-click on **bottomplate** and select **Remove Row**.
6. Click **Yes** to confirm the removal of the row.
7. Toggle some rows on or off by clicking on the light-bulb icons in the *On/Off BOM Row* column.
8. Click **Save**.

Task 3: Create a new item in the BOM.

1. In the *Bill of Materials* tab, right-click on **Final Mold Assy**, then select **Add Row>From New Item**, as shown in Figure 10–30.

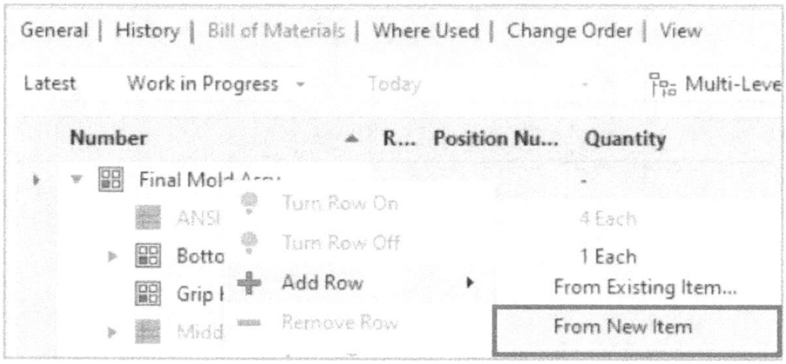

Figure 10–30

2. For the category, select **Purchased**, then click **OK**.
3. The new item is created successfully and displayed at the bottom of the list.
4. Click **Save**.

Task 4: Save a BOM view.

In this task, you will save the BOM view details to an Excel file.

1. Select **File>Save BOM View.**
2. Navigate to the folder where you want to save the file and enter **Final Mold Assy BOM View** as the filename. Click **Save**, as shown in Figure 10–31.

Figure 10–31

3. Navigate to the folder where the saved file is located. Open it in Excel to view the details, as shown in Figure 10–32. Note that rows that are toggled on and off are both displayed.

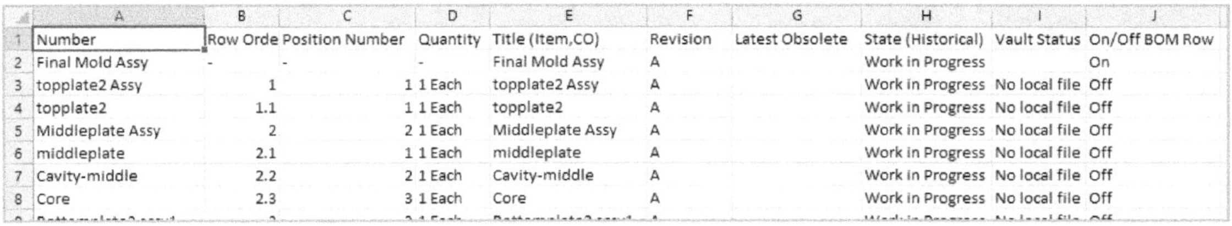

	A	B	C	D	E	F	G	H	I	J
1	Number	Row Orde	Position Number	Quantity	Title (Item,CO)	Revision	Latest Obsolete	State (Historical)	Vault Status	On/Off BOM Row
2	Final Mold Assy	-	-	-	Final Mold Assy	A		Work in Progress		On
3	topplate2 Assy	1	1	1 Each	topplate2 Assy	A		Work in Progress	No local file	Off
4	topplate2	1.1	1	1 Each	topplate2	A		Work in Progress	No local file	Off
5	Middleplate Assy	2	2	1 Each	Middleplate Assy	A		Work in Progress	No local file	Off
6	middleplate	2.1	1	1 Each	middleplate	A		Work in Progress	No local file	Off
7	Cavity-middle	2.2	2	1 Each	Cavity-middle	A		Work in Progress	No local file	Off
8	Core	2.3	3	1 Each	Core	A		Work in Progress	No local file	Off

Figure 10–32

4. Close the file and Microsoft Excel.

Task 5: Compare BOM structure views and export a BOM.

In this task, you will compare the BOM structure views.

1. In the *Bill of Materials* tab, select **First-Level**, as shown in Figure 10–33.

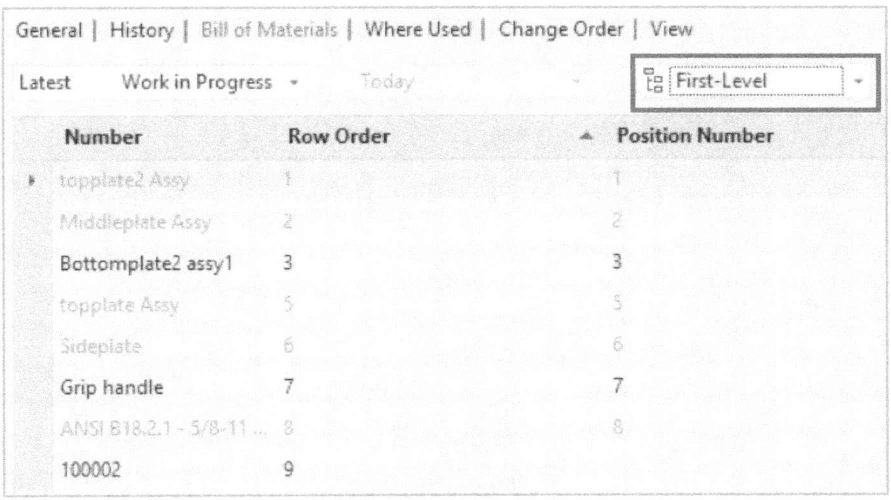

Figure 10–33

2. Select **Parts Only** and **Multi-Level** to compare their results, as shown in Figure 10–34. Note that you can only modify while in the Multi-Level structure view.

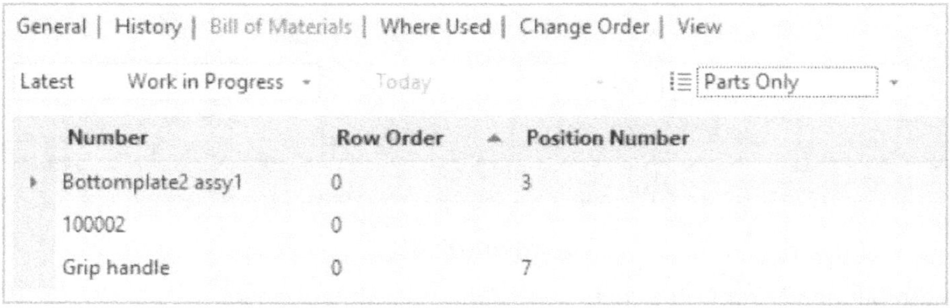

Figure 10–34

3. Click **Exit Edit Mode**. Right-click on **Final Mold Assy** and select **BOM Export...**, as shown in Figure 10–35.

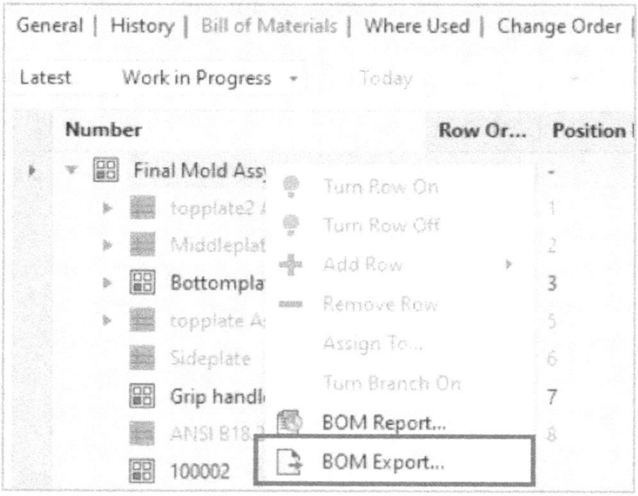

Figure 10–35

4. In the *Export Wizard* dialog box, select **Next>**, then select **CSV (Comma Separated Values .CSV)** for the file type. Select **Browse** to select a folder and enter a file name for the .CSV.
5. Click **Next**.
6. Drag and drop attributes, including **Number**, from the *Attributes* list to the *Export file* list. Click **Export**, then click **Finish** to create the .CSV file. Review the file and note that only the rows that were toggled on are exported.

End of practice

Chapter Review Questions

1. When items are created in the Item Master first, and then associated with design files second, it is known as the “BOM first” workflow.
   a. True
   b. False

2. In order to make changes to a bill of materials, what do you need to do?
   a. Toggle all rows to On.
   b. Select First-Level for the BOM Structure View.
   c. Click Edit.
   d. Reorder the BOM rows.

3. A bill of materials can only be edited when it is in the Multi-Level structure view.
   a. True
   b. False

4. To save a BOM to a file that shows only the rows that are toggled On, use the ____________ command.
   a. Save BOM View
   b. BOM Export
   c. Multi-Level
   d. BOM Report

Command Summary

Button	Command	Location
	Assign/Update Item	• **Shortcut:** (right-click on selected file) • Standard toolbar
	Add Row	• **Item** dialog box on *Bill of Materials* tab: Toolbar • Shortcut: right-click on object on *Bill of Materials* tab
	BOM Report	• **Item** dialog box on *Bill of Materials* tab: Toolbar • Shortcut: right-click on object on *Bill of Materials* tab
	BOM Export	• **Item** dialog box on *Bill of Materials* tab: Toolbar • Shortcut: right-click on object on *Bill of Materials* tab
	Compare	• **Item** dialog box on *Bill of Materials* tab: Toolbar
	New Item	• Standard Toolbar when in Item Master
	Remove Row	• **Item** dialog box on *Bill of Materials* tab: Toolbar (with BOM row selected)
	Save BOM View	• **Item** dialog box: File menu

Chapter 11

Change Management

The Change Order object in Autodesk Vault enables you to manage the Change Order process of a design. You will learn about the components of the Change Order object and how to create and approve a Change Order.

Learning Objectives

- Use the **Add to Change Order** command to create a Change Order for an item or file.
- Review and approve a Change Order.

11.1 Change Order Object Overview

The Change Order is an object in Autodesk Vault Professional that enables you to manage the changes for your design.

Select the **Change Order List** in the Navigation pane to view the interface, as shown in Figure 11–1.

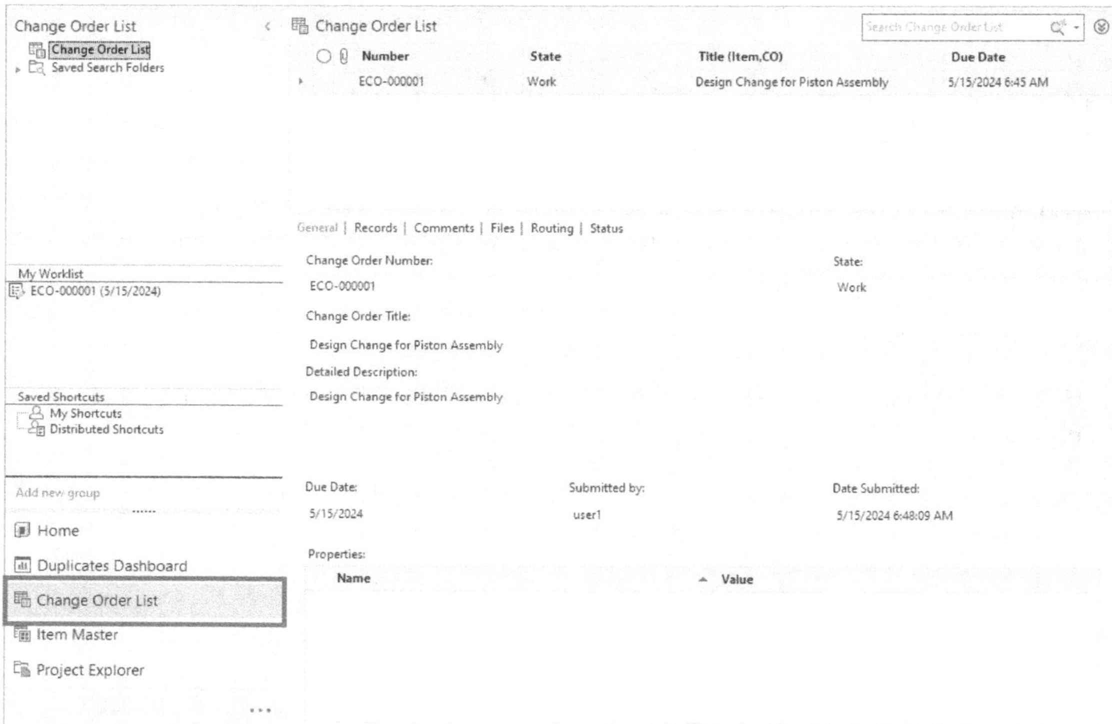

Figure 11–1

General Tab

The *General* tab displays the properties of a Change Order, as shown in Figure 11–2.

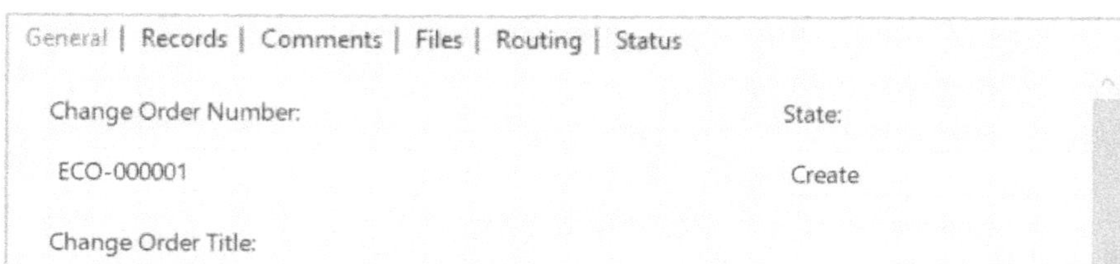

Figure 11–2

Records Tab

The *Records* tab displays the list of files and items associated with the Change Order, as shown in Figure 11–3.

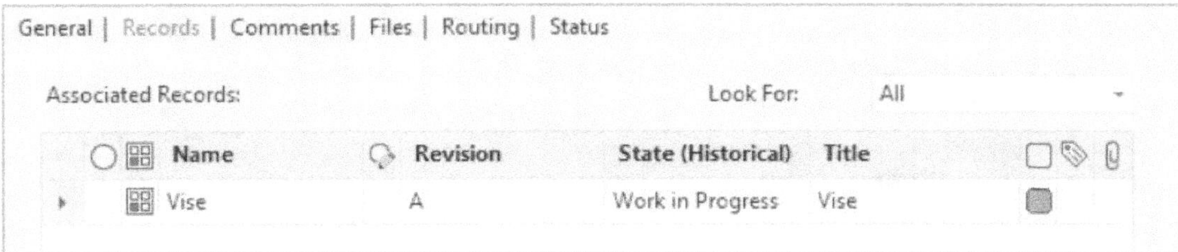

Figure 11–3

Comments Tab

The *Comments* tab contains the details of change order decisions in the form of comments, attachments, and markups, as shown in Figure 11–4.

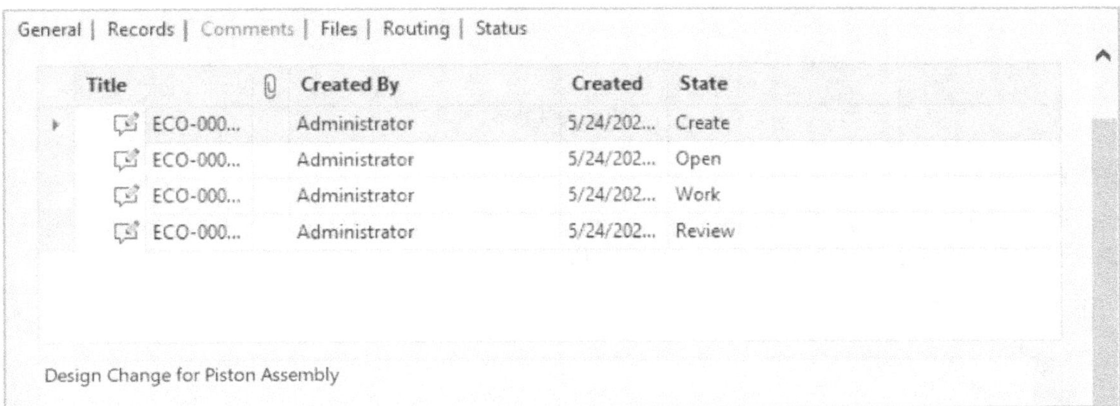

Figure 11–4

Files Tab

The *Files* tab lists all of the files attached to the change order. Any associated items are displayed in the *Associated Items* subtab, and the files can be viewed from the *Preview* subtab, as shown in Figure 11–5.

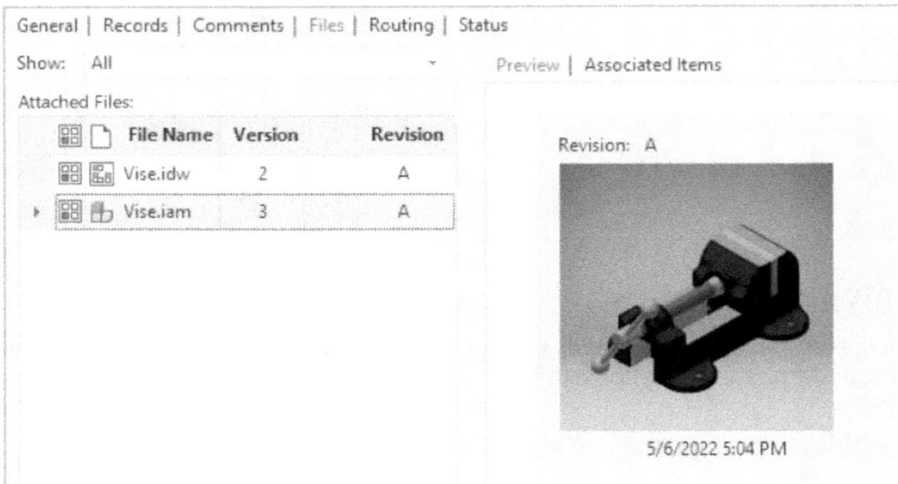

Figure 11–5

Routing Tab

The *Routing* tab displays the routing list used to control which users are notified when a Change Order moves to a specific state, as shown in Figure 11–6.

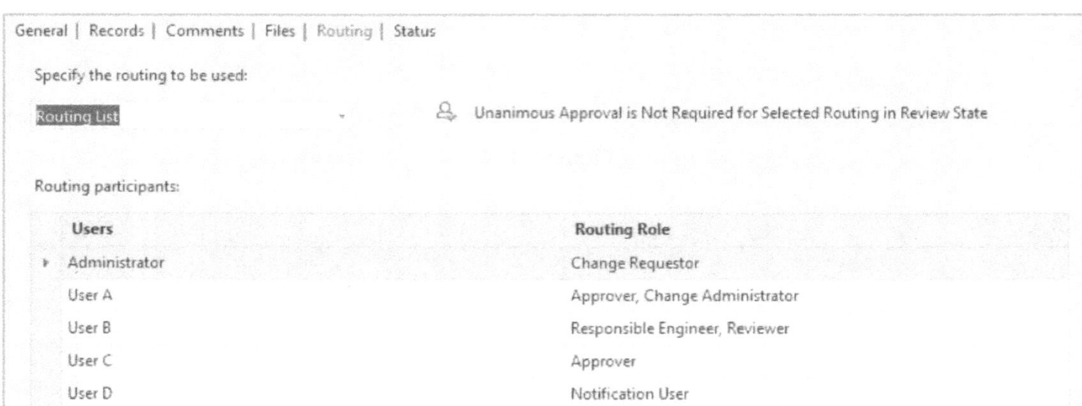

Figure 11–6

Status Tab

The *Status* tab shows the current lifecycle state of the Change Order. An example is shown in Figure 11–7.

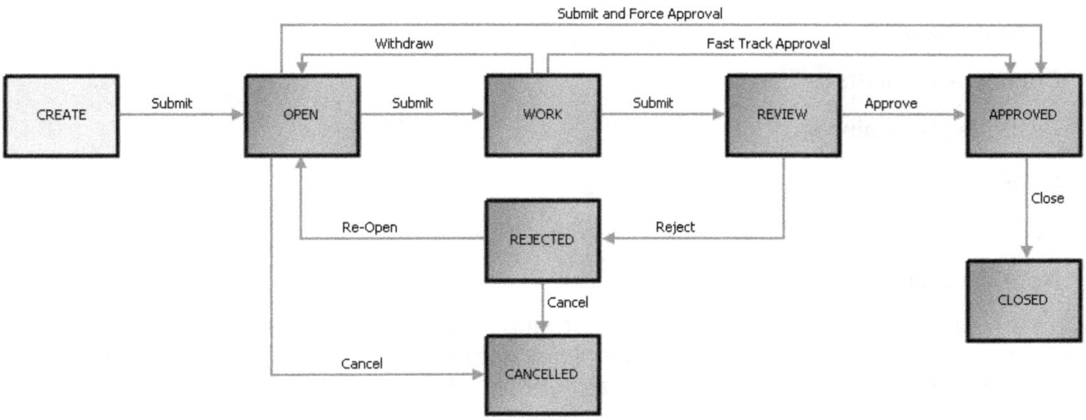

Figure 11–7

11.2 Change Order Process

The Change Order Process begins with a Change Requestor creating a Change Order. The standard roles in the Change Order process are:

- Change Requestor
- Change Administrator
- Responsible Engineer
- Reviewer
- Approver
- Notification User

Users are assigned to each of these roles. A routing list is used to control which users are assigned to each role, and when a user should be notified when a Change Order enters a certain state. The main states for a default standard Change Order are shown in Figure 11–8.

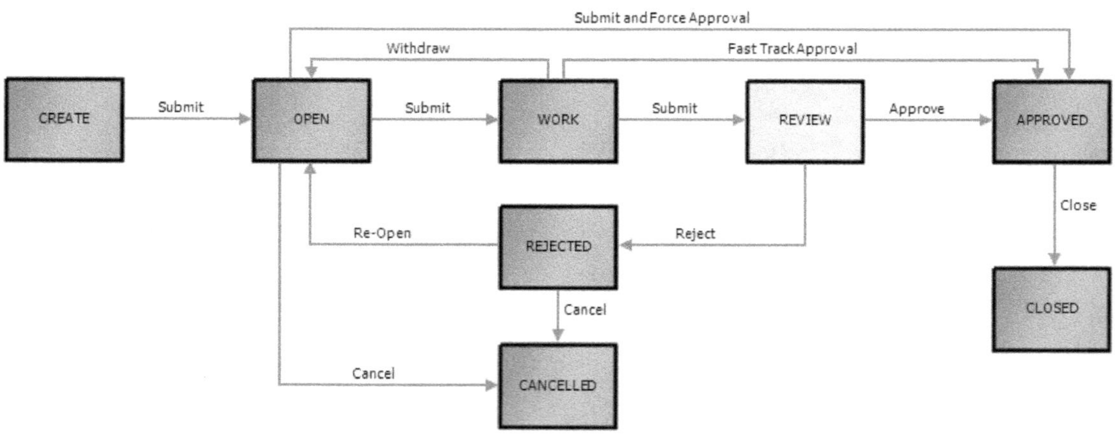

Figure 11–8

The roles and actions that occur at each stage of the Change Order Process are described below.

Create

The Change Requestor creates the change order, adds comments, attaches files, and selects the routing participants. The Change Requestor also automatically becomes a reviewer.

Open

The Change Administrator can edit the change order, if required. They can edit all values as in the Create state except the ECO number.

Work

The Responsible Engineer is notified and the Change Order Number is added to their work list. The Responsible Engineer can edit the change order and make any required changes, and then submits the change order for review.

Review

The Reviewer can view, add, and reply to comments.

> **Note:** *Any participant can add additional Reviewers to the routing, as required.*

Approved or Rejected

The Approver can review, approve, and reject a change order.

Canceled

The Change Administrator can cancel the change order or reopen a closed change order, as required.

Closed

The Notification User receives notification when the change order is closed.

> **Note:** *If Check State is enabled, a Checker is added to the list of routing participants when a work order is rejected. The checker can review, approve, or reject the change order. A standard workflow does not include the Check State or Checker role.*

Creating a Change Order

Create State (Change Requestor)

1. With a file or item selected, right-click on the file and select **Add to Change Order>To New...** as shown in Figure 11–9.

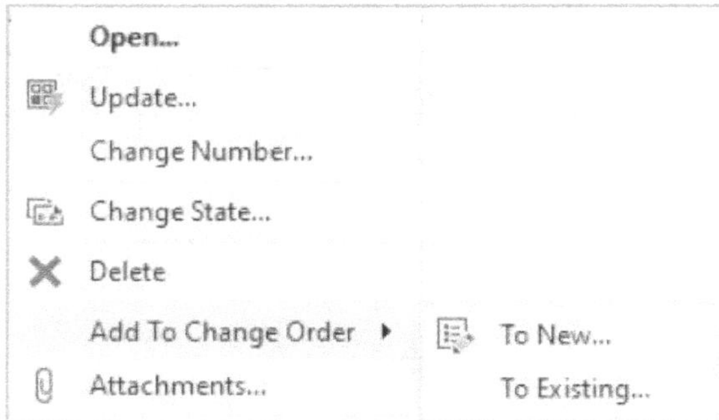

Figure 11–9

2. A window opens with the new ECO object displaying an automatically-generated Change Order Number and a State of **Create**.
3. In the *General* tab, enter a *Change Order Title* and *Detailed Description*.
4. Select the *Files* tab and attach any additional objects to the Change Order.
5. Select the *Routing* tab and click **Edit** to make any changes to the routing.
6. Select the *Status* tab and note that the next state is **Open**.
7. Select **Save** to save the ECO.
8. If no other changes are required to promote the ECO to the Open state, click  (Submit).
9. Enter comments in the *Comment* field and click **OK**.

10. In the Main table, hold <Ctrl> and select the change order icon to go to the change order. In the *Status* tab, note that its state is **Open**, as shown in Figure 11–10.

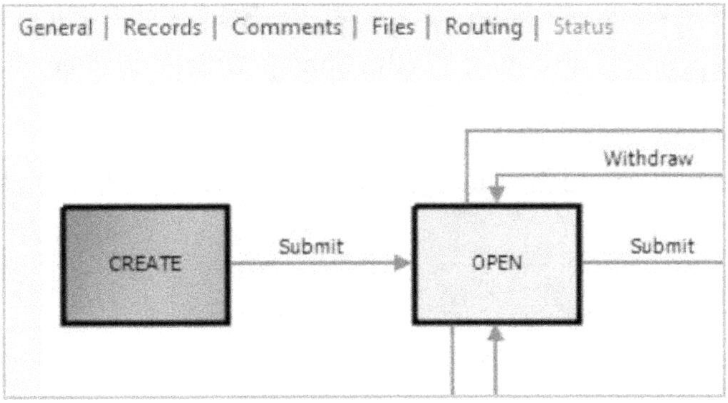

Figure 11–10

Open State (Change Administrator)

1. The Change Administrator is notified and can now edit the Change Order, if required. The Change Administrator can also determine whether the ECO should be canceled.

2. Click (Submit) to move the Change Order to the **Work** state, as shown in Figure 11–11.

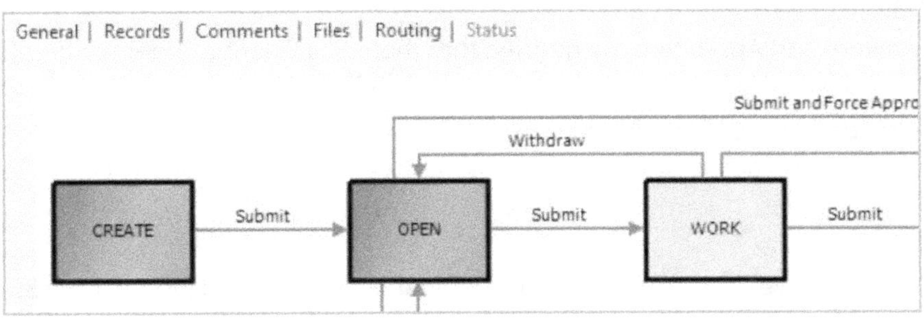

Figure 11–11

Work State (Responsible Engineer)

1. The Responsible Engineer is notified and the ECO is placed in their Worklist. If the files or items are not in the Work In Progress state yet, the Responsible Engineer will do this.
2. Make the design changes as outlined in the Change Order and check the files back into the vault. Note that the items are now listed as being updated.
3. Click  (Submit) to move the Change Order to the **Review** state, as shown in Figure 11–12.

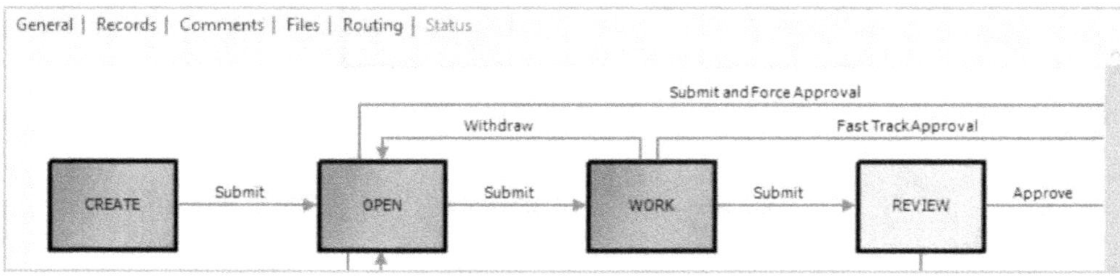

Figure 11–12

Approving a Change Order

Review State (Reviewers)

1. The Reviewers and Approvers are notified that there is a Change Order waiting for approval. They review files with the design changes and add their comments.

   Note: *If* ***Unanimous Approval for Review State Required*** *is selected in the Routing Settings dialog box, all Approvers must review and submit their acceptance of the Change Order.*

2. Click  (Approve) or  (Reject), as applicable, as shown in Figure 11–13.

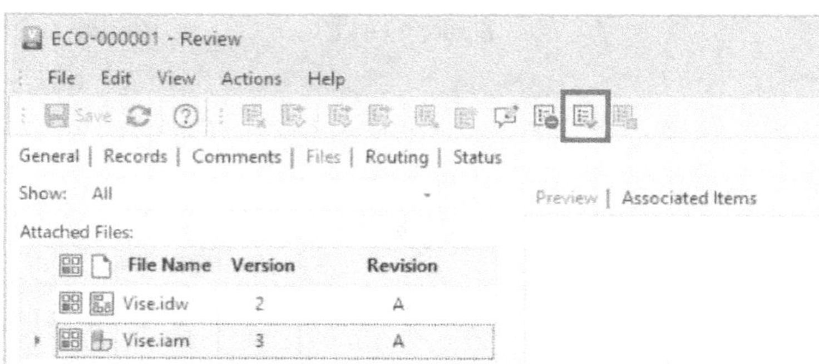

Figure 11–13

3. The Change Order moves to the **Approved** state as shown in Figure 11–14.

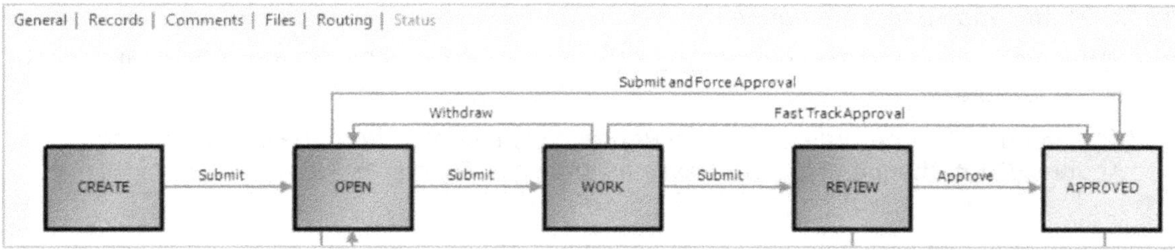

Figure 11–14

Approved State (Approvers/Change Administrator)

1. The Approver can review, approve, and reject a change order. The Change Administrator is notified. and any Work In Progress or In Review/For Review items and files on the change order are set to **Released**.

2. Click  (Approve). The Change Order moves to the Closed state, as shown in Figure 11–15.

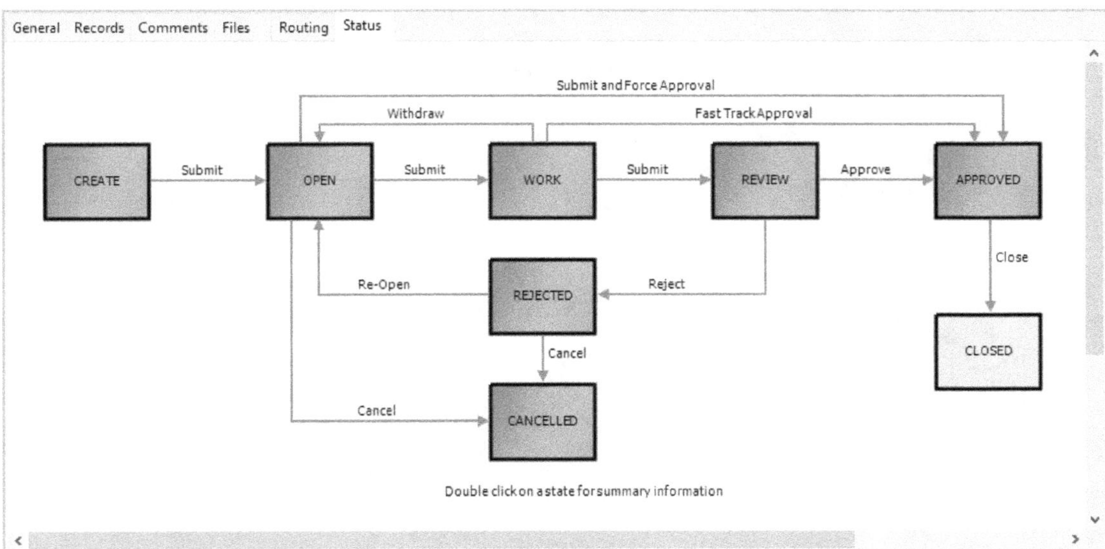

Figure 11–15

Closed State (Notification Users)

1. All Notification Users are notified.
2. In the ECO, select the *Records* tab and note the incremented *Revision* and *State* of the item or file as **Released**.
3. If required, a Change Order Summary Report can be printed from the ECO by selecting **Actions>Print Change Order Summary**, as shown in Figure 11–16.

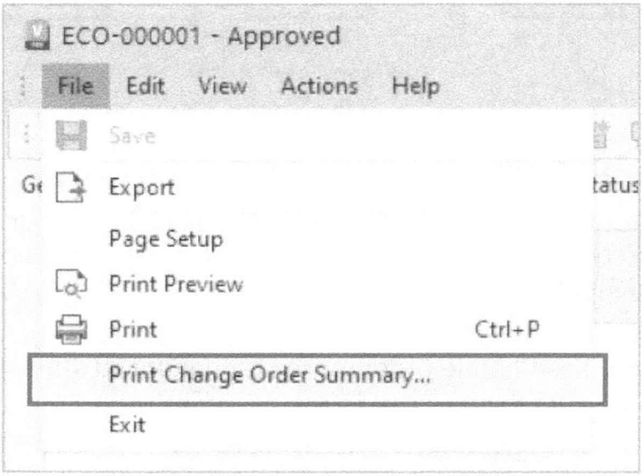

Figure 11–16

Practice 11a
Create and Approve a Change Order Using Items

Practice Objectives

- Create a Change Order using items.
- Review, approve, and close a Change Order using items.

In this practice, you will create, review, and approve an Engineering Change Order (ECO) using items. For instructional purposes, **user1** will have permissions to create, review, and approve a Change Order. Note that a company will typically have different users set up for these various roles.

Task 1: Create an ECO (Create state: Change Requestor).

1. Log in as **administrator** to the **Vault_Training** vault (no password is required for this account).
2. In Project Explorer, locate the Vise folder. Use <Ctrl>+<A> to highlight all files in the folder, right-click and select **Assign/ Update Item**
3. In the Item Master, locate the **Vise** item.
4. Right-click on the **Vise** item and then select **Add to Change Order>To New...**, as shown in Figure 11–17.

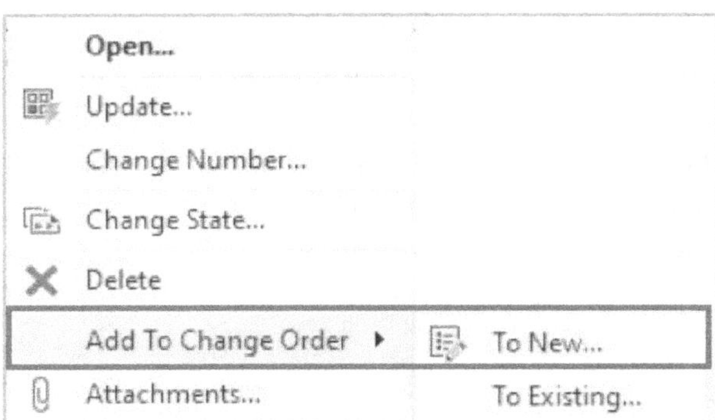

Figure 11–17

5. A window opens with the new ECO object displaying an automatically-generated *Change Order Number* and a *State* of **Create** as shown in Figure 11–18.

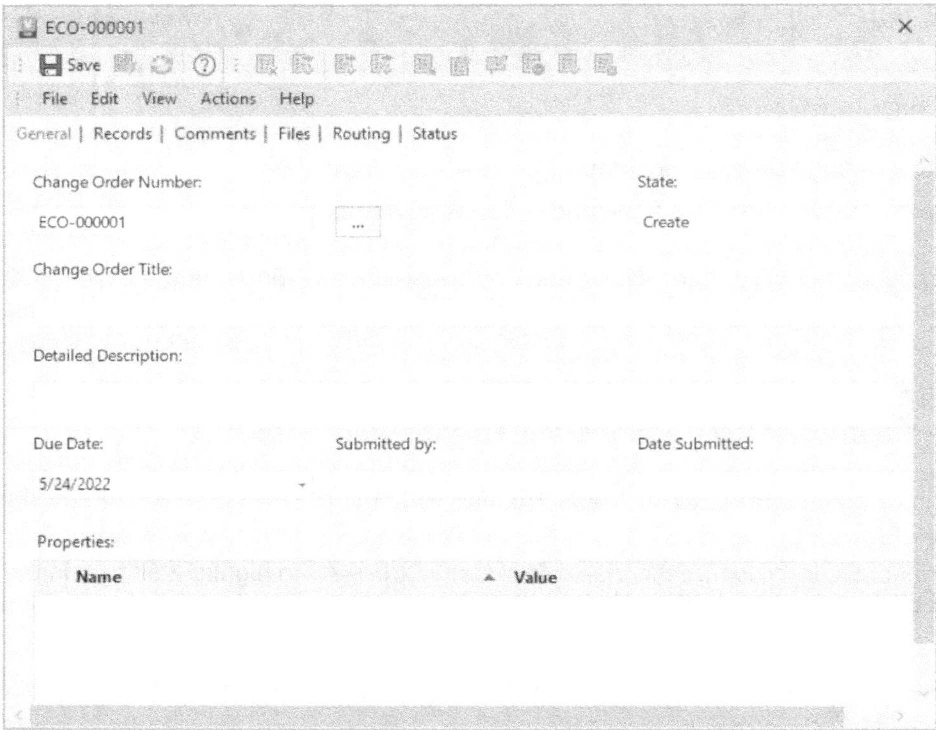

Figure 11–18

6. In the *General* tab, enter **Design Change for Piston Assembly** for the *Change Order Title* and *Detailed Description*.
7. Select the *Routing* tab to view the roles assigned to **user1**, such as *Change Administrator* and *Responsible Engineer*, as shown in Figure 11–19.

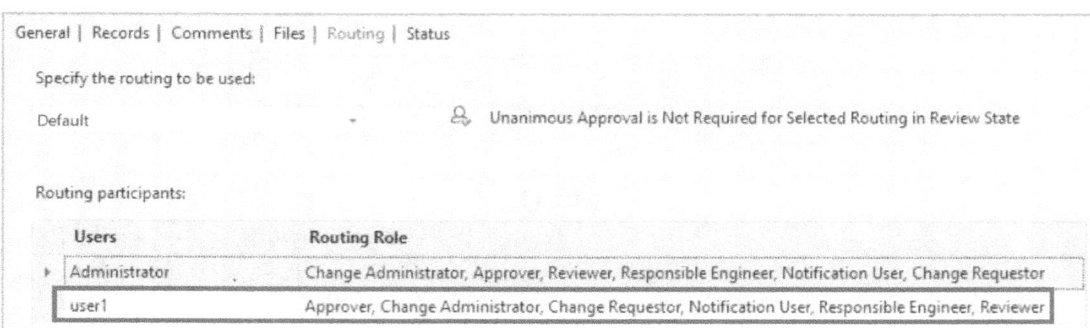

Figure 11–19

8. Select the *Status* tab to see that the current state is **Create** and the next state is **Open** as shown in Figure 11–20.

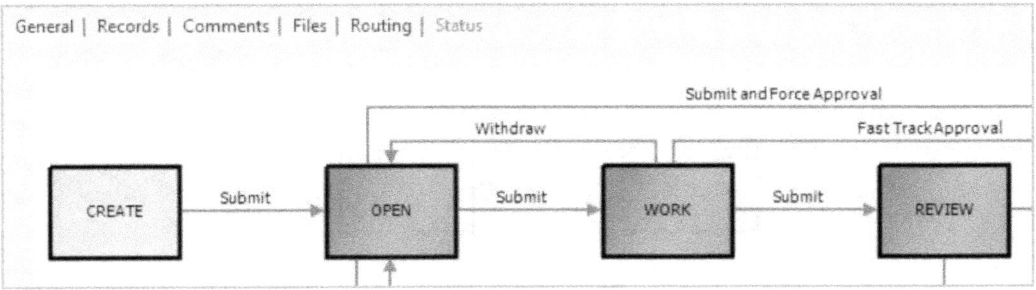

Figure 11–20

9. Select **Save** to save the ECO.

10. Select (Submit) to promote the ECO to the **Open** state, as shown in Figure 11–21.

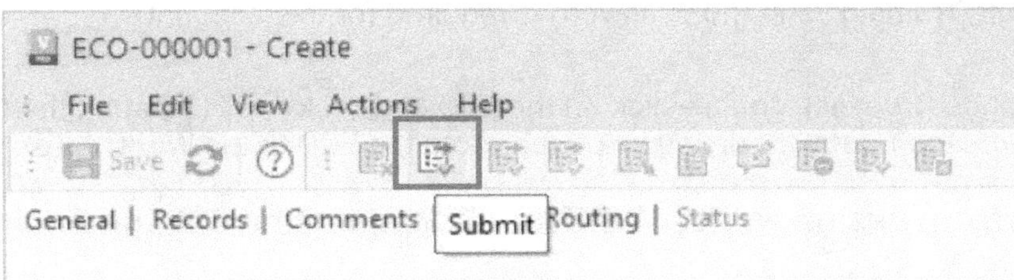

Figure 11–21

11. In the *Comment:* field, type, "Redesign shaft" and click **OK**.

12. In the Item Master, select **Vise**, then hold <Ctrl> and select the change order icon to open the change order, as shown in Figure 11–22.

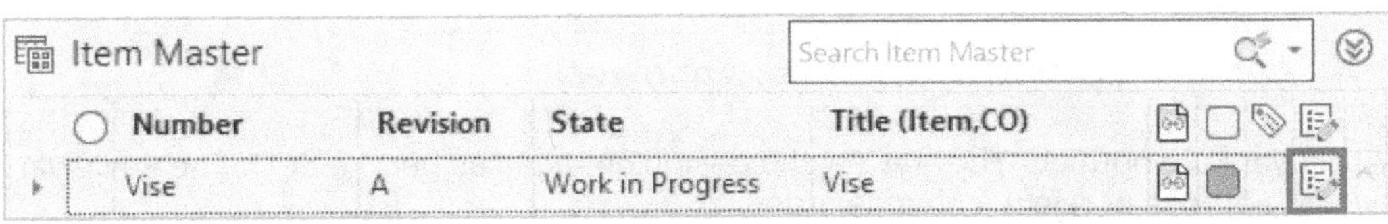

Figure 11–22

13. Select the *Status* tab and note that the state is now **Open**, as shown in Figure 11–23.

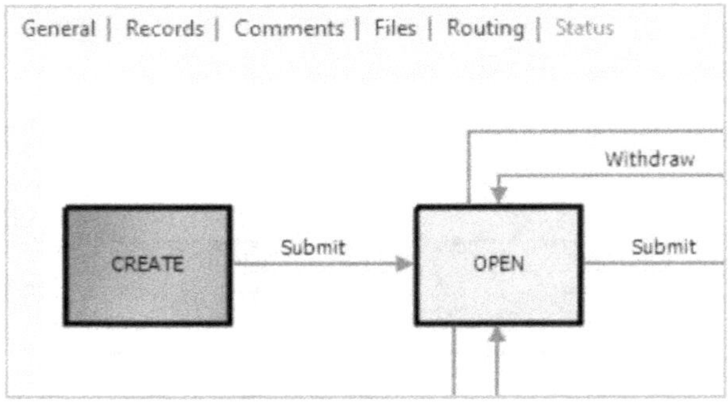

Figure 11–23

Task 2: Edit ECO (OPEN state: Change Administrator).

1. The Change Administrator is now notified and can edit the ECO if required. Log in as **user1** to the **Vault_Training** vault (no password is required for this account).

2. In the Change Order list, double-click on the ECO and click  (Submit), then click **OK** in the *Submit - Add Comment* dialog box to promote the ECO to the **Work** state.

Task 3: Perform design work (WORK state: Responsible Design Engineer).

The Responsible Engineer is notified and the ECO is placed in their Worklist. The Responsible Engineer makes the design changes as outlined in the Change Order. Once complete, they check the files back into the vault, and the items are updated.

1. Click  (Submit), then click **OK** in the *Submit - Add Comment* dialog box to promote the ECO to the **Review** state.

Task 4: Approve ECO (REVIEW state: Approver).

The Approvers are notified. They review the design changes as per the ECO. The Reviewer can review and approve or reject a change order.

1. Click  (Approve), then click **OK** in the *Submit - Add Comment* dialog box to promote the ECO to the **Approved** state.

Task 5: Release the design and close the ECO (APPROVED state: Change Administrator).

The Change Administrator is notified and any Work In Progress or In Review or For Review items and files on the change order are set to **Released**.

1. Click  (Close Change Order), then click **OK** in the *Close - Add Comment* dialog box.
2. A *Change State* dialog box opens. Select **Released** from the list, as shown in Figure 11–24.

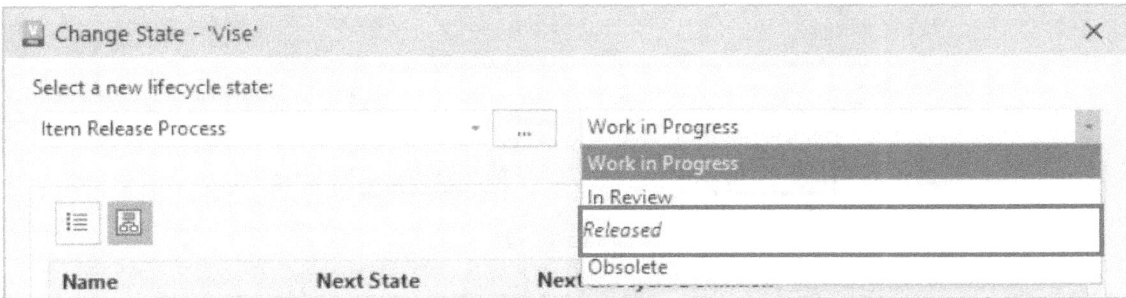

Figure 11–24

3. The *Comments* are entered automatically as **Released to manufacturing**. Click **OK**. The Change Order moves to the **Closed** state, as shown in Figure 11–25.

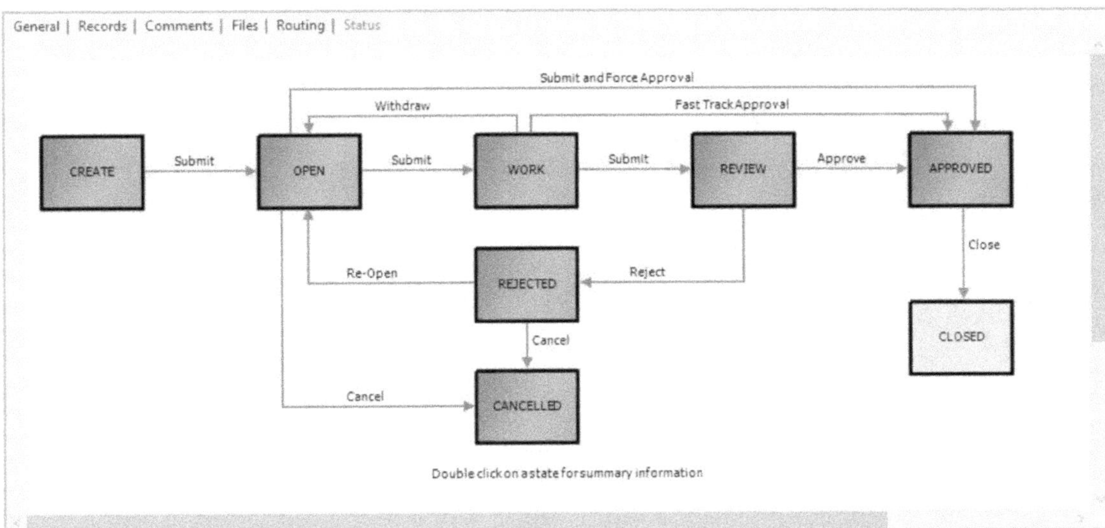

Figure 11–25

4. Select the *Records* tab of the ECO and note the *State* of the item is **Released**.

5. Print a Change Order Summary Report by selecting **File>Print Change Order Summary**, as shown in Figure 11–26.

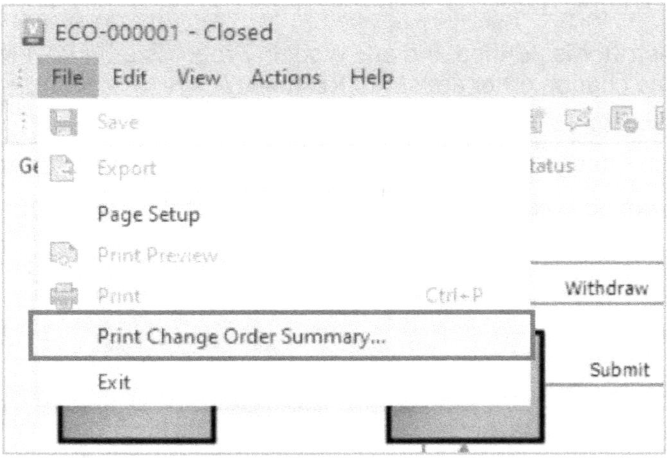

Figure 11–26

End of practice

Practice 11b
Create and Approve a Change Order Using Files

Practice Objectives

- Create a Change Order using files.
- Review, approve, and close a Change Order using files.

In this practice, you will create, review, and approve an Engineering Change Order (ECO) using files. The steps are the same as the previous practice. Again, for instructional purposes, **user1** will have permissions to create, review, and approve a change order.

Task 1: Create an ECO (Create state: Change Requestor).

1. Log in as **user1** to the **Vault_Training** vault (no password is required for this account).
2. Locate **piston_assem.iam**.
3. Right-click on **piston_assem.iam** and then select **Add to Change Order>To New**, as shown in Figure 11–27.

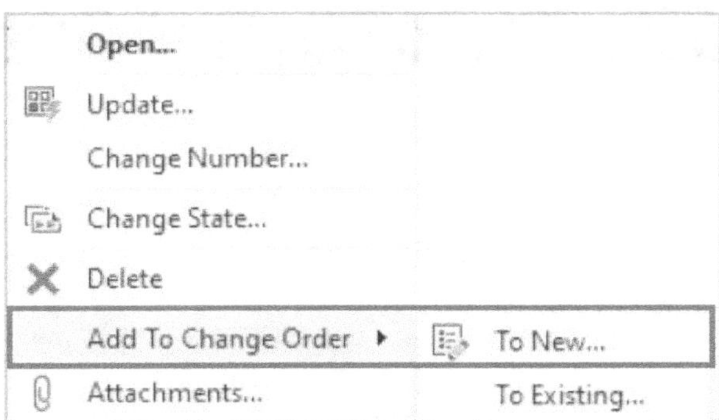

Figure 11–27

4. Edit the ECO by adding a Change Order Title, save it, and click (Submit) to promote to the **Open** state.

Task 2: Edit ECO (Open state: Change Administrator).

1. Edit the ECO and click (Submit) to promote to the **Work** state.

Task 3: Perform design work (Work state: Responsible Design Engineer).

1. Perform the design work and click (Submit) to promote to the **Review** state.

Task 4: Review and approve ECO (Review state: Approver).

1. Review the ECO and click (Approve) to promote it to the **Approved** state.

Task 5: Release the design and close the ECO (Approved state: Change Administrator).

1. Click (Close Change Order) to promote it to the **Closed** state.

End of practice

Chapter Review Questions

1. When viewing a Change Order object, what tab enables you to view which users can approve the change order?
   a. General
   b. Records
   c. Files
   d. Routing

2. While moving through the standard Change Order lifecycle states of **Create>Open>Work>Review>Approved>Closed**, it is at the **Work** state that the Responsible Engineer can edit the change order and make design changes.
   a. True
   b. False

3. What tab of a Change Order object is used to attach additional files to a change order?
   a. General
   b. Records
   c. Files
   d. Status

4. What does Unanimous Approval mean?
   a. Only the Administrator needs to review and submit their acceptance of the change order.
   b. All Approvers must review and submit their acceptance of the change order.
   c. Only one Approver needs to review and submit their acceptance of the change order.
   d. The Approved lifecycle state is skipped.

5. The Approver cannot reject a change order.
   a. True
   b. False

Command Summary

Button	Command	Location
	**Approve**	• **ECO dialog box:** Toolbar
	**Close Change Oder**	• **ECO dialog box:** Toolbar
	**Reject**	• **ECO dialog box:** Toolbar
	**Submit**	• **ECO dialog box:** Toolbar

Chapter

12

Customizing the User Interface

There are several ways you can customize the user interface of the Autodesk® Vault software to improve productivity and efficiency.

Learning Objectives

- Customize the Autodesk Vault interface using the **View** menu.
- Change the column display in the Autodesk Vault software using the **Customize View** option.
- Apply a filter to the main table using the filter options.
- Create a custom view using the **Define custom views** menu.
- Create a shortcut to access frequently used designs.

12.1 Autodesk Vault Customization

The **View** menu options control the display of the Autodesk Vault window. The menu is shown in Figure 12–1.

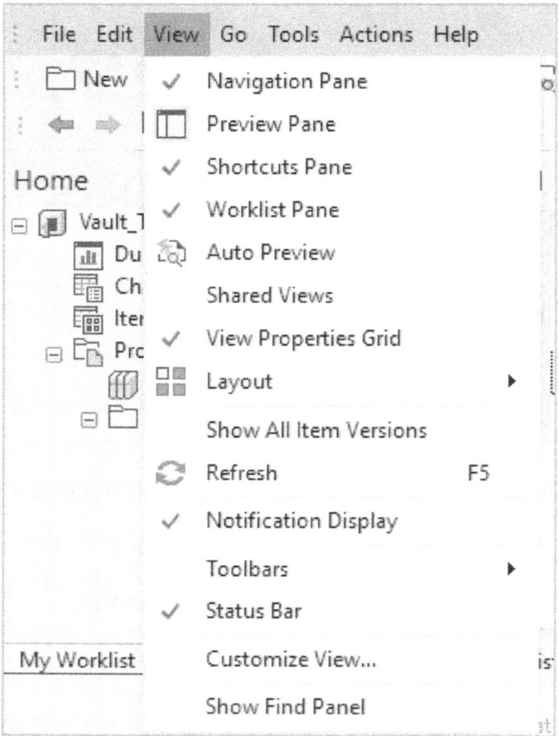

Figure 12–1

Pane Display

You can toggle the interface items shown in Figure 12–2 on and off.

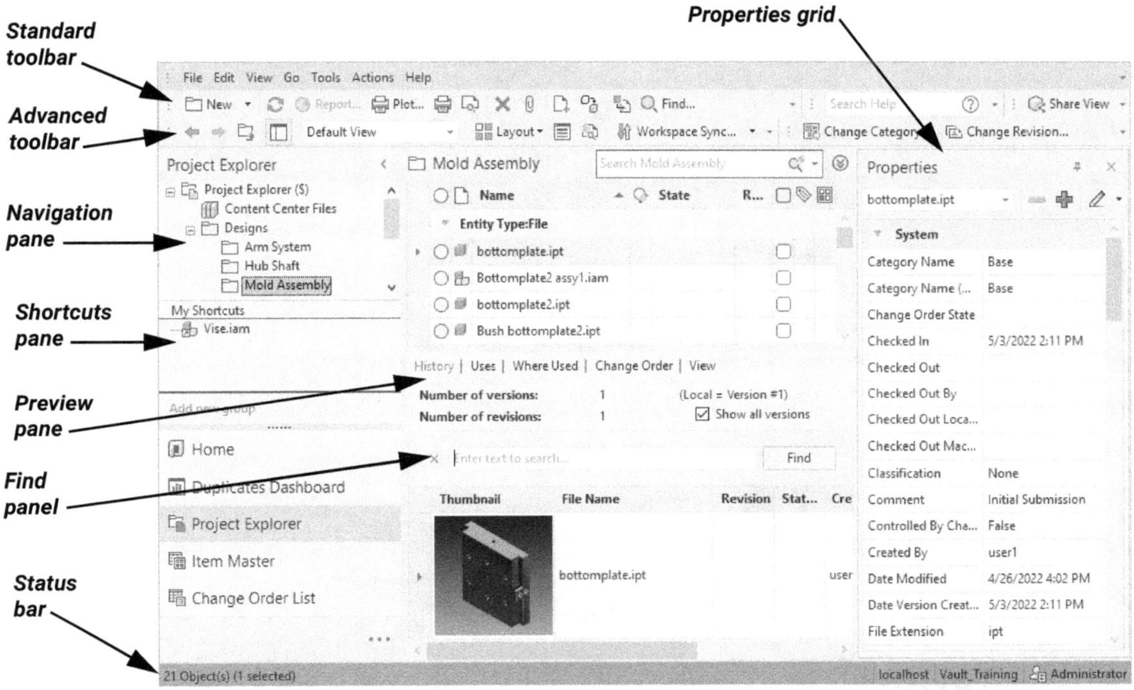

Figure 12–2

Note: *(Preview pane) is also located in the Advanced toolbar.*

If a window pane is on (displayed), you can toggle it off (hide it) by selecting its option in the **View** menu. For example, you can toggle the Navigation pane and the Properties grid off so that the Main table and Preview pane fill the extra space, as shown in Figure 12–3.

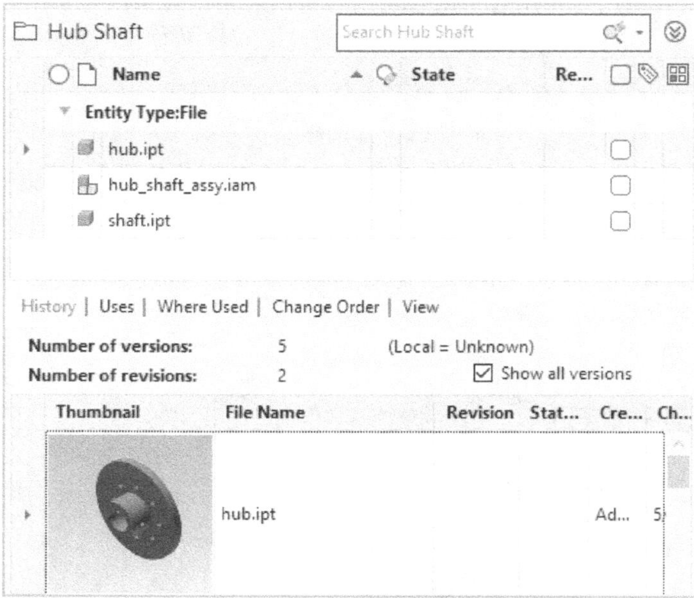

Figure 12–3

Auto Preview

Auto Preview can also be toggled on or off in either the View menu or from the Advanced toolbar ( ). When on, objects display in the Main table with comments directly below them, as shown in Figure 12–4.

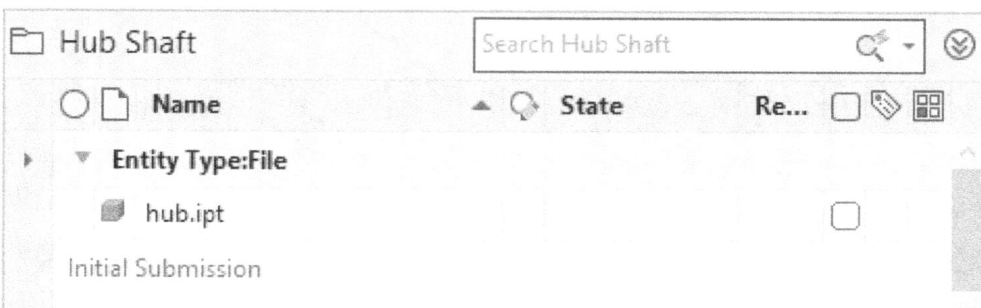

Figure 12–4

12.2 Customizing Columns

The **Customize View** option enables you to customize the column display in the Main table, Preview pane, and search results window. This can increase your productivity by displaying only the required file property information in an easy-to-view display.

The **Customize View** option is available when you right-click on a column heading, as shown in Figure 12–5.

> ***Note:*** *The* ***Customize View*** *option is also available when you right-click in any white space in the Main table or Preview pane.*

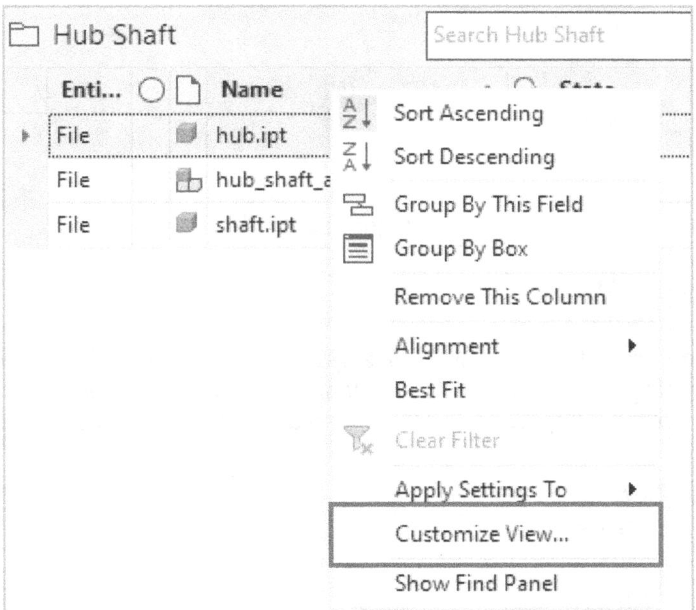

Figure 12–5

When you select **Customize View**, the *Customize View* dialog box opens as shown in Figure 12–6. The options available vary depending on whether you click **Customize View** in the Main table, Preview pane, and search results window.

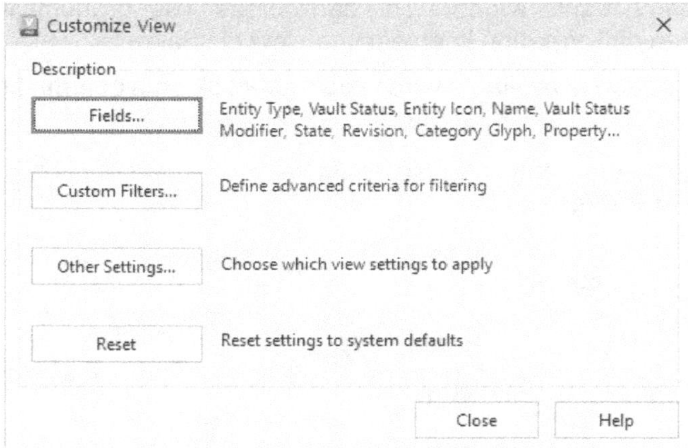

Figure 12–6

Column Display

To customize the columns that display, click **Fields...** in the *Customize View* dialog box. The *Customize Fields* dialog box opens. The *Show these fields in this order* area contains the columns that are currently displayed and their display order, as shown in Figure 12–7.

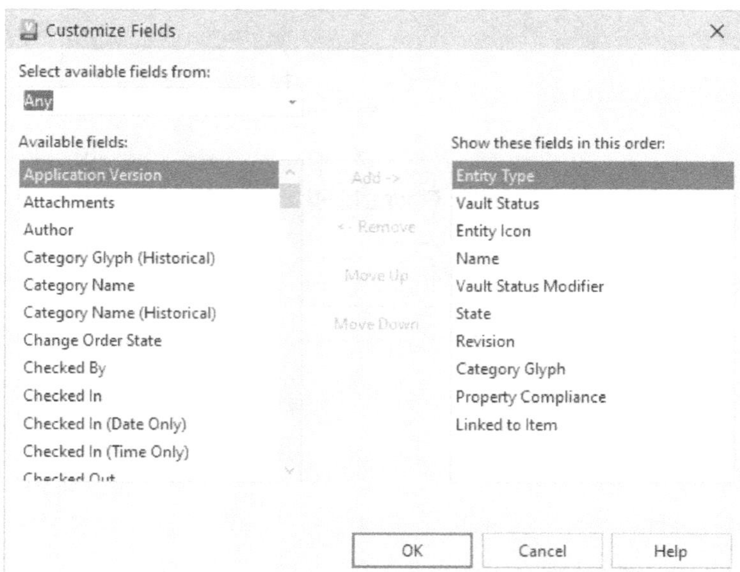

Figure 12–7

Adding Columns

You can add columns to the Main table and customize the order in which they display.

How To: Add Columns to the Main Table

1. In the *Customize Fields* dialog box, in the *Select available fields from* drop-down list, select one of the options as shown in Figure 12–8.

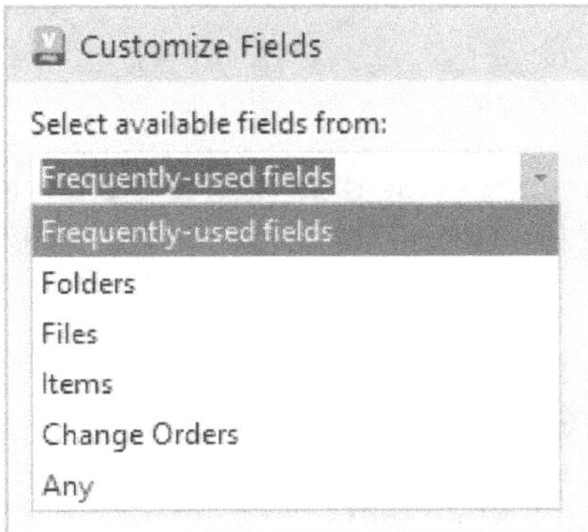

Figure 12–8

2. In the *Available fields* area, select a property as shown in Figure 12–9. Click **Add** to move the property to the *Show these fields in this order* area.

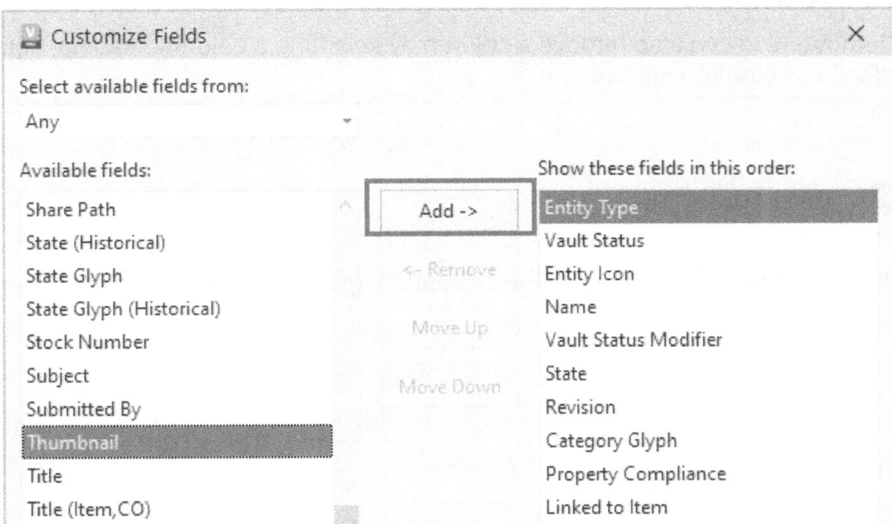

Figure 12–9

3. Click **OK**.

Changing Column Order

In the *Customize Fields* dialog box, the order in which the columns are shown is the order in which they display in the Main table.

How To: Change the Column Order

1. In the *Customize Fields* dialog box, in the *Show these fields in this order* area, select the property field to reorder.

   Note: *You can also change the column order by dragging and dropping a column heading to a new position in the Main table.*

2. Click **Move Up** to move the property field up (i.e., to the left in the Main table). Click **Move Down** to move the property field down (i.e., to the right in the Main table).
3. Click **OK**.

Removing Columns

You can remove columns from the Main table.

How To: Remove a Column

1. In the *Customize Fields* dialog box, in the *Show these fields in this order* area, select the property to remove.
2. Click **Remove**. You can also remove a column by selecting a column heading, right-clicking, and selecting **Remove This Column**.
3. Click **OK**.

Text Alignment

You can modify the alignment of the text displayed in the columns in the Main table.

How To: Align the Text in a Column

1. Select the column heading, right-click on **Alignment** to display the alignment options as shown in Figure 12–10.

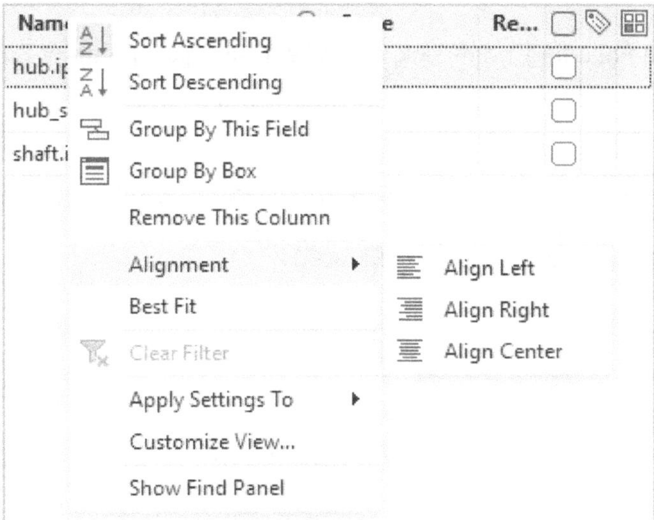

Figure 12–10

2. Select the required type of alignment: **Align Left**, **Align Right**, or **Align Center**. The text in the column updates accordingly.

Column Size

You can modify the width of the columns in the Main table.

How To: Resize a Column

1. Hover over the right edge of the column heading border so that the double arrowheads display (↔).
2. Drag the border to manually resize the column.

You can also resize columns as follows:

- Select the column heading, right-click, and select **Best Fit** to automatically resize the column to fit the data.
- Double-click on the right edge of the column heading border to automatically fit the column width to the data.

Sorting

You can sort the data that displays in the columns in the Main table.

How To: Sort Data in a Column

1. Select the column heading, right-click, and select **Sort Ascending** or **Sort Descending**.

   Note: *You can also select the column heading to switch between the ascending and descending sort type.*

   - **Sort Ascending:** Sorts columns from A to Z, reading from top to bottom (or from the lowest to highest number). If a column is sorted in ascending order, an up arrow displays in the column heading, as shown in Figure 12–11.

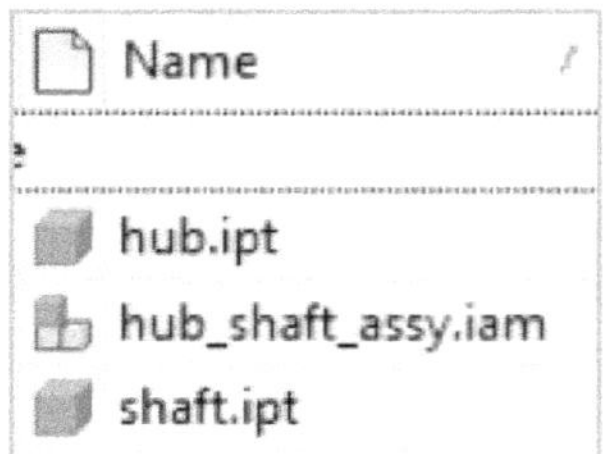

Figure 12–11

   - **Sort Descending:** Sorts columns from Z to A, reading from top to bottom (or from the highest to lowest number). If a column is sorted in descending order, a down arrow displays in the column heading as shown in Figure 12–12.

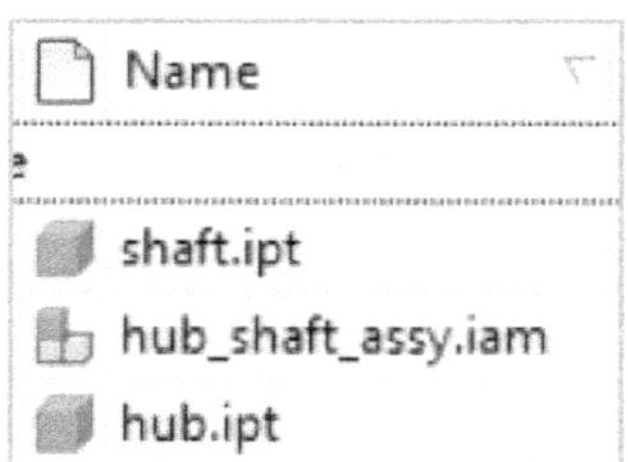

Figure 12–12

Grouping

You can sort the contents of the Main table and Preview pane by any combination of column headings. Objects that have the same values for the selected properties are then listed together. For example, you can group a folder by designer, version, date, etc. for a more manageable view of the folder.

How To: Group by Column Headings

1. Select the column heading, right-click, and select **Group By This Field**. The column heading is moved to the *Group By Box* area and the contents are grouped and collapsed, as shown in Figure 12–13.

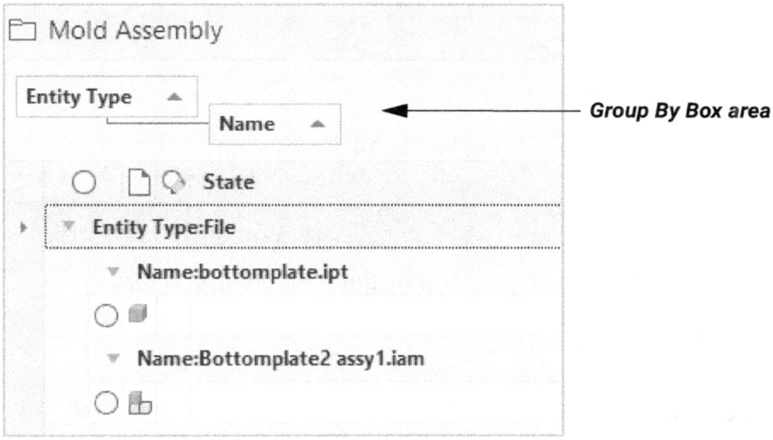

Figure 12–13

Note: You can also drag the column heading next to the first one in the Group By Box area to add a sub-group. Drag it back to the other column headings to remove the sub-group.

 *(Group By Box) is also located in the Advanced toolbar.*

2. If you need to place another group in the first one (a sub-group), right-click on another column heading, and select **Group By This Field**.
3. To expand all of the groups, right-click in the *Group By Box* area, and select **Full Expand**.
4. To collapse all of the groups, right-click in the *Group By Box* area, and select **Full Collapse**.
5. To clear the group so that the files display as a flat list without any groups, right-click in the *Group By Box* area, and select **Clear Grouping**.
6. To remove the *Group By Box* area, right-click on a column heading, and select **Group By Box** to toggle it off.

Additional Settings

Additional settings can be found by clicking **Other Settings...** in the *Customize View* dialog box. The settings are shown in Figure 12–14.

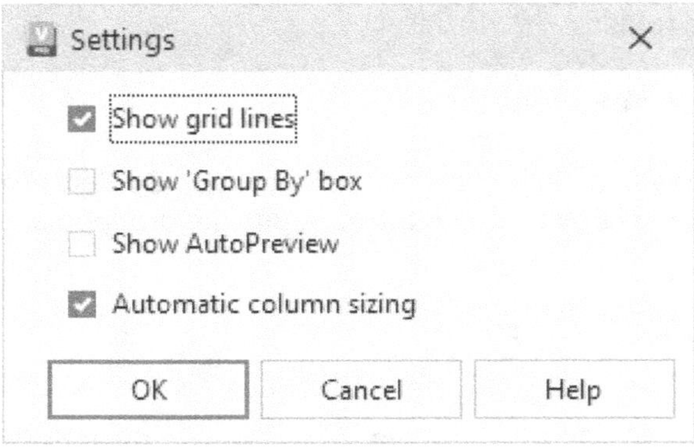

Figure 12–14

Filters

You can hide contents based on specific criteria by defining column filters.

How To: Create a Column Filter

1. In the Main table or Preview pane, hover the cursor over a column heading. A filter icon displays, as shown in Figure 12–15.

Figure 12–15

Note: Filters can also be created by clicking ***Custom Filters...*** *in the Customize View dialog box.*

2. Click the filter icon and select either the *Values* tab or *Text Filters* tab, as shown in Figure 12–16.

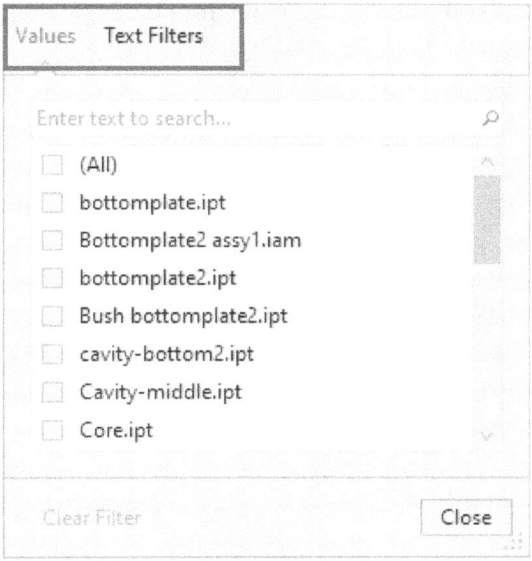

Figure 12–16

3. To create a filter from column values, in the *Values* tab, select checkboxes next to the files whose data you would like displayed, as shown in Figure 12–17. Note that the files are displayed immediately and the filter is shown at the bottom of the main table. Click **Close** when finished.

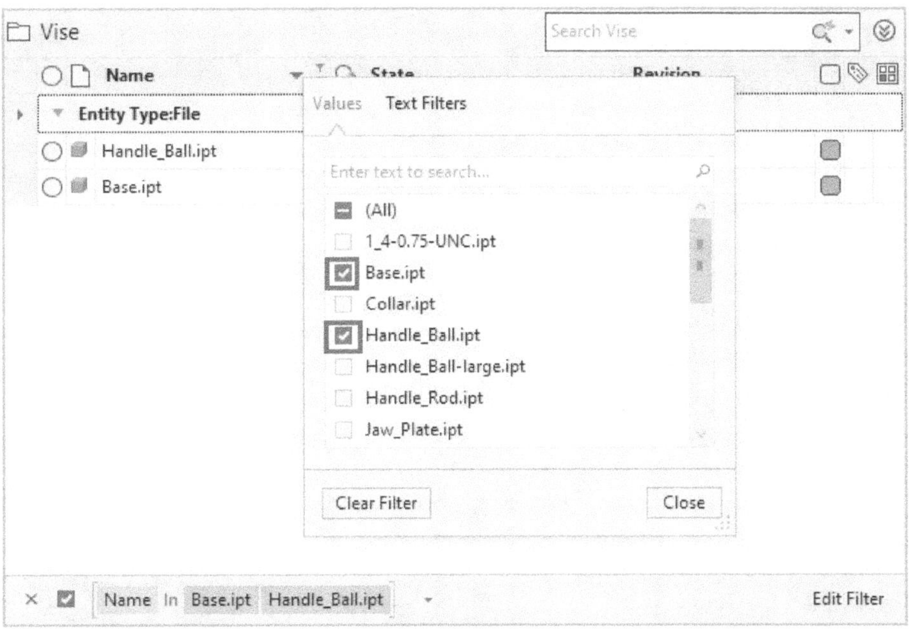

Figure 12–17

4. To create a filter using text filters, in the *Text Filters* tab, select an operator from the drop-down list, as shown in Figure 12–18.

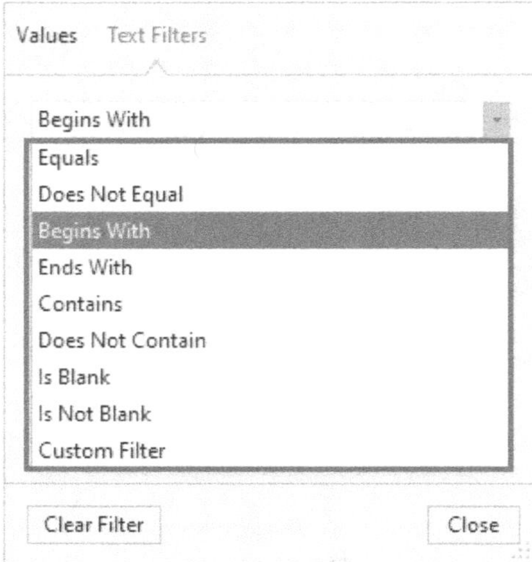

Figure 12–18

5. Enter a value for the condition, as shown in Figure 12–19. The filtered list displays immediately. Click **Close** when finished.

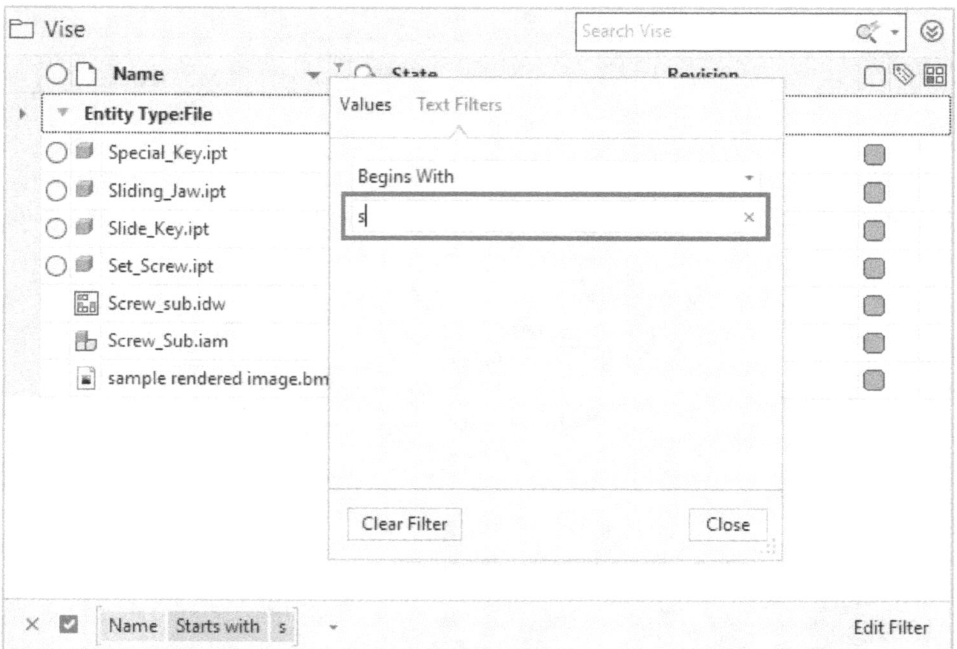

Figure 12–19

6. To create a custom filter, select the *Text Filters* tab and select **Custom Filter** in the drop-down list, as shown in Figure 12–20.

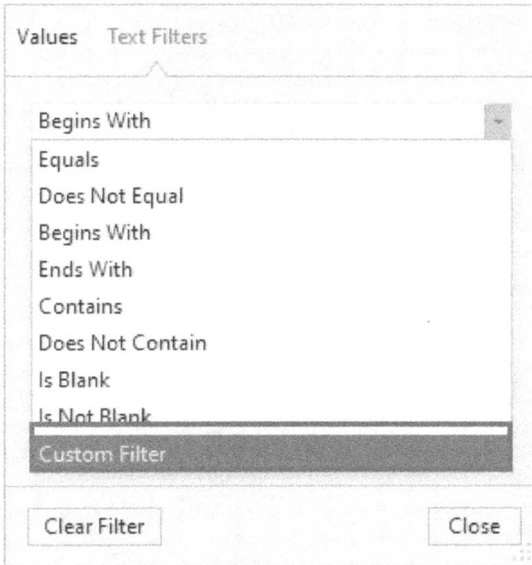

Figure 12–20

7. In the *First* search criteria section, select an operator from the drop-down list and enter a value for the condition, as shown in Figure 12–21.

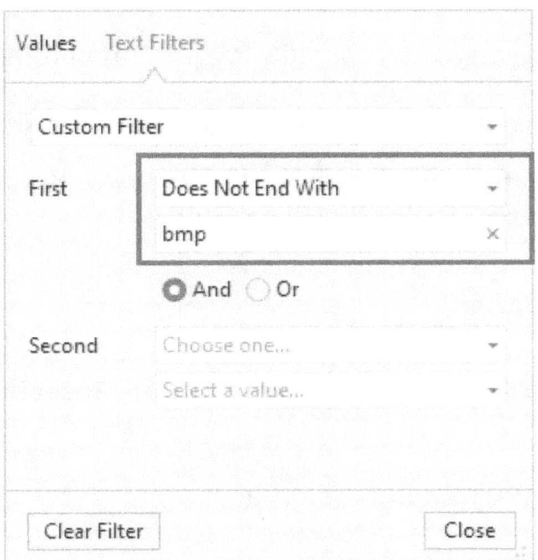

Figure 12–21

8. You can specify up to two types of search criteria. Select **And** to combine the criteria or select **Or** to contain either criteria.

9. Click **Close** to complete the custom filter definition. The line at the bottom of the pane indicates that a custom filter is being used, as shown in Figure 12–22.

Figure 12–22

10. Click **Edit Filter** to view the Filter Editor and to modify the filter's definition, as shown in Figure 12–23.

Figure 12–23

__Note:__ The filter can also be removed by right-clicking on the column heading, and selecting __Clear Filter__.

11. When a filter is created, you can temporarily toggle it off or remove it. To toggle off a filter, click [checkbox icon] at the bottom of the Main table list. To remove the filter, click [X icon]. Toggling off or removing a filter causes the complete list of files to be displayed. Click [drop-down arrow icon] to select from the list of available filters.

Reset Current View

To reset the column view to the default configuration, click **Reset** in the *Customize View* dialog box.

12.3 Custom Views

Custom views enable you to create your own configuration of the interface. Once created, you can modify, rename, copy, delete, or reuse it.

How To: Create a Custom View

1. In the Advanced toolbar, expand the drop-down list and select **Define custom views...** as shown in Figure 12–24.

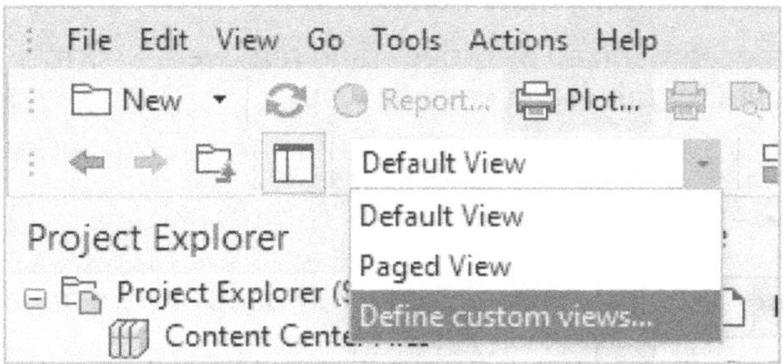

Figure 12–24

2. In the *Manage Custom Views* dialog box, click **New...**.
3. For *View Name*, enter a name for the custom view and click **OK**.
4. In the *Manage Custom Views* dialog box, click **Modify...**.
5. In the *Customize View* dialog box, click **Fields...**.
6. In the *Customize Fields* dialog box, select the columns that you want to display in the custom view.
7. Click **Close** to close the dialog box and apply the settings.

12.4 Shortcuts

Shortcuts can be used to quickly access specific folders or objects. When the shortcut is selected, the associated folder or object displays in the Main table. Vault shortcuts can also be accessed in the Autodesk Inventor *Open* and *Place From Vault* dialog boxes for quick retrieval of components and designs.

When created, shortcuts are added to the *Saved Shortcuts>My Shortcuts* folder in the Shortcuts pane, which is part of the Navigation pane. The Shortcuts pane is hidden when the Navigation pane is hidden but can also be hidden independent of the Navigation pane. To hide the Shortcuts pane, clear the **View>Shortcuts Pane** option.

Shortcuts can be renamed, organized by groups, and removed. Shortcut groups can be created to organize your shortcuts for quick and easy access.

Create Shortcut

You can create shortcuts to quickly access frequently used folders or objects.

How To: Create a Shortcut

1. In the Navigation pane or Main table, select a folder or file.
2. Right-click and select **Create Shortcut>My Shortcut**. A shortcut displays in the *My Shortcuts* folder, as shown in Figure 12–25. In this example, shortcuts were created to the *Hub Shaft* folder and to the **Operating instructions.doc** file.

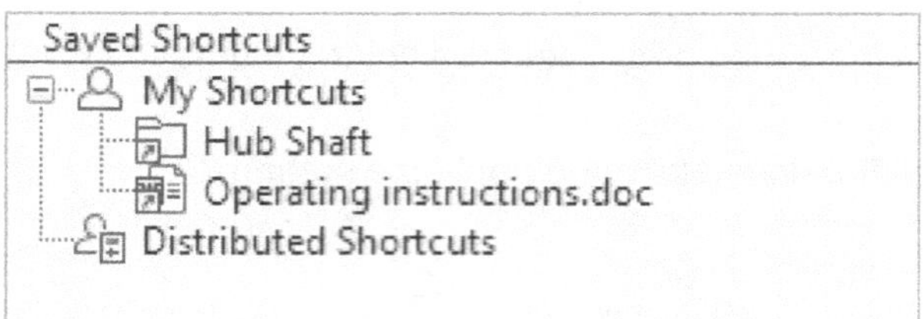

Figure 12–25

__Note:__ Administrators can select __Create Shortcut>Distributed shortcut__ to create a new shortcut to be made available for all users under the Distributed Shortcuts folder.

3. To rename a shortcut, right-click on it and select **Rename**. Enter a new name.
4. To remove a shortcut, right-click on it and select **Delete**. Only the shortcut is removed and not the associated folder or object.

Create Shortcut Groups

You can organize your shortcuts using groups to make them easier to locate.

How To: Create a Shortcut Group

1. In the Shortcuts pane, right-click on *My Shortcuts* and select **New Group**. Enter a name for the group.
2. Drag existing shortcuts to the new group and drag them in the group to change their order. An example of a group is shown in Figure 12–26.

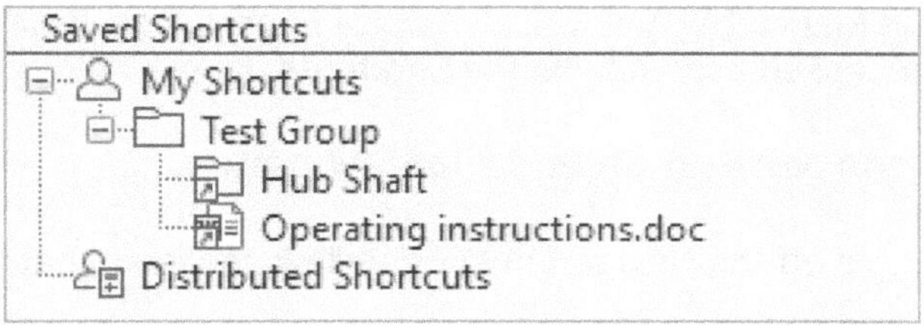

Figure 12–26

3. To rename a shortcut group, right-click on it and select **Rename**. Enter a new name.
4. To remove a shortcut group, right-click on it and select **Delete**. This also removes any shortcuts in the group.

Practice 12a
Customize the User Interface

Practice Objectives

- Use the View menu and Customize View option to customize the Autodesk client interface.
- Apply a filter to the main table.
- Create a shortcut.

In this practice, you will customize the user interface to display only the Main table and thumbnail images in the Main table. You will also use a filter to hide .BMP files in the Main table and add a frequently accessed assembly to the Shortcuts pane.

Task 1: Toggle off the Navigation and Preview panes.

In this task, you will toggle off the Navigation and Preview panes so that only the Main table displays.

1. In the Autodesk Vault software, select the *Hub Shaft* folder.
2. Select **View>Navigation Pane** and **View>Preview Pane** so that these panes are no longer displayed.

Task 2: Add a new column to the Main table.

In this task, you will add a new column to the Main table so that you can display a thumbnail image.

1. In the Main table, right-click on a column heading and select **Customize View**.
2. In the *Customize View* dialog box, click **Fields...**.
3. In the *Customize Fields* dialog box, expand the *Select available fields from* drop-down list, and select **Files**.
4. In the *Available fields* area, select **Thumbnail** and click **Add** to add it to the *Show these fields in this order* area.
5. In the *Show these fields in this order* area, select **Thumbnail** and click **Move Up** so that it is first in the list. Click **OK**.

6. Click **Close** to close the *Customize View* dialog box and complete the change. The thumbnail images display in the first column for each applicable file in the Main table, as shown in Figure 12–27.

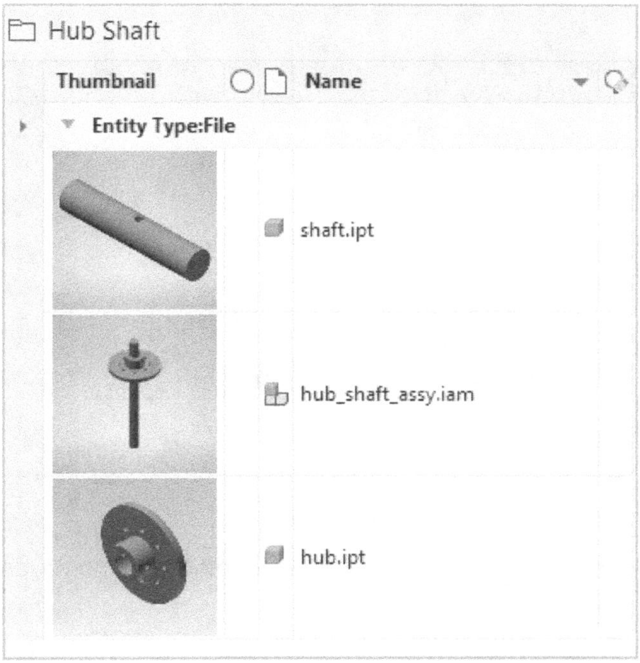

Figure 12–27

Task 3: Adjust the Name column.

1. Double-click on the border on the right side of the *Name* column heading to adjust the column size to fit the data.
2. Click the *Name* column to sort the list of files alphabetically, in ascending order.

Task 4: Apply a filter to the Main table.

In this task, you will create a custom filter to exclude all .BMP files from the display.

1. Select **View>Navigation Pane** to display the Navigation pane.
2. Select the *Vise* folder.
3. Identify the *sample rendered image.bmp* file. This is the file that you will filter out of the display.
4. Hover the cursor over the *Name* column and click .
5. Select the *Text Filters* tab.

6. In the *Text Filters* tab, select **Custom Filter** in the drop-down list, as shown in Figure 12–28.

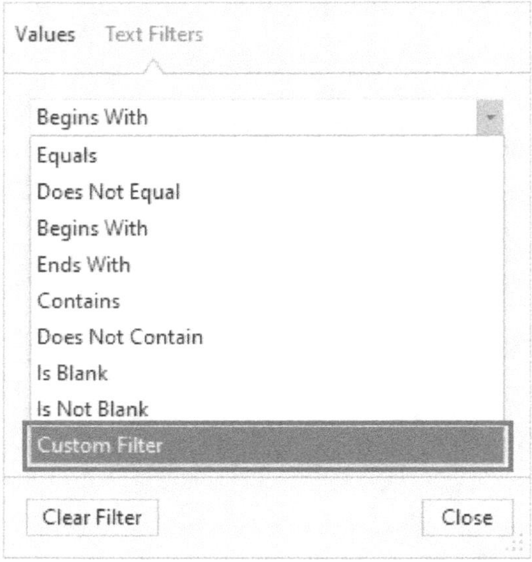

Figure 12–28

7. Select the **Does Not End With** operator. For the condition, type **bmp**, as shown in Figure 12–29.

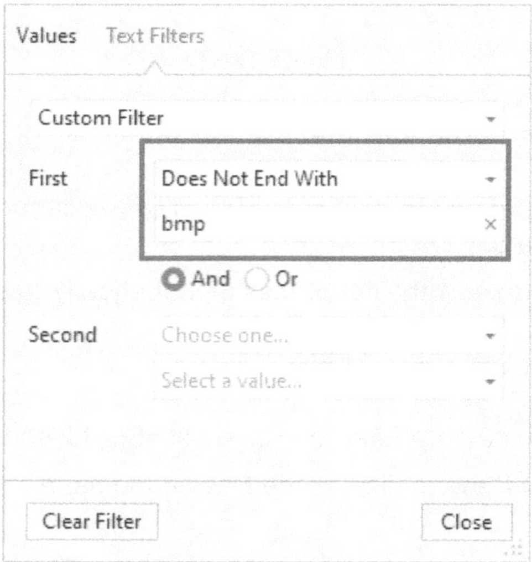

Figure 12–29

Note: *Once a filter is created, it is available for use in all folders.*

8. Click **Close**. The .BMP file is removed from the display and the filter displays at the bottom of the pane, as shown in Figure 12–30. You can disable the filter by clearing the checkmark.

Figure 12–30

Task 5: Undo/delete the customizations.

In this task, you will undo the user interface customizations.

1. Select **View>Preview Pane** to toggle on the Preview pane.
2. To delete the thumbnail image from the Main table, select the Thumbnail column heading, right-click, and select **Remove This Column**.
3. Click × at the bottom of the Main table to remove the filter and see the *rendered image.bmp* file return to the list.

Task 6: Add a shortcut.

1. Select **vise.iam**, right-click, and select **Create Shortcut>My Shortcut** to add the assembly to the Shortcuts pane, as shown in Figure 12–31. You can also drag the file to *My Shortcuts*. If the Shortcuts pane is not displayed, click **View>Shortcuts Pane**.

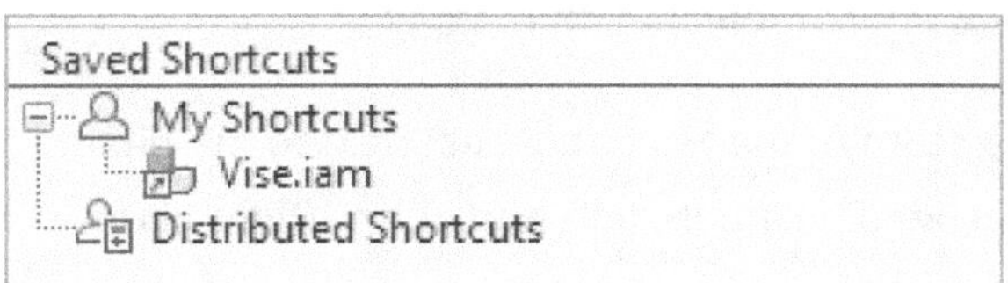

Figure 12–31

End of practice

Chapter Review Questions

1. In the Autodesk Vault interface, what are some of the ways in which you can customize the window display? (Select all that apply.)
   a. You can toggle on and off the Navigation and Preview panes.
   b. You can apply a filter to a column to only display objects with specified file formats, for example.
   c. You can change the font size in the main table.
   d. You can resize and reorder the columns.

2. How can you resize columns to fit the data? (Select all that apply.)
   a. Drag the border to manually resize the column.
   b. Select the column heading, right-click, and select Alignment.
   c. Select the column heading, right-click, and select Best Fit to automatically resize the column to fit the data.
   d. Double-click on the right edge of the column heading border to automatically fit the column width to the data.

3. How do you remove a filter? (Select all that apply.)
   a. Click × at the bottom of the Main table list next to the filter.
   b. Select the column heading, right-click, and select Clear Filter.
   c. Click ☐ at the bottom of the Main table list to place a checkmark for the filter.
   d. Click Reset in the *Customize View* dialog box.

4. When you remove a shortcut, you also remove the associated folder or object.
   a. True
   b. False

Command Summary

Button	Command	Location
	**Auto Preview**	• **Advanced Toolbar**
	**Group By Box**	• **Advanced Toolbar**

Chapter

13

Managing Prompts and Dialog Boxes

While interacting with files in the Vault, prompts and dialog boxes display to confirm your intentions or notify you of secondary functions that might or can be performed. These prompts and dialog boxes are useful when you are beginner but can become redundant when you are more familiar with the software. You can disable or enable prompts and dialog boxes.

Learning Objective

- Differentiate between prompt and dialog box settings for streamlining the file check out and check in processes.

13.1 Managing Prompts and Dialog Boxes in Vault Client

To streamline the workflow process, you can manage the prompt and dialog box defaults that are related to lifecycle operations. In addition, you can specify which operations are performed automatically without prompting for input.

Managing prompts and dialog boxes in the Vault Client controls how all prompts and dialog boxes respond regardless of the application that is launched, such as Word. To control the applications individually, use the Add-in options discussed in ***13.2 Managing Prompts and Dialog Boxes in Vault Add-in***.

In the Autodesk Vault Client software, select **Tools>Options** to open the *Options* dialog box, as shown in Figure 13–1.

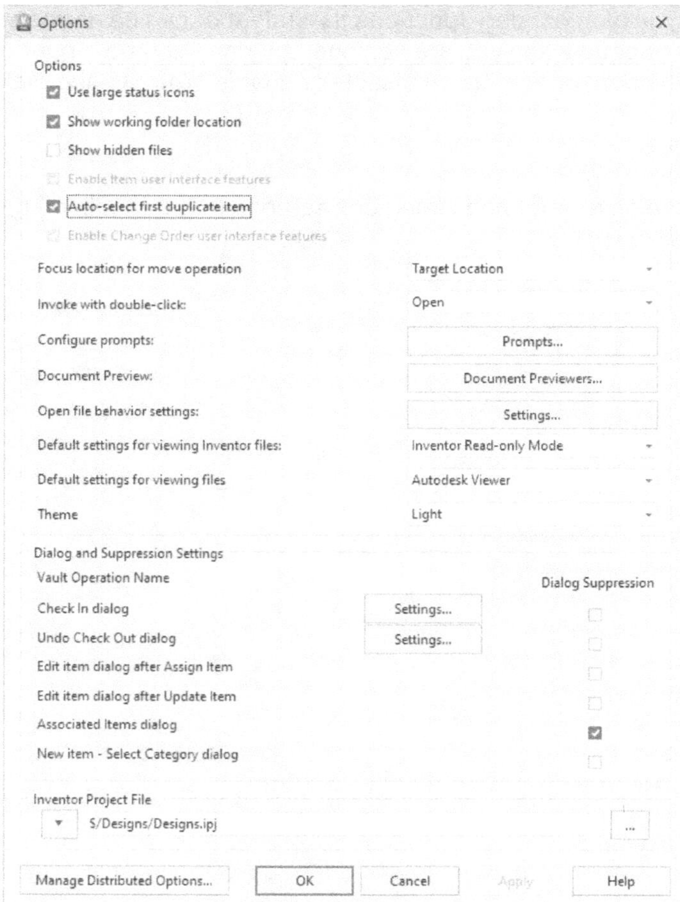

Figure 13–1

Prompts

To manage the default prompt settings, click **Prompts...** in the *Options* dialog box. The *Manage Prompts* dialog box opens as shown in Figure 13–2.

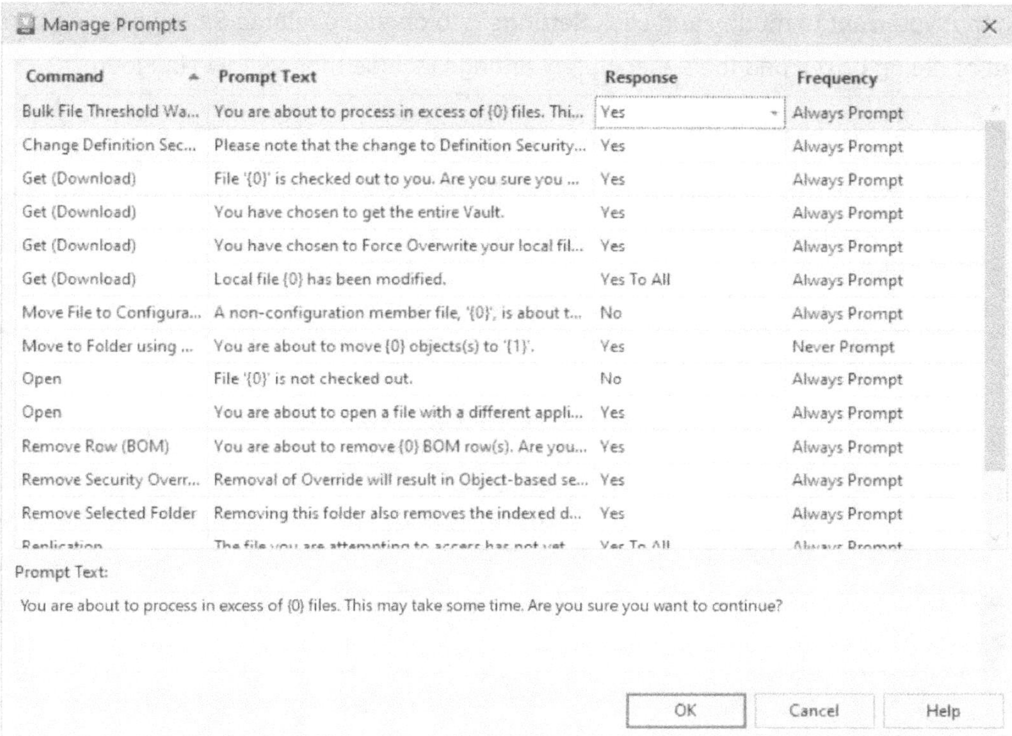

Figure 13–2

The dialog box displays four columns:

Command	Displays the command name.
Prompt Text	Displays the text that is displayed in the Warning box related to the selected command.
Response	Set the default response to the prompt.
Frequency	Set the frequency at which the prompt displays. • **Always Prompt** - This is the default prompt setting. Leave the default setting as is, if you require the prompt dialog box to display each time. • **Never Prompt** - Set it to **Never Prompt**, if you require automatic processing of the prompt request and do not want the prompt dialog box to display. The response you select will determine how the prompt will be automatically processed.

Dialog Boxes

Dialog boxes associated with lifecycle operations can be customized and suppressed. If a dialog box is suppressed, it is not displayed when the operation is performed. This streamlines and automates the workflow process. In the *Dialog Suppression* area, select the dialog box option that you want to modify and click **Settings...** to open the related *Settings* dialog box.

The list of dialog boxes and their associated settings include those shown in Figure 13–3:

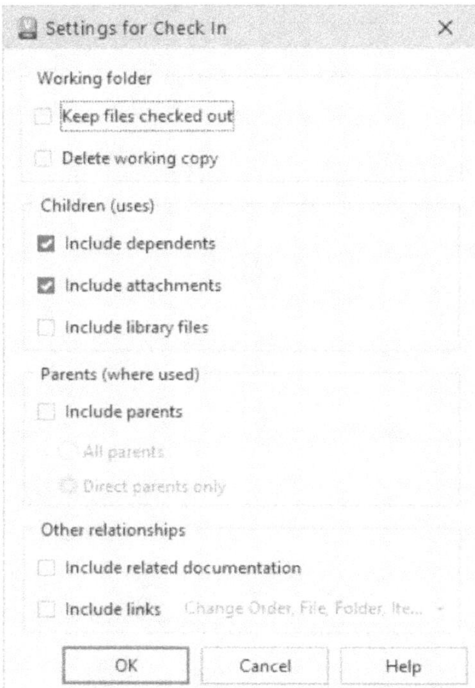

Settings for Check In dialog box

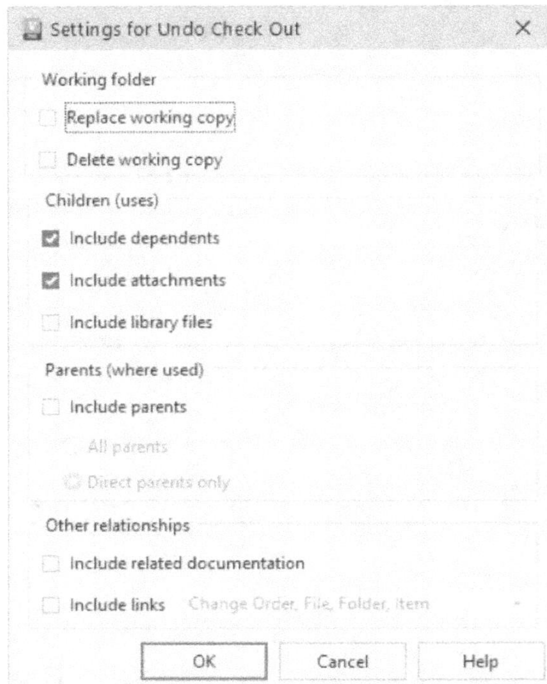

Settings for Undo Check Out dialog box

Figure 13–3

Document Preview

Use the *Document Preview* area to control document previews. Click **Document Previewers...** to open the *Document Previewer Options* dialog box, shown in Figure 13–4. Toggle a specific previewer by selecting the checkbox next to the option.

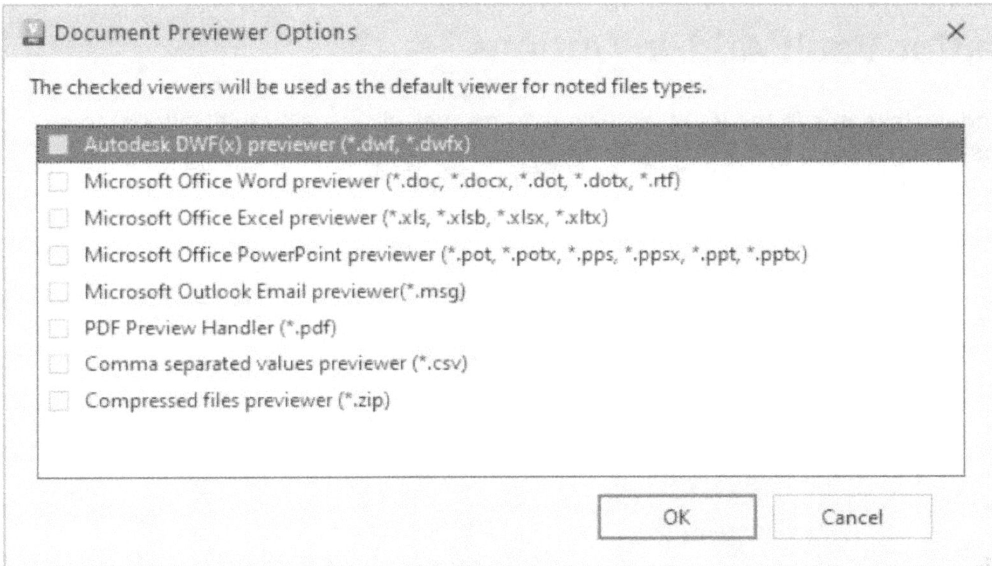

Figure 13–4

13.2 Managing Prompts and Dialog Boxes in Vault Add-in

Each application has its own options for controlling how it will respond to Vault prompts. Open the desired application, such as AutoCAD, and access the options via the *Vault* tab.

Inventor Vault Add-in Options

In Autodesk Inventor, in the *Vault* tab>*File Status* panel, click (Vault Options) to open the *Options* dialog box, as shown in Figure 13–5.

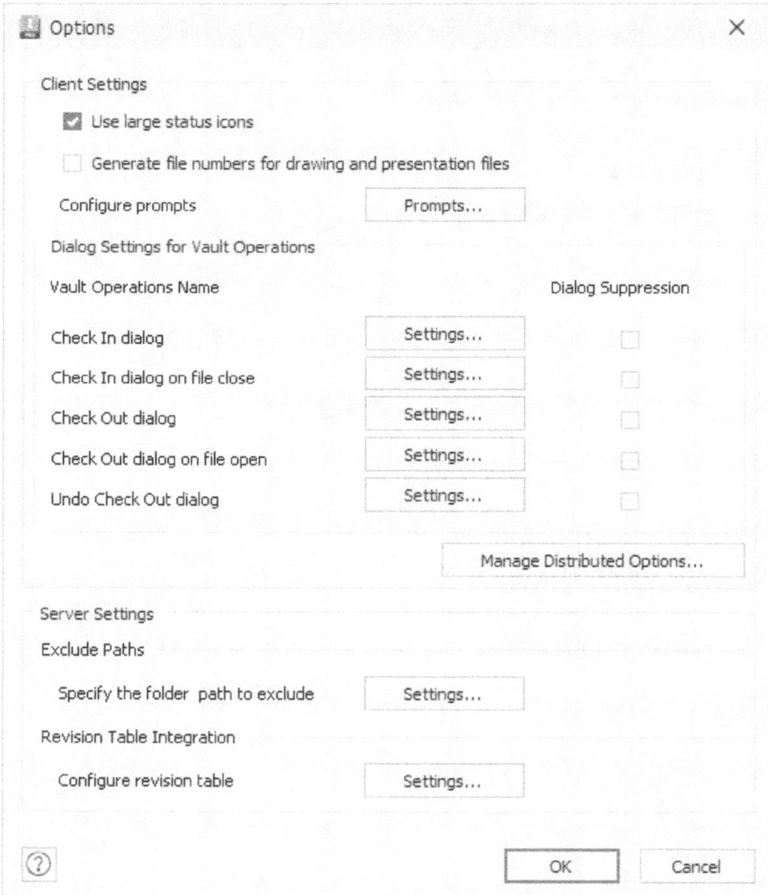

Figure 13–5

Prompts

To manage the default prompt settings, click **Prompts...** in the *Options* area. The *Manage Prompts* dialog box opens as shown in Figure 13–6.

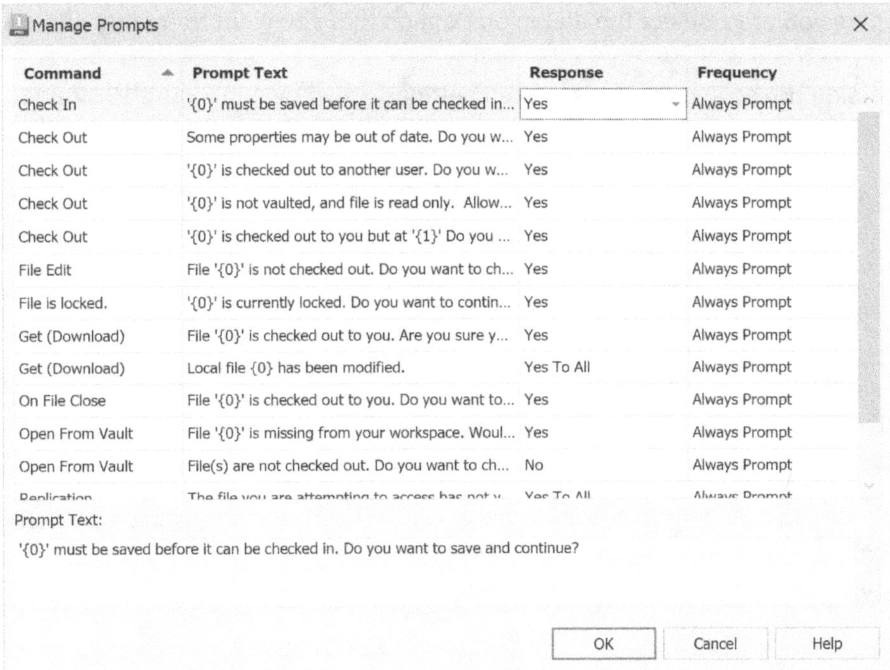

Figure 13–6

The dialog box displays four columns:

Command	Displays the command name.
Prompt Text	Displays the text that is displayed in the Warning box related to the selected command.
Response	Set the default response to the prompt.
Frequency	Set the frequency at which the prompt displays. • **Always Prompt** - This is the default prompt setting. Leave the default setting as is, if you require the prompt dialog box to display each time. • **Never Prompt** - Set it to **Never Prompt**, if you require automatic processing of the prompt request and do not want the prompt dialog box to display. The response you select will determine how the prompt will be automatically processed.

Dialog Boxes

Dialog boxes associated with Check In, Check Out, Undo Check Out, and File Open and Close operations can be customized with default settings and suppressed. When the operation is performed, no dialog box opens, thereby streamlining and automating the workflow. In the *Dialog Suppression* area, select the dialog box option that you want to modify and click **Settings...** to open the related *Settings* dialog box.

The list of dialog boxes and their associated settings are shown in Figure 13–7 and Figure 13–8:

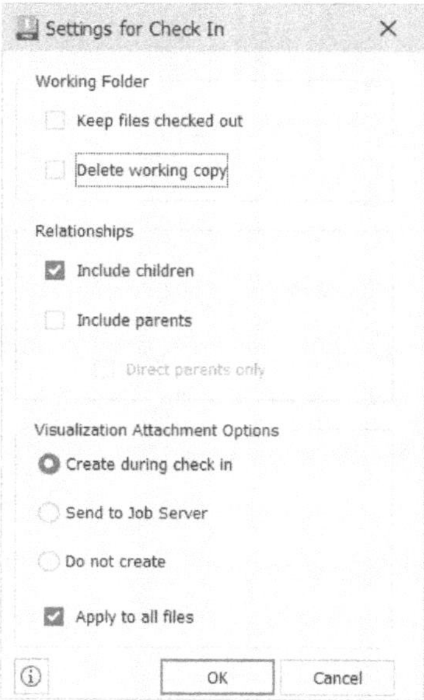

Settings for Check In dialog box

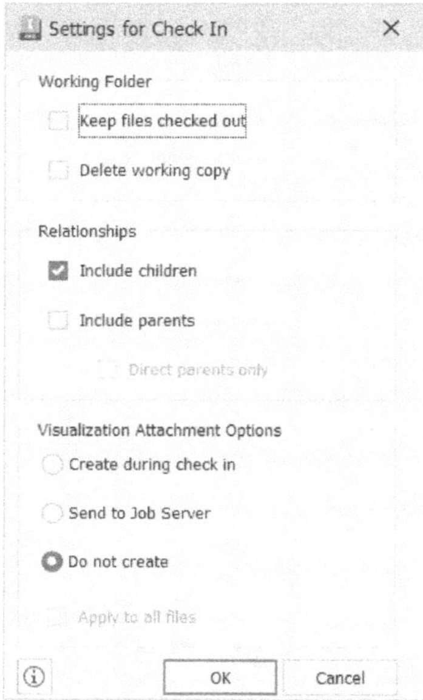

Settings for Check In dialog box on file close

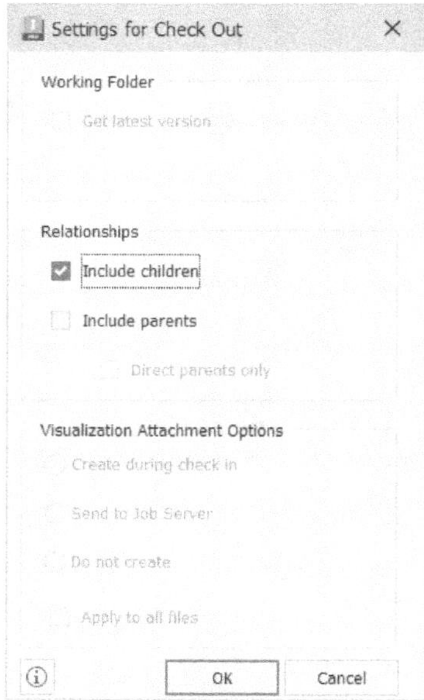

Settings for Check Out dialog box

Figure 13–7

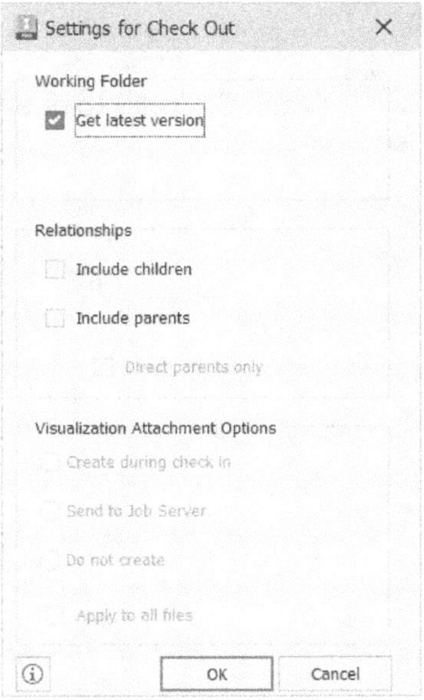

Settings for Check Out dialog box on file open

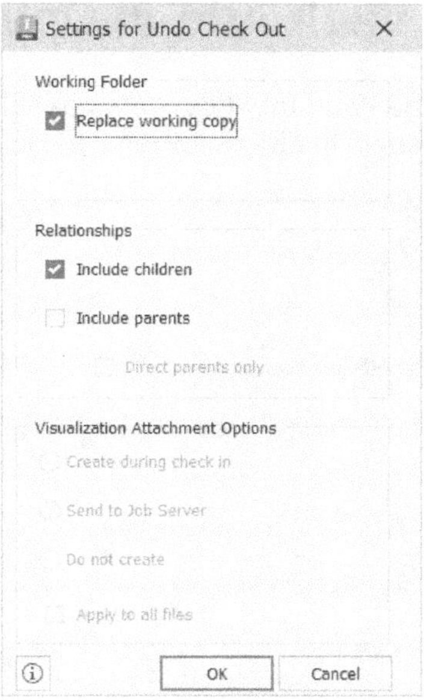

Settings for Undo Check Out dialog box

Figure 13–8

AutoCAD Vault Add-in Options

In AutoCAD, in the *Vault* tab>*File Status* panel, click (Vault Options) to open the *Options* dialog box, as shown in Figure 13–9.

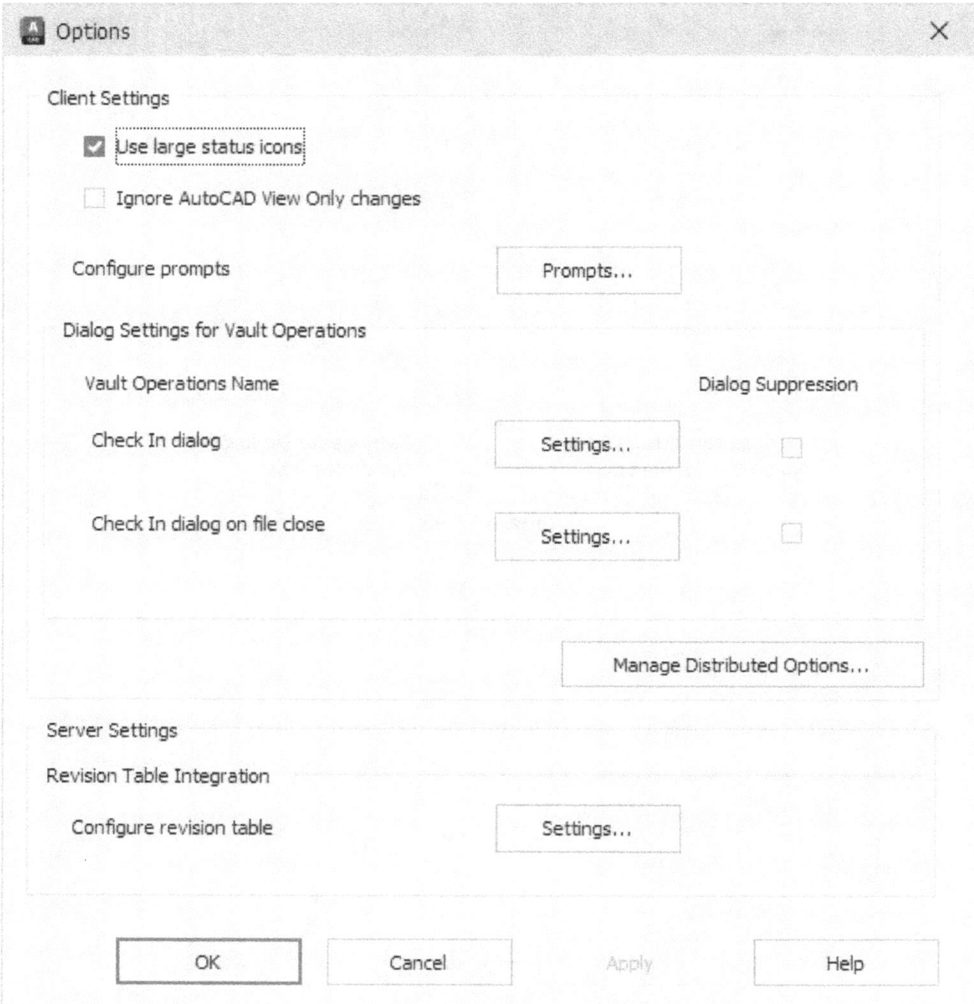

Figure 13–9

Prompts

To manage the default prompt settings, click **Prompts...** in the *Options* area. The *Manage Prompts* dialog box opens as shown in Figure 13–10.

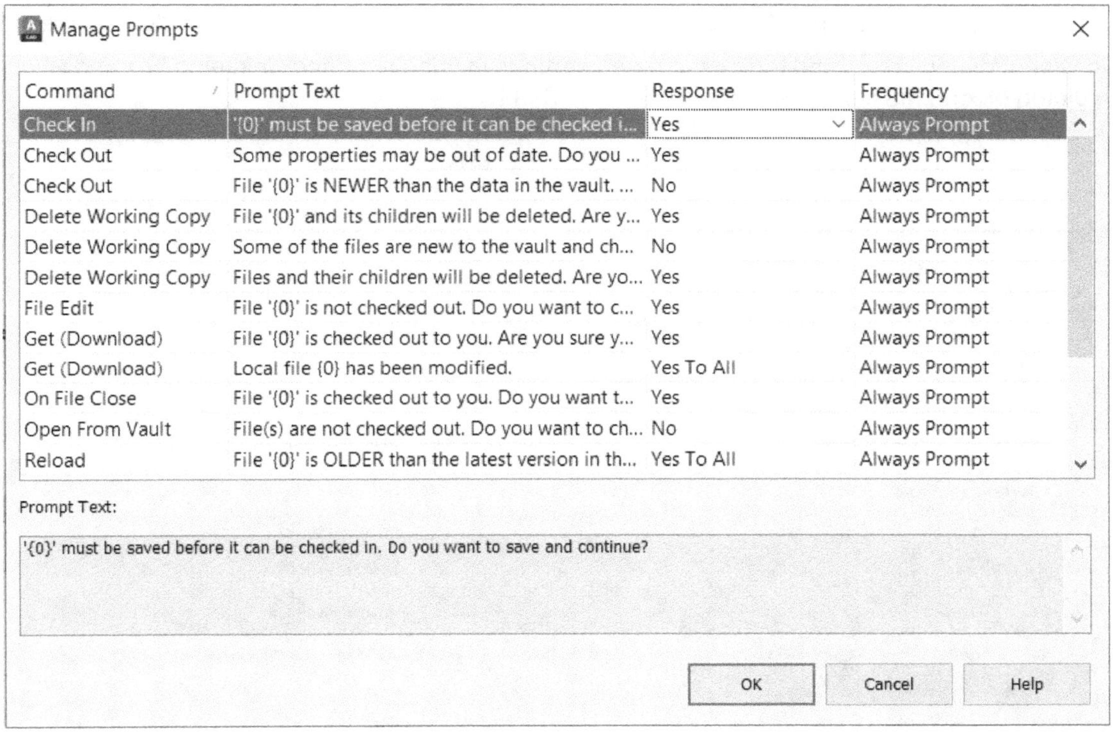

Figure 13–10

The dialog box displays four columns:

Command	Displays the command name.
Prompt Text	Displays the text that is displayed in the Warning box related to the selected command.
Response	Set the default response to the prompt.
Frequency	Set the frequency at which the prompt displays. • **Always Prompt** - This is the default prompt setting. Leave the default setting as is, if you require the prompt dialog box to display each time. • **Never Prompt** - Set it to **Never Prompt**, if you require automatic processing of the prompt request and do not want the prompt dialog box to display. The response you select will determine how the prompt will be automatically processed.

Dialog Boxes

Dialog boxes associated with vault operations such as Check In can be customized with default settings and suppressed. When the operation is performed, no dialog box opens, therefore streamlining and automating the workflow. In the *Dialog Suppression* area, select the dialog box option that you want to modify and click **Settings...** to open the related *Settings* dialog box.

The list of dialog boxes and their associated settings include the *Check In* dialog box and *Check In* dialog box on file close, as shown in Figure 13–11.

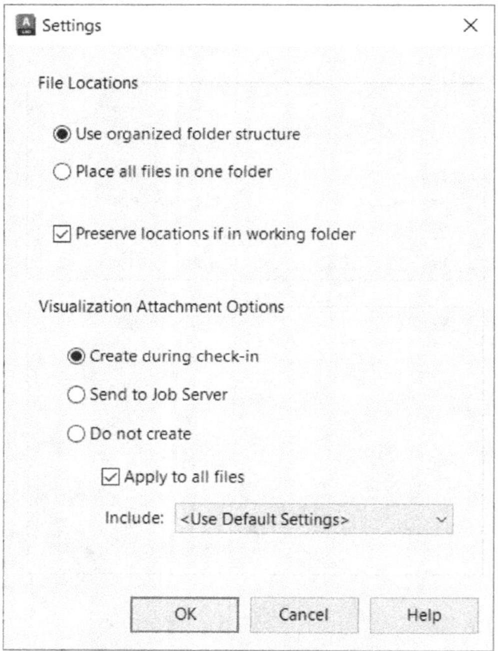

Settings for Check In dialog box

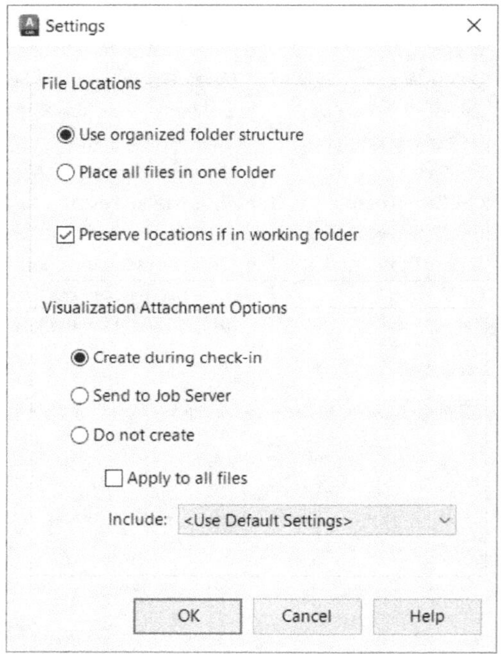

Settings for Check In dialog box on file close

Figure 13–11

Non-CAD Add-in Options

In the desired Microsoft application, such as Microsoft Word or Excel, in the *Autodesk Vault* tab>*File Status* panel, click (Options) to open the *Options* dialog box, as shown in Figure 13–12.

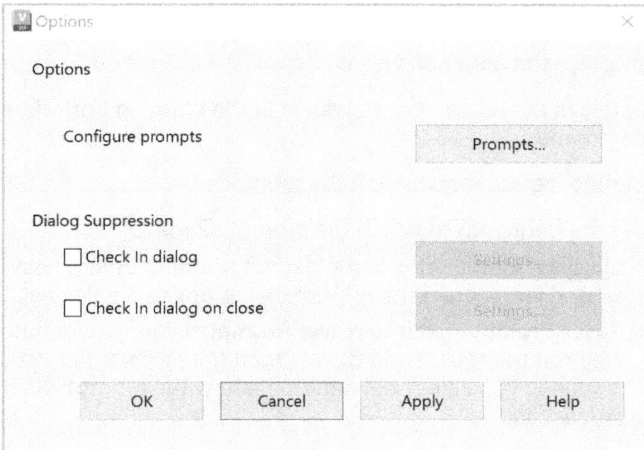

Figure 13–12

Prompts

To manage the default prompt settings, click **Prompts...** in the *Options* area. The *Manage Prompts* dialog box opens as shown in Figure 13–13.

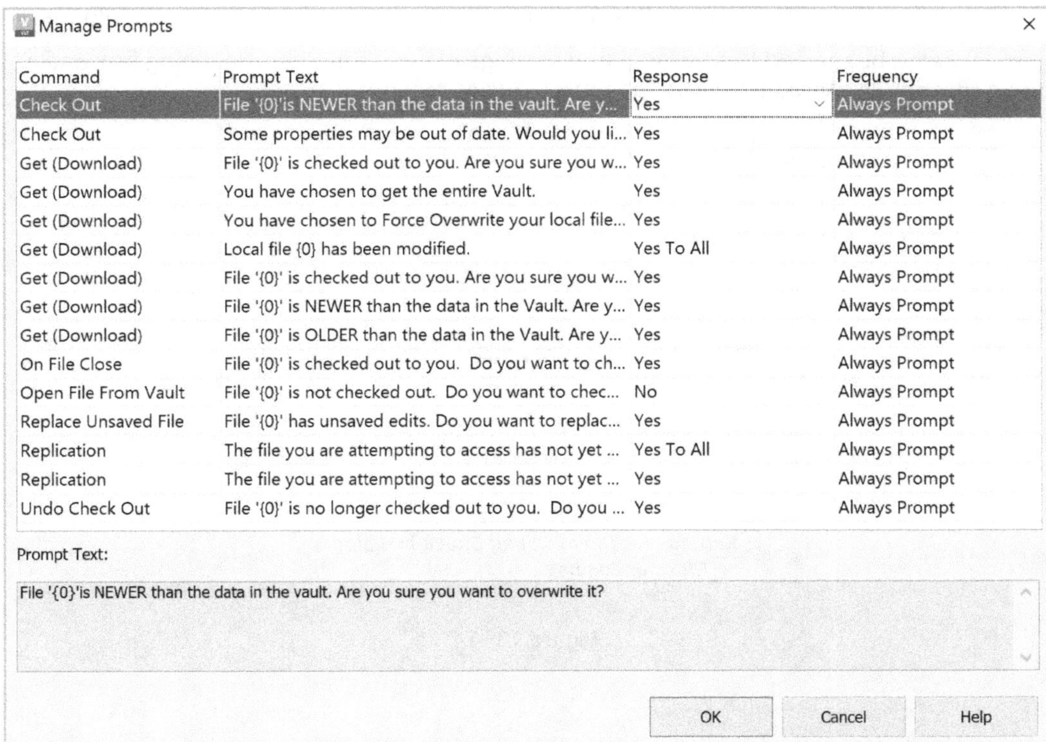

Figure 13–13

The dialog box displays four columns:

Command	Displays the command name.
Prompt Text	Displays the text that is displayed in the Warning box related to the selected command.
Response	Set the default response to the prompt.
Frequency	Set the frequency at which the prompt displays. • **Always Prompt** - This is the default prompt setting. Leave the default setting as is, if you require the prompt dialog box to display each time. • **Never Prompt** - Set it to **Never Prompt**, if you require automatic processing of the prompt request and do not want the prompt dialog box to display. The response you select will determine how the prompt will be automatically processed.

Dialog Boxes

Dialog boxes associated with vault operations such as Check In can be customized with default settings and suppressed. When the operation is performed, no dialog box opens, therefore streamlining and automating the workflow. In the *Dialog Suppression* area, select the dialog box option that you want to modify and click **Settings...** to open the related *Settings* dialog box.

The list of dialog boxes and their associated settings include the *Check In* dialog box and *Check In* dialog box on file close, as shown in Figure 13–14.

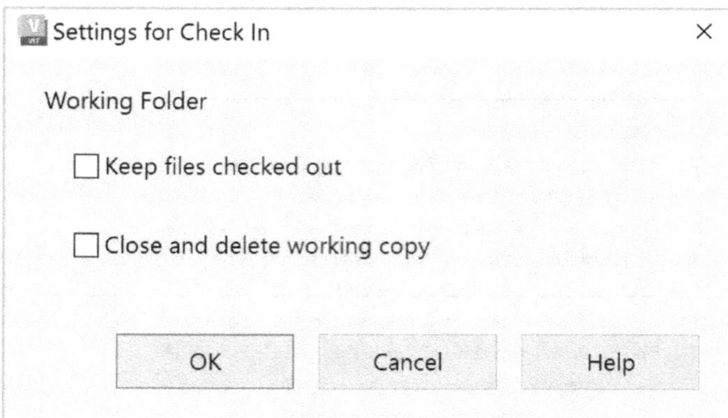

Settings for Check In and Check In dialog on Close dialog box

Figure 13–14

Chapter Review Questions

1. Dialog boxes associated with vault operations such as Check In can be customized with default settings and suppressed.
    a. True
    b. False

2. To manage the default prompt settings, click ____ in the *Options* dialog box.
    a. Options...
    b. Settings...
    c. Prompts...
    d. File Edit

Chapter 14

Thin Client

Autodesk® Vault Thin Client enables you to access vaulted files and items with a browser. You can view, search, and print details of items and files.

Learning Objectives

- Sign in and out of Thin Client.
- Navigate the folders and files in the Thin Client.
- Search for files and items using the Thin Client.
- Configure view display settings.
- Navigate between the tabs to view details of a selected file and item.
- Download files from the vault.

14.1 Sign In and Sign Out of the Thin Client

The supported browsers for Thin Client are Microsoft Edge, Google Chrome, Mozilla Firefox, and Apple Safari. You must sign in using a unique user name and password assigned by the vault administrator. Your administrator can also import a Windows Active Directory account. With an Active Directory account, you can sign in using your Windows account credentials. If an account has not been set up for you, contact your vault administrator.

> ***Note:*** *The Thin Client is compatible with Vault Professional only.*

How To: Sign In to the Thin Client

1. In the browser address field, enter the URL for Thin Client. **http://<servername>/AutodeskTC/<vaultname>**, where server name is either the IP address or the name of the server hosting the Autodesk Data Management Server (for this class, it is '**localhost**'). Note: After signing in to the Thin Client, you can change vaults in the Thin Client interface, if required.
2. On the Sign in page, as shown in Figure 14–1, enter your user credentials, depending on the authentication method:
   - **Sign in to Vault (Autodesk Vault Account):** Enter the username and password for the Autodesk Data Management Server account assigned to you by your vault administrator and click **Sign in to Vault**.
   - **Windows Account (Windows Authentication):** Click **Windows Account**, enter your Active Directory username and password in the window that appears, and click **OK**.

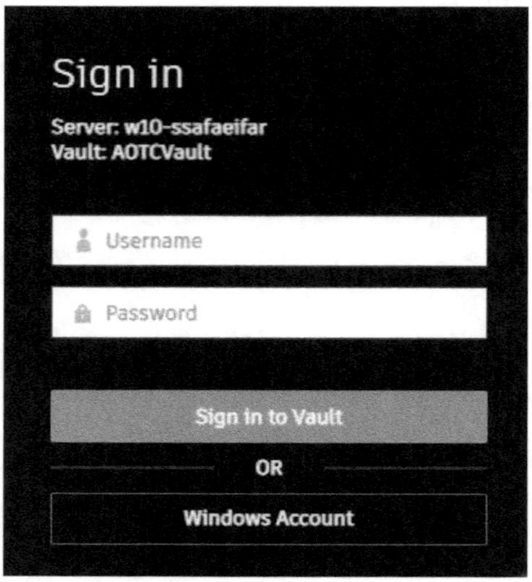

Figure 14–1

3. The Thin Client interface displays, as shown in Figure 14–2. Your folders may look different than those shown.

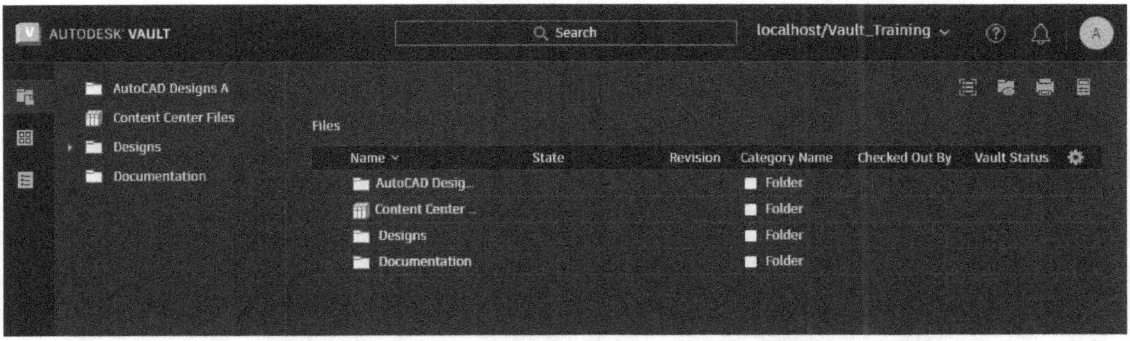

Figure 14–2

How To: Sign Out of the Thin Client

1. To sign out of the session, click (Profile icon) in the upper-right corner of the page then select **Sign Out**.

14.2 The Thin Client Interface

The Thin Client Interface is shown in Figure 14–3.

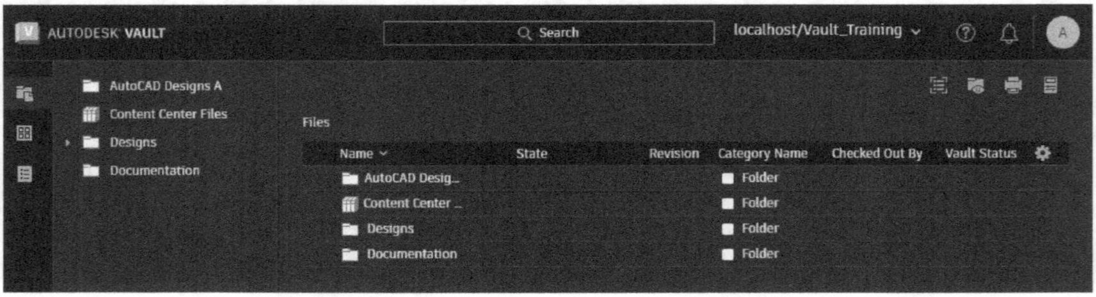

Figure 14–3

Navigation Bar

The navigation bar at the top of the window contains several icons. It also contains a search bar. The icons and areas of the navigation bar are described below.

Vault Selector: Displays a list of available vaults.

- To switch to a different vault:

a. Select the Vault selector drop-down list, displaying the current server/vault name.

b. Select a vault.

c. Click **OK** to change the vault and be directed to the Sign In page. You must sign in again to access the selected vault.

Help Icon: Displays a menu containing the following options:

- **Help and Support:** Opens the Autodesk Help pages for Autodesk Vault.
- **About:** Displays the Thin Client's version information.
- **Contact Us:** Opens Autodesk's Vault Forums, where you can share knowledge, ask questions, collaborate on ideas, and explore Vault topics.

Notification Icon: Displays unread notifications. When you have a new notification, a badge appears on the icon.

Profile Icon: Displays the following options:

- **Settings:** Displays settings for display and viewing data in the Thin Client.
- **Sign Out:** Ends your session in the Thin Client and signs out the current account.

Workspace Navigation

The workspace navigation pane, on the left of the Thin Client window, contains icons for **Files**, **Items**, and **Change Orders**., as shown in Figure 14–4. These are the types of objects that you can work with in the Thin Client.

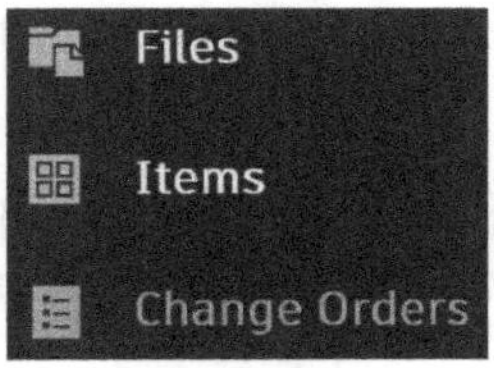

Figure 14–4

Click a workspace icon to display that workspace view. If a workspace contains folders, you can navigate the folder tree by clicking folder names in the workspace navigation pane.

Search Bar

The search bar searches in the current workspace, by default.

Data Tables

Click an object or a folder in the data table of a workspace to display its contents and to view more details. A checkbox displays to the left of the items in a data table. Select a checkbox to display icons at the top of the table. Each icon represents an action available for that type of object. An example showing the **View**, **Download**, and **Share** icons is shown in Figure 14–5.

Figure 14–5

Properties Tab

The properties panel shows the properties associated with a selected object in the vault.

Click the  (Open Properties Panel) icon to open the panel. Select an object to display its properties. An object is selected when its checkbox is marked.

Details Page

Every object in the vault has specific data and relationships associated with it displayed in the *History*, *Uses*, *Where Used*, *Item*, and *Change Order* tabs.

View Tab

The Thin Client displays files with viewable geometry in an integrated viewer.

14.3 Working with Files

The File Details page in the Thin Client provides information about the selected file in the vault such as its user-defined properties, file *History*, *Uses*, and *Where Used* information. The **Files** workspace displays files and folders in your vault. A breadcrumb trail, displayed above the data table, represents the location of the current folder. Click a folder name in the breadcrumb trail to view its contents.

Files are listed in a data table. Click the (Configure Columns) icon to modify the column headers in the Files workspace. You can reorder or add user- and system-defined headers to the data table in the *Configure Columns* drop-down list. The default order contains headers for the following data:

- Name (required)
- State
- Revision
- Category Name
- Checked Out By
- Vault Status

How To: View the Details of a File

1. Select the **Files** workspace in the workspace navigation panel.
2. Navigate the folder tree to find your file. You can click folders in the workspace navigation pane or in the table. Alternatively, you can search the vault to find the file with the search bar.

3. Click the file name in the table to view detailed information about the selected file on the File Details page, as shown in Figure 14–6.

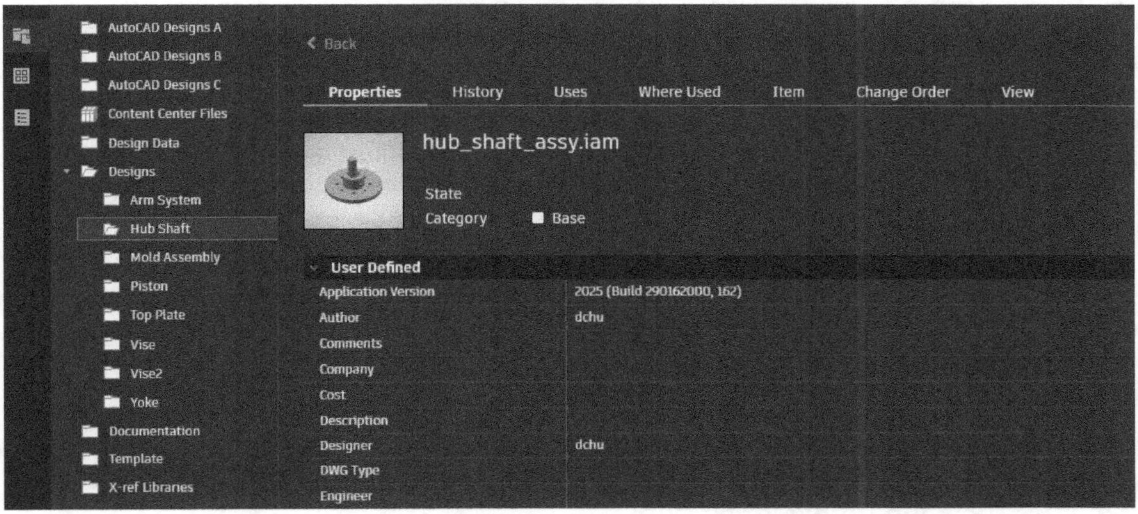

Figure 14–6

4. The file details view contains several tabs that display file information and viewing functions. The following tabs are available in the details view of a file:

- *Properties* tab
- *History* tab
- *Uses* tab
- *Where Used* tab
- *Item* tab
- *Change Order* tab
- *View* tab

14.4 Working with Items

The **Items** workspace displays the Item Master list of all items and the Item Details page provides information about the selected item in the vault such as its' user-defined properties, *Bill of Materials*, *History*, *Where Used*, *Associated Files*, and *Change Order* information. Similar to working with files, click the (Configure Columns) icon to modify the column headers in the Items workspace. You can reorder or add user- and system-defined headers to the data table in the *Configure Columns* drop-down list. The default order contains headers for the following data:

- Name (required)
- State
- Revision
- Vault Status
- Category Name
- Title (Item, CO)

How To: View the Details of an Item

1. Select the **Items** workspace in the workspace navigation panel.
2. Scroll through the Items list (shown in Figure 14–7) to find your item. Alternatively, you can search the vault to find the item using the search bar.

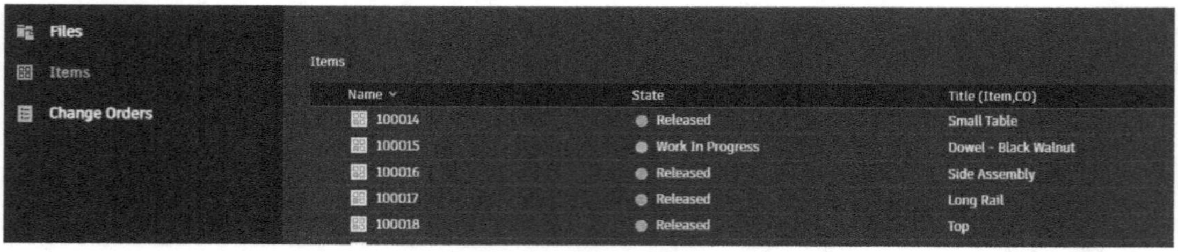

Figure 14–7

3. Select the item name in the data table to view its information in the following tabs:

- *Properties* tab
- *History* tab
- *Bill of Materials* tab
    - The BOM view supports Multi-Level and Parts Only views. To change the BOM view, click the view icon (either or , depending on the current view) in the upper-right corner of the table.
    - If **Show released files only** is toggled on in Administrator Settings, non-released versions of the item don't display.
- *Where Used* tab
- *Associated Files* tab
- *Change Order* tab

14.5 Change Orders

The **Change Orders** workspace displays change orders in your vault in a data table. The Change Order Details page provides information about the selected change order in the vault such as its user-defined properties, *Records*, and *Attachments*, displayed in their respective *Properties*, *Records*, and *Attachments* tabs.

Similar to working with files, click the (Configure Columns) icon to modify the column headers in the Change Orders workspace. You can reorder or add user- and system-defined headers to the data table in the *Configure Columns* drop-down list. The default order contains headers for the following data:

- Number (required)
- State
- Due Date
- Vault Status
- Title (Item, CO)
- Number of File Attachments

How To: View the Details of a Change Order

1. Select the **Change Orders** workspace in the navigation panel.
2. Scroll through the Change Orders list to find your change order. Alternatively, you can search the vault to find the change order using the search bar.
3. Select the change order number in the data table to display its change order information in the following tabs:
    - *Properties* tab
    - *Records* tab
    - *Attachments* tab

14.6 Viewer

The Thin Client includes a browser version of the viewer, Autodesk's tool for exploring, examining, and reviewing the contents of CAD files.

The Thin Client viewer implements the same controls and features as the viewer available in the Vault Client.

How To: Open the Viewer in the Thin Client

1. Select the **Files** workspace in the navigation panel.
2. Navigate the folders to find your file. You can click folders in the workspace navigation pane or in the data table. Alternatively, you can search the vault to find the file with the search bar.
3. Select the file by clicking, or tapping on touchscreen devices, the checkbox to the left of the file name. The file is selected when its checkbox is marked.

   Note: *You can select multiple files to open at once.*

4. Select the  (View) icon above the data table to open the viewer displaying the file, in a new browser tab.
   - Alternatively, you can view a file's details, select the *View* tab to open the viewer and display the file, as shown in Figure 14–8.

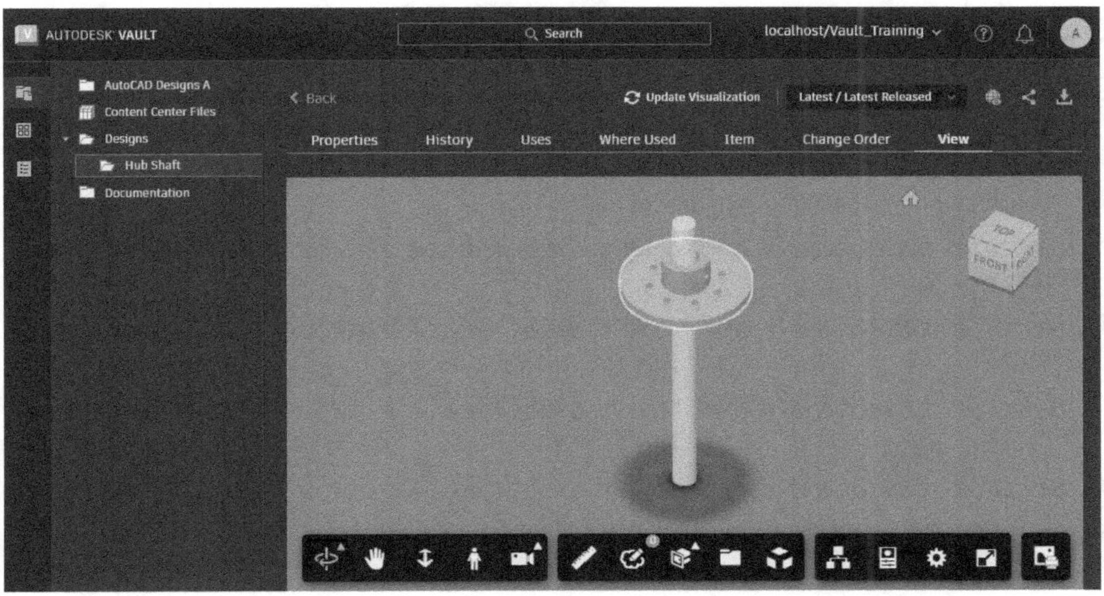

Figure 14–8

14.7 Working with Vault Data

The Thin Client enables you to share links to vaulted data, download files, view file contents, and more to effectively work with your vault data.

Downloading a File

When downloading multiple files at once, the Thin Client limits the download to 500mb. Downloading files individually doesn't have a maximum limit.

How To: Download a Local Copy of a File from the Vault

1. Select the **Files** workspace in the navigation pane.
2. Locate the file to download by navigating the folders or searching the vault using the search bar.
3. Select the file name to view its details or select the checkbox to the left of the file name.

   Note: *You can select multiple files to download at once.*

4. Select the (Download) icon to display a drop-down list with the following options:
   - Select **Download File** to download a local copy of the file.
   - Select **Download Visualization File** to download a local DWF of the file.

Sharing Links

How To: Generate a Link That You or Others Can Open in the Vault Client or Thin Client

1. Select a workspace in the navigation pane.
2. Locate the object to share by navigating the folders or searching the vault using the search bar.
3. Select the object name to view its details or select the checkbox to the left of the object name.

   Note: *You can select multiple files to share at once.*

4. Select the (Share) icon.
5. Select the *Desktop Client* tab or the *Web Client* tab in the *Share* window.

   Note: *Links for the Vault Client and the Thin Client are not interchangeable. The type of link that you select can only be viewed in the specified client.*

6. To share the link, use either of the following methods:
   - Enter an email address in the open field and select **Send**. An email is automatically generated by your computer's default email client.
   - Select **Copy Link** to copy the link to your clipboard.

Update File Visualization

Visualization files can be updated so that the latest DWF of a CAD file is available. When a visualization file is updated, the job is sent to the job server for processing. The **Update Visualization** command is only available if the Job Server is enabled and turned on.

How To: Update Visualization Files

1. Select the **Files** workspace in the navigation pane.
2. Hover over a row and select the ••• icon of the file to update.

   Note: *On touch screen devices, tap a row to the right of the file name to reveal this icon.*
3. Select **Update Visualization** to send the job to the Job Processor.

Sort Data Tables

Select a header in a data table to sort the table. Number-based fields sort numerically in ascending or descending order. Text-based fields sort alphabetically from A-Z or Z-A. Date-based fields sort from older to newer or newer to older.

View Historical Versions and Revisions

In object details, select the *Latest / Latest Released* drop-down list to browse and select historical versions or revisions. You can also select past versions in the *History* tab.

Version and revision apply when you share a link to the Thin Client. Links redirect to the version and revision selected in the drop-down list or *History* tab.

Filter Data in the History Tab

When you're viewing file or item details, the *History* tab can be filtered. Select the **Filter** icon to the far right of the table header to display filter options. Filter options include **Show Latest Versions Only** and **Show All Versions**.

Modify Data Table Headers

Data tables display in a default header configuration that can be modified. You can rearrange the display order of headers and also add system-generated or user-generated properties to the header.

How To: Modify Table Headers

1. Select the (Configure Columns) icon to the far-right of the table header.
2. Click, or tap and hold on touchscreen devices, to drag a header and rearrange the display order.
3. To hide a header, unselect its checkbox.

14.8 Searching

Use the Thin Client to search for specific data in your vault.

Search Bar

The current workspace, indicated by the drop-down list to the left of the search field, is automatically selected when you click the search bar. Click the menu to select a different workspace, as shown in Figure 14–9.

Figure 14–9

Basic Search

Basic searches are keyword searches run from the search bar, as shown in Figure 14–10, or from the search results page in the *Basic Search* tab, as shown in Figure 14–11.

Basic searches are performed within the folder you are currently in (and its subfolders) when in the Files workspace, but do not search folders above it.

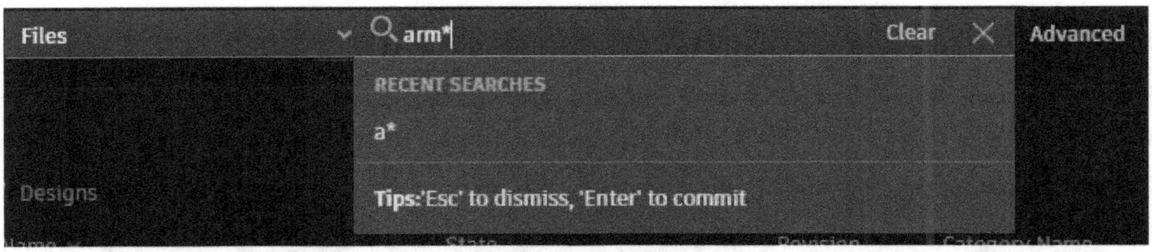

Figure 14–10

Figure 14–11

Advanced Search

You can create advanced searches by specifying property criteria. Advanced searches can be accessed by clicking the **Advanced** link after selecting in the search field, as shown in Figure 14–12, or by selecting the *Advanced Search* tab in the search results page, as shown in Figure 14–13.

Figure 14–12

Figure 14–13

How To: Search in the Thin Client

1. Click **Search** in the navigation bar to expand the search bar.
2. Select a workspace (**Files**, **Items**, or **Change Orders**) to search. By default, only the latest versions are searched, as shown in Figure 14–14.

Figure 14–14

3. For a basic search, enter your search term(s) in the search field and press <Enter> to search in the selected workspace (and folder for the Files workspace searches), as shown in Figure 14–15.

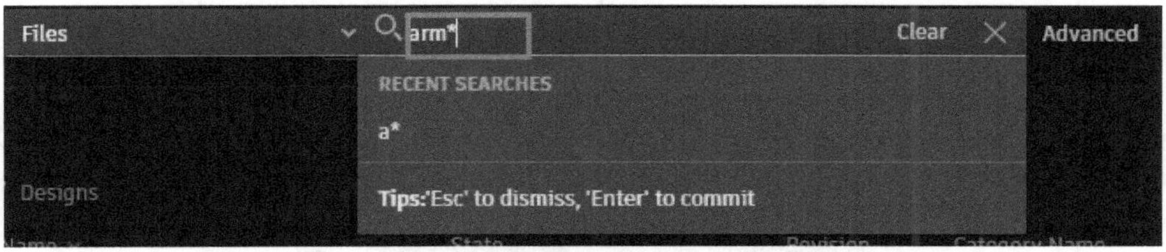

Figure 14–15

4. The search results display, as shown in Figure 14–16.

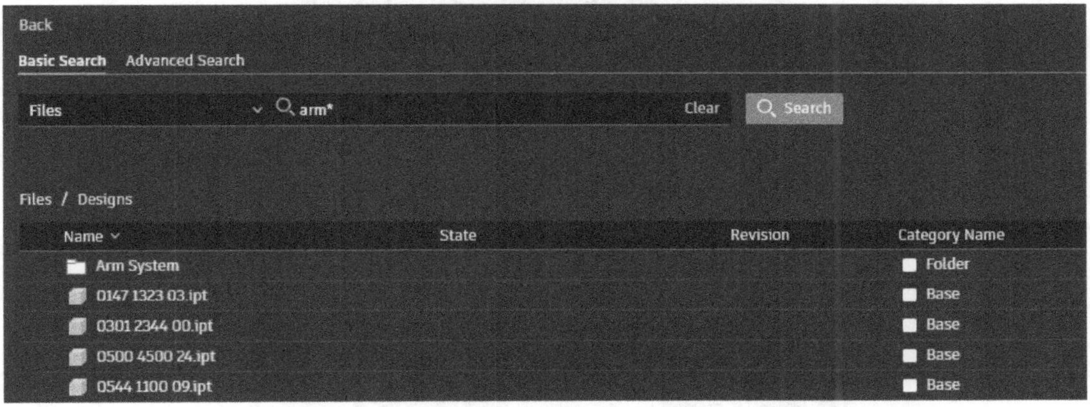

Figure 14–16

5. Click **Clear** to run another basic search, or you can select the *Advanced Search* tab to run an advanced search.

6. For an advanced search, select a property from the *Properties* drop-down list, select an operator from the *Operator* drop-down list, enter a value in the *Value* field, and click + to add the search criteria, as shown in Figure 14–17. You can add multiple search criteria. When finished, click **Search**.

Figure 14–17

7. The search results display.

14.9 Settings

Administrators can customize display settings in the Thin Client.

File and Item Display Settings

You can modify which files and items are displayed on the page by selecting **Settings** in the Profile menu, as shown in Figure 14–18. The *General* tab, *Files* tab, *Items* tab, and *Change Order* tab settings are shown in Figure 14–19, Figure 14–20, Figure 14–21, and Figure 14–22.

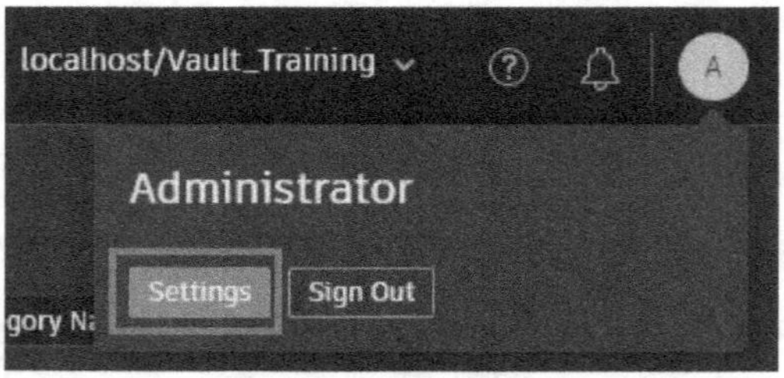

Figure 14–18

General

- Default image or Custom image
- Enforce admin default properties headers

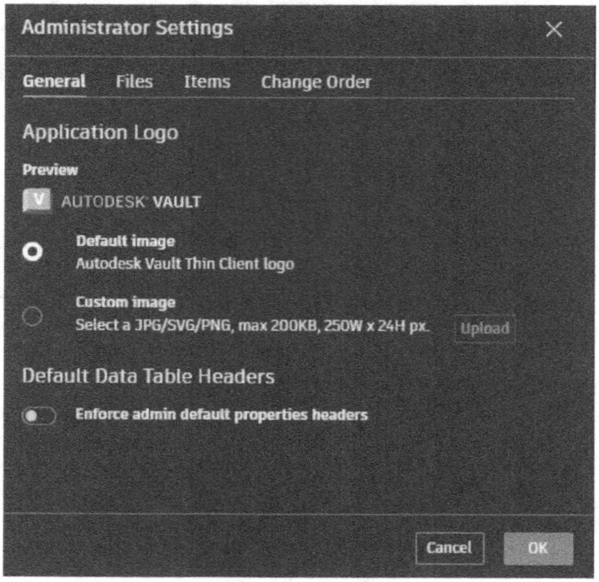

Figure 14–19

Files

- Hide Files workspace
- Make default landing page
- Show released files only
- Show latest version of file only

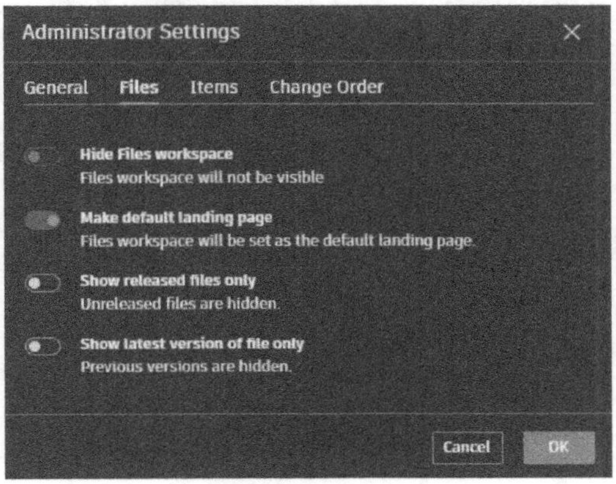

Figure 14–20

Items

- Hide Items workspace
- Make default landing page
- Show released items only
- Show latest version of item only

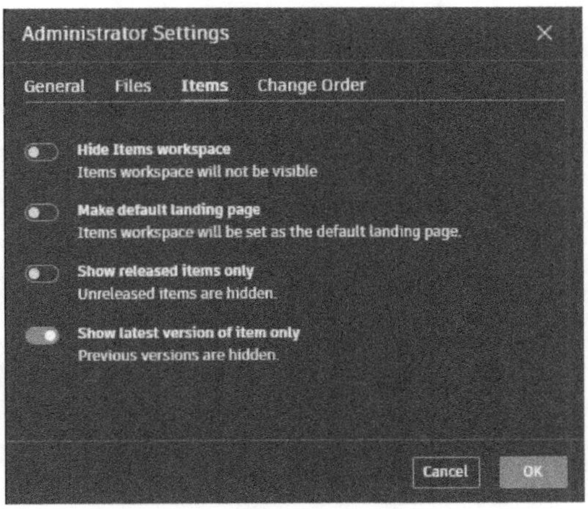

Figure 14–21

Change Order

- Hide Change order workspace
- Make default landing page

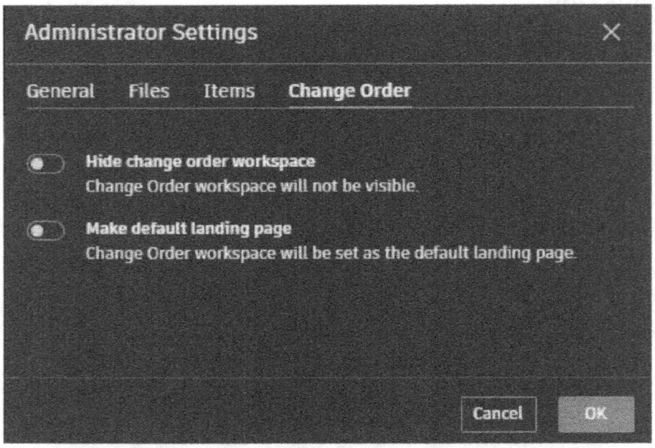

Figure 14–22

14.10 Printing

You can print data tables and object details in the Thin Client.

How To: Print a Page from the Thin Client

1. Select a workspace (**Files**, **Items**, or **Change Orders**). Alternatively, you can search the vault using the search bar.
2. To print the data table in your current workspace:
   a. Modify the table as necessary. The page will print as it appears in your browser.
   b. Select the (Print) icon in the upper-right corner of the page.
   c. Follow your browser's instructions to print the page.
3. To print the details of a specific object:
   a. Select the object name to view its details.
   b. Select the tab you want to print (e.g., *History*, *Bill of Materials*, etc).
   c. Modify the table as necessary. The page will print as it appears in your browser.
   d. Select the (Print) icon in the upper-right corner of the page.
   e. Follow your browser's instructions to print the page.

Practice 14a
Get Started with the Thin Client

Practice Objectives

- Sign in to the Thin Client.
- Configure view display settings.

In this practice, you will sign in to the vault using the Thin Client, navigate the vault, change the layout and configuration of the properties displayed in a view, and search the vault.

1. Open a browser to access the Autodesk Vault Thin Client.
2. Type in the URL to access the Thin Client Login page (**http://localhost/AutodeskTC/Vault_Training** for this class).
3. Enter your user name (**administrator**) and password (leave blank), as shown in Figure 14–23) and press <Enter> or click **Sign in to Vault**.

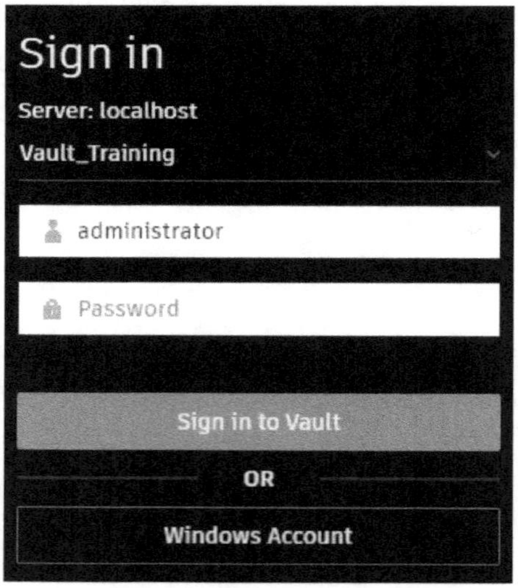

Figure 14–23

4. Select the **Files** icon on the left side on the Thin Client page, as shown in Figure 14–24.

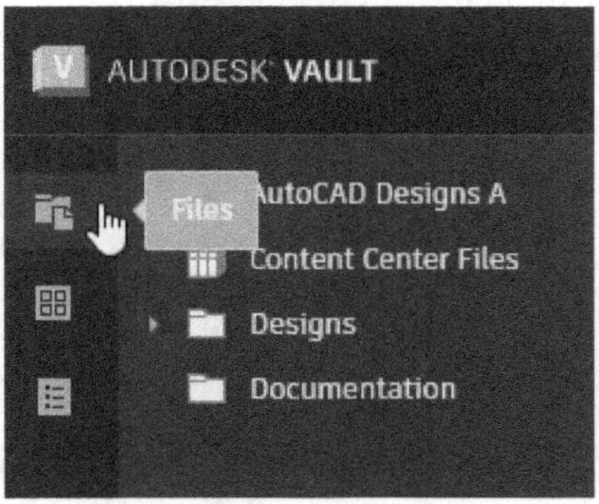

Figure 14–24

5. Navigate to the *Designs>Hub Shaft* folder. Note that there are no files displayed in the folder, as shown in Figure 14–25. This is because the default setting for the Thin Client is to only show released items and files. Currently there are no released items or files in this folder.

Figure 14–25

6. Click the **Profile** icon and select **Settings**, as shown in Figure 14–26.

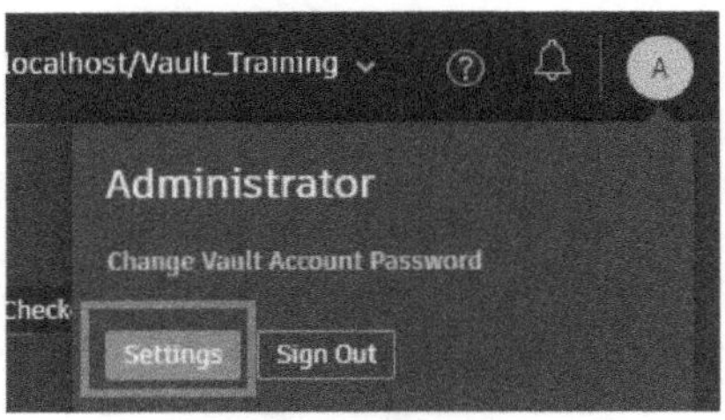

Figure 14–26

7. In the *Administrator Settings* window, select the *Files* tab and disable the option for **Show released files only**, as shown on the left in Figure 14–27.
8. Select the *Items* tab and disable the option for **Show released items only**, as shown on the right in Figure 14–27.

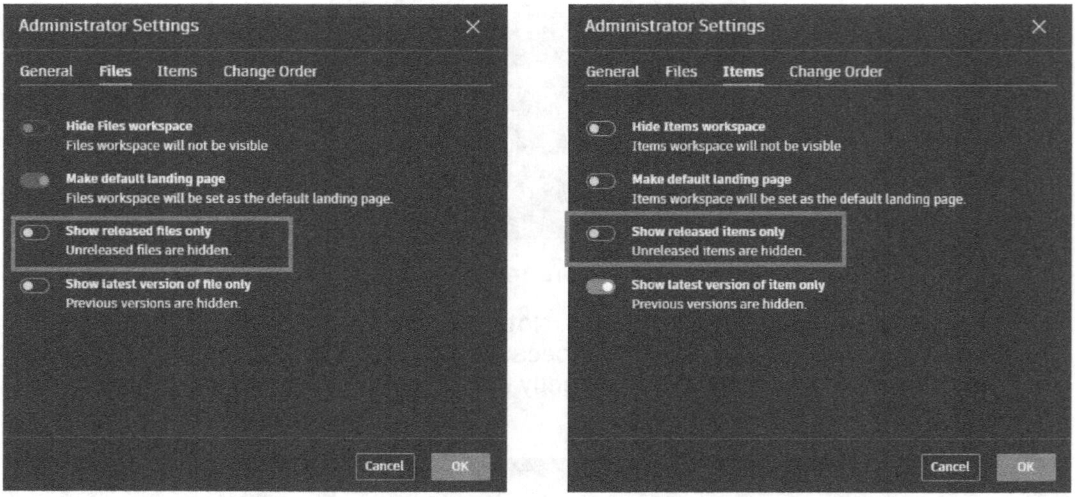

Figure 14–27

9. Click **OK** to close the *Administrator Settings* window. Note how all the files are now displayed in the view in the Thin Client.
10. Select the arrow beside the *Name* column header to change the sort order for the names.
11. Select the (Configure Columns) icon, as shown in Figure 14–28.

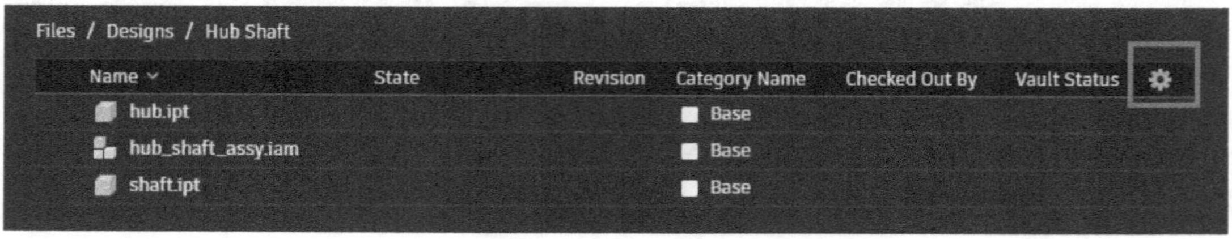

Figure 14–28

12. Select **Vault Status** in the *SELECTED HEADERS* section and drag it up until it is listed under **Name**, as shown in Figure 14–29.

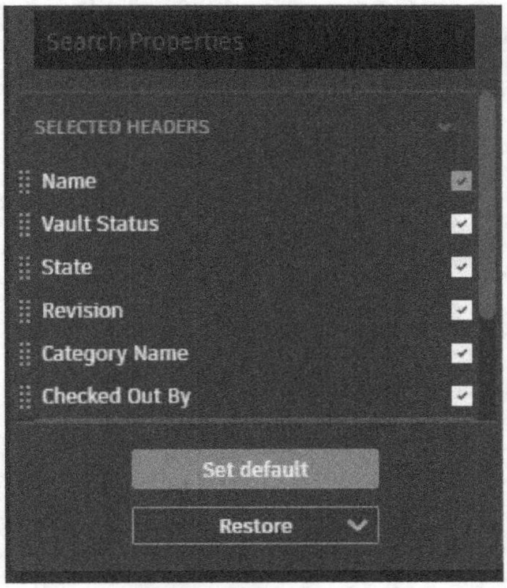

Figure 14–29

13. In the *SYSTEM DEFINED PROPERTIES* section, select the **Category Glyph** checkbox. It will be added to the *SELECTED HEADERS* section.
14. Note that the display for the current folder has changed. Switch to other folders and note that the column properties displayed have also changed.
15. Select (Configure Columns). In the *Restore* drop-down list, select **Default order** to return to the default column display.
16. Select the *Designs* folder.
17. In the search field, click on the drop-down list to expand the search options. Select **Files**. Enter **arm*** in the search bar and press <Enter>.

18. The results are displayed, as shown in Figure 14–30. Click **Back** to return to the Files view.

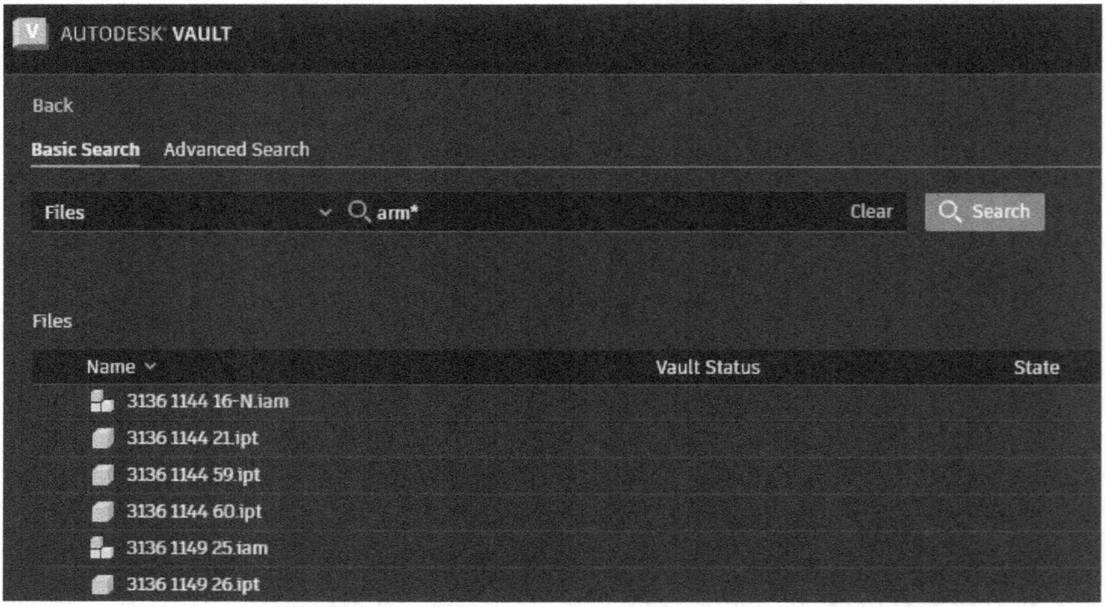

Figure 14–30

End of practice

Practice 14b
Work with Files

Practice Objectives

- Navigate the folders and files in the Thin Client.
- View the details of a file.

In this practice, you will navigate through the file structure to locate a file. Once located, you will access the File Details page and view the details of the file using the *History*, *Uses*, and *Where Used* tabs. You will also open the DWF preview of the file.

1. In the Project Explorer, navigate to the *Designs>Mold Assembly* folder.
2. In the Files list, select **Final Mold Assy.iam** to view the detailed information about the file on the File Details page.
3. The thumbnail for the selected file displays in the File Details page. Below the thumbnail is the detailed summary of the *User Defined* and *System Defined* properties, as shown in Figure 14–31. Scroll through the list to review the details.

Figure 14–31

4. Select the *History* tab, as shown in Figure 14–32.

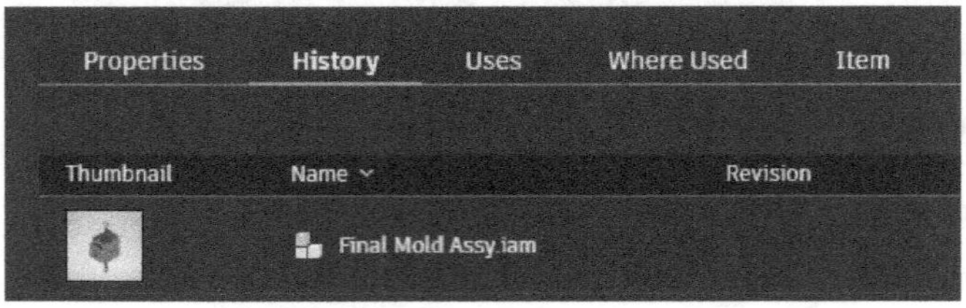

Figure 14–32

5. Select the *Uses* tab to display all the files that are used in the Final Mold Assy.iam file, as shown in Figure 14–33.

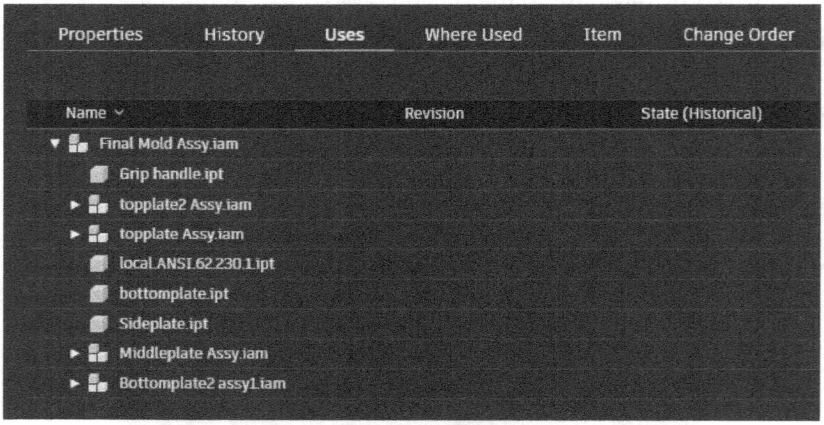

Figure 14–33

6. Select **Grip handle.ipt** in the *Uses* tab. This is now the active file listed on the File Details page.
7. Select the *Where Used* tab to display where the Grip handle is used, as shown in Figure 14–34. This part is only used in Final Mold Assy.iam.

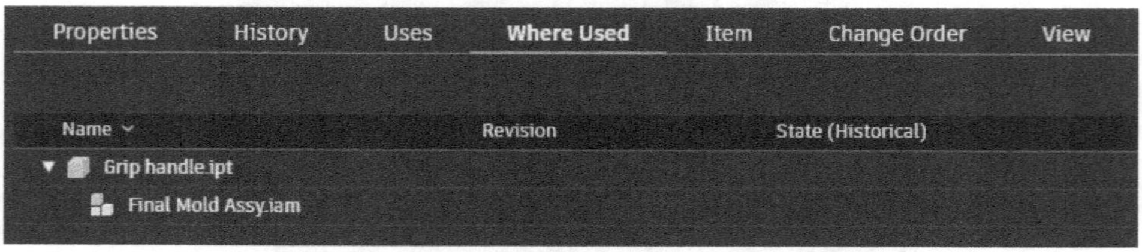

Figure 14–34

8. Select **Final Mold Assy.iam** in the *Where Used* tab to make it the active file.

9. Select the *View* tab to view the file in Autodesk Viewer, as shown in Figure 14–35.

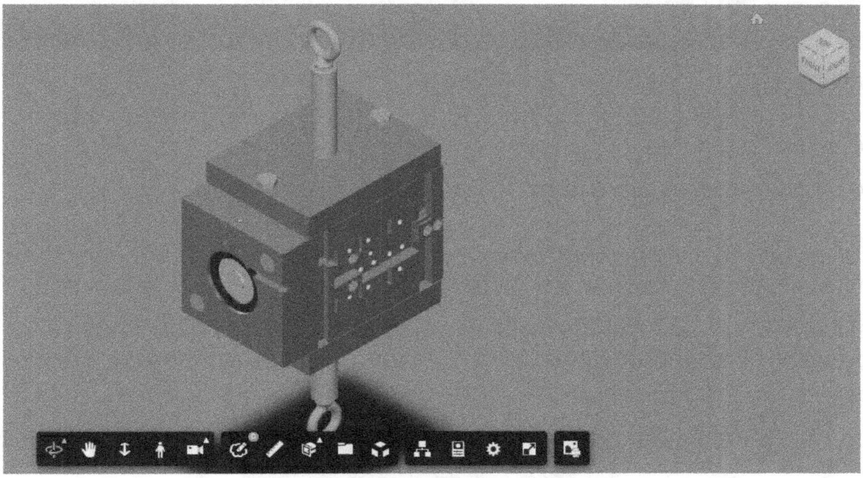

Figure 14–35

- When viewing a visualization file in the viewer, you can use markup to superimpose annotations on the 2D or 3D representation of the file. Markup tools in the viewer include freehand drawing, text, and callouts, among others.
- The **Save Snapshot** function downloads a local copy of the current markup in the viewer as a PNG.

10. Use the toolbar and the ViewCube to navigate the assembly. Select the **Home** icon to return the model to its default orientation.
11. In the Viewer toolbar, select **Explode Model** and separate the model's geometry to see individual parts of the design. Select **Markup** and select the **Callout** icon.
12. Enter **Please Review** in the text box to add this markup to the file.
13. Click **Save Snapshot** to save and download the current markup as a .PNG file.
14. Select **Download Visualization File** from *Download* tab at the top-right of the toolbar, as shown in Figure 14–36, to save a local copy of the DWF file.

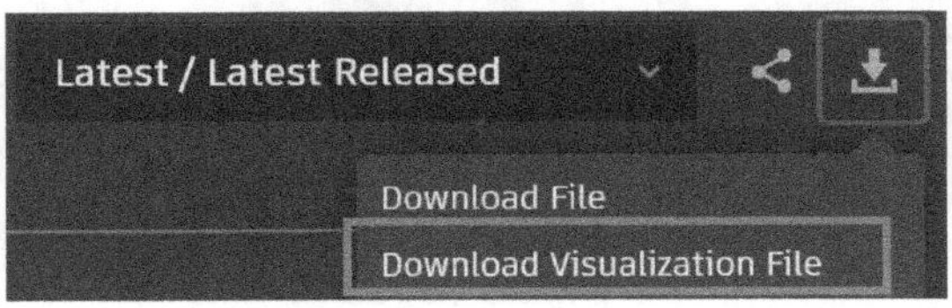

Figure 14–36

End of practice

Practice 14c
Work with Items

Practice Objectives

- View the details of an item.
- View the bill of materials of an item.

In this practice, you will activate the **Items** view and review the information and tabs available on the Item Details page for a selected item.

1. To display the list of items in the vault, select **Items** in the menu on the left side of the Thin Client browser, as shown in Figure 14–37. All items that exist in the vault display in the Items list.

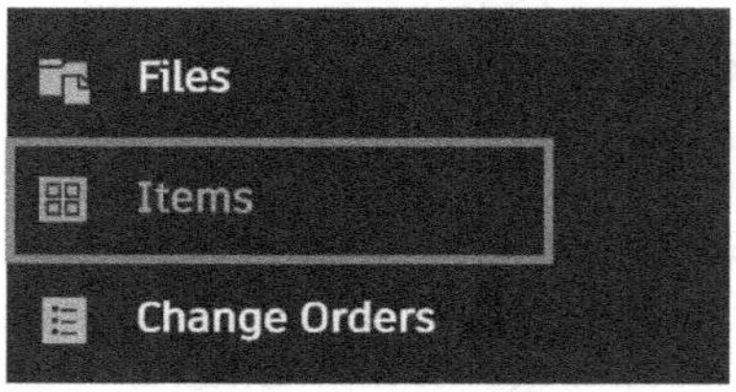

Figure 14–37

Note: *If no items are listed in the Item view, check the settings for the Thin Client and ensure that the* ***Show released items only*** *option is disabled.*

2. Select the arrow beside the *Name* property header to change the sort order for the items.
3. With the Items view still active, use the search functionality to search for **Work in Progress** items. Click **Advanced** and enter the criteria as shown in Figure 14–38.

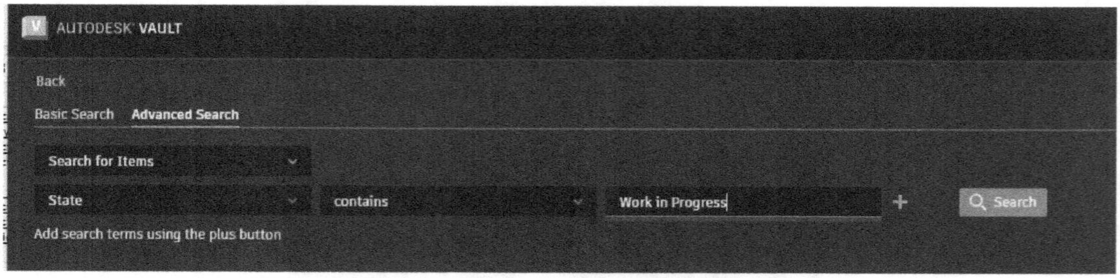

Figure 14–38

4. Click **Search**, then click **OK** to add the criteria you entered to your search. The results of the search are returned in the Items view showing only those items identified in this view as Work in Progress.

5. Click **Clear**, then click **Clear** again to confirm that you want to clear all search parameters. Click **Back** to return to the Items view.
6. Select the **Final Mold Assy** item to open the Item Details page, as shown in Figure 14–39.

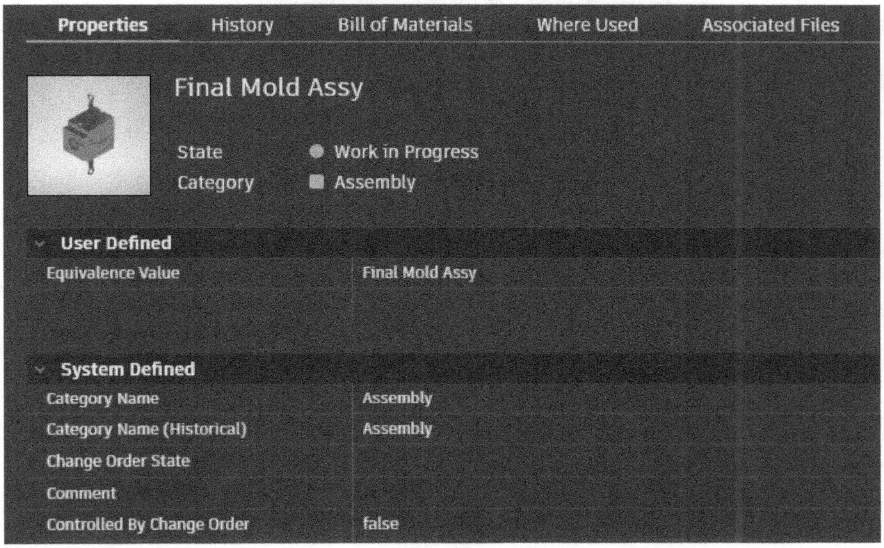

Figure 14–39

7. Select the *History* tab and note the history of this item.
8. Select the *Bill of Materials* tab. The default display option for the *Bill of Materials* tab is **Multi-Level**, as shown in Figure 14–40.

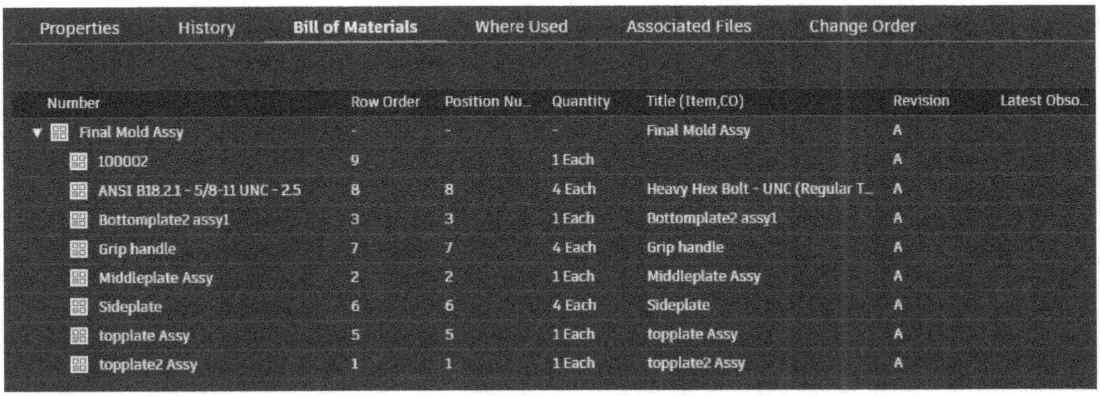

Figure 14–40

9. Change the display to **Parts Only**, as shown in Figure 14–41.

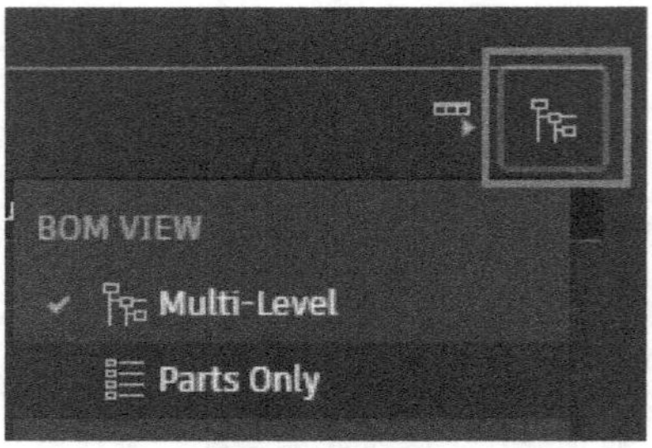

Figure 14–41

10. Note the **Print**, **Share**, and **Open Properties Panel** icons are available in the top-right corner, as shown in Figure 14–42.

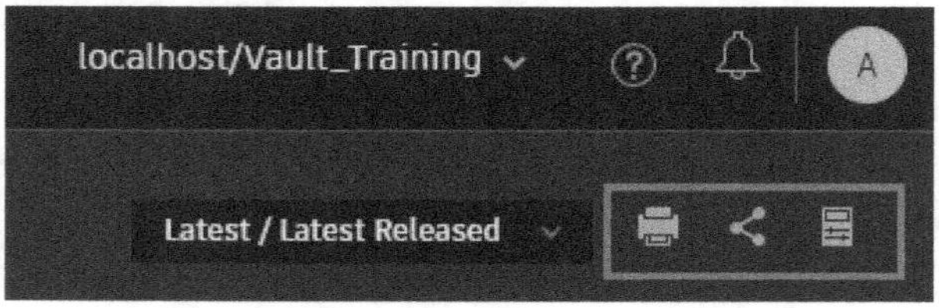

Figure 14–42

End of practice

Chapter Review Questions

1. Which option must be disabled to view non-released files in Vault Thin Client?
   a. Hide Files workspace
   b. Show released items only
   c. Show latest version of file only
   d. Show released files only

2. Which of the following tabs can you select from the Details view of a file? (Select all that apply.)
   a. Properties
   b. History
   c. Uses
   d. Where Used
   e. Item
   f. Change Order
   g. View

3. Which workspace displays bill of materials information?
   a. Files
   b. Items
   c. Change Orders

4. The basic search searches within the folder you are currently in and its subfolders, but does not search folders above it.
   a. True
   b. False

5. The basic search allows you to specify multiple search criteria based on properties.
   a. True
   b. False

6. Which of the following actions can you perform when viewing an assembly in Autodesk Viewer? (Select all that apply.)

a. Markup

b. Pan

c. Zoom

d. Explode Model

Index

www.ingramcontent.com/pod-product-compliance
Lightning Source LLC
LaVergne TN
LVHW082025200926
848481LV00010B/2927